Music is Love in search of a word—SYDNEY LANIER.

TWENTY-FIFTH ISSUE

*Thoroughly Revised, and Augmented by an Appendix
of 700 Additional Words and Phrases*

A

DICTIONARY

OF

MUSICAL TERMS

*Containing upwards of 9,000 English, French, German, Italian,
Latin and Greek words and phrases used in the art and
science of music, carefully defined, and with the accent
of the foreign words marked; preceded by rules for
the pronunciation of Italian, German and French.*

WITH A

SUPPLEMENT

CONTAINING

An English-Italian Vocabulary for Composers

COMPILED AND EDITED

BY

Dr. TH. BAKER

——

AMS PRESS
NEW YORK

Reprinted from the edition of 1923, New York
First AMS EDITION published 1970
Manufactured in the United States of America

International Standard Book Number: 0-404-00468-7

Library of Congress Card Catalog Number 75-124595

AMS PRESS, INC.
NEW YORK, N.Y. 10003

PREFACE.

It is the aim of this Dictionary of Musical Terms to furnish an accurate and concise explanation of any technical word or phrase which the student is apt to meet with. The English vocabulary will be found practically exhaustive. Want of space forbade making the foreign vocabulary equally so; but the editor has endeavored to preserve a proper balance by giving any term, appearing in either German, French, or Italian, in each of those languages, thus maintaining a consistent polyglot character so far as necessary limitations permitted.

The scope of the work, which is rather a dictionary than a lexicon, rendered the editor's task more that of a compiler than of an original investigator. Most of the material here presented has been gleaned from numerous standard works of reference, such as those of Grove (Dictionary), Riemann (Musik-Lexikon), Gevaert (Instrumentation), Weitzmann (History of Pianoforte-Playing), Stainer and Barrett, Ambros (Geschichte der Musik), Paul (Handlexikon), Soullier (Dictionnaire), Helmholtz (Tonempfindungen), Niecks, The Century Dictionary, many English, German, French, and Italian periodicals and musical journals, etc., etc. Literal quotations are duly credited to their sources; condensations and adaptations, however, are, for obvious reasons, not so credited, and must, therefore, be included under this general acknowledgment. The information so gathered has been carefully sifted, and supplemented by the personal researches of over ten years.

Due credit should be given to Dr. William Mason for suggesting the Supplement, containing an "English-Italian Vocabulary for Composers", to which Dr Mason also contributed valued additions.

HINTS ON PRONUNCIATION.*

ITALIAN.

Vowels:

General rule : The vowels are very open, and never to be pronounced as impure vowels or diphthongs ; they are *long* in accented syllables which they terminate,—*short* in unaccented syllables, or in accented ones ending with a consonant.

a like *ah* or *ăh* (never *ă*) ; e.g. *amare* [pron. ăh-mah'-rĕh].

e " *ay* in bay (without the vanish *ĭ*); *ĕ* in bed ; *a* in bare (before *r*).

i " *ee* in beet ; *ĭ* in bit ; *i* before a vowel, like *y* (consonant).

o " *aw*, or *oh* (without the vanish *ŭ*) ; *ŏ* in *ŏ*pinion.

u " *oo* in boot ; *u* in bull.

Consonants:

General rule : Even the hard consonants are somewhat softer than in English ; the soft consonants are very delicate.

b, d, f, l, m, n, p, qu, s, t, v, as in English.

c like *k*, before *a*, *o*, *u*, or another consonant except *c*, as below.

c " *ch* in chair before *e* or *i ;* **cc** like *t-ch* before *e* or *i*.

g " *g* hard before *a*, *o*, *u*, or another consonant ; except before *l* (pronounce *gl* like *l-y* [consonant], e.g. *sugli*, [pron. sool'-yē]), and *n* (pronounce *gn* like *ñ* in cañon [kan'-yon]).

g " *z* in azure (or a very soft *j*) before *e* or *i*.

h is mute.

j like *y* in you.

r, pronounce with a roll (tip of tongue against hard palate).

Where a doubled consonant occurs, the first syllable is dwelt upon ; e.g. in *ecco* [pronounce ek' -ko, not ek' - o]. — Accented syllables take a less explosive stress than in English, being prolonged and dwelt upon rather than forcibly marked.

sc like *sh*, before *e* and *i*.

z " *ds* (very soft *ts*).

GERMAN.

Vowels:

The simple vowels as in Italian ; **y** like German *i* or *ü*.

Modified vowels:

ä like *a* in bare, but broader ; *ĕ* in bed.

ö has no English equivalent ; long *ö* can be pronounced by forming the lips to say *oh*, and then saying *ā* (as in bay) with the lips in the first position ; short *ö*, by saying *ĕ* (as in bed) instead of *ā*. [N.B.—Long *ö* is the French *eu* (in *jeu*)].

ü has no English equivalent ; pronounce long *ü* by forming the lips to say *oo* (as in boot), and then saying *ee* (beet) with the lips in the first position ; short *ü*, by saying *ĭ* (as in bit) instead of *ee*. [N.B.—Long *ü* is the French *u*.]

Diphthongs:

ai and **ei** like long *ī* in bite.

ae like *ä*.

au " *ow* in brow.

eu and **äu** like *oi* (more exactly *ah'-ü*, closely drawn together).

Consonants :

f, h, k, l, m, n, p, t, as in English.

b and **d**, beginning a word or syllable, as in English ; ending a word or syllable, like *p* and *t* respectively.

c like *k* before *a*, *o*, and *u ;* like *ts* before *e*, *i*, and *ä*.

g usually hard, but like *z* in azure in words from the French and Italian in which *g* is so sounded ; —*ang*, *eng*, *ing*, *ong* and *ung* terminate, at the end of a word, with a *k*-sound (e.g. *Bĕ'-bung*ᵏ).

* These "hints" are offered as an aid for tyros, and not in the least as an exhaustive set of rules.

j like *y* (consonant).
qu " *kv.*
r either with a roll, or a harsh breathing.
s beginning a word or syllable, and before a vowel, like *z* (soft); ending a word or syllable, like sharp *s ;* before *t* and *p*, beginning a word, usually like *sh* (e.g. *stumm*, pron. shtŭm [*u* as in bull]) ; otherwise as in English.
v like *f.*
w " *v* (but softer, between *v* and *w*).
x " *ks* (also when beginning a word).
z " *ts.*

Compound consonants :
ch is a sibillant without an English equivalent ; when beginning a syllable, or after *e, i, ä, ö, ü, ai, ei, ae, eu*, and *äu*, it is *soft* (set the tongue as if to pronounce *d*, and breathe an *h* through it ; e.g. *Strich*, pron. shtrĭd-h); after *a, o, u*, and *au*, it ĭs *hard* (a guttural *h*).
chs like *x.*
sch " *sh.*
sp and **st**, see *s*, above.
th like *t.*
Accented syllables have a forcible stress, as in English. In compound words there is always a secondary accent("), sometimes a tertiary one("'), depending on the number of separate words entering into the composition of the compound word ; e.g. *Zwi'schen-akts"'musik"*, *Bo'genham"merkla-vier"'*. The principal accent is regularly marked (') in this work.

FRENCH.

Vowels :
a as in Italian, but shorter, often approaching English *ă.*
â like *ah.*
e " *u* in but ; *e*-final is almost silent in polysyllabic words.
é " *ay* in bay.
è " *e* in there.
ê " German *ä*, and always long.

i or **î** like *ee* in beet ; short *i* as in English.
o as in Italian.
u like the German *ü.*

Diphthongs :
ai like *ai* in fair; but before *l*-final, or *ll*, is pronounced as a diphthong (*ah'-ee*, drawn closely together).
aî and **ei** like *é.*
eu, eû and **œu** like German *ö.*
oi like *oh-ăh'* (drawn closely together).
ou and **où** like *oo* in boot.
eau like *ō* long, without the vanish *u.*
Modified by a following *n, m, nd, nt* or *mt* at the end of a syllable, the vowels and diphthongs are nasal (exception,—verbal ending of 3rd pers. plural).

Consonants as in English, with the following exceptions :
c like *s* in song before *e, é, è, ê,* and *i.*
ch " *sh.*
g " *z* in azure before *e, é, è, ê,* and *i.*
gn as in Italian.
h is mute ; the treatment of initial *h* cannot be explained here.
j like *z* in azure.
ll after *i* is usually sounded like English *y* (consonant), and frequently prolongs the *i* (*ee*) ; e.g. *travailler* [träh-väh-yay'], *tranquille* [trähngkee'ʸ].
n nasal, see above ; otherwise as in English. [The nasal effect is accurately obtained by sounding *n* (or *m*) *together with* (instead of *after*) the preceding vowel ; but the sound of *e* is changed to äh, *i* to *ă* (in bat), and *u* to *eu*.]
m, nasal in certain situations.
r with a roll.
s-final is silent.
t-final is silent.
er, et, es, est, ez, as final syllables, are pronounced like *é.*

Accentuation. The strong English stress on some one syllable of a polysyllabic word is wanting in French ; the general rule is *slightly* to accent the *last syllable.*

A

DICTIONARY

OF

MUSICAL TERMS.

A—ABBREVIATIONS.

A.

A. 1. (Ger. *A;* Fr. and It. *la.*) The sixth tone in the typical diatonic scale of *C*-major. The tone a^1 (see *Pitch, absolute*) is that sounded by the oboe or other fixed-tone instr. (pfte., organ) to give the pitch for the other instr.s of the orchestra or military band.—2. In mus. theory, capital *A* often designates the *A*-major triad, small *a* the *a*-minor triad.—3. In scores, the capitals, or doubled letters (A a—Z z), are often set at the head of main divisions or at any critical point to facilitate repetition at rehearsal —4. As an Italian (or French) preposition, *a* (or *à*) signifies to, at, for, by, in, etc.—5. A♯, a♭, a♮, see *Sharp, Flat, Natural.*—6. At the head of Gregorian antiphones, etc., *A* means that the first mode is to be employed.—7. In this Dictionary, an –*a* appended to an Italian word signifies, that in the feminine form *a* is substituted for the masculine termination *o*.

Ab (Ger.) Off (organ-music).

Ab'acus harmon'icus (Lat.) 1. A diagram of the notes, with their names.—2. The structure and disposition of the digitals and pedals of a mus. instr.

Abandon (Fr.) Unrestrained abandonment to natural emotion ; *avec a.*, same as *con abbandono.*

Abbandonatamen'te { (It.) In an im
Abbando'no, con } passioned style as if carried away by emotion ;—subordi nation of rhythm and tempo tc expres sion.

Abbassamen'to (It., abbr. *abb.*) " Lowering " ; indicates in pfte.-playing that one hand is to play below the other ; opp. to *alzamen'to...A. di ma'no*, sinking of the hand in beating time ; *A. di vo'ce*, diminution (in volume) of the voice.

Abbattimen'to (It.) Falling of the hand in beating time ; the down-beat.

Abbellimen'to } (It.) Embellishment,
Abbellitu'ra } ornament, grace ; from *abbelli're*, to embellish.

Ab'betont (Ger.) With *final* accent.

Abbreviation. (Ger. *Abbreviatur', Ab'-kürzung;* Fr. *abréviation;* It. *abbreviatu'ra.*) [In this Dictionary, any keyword recurring in the article which it heads will be represented by its initial letter or letters ; for instance, *Abbassamento* above by *A*. Also, various other abbreviations are used, such as *abbr.* for abbreviation, *instr.* for instrument, *mus.* for musical, *pfte.* for pianoforte, *opp.* for opposed, etc.]

1. The commonest abbreviations **of** musical technical terms are the following :

A. See A.
Abb. Abbassamento
Accel. } Accelerando
Accel°. }
Acc. }
Accom. } Accompaniment
Accomp. }
Accres. Accrescendo
Adg°. or Ad°. Adagio
Ad lib. Ad libitum
Aevia Alleluia
Affett. Affettuoso
Affrett. Affrettando
Ag°. or Agit°. Agitato
All°. Allegro

Allgtt° } Allegretto
Alltt° }
All'ott. } All'ottava
All'8va }
Al seg. Al segno
Alz. Alzamento
Andⁿ°. Andantino
And^te. Andante
Anim°. Animato
Arc. Coll'arco, or Arcato.
Ard. Ardito
Arp°. Arpeggio
A t. }
A tem. } A tempo
A temp. }

Aug. By augmentation

B. See B.
B. C. Basso continuo
B. G. Basso generale, or Bassus generalis
Bl. Blasinstrumente
Br. Bratschen
Brill. Brillante

C. See C.
C. a. Coll'arco
Cad. Cadenza
Cah. Cahier
Cal. Calando

Calm. Calmato
Cant. Canto
Cantab. Cantabile
C. b. Contrabasso
C. B. Col basso
Cb. Contrabässe
C. D. Colla destra
'Cello. Violoncello
Cemb. Cembalo
Ch. Choir-organ
Chal. Chalumeau
C. Iº. Canto primo
C. L. Col legno
Clar. Clarinet
Clarº. Clarino
Clartto. Clarinetto
Col c. Col canto
Coll' ott. } Coll'ottava
C. 8va }
Con espr. Con espressione
Cont. Contano
Cor. Cornet or Corno
Co. So. Come sopra
C. P. Colla parte
Cres. } Crescendo
Cresc. }
C. S. Colla sinistra
C. S., or Co. So. Come sopra
Cto. Concerto
C. voc. Colla voce

D. See D.
Dal S. Dal segno
D. C. Da capo
Dec. Decani
Decresc. Decrescendo
Delic. Delicatamente
Dest. Destra
Diap. Diapason(s)
Dim. By diminution, or Diminuendo
Div. Divisi
Dol. Dolce
Dolcis. Dolcissimo
Dopp. Ped. Doppio pedale
D. S. Dal segno

Energ. Energicamente
Espr., or Espress. Espressivo
Exp., or Expr. Orgue expressif (b)

F. See F.
f, or for. Forte
Fag. Fagotto
Falset. Falsetto
ff, or fff Fortissimo
Fl. Flauto
Flag. Flageolet
F. O. } Full organ
F. Org. }
fp Forte piano
Fz., or Forz. Forzando

G. See G.
Ged. Gedämpft
G. O. } Great organ
G. Org. } Grand-orgue
Grand. Grandioso
Graz. Grazioso
Gt. Great organ

Hauptw. Hauptwerk
Haut. Hautboy
H. C. Haute-contre
Hlzbl., or Hzbl. Holzbläser

Hptw., or H. W. Hauptwerk
Hr., or Hrn. Hörner

Intro. Introduction
Inv. Inversion

K. F. Kleine Flöte

L. See L.
Leg. Legato
Legg. Leggero, Leggiero
L. H. Left hand, linke Hand
Lo. Loco
Luo. Luogo
Lusing. Lusingando

M. See M.
Maestº. Maestoso
Magg. Maggiore
Man. Manual
Man. 1+2. Couple Ch. to Gt.
Manc. Mancando
Marc. Marcato
M. D. Mano destra, or main droite
Men. Meno
Mez. Mezzo
mf Mezzo forte
mfz Mezzo forzando
M. G. Main gauche
M. M. Maelzel's metronome
Mod., or Modtº. Moderato
Mor. Morendo
mp Mezzo piano
M.S. Manuscript, or Mano sinistra
Mus. B., or Mus. Bac. Musicæ baccalaureus
Mus. D., or Mus. Doc. Musicæ doctor
M. V. Mezza voce

Ob. Oboe
Obbl. Obbligato
Oberst. Oberstimme
Oberw., or Obw. Oberwerk
Oh. Ped. Ohne Pedal
O. M. Obermanual
Op. Opus
Opp. Oppure
Org. Organ
Ott., Ova., or 8va Ottava
O. W. Oberwerk

P. See P.
Ped. Pedal
Perd. Perdendosi
pf più forte
P. F. } Pianoforte
Pfte. }
Piang. Piangendo
Pianiss. Pianissimo
Pizz. Pizzicato
pmo., pp, ppp, pppp Pianissimo
Prin. Principal

Raddol. Raddolcendo
Rall. Rallentando
Recit. Recitative
rf, rfz, rinf. Rinforzando
R. H. Right hand, or rechte Hand
Rip. Ripieno
Ritard. Ritardando
Rit., Riten. Ritenuto

S. See S.
Salic. Salicional
Scherz. Scherzando
Seg. Segue
Sem. or Semp. Sempre
sf, sfz, sff Sforzando
Sim. Simile
Sin. Sinistra
Sinf. Sinfonia
S. int. Senza interruzione
Smorz. Smorzando
Sos., Sost. Sostenuto
Sp. Spitze
S. P. Senza pedale
Spir. Spirituoso
S. S., or S. Sord. Senza sordini
S. T. Senza tempo
Stacc. Staccato.
St. D., or St. Diap. Stopped diapason
Stent. Stentando
Str. Streichinstrumente
String. Stringendo
Sw. Swell-organ
Sym. Symphony

T. See T.
T. C. Tre corde
Temp. Tempo
Tempo I. Tempo primo
Ten. Tenuto
Timb. Timbales
Timp. } Timpani
Tp. }
T. P. Tempo primo
Tr. Trillo, Trumpet
Tratt. Trattenuto
Trem. Tremolando, Tremulant
Tromb. Trombe, Tromboni
Tromp. Trompete
T. S. Tasto solo

U. C. Una corda
Unis. Unisono

V. See V.
Va. Viola
Var. Variation
Vc., Vcllo., Vllo. Violoncello
Viol., Vl., Vno. Violino
Viv. Vivace
V. S. Volti subito
Vv., Vni. Violini

Abbreviations by Numerals.

1. or I. Prima volta
2. or II. Seconda volta
① ② etc. See Harmonium-music
Man. 1. (2.) Great (Choir-)organ

2-time } or } Duple time
3-time } } Triple time

4tette. Quartette
5tette. Quintette
Also compare art. Numerals.
For single figures over groups of notes, compare (2) Couplet, (3) Triplet, (4) Quadruplet, (5) Quintuplet, (6) Sextuplet, (7) Septuplet, (8) Octuplet, (9) Nonuplet, (10) Decuplet, etc.

2. Abbreviations in manuscript or printed music by means of conventional **signs**.

(A) Of **rests**: 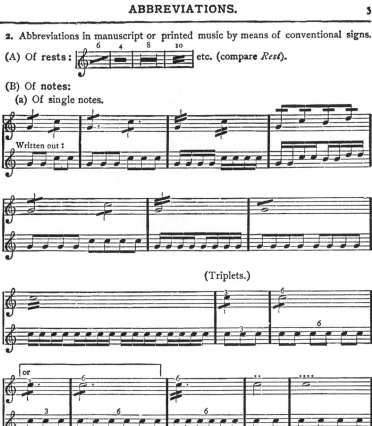 etc. (compare *Rest*).

(B) Of **notes**:
   (a) Of single notes.

(Triplets.)

(b) Of doubled notes (see *Tremolo*). **[Note to** (b). When the abbreviation consists of two *consecutive* notes, the sum of the notes in the solution is equal to only *one* of them, unless specially marked.]

(c) Of figures and phrases.

(Also compare *Arpeggio, Bis, Repeat, Segue, Simile, Ter, Tremolo.*)

A B C, musika′lisches (Ger., "musical A b c.") See *Alphabetical notation.* ...*A-b-c-dieren*, to use, in singing exercises, the letter-names of the notes.

A′bendglocke (Ger.) Evening bell, curfew.—*A′bendlied*, evening song.

A′benteuerlich (Ger., "Adventurous.") Strange, singular, uncouth; an epithet sometimes applied to music having no settled or recognized form, especially to that of the neo-German school.

Ab′fallen (Ger.) To deteriorate; said of any part of the compass of an instr. or voice showing a falling-off, in quality or volume of tone, as compared with other parts.

Ab′gebrochene Kadenz′ (Ger.) See *Kadenz.*

Ab'geleitet (Ger.) Derived, derivative.

Ab'gesang (Ger) See *Strophe*.

Ab'gestossen (Ger.) Detached, staccato.

Ab'gleiten (Ger.) To slip or slide any finger, on the keyboard, from a black digital to the next white one.

Ab'hub, abub. Hebrew wind-instr. resembling the cornet.

Ab ini'tio (Lat) Same as *Da capo*.

Ab'kürzung (Ger.) Abbreviation.

Ab'leiten (Ger.) To derive from.

Ab'lösen (Ger.) To change fingers quietly on a digital of the pfte. or organ.

Ab'nehmen, Ab'nehmung (Ger.) Diminuendo.

Abrégés (Fr.) Trackers.

Ab'reichen (Ger.) In violin-playing, to take a tone by extending the little finger (see *Extension*), or by drawing back the forefinger.

Ab'reissung (Ger.) See *Abruptio*.

Abrup'tio (Lat. " a breaking-off.") The sudden stopping of a melody before reaching the actual close, it being continued after a pause.

Ab'satz (Ger.) 1. A thematically or rhythmically well-defined division of a piece or movement. — 2. A melodic phrase.

Ab'schwellen (Ger.) Decrescendo.

Ab'setzen (Ger., "to lift from".) To strike two digitals in succession with the same finger, to lift ; e.g.

Absolute Music. In contradistinction to " program-music," which is supposed or intended to express (depict, portray) something tangible, absolute music subsists in and for itself, without being in any way derived from concrete conditions or objects. Program - music seeks its inspiration in poetry, in art, in living realities ; absolute music is itself the inspiration, awakening emotion through emotion without the interposition of or definite interpretation by the intellect, infecting and influencing the soul directly...*Absolute Pitch*, see *Pitch*.

Ab'stammen (Ger.) To be derived from.

Ab'stand (Ger.) See *Tonabstand*.

Ab'stimmen (Ger.) 1. To tune.—2. To lower the pitch (of instr.s)...*Ab'stimmend, Ab'stimmig*, discordant, dissonant.

Ab'stossen (Ger.) To play staccato, to detach...*Ab'stosszeichen*, staccato-mark.

Abstrak'ten (Ger.) Trackers.

Ab'stufung (Ger., "graduation.") The shading of a passage or piece, either emotionally or dynamically.

Abun'dans (Lat.) Superfluous.

Ab'wechseln (Ger.) To alternate ; *mit ab'wechselnden Manua'len*, with alternating manuals.

Ab'weichung (Ger.) A variant ; a different reading or notation ; specifically, the measure or measures marked *secunda volta* in a repeat.

Ab'ziehen (Ger.) 1. See *Abgleiten*.—2. To unstring (in the sense of taking off worn-out strings) a violin, harp, etc.

Ab'zug (Ger.) 1. See *Abgleiten*.—2. The lifting of the fingers in playing wind-instr.s, or of the bow from the strings.

Acathis'tus (Gk.) In the Gk. Church, a long canon or hymn in praise of the Virgin, sung by all standing.

Accarezze'vole } (It.) Caressful-
Accarezzevolmen'te } ly, caressingly, coaxingly.

Acceleran'do (It.) " Accelerating," gradually growing faster...*Accelera'to*, accelerated, livelier.

Accent. (Ger. *Accent'*, *Beto'nung ;* Fr. *accent ;* It. *accen'to*.) 1. The natural stress or emphasis regularly recurring on certain tones in each measure, called the *grammatical, metrical*, or *regular* accent ; e.g. that on the first beat in every species of time

(*primary accent*), and on the third beat in triple or compound duple time

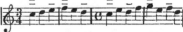

(*sub-accent*).—2. The monotony of the regular accent is varied by the *rhythmical* accent, which brings out more prominently the broader musical divisions of a composition by special emphasis at the entrance or culminating points of motives, themes, phrases, passages, sections, etc.; the *rhythmical a.* is nearly synonymous with the *pathetic* or *poetic a.*, as an aid in interpreting the meaning and making plain the construction of a work.—3. An irregular stress laid upon any tone or beat at the composer's pleasure, is the *rhetorical* or *æsthetic a.*, indicated either by a special sign (*sfz, fz,* >, ∧), or by an interruption of the natural rhythmical flow (syncopation), whereby the *natural a.* is thrown back to an otherwise less accented or non-accented beat.—4. See *Accentus.*—5. An obsolete harpsichord-grace resembling the appoggiatura ;

written :

played :

Accen'tor. The leading singer in a choir or vocal performance.

Accentuie'ren (Ger.) To accent...*Accentuier'ter Durch'gang,* a passing-note or -chord on a strong beat.

Accen'tus (Lat.) In the R. C. Church, that part of the service which is chanted or intoned at the altar by the officiating priest and his assistants ; opp. to *Concentus,* the part taken by the choir,

Accen'tus ecclesias'tici (Lat.) The musical inflections observed in intoning the gospels, epistles, etc., corresponding to a certain extent with the punctuation. There are 7 accents : (1) *accentus immuta'bilis,* the voice neither rising nor falling ; (2) *a. me'dius,* falling a third ; (3) *a. gra'vis,* falling a fourth ; (4) *a. acu'tus,* first falling a third, then rising to the reciting-note ; (5) *a. modera'tus,* first rising a second, then falling to the reciting-note ; (6) *a. interrogati'vus,* at a question, first falling a second, then rising to the reciting-note ; (7) *a. fina'lis,* falling at the end of a sentence by a fourth, by a diatonic passage through the intervening tones.

Accessis'ten (Ger.) Unpaid choir-singers, supernumeraries.

Accessory note. In a trill, the higher auxiliary.

Acciacca'to,-a (It.) Vehemently.

Acciaccatur' (Ger.) In organ-playing, the doubling by the left hand of the $\frac{6}{4}$ chord on the dominant, its resolution to the dominant chord being effected by the right hand alone.

Acciaccatu'ra (It.) 1. (Ger. *Zusam'menschlag;* Fr. *pincé étouffé.*) A grace on keyboard instr.s, the semitone below

a melody-note or chord-note being struck with the latter, but instantly released :

written :   played :

2. Same as short appoggiatura.—3 (in Ger. usage). Same as *Acciaccatur.*

Accident (Fr.) Accidental.

Accidental. (Ger. *zu'fälliges Verse'-tzungszeichen;* Fr. *accident,* or *signe accidentel;* It. *acciden'te.*) A chromatic sign not found in the signature, set before a note in the midst of a composition. (See *Chromatic Signs.*)

Accolade (Fr.) Brace.

Accompaniment. (Ger. *Beglei'tung;* Fr. *accompagnement;* It. *accompagnamen'to.*) The accessory part or parts attending the voices or instr.s bearing the principal part or parts in a musical composition. Its intention may be to enhance the general effect, or to steady the soloists either as regards rhythm or pitch. Either one or more instr.s, or a vocal chorus, may carry out an *acc.*—An *acc.* is *ad li'bitum* when the piece can be performed without it, and *obbliga'to* when of vital importance to the latter.—*Acc. of the scale,* the harmonies assigned to the successive tones of the ascending or descending diatonic scale.—*Additional accompaniments,* parts added to a composition by some other than its original author.

Accompanist. (Ger. *Beglei'ter;* Fr. *accompagnateur* m., *-trice* f.; It. *accompagnato're* m., *-tri'ce* f.) One who executes an accomp.

Accompany. (Ger. *beglei'ten;* Fr. *accompagner;* It. *accompagna're.*) To perform an accompaniment.

Accoppia'to (It., "coupled.") Tied... *Accoppiamen'to, pedale di,* see *Pedal, sustaining.*

Accord (Fr.) 1. A chord.—*A. à l'ouvert,* chord produced by sweeping only open strings...*A. fondamental,* or *naturel,* fundamental chord...*A. parfait* (or *triade harmonique*), common chord, triad...*A. plaqué,* a solid chord (not arpeggio'd)...*A. renversé,* inverted chord.—2. Tune (i.e. the state of being in tune)...*Être d'accord,* to be in tune. —3. *Accords* (pl., poetical). Strains, harmonies.—4. Accordatura.

Accordable (Fr.) Tunable, that may be tuned.

Accordamen'to (It.) Accordance; consonance.

Accord'ance. An English equivalent for *Accordatura;* used in GROVE, vol. IV, p. 187*b*, l.9–10, and foot-note.

Accordan'do (It.) Accordant, in tune, tuned together; applied also to comic scenes in which the tuning of an instr. or instr.s is imitated by the orchestra.

Accordant (Fr.) Consonant.

Accorda're (It.) To tune, tune together.

Accordato'io (It.) Tuning-key, tuning-hammer.

Accordatu'ra (It.; see *Accordance.*) The series of tones according to which a stringed instr. is tuned; thus g-d^1-a^1-e^2 is the *a.* of the violin.

Accorder (Fr.) To tune... *S'accorder*, to tune together, get the pitch (as an orchestra).

Accordeur (Fr.) 1. Tuner.—2. The monochord.—3. A small instr. containing 12 steel tuning-forks set on a sound-board and yielding the 12 tones of the equally tempered scale.

Accor'dion. (Ger. *Accor'deon*, *Akkor'dion*, *Zieh'harmonika;* Fr. *accordéon;* It. *accor'deon.*) A free-reed instr. invented by Damian, of Vienna, in 1829. The elongated body serves as a bellows, which can be drawn out or pushed together at will; the bellows is closed at either end by a keyboard, that for the right hand having a diatonic (or incomplete chromatic) scale, while that for the left has 2 or more keys for harmonic bass tones. There are two sets of reeds, one sounding when the bellows is opening, by suction, the other when it is closing. (Compare *Concertina.*)

Accor'do (It.) 1. A chord... *A. con'sono* (*dis'sono*), a consonant (dissonant) chord.—2. An instr. formerly used in Italy, resembling the bass viol, having from 12 to 15 strings, and played with a bow in such a way that several strings were caused to vibrate at once; employed where powerful harmonies were required. (Also called the *modern lyre*, and *Barbary lyre.*)

Accordoir (Fr.) Tuning-hammer, tuning-key; (org.) tuning-cone or -horn.

Accoupler (Fr.) To couple... *Tirant à a.*, coupler... *Accouplez*, "couple," (i.e. "draw coupler").

Accrescen'do (It.) Same as *Crescendo.*

Accrescimen'to (It.) Augmentation (of a fugal theme)... *Pun'to d'accr.*, dot of prolongation (♩.).

Accresciu'to (It.) Augmented.

Aceta'bulum. Latin name for an ancient Gk. instr., of percussion. The *acetabula* were earthen or metallic vessels struck with sticks, like a carillon, or clashed together, like cymbals.

Acht (Ger.) Eight... *Acht'füssig*, 8-foot ... *Acht'stimmig*, in or for 8 parts, 8-part.

Ach'tel, Ach'telnote (Ger.) An eighth-note... *Ach'telpause*, eighth-rest.

Ac'ocotl. A wind-instr. of the Mexican aborigines, consisting of a thin tube 8 or 10 feet long made of the dried stalk of the plant *acocotl*, and played by inhaling the air through it. (Also called *Clarin.*)

Acoustic color. The timbre (character or quality) of a mus. tone.

Acoustics. (Ger. *Aku'stik;* Fr. *acoustique;* It. *acu'stica.*) The science of the properties and relations of sounds. §1. *Musical acoustics*, the science of mus. tones, distinguishes between tones and noises. A tone of sustained and equal pitch is generated by regular and constant vibrations of the air, these being generated by similar vibrations in the tone-producing body; whereas a noise is caused by irregular and fluctuating vibrations. Briefly, "the sensation caused by a tone is produced by rapid periodic movements; that caused by a noise, by imperiodic movements" (HELMHOLTZ). But a sonorous or tone-producing body vibrates not only as a whole, but in its various fractional parts as well. Take a pfte.-string, for instance; when struck by the hammer it vibrates, not simply as a whole in its entire length, but each half, each $\frac{1}{3}$, $\frac{1}{4}$, $\frac{1}{5}$ etc., of the string vibrates by itself, as it were (comp. *Node*), and produces a tone of a pitch corresponding to its own length; the *C*-string thus produces, besides the fundamental tone or generator, *C*, its octave *c* ($\frac{1}{2}$ of string), its twelfth *g* ($\frac{1}{3}$), fifteenth c^1 ($\frac{1}{4}$), seventeenth e^1 ($\frac{1}{5}$), nineteenth g^1 ($\frac{1}{6}$), etc. The points of rest in the string (or other tone-producing body) where such vibrating portions meet, are called *nodes*, or *nodal points ;* the tones produced by the vibrating divisions are called *harmonics*, or *overtones ;* and the entire series, including the generator, are called *partial tones*, being considered parts of the composite tone (clang) named after the generator. The series of partial tones may be given in notes as follows, numbered consecutively from *C* upward ·

1 ◠ 2 3 4 ◡ 5 6 7 8   9 10 11 12 13 14 15 16

C: I ——V———III (= major triad).

(Notes marked * are only approximately correct.)

The intensity of the harmonics ordinarily decreases rapidly as their pitch becomes higher.

§2. The harmonics are important in many ways. (*a*) Their presence in varying degrees of intensity produces the timbre peculiar to the several instr.s; thus the tone of the stopped diapason (organ), in which they are weak, is soft and " hollow " ; the tone of an old violin, in which the lower harmonics are well-developed and evenly balanced, is mellow, round, and sonorous; that of the trumpet, in which the high dissonant harmonics also make themselves felt, is ringing, "metallic," and brilliant. (Compare *Scale.*).—(*b*) On bowed instr.s they yield an additional and highly characteristic register (see *Harmonic* 2).—(*c*) On wind-instr.s, from which they are obtained by varying the intensity and direction of the air-current, they are indispensable for extending and completing the natural scale ; thus the bugle and French horn, which yield but one fundamental tone (without keys or valves), depend entirely on the harmonics for the production of their scale ; the flute depends upon overblowing, which produces the harmonics of its tube, for its upper register ; etc., etc.—(*d*) Musical theory owes highly important discoveries to the investigation of the harmonics, of which discoveries practical music in turn reaps the benefit (improved construction of many instr.s). (Comp. *Scale.*)

§3. By sounding two tones together, various phenomena are produced. (*a*) 2 tones of nearly the same pitch produce *beats*. E. g. if the one makes 442 vibrations per second and the other 440, the difference, 2, represents the number of *beats* per second, a beat being the pulsation or throb caused by the coincidence of, and consequent momentary increase of the intensity in, the soundwaves of the two tones ; this coincidence recurring regularly at every 221st vibration of the first tone and 220th vibration of the second.—(*b*) As soon as the number of beats per second amounts to about 32, the ear no longer distinguishes them as separate throbs, and they unite to form a very low tone (32 v. = C_2), called a *combinational, summational,* or *resultant tone;* in fact, the various combinations of interfering vibrations produce, in their different combination, a series of harmonics, the lowest and chief among which is always the generator of the series to which the two original tones belong. Thus, according to Tartini, the interval g-e^1 produces the following series of resultant tones :

1 ◠ 2   4 ◡ 6   7   8 etc.

—(*c*) In the series of partials given in §1, those belonging to the major scale of the generator *C* are written as half-notes ; the consonance of the **major triad** is derivable from and based upon the principal partial tones. In like manner, the consonance of the **minor triad** is derived from a *reverse* series of *lower partials*, the existence of which is proved by the phenomena of sympathetic vibration and of the resultant tones. In this series of *lower* partials (undertones),

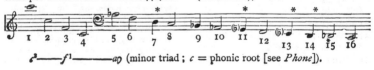

1 2 3 4 5 6 7 8 9 10 11 12 13 14 15 16

c^3——f^1———*a͡p* (minor triad ; *c* = phonic root [see *Phone*]).

the numerals also represent the relative length of the strings necessary to yield the several tones ; while in the series of higher partials (overtones) the string-lengths are represented by the simple fractions formed by the numerals.—(*d*) From the relative number and importance (intensity) of the first 6 partials in either series, it follows, that the only *consonant chords* are the *major* and *minor triads*, and that the only *consonant intervals* are such as are derived from these chords or their inversions ; the addition of any further tone, either found in or foreign to the series of partials, produces a *dissonance*.

Act. (Ger. *Akt, Auf'zug ;* Fr. *acte ;* It. *at'to.*) One of the principal divisions of a dramatical performance.

Acte de cadence (Fr.) A progression in one of the parts, particularly the bass, which forces the others to join either in forming a cadence, or in avoiding one apparently imminent.

Actin'ophone. An apparatus for the production of sound by actinic rays.

Action. (Ger. *Mecha'nik ;* Fr. *méca-nique ;* It. *mecca'nica.*) In keyboard instr.s, the mechanism directly actuated by the player's finger, or set in motion by the organ-pedals.—In the harp, the *action* (pedals) does not directly produce the sound, but effects a change of key by shortening the strings, whereby chromatic alterations of a semitone or a whole tone result. (See *Pianoforte, Organ.*)

Act-tune. Music performed between the acts of a drama ; an entr'acte.

Acu'ta (Lat., " sharp, shrill.") In the organ, a mixture-stop having 3 to 5 ranks of from 1⅗ to 1 foot, usually including a Third ; its compass is higher than that of the ordinary Mixture.

Acu'tæ cla'ves (Lat.; also *acuta loca, acutæ voces.*) Literally, acute keys (pitch, voices) ; the tones from *a* to *g*[1] inclusive ; so termed by Guido d'Arezzo.

Acute. (Ger. *scharf, hoch ;* Fr. *aigu ;* It. *acu'to.*) High in pitch, sharp, shrill ; said of tones ; opp. to *grave.*

Acutez'za (It.) Acuteness ; sharpness (of pitch).

Acu'tus (Lat.) See *Accentus eccl.*, 4.

Adagiet'to (It.) 1. A movement slightly faster than adagio.—2. A short Adagio.

Ada'gio (It., " slow, leisurely.") A slow

movement (comp. *Tempo-marks*)...*A. assa'i, A. mol'to,* very slow...*A. non tan' to, non molto,* not too slow...*Adagio adagio,* very slow...Superlative *adagissimo.*

Adaptation. Same as *Arrangement.*

Ada'sio (It.) Same as *Adagio.*

Added sixth. See *Sixth.*

Addita'to (It.) Provided with a fingering, fingered.

Addition. Obsolete term for the dot (♩.).

Additional accompaniments. See *Accompaniment...Additional keys,* those above *f*[3]

Addolora'to (It.) Plaintive ; in a style expressive of grief.

Adi'aphon. See *Ga'belklavier.*

Adi'aphonon. A keyboard instr. invented by Schuster of Vienna in 1820.

Adira'to (It.) Angry, wrathful.

Ad'junct. Closely related, as one key or scale to another...*A. note,* an auxiliary note, unaccented, and unessential to the harmony.

Ad'juvant. The cantor's assistant, assistant teacher.

A'dler (Ger.) An obsolete organ-stop.

Ad li'bitum (Lat., " at pleasure," " at will.") A direction signifying (1) that the performer is free in choice of expression or tempo ; (2) that any vocal or instrumental part so marked is not absolutely essential to a complete performance of a piece...*Caden'za ad lib.* thus means, that a given cadenza may be performed or not, or another substituted, at the executant's discretion.

Ad lon'gam (Lat., " with the long.") A term applied to certain ancient church-music written entirely in equal notes, generally the longest in use.

Adornamen'to (It.) A grace.

Adquis'ta or **adsum'ta** (**vox**) (Lat., " the added tone.") The lowest tone of the scale, the *Proslambanom'enos.*

Æ'erophon. See *Harmonium.*

Æolharmon'ica. See *Seraphine.*

Æolian attachment. An attachment to a pfte. for directing a current of air against the strings, reinforcing their vibration and thus prolonging and sustaining the tones...*Æolian harp* or *lyre.* (Ger. *Ä'olsharfe, Wind'-, Wet'-*

ter- or *Gei'sterharfe ;* Fr. *harpe éoli-enne, harpe d'Éole ;* It. *ar'pa d'E'olo.*) A stringed instr. sounded by the wind. It consists of a narrow, oblong wooden resonance-box, across the low bridges at either end of which are stretched gut strings in any desired number and of different thickness and tension, but all producing the same fundamental tone. When adjusted in an appropriate aperture, like a window through which the air passes freely, the latter causes the strings to vibrate and to produce, if the tension be properly adjusted (rather slack than otherwise), full chords composed of the harmonics of the fundamental tone common to all the strings ; and rising, according to the force of the wind, from pure, dreamy, deliciously vague harmonies to a plaintive wail or a thrilling *forte.*...*Æolian mode,* see *Greek music*...*Æolian piano,* see *Äolsklavier.*

Æolina. 1. A small instr. consisting of a graduated series of free reeds set in a metal plate and blown by the mouth ; invented by the Messrs. Wheatstone in 1829. As the first practical attempt to use free reeds in this way, it may be regarded as the precursor of the accordion and melodion. The Germans, however, claim the invention for Eschenbach, of Hamburg, about 1800.—2. An organ-stop constructed on the same principle as the above, without (or with very short) pipe-bodies, and of very soft tone.

Æolo'dicon. A keyboard instr. embodying the principle of the *Æolina,* and the direct precursor of the harmonium. (Also *Æolodion, Klaväoli'ne,* etc.)...A further modification was the *Æolomelo'dicon,* invented by Prof. Hoffmann of Warsaw about 1825, in which short brass tubes were added to the reeds.

Æolopan'talon. An Æolomelodicon combined with a pfte., constructed about 1830 by Dlugosz of Warsaw.

Aequal' (Ger.) Formerly, an independent 8-foot organ-stop (*Aequal'stimme*) ; still used as prefix to names of organ-stops, indicating that they belong to the standard 8-foot registers; as *Aequal'-prinzipal,* etc.

Æquiso'nus (Lat.; Ger. *äquison'.*) Unison (of either primes or octaves).

Æquiva'gans (Lat.) Denotes simultan

eous syncopation, or "deviation from the natural order " of the measure, in all the parts.

AEVIA. A frequent abbr. of *Alleluia* in MS. music of the middle ages.

Affa'bile (It.) Sweetly and gracefully gently.

Affanna'to (It.) Uneasily, distressfully

Affannosamen'te (It.) Anxiously, restlessly...*Affanno'so,* anxious, restless.

Affet'to (It.) Emotion, passion, tenderness...*Con a.,* or *affettuosamen'te, affettuo'so,* with emotion or feeling, very expressively. (Compare *Innig.*)

Affezio'ne, con (It.) In a style expressive of tender emotion.

Affilar' (or **filar'**) **il tuo'no** (It.) In the Italian school of singing, to produce a long-sustained and uniform tone ; nearly the same as *metter la voce, messa di voce,* except that with these a *crescendo* or *decrescendo* is usually to be combined.

Affinité (Fr.) Affinity, relationship.

Afflit'to (It.) Melancholy, sad...*Afflizio'ne, con,* sorrowfully, mournfully.

Affrettan'do (It.) Hurrying (*stringendo*)...*Affretto'so,* hurried (*più mosso*).

After-beat. (From Ger. *Nach'schlag;* Fr. *note de complément, terminaison.*) An ending added to a trill, comprising 2 notes, the lower auxiliary and the main note ; compare *Trill.*

After-note. 1. Occasional for *unaccented appoggiatura.*—2. The unaccented note of a pair.

After-striking. (Ger. *Nach'schlagen.*) The reverse of anticipation by the bass ; e.g.

(Compare *Anticipation.*)

Agen'de (Ger., from Lat. *agen'da.*) Breviary, more especially of the Ger. Reformed Church, containing in regular order the formularies, prayers, responses, collects, etc., employed in religious exercises.

Age'vole (It.) Easy, light...*Agevolez'za, con,* easily, lightly.

Aggiustatamen'te (It.) Strictly in time

Aggraver la fugue (Fr.) To augment the theme of a fugue.

Agiatamen'te (It.) Easily, indolently.

Agilità' (It.)) Agility, sprightliness, vi-
Agilité (Fr.)) vacity; *con a.*, in a light and lively style.

Agilmen'te (It.) Nimbly, lightly, vivaciously.

Agitamen'to (It.) Agitation...*Agitatamen'te, con agitazio'ne*, excitedly, agitatedly...*Agita'to*, agitated ; *a. con passio'ne*, passionately agitated...*Agitazio'ne*, agitation.

Ag'nus De'i (Lat., "Lamb of God.") Closing movement of the mus. Mass.

Ago'ge (Gk.) The order, with reference to pitch, in which the tones of a melody succeed each other...*A. rhyth'mica*, their succession with reference to accent and rhythm ; tempo.

Ago'gik (Ger.) Theory of the *tempo rubato*...*Ago'gisch*, relating to such deviations from the tempo...*Ago'gischer Accent'* (RIEMANN), a sign (∧)over a note indicating the slight prolongation of its value required, in certain rhythms, to mark the culminating point of the measure-motive.

Agraffe'. In the pfte., a small metallic support of the string, between bridge and pin, serving to check vibration in that part.

Agrémens (Fr., pl.) Harpsichord-graces.

Aigu, aiguë (Fr.) Acute ; also used substantively, e. g. *passer de l'aigu au grave.*

Air. (Ger. *Melodie', Wei'se, Sing'weise ;* Fr. *air, mélodie ;* It. *a'ria.*) 1. A rhythmical melodious series of single tones in a metrical (symmetrical) grouping easily recognizable by the ear ; a tune or melody.—2. The highest part in a harmonized composition...*National air*, a melody become thoroughly popular through long usage and peculiar fitness, recognized as a national emblem, and performed at public festivals, etc.

Air (Fr.) Air, melody, tune ; also song, as *Airs à boire*, drinking-songs...Also, instrumental melody, as *air de violon, de flûte ; air de ballet, de danse*, etc... Also, aria ; *air détaché*, any single aria taken from an opera.

A'ïs (Ger.) A♯.—*A'ïsis*, A×.

Ajouté,-e (Fr.) Added. (See *Ligne, Sixte.*)...*Ajoutez*, "add" (organ-mus.) ; abbr. *ajout.*

Ajuster (Fr.) See *Accorder.*

Akkord' (Ger.) 1. A chord...*Akkord'-passage*, arpeggio...*Akkord'zither*, the autoharp.—2. A set of several instr.s of one family, but different in size, as made from the 15th to the 18th century (comp. Engl. *chest* or *consort* of viols). (Also *Stimm'werk.*)

Akkor'dieren (Ger.) 1. To tune an instr.,with reference to the harmony of its principal chords.—2. To get the pitch (said of the orchestra).

Akroama'tisch (Ger.) Pleasing to the ear ; said of music depending more upon outward effect than on depth.

Akt (Ger.) Act.

Aku'stik (Ger.) Acoustics ; *aku'stisch*, acoustic.

Al (It.) To the, up to the, at the, in the, etc...*ppp al* (or *alla*) *fine*, pianissimo to the end

Alber'tischer Bass (Ger.) Alberti bass. (See *Bass*.)

Alcu'no (It.) Some, certain.

Alexandre organ. See *American organ.*

Al'iquot (Lat.) Forming an exact measure of something ; a factor, or even divisor...*A'liquotflügel* (Ger.) A grand piano, invented by Julius Blüthner of Leipzig, the tone of which is reinforced and enriched by an additional sympathetic string stretched over, and tuned in the higher octave to, each unison. These added strings are not struck by the hammers, and are called *A'liquotsaiten*...*A'liquottheorie*, theory of overtones produced by the vibration of strings or of wind-instr.s. Such overtones or harmonics are called *A'liquottöne.*

All', al'la (It.) To the, at the, in the ; in the style of.

Allabre've (Ger.) See *Alla breve*, under *Breve*...*Allabre'vetakt*, alla breve time.

Allargan'do (It.) Same as *Largando.*

Allegramen'te (It.) Nimbly, lightly, vivaciously.

Allegretti'no (It.) A short Allegretto ; also, a movement slower than allegretto.

Allegret'to (It., abbr. *all⁰.*) Dimin.

of allegro; moderately fast, lively; faster than *andante*, slower than *allegro*.

Allegrez'za (It.) Liveliness, vivacity.

Allegris'simo (It.) Superl. of allegro; extremely rapid, as quick as possible; =*presto assai.*

Alle'gro (It., abbr. *all°.*) Lively, brisk, rapid. Used substantively to designate any rapid movement slower than presto...*A. assa'i, a. di mol'to*, very fast (usually faster than the foregoing movement)...*A. di bravu'ra*, a technically difficult piece or passage to be executed swiftly and boldly...*A. giu'sto*, a movement the rapidity of which is conformed to the subject...*A. risolu'to*, rapidly and energetically; etc., etc.

Allein' (Ger.) Alone.

Allelu'ia (Hebr.) Lit. "Praise ye the Lord," an exclamation closing various Psalms, or introduced in their midst. Taken, by the early Christian Church, from the ancient Hebrew ritual, it developed into the long jubilations (see *Jubilatio*) of the early middle ages (on the vowels AEVIA), to the melodies of which were set, after the adoption of the *cantus planus*, special words. (Also, *Hallelu'jah*.)

Allemande (Fr.; It. *alleman'da*.) 1. A Ger. dance in 3-4 time, like the *Ländler.*—2. A lively Ger. dance in 2-4 time.—3. A movement in the Suite, either the first or immediately following the prelude, in 4-4 time and moderate tempo (*andantino*), commencing with a short note in the *auf'takt.*—4. A figure in dancing.

Allentamen'to (It.) Same as *Rallentando.* (Also *allentan'do, allenta'to*.)

Al'le Sai'ten (Ger.) Same as *Tutte corde.*

All'gemeiner Bass (Ger.) Thorough-bass. (Now *General'bass*.)

Allmäh'lich (Ger.) Gradually, by degrees. (Also *allmäh'lig, allmä'lig*.)

Allonger l'archet (Fr.) To prolong (the stroke of) the bow.

Allo'ra (It.) Then.

Almain', Almand', Almayne'. Same as *Allemande.*

Al'penhorn, Alp'horn (Ger.) The alp-horn, an instr. made of strips or staves of wood firmly bound together to form a conical tube from 3 to 8 feet long, the bell slightly curved upward, and with a cupped mouthpiece of hard

wood. The scale of the tube is narrow, and the tones produced are its natural harmonics. The alpine herdsmen use this horn to play the *Ranz des vaches* and other simple melodies.

Alphabetical notation. Any method of writing music which uses the letters of the alphabet.—The earliest known method was the ancient Greek, which employed two parallel series of letters, one for vocal and the other for instrumental music, the letters being variously inverted, accented, or mutilated to indicate the several octaves and chromatic tones. This method was retained, at least by theorists, down to the 10th century (see *Neumes*), when the beginnings of a new method appeared, employing the first 7 letters of the Latin alphabet *A B C D E F G* for the major diatonic scale now represented by *C D E F G A B*, and repeating the same series for the higher octaves. These Latin letters were at first used for instrumental notation (psaltery or rotta, later the organ). Their signification was soon altered, however, to conform to that of the earlier Greek system (*minor*), the series then agreeing with our present one; the Greek *Γ* (*Gamma, G*) was added as the lowest tone, and the octaves above *Γ* were written *ABCDEFG abcdefg aabbccdd eeffgg* etc. (or $\begin{smallmatrix}a&b&c&d\\a&b&c&d\end{smallmatrix}$ etc.); though sometimes, instead of small letters, the capitals ran on (*HIKLMNOP*), in which latter system *A* was equivalent to our modern *C*, as at first. Arbitrary innovations led to great confusion in the alphabetical notation, which was in reality rendered superfluous, as a method of writing music, by Guido d'Arezzo's invention or systematization (about 1026) of line-notation (see *Notation*). When letters were used, without staff-lines, instead of neumes, they were often written above the words in this wise:

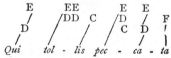

Qui   tol - lis   pec - ca - ta

i.e., in notes:

Qui   tol - - lis   pec - ca - ta

ascending or descending as the voice was to rise or fall.—Our present theoretical division of the octave is first found fully developed in the works of Praetorius (1619); side by side with which the old method of writing music (*A–G, a–g* etc.) still occurred, until the various systems of tablature were given up (comp. *Tablature*).—Letters are no longer used in practical mus. notation, except by Tonic Sol-fa, in which, however, they represent no fixed pitch, as formerly, but are mere abbreviations of the movable solmisation-syllables. In modern theory, letters are variously employed (comp. *Pitch, absolute*).

Alt (Ger.) Alto (voice or part)...In compound words, the alto instr. of any family, as *Alt'geige, Alt'horn, Alt'-klarinette, Alt'oboe, Alt'viole*, etc.— (Engl.) Hence, the same employment in English usage [alt-clarinet, alt-horn]...Notes "in alt" are those of the next octave ($g^2–f^3$) above f^2 ; notes in the octave above this are said to be "in altissimo".

Altera're (It.) To alter, change.

Altera'tio (Lat.) See **Notation**, §3.

Alteration. 1. Same as *Alteratio.*—2 Chromatic alteration of the pitch of a note.

Altera'to (It.), **Altéré** (Fr.) Chromatically altered.

Alterez'za (It.) Pride, loftiness.—*Con a.*, in a lofty and dignified style.

Alternamen'te (It.) Alternatively... *Alternan'do*, alternating.

Alternati'vo (It.) See *Trio* 2.

Alt-horn. (Fr. *saxhorn;* Ger. *Alt'-horn.*) One of the Saxhorns.

Altieramen'te (It.) In a lofty and majestic style.

Alti natura'li (Lat.) Natural (male) altos, or counter-tenors. (See *Alto.*)

Altis'simo (It.) Highest. (See *Alt.*)

Alti'sta (It.) An alto or contralto singer.

Alt'klausel (Ger.) The leading of the alto part in a perfect close.

Alto. 1. (Fr. *haute-contre ;* Ger. *Alt, Alt'stimme;* It. *al'to.*) The deeper of the two main divisions of women's or boys' voices, the contralto ; (in Germany a distinction is sometimes made between *Alt* and *Kon'traalt*, the latter

term being reserved for the lower alto voice). Ordinary compass from *g* to c^2 which, in voices of unusual range, may be extended down to *d* and up to f^2, or even higher.—2. A high head-voice in men (It. *al'ti natura'li*) formerly cultivated for the performance of church-music (in England for secular music as well, e. g. glees), but now generally superseded by the female alto or high tenor.—3. (Ger. *Bra'tsche, Alt'-viole;* Fr. *alto, quinte, basse de violon;* It. *al'to, vio'la.*) The tenor violin, or viola.

Al'to,-a (It.) High...*Otta'va alta*, an octave higher...*Alta vio'la*, tenor violin. ...*Alto bas'so*, an obsolete variety of dulcimer, consisting of a square wooden box set on legs and strung with gut. It was generally employed to accompany simple melodies played by the performer on a flageolet held in his right hand, the left striking the strings.

Alto-clef. See *Clef.*

Alt'posaune (Ger.) Alto trombone.

Al'tro,-a (It.) Other...*Altra vol'ta*, "encore !"

Alt'schlüssel (Ger.) Alto-clef.

Alt'viole (Ger.) Viola.

Alzamen'to (It.) A raising or lifting (opp. to *Abbassamento*). Abbrev. *Alz.*

Ama'bile (It.) Sweet, tender.

Amare'vole (It.) Bitterly, mournfully. (Sometimes written mistakenly for *Amore'vole*, lovingly.)...*Amarez'za*, bitterness, sadness ; *con a.*, grievingly.

Amateur (Fr.) A "lover" of art, who, while possessing an understanding for and a certain knowledge of it, does not pursue it as a profession.

Am'bitus (Lat.) Compass.

Ambrosian chant. The style of church-music introduced by St. Ambrose (d. 397) from the Eastern Church, and established by him in the cathedral at Milan, towards the end of the 4th century. It was based on the 4 authentic modes

$$d\ e\ f\ g\ a\ b\ c^1\ d^1$$
$$e\ f\ g\ a\ b\ c^1\ d^1\ e^1$$
$$f\ g\ a\ b\ c^1\ d^1\ e^1\ f^1$$
$$g\ a\ b\ c^1\ d^1\ e^1\ f^1\ g^1$$

and was thus essentially diatonic, although embellished with occasional chromatic graces ; it was probably rhythmical, in contrast to the later development of Plain Chant. Nothing positive is known about these melodies, except that St. Ambrose introduced the antiphonal songs and hallelujahs of the Eastern Church, and himself composed numerous hymns. (Comp. *Gregorian Chant.*)

Ambrosian hymn (*hym'nus Ambrosia'-nus*). The "Te deum laudamus," of which St. Ambrose is the reputed author.

Âme (Fr.) Soundpost.

American organ. See *Reed-organ.*

Amo're (It.) Love... *Con a.*, with devotion, fondly, devotedly; tenderly... *Amore'vole, amorevolmen'te,* lovingly, fondly, etc... *Amorosamen'te,* amorously, lovingly, fondly... *Amoro'so,* amorous, loving.

A'morschall, A'morsklang (Ger.) A French horn with valves, invented by Kölbel, of St. Petersburg (1760); its tone was lacking in purity, and the valve-mechanism did not quite do away with "stopping."

Am'phibrach. A metrical foot of 3 syllables (ᴗ—ᴗ); opp. to *amphim'acer.* Also *amphibra'chys.*

Am'phichord. See *Lira barberina.*

Amphim'acer. A metrical foot of 3 syllables (—ᴗ—); opp. to *am'phibrach.* [Also *amphimacrus.*]

Ampho'ter (Ger.) Amphoteric; said of a series of tones "common to two" registers of the same voice.

Amplitude of vibration. See *Vibration.*

Amts'pfeiffer (Ger.) See *Stadtpfeiffer.*

Amusement (Fr.) See *Divertissement.*

An (Ger.) On; add (i.e. *draw*).

Anacru'sis (Gk.; Ger. *Anakru'sis* [*Auf'-takt*]; Fr. *anacrouse.*) An up-beat beginning a verse, containing 1 or 2 unaccented syllables; hence transferred to musical rhythms, for which, in English usage, the term *auftakt* is often met with.

Analytical programs are an English invention; analyses of the mus. form of compositions on the concert-program, with quotations from the music, date from 1845 (Ella, matinées of Mus. Union). The most ambitious attempts of this kind are probably H. v. Wolzo-gen's "*Führer*" (Guides) "through" Wagner's mus. dramas.

An'apest. A metrical foot of 3 syllables,

the first 2 short, the last long (ᴗ ᴗ —́); the reverse of the *Dactyl.*

Anche (Fr.) Reed (of any instr.)....*A. libre,* free reed...*Jeu d'anche,* reed-stop.

An'che (It.) Also, too, likewise; even.

An'cia (It.) Reed.

Anco'ra (It.) Again, also, yet, still, even...*Ancor' più mos'so,* still faster.

An'dacht (Ger.) Devotion...*An'dächtig,* or *mit Andacht,* devotionally (It. *devo'to, con devozio'ne*).

Andamen'to (It.) 1. Movement, rate of speed.—2. A passage, especially an episode in a fugue.—3. Specifically, an extended fugal theme, usually consisting of two distinct and contrasting members. (See *Soggetto.*)

Andan'te (It., lit. "going, moving.") A tempo-mark indicating, in modern usage, a moderately slow movement, between Adagio and Allegretto; often modified by qualifying words, as *A. maesto'so, A. sostenu'to,* a stately and tranquil movement; *A. con moto, A. un poco allegretto,* a comparatively animated movement; *A. canta'bile,* a smoothly flowing and melodious movement; etc.—In earlier usage often employed in its more literal sense, as *A. allegro,* "moving rapidly;" *me'no andante* ("less moving"), slower.

Andantemen'te (It.) Flowingly, uninterruptedly.

Andanti'no (It.) Dimin. of *Andante;* strictly, *slower* than andante, but often used in the reverse sense.

Anda're (It.) To move on... *A. dirit'to,* go straight on; *a. in tempo,* keep to the tempo.

Än'derungsabsatz (Ger.) Half-cadence, ending on the dominant triad.

Anem'ochord. (Fr. *anémocorde.*) A keyboard wind-instr. with strings, invented by J. J. Schnell, of Paris, in 1789, as an attempt to imitate the tone of the Æolian harp by means of small bellows forcing a current of air against the strings: a pneumatic harpsichord. —The *piano éolienne* of Henri Herz (1851) was a similar instr.—(Also *Anim'ocorde.*)

Ane'sis (Gk.) The passage from a high tone to one lower in pitch; also, the tuning of strings to a lower pitch.—Opp. to *epit'asis.* [STAINER AND BARRETT.]

An'fang (Ger.) Beginning.— *Vom A.*, same as *Da capo.*

An'geben (Ger.) To sound, to strike... *Den Ton a.*, to give the pitch (as for an orchestra).

Angelic hymn. The hymn sung by the angels upon the announcement of Christ's birth ; sung in both the Eastern and Western Churches, extended in the latter to the " Gloria in excelsis ; " also in the Anglican and Episcopal Churches, as a song of thanksgiving after communion.

Ange'lica (Lat., " angelic.") See *Vox a.*

Angelique'. (Fr. *angélique.*) A keyboard instr. having 17 strings tuned in chromatic order ; inv. early in the 17th century.—Also, a kind of guitar.

Angelophone. An earlier name for the harmonium or parlor-organ.

An'gemessen (Ger.) Suitable, appropriate.

Anglaise (Fr.) The English country-dance (*contredanse*), of lively character, sometimes in 2–4, at others in 3–4 or 3–8 time. It closely resembles the *Écossaise*, and most probably took its origin from the older form of the French Rigaudon. [GROVE.]

Angosciosamen'te ⎱ (It.) Expressive of
Angoscio'so ⎰ anguish, agony.

Ängst'lich (Ger.) Fearfully (It. *timidamen'te*, wrongly *tramidamente*).

An'hang (Ger.) Appendix ; coda, codetta.

A'nima (It.) 1. Spirit ; *con a.*, with spirit, animation.—2. Soundpost.

Animan'do (It.) With growing animation ; livelier...*Anima'to*, in an animated, spirited style.

Animocor'de (It.) See *Anemochord.*

Animo'so (It.) Animated, spirited... *Animosis'simo*, *animosissimamen'te*, with the utmost animation, spirit, boldness.

An'mut(h) (Ger.) Grace, sweetness, charm, suavity...*An'mut(h)ig*, gracefully, etc.

Anom'aly. The slight deviation from the exact pitch caused by tempering intervals on fixed-tone instr.s ;—hence, an *anomalous chord* is one containing an interval rendered by tempering, extremely sharp or flat.

Anonner (Fr.) To perform in a hesitating, stumbling manner ; to read music haltingly.

An'satz (Ger.) 1. Lip, embouchure (in playing wind-instr.s).—2. The method of attacking a vocal phrase.

An'schlag (Ger.) 1. Touch (on a keyboard instr.)—2. A kind of double appoggiatura :

written : played :

An'schwellen (Ger.) To increase in loudness, swell.

Ansiosamen'te (It.) In a style expressive of anxiety or hesitation.

An'sprache (Ger.) The "speaking" of an organ-pipe, wind-instr., string, etc...*An'sprechen*, to speak.

An'stimmen (Ger.) To intone, strike up.

Answer. (Lat. *co'mes ;* Ger. *Gefähr'te, Ant'wort ;* Fr. *réponse, réplique ;* It. *ripo'sta, conseguen'te.*) In a fugue, the taking-up of the subject, proposed by the first part, by the second part, at a different pitch. (See *Antecedent.*)

Antece'dent. (Ger. *Füh'rer ;* Fr. *thème ;* It. *anteceden'te, propo'sta, gui'da.*) The theme or subject of a fugue or canon, as proposed by the first part.— Also, any theme or motive proposed for imitation, or imitated later.

Antelu'dium (Lat.) Prelude, introduction.

Anthem. A piece of sacred music usually founded on biblical words, with or without instrumental accomp., and of various forms :—(1) *Anthems for double choir*, the choirs frequently answering each other...(2) *Full anthems*, consisting wholly of chorus, accompanied or not ...(3) *Full anthems with verses*, certain parts of which are sung by solo voices, although beginning and close are choruses (*Tutti*), and the chorus predominates throughout...(4) *Verse anthems*, in which the verses (soli, duets, trios, quartets) predominate over the choruses...(5) *Solo anthems*, in which a solo part predominates, though the chorus always concludes them...(6) *Instrumental anthems*, those accompanied by instr.s other than the organ ;—formerly so called.—The anthem, an integral part of the Anglican church-service, is essentially an English product, a motet developed on the lines of vocal variety and instrumental accomp., approximating to the Ger. *Kantate*.

Antholo'gium (Lat.) The book or collection of the hymns, etc., of the Eastern Church.

Antibac'chius (*Antibacchy*). A metrical foot of 3 syllables, 2 long and 1 short, with the ictus on the first (—́ — ⏑).

Anticipation. (Ger. *Antizipation'*, *Voraus'nahme;* Fr. *anticipation;* It. *anticipazio'ne.*) The advancing of one or more of the parts constituting a harmony before the rest, which part or parts would, if all the parts progressed simultaneously, enter later:

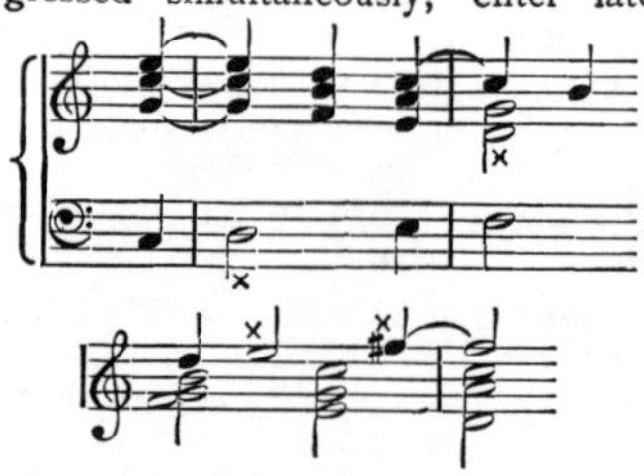

Anti'co (It.) Antique, ancient...*All'antico*, in the ancient style.

Antienne (Fr.) Antiphon.

An'tiphon, or **An'tiphone.** (Gk. *anti'phona*, *anti'phonon;* Ger. *Antiphonie';* Fr. *antienne;* It. *anti'fona.*) Originally, a responsive system of singing by two choirs (or a divided choir), one of the earliest features in the Catholic service of song; hence applied to responsive or alternate singing, chanting, or intonation in general, as practised in the Greek, Roman, Anglican, and Lutheran churches...Also, "a short sentence, generally from Holy Scripture, sung before and after the Psalms for the day, or the Canticles, selected for its appropriateness to the church season in which it is sung" [STAINER AND BARRETT].

Antiph'onal. 1. A book or collection of antiphons or anthems.—2. (adj.) In the style of an antiphon, responsive, alternating.

Antiph'onary. (Lat. *antiphona'rium;* Ger. *Antiphonar';* Fr. *antiphonaire;* It. *antifona'rio.*) Properly, a collection of antiphons, but extended to include the responsories, etc., sung at ecclesiastical celebrations.—The original collections embraced all the antiphonal songs both in the mass and the offices of the Latin Church; but now, by long-established custom, a separate book called the Gradual contains the liturgical antiphons (those proper to the mass); whereas the responsories of the office, formerly relegated to the Responsorial, now form the Antiphonary, together with the antiphons proper (i.e. the antiphons associated with the psalms of the office). (Also *Antiph'onal*, *Antiph'oner.*)

Antiph'onel. The planchette-mechanism devised by Alexandre Debain, of Paris, when attached to a pfte., organ, or harmonium; hence *Antiphonel-harmonium*, *Orgue-antiphonel*, etc.

Anti'phonon (Gk.) Antiphon, anthem.

Antiph'ony. Responsive singing by two choirs (or divided choir) of alternate verses of a psalm or anthem; opp. to *responsorial singing*, and also to *homophony* (see *Homophonic* 1).

An'tispast. A metrical foot of four syllables, the first and last being short and the two in the middle long (⏑ — — ⏑).

Antis'trophe. See *Strophe*.

Ant'wort (Ger.) Answer.

An'wachsend (Ger.) Same as *crescendo.*

Äoli'ne, etc. (Ger.) See *Æolina.*

Ä'olsharfe (Ger.) Æolian harp.

Ä'olsklavier (Ger.) "Æolian pfte.;" a keyboard instr. invented about 1825 by Schortmann of Buttelstedt, resembling the Physharmonica, but having, as tone-producing bodies, wooden wands instead of steel bars.

Aper'to (It., "open.") "Take the loud pedal" (in pfte.-music).—Clear, distinct; broad, ample; *Allegro aperto*, an allegro with broad, clear phrasing.

Aper'tus (Lat.) 1. Open; said of organ-pipes.—2. See *Aperto.*

Ap'felregal (Ger.) An obsolete reed-stop in the organ, the narrow pipes of which were furnished at the top with hollow perforated globes or buttons (hence also called *Knopf'regal*).

Aplomb (Fr.) Coolness, self-possession, steadiness.

Apoggiatura, Apogiatura. Occasional spellings of *Appoggiatura* (Fr. *appogiature*).

Apollo. (Fr. *Apollon.*) A large lute

(or theorbo) having 20 single strings, invented in 1678 by Prompt of Paris.

Apollo-Lyra. See *Psalmmelodicon.*

Apollonicon. An instr. finished in 1817 by Flight and Robson of London. It was a combined organ and orchestrion, containing about 1900 pipes in 45 stops, with 5 manuals played on by different performers, and kettledrums operated by a special mechanism, so that a full orchestral effect was obtainable ; it was likewise provided with various barrels actuated by machinery, for the automatic performance of several extended compositions. It was taken to pieces in 1840.

Apollonion. An instr. consisting of a pfte. with double keyboard, combined with an organ flue-work containing pipes of 2, 4, and 8-foot pitch, together with an automatic player the size of a boy ; inv. by J. H. Voller of Angersbach early in the 19th century.

Apos'trophe ('). Often employed as a breathing-mark.

Apo'tome (Gk.) In the Pythagorean system, the chromatic semitone—2048: 2187 ; the *limma*, or diatonic semitone, therefore being 243:256 ($\frac{243}{256} \times \frac{2048}{2187}$) $= \frac{8}{9} =$ the greater whole tone). This chromatic semitone (obtained by subtracting 2 whole tones 8:9 from a perfect fourth 3:4) was therefore a wider interval than the diatonic ; whereas *our* diatonic semitone is wider than the chromatic.

Appassiona'to,-a (It.) Impassioned, with passion...*Appassionamen'to,* passion, ardor, deep emotion...*Appassionatamen'te,* passionately, ardently.

Appel (Fr.), Appell' (Ger.) Assembly ; signal to troops to fall in.

Appena'to (It.) Distressed ; in a style expressive of distress or suffering.

Applica'tio (It.) Fingering.

Applikatur' (Ger.) Fingering (usually *Fing'ersatz*).

Appoggian'do (It., "leaning on, supported.") Said of a tone (note) gliding over to the next without a break, as in appoggiaturas and the portamento. (Also *Appoggia'to.*)

Appoggiatu'ra (It.; Fr. *appogiature;* Ger. *Vor'schlag, Nach'schlag.*) 1. The *accented appoggiatura* (Ger. *Vorschlag*) is a grace-note preceding its main note (melody-note), and taking the accent

and part of the time-value of the latter. (a) The *long appoggiatura,* now obsolete, often occurs in earlier music ; it was, in point of fact, a *suspension* written as a small note in order to evade, as it were, the rule against the entrance of unprepared dissonances. The duration of the small note properly corresponds to its time-value if written as a large note ; e. g.

written :

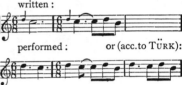

performed :   etc.

though cases may occur in which the appoggiatura takes more than its apparent value :

written :

performed :   or (acc. to TÜRK):

(b) The *short appoggiatura* is properly written as a small eighth-note or 16thnote with a slanting stroke through the hook ; the general rule for its execution is, to perform it very swiftly, giving it the accent of its principal note, and a portion of the latter's time-value differing according to the speed of the movement somewhat as follows :

written :

Adagio.   Andante.   Allegro.   Presto.

performed :

(c) The *double appoggiatura* contains 2 or more small grace-notes (commonly written as 16th-notes) before a principal note ; it is performed rapidly, its duration subtracted from the time-value of the principal note, with the accent on the first small note (compare *Anschlag, Slide*).—2. The *unaccented appoggiatura* (Ger. *Nachschlag*) is a rapid single or double grace-note *following* a principal note, from the time-value of which its duration must be subtracted, and with which it is connected by a slur: written :

performed :

Appresta're (It.) To set up and finish an instr.

Appretie'ren (Ger.) Same as *Apprestare...Appretur'*, the proper adjustment of the parts of an instr.

Äquivo'ken (Ger., pl.) Meistersinger melodies bearing like names.

Arabesque. (Ger. *Arabes'ke.*) 1. An occasional title for pfte.-pieces resembling a rondo in form.—2. *Arabesken* (Ger. pl.) Ornamental passages accompanying or varying a theme.

Arbi'trio (It.) Free will, absolute power; *a suo a.*, at pleasure (equiv. to *a piacere*).

Arca'to (It.) Bowed, played with the bow.

Archeggia're (It.) To play with the bow.

Archet (Fr.) Bow.

Ar'chi-[ar'kē] (Lat.), and **Ar'ci-[ar'-tchē]** (It.) (Engl. *Arch-*, Ger. *Erz-.*) A prefix signifying "chief, preëminent," formerly applied to names of instr.s in the sense of "largest" (of the family in question), and to official titles in the sense of "head."—E. g., *Archchanter* (Fr. *archichantre*), precentor ; *Archlute* (It. *arciliu'to*, Fr. *archiluth*, Ger. *Erz'laute*), a variety of the bass lute ; *Aricem'balo* (It.; Fr. *archicembalo*, Ger. *Archicym'bal*), a keyboard stringed instr. inv. by Niccolò Vincentino (16th century), with 6 keyboards, and keys and strings for all the tones of the three ancient Greek modes (diatonic, chromatic, and enharmonic); *Arcivio'la di lira* (It.), same as *Lirone.*

Ar'chi (It., pl. of *Arco.*) Bows ; *gli archi*, "the bows," i. e. bow-instr.s in the orchestra ; Engl. equivalent, "the strings."

Ar'co (It.) Bow ; *a pun'ta d'arco*, or *colla punta dell'arco*, with the point of the bow ; *coll'arco*, with the bow, i. e. resume the bow after a *pizzicato* passage...*Arco in giù*, down-bow ; *a. in su*, up-bow.

Arden'te (It.) Ardent, fiery, passionate.

Arditez'za, con (It.) Boldly, spiritedly...*Ardi'to*, bold, spirited.

Aretin'ian syllables. (Ger. *areti'nische Sil'ben.*) The syllables *ut, re, mi, fa, sol, la*, first used as solmisation-syllables by Guido d'Arezzo.

A'ria (It.; Ger. *A'rie.*) Primarily, an air, or rhythmic melody.—As a technical term, an aria is an extended lyrical vocal solo in various forms, with instrumental accompaniment. With the rise of homophonic music in the opera and oratorio, the aria developed, from a mere plain-song melody with *basso continuo*, into the *aria gran'de* (the *grand* or *da-capo aria* in 3 divisions preceded by an instrumental *ritornello* containing the principal melody ; division I being an elaborate development of a theme with frequent repetitions of the words ; II, a more tranquil and richly harmonized section ; followed by III, the repetition *da capo* of I, with still more florid ornamentation); the *aria di bravu'ra*, (similar to the foregoing, but overloaded with difficult passages and coloraturas for showing off the singer's skill); the *aria da chie'sa* (church-aria, differing from the sacred song chiefly in its greater breadth, and in being accompanied by full orchestra); and the *aria da concer'to* (concert-aria, differing from the others, which are portions of operas, oratorios etc., in being an independent composition intended for the concert-hall).— The modern aria is freer in form than the *aria grande* of the 18th century, the ritornello often being omitted, greater variety given to the *da capo*, and the thematic construction made to follow the sense of the words, so that it sometimes assumes the form of a rondo, or consists of 2 slow divisions separated by an allegro movement...*Aria parlan'te* (also *ario'so*), a vocal style combining the melody of an aria with the distinct enunciation of a recitative, the vowels being "thrown forward." —Smaller arias, nearly in song-form and with slighter accompaniments, are called *ariettas* or *cavatinas.*

Ariet'ta (It.) A small aria. (See *Aria.*)

Ariette (Fr.) Same as *aria grande*, the original signification being completely reversed.

Ario'so (It.) In vocal music, a style intermediate between aria and recitative (see *Aria parlante*); also, a short melodious strain interrupting or terminating a recitative.—Also signifies an effective dramatic style suitable for the *aria grande.*—In instrumental music, same as *cantabile.*

Armer la clef (Fr.) See *Clef.* Add sig.

Arm'geige (Ger.) *Viola da braccio.*

Armoni'a (It.) Harmony . . *Armonia milita're,* military band.

Armo'nica (It.) 1. Harmonic.—2. Harmonica.

Armonie (Fr.) Probably same as *Vielle.*

Armoniosamen'te (It.) Harmoniously; *armonio'so,* harmonious.

Armure (Fr.) 1. Mechanism, action.—2. Key-signature.

Ar'pa (It.) Harp... *A. dop'pia,* see *Spitzharfe.*

Arpanet'ta, Arpanel'la (It.) A small harp. (See *Spitzharfe.*)

Arpège (Fr.) Arpeggio... *Arpègement,* playing arpeggio, breaking a chord... *Arpéger,* to arpeggio.

Arpeggian'do (It.) Playing arpeggio, in harp-style, or in broken chords; from *arpeggia're,* to play on the harp... *Arpeggia'to,* (a) arpeggiated, arpeggio'd ; (b) as a noun, same as *Arpeggio.*

Arpeggiatu'ra (It.) A series of arpeggios.

Arpeg'gio (It., pl. *arpeg'gi,* Engl. pl. *arpeg'gios.*) [Lit." harping."] Playing the tones of a chord in rapid and even succession ; playing broken chords. Hence, a chord so played, or broken ; a broken or spread chord, or chord-passage. The modern sign for the *a.* calls for the following execution :

i. e. the first arpeggio-note falls on the accent; this is the rule for the accent, tho' there are occasional exceptions.

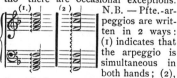

N.B. — Pfte.-arpeggios are written in 2 ways: (1) indicates that the arpeggio is simultaneous in both hands; (2), that all the notes are to be played in succession from lowest to highest.—In earlier music (Bach, Händel) the same sign calls for a more or less free spreading of the chords, generally according to a preceding pattern-chord in which

the *a.* is written out in full. Obsolete or unusual signs are as follows :

a, b, c, d are equivalent to the modern sign ; *e, f, g* call for a reversed (descending) arpeggio ; *h* means either an ascending arpeggio, or a combined *a,* and acciaccatura ; *i* and *k* signify a spreading in eighth-notes ; the appoggiaturas at *l* and *m* delay the performance of the notes to which they are attached by the time required for playing a long or short appogg. respectively.

Arpeggio'ne. An instr. like a small 'cello, with fretted fingerboard and 6 strings tuned ; inv. 1823 by G. Stauffer, of Vienna.

Arpicor'do (It.) Harpsichord.

Arpo'ne (It.) An instr. played like the harp, but having the strings adjusted horizontally instead of vertically; inv. by Barbieri of Palermo, towards the end of the 18th century.

Arrangement. (Ger. and Fr. ditto; It. *riduzio'ne*). The adaptation of a composition for performance on an instr., or by any vocal or instrumental combination, for which it was not originally intended; hence, the composition as so adapted or arranged.

Arranger (Fr.), **Arrangie'ren** (Ger.) To arrange. (See *Arrangement.*)

Ar'sis (Gk.) Up-beat.

Art (Ger.) Sort, kind; manner, style.

Articola're (It.; Fr. *articuler;* Ger. *artikulie'ren.*) To articulate, utter distinctly...*Articola'to,* articulated. ..*Articolazio'ne,* articulation.

Ar'tig(lich) (Ger.) Neatly, prettily, gracefully.

As (Ger.) A♭.—*As'as,* or *As'es,* A♭♭.

Aspira're (It.) To aspirate. Also, in singing, to quaver a vowel by audibly interpolating successive *h*'s. Also, to take breath.

Aspiration (Fr.) An obsolete grace (comp. *Grace*).

Asprez'za (It.) Harshness, roughness; bitterness.

Assa'i (It.) Very ; used to intensify a tempo-mark, as *allegro assai*, very rapid ; it has less intensifying force than *molto*.

Assembly. A signal by drum or bugle for soldiers to rally and fall in.

Assez (Fr.) Enough ; rather.

Assolu'to (It.) Absolute, positive ; *primo uomo assoluto*, a male singer for leading rôles.

As'sonance. (Ger. *Assonanz'*; Fr. *assonance;* It. *assonan'za.*) Agreement or resemblance in sound.

A'them (Ger.) Breath...*A'themlos*, breathless(ly).

Attac'ca (It.) Attack or begin what follows without pausing, or with a very short pause ; *a. su'bito* (or *attaca'te subito*), attack immediately.

Attacca're (It.), **Attaquer** (Fr.) To attack, or begin, at once.

Attac'co (It.), **Attaque** (Fr.) A motive in fugal imitation ; formerly, a very short fugue-theme.

Attache du cordier (Fr.) Loop.

Attack. The act or style of beginning a phrase, passage, or piece ; said both of vocalists or instrumentalists, either in solo or ensemble.

Attendant keys of a given key are its relative major or minor, together with the keys of the dominant and subdominant and their relative major or minor keys. (Comp. *Phone*, §4.)

At'to (It.) Act of a drama

Atto're, (**Attri'ce**) (It.) Actor (actress).

Au (Fr.) To the, in the, etc.

Aubade (Fr.) 1. Morning-music, generally addressed to some particular person ; opp. to *Serenade;*—specifically, a morning-concert by a military band.—2. Occasional title for short instrumental pieces in lyric style.—3. A callithumpian concert (ironical).

Audace (Fr.) Audacious, bold.

Auf'fassung (Ger.) Reading or conception (of a work).

Auf'führung (Ger.) Performance.

Auf'geregt (Ger.) Agitated(ly), excited(ly).

Auf'geweckt (Ger.) Lively, animated(ly), brisk(ly).

Auf'halten (Ger.) To suspend...*Auf'-haltung*, suspension (usually *Vor'halt*).

Auf'lösen (Ger.) To resolve...*Auf'-lösung*, resolution ; also, the breaking of a chord ; also, the solution of an enigmatical canon...*Auflösungszei, chen*, the natural (♮).

Auf'satz (Ger.) Tube (of a reed-pipe in the organ).

Auf'schlag (Ger.) Up-beat...*Auf'-schlagende Zung'e*, beating reed.

Auf'schnitt (Ger.) Mouth (of an organpipe).

Auf'strich (Ger.) Up-bow.

Auf'takt (Ger.) Up-beat, anacrusis ; a fractional measure beginning a movement, piece, or theme (in this sense often used by English writers without capital [*auftakt*]).

Auf'tritt (Ger.) Scene.

Auf'zug (Ger., lit. " raising [of the curtain]".) An act of a drama.

Augmentation. (Ger. *Vergrö'sserung*, *Verläng'erung*.) 1. Doubling or increasing the time-value of the notes of a theme or motive in imitative counterpoint.—2. See *Notation*, §3.—*Augmented intervals*, see *Interval*.

Augmenter (Fr.) To increase (in loudness) ; *en augmentant*=crescendo.

Aule'tes (Gk.) Flute-player...*Aulos*, flute.

Aumentan'do (It.) *Crescendo*...*Aumenta'to*, augmented.

Aus'arbeitung (Ger.) Working-out, development.

Aus'druck (Ger.) Expression...*Aus'-drucksvoll*, expressively.

Aus'führung (Ger.) Execution, performance ; exposition.

Aus'halten (Ger.) To sustain; sustain ! ..*Aus'haltung*, sustaining...*Aus'haltungszeichen*, see *Fermate*.

Aus'lösung (Ger.) Hopper, grasshopper, escapement.

Äu'ssere Stim'men (Ger.) Outer parts.

Äu'sserst (Ger.) Extreme(ly).

Aus'stattung (Ger.) Mounting (of an opera, etc.)

Aus'weichung (Ger.) Modulation transition.

Authentic. (Ger. *authen'tisch ;* Fr. *authentique ;* It. *auten'tico.*) Within the compass of an octave above the keynote...*Au. cadence, mode,* see *Ca-*

dence, Mode...Au. melody, one whose range extends through or nearly through the octave-scale above its tonic or final ; opp. to *plagal...Au. part of the scale,* that lying between a given keynote and its higher dominant, the part between the keynote and lower dominant being called *plagal.*

Auto-harp. (Ger. *Akkord'zither.*) A zither without fingerboard or accompaniment-strings, all the strings being plucked or swept by the plectrum and stopped by a series of from 4 to 8 compound dampers (called "manuals" or "pedals"), each of which when pressed down damps all the strings except those forming one particular chord ; the plectrum, rasping across all the strings, sounds this cord as an arpeggio ; the melody is brought out by special stress on the highest (or any other) tone of the chord.

Au'tophon. A form of barrel-organ, the tunes played being determined by perforations in a sheet of mill-board [heavy pasteboard] cut to correspond with the desired notes. (KNIGHT.)

Auxiliary note. (Ger. *Hilfs'note.*) A note not essential to the harmony or melody ; particularly, a grace-note or added note a second above or below a given melody-note...*Auxiliary scales,* those of attendant keys.

A've Mari'a (Lat.) "Hail, Mary!"; the salutation of the angel Gabriel at the annunciation ; followed by the words of Elizabeth to Mary (Luke I, 42), it has been a favorite subject of sacred composition since the 7th century ; concluded by a hymn of praise or prayer to the Virgin.

A've ma'ris stel'la (Lat., "hail, star of ocean!") Hymn of the Roman Catholic Church.

Avec (Fr.) With.

Avici'nium (Lat.) An organ-stop imitating the warbling of birds.

Avoided cadence. See *Cadence.*

Azio'ne sa'cra (It., "sacred drama"; equiv. to the Spanish "auto sacramentale".) An oratorio or passion.

B.

B. (Ger. *H;* Fr. and It. *si.*) The 7th tone and degree in the typical diatonic scale of *C*-major...*B cancella'tum,* the sharp (♯), formed originally by crossing

or cancelling the sign ♭ for *B rotun'- dum...B quadra'tum,* B♮...*B* is also an abbr. for *Bass* or *Basso* (c. B.=col Basso ; B. C.=basso continuo).

Baboracka, Baborak. Bohemian dances with changing rhythms.

Bac'chius (*Bacchy*). A metrical foot containing 1 short and 2 long syllables, with the ictus on the first long one (⌣ —́ —).

Baccioco'lo (It.) A Tuscan instr. of the guitar family.

Bachelor of Music. (Lat. *baccalau'reus mu'sicæ.*) The lower of the 2 musical degrees, Doctor of Music being the higher.

Back. (Ger. *Boden;* Fr. *dos;* It. *schiena.*) The lower side of the body of a violin, etc.; opp. to *Belly.*

Back-block. Same as *Wrest-block.*

Backfall. 1. An obsolete melodic ornament in lute or harpischord-music ;

written 🎵 or 🎵 ; played 🎵

(Also comp. *Grace.*)—2. A double lever in the organ-action, working between a sticker and a pull-down.

Backturn. See *Turn.*

Badinage (Fr.) Good-humored raillery, banter.

Bagana. The Abyssinian lyre, having 10 strings tuned to 5 tones and their octaves.

Bagatelle (Fr.) A trifle.

Bagpipe(s). (Ger. *Du'delsack, Sack'- pfeife;* Fr. *cornemuse;* It. *cornamu'sa.*) A very ancient wind-instr. of Eastern origin, known to the Greeks and Romans, in great vogue throughout Europe during the middle ages, and still popular in many countries, especially Great Britain. It consists of a leathern bag, filled with wind either from the mouth or from a small bellows worked by the player's arm, and of pipes inserted in and receiving wind from the bag. The commonest form has 4 pipes ; 3 *drones* (single-reed pipes tuned to a fundamental tone, its fifth and its octave, and sounding on continuously), and 1 *melody-pipe,* the *chanter* (a sort of shawm or double-reed pipe with from 6 to 8 finger-holes ; compass approximately :

).

PRAETORIUS enumerates several sizes used in the 17th century ; the *"Grosser Bock"* (drone in contra-*G* or great *C*), *" Schaperpfeif"* (drones in *b♭* and *f¹*), *" Hümmelchen"* (drones *f¹–c¹*), and *" Dudey"* (*e¹♭–b¹♭–e²♭*).

Baguette (Fr.) Drumstick ; fiddlestick.

Baisser (Fr.) To lower (as a tone by a ♭).

Bajadere. See *Bayadere.*

Balala′ika (also *Balaleïka, Balaleïga*). A rude stringed instr. of the guitar family, having 2, 3, or 4 strings tuned in minor. It is of Russo-Tartar origin, and now most often met with among the Gypsies.

Balancement (Fr.) See *Bebung.*

Balance-rail. A strip of wood running transversely beneath the middle of the piano-keys, which are balanced upon it...*Balance swell-pedal,* see Pedal.

Balg (Ger.) Bellows...*Bal′gentreter* ("bellows-treader"), calcant, a man employed to tread or stand on the old-fashioned German organ-bellows to fill them with wind...*Balg′klavis,* see *Clavis...Balg′werk,* bellows.

Bal′ken (Ger.) 1. Bass-bar.—2. The thick line connecting the stems of grouped hooked notes, substituted for the hooks.

Ballabi′le (It.) A composition intended for a dance-accomp.; any piece of dance-music.

Ballad. (Ger. and Fr. *Balla′de;* It. *balla′ta*.) Originally, a song intended for a dance-accomp.; hence, the air of such a song. In modern usage, it is a simple narrative poem, a mixture of the epic and lyric, generally meant to be sung.—As a purely musical term, it was originally applied to a short, simple vocal melody, set to one or more stanzas, and with a slight instrumental accomp.—In an extended application, it includes instrumental melodies of a similar character ; also compositions for single instr.s, for orchestra, etc., supposed to embody the idea of a narrative.

Balla′denmässig (Ger.) In ballad-style.

Ballad-opera. An opera chiefly composed of ballads and folk-songs (e. g. Gay's " Beggar's Opera ").

Balla′ta (It.) A ballad...*A ballata,* in ballad-style.

Balleri′na (It.) A female ballet-dancer.

Bal′let. (Ger. *Ballett′ ;* Fr. *ballet ;* It. *bal′lo, ballet′to*.) 1. A spectacular dance, often one introduced in an opera or other stage-piece.—2. An independent pantomimic representation, accompanied by music and dances setting forth the thread of the story.—3. A composition of a light character, but somewhat in the madrigal style, frequently with a " fa la " burden which could be both sung and danced to ; these pieces were commonly called " Fa las " [GROVE].—4. The corps of ballet-dancers (*corps de ballet*).

Ballet′to (It.) 1. Ballet.—2. Title employed by Bach for an Allegretto in common time.

Bal′lo (It.) A dance ; a ballet...*Balli ingle′si,* English dances; *balli ungare′si,* Hungarian dances...*Da ballo,* in dance-style, light and spirited.

Ballon′chio (It.) See *Paspy.* (Originally, a round dance of the Italian peasantry.)

Ballonza′re (It.) To dance wildly and recklessly, regardless of rule.

Band. 1. An orchestra.—2 (most commonly). A company of musicians playing martial music (brass-band, military band).—3. A company of musicians, or section of the orchestra, playing instr.s belonging to the same family or class (brass-band, string-band, wood-band, wind-band)...The 24 fiddlers of Charles II. were called "the king's private band."

Band (Ger.) A volume.

Ban′da (It.) The brass wind-instr.s, and the instr.s of percussion, in the Italian opera-orchestra.—Also, an orchestra appearing on the stage.

Bandalore, Bandelore. See *Bandore.*

Ban′de (Ger.; usually *Musik′-* or *Musikan′tenbande*.) A company of strolling musicians.—(Fr.) In earlier usage, the 24 violins at the royal court (" la grande bande ").

Band-master. The conductor of a military band...*Bandsman,* a member of such a band.

Bando′la (Span.; also *Bandolon, Bandora, Bandura*.) Instr.s of the lute family, with a greater or smaller number of steel or gut strings, and played with a plectrum ; like the *Pandora, Pandura, Pandurina, Mandora, Mandola, Mandoer, Mandura, Mandürchen,* all essentially identical with the *Mandolin*

still in vogue (see *Mandolin* and *Lute*).
[RIEMANN.] (Also comp. *Cither*.)

Bando'nion. A kind of Concertina with
square ends (keyboards), inv. by C. F.
Uhlig of Chemnitz, about 1830, and
since then much improved and enlarged.
It takes its name from Heinrich Band
of Crefeld, a dealer in the instr.—Comp.
art. *Harmonicum*.

Bandore. See *Bandola* and *Cither*.

Bandur'ria (Span.) A variety of guitar
having wire strings instead of gut.

Banger. The banjo. (" The Negroe-
Banger " [ADAIR].)

Bania, Banja (African.) Parent instr.
of the Banjo. (?)

Banjo. A variety of guitar ; its body is
formed by a circular hoop, over the
upper side of which is stretched parchment or skin ; it has a long neck with
or without frets, and from 5 to 9 strings,
the melody-string, which is the shortest
and played with the thumb of the right
hand, lying outside of and next to the
lowest bass string. The other strings
are plucked or struck with the right
hand, and all are stopped with the left.
It is variously tuned, the 5-stringed
banjo often as follows :

Bän'kelsänger (Ger.; " bench-singers,"
from their mounting on benches, the
better to gain a hearing.) Strolling
singers of a low class, who frequent
fairs and other places of public resort,
and recount, partly singing and partly
speaking, romantic tales taken from
history or adventure, stirring events of
the day, etc., usually explanatory of a
picture which they display.

Bar. (Ger. *Takt'strich ;* Fr. *barre ;* It.
li'nea, bar'ra, sbar'ra.) 1. A vertical
line dividing measures on the staff, and
indicating that the strong beat falls on
the note immediately following.—2.
Hence, the popular name for "measure".
... *Bar-line*, a barbarism evoked by the
familiar use of *bar* for *measure*.

Bar (Ger.) Compare *Strophe* 3.

Bar'baro (It.) Equiv. to *Feroce*.

Bar'biton, Bar'bitos. An ancient
Greek variety of the lyre.

Barcarole'. (Ger. ditto ; Fr. *barcarolle* ;
It. *barcaro'la, barcaruo'la*, "boatman's
song.") 1. A gondoliera (song of the
Venetian gondoliers).—2. A vocal or
instrumental solo, or concerted piece, in
imitation of the Venetian boat-songs,
and in 6-8 time (though Chopin's for
pfte. is in 12-8 time).

Bard. A poet and singer among the
ancient Celtic nations ; one who composed and sang, generally to the harp,
verses celebrating heroic achievements.
.. In earlier Scotch usage, a vagabond
minstrel.

Bardiet', Bardit' (Ger.) [A word coined
by Klopstock, who derived it from the
"barditus" (for *baritus*, a battle-song)
of Tacitus, whence the erroneous as-
sumption that the ancient Germans had
bards.] A bardic song.

Bardo'ne. 1 (It.) A barytone 2.—2
(Ger.) Occasional spelling for *Bourdon*
(organ-stop); also *Barduen*.

Bare fifth. See *Naked*.

Ba'rem (Ger.) Obs. name for the very
soft-toned organ-stop *Still'gedackt* or
Musicir'gedackt.

Bargaret, Barginet. Same as *Bergeret*.

Baribas'so (It.) A low barytone voice,
a bass-barytone.

Bariolage (Fr.) A medley.—A cadenza, or series of cadenzas, whose appearance forms a design upon the music-
paper, a " waistcoat pattern," as it is
called by performers. [STAINER AND
BARRETT.]

Bariteno're (It.) A low tenor voice, a
tenor-barytone (second tenor)

Ba'riton (Ger.), **Bariton** (Fr.), **Bari'-
tono** (It.) Barytone. [An attempt has
been made to confine the spelling *bari-
tone* to instruments, and *barytone* to the
voice ; the idea is not yet generally
accepted.]

Baroc'co (It.; Ger. *barock'* ; Fr. *baroque*.)
Eccentric, odd, strange, whimsical.

Barox'yton (Gk., " the deep and high-
toned.") A brass wind-in-
str. of broad scale, inv.
in 1853 by Cerveny of
Königgrätz; compass from
contra-D to a^1 :

Bär'pfeife (Ger., also *Bär'pipe, Barpyp;*
Dutch *Baar'pyp*.) A reed-stop in old
organs, with pipes nearly closed by
caps of a peculiar shape, and emitting
a humming, " growling" tone.

Barquarde (Fr.) Obs. for *Barcarolle*.

Bar'ra (It.) A bar (not measure).

Barre (Fr.) A bar (not measure); also *barre de mesure.*—Certain abbreviations are also termed *barres.*—Also, the low bridge of some stringed instr's... Also the accent mark (—)..*B. d' harmonie,* bass-bar...*B de répétition,* a dotted double-bar, indicating a repeat.

Barré (Fr.) In lute- or guitar-playing, the stopping of several or all the strings by laying the left-hand forefinger across them, the next fret then acting as a capotasto or temporary nut to raise their pitch...*Grand barré,* a stop of more than 3 strings...*C-barré,* see *Tranché.*

Barrel-organ. (Ger. *Drehorgel, Leierkasten;* Fr. *orgue à cylindre (noté), orgue de Barbarie ;* It. *organet' to.*) An instr. (often portable) consisting of a case containing pipes, a bellows, and a cylinder (the barrel) turned by a crank and studded with pins or pegs ; when the cylinder revolves, the pins open valves communicating with the bellows, which is worked by the same motion, and wind is thus admitted to the pipes. It generally plays a melody with an harmonic accomp. Larger forms (see *Orchestrion*) are used in dance-halls, restaurants, or even in churches.—In another variety, hammers striking wire strings (as in the pfte.) are similarly actuated by the revolving cylinder (*piano-organ, handle-piano*).

Bart (Ger.) Ear (of organ-pipe). Also *Flügel.*

Barytone. 1. (Ger. *Ba'ryton, Ba'riton ;* Fr. *baryton;* It. *bari' tono.*) The male voice intermediate between bass and tenor, and in quality partaking more or less of the characteristics of both ; thus the Germans distinguish between a *Bass'-bariton* and a *Tenor'bariton,* and the French had (in earlier usage) *basse-taille, seconde taille,* and *ténor concordant.* — Its mean compass is from *G* to *f¹*: 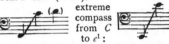—Hence, a singer having a barytone voice.—**2.** A bow-instr. (It. *vio'la di bardo'ne* or *bordone*) resembling the *viola da gamba,* in great favor during the 18th century, but now obsolete ; it had 6 or 7 gut strings, stopped by the left hand, *above* the fingerboard, and a widely varying number of brass or steel strings (from 9 to 24) *below* it, which acted as sympathetic strings, though sometimes plucked with the left thumb. The upper strings were tuned *B E A d f b e¹.* It dates from the 17th century.

—**3.** The euphonium.—**4.** Prefixed to instr.-names, *barytone* denotes the pitch of an instr. intermediate between bass and tenor (or alto); e. g. barytone clarinet...*Barytone-clef,* the (obsolete) *F*-clef on the 3rd line.

Ba'rytonhorn (Ger.) The euphonium... *Ba'rytonschlüssel,* barytone-clef...*Ba'rytonstimme,* barytone voice or part.

Bas-dessus (Fr.) Mezzo-soprano.

Base. Old spelling of Bass.

Bas'kische Trom'mel (Ger.) Tambourine.

Bass. (Ger. *Bass ;* Fr. *basse ;* It. *bas'-so.*) 1. The lowest tone in a chord, or lowest part in a composition.—2. The lowest male voice ; ordinary compass from *F* to *c¹* (or *d¹*):

extreme compass from *C* to *e¹*:

—3. A prefix indicating the lowest in various families of instr.s, as bass trombone.—4. (Ger.) (*a*) Abbr. for *Kontrabass* (double-bass)...(*b*) In earlier usage, a bow-instr. intermediate in size between the 'cello and double-bass, having from 5 to 6 strings...(*c*) As a suffix to the name of an organ-pipe, *bass* denotes that it belongs on the pedal ; e. g. *Gemshornbass.*—*Albertibass,* a bass in broken chords like the following: ...*Continued* or *figured bass,* bass notes provided with figures indicating the chords to be performed above the notes (*Basso continuo*)...*Fundamentalbass,* see *Fundamental...Ground bass,* a continually repeated bass phrase of 4 or 8 measures (*basso ostinato*)... *Murky bass,* see *Murky...Supposed bass,* a bass tone other than the root of a chord...*Thorough-bass,* see that word.

Bass-bar. (Ger. *Bal'ken;* Fr. *barre d' harmonie, ressort.*) In violins and the like, a long narrow strip of wood glued to the inner surface of the belly parallel with and just beneath the G-string, put in to strengthen the belly and equalize the vibration. [The violin-maker Held, of Beuel, Germany, gives the bass-bar a slight *diagonal* inclination, in accordance with a suggestion by Ole Bull.]

Bass-clef. *F*-clef on the 4th line. (See *Clef.*)

Basse (Fr.) Bass.—(Also applied to tl

thick lower strings of an instr., as *les basses d'un piano*)...*B. chantante*, the high "singing" (i. e. flexible) bass voice ; a barytone...*B. chiffrée*, figured bass...*B. continue*, basso continuo...*B. contrainte*, basso ostinato... *B.-contre*, a deep bass voice...*B. de cornet*, old term for the serpent, as the natural bass for the cornet family... *B. de cremone (cremorne, cromorne)*, the bassoon, or its precursor...*B. de flûte traversière, b. d'hautbois*, same as preceding...*B. d'harmonie*, the ophicleide...*B. de viole*, see *Barytone* 2... *B. de violon, b. double*, double-bass... *B. figurée*, figurate bass...*B. fondamentale*, (*a*) root of a cord, (*b*) a generator (see *Fundamental bass*)...*B. guerrière*, a species of bass clarinet...*Basse-orgue*, an instr. inv. by Sautermuiter of Lyons, in 1812...*B. récitante*, see *B. chantante*...*Basse-taille*, barytone voice.

Bas'set-horn. (Ger. *Bassett'horn* ; Fr. *cor de basset ;* It. *cor'no di basset'to*.) An alto or tenor clarinet in *F*, no longer in use ; compass from *F* to *c³ :* It has a single reed, and a wooden tube bent at the mouthpiece and bell. Timbre mellow, though of a sombre quality, like the bass clarinet, especially in the lower register.

Bassett' (Ger., also *Basset'l, Bass'l.*) 1. Old term for the 'cello.—2. As a prefix to the names of other instr.s, same as *Tenor*.—3. A 4-foot flute-stop on the organ-pedal.

Basset'to (It.) 1. A small bass viol with three strings (obs.)—2. When the bass rests, the lowest harmonic part.—3. Tenor violin (rarely).—4. An 8 or 16-foot reed-stop in the organ.

Bass'flöte (Ger. "bass flute.") See *Flötenbass.*)

Bass'geige (Ger.) Familiar term for the 'cello; *gro'sse Bassgeige*, the double-bass.

Bass'horn (Ger.) See APPENDIX.

Bass'klausel (Ger.) The cadence-like leading of the bass at a close, from dominant to tonic.

Bass'lade (Ger.) See *Windlade.*

Bas'so (It.) 1. Bass, either as the fundamental harmonic part, a bass voice, or a bass singer.—2. A bass instr., more especially the double-bass. —*B. buf'fo*, see *Buffo*...*B. cantan'te*, (*a*) a vocal bass ; (*b*) comp. *Basse chan-*

tante (opp. to *basso profon'do*)...*B. concertan'te*, the principal bass, as an accomp. to soli and recitatives...*B. conti'nuo* (or *continua'to*), a continuous bass provided with figures indicating the chords to be played above it ; also, thorough-bass...*B. figura'to*, (*a*) basso continuo ; (*b*) a figurate bass part... *B. fondamenta'le*, fundamental bass... *B. numera'to*, figured bass...*B. obbliga'to*, an indispensable bass part or accomp...*B. ostina'to*, ground bass... *B. profon'do*, a deep, heavy bass...*B. ripie'no*, see *Ripieno*.

Basson (Fr.) Bassoon...*B. quinte*, a tenor bassoon a fifth higher in pitch than the ordinary one ; compass :

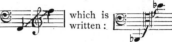

which is written :

Bassoon'. (Ger. *Fagott';* Fr. *basson ;* It. *fagot'to*.) A wood-wind instr. of the oboe family, serving as bass for the wood-wind. The tube is doubled upon itself, forming 2 parallel air-chambers ; the long, curving mouth-piece is of metal, with a double reed ; compass from $B_1\flat$ to c^2, on newer instr.s to $e^2\flat$, and extended by virtuosi to e^2 or even f^2: The unwieldy length of the parent-instr., the bombardo, led in 1539 to the idea of bending the tube back upon itself, and from the faggot-like appearance of the new instr. its Italian name is derived. The tone is far softer and mellower than that of the bombardo, and its expression is entirely under the player's control.

Bass'pommer (Ger.) See *Bomhart.*

Bass'posaune (Ger.) A bass trombone. (See *Trombone.*)

Bass'schlüssel (Ger.) Bass-clef.

Bass'stimme (Ger.) Bass voice.

Bass'tuba (Ger.) See *Tuba.*

Bass viol. See *Viol.*

Ba'thyphon (Gk.; "the deep-toned.") A wood-wind instr. inv. in 1829 by Wieprecht (or Skorra ?) of Berlin, having a clarinet mouthpiece, and a compass from contra-*D* to small $b\flat$: used for a short time in military bands.

Ba'ton. 1. (Fr. *bâton de mesure ;* Ger. *Taktstock, Taktstab, Taktierstock*, etc.;

It. *bacchet'ta* [di diretto're].) The staff or wand with which the conductor of a musical performance beats the time.— 2. A rest of 2 measures.

Bâton (Fr.) A thick vertical stroke traversing 1 or more spaces of the staff, and indicating, according to the number so traversed, a rest for an equal number of measures :

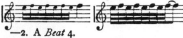

replaced in modern usage by signs like :

(see *Measure-rest*,under *Rest*)...*Bâton de mesure*, a *Baton* 1...*B. de reprise*, a repeat.

Battante (Fr.) Beating.

Battement (Fr.) 1. An obsolete grace, consisting of a short trill preceding the principal tone and beginning on the auxiliary a semitone below it. It had no sign, being always written out in small notes :   played :

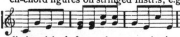

—2. A *Beat* 4.

Bat'tere (It.) Down-beat.

Batterie (Fr.) 1. A general term for broken-chord figures on stringed instr.s; e.g.

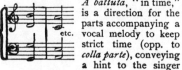

distinguished from the arpeggio (acc. to ROUSSEAU) by being played staccato instead of legato.—2. Striking instead of plucking the strings of a guitar.—3. A roll on a side-drum.—4. The percussion-group in the orchestra.

Battery. An effect in harpsichord-music;

written :   played :

Battimen'to (It.) *Battement.*

Battu'ta (It.) 1. A beat.—2. A measure or bar (*battuta* taken in the narrower sense of "down-beat"; see *Rit'mo di due battute*).—3. In medieval counterpoint, the forbidden progression from a tenth on the up-beat to an octave on the down-beat, between 2 outer parts ; e. g. *A battuta*, "in time," is a direction for the parts accompanying a vocal melody to keep strict time (opp. to *colla parte*), conveying a hint to the singer that his delivery should not be too free.

Bau (Ger.) Structure, construction.

Bäu'erlein (Ger.) *Bauernflöte.*

Bau'ernflöte,-pfeife (Ger.; "rustic flute"; Lat. *ti'bia rures'tris.*) A pedal-register not uncommon in old organs, consisting of stopped pipes of 1 or 2-foot pitch.

Baxoncil'lo (Span.) 1. An organ-stop like the open diapason.—2. A small bassoon.

Bayadere', Bayadeer'. East-Indian dancing-girl.

Ba'yla, Ba'yle (Span.) A dance ; *bayle* has the more comprehensive signification.

bb (Ger.) Double-flat (see *Doppel-b*).

B cancella'tum, B du'rum. See *B.*

Bear'beiten (Ger.) To revise, work over, adapt, arrange, rearrange, touch up...*Bear'beitung*, an adaptation or revision, a working-over.

Bearing-notes, Bearings. The tones first carefully tuned by the tuner of a pfte. or organ, serving to regulate its entire compass by.

Beat. 1. (Ger.; *Takt'schlag, Takt'teil;* Fr. *battement de mesure, temps ;* It. *battu'ta.*) The motion of the hand or foot in marking time (the equal divisions of the measure).—2. A division of a measure so marked.—3. In a trill, a pulsation embracing 2 consecutive tones.—4. In acoustics, see *Acoustics*, §3.—5. An old grace, consisting of a short trill before the principal note ;

written :   played :
= or ↝

Beating. Same as *Beat* 4.

Bebisa'tion. Compare *Solmisation.*

Be'bung (Ger.; Fr. *balancement ;* It. *tre'molo.*) 1. A rapid pulsation or tremulous effect, either vocal or instrumental, given to a sustained tone for the sake of expression.—2. Specifically, an effect obtained on the clavichord by holding down a key after striking it, and balancing the finger upon it in such a way as to produce a prolonged, tremulous tone. (On modern pianofortes having the Erard action, a *sustained* tone can be produced in a somewhat similar manner.)

Bec (Fr., "beak.") A mouthpiece (of a flageolet, clarinet).

Bécarre (Fr.) The natural (♮).

Bec'co (It.) Same as *Bec...Becco po-lac'co*, a large species of bagpipe.

Bech'er (Ger., "beaker, cup.") 1. The bell (of various wind-instr.s ; also *Schall'trichter*).—2. The tube (of a reed-pipe in the organ; also *Auf'satz*, *Schall'becher*).

Beck'en (Ger.) Cymbals.

Bedeckt' (Ger.) Stopped, as strings ; opp. to *leer*, open.

Bedon (Fr.) Old name for drum...*Bedon de Biscaye*, a tambourine.

Bee moll. (Obs., from Lat. *B molle*, soft B.) Be mol, Bemol.

Beffroi (Fr.) Gong (tam-tam)...Also, an alarm-bell, a tocsin.

Befil'zen (Ger.) To felt (put felt on pfte.-hammers)...*Befil'zung*, felting.

Begei'sterung (Ger.) Enthusiasm, spirit.

Beglei'ten (Ger.) To accompany... *Begleit'stimmen, Beglei'tung*, accompaniment ; accompanying parts subordinate to a principal melody.

Bei'sser (Ger.) A mordent.

Bei'töne (Ger.) Harmonic overtones or undertones...Also, auxiliary tones.

Bekie'len (Ger.) To furnish with quills, as the jacks of a harpsichord.

Beklemmt' (Ger., properly *beklom'men*.) Anxious, oppressed [Beethoven].

Bele'bend (Ger.) Ravvivando.

Bele'dern (Ger.) To cover with leather. ...*Bele'derung*, formerly, the *leather*, now, the *felt*, used in covering pfte.-hammers...Also, the strips of leather covering the treble hammers.

Belegt' (Ger.) Hoarse, not clear ; veiled (of the voice).

Bell. 1. (Ger. *Glock'e ;* Fr. *cloche ;* It. *campa'na.*) A hollow metallic instr. of percussion, set in vibration by a swinging clapper hung within, or by hammers actuated from without. — 2. (Ger., *Schall'trichter;* Fr. *pavillon;* It. *paviglio'ne.*) The flaring end of various wind-instr.s.

Bell-diapason. An organ-stop, usually of 8-foot pitch, with open bell-mouthed pipes.

Bellez'za (It.) Beauty, grace.

Bell-gamba. An organ-stop having conical pipes surmounted by a bell ; also called *cone-gamba.*

Bell-harp. An old variety of harp with 8 or more steel strings and enclosed in a wooden box which the player swung to and fro like a bell while twanging the strings with the thumbs of both hands inserted tnrough holes in the cover.

Bellicosamen'te (It.) In a bellicose, martial, warlike style...*Bellicoso*, martial, warlike.

Bell-met'ronome. A metronome with a bell-attachment which can be set so as to strike with every second, third, fourth, or sixth beat of the pendulum.

Bello'nion. An instr. consisting of 24 trumpets and 2 drums played by a mechanism ; inv. in 1812 at Dresden.

Bell open diapason. Same as *Bell-dia-pason.*

Bellows. (Ger. *Balg ;* Fr. *soufflet ;* It. *soffiet'to.*) The mechanical contrivance for gathering and propelling the wind supplying the pipes or reeds of the organ, harmonium, concertina, bagpipe, and the like. See *Organ.*

Bell-piano. See *Glockenspiel (2).*

Belly. 1. (Ger. *Deck'e ;* Fr. *table ;* It. *ta'vola, pan'cia.*) The face (upper side) of the resonance-box of the violin etc. —2. (Ger. *Resonanz'boden ;* Fr. *réson-nance, table d'harmonie ;* It. *ta'vola armo'nica.*) Soundboard of the pfte.

Bemol. B-flat.

Bémol (Fr.), **Bemol'le** (It.) The flat (♭)...*Bémoliser (bemollizza're),* to flat (set a flat before a note).

Ben, Be'ne (It.) Well ; as *ben marcato*, well marked ; *a bene placito*, at pleasure, ad libitum; *ben ritmato*, see *Bien rythmé; ben tenuto*, well sustained or held.

Benedic'tus. See *Mass.*

Bequa'dro (It.) The natural (♮).

Berceuse (Fr.) A cradle-song, lullaby ; hence, a piece of instrumental music imitating the effect of a lullaby.

Ber'gamask. (Fr. *bergamasque;* It. *bergama'sca.*) A clownish dance in derisive imitation of the rustics of Bergamasca in Northern Italy. (Also *ber-gomask, burgomask.*)

Bergeret'. A pastoral or rustic song or dance. (Also *bargaret, bargeret.*)

Bergk'reyen, Berg'reihen (Ger.) "Dance-tunes from the mountains ;" the title of various collections of dance-music.

Bes (Ger.) B double-flat; generally called *bb*.

Besai'ten (Ger.) To string, put strings on.

Bestimmt' (Ger.) With decision, energy.

Beto'nen (Ger.) To accent, emphasize. ..*Betont'*, accented...*Beto'nung*, accênt, stress, emphasis.

Bet'tlerleier (Ger.) Hurdy-gurdy... *Bet'tleroper*, Beggar's Opera.

Bewe'gen (Ger.) To move, stir, agitate. ..*Bewegt*, moved; *con moto*...*Bewe'-gung*, movement, agitation (comp. *Motion*)...*Bewe'gungsart*, see *Movement* 1, 2, 3.

Bezif'fern (Ger.) To figure (as a bass). ...*Bezif'fert*, figured...*Bezif'ferung*, figuring.

Bezug' (Ger.) All the strings of, or a set of strings for, any stringed instr.

Bian'ca (It., " white.") A half-note... *Voce bianca*, see *Voce*.

Bibi (Fr.) A pianette.

Bibrev'is (Lat.) See *Pyrrhic*.

Bi'chord. 1. Having 2 strings.—2. The technical term for an instr. having a pair of strings, tuned in unison, for each tone (as the mandolin, lute, and certain pftes).

Bici'nium (Lat.) A 2-part composition, especially a vocal one.

Bi'fara (also *bif'fara*, *bi'fra*, *pif'fara*, *pif'fero*). An organ-stop, the pipes of which are either double-mouthed or paired; the two members of each pair being tuned at slightly different pitches, the interference of the sound-waves produces a gentle tremolo. (Also *Celestina*, *Unda maris*, etc.)

Bifari'a. Title of a Presto in 3-measure rhythm, in an Invention or Suite ascribed to J. S. Bach.

Biju'ga (Lat.) The " 2-necked " cither.

Bimol'le (It.) Same as *Bemolle*.

Bi'na. See *Vina*.

Bi'nary. Dual; two-part...*Binary form*, a form of movement founded on 2 principal themes (comp. *Sonata*), or divided into 2 distinct or contrasted sections... *Binary measure*, that of common time, the first of every 2 members taking the accent; i. e. the regular and equal alternation of the down-beat and up-beat.

Bind. 1. Properly, a tie (a curved line connecting 2 notes of like pitch, or

enharmonically changed; written by Sterndale Bennett in bracket-form :—→ and by ⁓ to distinguish it Morley in from the *Slur*). 1597 thus : —2. The brace binding together the several staves of a score.

Bin'debogen (Ger.) A slur, or a tie.

Bin'den (Ger.) To bind, tie; to connect, play or sing smoothly and connectedly (legato)...*Gebun'den*, bound, tied; legato...*Gebun'dener Stil*, strict style of composition, in which dissonances are prepared (tied over)...Also see *Gebunden*.

Bin'dung (Ger.) A ligature, bind, tie, or slur; hence, a suspension or syncopation; also, the legato...*Bin'dungszeichen*, a sign used to express any of the above.

Biqua'dro (It.) Same as *Bequadro*.

Birn, Bir'ne (Ger.) Socket.

Bis (Lat., " twice".) 1. Signifies that a measure, passage, or section is to be repeated; often written over or under a slur embracing the music to be repeated. —2. Used by the French as an exclamation of applause (" again !"), like the French word " encore " in English usage. (See *Bissare*.)—3. The second part, or a continuation, of a scene on the stage; e. g., 16bis; 16ter and 16^quater then mean the *third* and *fourth* parts, respectively, of such a scene.

Bis'chero (It.) Peg (tuning-peg) of a violin, lute, etc.

Biscro'ma (It.), **Biscrome** (Fr.) A 16th-note.

Bisdiapa'son. The interval of a fifteenth, or double-octave.

Biso'gna (It.) " Is necessary," "must"; as *si bisogna da capo al segno*, must be repeated from the beginning to the sign.

Bisqua'dro (It.) Same as *Bequadro*.

Bissa're (It.), **Bisser** (Fr.) To encore.

Bissex (Lat., " twice six "; Ger. *Zwölf'-saiter*.) A kind of guitar having 12 strings, of which the 6 highest ones could be stopped on a fretted fingerboard; compass 3½ octaves; invented 1770.

Bis unca (Lat., " twice hooked.") A sixteenth-note.

Bit. A short additional piece of tube used to lengthen a crook in the *cornet à* *pistons*, etc., for slightly modifying the pitch.

Bizzarramen'te (It.) Bizarrely, whimsically, fantastically...*Bizzarri'a*, a freak, whim, fancy, extravagance... *Bizzar'ro,-a*, bizarre, fantastic, etc.

Blanche (Fr., "white".) A half-note.

Blä'ser (Ger., "blower.") A player on any wind-instr.

Blas'instrument (or *Bla'seinstrument*) (Ger.) Wind-instrument...*Bla'sebalg*, bellows.

Blatt (Ger.) Reed (of a wind-instr.; also *Rohr'blatt*)...*Dop'pelblatt*, double reed.

Blech'instrument (Ger.) Brass instrument, metal wind-instr.

Blind (Ger.) "Blind"...*Blinde Pfeife*, dummy pipe (organ)...*Blinder Doppeltriller*, a simulated or imperfect double trill ; e. g. etc.

Bloch'flöte, Block'flöte (Ger.) 1. A small kind of *flûte à bec*, in vogue in the 16th century.—2. An organ-stop having pyramid-shaped flue-pipes of 2, 4, 8, or 16-foot pitch, and sometimes stopped.

Block. In violins, etc., the blocks are small pieces of wood within the body, glued vertically to the ribs between belly and back to strengthen the instr.

Blower. (Ger. *Bal'gentreter, Kalkant'*; Fr. *souffleur* ; It. *tiraman'tici*.) A person working the bellows of an organ.

B molle. See *B*.

Boat-song. 1. A song intended to be sung in a boat, especially in time with the oars.—2 A vocal or instrumental composition imitative of 1. (*Barcarole, Gondoliera*.)

Bob. A term in change-ringing applied to the various sets of changes which may be rung on 6 bells (bob minor), 8 bells (bob major), 10 bells (bob royal), or 12 bells (bob maximus).

Bobisa'tion. A collective term for the various methods proposed, during the 16th and 17th centuries, for naming the tones of the scale by syllables. (See *Solmisation*.)

Bocal (Fr.) Mouthpiece of the horn, trombone, serpent, etc.—Also, the crook of the bassoon.

Boc'ca (It.) Mouth...*Con bocca chiu'sa*, with closed mouth (comp. *Brummstimmen*)...*Bocca riden'te*, "smiling

mouth," the position necessary for the production of beautiful tones.

Bocchi'no (It.) Mouthpiece of a wind-instr.

Bocedisa'tion. See *Solmisation*.

Bock (Ger.; also *pol'nischer Bock, Gross-Bock*.) The bagpipe.

Bocks'triller (Ger., "goat's-trill"; Fr. *chevrotement* ; It. *tril'lo capri'no*.) A trill like a goat's bleat ; the repeated interruption of *one* tone instead of the alternation of *two*.

Bo'den (Ger.) Back (of violin, etc.)

Body. 1. (Ger. *Cor'pus, Schall'kasten;* Fr. *coffre, corps* ; It. *cor'po*.) The resonance-box of a stringed instr.—2. That part of a wind-instr. remaining after removing the mouthpiece, crooks, and bell.—3. The tube of an organpipe above its mouth.—4. A tone is said to have "body" when it is full and sonorous ; the resonance of a tone is also called the *body*.

Boehm Flute. See *Flute*.

Bo'gen (Ger.) 1. A bow.—2. A slur or tie (*Hal'tebogen, Lega'tobogen, Bin'-debogen*)...*Bo'genflügel*, piano-violin (*Bo'genhammerklavier,Bo'genklavier*). ...*Bo'genführung*, see *Bowing* 1... *Bo'genstrich*, stroke of the bow.

Bois (Fr.) Wood...*Les bois* (pl.), woodwind.

Boîte (Fr.) Box ; swell-box (*boîte d'expression*)...*Ouvrez la boîte*, or *boîte ouverte*, open swell ; *fermez la boîte*, close swell.

Bole'ro (Span.) 1. A Spanish national dance in 3-4 time and lively tempo (allegretto), in which the dancer accompanies his steps with castanets ; also called *Cachucha*. The castanet-rhythm runs as follows : alternating with the melody-rhythm : —2. A composition in the style of a bolero.

Bom'bard. (Ger. *Bom'hart, Bom'mert, Pom'mer;* Fr.*bombarde;* It. *bombar'do*.) A wind-instr. of the oboe family, with a wooden tube and double reed ; properly, the bass instr. of the shawms, though sometimes made as a smaller instr. The unwieldy length of the larger sizes led to the invention of the bassoon, which is a bombard with the tube doubled upon itself, and thus shortened by half. The *bombardo'ne* or *contra-bombard* (Ger. *Bass'bomhart*) was the deepest, followed by the *bass bombard* (*Bomhart*), the *tenor* or *basset-bombard* (*Bassett'bomhart*), and the *alto* or *bombar'do pic'colo.*

Bombarde (Fr.) 1. Bombard.—2. *Posaune* 2.

Bombar'don. 1. A large instr. of the trumpet family, used as a bass in military music, and belonging, in its modern forms, to the saxhorn group; the usual sizes are in *B♭*, *F*, *C*, and contra-*B♭*; but the bombardon proper, old model, is in *F*, having 3 valves and a compass from contra-*F* to *d*[1] : It is non-transposing.—2. The bass of the saxhorns.—3. A deep-toned reed-stop in the organ.

Bom'bo (It.) A figure in repeated notes.

Bom'byx (Gk.) An ancient Greek wind-instr., presumably with a reed.

Bon (Fr.) Good...*Bon temps de la mesure,* strong beat.

Bonang. A Javanese instr. consisting of gongs mounted on a frame.

Bones. A set of 4 pieces of bone, wood, or ivory, held pairwise between the fingers, and used to mark time as a rattling accompaniment to a dance, song, or instrumental performance.

Book. 1. (Ger. *Heft;* Fr. *cahier;* It. *li'bro.*) A part of a series of songs, exercises, etc., under a separate paper cover.—2. The words (libretto) of an opera, oratorio, etc.

Boot. The foot of a reed-pipe (organ).

Bordun' (Ger.) Bourdon. (The 2 free strings on either side of the fingerboard of the hurdy-gurdy, that kept up a continual humming, were called *Bordune; bordunus* occurs as the name of the bass strings stretched beside the fingerboard of the ancient *viella.*)

Bouche (Fr.) Mouth ; *à bouche fermée,* with closed mouth (comp. *Brummstimmen*).

Bouché(e) (Fr.) Muted (of wind-instr.s) ; stopped (of organ-pipes).

Bouffe (Fr.) Same as *Buffo...Opéra bouffe,* comic opera.

Bourdon. (Fr.) 1. A drone bass.—2. An organ-stop of 16 or 32-foot pitch,

having stopped wooden pipes, sometimes with metallic tops ; tone usually hollow or "fluty," i. e. deficient in harmonics. The French also have open bourdons of 8 and 4-foot pitch (*bourdons de huit, de quatre ouverts*).—3. In French usage, the lowest string of the 'cello and double-bass ;—also, a great bell, as the *bourdon* of Notre-Dame...*Faux-bourdon,* see *Faburden.*

Bourrée (Fr.) 1. A dance of either French or Spanish origin, from Auvergne or Biscaya, in rapid tempo, consisting of 2 parts of 8 measures each and in 4-4 or 2-4 time.—2. A movement in the earlier Suites, in *alla breve* time.

Boutade (Fr.) 1. A short ballet performed, as it were, impromptu.—2. An instrumental impromptu or fantasia. —3. An old French spectacular dance.

Bow. (Ger. *Bo'gen;* Fr. *archet;* It. *ar'co.*) An implement originally curved outward, though now slightly inward, consisting of an elastic wooden rod (the *stick*), and of from 175 to 250 horsehairs [GROVE] (the *hair*) attached to the bent *point* or *head,* and drawn into proper tension by the sliding *nut,* which is actuated by the *screw.* (Schuster & Otto, Markneukirchen, have recently [1893] manufactured bows with *fine gut threads* in lieu of hairs.) After rubbing the hair with rosin, the bow is drawn across the strings (of the violin, bow-zither, etc.), setting them in vibration ; the vibration is communicated to the resonance-box, which latter reinforces the weak tone of the strings...*Bow-arm* or *-hand,* the right arm or hand... *Bow-guitar* (It. *chitar'ra coll' arco*), a species of violin with a guitar-shaped body...*Bow-clavier, Bow-harpsichord,* see *Piano-violin...Bow-instrument,* one played with the aid of a bow, as the violin or bow-zither...*Bow-zither,* see *Zither.*

Bow (*verb.*) 1. To execute with a bow. —2. To mark (a passage or piece) with signs indicating the bowing.

Bowing. 1. (Ger. *Bo'genführung.*) The art of handling the bow ; the style or method of a player,—"his bowing as shown in his management of the bow."—2. (Ger. *Strich'art.*) The method of, and signs for, executing any given passage ; "the *bowing* of the passage."

Boyau (Fr.) Gut ; hence, gut string.

Bozzetto (It.) Sketch.

B quadra'tum, B qua'drum. See *B*.

Brabançonne. The Belgian national hymn.

Brac'cio (It.) The arm... *Viola da braccio*, see *Viola*.

Brace. 1. (Ger. *Klam'mer ;* Fr. *accolade ;* It. *grap'pa*.) A bracket connecting the heads of 2 or more staves. —2. One of the leathern slides on the cords of a side-drum.

Branle, Bransle (Fr.) A brangle or brawl ; an old French dance in 4-4 time, in which several persons joined hands and took the lead in turn. *Branle* was the generic name of all dances in which, like the *Cotillon* or *Grossvater*, one or two dancers led the rest, who imitated all the evolutions of their leaders. (Also *Brantle*.)

Brass-band. See *Band* 2 ; distinguished from full military band by omission of reed-instr.s...*Brass-wind*, collective term for the players on metal wind-instr.s in an orchestra.

Bra'tsche (Ger.) The tenor violin (comp. *Viola*).

Bra'vo (It., masc. adj., pl. *bravi ;* fem. *brava*, pl. *brave*.) Used as an interjection, signifying "well done !" and the like ; superlative *bravissimo,-a*, etc.

Bravour' (Ger.) See *Bravura*...*Bravour'arie*, aria di bravura...*Bravour'stück*, a vocal or instrumental piece of a brilliant and florid character.

Bravoure (Fr.) See *Bravura*...*Valse de bravoure*, an instrumental waltz of a brilliant, showy character.

Bravu'ra (It.) Boldness, spirit, dash, brilliancy...*A'ria di bravura*, a vocal solo consisting of difficult runs and passages, designed to show off the singer's voice or skill...*Con bravura*, with boldness, etc.

Brawl. See *Branle*.

Break. 1. The point at which one register of a voice or instr. passes over into another ; in the voice, the junction of the head- and chest-registers ; in the clarinet, between the notes :
...*Breaking of voice*, see *Mutation*. —2. A false or imperfect tone produced by incorrect lipping of a horn or trumpet ; or by some difficulty with the reed of the clarinet (the "goose") ; or, in singing, by some defect in the vocal

organs.—3. In an organ-stop, when playing up the scale, the sudden return (caused by an incomplete number of pipes) to the lower octave ; also, in compound stops, any point in their scale where the relative pitch of the pipes is changed.

Breakdown. A negro dance (U. S.) of a noisy, lively character.

Breathing-mark. A sign set above a vocal part to show that the singer may (or must) take breath at that place ; written variously (', *, √, ∨, //).

Breit (Ger.) Broad, stately, slow.

Brett'geige (Ger.; also *Sack'geige, Spitz'violgeige, Stock'geige, Ta'schengeige*.) A kit.

Breve. 1. (Lat. and Ger. *Brev'is ;* Fr. *brève ;* It. *bre've*.) A note equivalent to 2 whole notes or semibreves; the longest employed in modern music. It is written thus : —2. In medieval music, a note having ½ or ¼ the time-value of the *longa* (comp. *Mensurable music*)...*Alla breve* (It.), (*a*) originally, a time of 4 minims (= 1 breve) to the measure ; time-signature ₵, later ₡ ; this is *2-1* or *great alla breve time.* (*b*) Now, 4-4 time with 2 beats instead of 4 to the measure, and in quicker tempo ; time-signature ₵ ; also called *alla cappella;*—opp. to *Tempo ordinario* 1.

Brev'is (Lat.) A breve.

Bridge. (Ger. *Steg ;* Fr. *chevalet ;* It. *ponticel'lo*.) 1. In bow-instr.s, a thin, arching piece of wood set upright on the belly to raise and stretch the strings above the resonance-box, and to communicate to it their vibrations, which the bridge also cuts off from the rear ends of the strings.—2. In the pfte. and other stringed instr.s, a strip or rail of wood or metal over which the strings are stretched.

Brief. Obsolete for *Breve*.

Brillant,-e (Fr.), **Brillan'te** (It.) Brilliant, showy, sparkling.

Bril'lenbässe (Ger.) "Spectacle-basses," familiar term for the abbreviated notation of alternating eighth-notes or 16th-notes, e. g.

Brin'disi (It.) Drinking-song, sometimes in style of *Jodler*.

Bri'o (It.) Vivacity, spirit, fire...*Con*

brio, or *brio'so,* with fire and vivacity, spiritedly.

Brisé,-e (Fr.)   Broken (as chords)... *Cadence brisée,* a grace consisting of a short trill beginning on the higher auxiliary note:

Broderies (Fr., pl.) Ornaments, embellishments.

Broken cadence. See *Cadence...Broken chords,* chords the tones of which are sounded in succession instead of together (see *Arpeggio*)... *Broken music,* music for the harp, guitar, and other instr.s on which the chords are generally arpeggio'd or broken... *Broken octaves,* series of octaves in which the higher tones alternate with the lower, thus:

B rotun'dum. See *B.*

Brumm'eisen (Ger.) A jew's-harp (usually *Maul' trommel*).

Brum'mer (Ger.) Drone.

Brumm'stimmen (Ger.) "Humming voices"; production of tone without words, through the nose, with closed mouth (*a boc'ca chiu'sa*); a 'not infrequent effect in male quartets, especially as an accomp. to a solo part.

Brumm'ton (Ger.) Drone.

Bruscamen'te (It.) "Brusquely" or forcibly accented.

Brust (Ger.) Breast; chest... *Brust'-stimme,* chest-voice... *Brust' ton,* chesttone... *Brust'werk,* (usually) the pipes of the swell-organ or choir-organ as set up together in the middle of the instr.

Bu'ca (It.) Sound-hole of lute, mandolin, etc.

Bucci'na (Lat.) Either a curved trumpet, originally the horn of an ox; or a straight trumpet (*tuba*), the prototype of the trombone or posaune.

Bucco'lico,-a (It.), **Bucolique** (Fr.) Bucolic, pastoral, rustic.

Büch'se (Ger.) Boot (of a small reed-pipe in the organ); also *Hose.*

Buch'stabentonschrift (Ger.) Alphabetical notation.

Buffa're (It.) To play the wag or buffoon, to jest, trifle.

Buffet (Fr.) Organ-case, or case of any partial organ... *Buffet d'orgues,* a small organ complete, its case and all within.

Buf'fo,-a (It.) Comic, humorous; hence *Buffo, Buffo-singer,* the comic actor in an opera; a comic singer... *Aria buffa,* comic air or aria... *Opera buffa,* comic opera... *Buffone,* comic opera-singer.

Buffone'sco,-a (It.) Droll, ludicrous... *Buffonescamen'te,* drolly, etc.

Bugle, Bugle-horn. (Ger.) *Bü'gelhorn, Flü'gelhorn;* Fr. *bugle;* It. *trom'ba.*) 1. A wind-instr. of brass or copper, with cupped mouthpiece, used for infantry calls and signals, having 7 harmonic tones:

and made in various pitches (*Bb, C, Eb*).—2. The key-bugle (*Kent bugle, Regent's bugle*) (Ger. *Bügelhorn mit Klappen;* Fr. *bugle à clés*); it has 6 keys and ; inv. by Halliday in 1815.— a compass of over 2 3. Valve-bugle octaves: (see *Saxhorn*).

Büh'nenweihfestspiel (Ger.) "Stage-consecrating festival play;" the epithet bestowed by Wagner on *Parsifal,* his last musical drama.

Bund (Ger.) A space between frets, on a fretted fingerboard. [*Bund* is used as effectively synonymous with *fret;* e. g., *Bund 1.* means *1st fret,* the string being stopped *on the fret* by pressure *in the space* just behind it.]... *Bundfrei* ("unfretted," i. e. not spaced off by 2 or more frets or tangents), a term designating a clavichord in which each key had its own string; opp. to *gebunden.*

Buonaccor'do (It.) A small spinet with narrow keys, for children.

Buo'no,-a [boo-ô'no] (It.) Good... *Buona nota,* an accented note (one on a strong beat); *buon gusto,* good taste... *Buonamen'te,* well, accurately.

Burden. 1. A refrain or chorus recurring after each stanza of a song.—2. The drone of the bagpipe.—3. The bass part.

Bur'la (It.) A joke, jest... *Burlan'do,* joking, jesting, romping... *Burle'sca.* a burlesque... *Burle'sco,-a,* burlesque, farcical, comic... *Burlescamen'te,* in burlesque style.

Burlesque. (It. *burle'sca.***)** A dramatic

extravaganza, or farcical travesty of some serious drama or subject, with more or less music.

Burlet′ta (It.) A comical operetta or musical farce.

Busain (*Busaun, Buzain*). A reed-stop in the organ, generally of 16-foot tone, and on the pedal.

Button. 1. A small round disk of leather screwed on the tapped wire of a tracker to keep it in place.—2. A key of the accordion, etc.—3. The round knob at the base of the violin, etc.

Bux′ea tib′ia, Bux′us (Lat.) An ancient ᴐox-wood flute with 3 finger-holes, resembling the Phrygian flute.

C.

C. 1. (Ger. *C;* Fr. *ut;* It. *do.*) The first tone, 1st degree, or key-note of the typical diatonic scale of *C*-major. (Compare *Alphabetical notation*, and *Solmisation.*)... on the pfte.-Middle-*C*, the keyboard; *Tenor* note *c*¹ —> or *C* is small *c*. —2. Abbr. for *Capo* (D. C.=da capo); *Cantus, Canto* (c. f. = cantus firmus or canto fermo); *Col* (c. B.=col basso, c. 8va = coll'ottava); C.-B. (Cb.) = *contrabbasso.*

Cabalet′ta (It.) A song in rondo-form, with variations, often having a triplet accomp. imitating the hoofbeats of a cantering horse.

Cabinet d'orgue (Fr.) Organ-case.

Cabinet organ. See *Reed-organ.*

Cabinet pianoforte. An old style of upright pfte.; a grand pfte. set on end.

Cabis′cola (Lat.) Precentor of a choir.

Cac′cia (It.) The chase ; a hunt...*Alla c.*, in the hunting style (i. e. accompanied by horns).

Cachée (Fr.) Hidden, concealed, covered ; said of fifths and octaves.

Cachu′cha (Sp.) A dance similar to the Bolero.

Cacoph′ony. (Fr. *cacophonie;* It. *cacofoni'a.*) Discord ; harsh or discordant music.

Cadence. (Ger. *Kadenz';* Fr. *cadence;* It. *caden'za.*) 1. See *Cadenza.*—2. The measure or pulsation of a rhythmical movement.—3. (*a*) In general, the closing strains of a melody or harmonic movement. (*b*) Specifically, an harmonic formula (i. e. succession of chords) leading to a momentary or complete musical repose ; the close or ending of a phrase, section, or movement...*Amen c.*, popular term for *plagal c.*, to which the word amen is often sung...*Authentic c.*, see *Perfect c....Avoided, Broken, Deceptive*, or *False c.*, see *Interrupted c...Complete c.*, a perfect c...*Half-cadence* (half-close), or *Imperfect c.*, the chord of the tonic followed by that of the dominant...*Interrupted c.*, an unexpected progression avoiding some regular cadence...*Irregular c.*, an interrupted c...*Medial c.*, in ancient church-music, one in which the mediant was peculiarly prominent...*Mixed c.*, that formed by the succession of the subdominant, dominant, and tonic chords, it thus being a "mixture" of the authentic and plagal cadences... *Perfect c.*, the dominant triad or chord of the 7th followed by the tonic chord ; the *authentic cadence* of the ecclesiastical modes...*Plagal c.*, that formed by the chord of the subdominant followed by the tonic chord ; opp. to *authentic c...Surprise c.*, an interrupted c...*Radical c.*, a close, either partial or complete, formed with two fundamental chords... *Whole c.*, a perfect c.—A few examples are given below :

Authentic.   Plagal.   Interrupted.   Mixed.

Cadence (Fr.) 1. A cadence 2 and 3.— 2. A trill (as *c. brillante, c. perlée*).—*C. brisée*, see *Brisée...C. évitée*, avoided cadence... *C. imparfaite* (or *sur la dominante*), half-cadence. *C. interrompue,* interrupted cadence...*C. irrégulière,* half-cadence...*C. parfaite* (or *sur la tonique*), perfect cadence...*C. plagale,* plagal cadence...*C. pleine,* (*a*) a trill preceded by the higher auxiliary as ᴣ long appoggiatura ; (*b*) the progression from a dissonant chord to a consonant one...*C. rompue*, broken cadence.

Cadent. An obsolete grace (see *Grace*).

Cadenz (Ger.) See *Kadenz*.

Caden'za. 1. A brilliant passage in a vocal solo, usually at its conclusion, having the effect of an extemporization, but commonly prepared beforehand. As an interpolation on the singer's part, such *c. s* are no longer in vogue.—2. An elaborate and florid passage or fantasia introduced in, and interrupting, the closing cadence of the first or last movement of a concerto ; the orchestral accomp. generally pauses after a hold on the $\frac{6}{4}$ chord of the tonic, leaving the field clear for the performance, by the solo instr., of the cadenza. This is either a more or less original effort of the soloist, or a supplementary passage written out by the composer himself or some other musician. Such cadenzas are for the most part built up of themes or reminiscences from the work to which they are appended, and are always calculated to display the soloist's proficiency in the most brilliant light.

Caden'za (It.) A cadence... *C. fin'ta* or *d'ingan'no*, a deceptive cadence... *C. fioritu'ra*, an ornamented cadence.

Cæsura. See *Cesura*.

Caisse (Fr.) A drum... *C. plate*, the shallower side-drum... *C. roulante*, drum with wooden cylinder, that of the ordinary *caisse* being of copper... *Grosse c.*, bass drum (also *Gros-tambour*).

Calamel'lus. See *Calamus*.

Ca'lamus (Lat.) A reed-flute or reed-pipe (chalumeau ; shawm)... *C. pastora'lis*, or *tibia'lis*, a very ancient wood-wind instr., a reed with 3 or 4 finger-holes.

Calan'do (It.) Decreasing. An expression-mark denoting a decrease in loudness, usually coupled with a slackening of the tempo.

Calandro'ne (It.) A small variety of chalumeau or clarinet, a favorite among the Italian peasantry.

Calascio'ne (It.) A variety of lute or guitar with fretted fingerboard, and 2 gut strings, tuned a fifth apart and twanged with a plectrum ; found in lower Italy.

Cala'ta (It.) A lively Italian dance in 2-4 time.

Calcan'do (It.) Hastening the tempo.

Calichon (Fr.) Calascione.

Calisonci'no (It.) Calascione.

Call. A signal given by the fife, bugle or drum, calling soldiers to some special duty.

Calli'ope (also *Kalli'ope*). A steam-organ ; a species of pipe-organ having a harsh tone produced by steam under pressure instead of wind.

Callithum'pian concert. (Ger. *Katz'-enmusik ;* Fr. *charivari ;* It. *chias'so, scampana'ta.*) A boisterous serenade given to some person who has become an object of popular hostility or ridicule ; characterized by the blowing of horns, beating on tin pans, derisive cries, groans, hoots, cat-calls, etc.

Cal'ma (It.) Calm, tranquillity... *Cal-man'do*, calm, growing quieter... *Cal-ma'to*, calmed, tranquilized.

Calo're (It.) Warmth, passion ; *con c.*, with warmth, etc... *Caloro'so*, warmly, passionately.

Cambia're (It.) To alter, change... *Nota cambia'ta*, changing-note.

Ca'mera (It.) Chamber, room... *Mu'sica di c.*, chamber-music... *Sonata di c.*, chamber-sonata... *Alla c.*, in the style of chamber-music.

Camminan'do (It.) "Walking," moving, flowing. (See *Andante*.)

Campa'na (It.) A bell ; in eccles. usage, a church-bell... *Campanel'lo,-a*, a small bell... *Campanelli'no*, a very small bell. ..*Campani'sta*, a bell-ringer.

Campanet'ta (It.) See *Glockenspiel*.

Campanology. Theory of the construction and use of bells.

Canarder (Fr.) To produce a "couac" on the clarinet or oboe.

Canarie (*Canaries, Canary ;* It. *Cana'rio*). A lively dance of French or English origin, the melody being in 6-8 or 4-4 time and having 2 phrases.

Cancel. See *Natural* 1.

Cancrizans (Lat.) Retrogressive. (It. *cancrizzamen'te, cancrizzan'te*.)

Can'na (It.) A reed or pipe... *Canne d'a'nima*, flue-pipes ; *canne a lin'gua*, reed-pipes.

Canon. (Ger. *Ka'non ;* Fr. *canon ;* It. *ca'none.*) 1. The strictest form of mus. imitation, in which two or more parts take up in succession exactly the same subject.—The part taking the lead is called the *antecedent*, and the following part the *consequent*. Canons are now usually written out in full, but during the high tide of medieval counterpoint it was customary to write only the antecedent, and to mark the successive entrances of the other parts by signs or merely by mysterious superscriptions (*enigmatical canons*); the superscription was then called the *canon* (i. e. rule, direction), while the composition was called the *fu'ga* or *conseguen'za*.—According to the interval from the antecedent at which the consequent enters, the canon is called a *C. in unison* (the consequent taking the very same notes as the antecedent, but of course entering later); *C. at the octave* (the consequent entering an octave above or below); *C. at the fifth, fourth*, etc. The *c.* could also be varied, like the fugue, by the diminution or augmentation of the theme, by inversion or retrogression, etc. (Comp. *Fugue*.) When the parts entered at the time-interval of a minim one after the other, the canon was called a *fuga ad minimam*.—2. Ancient Greek name for the Monochord.

Ca'none (It.) A canon...*C. aper'to*, an "open" canon, i. e. one written out in full...*C. cancrizzan'te*, canon by retrogression...*C. chiu'so*, a "close" canon, in which only the leading part is written out in full; an enigmatical canon...*C. enigma'tico*, enigmatical canon (see *Canon*)...*C. infini'to* or *perpe'tuo*, an infinite canon; one which, without a specially added close, can be sung on for ever...*C. sciol'to*, a canon in free imitation.

Canonical hours. The 7 canonical hours of the R. C. Church are the established times for daily prayer; called *matins* (incl. *nocturns* and *lauds*), *prime, terce, sext, nones, vespers*, and *complin*. Those from prime to nones are named after *the hours of the day*, prime (the first hour) being at or about 6 A. M., terce (the third) at 9, sext (the sixth) at noon, and nones (the ninth) at 3 P. M.

Cano'nici. See *Harmonici*.

Canonic imitation, strict imitation of one part by another (see *Canon*).

Canta'bile (It.) In a singing or vocal style. Where a passage is so marked,

the leading melody should stand out well from the accomp., and the general effect should be free and flowing.

Cantamen'to (It.) Same as *Cantilena, Canto*.

Cantan'do (It.) See *Cantabile*.

Cantan'te (It.) A singer; also, singing, gay.

Canta're (It.) To sing...*C. a a'ria*, to sing with more or less improvisation... *C. a orec'chio*, to sing by ear...*C. di manie'ra* or *maniera'ta*, to sing in a florid or ornamental style.

Canta'ta (It.) Originally, a vocal piece, as opp. to an instrumental one, or *sonata*. But *cantata* has come, like sonata, to mean a definite form of composition, with the difference, that all earlier forms once called *cantate* must still be taken into account in defining the word *cantata*, whereas no one would now think of calling a short and simple prelude a *sonata*.—In modern usage, a cantata is a more or less extended vocal work with instrumental accomp., consisting of chorus and solos, recitative, duets, etc.; distinguished from the oratorio and opera by the exclusion of scenic effects and the epic and dramatic element; though the latter can, of course, not be entirely excluded, as even the purest lyrical emotion may often be intensified to dramatic pathos.—In the *sacred cantata* this form of composition finds its finest and most unequivocal expression.

Cantatil'la, Cantati'na (It.) A short cantata. (Fr. *cantatille*.)

Cantato're (It.) A male singer; *Cantatri'ce*, a female singer.

Cantato'rium (Lat.) A music-book, book of song; a service-book of the R. C. Church containing the music of the Antiphonary and Gradual.

Canterellan'do (It.) Singing softly; trilling, warbling; from *canterella're*, to hum, etc.

Can'ticle (Lat. *can'ticum ;* Ger. *Lob'gesang ;* Fr. *cantique ;* It. *can'tico*.) 1. One of the non-metrical hymns of praise and jubilation in the Bible.—2. A sacred chant based on or similar to 1.—The Evangelical canticles (*Cantica majora*) of both the Catholic and Anglican church are taken from the Gospels, and embrace the Magnificat ("Magnificat anima mea"), the Benedictus ("Benedictus dominus deus Israel "), and the Nunc dimittis (" Nunc dimittis servum tuum").—The 7 *Cantica minora* are taken from various parts of the Old Testament.

Can'tico (It.) See *Canticum.*

Can'ticum (Lat.) 1. In the ancient Roman drama, any passage sung by the actors.—2. A canticle.—*Can'tica gra'duum*, the Gradual...*Canticum Cantico'rum*, Solomon's Song.

Cantile'na (It., "a little song"; Ger. *Cantilene;* Fr. *cantilène.*) 1. In medieval music, a solfeggio; also, a *cantus firmus* as used in church-music.—2. Formerly, the higher or solo part of a madrigal; also, a small cantata or short vocal solo.—In modern usage, a ballad or light popular song; also, in instrumental music, a flowing melodious phrase of a vocal character; often used to define a smooth and voice-like rendering of slow melodic passages.

Cantilenac'cia (It.) A vile song.

Cantilena're (It.) To sing in a low voice.

Cantilla'tio (Lat.) See *Intonation* 1.

Canti'no (It.) Same as *Chanterelle.*

Can'tio (Lat.) A song, an air.

Cantique (Fr.) A canticle; also, a choral, or hymn-tune.

Can'to (It.) 1. The soprano; the highest vocal or instrumental part...*Col c.* same as *colla parte.*—2. See *Cantino.*—3. A melody, song, chant.—*C. a cappella*, same as *Cappella, a...C. Ambrosia'no*, Ambrosian chant...*C. armo'nico*, a part-song...*C. croma'tico*, a melody in chromatic style...*C. fer'mo*, see *Cantus firmus...C. figura'to*, figurate melody...*C. Gregoria'no*, Gregorian chant...*C. pla'no*, plain chant...*C. pri'mo*, first soprano...*C. recitati'vo*, recitative or declamatory singing...*C. ripie'no*, see *Ripieno...C. secon'do*, second soprano.

Can'tor 1. (Lat.) A singer, a precentor. ..*C. chora'lis*, chorus-master.—2. (Ger.) See *Kantor* (on p. 238).

Canto're (It.) A singer; a chorister.

Canto'ris (Lat., "of the cantor.") Term designating the side of a cathedral choir on which the precentor (cantor) sits, i. e., on the left or north side of a person facing the altar; opp. to the *deca'ni* (" of the dean") side.

Can'tus (Lat.) A song, a melody...*C. corona'tus*, see *C. fractus...C. du'rus*...

see *Dur...C. ecclesiasticus*, (a) church-music in general; (b) plain song; (c) the musical rendering of a liturgy, opp. to merely reading it...*C. figura'lis*, mensurable music...*C. figura'tus*, a melody with a florid or figurate contrapuntal accomp...*C. fir'mus*, a fixed or given melody; (a) plain song; (b) in modern counterpoint, a given melody, usually in imitation of a, to which other parts are to be set according to rule... *C. frac'tus*, a broken melody; a term applied to a tune which proceeded either by perfect or imperfect consonances. When accomp. by a *faux bourdon*, it was called *Cantus corona'tus*. [STAINER AND BARRETT.]...*C. Gregoria'nus*, Gregorian chant...*C. mensurabilis*, see *Notation*, §3...*C. mol'lis*, see *Moll...C. natura'lis*, see *Mutation... C. pla'nus*, plain song.

Canun'. See *Kanun.*

Canzo'ne (It., also *Canzo'na.*) Originally, a folk-song (Fr. *chanson*); later, a secular part-song in popular style, hence the *Canzo'ni Napolita'ni*, Sicilia'ni, etc.; many such songs closely resemble the madrigal. The name was sometimes applied to instrumental pieces in madrigal style.—*Canzonac'cia*, a vulgar song...*Canzonci'na, Canzonetta*, a little song, a canzonet...*Canzonie're*, a collection of lyric poems or songs.

Canzonet(te). A little air or song; a short part-song; a madrigal.

Capel'le (Ger.) See *K.*

Ca'po (It.) The head, beginning...*Da capo*, from the beginning...*Capolavoro*, master-work...*Capo-orchestra*, conductor.

Capodastre (Fr.) See *Capotasto.*

Capota'sto (It.; also *capo di tasto*, " head of the fingerboard.") 1. The nut of stringed instr.s having a fingerboard. —2. A piece of wood or ivory which can be fastened across a fretted fingerboard, like that of the guitar, to raise the pitch of all the strings at once.—Sometimes written, in Engl. usage, *Capo d'astro.*

Cappel'la (It., "chapel.") 1. A choir. —2. An orchestra. (Incorrectly written *capella.*)...*A cappella*, vocal chorus without instrumental accomp...*Alla c.*, (a) same as *a cappella*; (b) see *Alla breve...Da c.*, in church-style, i. e. in a solemn and devotional manner.

Capricciet'to (It.) A little capriccio.

Capric'cio (It.) Title frequently given to instrumental pieces of free, unconventional form, and distinguished by originality in harmony and rhythm. (Compare *Scherzo.*)...*A capriccio*, at pleasure, ad libitum...*Capricciosamen'te*, capriciously, fantastically...*Capriccio'so*, capricious, fantastic; *a capriccio*.

Caprice (Fr.) Capriccio.

Carat'tere (It.) Character, dignity; style, quality.

Caressant (Fr.)
Carezzan'do (It.) } Caressingly, soothingly.
Carezze'vole (It.)

Carica'to (It.) Overloaded as to graces, chromatics, peculiarities of instrumentation, or other means of mus. expression.

Carillon (Fr.) 1. A set of bells differing from those of a chime in being fixed, and in their greater number; played either by hand (on a keyboard) or machinery (on the principle of the cylinder in the barrel-organ).—2. A bell-piano, with pfte.-keyboard, and bells instead of strings.—3. A melody to be played on 1.—4. An instrumental piece imitating the peculiar character of carillon-music.—5. The "clashing" (ringing all at once) of several large bells.—6. See *Glockenspiel.*—7. A mixture-stop yielding the 3rd, 5th, and 8th partials of the fundamental represented by the digital pressed (c^1—g^2-e^3-c^4).

Carillonneur (Fr.) A performer on the carillon.

Carità' (It.) Lit. "charity." Same as *Affetto.*

Carmagnole (Fr.) A dance and song in great vogue during the Reign of Terror; it dates from the taking (1792) of Carmagnola, a town in Piedmont, though the connection between the town and the air is not clearly established.

Carol. 1. A circle-dance (obs.)—2. A joyous song or ballad, particularly one celebrating Christmas.

Caro'la (It.) A circle-dance similar to the *carmagnole.*

Carrée (Fr.) A breve.

Cartelle (Fr.) A large leaf (for writing) of prepared ass's-skin, on which the lines of the staff are traced to jot down notes while composing, the notes being afterwards erased with a sponge. All *cartelles* come from Rome or Naples. [ROUSSEAU.]

Ca'rynx (Gk.) An ancient Greek trumpet.

Cas'sa (It.) A bass drum. (Also *cassa gran'de.*)...*C. armonica*, body (of violin, etc.)

Cassation' (Ger.) See *K.*

Castanets. (It. *castagnet'te*; Fr. *castagnettes*; Ger. *Kastagnetten*; from Span. *castañetas.*) A pair of small concave pieces of hard wood or ivory, each having a projection on one side, by means of which they are fastened together with a cord long enough also to pass over the performer's thumb, or thumb and forefinger. Generally used (especially in Spain) by dancers as a dance-accomp. They yield no mus. tone, but merely a hollow click or rattle.

Castra'to (It.) A eunuch (adult male singer with soprano or alto voice).

Catalectic. Lacking part of the last foot; e. g. the second of the following lines is catalectic:

Lives of great men all remind us
We can make our lives sublime.

($-\smile|-\smile|-\smile|-\smile||-\smile|-\smile|-\smile|-\smile|-\wedge$)

Catch. Originally, an unaccomp. round for 3 or more voices, written as a continuous melody, and not in score; the "catch" was for each succeeding singer to take up or catch his part at the right time. Later, a new element was introduced, and words were selected in such sequence that it was possible, either by mispronunciation or by interweaving the words and phrases apportioned to the different voices, to produce the most ludicrous and comical effects.

Cate'na di tril'li (It.) A chain of trills.

Catgut. Popular term for *Gut strings* (q.v.)

Catlings. Lute-strings of the smallest size.

Catti'vo (It., "bad.") *Cattivo tempo* the weak beat.

Cau'da (Lat., "tail.") The stem of a note.

Cavallet'to (It., "little horse.") 1. bridge (usually *ponticello*).—2. The break in the voice.

Cavalquet (Fr.) A piece played by a cavalry trumpeter-corps when approaching or marching through a town.

Cava'ta (It.) 1. Production of tone.—2. Cavatina —3. Stroke (of a bow).

Cavati'na (It.) 1. A short song of any description.—2. A vocal air, shorter and simpler than the aria, and in one division, without *Da capo.*—3. Title given by Beethoven to the 2nd movement of his B♭ Quartet.

C barré (Fr.) The "barred C" (₵), indicating alla breve time.

C-clef. See *Clef.*

Cebell. A theme for variation on the lute or violin, in 4-4 time and 4-measure phrases, characterized by the alternation of very high and low notes in the successive strains. (Obs.)

Céciiium (Fr.) A free-reed keyboard instr. inv. by Quantin de Crousard, exhibited at Paris in 1867. It has the shape and nearly the size of the 'cello, and is held in the same way. The keys are pressed by the left hand, while the right operates the bellows by means of a handle like a bow. Compass about 5 octaves; tone sweet and sonorous.

Cédez (Fr.) Go slower; *rallentate.*

Célamustel (Fr.) A kind of reed-organ having fundamental stops similar to those of the harmonium, and various additional effects, such as bells, harp, echo, thunder, dove- and cuckoo-notes, etc.

Ce'lere (It.) Rapid, swift... *Celeritā',* celerity, rapidity; *con celeritā,* with celerity, etc.

Céleste (Fr., "celestial, divine".) *Jeu c., pédale c.,* organ-stops producing a sweet, veiled tone; *Pédale c.* is also a pedal-mechanism on the pfte. for obtaining a sweet, veiled tone... *Voix c.,* the organ-stop *vox angelica.*

'Cello,-i. Abbr. of *Violoncello,-i.*

Cembal d'amour (Fr.) A species of clavichord, twice as long as the ordinary instr.s, the strings of which were struck in the middle by the tangents, the vibration of *both* sections of the string thus yielding a double volume of tone; inv. by G. Silbermann, 1st half of 18th century.

Cembalist, (It. *cembali'sta.*) A player on the cembalo (either harpsichord or pfte.)

Cem'balo (It.) 1. Originally, a dulcimer; a general name for various instr.s having several wire strings struck by hammers.—2. A harpsichord.—3. A pianoforte... *A cembalo,* for harpsichord (or pfte.)... *Tutto il cembalo,* see *Tutte corde... Cembalo onnicor'do,* a keyboard stringed instr. inv. by Nigetti about 1650; also called *Proteus.*

Cembanel'la, Cennamel'la (It.) A pipe or flute.

Cen'to (It.), **Centon** (Fr.) 1. The antiphonary of Pope Gregory the Great.—2. (Also *cento'ne,* "a patchwork".) A medley of extracts from the works of one composer, worked up into an opera or similar composition. (*Pasticcio.*) Hence the verb *centoniza're* (Fr. *centoniser*), meaning "to put together."

Cercar' la no'ta (It.) To seek the note; i. e. to sing in the same breath the tone belonging to the next syllable like a light grace-note, before its proper time of entrance, in portamento style; e. g.

written: sung:

Cervalet', Cervelat'. Species of clarinet with bassoon-like tone (obs.)

Ces (Ger.) C♭...*Ces'es,* C♭♭.

Cesu'ra, Cæsu'ra. A term in prosody sometimes used in music to designate the dividing line between two melodic and rhythmic phrases within a period; called *masculine* or *feminine* according as it occurs after a *strong* or a *weak* beat.

Ce'tera or **Ce'tra** (It.) A cither...*C. tede'sca,* "German cither," a 10-stringed instr. of the lute class.

Chaconne', Chacone'. (It. *ciacco'na;* Span. *chaco'na;* Fr. *chaconne.*) 1. Originally, a Spanish or Moorish (possibly Italian) dance or sarabande.—2. An instrumental composition consisting of a series of variations, above a ground bass not over 8 measures in length, in 3-4 time and slow tempo. (See *Passacaglia.*)

Chair-organ. Variant of *Choir-organ.*

Chalameau. Variant of *Chalumeau.*

Chalil. Ancient Hebrew instr., either a flute (flageolet) or reed-pipe.

Chalumeau (Fr.; Engl. *chalameau;* Ger. *Chalümau, Chalamaus;* It. *scia-lumò, salmò.*) 1. See *Shawm, Clarinet.*—2. The "chalumeau" register is the lowest register of the clarinet and basset-horn; as a direction in clarinet-playing, *chalumeau* signifies "play an octave lower."—3. (In French usage.) The chanter of the bagpipe; also, occasional for Pan's-pipe.

Chamber-music. Vocal or instrumental

music suitable for performance in a room or small hall ; opp. to concert-music, church-music, operatic music, etc.; ordinarily applied to quartets and similar concerted pieces for solo instr.s.

Chamber-organ. A cabinet organ.

Change. 1. In harmony, see *Modulation.*—2. In the voice, see *Mutation.* —3. Any melodic phrase or figure executed on a chime of bells.

Changer de jeu (Fr.) To change the stops of an organ, etc.

Change-ringing. The art and practice of ringing a peal of bells in varying and systematic order.

Changing-chord. A chord containing a number of tones (" changing-notes ") dissonant to the bass, and entering on the strong beat... *Changing-note.* (Ger. *Wech'selnote, Durch'gangston, durch'-gehende Note ;* Fr. *note d'appogiature ;* It. *nota cambia'ta.*) A dissonant note (tone) entering on the strong beat and generally progressing by a step to a consonance within the same chord ; sometimes by a skip to a chord-note or note belonging to another chord.—A *passing-note* differs from a *changing-note* by entering on a weak beat.

Chanson (Fr.) A song ; originally, a ballad-like song ; now rather a vocal solo (*Lied*) with pfte.-accomp... *Chansonnette,* a short chanson. (*Canzonet.*)

Chansonnier (Fr.) 1. A composer of songs.—2. A book or collection of songs.

Chant. 1. A Gregorian melody repeated with the several verses of a prose text, a number of syllables being intoned on each reciting-note ; its 5 divisions are : (1) the intonation ; (2) the first dominant, or reciting-note ; (3) the mediation ; (4) the second dominant or reciting-note ; (5) the cadence. —2. A melody similar in style to the above, and non-rhythmical ; a tone ; called *cantus firmus* in contrapuntal composition.—3. The so-called *Anglican chant,* that employed in chanting the canticles and Psalms ; it consists of 7 measures, harmonized, the time-value of the single note constituting the first and fourth measures being expanded or contracted to fit the words, whereas the others are sung in strict time. It has 2 divisions of 3 and 4 measures respectively, each commencing on a reciting-note and ending with a cadence : the first

cadence is called the *mediation,* and the arrangement of the words to the music is called *pointing.* Any short piece of like character is also called a chant... *Double chant,* one twice as long as the usual chant, having 14 measures, 4 reciting-notes, and 4 cadences... *Changeable chant,* one that can be sung either in major or minor... *Free chant,* one having but 2 chords to each half-verse, for the declamatory singing of the canticles, etc.

Chant (Fr.) Song ; singing ; melody, tune ; voice (i. e. vocal part in contradistinction to the accomp.)... *Ch. composé,* plain song... *Ch. d'église* (or *grégorien*), Gregorian chant... *Ch. en ison,* or *ch. égal,* a chant sung on only 2 tones, thus having but one interval... *Ch. figuré,* figurate counterpoint... *Ch. royal,* mode (*ton*) in which the prayer for the sovereign is chanted... *Ch. sur le livre,* an extemporized counterpoint sung by one body of singers to the plain-song melody (a *cantus firmus*) sung by the others.

Chanter. The melody-pipe of the bag-pipe.

Chanter (Fr.) To sing... *Ch. à livre ouvert,* to sing at sight.

Chanterelle (Fr.) The highest string of an instr. belonging to the violin or lute family, especially the E-string of the violin ; the *soprano string.*

Chanteur (Fr.) A male singer... *Chanteuse,* a female singer.

Chantonner (Fr.) Same as *Canterellare.*

Chantre (Fr.) Leader of a choir... *Grand ch.,* precentor, cantor... *Second ch.,* choir-singer, chorister, choir-boy.

Chapeau (Fr.) A tie ⌒ (usually *liaison*)... *Ch. chinois,* a crescent.

Chapel. A company of musicians attached to the establishment of any distinguished personage. (See *Kapelle.*)

Character, individual, of the several keys.—Theoretically, each major or minor key is precisely like every other major or minor key, the intervals in all being precisely similar. Practically, there subsist recognized differences, due (1) to the system of equal temperament as applied to instruments with keyboard or frets, and (2) to a more or less perceptible tendency towards " forcing up " the sharp keys (thus lending them a brighter and intenser character), and towards " letting down " or relaxing the flat keys (rendering them darker or, as it were, lending them a minor character). The Theoreticians seem disposed to deny *in toto* the possibility of characteristic differences ; while many highly cultivated practical musicians (not to speak of æsthetic enthusiasts of all stripes) are equally positive that such differences exist.

Characteristic piece. A character-piece ; one depicting a definite mood, impression, scene, or event... *Characteristic tone*, (1) the leading-tone ; (2) that tone in any key which specially distinguishes it from nearly related keys, as *F♯* in the key of *G*, distinguishing it from *C*-major.

Characters. See *Signs.*

Charak'terstimme (Ger.) Solo-stop (organ)... *Charak'terstück*, a characteristic piece.

Charivari (Fr.) A callithumpian concert.

Chasse, à la (Fr.) *Alla caccia.*

Chef d'attaque (Fr.) The leader of an orchestra, or of any division of a chorus. ..*Chef d'orchestre,* conductor of an orchestra... *Ch. du chant,* see *Repetitor.*

Chelys (Gk., "tortoise.") 1. The lyre of Mercury, fabled to have been a tortoise-shell with strings stretched over its hollow.—2. Name for both the bass viol and division viol in the 16th and 17th centuries.

Cheng. The Chinese mouth-organ, the wind-chest of which is formed by a gourd into which the air is blown through a curving tube, and bears on its upper side from 12 to 24 free-reed pipes. Its introduction into Europe led to the invention of the accordion and harmonium.

Chest of viols. A set of viols, i. e. 2 trebles, 2 tenors, and 2 basses, which formed the nucleus of the 17th century orchestra. (Also *Consort of viols.*)

Chest-register. The lower register of the male or female voice, the tones of which produce sympathetic vibration in the chest... *Chest-tone, chest-voice,* a vocal tone possessing the quality of the chest-register ; opp. to *Head-register, head-tone.*

Chevalet (Fr.) Bridge.

Cheville (Fr.) Peg... *Cheviller,* peg-box.

Chevrotement (Fr.) See *Bockstriller...* *Chevroter,* to execute a *chevrotement.*

Chiari'na (It.) A clarion.

Chia'ro,-a (It.) Clear, pure... *Chiaramen'te,* clearly, limpidly, distinctly... *Chiarez'za,* clearness, etc.

Chia've (It.) 1. A clef.—2. Key of an instr.—3. Tuning-key.

Chiavet'te, or **Chiavi trasporta'ti** (It., " transposed clefs.") A system of transposing clefs, freely used in the 16th century. As it was then a rule, but seldom infringed, that no vocal part should overstep the limits of the 5-line staff, and the modern system of chromatic transposition being undeveloped, composers often employed, in the notation of the various parts, clefs differing from those customarily used for the several voices, these unusual clefs indicating to the practised singers a transposition of their respective parts to a higher or lower pitch :

1. High chiavette.

Discant.   Alto.   Tenor.   Bass.

2. Ordinary clefs.

3. Low chiavette.

The *high chiavette* had the effect of transposing the parts (and consequently the entire composition) into a key a major or minor third higher, i. e. their effect was equivalent to writing *3 flats* or *4 sharps* in a signature headed by the ordinary clef ; the *low chiavette* had a precisely opposite effect, as if *3 sharps* or *4 flats* had been written after the ordinary clef.—Though not recognized as such, this system was tantamount to a pretty free use of the transposing scales.

Chi'ca. An old Spanish dance, modifications of which are the Fandango, Chaconne, Cachucha, Bolero, and possibly the English Jig.

Chie'sa (It.) Church... *Concer'to da ch.,* a sacred concert... *Sonata da ch.,* a sacred sonata... *Da chiesa,* for the church, in church-style.

Chiffre (Fr.) A figure, as in thorough-bass.

Chifonie (Fr.) Old name of the hurdy-gurdy.

Chikara. A Hindu violin having 4 or 5 horsehair strings.

Chime. 1. A set of from 5 to 12 bells tuned to the tones of the scale, and employed in playing the chimes by swinging either the bells themselves, or clappers hung within them.—2. A set of bells and strikers (hammers) in a musical box, organ, etc. (See *Carillon*.)

Chiming-machine. A revolving drum with pins so set as to pull the ropes of a chime of bells and ring the chime mechanically.

Chirogym'nast. An apparatus for exercising the hands of players on the pfte. or organ, consisting of a set of rings attached by springs to a cross-bar.

Chi'roplast. (Ger. *Hand'leiter*, i. e. hand-guide.) An apparatus inv. by Logier about 1814, consisting of 2 smooth wooden rails attached in front of and parallel with the pfte.-keyboard, and a pair of open gloves, the whole serving to hold both hands in the proper position for playing, by hindering the wrist from sinking and obliging the fingers to strike vertically. Simplified later by Kalkbrenner.—Termed by Liszt "ass's guide" (*guide-âne*) for the French "hand-guide" (*guide-main*).

Chitar'ra (It.) A guitar.—The Italian guitar, like the English cither, was strung with wire instead of gut strings. ..*Ch. coll'arco*, a bow-guitar...*Chitarri'na*, a small Neapolitan guitar...*Chitarro'ne*, "great guitar;" a kind of theorbo differing from the arciliuto in having a longer neck, a wider space between the 2 sets of pegs, and a smaller body. It had 20 wire strings, 12 being over the fingerboard. (See *Lute*.)

Chiu'so,-a (It.) Closed; hidden...*Ca'none chiuso*, see Canone...*Con bocca chiusa*, with closed mouth (comp. *Brummstimmen*).

Chœur (Fr. [*ch* like *k*.]) Choir, chorus. ..*À grand chœur*, for full chorus.

Choice-note. An alternative note written above or below another in a vocal part, which the singer may take in preference if he choose.

Choir. (Ger. *Chor;* Fr. *chœur;* It. *co'ro*.) 1. A company of singers, especially in a church; hence, the part of the church which they occupy.—2. A choral society.—3. (In the Anglican Church.) A body of officials whose function is the performance of the daily choral service, sitting divided on the *decani* and *cantoris* sides of the chancel.—4. A subdivision of a chorus, e. g. the 1st and 2nd choirs (*coro primo e secondo*) in 8-part music.—5. Same as *Band* 3.

Choir-organ. (See *Organ*.)...*Choir-pitch*, (see *Chorton*).

Chor (Ger.) 1. Chorus; choir.—2. On the pfte., a unison (the 2 or 3 strings belonging to one tone).—3. On the organ, those pipes belonging to a mixture which are sounded by one key.—4. A combination of instr.s of the same family, but different pitch, e. g. *Trompetenchor*.

Chora'gus, Chore'gus (Gk.) The leader or superintendent of the ancient dramatic chorus. Hence, in Oxford (England), the title of a functionary who has charge of the mus. services in church.

Cho'ral (*adj.*) Relating or pertaining to a chorus or vocal concerted music... *Choral notes*, see *Note*...*Choral service*, a church-service consisting chiefly of music by the choir.

Cho'ral (*noun.*) 1. (Ger. *Choral'*; Fr. *cantique, plain-chant;* It. *can'tico, canzo'ne sa'cra*.) A hymn-tune of the early German Protestant Church; also, a hymn-tune similar in style to the above. (Sometimes spelled *Chorale*.) —2. (In the R. C. Church.) Any part of the service sung by the choir.

Chora'leon. See *Æolomelodicon*.

Chora'liter (Lat.) } In the style of a
Choral'mässig (Ger.) } choral.

Choral'note (Ger.) A choral note.

Chor'buch (Ger.) See *Part-book* 2.

Chord. 1. (Ger. *Akkord'*; Fr. *accord;* It. *accor'do*.) In a general sense, the harmony of 2 or more tones of different pitch produced simultaneously.—As a technical term, a combination of from 3 to 5 different tones, formed by erecting, upon a fundamental tone or root, an ascending series of diatonic th'rds. A 3-tone chord is called a *triad*, a 4-tone chord a *chord of the 7th*, and a 5-tone chord a *chord of the 9th*. The term *chord* is often applied specifically to the triads, as *major chord, minor* *chord, fundamental chord,* etc.—A View of the fundamental diatonic chords follows, with the ordinary figuring in thorough-bass and theory :

Triads in Major.

C: I II III IV V VI VII⁰

Triads in Minor.

c: I II⁰ III′ IV V VI VII⁰

Chords of the Seventh in Major.

C: I₇ II₇ III₇ IV₇ V₇ VI₇ VII₇⁰

Chords of the Seventh in Minor.

c: I₇ II₇⁰ III₇′ IV₇ V₇ VI₇ VII₇⁰

Chords of the Ninth :

in major :   in minor :

etc.

When the root of a chord is the lowest tone, the chord is said to be in the *fundamental position;* when some other tone is the lowest, the chord is *inverted.* Each triad has 2 *inversions,* and each chord of the 7th has 3. The inversions are limited neither to the given number of tones, nor to any particular order of the intervals above the bass ; e. g. a chord of the sixth may be written

C: I I I I I I I

6 6 6 6 6 6 6 etc.

that is, it remains a chord of the *sixth* so long as the *third* of the triad remains the *lowest tone,* above which the (octave of the) *root* forms the interval of a

sixth. The **Arabic numerals** over the bass form what is called thorough-bass figuring ; each figure marks the interval of some tone above the bass (or lowest tone), the order of the figures depending, not upon the order of the notes, but upon the width of the intervals, the widest interval always being written at the top. The simple figures invariably call for the diatonic intervals as established by the key-signature. O calls for *tasto solo* (see *Tasto*) ; 2 or $\frac{4}{2}$ or $\frac{4}{2}$, for the chord of the second (in full, chord of the second, fourth and sixth) ; 3 or $\frac{5}{3}$ or $\frac{8}{5}$, (*a*) for the simple triad, (*b*) 3 alone over the first bass note signifies that the soprano takes the third of the root ; $\frac{4}{3}$ or $\frac{6}{4}$ calls for the chord of the third and fourth (and sixth) ; 5, for the fifth in the soprano ; $\frac{5}{3}$, for the simple triad ; 6, for the chord of the sixth ; $\frac{6}{4}$, for the chord of the fourth and sixth ; $\frac{6}{5}$, or $\frac{6}{5}$, for that of the fifth and sixth ; 7 ($\frac{7}{5}$), for the chord of the seventh ; 8, for the octave in the soprano, $\frac{8}{3}$, for the simple triad ; 9, ($\frac{9}{7}$ or $\frac{9}{3}$, according as the fifth or seventh is dropped), for the chord of the ninth. $\frac{10}{8}$ $\frac{11}{9}$ $\frac{12}{10}$ were formerly used to show that the tenth and octave, eleventh and ninth, etc. of the bass note were to be taken instead of the third and prime, fourth and second, etc. Where there is a choice, the simpler figuring is preferable, unless some interval is chromatically altered. A ♯, ♭, ♮, ×, or ♭♭ *alone* over a bass note signifies that the *third* in the chord is correspondingly altered chromatically. A crossed figure (*4, 4, 5,* etc.) indicates that the interval is sharped. A dash (–) after a figure prolongs the tone into the next chord.—The **Roman numerals** under the bass form no part of the thorough-bass figuring ; they indicate on what degree of the scale the given chord (i. e. the *root* of the chord) has its seat, the key or scale itself being marked by a capital letter for major and a small letter for minor. A large numeral indicates a triad with major third ; a small numeral, a triad with minor third ; with an accent (III′), the augmented fifth ; with a cipher (VII⁰), the diminished fifth ; with a 7 (V₇), the chord of the seventh. [This is the system generally accepted ; its prime defect (clumsiness in following chromatic alterations, and consequent inability to cope with the exigencies of free tonality) is felt by all theorists ; *Jadassohn* solves the problem empirically by stretching his highly elastic theory of altered chords to the utmost ;—e. g. he writes $C:IV$ ($=f\sharp$-*a*♭-*c* as the major triad on the 4th degree of *C*-major !)—*Riemann*, on the other hand, has devised an entirely new system, explained under art. *Phone.*] (Also comp. *Thorough-bass.*)

Altered chord, a chord chromatically changed, but not effecting a modulation ; the commonest *altered chords* are the triads on the 1st, 2nd, 4th and 5th degrees in major and on the 4th and 6th degrees in minor (with altered fifth) ; on the 2nd degree in major and 6th in minor (with altered root) ; the chords of the 7th on the same degrees, excepting the 6th in minor (with altered fifth), and on the 7th degree in major and 2nd in minor (with altered root)...*Anomalous ch.*, see *Anomaly*...*Augmented ch.*, one having major third and augm. fifth...*Broken ch.*, an arpeggio...*Chromatic ch.*, one chromatically altered...*Common ch.*, a triad peculiar to any given scale...*Derivative ch.*, one derived by inversion from another...*Diatonic ch.*, a common chord...*Diminished ch.*, one having both 5th and 7th diminished...*Dominant ch.*, (*a*) the dom. triad, (*b*) the dom. ch. of the 7th...*Doubtful* or *Equivocal ch.*, a dissonant chord of uncertain resolution, like that of the dimin. 7th, which belongs to various keys, and may resolve to any one of them...*Fundamental chord*, (*a*) one in the fundamental position, i. e. with the root lowest ; (*b*) the tonic triad ; (*c*) one of the 3 principal triads of a key (tonic, dominant, and subdominant) ; (*d*) a common chord...*Imperfect* or *incomplete ch.*, a chord, one of whose tones is omitted. ..*Inverted ch.*, see *Inversion*...*Leading ch.*, the dominant ch. of the 7th. ..*Major, minor ch.*, see *Major, Minor*. ..*Related* or *relative ch.*, see *Relation*. ..*Seventh-chord*, ch. of the 7th...*Solid ch.*, one whose tones are produced simultaneously ; opp. to *broken*...*Transient ch.*, one used in modulating from one key to another, and foreign to both. —2. A string.

Chor′da (Lat.) 1. A string.—2. A tone or chord... *Ch. characteri′stica*, a chord of the 7th containing a leading-note...

Chordæ essentia′les, the key-note with its third and fifth, the tonic triad.

Chordaulo′dion, or **Chordomelo′dion**. A kind of automatic barrel-organ having pipes and strings combined ; inv. by Kaufmann of Dresden, in 1812.

Chordom′eter. A string-gauge.

Cho′ree, Chore′us. A metrical foot identical with the trochee.

Cho′riamb, Choriam′bus. A metrical foot having 2 short syllables between 2 long ones, the ictus being on either of the latter ($-\!\!\smile\smile-$, or $-\!\smile\smile-\!$).

Chor′ister. 1. A singer in a choir.—2. A precentor.

Chor′ton (Ger.) "Choir-pitch," i. e. the pitch at which church-choirs formerly sang in Germany, as set by the organs. (See *Pitch, absolute*.)

Cho′rus. (Ger. *Chor;* Fr. *chœur;* It. *co′ro*.) 1. A company of singers.—2. In an opera, oratorio, etc., the main body of singers, as distinguished from the soloists and orchestra.—3. A refrain. —4. A composition, or any part of one, oftenest in 4 parts, intended to be sung in chorus ; a *double chorus* has 8 parts. —5. The compound stops of an organ. —6 (obs.) The bagpipe ; the drone of the bagpipe, or the free sympathetic strings of the crowd.

Chorus-master. The leading singer in a chorus.

Chri′ste ele′ison (Gk.) Part of the Kyrie in the Mass (see *Mass*).

Chro′ma (Gk., "color"). 1. In Greek music, a chromatic modification of the tetrachord.—2. A sign altering the pitch of a note by a semitone ($\sharp$ or ♭) ; also, a chromatic semitone.—3. An eighth-note or quaver (♪); *ch. simplex*, (*a*) an eighth-note, (*b*) a $\sharp$ or ♭ ; *ch. duplex*, (*a*) a 16th-note (♬), (*b*) a × or ♭♭.—4. A semitone.

Chromat′ic. (Ger. *chroma′tisch*, Fr. *chromatique;* It. *croma′tico*.) Relating to tones foreign to a given key or chord ; opp. to *diatonic*...*Chr. alteration*, raising or lowering the pitch of a note by means of a chromatic sign ; *of a chord*, or *melody*, the introduction into it of one or more tones foreign to the ruling diatonic key, but not effecting a modulation (then sometimes called a chromatic chord or melody)...*Chr. harmony*, a succession of chromatically altered chords...*Chr. instrument*, one producing the tones of the chr. scale... *Chr. interval*, an interval chromatically augmented or diminished... *Chr. scale*, see *Scale*... *Chr. semitone*, an interval formed by altering a note of the natural scale by a sharp or flat, or by further altering such a sharped or flatted interval by a × or ♭♭. (See *Semitone*.)... *Chromatic signs*, the characters used in mus. notation for raising or lowering the pitch of (*a*) natural notes, (*b*) notes already raised or lowered (comp. Table, art. *Interval*). Those now in use are the *Sharp* (♯), *Flat* (♭), *Natural* (♮), *Double-sharp* (×), *Double-flat* (♭♭); the *Great Flat* (♭) is obsolete; the combined sign ♯♮ (or ♮♭) signifies that a note previously sharped (or flatted) is first restored to its natural pitch on the staff and then sharped (or flatted); the *Double-natural* (♮♮) is superfluous and incorrect.—The chromatic signs at the head of the staff are called the *key-signature* (see *Key* 1); such as occur irregularly in the course of a composition are called *accidentals*. An accidental, as a general rule, affects its note only during the measure in which it is written, unless the note be tied into the next measure or measures:

higher or lower octaves of the note are not affected, and must therefore likewise take an accidental.

Chromatic (*noun*.) A chromatically altered note.

Chronom′eter. Occasional for *Met′ronome.*

Chronomètre (Fr.) A species of monochord, made to sound by means of a keyboard like that of the pfte., to teach the tuning of the latter; inv. in 1827 by Raller, pfte.-maker in Paris.

Chrot′ta. See *Crowd.*

Church-modes. See *Mode.*

Chute (Fr.) A grace-note or appoggiatura either above or below the melody-note;
written:

played:

—Also, a slide descending by a third:

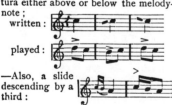

Ciacco′na (It.) Chaconne.

Cico′gna (It., lit. "stork.") The mouthpiece of a wind-instr.

Cicu′ta (Lat.) A sort of flute, or Pan's-pipe.

Cifra′to (It.) Figured.

Cim′bal. See *Cymbal.*

Cim′balo (It.) 1. A cymbal.—2. A harpsichord.—3. A tambourine.

Cim′balon. Same as *Zimbalon.*

Cim′bel (Ger.) See *Cymbal* 2... *Cim′belstern*, see *Zimbelstern.*

Cinel′le (It., pl.) Cymbals.

Cink (Ger.), **Cinq** (Fr.) See *Zink* 2.

Cin′que (It.) A fifth part in concerted music... *A cinque*, for or in 5 parts.

Cinque-pace. An old (presumably French) dance, with a 5-step movement.

Cipher. A tone is said to "cipher" on the organ when, owing to some derangement in the action, it persists in sounding.

Circle-(or circular) canon. See *Canon*... *Circle of fifths*, see *Temperament.*

Cir′colo mez′zo (It.) A turn. (Now *Gruppetto.*)

Cir′culus (Lat., "circle".) A time-signature in medieval music. (See *Notation*, §3.)

Cis (Ger.) C♯.—*Cis′is*, C×.

Cistel′la (Lat., "little box.") A dulcimer.

Cistole, Cistre, Citole. See *Zither.*

Cistrum. See *Sistrum.*

Ci′thara (Lat.; It. *ci′tara*.) An ancient instr. of the lyre family, from which many medieval and several modern instr.s (guitar, zither) derive their names and, in part at least, their construction. See *Cither*... *C. biju′ga*, a two-necked cither.

Cith′er (also *cithern, cittern*; Fr. *cistre, sistre*; It. *ce′tera, ce′tra*). An instr. strung with wire and played with a plectrum; a variety of lute or guitar, in vogue during the 16th and 17th centuries. (See *Zither.*)

Citole. A small dulcimer.

Civetteri′a (It.) Coquetry... *Con c.*, in a coquettish, trifling style.

Clairon (Fr.) 1. A clarion (either the instr. or the organ-stop)... *Cl. chromatique*, a species of valve-trumpet made in 6 different pitches, (as a contrabass, bass, barytone, tenor, alto and soprano.)—2. *Clarinetto register* of the clarinet.—3. Bugler (for infantry).

Clang. See *Klang*.

Clang-color, Clang-tint. Timbre, "tone-color ;" the quality of a tone, dependent on the number and intensity of its harmonics.

Claquebois (Fr.) Xylophone.

Clarabella. An organ-stop having open wooden pipes of 8-foot pitch and soft, mellow tone.

Claribel-flute. A 4-foot *Clarabella*.

Clarichord. An instr. of the late middle ages, apparently a variety of harp, though thought by some to have been identical with the clavichord.

Clarin (Fr.) See *Clarion*.

Clarinet'. 1. (Ger. *Klarinet'te;* Fr. *clarinette;* It. *clarinet'to*.) The parent instr. of the clarinet family was the chalumeau, a primitive wind-instr. having a cylindrical tube with 9 finger-holes, and a beating reed ; its entire scale

was composed of the prime tones produced by successively opening the holes.—The modern clarinet differs from the chalumeau chiefly in its ability to reproduce the prime tones of its scale (or rather their third partials) *a twelfth higher;* this result is due to the addition of a small hole, covered by an extra key, at the nodal point dividing the air-column into 3 equal portions,—an improvement attributed to Joh. Chr. Denner of Nuremberg about 1700. The higher scale or register thus obtained was termed, by reason of its bright and piercing quality, *clarinetto* (whence the name of the modern instr.); the original lower scale retained the name of the old chalumeau.—The soprano clarinet in *C* is the typical instr. of the family ; compass 3 octaves and a sixth (with chromatic intermediate tones):

It has a cylindrical wooden tube pierced by 18 holes, 13 of which are closed by keys, yielding a chromatic series of 19 prime tones (*e* to *b¹♭*); it is composed of 5 pieces or joints, namely, the *mouthpiece* with the reed, the *socket* (Ger. *Birne*), the "*right-hand*" and "*left-hand*" joints of the tube proper, and the *bell;* its higher registers are simply the third, and fifth or ninth, partials of the prime tones (from *b¹♭* to *f³*, and *f³♯* to *c⁴*.) The quality of the tone differs greatly in the four registers, the "chalumeau" and "clarinetto" being comparable to the female contralto and soprano respectively, while the medium is weak and veiled, and the highest shrill and piercing. Several sizes are made : (1) The *large soprano cl.* in *C, B♭*, and *A*, and (2) the *small soprano clarinets* in *D, E, F* and *A♭*, these last being mostly used in military music, in which their position is similar to that held by the violins in the orchestra. There are also *alto* (or *barytone*) *clarinets* in *F* and *E♭*, and *bass clarinets* in *C, B♭*, or *A* (octave below the soprano instr.s of the symphony-orchestra). The *cl.* is a transposing instr., and its music is written in the *C*-clef. The fingering is very complicated and the reed difficult to manage, a slight error of judgment sufficing to produce the fatal " couac."—2. See *Clarionet* 2.

Clarinet-stop. See *Krumm'horn*.

Clarinet'to (It.) See *Clarinet*.

Clari'no (It.) 1. Clarion 1 and 2.—2. A name loosely applied to the trumpet and bugle.—3. Used for *tromba*, in some old scores.

Clarion. 1. A small, shrill-toned trumpet.—2. In the organ, a 4-foot reed-stop of a shrill, piercing tone.

Clarionet. 1. A clarinet.—2. In the organ, an 8-foot reed-stop of soft tone. ..*Clarionet-flute*, a flue-stop with perforated cover.

Classic. In a restricted sense, a composition is called classic when it belongs to an acknowledged style in art, and is by an acknowledged master of that style.—In a broader sense, any composition may be termed classic which, in its kind, might be taken as a model for imitation, and in which the form :s in perfect harmony with the ·spirit or subject-matter.—*Classic* is also often used as a distinctive epithet for the works of the earlier masters, including Beethoven, and their imitators, in contrast to those of the *romantic* school ; *classic forms* being the aria, rondo, sonata, symphony, etc.

Clau′sula (Lat.) A cadence.

Clavecin (Fr.) A harpsichord...*Cl. acoustique*, a French invention of the 18th century, imitating several stringed and wind-instruments.

Claviatur′ (Ger.) Keyboard (*Klaviatur*).

Clavicem′balo (It.) Harpsichord.

Clavichord. (Ger. *Kla′vichord, Klavier′;* Fr. *clavicorde;* It. *clavicor′do.*) One of the precursors of the pfte. (see *Pianoforte*), differing in action from the latter in having, instead of hammers, upright metal wedges called tangents on the rear end of the digitals; on depressing a digital the tangent struck the wire and remained pressed against it till the finger was lifted, causing only one section of the string to vibrate. (Compare *Gebunden.*)

Clavicithe′rium(-cythe′rium.) An obsolete instr., supposed to have been a kind of harpsichord, but with the strings stretched in a vertical frame instead of horizontally.

Clavicor (Fr.) A kind of *cor à pistons.*

Clavicylin′der (Ger.) A keyboard instr. inv. by Chladni about 1800, containing a glass cylinder caused to revolve by a treadle, and steel wands or bars instead of strings, which were pressed against the revolving cyiinder on touching the digitals, and thus made to sound ; compass 4½ octaves.

Clavier′ [*-veer′*]. (Ger. *Klavier′.*) 1. A keyboard (*Klaviatur*).—2. (Ger.) Generic name for all keyboard instr.s except organs ; especially (formerly) for the clavichord, and (at present) for the pianoforte. See *Klavier.*

Clavier (Fr.) 1. A keyboard...*Posséder son cl.*, to know one's keyboard... *Cl. de récit, Récit expressif*, swell-manual (organ).—2. The range or scale of notes comprised on the grand staff without leger-lines.

Claviglissan′do. A keyboard instr. consisting of a combination of mechanisms for producing various harmonium effects, and also the *portamento* of the violin ; inv. by Le Jeune.

Cla′vis (Lat.) 1. A key (digital), clef, or note.—2. Bellows-handle.

Clé, Clef (Fr.) 1. Clef ; *armer la clef*, to furnish the clef with the key-signatures.—2. Key (of a wind-instr.)

Clef. (Ger. *Schlüs′sel :* Fr. *clé, clef;* It. *chia′ve.*) A character set at the head of the staff to fix the pitch or position of one note, and thus of the rest. The 3 now in use are the *F*-clef, *C*-clef, and *G*-clef ; the *F*-clef and *G*-clef are also called the *Bass*-clef and *Treble*-clef respectively, because they fix the position of the bass and treble notes. The *C*-clef is variously called the *Tenor-*, *Alto-*, and *Soprano*-clef, according as it is set on the 4th, 3d, or 1st line of the staff ; wherever placed, it marks the position of Middle-*C* (Tenor-*C.*) A view of the clefs used at present is appended.

Bass-clefs.   C-clefs.   Treble-clef.   Tenor-clef (recen).

The *F*-clef on the 3rd line (*Barytone*-clef), the *C*-clef on the 2nd (*Mezzo-Soprano*-clef), the *G*-clef on the 1st line (*French violin*-clef), or on the 3rd line, are no longer used (the *C*-clef on the 2nd line occasionally). The ⨎ is sometimes used in vocal double G-clef : ⨎ music as a tenor-clef, signifying that the part lies an octave lower than written.—Our modern forms of the clefs are corruptions of the letters *f, c,* and *g,* formerly plainly written.

Cliquette (Fr.) The bones.

Close (noun; Ger. *Schluss*). See *Cadence* 3.

Close harmony or **position.** See *Harmony*...*Close play,* a style of lute-playing in which the fingers were kept on the strings as much as possible.

Co′da (It., "tail.") Specificaily, a passage finishing a movement, and beginning where the repetition of the first subject ends. Originally, it was a few chords (or a short passage) intended as a winding-up ; it became of growing importance in the canon, sonata, rondo, etc., and is frequently developed into an almost independent concluding division. —Also, the stem or tail of a note (*cauda*)... *Codetta*, a short coda. (See *Fugue*.)

Cœlestina (or -o). A name bestowed in the 18th century on several modifications of keyboard stringed instr.s, in which alterations of the tone could be produced by mechanisms under the player's control.

Coffre (Fr.) Case (of a pfte.) ; body (of a violin).

Co'gli stromenti (It.) With the instruments.

Coi, col, coll', col'la, col'le, col'lo (It.) With the.

Colascio'ne (It.) See *Calascione*.

Collet de violon (Fr.) Neck of a violin.

Collinet (Fr.) A flageolet ; named after a celebrated player.

Col'ophony. (Ger. *Kolophon' ;* Fr. *colophane ;* It. *colofo'nia ;* from Lat. *colopho'nium*.) Resin or rosin.

Color. 1. Timbre (tone-color).—2. The characteristic rhythms, harmonies, and melodies of a composition.—3. (Lat.) See *Notation*, §3.

Colora'to (It.) Florid, figurate.

Coloratu'ra (It.) Coloratore, i. e. vocal runs, passages, trills, etc., enhancing the brilliancy of a composition and displaying the vocalist's skill.—Also applied to similar instrumental music.

Coloris (Fr.; Ger. *C(K)olorit' [Far'ben-gebung]*). The tonal "color-scheme," vocal or instrumental, of a composition, movement, or scene ; i. e. the modifications in vocal or instrumental timbre, or in the instrumentation, employed for obtaining special effects.

Col'po (It., "blow".) *Di colpo*, at a blow, suddenly, at once.

Combination pedal. See *Pedal*... *Combination tones* (combinational tones), see *Acoustics*.

Combined mode. See *Dur Moll-Tonart*.

Co'me (It.) As, like... *C. prima*, as at first, as before... *C. sopra*, as above... *C. sta*, as it stands, as written.

Co'mes (Lat.) Answer (in a fugue) : consequent (in a canon).

Comma. 1. A comma (,) is often used as a breathing-mark.—2. (*a*) *Didymic* or *syntonic c. :* The difference between the greater and lesser whole tone, or 80:81 ; (*b*) *Pythagorean c.*, or *c. maxima :* The difference between the octave of a given tone and a tone 6 whole tones higher than the given tone, or 524288:531441.

Com'modo (It. ; also *co'modo*.) Easy, leisurely, at a convenient pace ; as *allegro commodo... Commodamen'te*, easily, quietly, leisurely... *Commodet'to*, rather easy or leisurely.

Common chord. A major or minor triad... *Common hallelujah metre*, or *Common long metre*, a 6-line stanza formed of a common-metre stanza with half a long-metre stanza added ; thus, 8 6 8 6 8 8... *Common measure*, see *C. time*... *Common metre*, a form of iambic stanza, of 4 lines containing alternately 8 and 6 syllables ; thus, 8 6 8 6... *Double common metre*, a stanza formed of 2 common-metre stanzas... *Common particular metre*, a 6-line stanza, the 3rd and 6th lines having 6 syllables, and the others 8 each ; thus, 8 8 6 8 8 6... *Common time*, a measure containing 2 (or 4) half-notes or 4 quarter-notes, with 2 or 4 beats respectively ; duple or quadruple time. (Ordinarily, *common time* is understood to mean 4 quarter-notes [and as many beats] to a measure.)

Compass. (Ger. *Um'fang ;* Fr. *diapason ;* It. *estensio'ne*.) The range of a voice or instr., i. e. the scale of all the tones it can produce, from the lowest to the highest.

Compiace'vole (It.) Pleasing, delightful.

Com'plement. An interval which, added to any given interval not wider than an octave, completes the octave ; thus a fourth is the *c.* of a fifth, a minor sixth of a major third, etc. Also *complementary interval*.

Comple'tory. (Lat. *completo'rium*.) 1. An anthem supplementary to an antiphon in the lauds and vespers of the Ambrosian rite.—2. See *Complin*.

Com'plin(e). The last of the 7 canonical hours.

Componi'sta (It.) Composer.

Composition pedal. In the organ, a pedal which draws out or pushes in several stops at once. (Comp. *combination pedal.*)

Composizio'ne (It.) Composition... *C. di tavoli'no*, table-music.

Compound interval. See *Interval*... *C. measure, rhythm, time*, see *Time*... *C. stop*, an organ-stop having more than one rank of pipes.

Con (It.) With.

Concave pedals. See *Radiating*.

Concen'to (It.) 1. Concord, harmony. —2. The simultaneous sounding of all the tones of a chord ; opp. to *arpeggio*.

Concen'tus (Lat.) 1. Concord, harmony.—2. Part-music.—3. See *Accentus*.

Con'cert. 1. A set of instr.s of the same family but different in size (see *Chest, Consort*).—2. A concerto.—3. (Ger. *Konzert'*; Fr. *concert*; It. *concer'to*.) A public mus. performance...*Dutch concert*, the singing of an entire company in which each person sings whatever he pleases ; or the persons present sing in alternation any verse that comes into their heads, the refrain by the whole company being a regular repetition of some popular verse... *Concert spirituel* (Fr.), sacred concert.

Concertan'te (It.) Concordant, harmonious.—Hence : 1. A concert-piece. —2. A composition for two or more solo voices or instr.s with accomp. by organ or orchestra, in which each solo part is in turn brought into prominence —3. A composition for 2 or more solo instr.s without orchestra... *Concertante parts*, parts for solo instr.s in orchestral music... *Concertante style*, a style of composition admitting of a brilliant display of skill on the soloist's part... *Concerta'to*, concerted.

Concerted music. Music written in parts for several instr.s or voices, as trios, quartets, etc.

Concert-grand. See *Pianoforte*.

Concerti'na. The improved accordion inv. by Wheatstone in 1829. The keyboards are hexagonal ; the compass of the *treble c.* is 4 octaves: including all chromatic tones ; it is 8*va* a double action instr., producing the same tone on drawing out and on pushing in the bellows. *Tenor, bass,* and *double-bass concertinas* are also made. A great variety of music can be played, and the literature is quite extensive ; the instr. is likewise capable of great expression, and the tone is susceptible of considerable modification.

Concerti'no (It.) 1. A small concert. —2. Equiv. to *concertan'te*, i. e. leading, principal ; as *violino concertino*, principal violin ;—here opp. to *ripie'no*.

Concerti'sta (It.) Concert-player, solo performer, virtuoso.

Concert-master. See *Konzert'meister*.

Concer'to. (Ger. *Konzert'*.) An extended composition for a solo instr., commonly with orchestral accomp., in sonata-form modified to suit the character of the solo instr. (e. g. the *cadenza*); pfte.-concertos in which the pfte.-part is comparatively inconspicuous are jocularly called "symphonies with pfte.-accomp."—The earlier concertos were in *concertante* style, 2 or more instr.s or voices bearing leading parts ; Viadana's *concer'ti ecclesia'stici*, or *da chie'sa*, were simply motets with organ-accomp.; Torelli was the first (1686) to write *concerti da ca'mera* (for 2 violins and double-bass).

Concert-pitch. See *Pitch*.

Concert'stück (Ger.) A concert-piece ; a concerto.

Concita'to (It.) Moved, excited, agitated.

Concord. 1. Harmony ; opp. to *discord*.—2. See *Consonance*.

Concor'dant. 1. Consonant—2. (Fr.) A barytone voice.

Conductor. (Ger. *Kapell'meister, Dirigent'*; Fr. *chef d'orchestre*; It. *capo d'orchestra, mae'stro di cappel'la*.) The director of an orchestra or chorus.

Conduc'tus (Lat.) A form of polyphonous composition (12th century) in which the tenor to the contrapuntal variations was not borrowed from plain song (as in the *or'ganum* and *discan'tus*), but, like the counterpoint, was original with the composer... *C. du'plex*, 3-part counterpoint ; *C. sim'plex*, 2-part counterpoint.

Conduit (Fr.) 1. Conductus.—2. A wind-trunk (organ).

Cone-gamba. Bell-gamba.

Conjunct'. (Fr. *conjoint*; It. *congiun'to*.) A degree of the scale immediately succeeding another is called a *conjunct* degree ; opp. to *disjunct.*

Consecutive intervals. Intervals of the same kind following each other .in immediate succession ; " consecutives " are progressions of parallel fifths or octaves, forbidden in strict harmony. See *Parallel.*

Conseguen'te (It.) Consequent... *Conseguen'za*, a canon.

Consequent. (It. *conseguen'te.*) See *Canon.*

Conser'vatory. (Ger. *Konservato'rium;* Fr. *conservatoire;* It. *conservato'rio.*) A public institution for providing practical and theoretical instruction in music.

Consolan'te (It.) Consoling, soothing.

Con'sonance. (Ger. *Konsonanz';* Fr. *consonance;* It. *consonan'za.*) A combination of 2 or more tones, harmonious and pleasing in itself, and requiring no further progression to make it satisfactory ; opp. to *dissonance.* (Comp. *Acoustics*, §3.)...*Imperfect consonances,* the major and minor thirds and sixths. ..*Perfect consonances,* the octave, fifth, and fourth.

Consonant chord. One containing no dissonant interval... *C. interval*, a consonance.

Con'sort. 1. See *Chest* (of viols).—2. A band, or company of musicians.

Con'tano (It., "they count.") Direction in scores, that parts so marked are to pause.

Continua'to (It.) Continued (see *Basso continuo*) ; held, sustained.

Continued bass. See *Bass.*

Conti'nuo. A *Basso continuo.*

Contra (Lat., It.) Compounded with names of instr.s, it signifies an octave below ; e. g. *contrabbas'so,* a double-bass... *Contra-octave,* see *Pitch.*

Contrabass. (It. *contrabbas'so.*) 1. A double-bass.—2. The lowest bass instr. in a family of instr.s... *Contrabassist,* a player on the double-bass.

Contraddan'za (It.) Contra-dance or country-dance.

Contraffagot'to (It.) 1. A double-bassoon.—2. A reed-stop in the organ imitative of 1.

Contral'to (It.) The lowest female voice, having a compass from about f to e^2, the extremes being $e—g^2$:

(Also *Alto.*)—Male voices were exclusively employed in the old church-music, the tenor being called *altus;* hence the term *"contr'alto"*, i. e. opposed to or contrasted with the *altus.*

Contrappunti'sta (It.) A contrapuntist.

Contrappun'to (It.) Counterpoint... *C. alla men'te,* see *Chant sur le livre...C. alla zop'pa,* "limping", i. e. syncopated, counterpoint...*C. dop'pio,* double or invertible counterpoint...*C. synco-pa'to,* syncopated counterpoint...*C. so'pra (sot'to) il sogget'to,* counterpoint above (below) the theme.

Contrapunc'tus (Lat.) Counterpoint... *C. ad viden'dum,* counterpoint written out ; opp. to *contrappun'to alla men'te,* improvised counterpoint...*C. æqua'lis,* equal counterpoint...*C. diminu'tus* or *flor'idus,* florid or figurate counterpoint...*C. inæqua'lis,* unequal counterpoint.

Contrapun'tal. Pertaining to the art or practice of counterpoint.

Contrapun'tist. One versed in the practice and theory of counterpoint.

Contr'ar'co (It.) "Against the bow," up-bow for down bow. or *vice versu*

Contrary motion. See *Motion.*

Contrasogget'to (It.) Countersubject.

Contra-tenor. Countertenor.

Contrattem'po (It.) 1. A tone entering on a weak beat and ending on a strong beat ; a syncopation.—2. A sustained melody, as contrasted with its figurate accomp.

Contravioli'no, -violo'ne (It.) A double-bass.

Contre- (Fr.) Contra-, counter-... *Contre-basse,* double-bass... *Contredanse,* a French dance deriving its name from the position of the dancers opposite to or facing each other. Originally there were but 2 dancers ; there are now 8, and the dance is known in English as the *Quadrille.*—Also, dance-music for a quadrille... *Contre-éclisses,* linings... *Contre-partie,* a mus. part opp. to or contrasted with another, as bass and soprano ; said especially of either of the parts in a duet... *Contrepoint,* counterpoint ; *contrepointiste,* contrapuntist.

..*Contre-sujet*, countersubject...*Contre-temps*, see *Contrattempo*.

Conver'sio (Lat.) Inversion.

Coper'to (It.) "Covered," muffled ; as *tim'pani coper'ti*, muffled kettledrums.

Co'pula (Lat.) 1. (also Fr.) A coupler (organ).—2. A name for certain flue-stops ; (*a*) the 8-foot open diapason ; (*b*) the 8-foot *Hohl'flöte* or *Kop'pelflöte*.

Cor (Fr.) A horn...*Cor-alt, cor-basse*, see *Corno alto (basso)*...*C. anglais*, see *Oboe*...*C. de basset*, basset-horn...*C. de chasse*, a hunting-horn ; in particular, the large horn, whose tube is bent to form a circle of about $1\frac{1}{2}$ turns...*C. de signal*, a signal-horn or bugle...*C. de vaches*, a cow-horn, used by herdsmen...*C. omnitonique*, a chromatic valve-horn inv. by Sax.

Cora'le (It.) A choral.

Coran'to (It.) 1. A courante.—2. A country-dance.

Cor'da (It.) A string...*Sopra una c.*, direction to play a passage on one string...*Una Corda*, direction to use the soft pedal of the pfte...*Due corde*, (*a*) release soft pedal ; or, when the soft pedal shifts the keyboard, "play with the pedal pressed halfway down" [RIEMANN] ; (*b*) in violin-playing, a direction to double a note by playing it simultaneously on 2 strings...*Tutte (le) corde* (all the strings), release the soft pedal.

Cordatu'ra (It.) Same as *Accordatu'ra*.

Corde (Fr.) A string...*C. à jour*, or *à vide*, an open string...*C. fausse*, a string out of tune...*C. sourde*, a mute string...*Sur une corde*, Sopra una corda.

Cordier (Fr.) Tailpiece.

Cordomètre (Fr.) String-gauge.

Corife'o (It.) See *Corypheus*.

Cori'sta. (It.) 1. Chorister, either male or female.—2. Tuning-fork ; pitch-pipe

Cormorne (Fr.) See *Cromorne*.

Cornamu'sa (It.), **Cornemuse** (Fr.) A bagpipe in which the wind is supplied by the lungs (see *Musette*).

Cor'net. [See *Cornet à pistons*, in following art.] 1. (Ger. *Zin'ke*.) An obsolete wind-instr. much used during the 15th and 16th centuries, with a narrow cupped mouthpiece of ivory or wood,

and a wooden tube furnished with fingerholes.—There were two classes, the *straight cornet* (in 3 varieties, *cornetto dirit'to, c. muto*, compass a—a^2 · and *cornetti'no*, compass d^1—g^3), and the *bent cornet* (*cornetto cur'vo*, compass a—a^2 ; and *c. tor'to* [or *corno, cornon*], compass d—d^2). The *cornon* (*cornetto basso*) was the prototype of the *Serpent.*—2. A reed-stop in the organ, imitating the blaring tone of *C.* 1 (see 4), and of varying dimensions: 8-foot pitch, (or 2' or 4'), also called *Cornet-tino* ; 16-foot pitch (*Grand cornet*)... *Bass cornet*, a large deep-toned brass instr. (obs.)—3. (*Kornett'.*) A compound organ-stop of from 3 to 5 ranks and 8-foot or 4-foot pitch, differing from the Mixture in producing the Third among the harmonics...*Echo cornet*, a soft-toned cornet-stop enclosed in a wooden box...*Mounted cornet*, a cornet stop mounted on a separate soundboard to render its tone more prominent.—4. A reed-stop of 2 or 4-foot pitch, on the pedal.

Cornet à bouquin (Fr.) See *Cornet* 1. ..*Cornet à pistons* (Fr.; Ger. *Ventil'-kornett*), a brass instr. of the trumpet family, having a conical tube and cupped mouthpiece ; improved from the old post-horn by the addition of 3 valves ; tone apt to be loud and "brassy" ; medium compass 2 octaves and 3 tones. It is a transposing instr. noted in the *G*-clef :

this being for the cornet in $B\flat$, the one most in use.

In rapidity and lightness of execution, the cornet almost vies with the flute and clarinet ; a certain lack of refinement in its tone alone prevents its entrance into the symphony-orchestra...*Cornet d'écho* or *de récit*, cornet-stop.

Cornet-stop. See *Cornet* 2, 3, 4.

Cornet'to (It., dimin. *cornetti'no*.) 1. A small horn.—2. A cornet 1.

Cor'no (It.) A horn...*C. alto*, high horn in B; *C. basso*, low horn in B [STAINER AND BARRETT].—*C. alto (basso)* also signify, respectively, one of the two horn-players, in the orchestral group of four, who take the highest (lowest) horn-parts...*C. di bassetto*, basset-horn. ..*C. da caccia*, hunting-horn...*C. inglè'se*, English horn.

Cornon (Fr.) 1. A cornet.—2. A brass wind-instr. of broad scale, inv. in 1844.

Corno'pean. 1. Cornet à pistons.—2. An organ-stop on the swell-manual.

Co'ro (It.) Chorus ; choir... *C. favori'to*, a selected chorus, as opp. to the full chorus... *C. spezza'to*, a divided chorus (sung by several choirs in different parts of the church)... *A cori batten'ti*, for divided chorus, one half imitating, in parallel or reverse progression, what the other half sings.

Coro'na (It.) A hold (⌒).

Cor'onach (Gaelic.) A funeral lament ; a dirge.

Corps (Fr.) Body (of a tone)... *C. d'harmonie*, a fundamental chord... *C. de musique*, a wind-band... *C. de rechange*, a crook... *C. de voix*, the range and volume of a voice, taken collectively.

Correcto'rium (Lat.) Tuning-cone.

Corren'te (It.) Courante.

Coryphæ'us (Lat.) (Engl. *coryphe'us ;* Ger. *Koryphä'e ;* Fr. *coryphée ;* It. *corife'o*.) In the ancient Greek drama, the leader of the chorus ; hence, in modern usage, the leader of an opera-chorus or other company of singers.

Cotil'lion. (Fr. *cotillon*.) A French dance, the same as the german, to quadrille-music.

Cottage organ. The ordinary portable parlor organ (reed-organ)... *Cottage piano.* 1. A small style of upright pfte. —2. A small grand pfte. in upright form, inv. by Wilhelm Kress of Vienna in 1891.

Couac (Fr.) The "goose."

Couched harp. A spinet.

Coulé (Fr.) 1. Legato.—2. (Also *Dash*.) A harpsichord-grace ;
written :   played :

Coulisse (Fr.) Slide (of trombone or trumpet).

Count. An accent, beat, or pulse of a measure... *Counting*, the marking of the successive beats of the measure by counting aloud.

Counter. Any vocal part set to contrast with the principal part or melody ; specifically, the *counter-tenor* (high tenor, or alto), sometimes sung in the higher octave as a high soprano... *Bass counter*, a second bass part, either vocal or instrumental... *Counter-exposition*, re-entrance of the subject or subjects of a fugue, either directly following the exposition, or after the first episodes... *Counter-subject*, a fugal theme following the subject in the same part, as a contrapuntal accomp. to the answer ; often used independently as an episodal theme... *Counter-tenor*, a high tenor or alto voice ; hence, the part sung by such a voice, or the singer. It is the highest adult male voice; compass: being nearly the same as that of the contralto... *Counter-tenor clef*, the C-clef on the 3rd line ; used for the counter-tenor or alto voice, the viola, etc.

Counterpoint. (Ger. *Kon'trapunkt ;* Fr. *contrepoint ;* It. *contrappun'to*.) [From the Latin "punctus contra punctum" (point against point), i. e. note against note.] 1. In a wider sense, the art of polyphonic composition ; opp. to *homophony*. The canon and fugue are the most highly developed contrapuntal forms.—2. In a restricted sense, the art of adding one or more melodies to a given melody (*cantus firmus*) according to certain rules ; hence, one of, or all, the parts so added.—The Theory of Counterpoint generally recognizes 5 species, which, in practical instruction, are variously combined : (1) Note against note, whole notes in the counterpoint against whole notes in the *c. f.* (*cantus firmus*); (2) 2 against 1, half-notes in the counterpoint against whole notes in the *c. f.*; (3) 4 against 1, quarter-notes in the counterpoint against whole notes in *c. f.*; (4) with syncopation, syncopated half-notes in counterpoint against whole notes in the *c. f.*; (5) *florid*, *figurate*, or *figured*, the counterpoint written in irregular rhythms... *Double c.*, that in which 2 parts are so written as to be capable of mutual inversion by an interval (octave, tenth, etc.) determined beforehand... *Quadruple c.*, that written in 4 mutually exchangeable or invertible parts... *Single c.*, that in which the parts are not intended to be mutually invertible... *Strict c.*, that in which the entrance of (most) unprepared dissonances is forbidden. [The correctness of this definition largely depends upon what is meant by "preparation". The dissonant intervals included in the chord of the dimin. 7th—dimin. 7th and 5th, augm. 2nd and 4th—and also the dominant 7th, are now allowed to enter freely even in "strict" counterpoint; and preparation is often effected by a tone in a different part and octave from the one in which the following dissonance enters.]... *Triple c.*, counterpoint in 3 mutually invertible parts... *Two-part, Three-part, Four-part counterpoint*, that in which 2, 3, or 4 parts are employed.

Country-dance. A dance in which the partners form two opposing lines, which advance and retreat, the couples also dancing down the lines and returning to their places. The time varies, some tunes being in 2-4, others in 3-4 time; the essential thing is, for the strains to be in phrases of 4 or 8 measures, to accompany the several evolutions.

Coup d'archet (Fr.) A stroke of the bow... *Coup de (la) glotte*, see *Kehlschlag*... *Coup de langue*, a thrust or stroke of the tongue, tonguing; *double coup de langue*, double-tonguing.

Couper le sujet (Fr.) To cut or curtail the subject.

Coupler. (Ger. *Koppel;* Fr. *copula;* It. *unione.*) See *Organ.*

Couplet. 1. Two successive lines forming a pair, generally rhymed.—2. In triple times, 2 equal notes occupying the time of 3 such notes in the regular rhythm; thus :

Cou'rant [*Koo'-*]. (Fr. *courante;* It. *corren'te.*) An old French dance in 3-2 time; hence, the instrumental piece called *courante*, forming a part of the Suite, in which it follows the *Allemande*. Though the time-signature calls for 3-2 time, measures in 6-4 time often occur, especially at the close; the tempo is moderately rapid, and dotted rhythms abound.—The Italian *corrente* is quite different from the above, its chief feature being swift passages of equal notes, whence the name *corrente* ("running"). The tempo is rapid; time 3-8 or 3-4.

Couronne (Fr.) A hold (⌢).

Course. A group or set of strings tuned in unison.

Covered. See *Octave....Covered strings*, strings of silk, wire, or gut, covered by a machine with spiral turns of fine silver or copper wire, the process being termed " string-spinning."

Crackle. In lute-playing, to play the chords brokenly (*en batterie*) instead of simultaneously.

Cracovienne (Fr.) A Polish dance for a large company; hence, the music or an imitation of the music employed, which is in duple time with frequent syncopations (rhythm

Also *Krakowiak, cracoviak.*

Cre'do. The third main division of the Mass.

Crem'balum (Lat.) Jew's-harp.

Cremo'na. 1. A name ordinarily applied to any old Italian violin made by the Amatis, Stradivarius, or Guarnerius, at Cremona.—2. See *Krummhorn.*

Crescen'do (It.) Swelling, increasing in loudness... *Cr.-pedal*, see *Pedal.*

Crescen'dozug (Ger.) 1. Crescendo-pedal.—2. A kind of organ-swell with shutters, a contrivance inv. by Abbé Vogler.

Crescent; also **Chinese crescent, or pavilion.** (Ger. *Halb'mond;* Fr. *chapeau chinois;* It. *cappel'lo chine'se.*) An instr. of Turkish origin used in military music, consisting of several crescent-shaped brass plates hung around a staff and surmounted by a cap or pavilion; around the plates little bells are hung, which are jingled in time with the music.

Cre'ticus (Lat.) A metrical foot consisting of a short syllable between 2 long ones (— ◡ —).

Cri'brum (Lat.) Soundboard (organ).

Croche (Fr.) An eighth-note... *Croches liées*, eighth-notes having the hooks joined ( ).

Crochet (Fr.) The stroke of abbreviation across the stems of notes.

Croche'ta (Lat.) A crotchet, or quarter-note (♩).

Croisement (Fr.) Crossing (of parts).

Cro'ma (It.) An eighth-note.

Croma'tico (It.) Chromatic.

Cromor'na. (Fr. *cromorne.*) See *Krummhorn.*

Crook. 1. (Ger. *Bo'gen, Stimm'bogen;*

Fr. *corps de rechange, ton;* It. *pezzo di reserva.*) A supplementary tube, which can be rapidly fitted to the main tube (or body) of a horn or trumpet, for the purpose of lowering the pitch. Each crook is named after the fundamental tone to which it lowers the pitch of the tube ; e. g. the *D*-crook of an instr. in *E♭.*—2. The S-shaped tube forming the mouthpiece of a bassoon, and containing the reed.—3. In the old harp-action, a crotchet engaging a string and raising its pitch by a semitone.

Croque-note (Fr.) A player of facile execution, but little taste and judgment.

Cross-relation. See *False relation.*

Cro′talum (Lat.) A kind of clapper used by the ancient Greeks to mark the time of a dance.

Crotchet. I. A quarter-note ; *cr. -rest,* a quarter-rest.—2. See *Crook* 3.

Crowd ; also **Croud, Crouth.** (Welsh *crwth;* Lat. *chrot′ta.*) An ancient bow-instr., apparently of Welsh or Irish origin, and regarded as the oldest European instr. of the class ; still found early in the 19th century among the peasantry of Wales, Ireland and Britany. Its body was square, and terminated, instead of by a neck, by 2 parallel arms connected at the end by a cross-bar, the centre of which supported the end of the narrow fingerboard ; it had originally 3, in modern times 6, strings, 4 lying over the unfretted finger board and 2 beside it. The strings passed over a bridge, which rested on the belly between 2 sound-holes ; the accordatura [GROVE] was as follows :

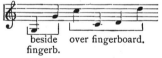

beside over fingerboard.
fingerb.

Crucifixus (Lat.) Part of the Credo.

Crush-note. An acciaccatura.

Crwth. See *Crowd.*

C-Schlüssel (Ger.) *C*-clef.

Cue. A phrase, from a vocal or instrumental part, occurring near the end of a long pause in another part, and inserted in small notes *in the latter* to serve as a guide in timing its re-entrance.

Cuivre (Fr., "copper.") Brass ; *les cuivres* (pl.), the brass-wind...*Faire cuivrer,* to obtain a metallic, ringing

tone by half-stopping the bell of the French horn with the right hand.

Cum sancto spi′ritu (Lat.) Part of the Gloria.

Cu′po (It.) Dark, deep, obscure ; reserved.

Curran′to. See *Courant.*

Cushion-dance. A Scotch and English round dance, in triple time, and performed in single file ; each dancer in turn drops a cushion before one of the opposite sex, at a regularly recurring strain of the music, whereupon the two kneel and kiss each other, after which the dance proceeds as before.

Cus′tos (Lat.) A direct.

Cuvette (Fr.) Pedestal (of a harp).

Cyclical forms. (Ger. *cyclische Formen.*) Forms of composition embracing a cycle or series of movements, such as the old suite or partita, or the sonata, symphony, and concerto.

Cylin′der (Ger.) Valve (in horns, etc.; usually *Ventil*).

Cymbale (Fr.) I. Cymbal.—2. A steel rod bent to a triangle, and bearing a number of rings, which are struck by a steel wand, the *cymbale* itself being dangled on a cord.

Cymbals. I. (Ger. *Beck′en;* Fr. *cymbales ;* It. *piat′ti, cinel′li.*) A pair of concave plates of brass or bronze, varying in size from finger-cymbals something over an inch in diameter to the large orchestral cymbals, which have broad, flat rims, and holes toward the middle for the insertion of the straps by which they are held ; used in orchestral music to mark time strongly, or to produce peculiar—often weird and thrilling—effects. One of the cymbals is often attached on top of the bass drum, so that one player can manipulate both drum and cymbals.—2. In the organ, a mixture-stop of very high pitch.—3. See *Cymbale* 2.

Cym′balum (Lat.) I. Cymbal.—2. A small drum of the medieval monks ; several such drums were tuned to form a scale of an octave, and played like a *Glockenspiel.*

Cym′bel. See *Cymbal.*

Čzakan (Bohemian.) A flute of cane or bamboo.

Čzardas (Hung.; pron. *tchar′dash.*) A national Hungarian dance, distinguished by its passionate character and changing tempo.

Czimbal (Hung.) A dulcimer.

Czimken (Pol.) A dance similar to the country-dance. [STAINER AND BAR-RETT.]

D.

D. 1. (Ger. *D ;* Fr. *ré ;* It. *re.*) The 2nd tone and degree in the typical diatonic scale of *C*-major. (Comp. *Alphabetical notation,* and *Solmisation.*)—2. Abbr. of *Da* (D. C.=da capo), and *Dal* (D. S.=dal segno).

Da (It) By, for, from, of... *Da ca'po,* (*a*) from the beginning ; (*b*) as an exclamation, "encore !"...*D. C. al fi'ne,* (repeat) from the beginning to the end (i. e. to the word *Fine,* or to a hold ⌒). ..*D. C. al se'gno,* (repeat) from the beginning to the sign (𝄋, ⊕, ⌒)...*D. C. al segno, poi* (*se'gue*) *la coda,* (repeat) from the beginning to the sign, then (follows) the coda...*D. C. dal segno,* **repeat** from the sign...*D.C. sen'za re'plica* (or *senza ripetizio'ne*), play through from the beginning without noticing the repeats...*Da eseguir'si,* to be executed. ..*Da tirar'si* ("for drawing out"), means "with slide"; as *tromba da tirarsi,* slide-trumpet.

D'accord (Fr.) In tune.

Dach (Ger., "roof.") The belly of a violin(usually *Decke*)...*Dach'schweller,* see *Crescendozug* 2.

Dac'tyl(e). (Lat. *dac'tylus,* a finger.) A metrical foot of 3 syllables arranged like the finger-joints, one long and two short, with the ictus on the first (—‿‿).

Dactyl'ion. An apparatus inv. by Henri Herz in 1835, consisting of 10 rings hanging over the keyboard and attached to steel springs ; used by pianists for finger-gymnastics.

Daddy-mammy. A familiar name for the roll on the side-drum.

Da'gli, dai, dal, dall', dal'la, dal'le, dal'lo (It.) To the, by the, for the, from the, etc.

Dal se'gno (It.) See *Segno.*

Damenisa'tion. (See *Solmisation.*) Graun's system of sol-faing with the syllables *da, me, ni, po, tu, la, be,* which are not (like *do, re, mi,* etc.) attached to special scale-degrees, but sim-

ply repeated over and over in the above order, whatever may be the notes sung.

Damper. 1. (Ger. *Däm'pfer ;* Fr. *étouffoir ;* It. *sordi'no.*) A mechanical device for checking the vibration of a pfte.-string (see *Pianoforte*)...*Damperpedal,* the right or loud pedal of the pfte.—2. The *mute* of a brass instr., e. g. a horn.

Däm'pfer (Ger.) A damper or mute... *Däm'pfung* ("damping"), the damping-mechanism of the pfte.

Dance. (Ger. *Tanz ;* Fr. *danse ;* It. *dan'za.*) A succession of rhythmical steps, skips, or leaps, accompanied by varying movements of the body, and generally timed by music (in primitive nations, simply by beating on a drum or the like).

Darm'saite (Ger.) Gut string.

Dash. 1. A staccato-mark (𝅘𝅥 or 𝅘𝅥).—2. In thorough-bass, a stroke through a figure, indicating the raising of the interval by a semitone (2 ♯, etc.)—3. Same as *Coulé* 2.

Dasian'-Notie'rung (Ger.) Hucbald's system of noting a scale of 18 tones by twisting and turning the letter F into 14 different positions and shapes, with 4 additional signs.

Dau'men (Ger.) Thumb...*Dau'menaufsatz,* thumb-positions (in 'cello-playing).

Dead-march. A funeral march.

De'bile, De'bole (It.) Feeble, weak.

Début(Fr.) A first appearance...*Débutant*(*e*), a male (female) performer or singer appearing for the first time.

Dec'achord. (Fr. *décacorde.*) 1. A 10-stringed instr., an ancient species of harp or lyre.—2. An obsolete French instr. of the guitar kind, 1 ‥ ‥ing 10 strings.

Dec'ad(e). See *Duodene.*

Deca'ni. Comp. *Cantoris.*

De'cem (Ger.) See *Decima* 2

Déchant (Fr.) Discant.

Décidé (Fr.) See *Deciso.*

De'cima (Lat. and It.) 1. The interval of a tenth.—2. An organ-stop pitched a tenth higher than the 8-foot stops ; also called *Tenth,* or *Double* ‥ ‥.

De'cime. See *Dezime.*

Decimo'le (Ger.) See *Decuplé.*

Deci'so (It.) Decided, energ ‥ ‥ with decision.

Deck'e (Ger.) Belly (of the violin, etc.); belly or soundboard (of the pfte.)

Declaman'do (It.) "Declaiming"; in declamatory style.

Declamation. In vocal music, the correct enunciation of the words, especially in recitative and dramatic music. (Comp. *Deklamation.*)

Décomposé (Fr.) Unconnected.

Décompter (Fr.) To sing with a portamento.

Découplez (Fr.) In organ-music, "uncouple," "coupler off."

Decrescen'do (It.) Growing softer; diminishing in force. Sign ⟹

Dec'uplet. A group of 10 equal notes executed in the time proper to 8 notes of like value, or to 4 notes of the next highest value; marked by a slur over or under which a figure 10 is set. (Also *Decimole, Dezimole.*)

Deduc'tio (Lat.) 1. The ascending series of syllables or tones in the hexachords of Guido d'Arezzo.—2. Acc. to later theoreticians, the resolution of a dissonance to a consonance.

Defective. Same as *Diminished.*

Deficien'do (It.) Dying away.

De'gli (It.) Of the; than the.

Degree. (Ger. *Stu'fe, Ton'stufe;* Fr. *degré;* It. *gra'do.*) 1. One of the 8 consecutive tones in a major or minor diatonic scale. Degrees are counted from below upward, the key-note being the first degree.—2. A line or space of the staff.—3. A step. (The prevailing confusion of the terms *degree* and *step* might be obviated by applying *degree* only to the tones, and *step* only to progression between conjunct tones, of the scale; the expressions whole step, half-step, and step and a half, are quite superfluous.)...*Scale-degree,* a degree of a scale... *Staff-degree,* a degree on the staff.

Deh'nen (Ger.) To expand, extend; to prolong... *Deh'nung,* expansion, extension, prolongation; *Deh'nungsstrich,* in vocal music, a line of continuation after a syllable, indicating that it is to be sung to all notes over the line; dots are sometimes used instead... *Gedehnt',* extended, prolonged; hence, slow, stately.

Dei (It.) Of the; than the.

Deklamation' (Ger.) Musico-poetical scansion.—"In vocal composition, the transformation of the poetic rhythm (metre) into a musical one; a song is badly *deklamiert* when an unaccented syllable receives a strong musical accent or a long note; or when an accented syllable, or a word rendered prominent by the sense, receives a subordinate position in the melody on a weak beat or in short notes." [RIEMANN.]

Del, dell', del'la, del'le, del'lo (It.) Of the; than the.

Délassement (Fr.) A piece or performance of a light and trifling character.

Deliberatamen'te (It.) Deliberately... *Delibera'to,* deliberate.

Delicatamen'te, con delicatez'za (It.) Delicately... *Delica'to,* delicate; in a delicate, refined style.

Délié (Fr.) *Non legato; leggero.*

Deli'rio (It.) Frenzy; *con d.,* with frenzied passion.

Delivery. Style (method and manner of singing); restrictedly, the enunciation of a singer.

Démanché, Démanchement (Fr.) "Off the neck"; the thumb-positions in 'cello-playing... *Démancher,* to quit the neck of the 'cello.

Demande (Fr.) "Question," i. e. the subject of a fugue. (Usually *sujet.*)

Demi (Fr., "half"). *Demi-bâton,* 2-measure rest... *Demi-cadence,* half-cadence... *Demi-croche,* a 16th-note... *À demi-jeu* (a direction found mostly in reed-organ or harmonium-music), with half the power of the instr., *mezzo forte.* ...*Demi-mesure,* half-measure... *Demi-pause,* half-rest. . *Demi-quart de soupir,* a 32nd rest . *Demi-soupir,* an eighth-rest.. *Demi-temps,* a half-beat...*Demi-ton,* a semitone.

Demiquaver. A 16th-note... *Demisemiquaver,* a 32nd-note... *Demitone,* rare for Semitone.

Demoiselle (Fr.) Tracker.

Dependent chord, harmony, triad. One which is dissonant, requiring resolution to a consonant one; opp. to *Independent.*

Depress. To lower (as by a ♭ or ♭♭)...*Depression,* chromatic lowering of a tone.

Derivative. 1. Same as *derivative chord,* i. e. the inversion of a fundamental chord.—2. The root of a chord.

Dérivé(e) (Fr., "derived, derivative".) *Accord dérivé,* inverted chord (also simply *dérivé,* an inversion)...*Mesure* *dérivée*, any measure indicated by 2 figures (2-4, 3-8, etc.) as being derived from, i. e. a fractional part of, a whole note.

Des (Ger.) D♭...*Des'es*, D♭♭.

Des'cant. See *Discant.*

Descend. To pass from a higher to a lower pitch...*Descent*, descending progression.

Deside'rio (It.) Desire, longing...*Con d.*, in a style expressive of longing, yearning.

Désinvolture, avec (Fr.) See *Disinvolto.*

Dessin (Fr.) The design, plan, or structure of a composition.

Dessus (Fr.) 1. Soprano or treble, i. e. the highest vocal part.—2. Earlier name for the violin (*dessus de viole*).

De'sto (It.) Sprightly.

De'stra (It.) Right...*Ma'no destra*, right hand (also *destra mano, colla destra*) ; a direction in pfte.-playing, signifying that the passage is to be played with the right hand. (Abbr. *m. d.*, or *d. m.*)

Détaché (Fr.) In violin-playing, detached, i. e. playing successive notes with alternate down-bow and up-bow, but not staccato...*Grand détaché*, a whole (stroke of the) bow to each note.

Determina'to (It.) Determined, resolute.

Detonation' (Ger.), **Détonnation** (Fr.) False intonation, singing out of tune... *Detonieren* (*détonner*), to sing false ; especially, to flat (gradually lower the pitch) in *a cappella* singing.

Det'to (It.) Aforesaid ; the same.

Deutsch (Ger.) German...*Deu'tsche Flöte*, the orchestral flute...*Deu'tscher Bass*, an obsolete kind of double-bass, having from 5 to 6 gut strings...*Deutsche Tabulatur'*, see *Tablature*... *Deutsche Tän'ze*, German dances, i. e. the old-fashioned slow waltzes.

Deux (Fr.) Two...*À deux mains*, for 2 hands...*Deux-quatre*, 2-4 (see *Mesure*)...*Deux-temps*, or *Valse à deux temps*, a quick waltz, with 6 steps to every 2 of the ordinary waltz (*trois temps*).

Deuxième position (Fr.) Half-shift.

Development. (Ger. *Durch'führung.*) The working-out or evolution of a theme by presenting it in varied melodic, harmonic, or rhythmic treatment ;

ordinarily applied to formal compositions like the fugue or sonata. (See *Form.*)

Devo'to (It.) In a devotional style (*con devozio'ne*).

Dex'tra (Lat.) Right...*Manus d.*, right hand...*Manu d.*, with the right hand.

De'zem (Ger.) See *Decima.*

De'zime (Ger.) The interval of a tenth.

Di (It.) Of, from, to, etc.

Diagram'ma (Gk.) A diagram. 1. The Greek written scale of 15 notes, divided into the various tetrachords.—2. In old music, the staff and the scale written on it ; also, a score or partition.

Dia'logo (It.), **Dialogue** (Fr.) A duet for 2 solo voices or divided chorus ; or a similar instrumental piece.

Diapa'son (Gk.) An octave (in ancient Greek and in medieval music)...*Diapason diapente*, or *diapason con diapente*, an octave plus a fifth, a twelfth. ..*Diap. diatessaron* (*diap. con diatessaron*), an octave plus a major fourth, a major eleventh...*Diap. ditone*, an octave plus a major third, a major tenth. ..*Diap. semi-ditone*, an octave plus a minor third, a minor tenth.

Diapa'son (Engl.) 1. An octave.—2. Either of the 2 principal foundation-stops of the organ, the open diapason and the stopped diapason, both commonly of 8-foot pitch; if there are 2 op. diap.s on a manual, one is sometimes of 16' pitch ; pedal-diapasons are generally 16' stops.—The *open d.* has metal pipes open at the top, and usually of large scale, though the scale differs when 2 or more diapasons are on one manual ; the tone is bright, full, and sonorous. ..The *stopped d.* has wooden pipes of large scale, closed at the top by wooden plugs, and yielding a powerful fluty, and somewhat hollow, tone.—3. Compass of a voice or instr.; chiefly poetical.

Diapason (Fr.) 1. Compass of a voice or instr.—2. A rule or scale, acc. to which makers of various instr.s regulate the size of the latter, and that of their parts.—3. An organ-stop (diapason).—4. A tuning-fork or pitch-pipe. —5. Absolute pitch...*Diapason normal*, the standard pitch or scale adopted in 1859 by the French Academy, in which a^1 has 870 single or 435 double vibrations per second of time (so-called "international pitch ").

Diapen'te (Gk. and Lat.) The interval of a fifth...*D. cum ditono*, a major 7th. ...*D. cum semiditono*, minor 7th...*D. cum semitonio*, minor 6th...*D. cum tono*, a major 6th.

Diapenter (Fr.), **Diapentisa're** (It.) To progress by skips of a fifth.

Diaph'ony. (Gk. *diaphoni'a*.) 1. A dissonance.—2. See *Organum*.

Diaschis'ma (Gk.) The difference between the second tierce below the 4th quint in the descending circle of fifths, and the 3rd octave below the given tone (*c:d♭♭ :: 2025 : 2048*).

Diaste'ma (Gk.) An interval.

Diates'saron (Gk.) The interval of a fourth.

Diaton'ic. 1. See *Greek music*, §2.— 2. (In modern usage.) By, through, with, within, or embracing the tones of the standard major or minor scale... *Diatonic instr.*, one yielding only the tones of that scale of which its fundamental tone is the key-note...*Diatonic interval*, one formed by 2 tones of the same standard scale...*Diatonic harmony* or *melody*, that employing the tones of but one scale...*Diatonic modulation*, see *Modulation*...*Diatonic progression*, stepwise progression within one scale...*Diatonic scale*, see *Scale*.

Diau'los (Gk.) A double *aulos*, the tubes meeting in an acute angle, and connected by and blown through a common mouthpiece.

Diazeuc'tic (Gk.) Disjoined (see *Greek music*, §1)...*Diazeu'xis*, the separation of 2 neighboring tetrachords by the interval of a tone ; also, the tone itself.

Di'brach, Di'brachys. A metrical foot consisting of 2 short syllables ($\smile\smile$) ; a pyrrhic.

Di'chord. 1. An ancient species of harp or lute having 2 strings.—2. Any instr. having 2 strings to each note.

Dicho'ree, Dichore'us. A double choree or trochee ; a metrical foot consisting of 2 long and 2 short syllables in alternation ($-\smile-\smile$).

Dictée musicale (Fr., "musical dictation".) A modern method of training the faculty of musical apprehension, in which the teacher plays or sings short phrases which the pupils take down on paper.

Diecet'to (It.) A piece for 10 instr.s.

Diesa're (It.) To sharp...*Die'sis*, a sharp.

Diéser (Fr.) To sharp...*Dièse*, a sharp.

Dies iræ (Lat., "day of wrath".) The sequence of the *Missa pro defunctis ;* it now forms the 2nd division of the Requiem.

Di'esis (Gk.) 1. The Pythagorean semitone (later *Limma*), which is the difference between a fourth and 2 greater whole tones, $=256:243$.—2. In modern theory, the difference between an octave and 3 major thirds, the modern *enharmonic diesis* (128:125).

Diezeug'menon (Gk.) Disjoined (see *Greek music*, §1).

Difference-tone. See *Acoustics*.

Differen'tia (Lat.) The *differen'tiæ tono'rum* in the medieval Gregorian chants were the different forms of the cadences or tropes to the *Seculo'rum a'men*, according to the tone to which transition was to be effected. (Also *distinctio*.)

Diffi'cile (It.), **Diffici'le** (Fr.) Difficult.

Dig'ital. A key on the keyboard of the pfte., organ, etc.; opp. to pedal (*finger*-key opp. to *foot*-key).

Digito'rium. A small portable apparatus for exercising the fingers, resembling a diminutive piano in shape, and having 5 keys set on strong springs ; sometimes called *Dumb piano*.

Di gra'do (It.) (Progression) by degrees, step-wise.

Diiamb', Diiam'bus. A double iambus ; a metrical foot consisting of 2 short and 2 long syllables in alternation ($\smile-\smile-$).

Dilettart'. (It. *dilettan'te*.) An amateur.

Diligen'za (It.) Diligence, care.

Dilu'dium (Lat.) An interlude, especially that between the separate lines of chorals.

Diluen'do (It.) Decreasing in loudness, dying away.

Dim'eter. 1. Consisting of 2 measures ; divisible into 2 feet.—2. A verse or period consisting of two feet.

Diminished. (Ger. *verklei'nert;* Fr. *diminué(e)* ; It. *diminu'to*.) *Dim. interval*, a perfect or minor interval contracted by a chromatic semitone...*Dim. chord*, a chord, the highest and lowest tones of which form a dimin. interval. ..*Dim. subject* or *theme*, one repeated or imitated in diminution...*Dim. triad*, a root with minor third and dimin. fifth.

Diminuen'do (It) Diminishing in loudness...*Dim. pedal*, see *Pedal.*

Diminuer (Fr.) To diminish (in loudness)...*En diminuant beaucoup*,=diminuendo molto.

Diminution. (Ger. *Verklei'nerung ;* Fr. *diminution ;* It. *diminuzio'ne.*) 1. The repetition or imitation of a theme in notes of smaller time-value (½, ⅓, or ¼ that of the original).—2. See *Notation*, §2.

Dioxia (Gk.) Less common term for *Diapente.*

Dip. The vertical fall of a digital or pedal when depressed to the full extent ; also *key-fall.*

Dipho'nium (Lat) A composition for 2 voices.

Diphtho'nia. A vocal anomaly produced by inflammatory nodules seated on the vocal cords, which on closure of the latter divide the glottis into an anterior and a posterior half, so that 2 tones are sounded on singing, instead of one.

Diplas'ic. Two-fold...*D. foot* or *rhythm*, that in which the thesis has twice the length of the arsis.

Dip'ody. A group of 2 similar metrical feet, or double foot, especially when constituting a single measure.

Direct. 1. (Ger. and Lat. *Cus'tos ;* Fr. *guidon ;* It. *gui'da, mo'stra.*) The sign ∿ or ✓ set at the end of a staff to show the position of the first note on the next staff. (N. B. The Germans often use it as a mere mark of continuation equivalent to "etc.", without reference to the pitch of any note.)—2 See *Motion* and *Turn.*

Directeur (Fr.) Conductor, director

Dirge. A funeral hymn or similar music.

Dirigent' (Ger.) Conductor, director.

Diriger (Fr.), **Dirigie'ren** (Ger.) To direct, conduct.

Dirit'to,-a (It.) Direct, straight...*Alla diritt'ta*, in direct motion.

Dis (Ger.) D♯...*Disis*, D×.

Dis'cant. 1. (Lat. *discan'tus ;* Ger. *Diskant';* Fr. *déchant.*) The first attempts at polyphony with contrary motion in the parts, beginning in the 12th century ; opp. to the *organum*, in

which parallel motion was the rule. —2. (Fr. *dessus.*) Treble or soprano voice ; the highest part in part-music.

Discord. 1. A dissonance.—2. Cacophony.

Discre'to (It.) Discreet ; comparatively subdued...*Discrezio'ne*, discretion; *con discrezione*, with discretion or due reserve ; with judicious subordination to a leading part or parts.

Disdiapa'son (Gk., Lat.) In medieval music, the interval of a double octave.

Dis'dis (Ger.) D× (usually *Disis*).

Disinvol'to (It.) Free, easy, graceful. ..*Con disinvoltu'ra*, with ease, grace ;

Dis'is (Ger.) D×. [flowingly.

Disjunct'. (Fr. *disjoint,-e.*) See *Motion*, *Tetrachord (disjoined).*

Diskant' (Ger.) 1. Discant, treble.— *Diskant'geige*, the violin (the treble instr. of its class)...*Diskantist'*, treble singer...*Diskant'register*, *Diskant'-stimme*, in the organ, a half-stop (also *Hal'bestimme*)...*Diskant'schlüssel*, soprano-clef.

Dispar'te, in (It.) Aside.

Dispera'to (It.) Desperate, hopeless... *Disperazio'ne, con*, in a style expressive of desperation or despair.

Dispersed. See *Harmony.*

Dispon'dee, Disponde'us. A double spondee ; a compound metrical foot containing 2 spondees.

Disposition' (Ger.) The *D.* of an organ is properly the preliminary estimate of its cost, fixing the varieties of stops, number of manuals, etc.; but also signifies a concise description of the working parts of a finished organ, especially an enumeration of the stops, couplers, combination-stops, etc.

Disposition (Fr.) Gift, talent, genius.

Dis'sonance. (Ger. *Dissonanz';* Fr. *dissonance;* It. *dissonan'za.*) 1. In theory, the simultaneous sounding of tones so remotely related that their combination produces beats.—2. In practice, a combination of 2 or more tones requiring resolution ; opp. to *Consonance*...*Dissonant*, consisting of tones forming a dissonance 2 ; opp. to *consonant*...*Dissonant interval*, 2 tones forming a dissonance. The dissonant intervals are the seconds and their inversions, the sevenths, also all diminished and augmented intervals...*Dis* *sonant chord*, a chord containing one or more diss. intervals.

Dissona're (It.) To be dissonant, to form a dissonance.

Distance. Interval. [Seldom used.]

Distan'za (It.) An interval ; distance... *In distanza*, at a distance, marking music to be performed as if far away.

Dis'tich. A group of 2 lines or verses ; usually called *couplet* in modern rhyming versification.

Distinc'tio (Lat.) I. In Gregorian music, the pauses or breaks dividing vocal melodies into convenient phrases.—2. See *Differentia*.

Distin'to (It.) Distinct, clear... *Distintamen'te*, distinctly.

Distona're (It.) To sing or play out of tune ; also *stonare*.

Dit'al. A key which, on pressure with the finger or thumb, raises the pitch of a guitar-string or lute-string by a semitone ; opp. to *pedal*... *Dital harp*, a chromatic lute shaped like a guitar, having from 12 to 18 strings, each controlled by a dital to raise its pitch by a semitone ; inv. by Light in 1798, and later improved by him. (Comp. *Klavier-Harfe*.)

Diteggiatu'ra (It.) Fingering.

Dith'yramb, Dithyram'bus. A form of Greek lyric composition, originally a hymn in praise of Dionysus ; later greatly modified. Its leading characteristics were a lofty enthusiasm, frequently degenerating into bacchantic wildness (whence the adj. *dithyram'bic*), and the irregular form of its strophes, no two of which were identical.

Di'to (It.) Finger.

Ditone. (Lat. *di'tonus;* Fr. *diton*.) A Pythagorean major third of 2 greater whole tones (81 : 64); wider by a comma than a true major third (5 : 4).

Ditro'chee, Ditrochæ'us. A compound metrical foot consisting of 2 trochees ($- \smile - \smile$); also *Dichoree*.

Ditty. A short, simple song.

Divertimen'to (It.) } I. A short poem
Divertissement (Fr.) } set to music, and interspersed with songs and dances, for some special occasion.—2. Light and easy pieces of instrumental music, such as variations, potpourris, etc.—3. An instrumental composition in 6 or 7 movements, similar to a serenade or

cassation.—4. An entr'acte in an opera, or between compositions of considerable length, in the form of a short ballet or other entertainment.—5. Episode in a fugue ; development of a principal theme.

Divide. To play divisions.

Divi'si (It.) Divided. A direction in scores signifying that 2 parts appearing on one and the same staff are not to be played as double-stops, but by the division into two bodies of the instr.s playing from that staff. The return to the unison is marked by the direction *a due*, (or by *unis.*, or *a 2*).

Division. A "dividing-up" of a melodic series of tones, vocal or instrumental, into a rapid *coloratura* passage ; if for voice, the passage was to be sung in one breath. (Obsolete.)... *To run a division*, to execute such a passage... *Division-viol*, the *Viola da gamba*.

Division-mark. A slur connecting a group of notes, and provided with a figure indicating their number, showing that their rhythm differs from the ruling rhythm of the piece ; as for a quintuplet, triplet, etc.

Divo'to, Divotamen'te. See *Devoto*.

Dixième (Fr.) The interval of a tenth.

Do. The Italian name for *C;* supposed to have been introduced by Bononcini in 1673. It is now also generally adopted in France instead of the Aretinian *Ut*.

Do. In solmisation, the usual syllable-name for the 1st degree of the scale.— In the *fixed-Do* method of instruction, *Do* is the name for all notes bearing the letter-name *C*, whether key-notes or not.—In the *movable-Do* method, *Do* is always the key-note, whatever key is sung in or modulation reached.—In the *Tonic Sol-fa system*, spelled *Doh*.

Doch'mius. A metrical foot consisting of 5 syllables ($\smile - - \smile -$).

Doctor of Music. See *Bachelor*.

Dodecachor'don (Gk.) I. See *Bissex*. —2. A treatise by Glareanus (1547) on the theory of the 12 keys or modes.

Dode'cupla di cro'me (It.) 12-8 time: *di semicrome*, 12-16 time.

Dodec'uplet. A group of 12 equal notes to be performed in the time of 8 in the regular rhythm.

Doh. See *Do*.

Do'i (It.) Same as *Due*.

Doigt (Fr.) Finger...*Doigté*, fingered.
..*Doigté*, or *doigter*, fingering ; *doig-tés fourchus*, cross-fingerings.

Dol'can. See *Dulcia'na*.

Dol'ce (It.) 1. Sweet, soft, suave ; *dol-cemen'te*, sweetly, softly.—2. A sweet-toned organ-stop.

Dolcez'za (It.) Sweetness, softness ; *con d.*, softly, gently.

Dolcian' (Ger.), **Dolcia'na, Dolcia'no** (It.) 1. A species of bassoon in vogue during the 16th and 17th centuries.—2. In the organ, a reed-stop of 8 or 16-foot pitch ; a *fagotto*.

Dolcia'to (It.) See *Raddolciato*.

Dolcis'simo (It.) Very sweetly, softly. ..Also, a very soft-toned 8-foot flute-stop in the organ.

Dolen'do, Dolen'te (It.) Doleful, plaint-ive, sad...*Dolentemen'te*, dolefully, etc.

Dolo're (It.) Pain, grief ; *con dolore*, in a style expressive of pain or grief ; pathetically (also *dolorosamen'te, dolo-ro'so*).

Dolz'flöte (Ger.; Fr. *flûte douce ;* It. *fla'uto dol'ce*.) 1. An obsolete trans-verse flute, having a half-plug within the embouchure.—2. In the organ, an open flute-stop of rather narrow scale and 8-foot pitch.

Dom'chor (Ger.) Cathedral-choir.

Dom'inant. 1. (Ger., Fr., and It. *Dominan'te*.) The fifth tone in the major or minor scale...*D. chord*, (*a*) the dominant triad ; (*b*) the dom. chord of the 7th...*D. section*, of a movement, a section written in the key of the domi-nant, lying between and contrasting with two others in the key of the tonic. ..*D. triad*, that having the dominant as root.—2. The reciting-tone in the Gre-gorian modes.

Dona nobis pacem. See *Mass*.

Doodlesack. See Ger. *Dudelsack*.

Do'po (It.) After.

Dop'pel- (Ger.) Double...*Dop'pel-B, Dop'pelbe*, the double-flat...*Dop'pel-blatt*, double reed...*Dop'pelchor*, double chorus...*Dop'pelfagott*, double-bassoon. ..*Dop'pelflöte* (*Duiflöte*), (It. *fla'uto dop'pio*), an organ-register of 8-foot stopped pipes, each pipe having 2 mouths, 2 windways, etc., one on either side (behind and in front) like the *Bi-*

fara, but at exactly the same height, so that the tone does not beat, but is merely reinforced...*Dop'pelflügel*, see *Vis-à-vis*...*Dop'pelfuge*, a double fugue or canon...*Dop'pelgeige*, viola d'amore. ..*Dop'pelgriff*, double-stop (on the vio-lin), paired notes (on keyboard-instr.s ; e. g. thirds, sixths, and octaves)... *Dop'peloktave*, double octave...*Dop'-pelpunkt*, double dot (♩..)...*Dop'pel-quintpommer*, a large variety of bom-bard...*Dop'pelschlag*, a turn...*Dop'-pelzunge*, double-tonguing.

Dop'pio (It.) Double...*D. movimen'to*, twice as fast...*D. no'te, d. valo're*, twice as slow (absolute time-value of notes is doubled)...*D. peda'le* (in organ-playing), the pedal-part in octaves... *Doppio* signifies, with names of instr.s, larger in size and consequently deeper in tone.

Do'rian or **Dor'ic mode.** See *Mode*.

Dot. (Ger. *Punkt ;* Fr. *point ;* It. *pun'-to*.) 1. A dot set after a note prolongs its time-value by half (♩.=♩♪) ; a second dot or third dot prolongs the time-value of the dot immediately pre-ceding it by half (♩...=♩♪♪). (The dot after a *note upon a line* is pre-ferably written *above* the line when the next note is *higher, below* the line when it is *lower :*

The dot of prolongation was formerly often set in the next measure, quite away from the note ; e. g.

which we now write :

—2. A dot set over or under a note in-dicates that it is to be executed staccato (♩ ♪) ; a slur connecting several such dots calls for the mezzo-staccato. (Some-times, especially in earlier authors, the staccato-dot calls rather for a *sforzando* than a *staccato*)—3. In old music, sev-eral dots set above a note indicate that it is to be subdivided into so many short notes (♩ = ♬) ; now used over a tremolo-sign in violin-music to mark

the exact subdivision of the large note

$$\left(\underset{8}{\overset{......}{\equiv}} = \underset{\text{.........}}{......}\right).—4.\ \text{Two}$$

set in the spaces of the staff, before or after a double-bar, form a *Repeat.*

Double. 1. A variation.—2. A repetition of words in a song.—3. In organ-playing, a 16-foot stop (as accompanying or doubling the 8-foot stops in the lower octave).—4. In the opera, etc., a substitute singer.—5. (Also *Grandsire.*) In change-ringing, changes on 5 bells.—6. As an adjective with names of mus. instr.s, double signifies "producing a tone an octave lower"; e. g. *doublebassoon, double-bourdon,* etc.—7. The *verb* double signifies, to add (to any tone or tones of a melody or harmony) the higher or lower octave.

Double (Fr.) 1 (pl. *doubles*). See *Variation.*—2. The alternativo in a minuet, when merely a variation of the principal theme and retaining the harmonic basis of the latter.—3. As an adjective, double; as *double-barre,* double-bar ; *d. coup de langue,* doubletonguing ; *double-croche,* a 16th-note ; etc...*Double - corde,* double-stop... *Double-main,* an octave-coupler (organ). ..*Double-octave,* double octave..*Double-touche,* a mechanism in the keyboard of harmoniums, etc., for adjusting the key-fall at 2 different levels, with corresponding differences in the degree of loudness of tone produced...*Doubletriple,* 3-2 time.

Doublé (Fr.) A turn.

Double-bar. (Ger. *Dop'peltaktstrich, Schluss'striche;* Fr. *double-barre;* It. *dop'pio bar'ra.*) 1. The two thick vertical strokes drawn across the staff to mark the end of a division, (repeat), movement, or entire piece.—2. Two thin vertical lines (bars) dividing one (1) (2) section of a movement from the next section:

Double-bass. (Ger. *Kon'trabass;* Fr. *contre-basse; violonar;* It. *contrabbas'-so.*) The largest and deepest-toned instr. of the violin family (with the exception of the rare *contrabbasso doppio* and the *Octobass*), with either 3 strings (G_1-D-A being the Italian, A_1-D-G the English accordatura), or 4 strings (tuned E_1-A_1-D-G). Compass:

but written : (the German tuning).

Double-stop. (Ger. *Dop'pelgriff;* Fr. *double-corde;* It. *dop'pia ferma'ta.*) In violin-playing, to stop 2 strings together, thus obtaining 2-part harmony.

Double-tongue. (Ger. *Dop'pelzunge;* Fr. *double coup de langue.*) In playing the flute, and certain brass instr.s, applying the tongue in rapid alternation to the upper front teeth and the hard palate, to obtain a clear-cut and brilliant staccato. (Also *Double-tonguing.*)

Double-trouble. A step peculiar to the "breakdown."

Doublette (Fr.) A 2-foot organ-stop, octave of the principal.

Doublophone. A combined Euphonium and Valve-trombone, with one common mouthpiece ; a valve operated by the left thumb throws the current of air from the mouthpiece into the tube of either instr. at will. Inv. by Fontaine Besson of Paris in 1891.

Doublure (Fr.) See *Double* 4 (Engl.)

Doucement. (Fr.) Gently, softly... *Doux, douce,* soft, gentle, sweet.

Douzième (Fr.) The interval of a twelfth.

Down-beat. 1. The downward stroke of the hand in beating time, which marks the primary or first accent in each measure.—2. Hence, the accent itself (thesis, strong beat).

Down-bow. (Ger. *Herunterstrich;* Fr. *tirez;* It. *arco in giù.*) In violin-playing, the downward stroke of the bow from nut to point ; on the 'cello and double-bass, the stroke from nut to point ; usual sign ⊓.

Doxology (Gk.) A psalm or hymn of praise to God ; especially the *Greater D.*(Gloria in excelsis Deo), and the *Lesser D.*(Gloria Patri, etc.)

Drag. 1. A *rallentando.*—2. A descending *portamento* in lute-playing.

Draht'saite (Ger.) Wire string.

Dramatic music. 1. Same as *Programmusic.*—2. Music accompanying and illustrating an actual drama on the stage.

Dram'ma (It.) Drama.—*D. li'rico,* a lyric drama...*D. musica'le,* a music-

drama, opera...*D. per mu'sica*, a musical drama, opera...*Drammaticamen'te*, dramatically...*Dramma'tico*, dramatic.

Dräng'end (Ger.) Pressing, hastening, hurrying.

Draw-stop. In the organ, one of the projecting knobs within easy reach of the organist, which, when drawn out, shift the corresponding slides so as to admit wind to the grooves communicating with a set of pipes or a combination of stops, or else effect a coupling.— *Draw-stop action*, the entire mechanism controlled and set in operation by the draw-stops.

Dreh'er (Ger.) An obsolete variety of waltz resembling the *Ländler*, of Bohemian or Austrian origin, in 3-8 or 3-4 time.

Dreh'orgel (Ger.) A barrel-organ.

Drei (Ger.) Three...*Drei'chörig*, (*a*) for 3 choirs ; (*b*) trichord (said of a pfte.)...*Drei'gestrichen*, 3-lined, thrice-accented...*Drei'klang*, a triad... *Drei'stimmig*, three-part, in 3 parts, for 3 voices.

Drit'ta (It.) See *Diritta*.

Driving-note. Syncopated note. (Obsolete.)

Droit(e) (Fr.) Right...*Main droite*, right hand (abbr. *m. d.*)

Drone. (Ger. *Stim'mer*, *Bordun'* ; Fr. *bourdon* ; It. *bordo'ne*.) In the bagpipe, one of the continuously sounding pipes of constant pitch. (Also see *Drone-bass*.)...*Drone-bass*, a bass on the tonic, or tonic and dominant, which is persistent throughout a movement or piece, as in the *Musette* 2...*Dronepipe*, same as *Drone*.

Drück'balg (Ger.) Concussion-bellows.

Druck'er (Ger.) A specially brilliant (sometimes a forced) effect ; *einen Drucker auf'setzen*, to bring out such an effect.

Drü'cker (Ger.) See *Stecher*.

Druck'werk (Ger.) An organ-action operating by the pressure of stickers on the remoter parts of the mechanism. (See *Zugwerk*.)

Drum. An instr. of percussion, consisting of a hollow *body* of wood or metal, over one or both ends of which a membrane (the *head*) is stretched tightly by means of a *hoop*, to which is attached an endless *cord* tightened by leathern *braces*, or by a system of rods and screws. The two chief classes of drums are the *rhythmical* (those employed to vary and emphasize the rhythm), and the *musical* (those capable of producing a mus. tone distinct in pitch). The commonest forms of the first class in modern use are : (1) The *side-drum* (Ger. *Trommel;* Fr. *tambour;* It. *tamburo*); it has a cylindrical body of wood or metal, and 2 heads, is slung across the left thigh, and only the upper head is beaten with the 2 drumsticks; when gut strings (*snares*) are stretched across the lower head, the instr. is called a *snare-drum*. (2) The *bass drum* (Ger. *grosse Trommel;* Fr. *grosse caisse;* It. *gran cassa, gran tamburo*), similar in form to 1, but much larger, and beaten on one or both heads with a stick having a soft round knob at the end. (3) See *Tambourine*...The sole representative of the second class is the *Kettledrum* (which see).

Duc'tus (Lat.) A series of tones in stepwise progression ; as *d. rec'tus*, ascending ; *d. rever'tens*, descending ; *d. circumcur'rens*, first ascending and then descending.

Du'delsack (Ger.) Bagpipe.

Du'e (It.) Two...*A due*, signifies (1) for two ; as *a due voci*, for 2 parts or voices ; (2) both together (see *Divisi*). ..*Due corde*, "two strings"; see *Corda*...*Due volte*, twice...*I due pedali*, both (pedals.-) pedals at once.

Duet'. (Ger. *Duett';* Fr. *duo;* It. *duet'to*.) 1. A composition for 2 voices or instr.s.—2. A composition for 2 performers on one instr., as the pfte.—3. A composition for the organ, in 2 parts, each to be played on a separate manual.

Duetti'no (It., dimin. of *duetto*.) A short and simple duet.

Dulcian' (Ger.) See *Dolcian*.

Dulcian'a. 1. An organ-stop having metal pipes of narrow scale and yielding a somewhat sharp, thin tone.—2. A reed-stop of delicate tone.—3. A small bassoon.

Dul'cimer. (Ger. *Hack'brett;* Fr. *tympanon ;* It. *cem'balo*.) A very ancient stringed instr., greatly varying in construction and form ; typical characteristic, the wire strings stretched over a soundboard or resonance-box and struck with mallets or hammers. In the modern forms the string-tension is regulated by wrest-pins, and the mallet-heads have one soft and one hard face, which produce different effects of tone. Compass 2 to 3 octaves, *g* to *g³*: The dulcimer was the precursor, and is often called the prototype, of the pianoforte. See *Pantalon.*

Dumb piano. An instr. like a small piano in form, having a keyboard of narrow compass, but neither hammers nor strings ; intended for silent finger-practice, i. e. merely for increasing the mechanical dexterity of the fingers (Comp. *Digitorium*, and *Virgil Practice-Clavier*)...*Dumb spinet*, see *Manichord.*

Dummy pipes. Pipes which do not speak, displayed in the front of an organ.

Dump. An obsolete dance in slow tempo and common time.

Du'o (It. and Fr.) A duet. (In English usage, *duo* is sometimes distinguished from *duet* by applying the former term to a 2-part composition for 2 voices or instr.s of different kinds, and the latter to such a composition for 2 voices or instr.s of the same kind.)

Duode'cima (It.) 1. The interval of a twelfth.—2. A Twelfth (organ-stop).

Duodecimo'le (Ger.) Dodecuplet.

Du'odene. A 12-tone group composed of 4 *trines*, applied to the solution and correction of problems in temperament and harmony. A *duode'nal* is the symbol of the root-tone of a duodene. The term (as also *Trine, Decad, Heptad, Heptadecad*, etc.) is the invention of A. J. Ellis, a full explanation of whose system of acoustics will be found in his original Appendices to the Second English Edition of Helmholtz's work " On the Sensations of Tone," (1885, translated by Ellis himself).

Duodra'ma. (It. *duodram'ma*.) A kind of melodrama, or spoken dialogue accompanied by the orchestra.

Duo'i (It.) Same as *Due.*

Duo'le (Ger.) Couplet 2.

Duo'lo (It.) Grief, sadness, melancholy.

Du'pla (*proportio*). See *Notation*, §3.

Duple. Double...*D. rhythm*, rhythm of 2 beats to a measure.

Dur (Ger.) Major.

Dur,-e (Fr.) Harsh, unpleasing in tone.

Duramen'te (It.) Sternly, harshly.

Durch'führung (Ger.) In a general sense, the mus. construction or working-out of a movement ; specifically, the development of a theme, as in the fugue or sonata. (See *Development, Form.*)

Durch'gang (Ger.; Lat. *tran'situs.*) The " passage " or progression of one principal tone to another through a tone or tones foreign to the harmony or key... *Durch'gangston*, passing-tone, changing-tone ; *re'gelmässiger D.ton*, one falling on a weak beat ; *un'regelmässiger Durchgangston*, one falling on a strong beat, also called a *schwe'rer Durchgang*, " heavy passing - tone," though properly an anticipation or free suspension.

Durch'gehend (Ger.) 1. Passing, as *Durch'gehender Akkord'*, passing-chord.—2. Transitional, as *durchgehende Aus'weichungen*, the transitional or continuous modulations necessary in passing to a key harmonically remote. —3. Complete ; as *durch'gehende Stim'men*, complete (organ-) stops.

Durch'komponieren (Ger.) In song-writing, to set each strophe to different music, thus following the changing mood more closely than in the ballad or folk-song, where melody and harmony are generally the same for each verse. ..*Durchkomponiert*, " through-composed," progressively composed.

Durch'schlagende Zung'e (Ger.) Free reed.

Durch'stechen (Ger.) Running (of wind in an organ). Also said of a pipe which, when facing another, causes the latter to speak by the wind issuing from its mouth.—*Durch'stecher*, tones produced by the above defects.

Durée (Fr.) Duration, time-value (of a note).

Durez'za (It.) Sternness, harshness.

Dur Moll'-Tonart (Ger., " major-minor mode ".) The " combined " mode derived theoretically from the resolution of the dominant chord in minor to the tonic in major (mode with *major* third and *minor* sixth); expressed by the Hauptmann formula
D/F-a♭-C-e-G-b-D/F.

Du'ro,-a (It.) Stern, harsh.

Du'rus,-a,-um (Lat., " hard ".) Equivalent to *major* in the phrases *cantus durus, hexachor'dum durum;* i. e. a chant (vocal music) and hexachord with major third ; opp. to *Mollis.—B durum, B* natural.

Dü'ster (Ger.) Gloomy, mournful.

Dutch concert. See *Concert.*

Dux (Lat., "leader, guide".) Subject or theme of a fugue.

Dynam'ics. The theory of mus. dynamics is the scientific explanation of the varying and contrasting degrees of intensity or loudness in mus. tones.

E.

E. (Ger. *E;* Fr. and It. *mi.*) The 3d tone or degree in the typical diatonic scale of *C*-major. (Compare *Alphabetical Notation,* and *Solmisation.*)

E (It.) And ; (before a vowel, *ed*).

Ear. 1. (Ger. *Ohr, Gehör';* Fr. *oreille;* It. *orec'chio.*) A mus. ear is one impressionable to mus. tones, thus affording to its possessor, after more or less practice, the capability of accurately reproducing them, and of appreciating and correctly analyzing compositions performed by others.—2. One of the 2 projecting plates of metal on either side of the mouth of an organ-pipe.

Ebollimen'to, Ebollizio'ne (It.) Ebullition ; a sudden and passionate expression of feeling.

Écart (Fr.) A wide stretch on the pfte.

Ec'bole (Gk.) The raising or sharping of a tone ; opp. to *Ec'lysis.*

Ecceden'te (It.) Augmented (of intervals).

Ecclesiastical modes. See *Modes.*

Ec'co (It.) Echo.

Échappement (Fr.) The hopper or escapement in a double-action pfte.

Échelette (Fr.) Xylophone.

Échelle (Fr.) Scale.

Echo. 1. A subdued repetition of a strain or phrase.—2. An echo-stop.—3. A harpsichord-stop... *Echo-organ,* a separate set of pipes, either enclosed in a box within the organ, or placed at a distance from the latter, to produce the effect of an echo ; it has separate stops, and often a special manual... *Echo-stop,* one producing an echo-like effect, either by itself or in an echo-organ.

Éclisses (Fr.) Ribs (of a violin).. *Contre-éclisses,* linings.

Éclogue. See *Églogue.*

Ec'lysis (Gk.) The flatting or depression of a tone ; opp. to *Ec'bole.*

E'co (It.) Echo.

Écossaise (Fr.) Originally, a Scotch round dance in 3-2 or 3-4 time ; now, a lively contredanse in 2-4 time. (Compare *Schottische.*)

Écu (Fr.) Shield (on face of lute, mandolin, etc.)

Ed (It.) And.

E'del (Ger.) Noble ; refined, chaste.

Effekt' (Ger.) Effect... *Effekt'piano,* the effect of the *forte-piano* (*f p*).

Effet (Fr.), **Effet'to** (It.) Effect, impression.

Effort (Fr.) In singing, a rough and guttural attack.

Égalité (Fr.) Evenness, smoothness.

Églogue (Fr.) A pastoral, or idyl, though in somewhat more animated style than the latter.

Egua'le (It.) Equal ; even, smooth... *Egualmen'te,* evenly, smoothly.

Eidomu'sikon. See *Melograph.*

Ei'gentlich (Ger.) Proper, actual, true, real... *Ei'gentliche Fuge,* a strict fugue. ..*Ei'gentliche Kadenz',* perfect cadence... *Ei'gentlicher Drei'klang,* common chord.

Ei'genton (Ger.) Natural tone (of a wind-instr.) ; tone proper to, or produced by, a sonorous body or hollow space.

Eighteenth. An interval of 2 octaves and a fourth.

Eighth. 1. An octave.—2. An eighth-note... *Eighth-note,* a note representing one-eighth of the time-value of a whole note ; a quaver (♪)... *Eighth-rest,* a rest equal in time-value to an eighth-note.

Ei'len (Ger.) To hasten, accelerate, go faster... *Ei'lend,* hastening ; *accelerando, stringendo...Ei'lig,* hasty, in a hurried style; rapid, swift.

Ein, Eins (Ger.) One... *Ein'chörig,* (*a*) having one string to each note ; (*b*) for single (or undivided) chorus (choir)... *Ein'fach,* simple, plain... *Ein'gang,* introduction... *Ein'gestrichen,* one-lined. ..*Ein'greifen,* (*a*) to touch or sound (strings) ; (*b*) in pfte.-playing, to inter-

lace the fingers...*Ein'klang*, unison...
Ein'lage, a short piece introduced (*ein'-gelegt*) between 2 compositions or in the midst of a long one...*Ein'leitung*, introduction...*Ein'mal*, once...*Ein'-saiter*, monochord...*Ein'satz*, entrance (of a vocal or instrumental part) ; attack.
Ein'satzstück, a crook (usually *Bogen*). *Ein'satzzeichen*, in a canon, the *presa*. ..*Ein'schnitt*, a pause at the end of a melodic phrase or section...*Ein'setzen*, to enter (as a part) ; to attack ; to strike or fall in ; *ein'setzender Hornist'*, a horn-player who sets the mouthpiece rather within than against his lips ; a lipping sometimes necessitated by thick lips...*Ein'singen*, (*a*) to sing to sleep ; (*b*) to practise singing until confidence is attained...*Ein'spielen*, (*a*) to play on a new instr. till it works smoothly ; (*b*) to practise a part or piece until confidence is attained...*Ein'stimmen*, to tune (in concert with other instr.s)...*Ein'stimmig*, for one part or voice...*Ein'tritt*, entrance ; beginning.

E'ïs (Ger.) E♯...*E'ïsïs*, E×.

Ei'senvioline (Ger.) See *Nagelgeige*.

Eklo'g(u)e. Ger. spelling of *Églogue*.

Ela. Name of the highest note in the Aretinian scale :

Electric Organ. See *Organ*...*Electric Pianoforte* (Ger. *elektropho'nisches Klavier'*), inv. in 1891 by Dr. Eisenmann of Berlin. Over each unison of strings an electro-magnet is fixed ; on closing the circuit (by depressing a digital) each magnet attracts its strings, and (the magnetic action being duly controlled and limited by a set of microphones) causes their continuous vibration.— Tone (of the improved instr.) full, sweet, capable of the most various dynamic

shading ; timbre like that of the string-orchestra ; the ordinary hammer-action may be employed alone, or in combination with the above. A peculiar (sustaining) pedal-mechanism permits a given tone, a full chord, or any harmony, to sound on as long as desired, even after lifting the fingers. Numerous combined effects of tone are possible.

Élégamment (Fr.) Elegantly.

Elegan'te (It) Elegant, graceful... *Elegantemen'te*, elegantly, etc.

Elegie'zither (Ger.) See *Zither*.

El'egy. (Fr. *élégie ;* It. *elegi'a*.) A composition of a mournful cast, either vocal or instrumental ; a dirge...*Ele'-giac*, a pentameter, i. e. a verse composed of 2 dactylic penthemims or written in elegiac metre...*Elegiac verse*, that in which elegiac poems or verses are written, consisting of elegiac distiches ; an *elegiac distich* being one in which the first line is a dactylic hexameter, and the second a pentameter, thus :

Élément (Fr.) The entire range of tones embraced in the mus. scale... *Élément métrique*, a measure-note.

Eleva'tio (Lat.) 1. Up-beat ; unaccented count.—2. The rising of a melody over the ambitus of the mode.—3. A mus. composition accompanying the elevation of the Host.

Elevation. See *Elevatio*...Also, the name of 2 obsolete graces, the *elevation* and *shaked elevation :*

Elevation.   Shaked Elevation.

written :

played :

Élévation (Fr.) 1. Up-beat or weak beat (also *levé*) ; opp. to *Frappé*.—2. Same as *Elevatio* 2 and 3.

Eleva'to (It.) Elevated, lofty, sublime. ..*Elevazio'ne*, see *Elevation*.

Embellir (Fr.) To embellish, ornament.

Embellishment. See *Grace*.

Embouchure (Fr.) 1. The mouthpiece of a wind-instr., or the oval orifice of a flute.—2. See *Lip*.

Empâter les sons (Fr.) To produce a very smooth and suave *legato*...*Exécution* (*voix*) *empâtée*, an instrumental (vocal) style lacking in neatness and distinctness.

Empfin'dung (Ger.) Feeling, emotion...
Empfin'dungsvoll, full of feeling ; feelingly, with emotion.

Empha'se (Ger. and Fr.) Emphasis, stress.

Emporté,-e (Fr.) Carried away by feeling or passion.

Empressé,-e (Fr.) Urgent, eager ; in haste.

Enarmo'nico (It.) Enharmonic.

En badinant (Fr.) See *Scherzando.*

Enclavure du manche (Fr.) Space cut in belly (of violin) for insertion of neck.

Encore (Fr.) "Again!" (in English usage ; the French use the word "*bis*" when recalling an actor or performer). —Also used for *recall* (*noun* and *verb*), and for the piece or performance repeated.

End-man. In the "negro minstrels", a man who sits at the end of the semicircle formed by the company on commencing the performance. There are 2 or 4 such end-men, who provide a good part of the fun apart from the songs, and likewise perform on the "bones" and the tambourine.

Energi'a (It.), **Énergie** (Fr.) Energy... *Energicamen'te* (It.), or *con energia*, with energy and decision, energetically.

Ener'gico (It.), **Ener'gisch** (Ger.) Energetic, vigorous ; indicates that the passage so marked is to be vigorously accented and distinctly phrased.

Enfant de chœur (Fr.) A choir-boy.

En'fasi, con (It.) With emphasis, emphatically...*Enfa'tico*, emphatic.

Eng (Ger.) Narrow, close...*Eng'e Harmonie'* (*Lage*), close harmony.

Eng'elstimme (Ger.) *Vox angelica.*

Eng'führung (Ger.) The *stretto* in a fugue.

Eng'lisch (Ger.) English...*Englisch Horn*, cor anglais...*Eng'lische Mecha'nik*, English action (pfte.)...*Eng'-lischer Tanz*, anglaise ..*Englisch Violet'*, (*a*) an obsolete bow-instr. resembling the *viola d'amore*, with 14 sympathetic strings stretched below the fingerboard ; (*b*) a former tuning of the violin (*e–a–e¹–a¹*).

Enharmon'ic. (Ger. *enharmo'nisch ;* Fr. *enharmonique ;* It. *enarmo'nico.*) In Greek music, the *enh. genus* was distinguished by a tetrachord, the first 2 steps in which were (approximately)

quarter-tones, and the third step a major third.—In modern music, *enharmonic tones* are tones derived from different degrees, but practically identical in pitch, as *c♯* and *d♭* on the pfte. or organ...*Enharmonic change*, a change effected in the harmonic relations of a tone or chord by treating it as identical in pitch with another tone or chord of different notation ; thus: where the enharm. change of *b♭* to *a♯* brings about a different resolution of the diminished seventh-chord by changing its tonality:

(1) *d*-minor.   (2) *b*-minor.

..*Enharmonic chords*, chords (like 1 and 2 above) alike in pitch but unlike in notation and derivation...*Enharm. di'esis*, see *Diesis*...*Enharm. interval*, one derived from an enharm. change... *Enharm. modulation*, an enharm. change of chords, as above...*Enharm. organ, pianoforte, scale*, one in which the identity of the enharmonic tones is denied, and an attempt made to realize practically the minute differences in pitch between such tones, e. g. by adding an extra digital for *d♭* as distinct from *c♯* ; etc.

Ensemble (Fr.) Concert, in the sense of "agreement of 2 or more in a design or plan".—1. The unity of a composition ; the harmonious agreement of parts which forms a well-balanced whole.—2. The harmonious cooperation of the various factors in a performance ; of the actors, singers, musicians, or instruments, taken in groups or together...*Morceaux d'ensemble*, concerted music.

En serrant (Fr.) Stringendo.

Entr'acte (Fr., "interval between acts".) A light instrumental composition or short ballet, intended or adapted for performance between acts.

Entra'ta (It.) See *Entrée*, and *Intrada.*

Entrée (Fr.) 1. See *Intrada;* also, specifically, the orchestral prelude to a ballet, following the overture.—2. Entrance (of a part or actor).—3. A division of a ballet corresponding to a "scene" in a dramatic performance ; also, the dance-music accompanying it.—4. An old dance resembling the Polonaise in character, usually in 4-4 time ; often occurs as first movement in the Serenata.

Entry. An act of an opera, burletta, etc. (Obsolete.)

Entschlos'sen (Ger.) Resolute(ly), determined, in a determined manner.

Entwurf' (Ger.) Sketch, plan, design.

Eo'lian. See *Æolian.*

Ep'icede. (Lat. *epice'dium;* Fr. *epicède;* It. *epice'dio.*) A funeral song, dirge.

Epigo'nion (Gk.) The ancient Greek lyre with 40 strings, named after its reputed inventor Epigonos.

Épinette (Fr.) Spinet.

Epini'cion (Gk.) 1. A triumphal song in celebration of a victory.—2. In the Greek Church, the triumphal hymn, the Sanctus.

Epio'dion (Gk.) A funeral song.

Episode. (Ger. *Zwisch'ensatz;* Fr. *épisode;* It. *divertimen'to.*) An intermediate or incidental section ; a digression from and interpolation between the repetitions or developments of the principal theme or themes of a composition ; specifically, in the fugue, a passage of the above character ordinarily formed of motives taken from the subject or countersubject.

Epistle side (of the altar). That on the priest's left, when he is facing the congregation ; the south side ; opp. to the *gospel* or north side.

Epis'trophe (Gk.) In a cyclic composition, a refrain.

Epit'asis (Gk.) The raising of the voice, or the strings of an instr., from a lower to a higher pitch. (See *Anesis.*)

Epithala'mium (Lat.), **Epithala'mion** (Gk.) A nuptial song or poem.

Epito'nion (Gk.) A tuning-wrench ; a pitch-pipe.

Ep'itrite. Same as *Hippius.*

Ep'ode (Gk., "after-song".) 1. A refrain.—2. The concluding stanza of an ode, following the strophe and antistrophe.

Eptacorde (Fr.), **Eptacor'do** (It.) 1. Heptachord.—2. A scale of 7 notes.—3. The interval of a seventh.

Equa'bile (It.) Equable, even, uniform, similar... *Equabilmen'te,* equably, etc.

Equal counterpoint, temperament. See the nouns... *Equal voices,* voices of the same class, i. e. either women's

(or boys') voices (contralto and soprano), or men's voices (tenor, bass) ; opp. to "unequal voices," a term equivalent to *mixed chorus.*

E'quisonance. In medieval music, the unison (of primes or octaves).

Équisonnance (Fr.) The unison (of octaves, double octaves, etc.)

Equi'sono (It.) In unison or octaves.

Equiv'ocal or **doubtful chord.** See *Chord.*

Ergrif'fen (Ger.) Affected, stirred, moved... *Ergrif'fenheit,* emotion, agitation.

Erha'ben (Ger.) Lofty, exalted, sublime... *Erha'benheit,* sublimity, etc.

Erhöh'ung (Ger.) Raising (the pitch of); sharping... *Erhöh'ungszeichen,* sign of raising, as the ♯, or a ♮ after a ♭.

Ermat'tet (Ger.) Exhausted, wearied.

Ernie'drigung (Ger.) Lowering (the pitch of); flatting... *Ernie'drigungszeichen,* sign of lowering, as the ♭, or the ♮ after a ♯.

Ernst (Ger.) Earnest, serious, grave. (Also *adverb.*)

Ero'ico,-a (It.) Heroic ; strong and dignified.

Erot'ic. (It. *ero'tico.*) 1. Amatory.—2. An amatory poem, a love-song.

Er'ster,-e,-es (Ger.) First... *Er'ste Stim'me,* the highest part or voice.

Erwei'tern (Ger.) To extend, expand. *Erwei'terte Harmonie',* see *Lage, weite.* ..*Erwei'terter Satz,* a movement in which there is a full exposition of the subject by development, repetition, etc. ..*Erwei'terung* (of a fugal theme), the widening of any of its intervals.

Erzäh'ler (Ger.) The *Evangelist* or *Narrator* in a Passion-play.

Erz'laute (Ger.) Archlute.

Es (Ger.) E♭...*Es'es,* E♭♭.

Esacor'do (It.) 1. Hexachord.—2. The interval of a sixth.

Esat'to (It.) Exact, true.

Esecuzio'ne (It.) Execution.

Eserci'zio (It.) Exercise ; practice.

Espace (Fr.) Space (in staff).

Espiran'do (It.) Expiring, dying away.

Espressio'ne, con (It.) With expression, expressively... *Espressi'vo,* expressive.

Essential harmony. See *Harmony*...
Ess. notes, chord-notes...*Ess. 7th*, (*a*) the leading-note ; (*b*) the dominant chord of the 7th.

Estensio′ne (It.) Compass...*Esteso,-a* (pl. *estesi,-e*), extended.

Estinguen′do (It.) Extinguishing, dying away.

Estin′to (It.) Barely audible ; the extreme of *pianissimo*.

Estravagan′za (It.) Extravaganza.

Étalon (Fr.) *Scale* 3.

Étendue (Fr.) Compass.

Étoffé(e) (Fr.) Having " body"...*Voix étoffée*, a full, sonorous voice.

Étouffé,-e (Fr.) Stifled, damped, muffled...*Étouffoir*, damper (pfte.)

Ettacor′do (It.) See *Eptacordo*.

Étude (Fr.) A study ; especially, one affording practice in some particular technical difficulty...*Étude de concert*, an étude designed for public performance ; a species of characteristic piece.

Et′was (Ger.) Rather, somewhat.

Euharmon′ic. Producing harmonies perfectly pure ; opp. to *tempered*... *Euharmonic organ*, one having a sufficient number of keys to produce all the fundamental and the chief derivative tones.

EUOUAE. See *EVOVAE*.

Eupho′ne. 1. (Also *Euphon*.) See *Euphonium*.—2. In the organ, a 16-foot free-reed stop, with a soft sweet tone like that of the clarinet.

Eupho′nia (It.) Euphony.

Eupho′niad. A kind of orchestrion.

Eupho′nium. 1. An instr. inv. by Chladni in 1790, consisting of graduated glass tubes set in vibration with the moistened fingers, and connected with steel rods. (Also *Euphon*.)—2. The bass Saxhorn.

Euter′pe. One of the nine Muses, the inventress of the double flute, and patroness of flute-players and of primitive and simple melody.

Evacua′tio (Lat.) In mensurable notation, writing only the *outlines* of solid notes, thus reducing their value by one-half.

Evakuant′ (Ger.) The exhaust-valve or exhaust-pallet in the organ ; (Engl. also *evacuant*).

Evening-song, Even-song. In the Anglican Church, a form of worship appointed to be said or sung at evening ; known as Vespers in the R. C. Church.

Ever′sio, Evolu′tio (Lat.) The inversion of the parts in double counterpoint.

Evira′to (It.) See *Castrato*.

Évolution (Fr.) See *Renversement*.

EVOVAE. The vowels of S*e*c*u*l*o*r*u*m *amen*, the last two words in the Gloria Patri.—In Gregorian music, the trope closing the Lesser Doxology; in a wider sense, any trope.

Exercise. (Ger. *Ü′bung, Ü′bungsstück;* Fr. *exercice;* It. *eserci′zio*.) A short technical study, often consisting of but one repeated measure, for training the fingers (or vocal organs) to overcome some special difficulty ; also, a short study in composition, consisting of an outline (e. g. a figured bass, or a *cantus firmus*) to be filled out harmonically or contrapuntally by the student.

Exhaust-pallet or **-valve.** A valve opened by a draw-stop, to let off the wind in the bellows after playing ; an evacuant.

Exposition. 1. (Ger. *er′ste Durch′füh-rung*.) See *Fugue*.—2. (Ger.,[*-tion′*].) Development.

Expression (Fr.) 1. Expression.—2. The *vibrato* effect on bow-instr.s.

Expression. (Ger. *Aus′druck;* Fr. *expression;* It. *espressio′ne*.) The clear and effective presentation of the emotional and intellectual content of a work ; its proper reading and interpretation, rendering and execution...*Expression-mark*, a written direction (either a sign, word, or phrase) for the performance of a piece...*Expression-stop*, in the harmonium, a stop which closes the escape-valve of the bellows, so that the wind-pressure, and consequently the intensity of the tone, is partly under the control of the pedals.

Expressive organ. (Ger. *Expressiv′-orgel;* Fr. *orgue expressif*.) The harmonium.

Extem′pore. Without previous preparation ; on the spur of the moment ; off-hand.

Extem′porize. (Ger. *extemporie′ren*.) To improvise...*Extemporizing-ma-chine*, an apparatus for mechanically recording improvisations on the pfte. or organ by means of a mechanism placed in communication with the keyboard. See *Melograph.*

Extended compass, harmony, interval. See the nouns.

Extension (Fr.) 1. On the pfte., a stretch ; on the violin, the extension of the little finger or forefinger of the left hand.—2. Same as *Étendue.*

Extension-pedal. See *Pedal.*

Extraneous chromatic signs. Those not proper to the key...*Extraneous modulation,* one to a remote key.

Extravagan'za. A composition of an extravagant, whimsical, or fantastic character ; a burlesque.

Extreme. 1. Of intervals, augmented. The *chord of the extreme sixth* has a major third and sharp sixth, and occurs on the 6th degree in minor in 3 principal forms :

or with progression to major (E♭).— The first form is called the *Italian sixth;* the second, the *French sixth;* and the third, the *German sixth.*—2 (pl.) In part-music, the outer parts.— 3. *Extreme key,* a remote key.

improvised.—3. A drone-bass, a burden.—4. The intonation of the Psalms.

Face (Fr.) The position of a chord, either as a fundamental chord or inversion , e. g. a triad has 3 *faces.*

-fach (Ger.,"-fold ".) When compounded with a numeral, equivalent to *ranks,* i.e. in a mixture-stop ; *zwei'fach*=with 2 ranks, *drei'fach*=with 3 ranks, etc.

F.

F. (Ger. *F;* Fr. and It. *fà.*) The fourth tone and degree in the typical diatonic scale of *C*-major. (Comp. *Alphabetical notation, Solmisation.*)—*f*=*forte; ff* or *fff* (seldom *ffff*), *fortissimo.*

Fa. 1. The fourth of the Aretinian syllables.—2. Name of the tone *F* in Italy, France, etc...*Fa feint* (Fr.), *fa fic'tum* (Lat.), former term for any flatted note...*Fa mi,* in solmisation, the descending step of a semitone; originally that from *F* to *E,* thereafter from B♭ to *A, E♭* to *D,* etc.

Fabliau (Fr.) A versified tale or romance of the *trouvères,* in vogue chiefly during the 12th and 13th centuries. ...*Fablier* (Provençal), a *Trouvère.*

Fa'burden. (Fr. *faux bourdon;* It. *fal'so bordo'ne.*) 1. In medieval music, the primitive harmonization of a *c. f.* by adding the third and the sixth above, and progressing in parallel motion throughout, only the first and last chords having key-note, fifth, and octave.—2. Later, the setting of a simple (note against note) counterpoint to the *c. f.,* strict parallel motion being given up to some extent ; dissonances were avoided, various embellishments added, and the whole counterpoint frequently

Fäch'erförmiges Pedal' (Ger.) A " fan-shaped " or radiating pedal-keyboard.

Faci'le (Fr.), **Fa'cile** (It.) Facile, easy, fluent...*Facilement* (It. *facilmen'te*), easily, fluently...*Facilité* (It. *facilità'*), ease, easiness, facility, fluency ; *facilité(e)* also signifies *made easy,* as an easy arrangement of a difficult piece or passage.

Fack'eltanz (Ger.,"torch-dance".) A torch-light procession arranged at some German courts at the marriage of a member of the reigning family ; the music is a polonaise in march-time, for military band, and in minuet-form.

Facture (Fr. ; Ger. *Faktur';* It. *fattu'-ra.*) 1. The plan, build, structure, construction of a composition.—2. (Fr. and It.) Scale (of organ-pipes).

-fä'dig (Ger.) Equivalent to *threads* (of violin-strings), as *4'fädig,* having 4 threads.

Fad'ing. An Irish dance ; also, the burden of a song.

Fagott' (Ger.) Bassoon...*Fagott'zug* (or simply *Fagott*), a reed-stop in the organ.

Fagot'to (It.) Bassoon...*Fagotti'no,* a

" small bassoon " pitched a fifth higher than the ordinary one (Ger. *Quint'-fagott, Tenor'fagott*)...*Fagotti'sta*, a bassoonist, bassoon-player...*Fagotto'ne*, double-bassoon.

Fah. For *fa*, in Tonic Sol-fa.

Faible (Fr.) Weak...*Temps faible*, weak beat.

Faktur' (Ger.) See *Facture*.

Fa-la. See *Ballet* 3...Also, in Italy, a kind of arietta ending with a burden of fa-la.

Fall. 1. Same as *Fly*.—2. A cadence or close.—3. A lowering of the voice.

Fall (Ger.) See *Ton'fall*.

Falling rhythm. A descending rhythm.

Fal'sa (Lat. and It.; Ger. *falsch*.) False, wrong...*Mu'sica falsa*, see *Ficta*... *Quin'ta falsa* (Ger. *fal'sche Quin'te*), diminished fifth.

False. (Ger. *falsch*; Fr. *faux, fausse*; It. *falso,-a*.) Wrong; not true to pitch, out of tune...*False cadence, chord, fifth, harmony,* see the nouns... *False relation,* also *inharmonic rel., cross-rel.,* an harmonic discrepancy arising from the chromatic contradiction of a tone in one part by another part. In equal counterpoint it is apt to occur at a modulation, and consists in sounding, either simultaneously or successively, a tone and its chromatically altered octave. The former case is generally confined to passing-notes in figuration, and then has no ill effect; the latter case occurs when a chromatically changed tone, which might have been reached in one part by the step of a chromatic semitone, enters in another octave in another part; the effect is harshest in passing from a major chord to a parallel minor chord, or vice versa:

Falset'to (It.; Ger. *Falsett'*; Fr. *voix de fausset, fausset.*) The highest of the 3 vocal registers (chest-voice, head-voice, falsetto), so named from its forced or unnatural character; often reckoned to the head-register...*Falset'tist*, a falsetto singer.

Fal'so,-a (It.) False...*Falso bordone,* (*a*) see *Faburden*; (*b*) the reciting-note.

Fancy. A short piece of an impromptu character; a fantasy.

Fandango. (Span.) A lively Spanish dance in triple time, for 2 dancers of different sex, who accompany it with castanets, or sometimes (in the case of the man) with a tambourine. The dance alternates with vocal couplets, both dance and song having a guitar-accomp.; the following is the castanet-rhythm :

Fanfa'ra (It.), **Fanfare** (Fr.) 1. A brass-band.—2. A fanfare.

Fan'fare. A flourish of trumpets or trumpet-call, either in the orchestra, on a hunt, or at warlike gatherings.

Fantasi'a (It.; Ger. *Fantasie', Phantasie'*; Fr. *fantaisie.*) 1. An improvisation or impromptu.—2. In the 17th and 18th centuries, an instrumental composition in free imitation, as contrasting with one in strict imitation.—3. Later, a composition free in form and more or less fantastic in character.—4. A term loosely applied to potpourris and paraphrases...*Free fantasia*, that part of the first movement of a symphony or sonata which follows the double-bar (repeat of first part) and precedes the reintroduction of the principal theme; it consists chiefly of a free development of motives taken from the first part.

Fantasie'ren (Ger.) See *Phantasieren*. ..*Fantasie'stück,* see *Phantasiestück*.

Fanta'stico (It.), **Fantastique** (Fr.), **Fantas'tisch** (Ger.) Fantastic, giving free rein to the fancy.

Fan'tasy. See *Fantasia*.

Farando'la, Farando'le. A circle-dance of southern France and the adjoining Italian provinces, in 6-8 time and very rapid tempo.

Farce. 1. (It. *far'sa.*) A one-act opera or operetta of ultra-comical or burlesque character.—2. (It. *farsia.*) A canticle in the vernacular intermingled with Latin, formerly sung at the principal festivals of the R. C. Church, and later finding ludicrous imitation in the *farsa* or farce.

Fa'scia (It.) 1. A tie.—2 (pl., *fascie*). Ribs.

Fastosamen'te (It.) Pompously, in a stately style...*Fasto'so,* pompous, stately.

Fatigue-call. A signal to soldiers, calling them to fatigue-duty.

Fattu'ra (It.) See *Facture*.

Fausse (Fr., masc. *faux.*) False...*F.*

quinte, dimin. fifth...*F. relation,* false relation.

Fausset (Fr.) See *Falsetto.*

Faux (Fr.) False...*Faux-bourdon,* see *Faburden.*

F-clef. (Ger. *F-schlüssel ;* Fr. *clef de fa ;* It. *chiave di basso.*) See *Clef.*

Fe'derklavier (Ger.) Spinet.

Feeder. In the organ, see *Organ,* (1) *Wind-supply.*

Fei'erlich (Ger.) Festive ; solemn, grave, serious. (Also *adverb.*)

Fei'len (Ger.) To file, polish, refine, put the finishing touches to.

Fein (Ger.) Fine, delicate, refined.

Feint,-e (Fr.) See *Ficta.*

Feld'flöte,-pfeife (Ger.) 1. See *Bauern- flöte.*—2. A fife.—3. See *Schweizer- flöte 2.*

Feld'stück (Ger.) A cavalry-call or signal.

Female or **feminine rhyme.** A rhyme ending with an unaccented syllable, as fate'ful—ungrate'ful.

Fermamen'te (It.) Firmly, with de- cision.

Ferma're il tuono. See *Messa di voce.*

Ferma'ta (It.), **Ferma'te** (Ger.) 1. A pause, stop, or interruption, as that be- fore the cadenza of a concerto.—2. A hold (⌢).—3. A stop (on the violin).

Fermez'za, con (It.) In a firm, de- cided, energetic style *(deciso).*

Fer'mo (It.) Firm, decided ; fixed, un- changed (as *canto fermo*).

Fer'ne (Ger.) Distance... *Wie aus der Ferne,* as if from a distance.

Fern'flöte (Ger.) A covered 8' organ- stop of very soft tone.

Fern'werk (Ger.) Echo-organ.

Fero'ce (It.) Wild, fierce, vehement... *Ferocità',* wildness, vehemence... *Con ferocità,* wildly, vehemently.

Fer'tig (Ger.) Ready; done, finished ; prompt, skilful, dexterous... *Fer'tigkeit,* readiness, skill, dexterity ; technical finish.

Ferven'te (It.) Fervent, ardent, pas- sionate.

Fes (Ger.) F♭...*Fes'es,* F♭♭.

Fest (Ger.) 1. A festival... *Musik'fest,* mus. festival.—2. Firm, steady. (Also *adv.*)

Festivamen'te (It.) In a gay, festive manner .. *Festività',* festivity, mirth : *con f.,* in a gay and festive style... *Fes- ti'vo* (Ger. *fest'lich*), festive, festal (also *festo'so*).

Feu'er (Ger.) Fire, ardor, passion... *Feu'erig,* fiery ; with fire, ardently, pas- sionately.

F-holes. (Ger. *F'-löcher ;* Fr. *les F.*) The 2 *f*-shaped soundholes cut in the belly of the violin, etc.

Fiac'co (It.) Languishing.

Fia'sco (It.) Failure.

Fia'to (It.) Breath, breeze, wind... *Strumen'to da f.,* wind-instr.

Fic'ta,-um (Lat., "feigned".) *Fa fic'- tum,* see *Fa...Mu'sica ficta,* see *Mu- sica,* in APPENDIX.

Fiddle. (Ger. *Fi'del, Fie'del.*) See *Vio- lin...Fiddle-bow, fiddlestick,* see *Bow.*

Fi'des (Lat.) 1. The string of a mus. instr.—2. A lute, lyre, cithara.

Fi'dicen (Lat.; fem. *fidicina.*) A player on a stringed instr.

Fidic'ula (Lat.) Dimin. of *Fides.*

Fidu'cia (It.) Confidence, boldness.

Fie'del (Ger.) Fiddle... *Stroh'fiedel,* xylophone.

Fier, Fière (Fr.) Proud, haughty.

Fie'ro,-a (It.) Wild, fierce ; bold, vig- orous... *Fieramen'te,* wildly, boldly... *Fierez'za,* fierceness, boldness, vigor.

Fife. (Ger. *Quer'pfeife ;* Fr. *fifre ;* It. *pif'fero.*) 1. An octave cross-flute with 6 holes and without keys (thus differ- ing from the *Piccolo*) ; compass about ———→ used chiefly as a march-accomp. with the drum.—2. An organ-stop of 2-foot pitch ; a piccolo-stop.

Fifteenth. 1. (Ger. *Quint'dezime ;* Fr. *quinzième ;* It. *quindice'sima.*) A double octave.—2. An organ-stop of 2- foot pitch.

Fifth. (Ger. *Quin'te ;* Fr. *quinte ;* It. *quin'ta.*) An interval of 5 diatonic de- grees (see *Interval*) ; also, the 5th de- gree in the diatonic scale, the dominant. ..The typical or standard interval of this name is the *perfect* (or *major*) *fifth,* equal to the interval between the key- note and the fifth tone of the diatonic scale ; e. g. (*c-g*), the vibrational ratio being *c:g*::2:3. ..*Diminished (imperfect, defective.*

minor, or *false*) *fifth*, an interval narrower by a semitone than a perfect fifth.
...*Augmented* (*pluperfect*, *superfluous*, or *extreme*) *fifth*, one wider by a chromatic semitone than a perfect fifth...
Consecutive (or *parallel*) *fifths* see *Consecutive*...*Covered* (*concealed* or *hidden*) *fifths*, see *Octave*...*Circle of fifths*, see *Temperament*.

Fifthy. Having the second harmonic (fifth above the octave of the generator) specially prominent.

Figur' (Ger.) See *Figure* 2.

Figu'ra mu'ta (Lat. and It.) A rest.

Figu'ra obli'qua (Lat.) The "oblique figure" of Plain chant and mensurable music was a simple ligature formed by uniting 2 notes; (*a*) in Plain chant, it was written in 2 ways:

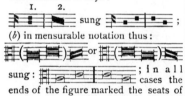

(*b*) in mensurable notation thus:

sung: ; in all cases the ends of the figure marked the seats of the 2 notes. In the midst of a ligature it possessed no special significance; but at the termination it denoted the *imperfection* of the final note.

Fig'ural. See *Figurate*...*Figural'gesang* (Ger.), cantus figuralis...*Figural'-musik*, unequal or figurate counterpoint.

Figurate. (Ger. *figuriert'*; Fr. *figuré*; It. *figura'to*.) Having, or consisting of, figurations. (Also *Figurative*.)

Figuration. 1. In counterpoint, the introduction of comparatively rapid figures or phrases, containing passing and changing-notes, into the counterpoint. —2. The variation of a theme by accompanying it with florid runs and passages, or by substituting for its own melody-notes more or less florid variations.—3. The writing-out of a figured bass.

Figure. 1. (Ger. *Figur'*; Fr. *figure*; It. *figura*.) A distinct group of notes, a motive.—2. (Ger. *Ziffer*; Fr. *chiffre*; It. *ci'fra*.) A numeral, as used in thorough-bass.

Figured. 1. (Ger. *bezif'fert*; Fr. *chiffré(e)*; It. *cifra'to*.) Provided with figures, as a bass (see *Thorough-bass*).— 2. Figurate.

Fil (Fr.) Thread (of a violin-string).

Filar' il tuo'no, la voce (It.) In the Italian method of singing, to produce an even, sustained tone, without *crescendo* or *diminuendo*. (Also *affilar' il tuono*; Fr. *filer un son, la voix*.)

Fil'pen (Ger.) See *Fistulieren*.

Fi'lum (Lat.) Stem (of a note).

Fin (Fr.) End, close.

Final. In Gregorian music, that tone (in any mode) on which the melody must end (equiv. to key-note or tonic); in the authentic modes it was the lowest tone; in the plagal modes, the 4th tone from below. Irregular final tones were called *confinals*...*Final close*, closing cadence.

Fina'le (It.) 1. A final.—2. The concluding movement of a sonata, symphony, etc., or the closing number of an act in an opera. An operatic *finale* is generally an ensemble for soloists and chorus, and intended to have a highly dramatic or otherwise striking effect.

Fina'lis (Lat.) See *Accentus*.

Fi'ne (It.) End, close; indicates either the end of a repeated section (after the *da capo* or *dal segno*), or the end of a piece in several divisions.

Fing'er (Ger.) Finger...*Fing'erbildner*, ("finger-developer"), see *Dactylion*. An apparatus of this name was also invented by Seeber, and consists of a separate attachment for each finger, whereby the bad habit of bending the last joint inwards is corrected...*Fing'erfertigkeit*, "finger-dexterity", agility and readiness of the fingers...*Fing'erleiter*, see *Chiroplast*...*Fing'ersatz*, *Fing'ersetzung*, fingering; *eng'er F.*, close fingering; *gedehn'ter F.*, spread fingering, stretches...*Fing'erwechsel*, change of fingers.

Fingerboard. 1. (Ger. *Griff'brett*; Fr. *touche*, *manche*: It. *tastie'ra*.) In the violin, guitar, etc., the thin, narrow strip of wood glued upon the neck, above which the strings are stretched, and on which they are stopped with the fingers of the left hand.—2. See *Keyboard*.

Finger-cymbals. Very small cymbals, held in pairs on the thumb and forefinger of both hands...*Finger-hole* (Ger. *Ton'loch*), in the flute, clarinet, etc., a hole in the tube, to be closed by a finger or by a lever operated by a finger, thus changing the pitch.

Fingering. (Ger. *Fing'ersatz, Appli-katur'*; Fr. *doigter*; It. *ditteggiatu'ra*.) 1. The method of applying the fingers to the keys, holes, strings, etc., of mus. instr.s.—2. The marks guiding the performer in placing his fingers...*English* (or *American?*) *fingering* (for the pfte.), that in which notes taken by the thumb are marked × (or +) with 1 2 3 4 for the fingers; *German* (or *continental*) *fingering*, that in which the thumb is marked 1, and the fingers 2 3 4 5. (An earlier German system resembled the English, merely using a o instead of the × for the thumb.)

Fini're il tuono. See *Messa di voce.*

Fini'to (It.) Finished.

Fi'no (It.) Till, up to, as far as.

Fin'to,-a (It.) Feigned...*Caden'za finta*, deceptive cadence...*Fa finto*, see *Fa feint.*

Fiochet'to (It.) Somewhat hoarse; faint, veiled...*Fiochez'za*, hoarseness. ..*Fio'co,-a*, hoarse, faint, veiled.

Fioreggia're (It.) To figurate.

Fioret'to (It.) Any melodic embellishment.

Fiori'to (It.) Florid, embellished... *Fioritu'ra*, an embellishment, an ornamental turn, flourish, or phrase introduced into a melody (commonly used in pl., *fioriture*).

First. 1. Of voices or instr.s of the same class, the *highest*; e. g. *first* soprano, *first* violin.—2. In the staff, the *lowest*; as *first* line, *first* space.—3. The *first* string of an instr. is the highest.—4. As the name of an interval, the prime or unison.

Fis (Ger.) F♯...*Fis'is*, F×.

Fis'telstimme (Ger.) Falsetto. (Also *Fistel.*)

Fis'tula (Lat.) Pipe.

Fistulie'ren (Ger.) 1. To sing falsetto. —2. Of an organ-pipe, to overblow in such wise as to sound (unintentionally) some harmonic tone instead of the fundamental.

Fixed Do. The *fixed-Do* system of solmisation is that in which the tone *C*, and all its chromatic derivatives (*C♯*, *C×*, and *C♭*, *C♭♭*) are called *Do*, *D* and its derivatives *Re*, etc., in whatever key or harmony they may appear: the

syllables are then termed *fixed syllables.* ..*Fixed-tone instr.*, (or *instr. of fixed intonation*), one (like the pfte. or organ) the pitch of whose tones cannot be modified at the player's pleasure like, for example, the tones of the violin.

Flag. 1. A hook (♮↓).—2. Abbr. for *flageolet* (*-tones*).

Flageolet. 1. (Ger. *Flageolett'*; Fr. *flageolet*; It. *flagiolet'ta*.) A modernized *flûte à bec*, a small wind-instr. of the whistle family. There are 2 species still in use, the English and the French; the latter is the more complicated, having 4 holes above and 2 below, various auxiliary keys, and a compass of 2 octaves and 3 semi-tones, *g*¹ to *b*³♭: an instr. inv. by Bainbridge about 1800, consisting of 2 flageolets of different size placed side by side and having a common mouthpiece; simple duets could be played on it, but it is no longer in use...*Flageolet-tones*, see *Harmonic* 2.—2. A small flute-stop in the organ, of 1 or 2-foot pitch.

It is not used in the orchestra... *Double flageolet*, an

Flageolett' (Ger.) 1. Flageolet.—2. General term for the harmonics (*Flageolet'töne*) produced on the violin, etc.

Flaschinet' (Ger.) Obs. spelling of *Flageolett.*

Flat. (Ger. *Be*; Fr. *bémol*; It. *bemol'le*.) The character ♭, which lowers the pitch of a note before which it is set by a semitone, and, when set in the signature, has a like effect on notes occurring on its line or space (and every octave of such line or space) unless cancelled.— Some earlier composers used the ♭ instead of a ♮ whenever a note was to be lowered by a semitone.—The *double flat* ♭♭ lowers a note by 2 chromatic semitones; for it the *great flat* 𝄫 was sometimes written...*Flat fifth*, a diminished fifth...*Flat tuning*, a method of tuning the lute (also called *French flat tuning*, by reason of the comparative lowness of the earlier French pitch)!

Flatter la corde (Fr.) "To caress the string," i. e. to play (on bow-instr.s) with graceful and tender expression.

Flautan'do, Flauta'to (It.) In violin music, to play over the fingerboard near middle of string and thus produce a somewhat flute-like tone...Also, occasional for *flageolet*.

Fla'uto (It.) Flute...*Fl. a becco*, flûte à bec...*Fl. pic'colo*, see *Piccolo...Fl. traver'so*, cross or transverse flute... *Flauto* also frequently occurs as a name for organ-stops, e. g. *flauto ama'bile*, *flauto dol'ce*, etc...*Flauti'no*, a small flute...*Flauti'sta*, a flute-player, flutist. ..*Flauto'ne*, a large or bass flute.

Fle'bile (It.) Tearful ; plaintive, mournful.

Flessi'bile (It.) Flexible.

Flick'oper (Ger.) See *Pasticcio*.

Fling. A spirited Scotch dance, resembling the Reel, and in quadruple time.

F'-löcher (Ger.) *f*-holes.

Florid. Embellished with figures, runs, passages, etc.

Flö'te (Ger.) Flute...*Flö'tenbass*, bass flute...*Flö'tenstimme*, a flute-stop (organ)...*Flö'tenwerk*, a small organ having only flue-pipes (opp. to *Schnarrwerk*, *Zungenwerk*, *Rohrwerk*, and *Regal*).

Flüch'tig (Ger.) Lightly, nimbly, airily ; fugitively, hastily, superficially. (Also *adj.*)

Flue-pipe. (Ger. *Labial'pfeife ;* Fr. *tuyau à bouche ;* It. *can'na d'a'nima.*) See *Pipe ;* also *Stop* 2.

Flü'gel (Ger., "wing".) 1. Formerly, a wing-shaped clavier (clavichord) ; now, a grand pfte...*Flü'gelharfe*, see *Spitzharfe...Flü'gelhorn*, bugle, keybugle.—2. See *Bart*.

Flute. (Ger. *Flö'te ;* Fr. *flûte ;* It. *fla'uto.*) 1. The orchestral flute (also called *German flute, cross-flute,* and *D-flute,* from its origin, the position in which it is held, and its—former—lowest tone respectively), in its present form as improved by Boehm, has a wooden tube of cylindrical bore, provided with 14 ventages closed by keys, and caused to sound by a current of air projected from the player's mouth against the feather-edge of an oval orifice near the upper end of the tube ; the air-column within the tube is set in vibration in the same way as that within a flue-pipe in the organ. Compass from c^1 to c^4 (rare extremes b and c^4♯) : the first octave is obtained by moderate

wind-pressure, the second and third by augmenting and forcing it, thus causing the tone to change (by overblowing) to the higher octave. It is a non-transposing instr., and its music is therefore written at the pitch at which it is to be played. Together with the *octave-flute* or *piccolo* it forms an incomplete family, made in 6 sizes :

Flute $\begin{cases} \text{in } C \\ \text{in } D♭ \\ \text{in } E♭ \end{cases}$ Piccolo $\begin{cases} \text{in } C \\ \text{in } D♭ \\ \text{in } E♭ \end{cases}$

the typical member of which is the *C*-flute. Its powerful and mellow tone (more reedy than that of the old flute), and extraordinary flexibility and agility, render it the leader of the wood-wind. —The *piccolos* in *D♭* and *E♭* are chiefly used in military music.—In the 15th and 16th centuries complete families of flutes were constructed, embracing bass, alto, and treble instr.s.—2. *Direct Flute,* the flageolet and *flûte à bec,* having a *mouthpiece* at the *end.*

Flûte (Fr.) Flute...*Fl. à bec*, a direct flute...*Fl. allemande*, a German flute. ..*Fl. à pavillon*, an 8-foot organ-stop. ..*Fl. d'amour,* (*a*) a flute in *B♭*; (*b*) a soft-toned organ-stop...*Fl. d'Angleterre,* flageolet...*Fl. douce*, flauto dolce. ..*Fl. du Poitou*, bagpipe (cornemuse). ..*Fl. harmonique, fl. octaviante,* see *Harmonic stop...Fl. traversière*, transverse flute.

Flute-work. In the organ, the *flute-work* includes all flue-stops not belonging to the *principal-work* and *gedact-work,* as well as various modifications of these two groups.

Fly. The hinged board or flap used as a cover for the keyboard of the pfte. and organ.

Fo'co (It.) See *Fuoco.*

Fogliet'to (It.) In orchestral music, the part for the leader ; it contains cues for, or the *obbligato* passages of, the other instr.s, and can therefore be used by the conductor in lieu of a score.

Foire des enfants (Fr.) See *Toy Symphony.*

Fois (Fr.) Time ; *première fois*, first time ; *seconde fois*, second time.

Foli'a (Span. ; It. *folli'a ;* usually in the plural, as Fr. "*folies d'Espagne*".) A Spanish dance for one person, in slow tempo and 3-4 time.

Folk-song. (Ger. *Volkslied.*) A song of the people, tinged by the musical peculiarities of the nation, and generally of a simple, unaffected character, and in ballad-form.—Also, a song imitative of the above.

Fondamental,-e (Fr.), **Fondamenta'le** (It.) Fundamental... *Son fondamental*, generator.—*Basse fondamentale*, see *Basse.*

Fondamen'to (It.) Fundament, fundamental part.

Fonds d'orgue (Fr.) The foundation-stops of the organ.

Foot. 1. (Ger. *Fuss;* Fr. *pied;* It. *pie'de.*) In prosody, a group of syllables, one of which is rendered specially prominent by an ictus (accent) ; it corresponds to the *measure* in music. —2. (Ger. *Stiefel.*) That part of an organ-pipe below the mouth.—3. (Obs.) A drone-bass; a refrain or burden.—4. The unit of measure in designating the pitch of organ-stops, and (by extension) that of other instr.s, and of the several octaves of the musical scale ; thus an 8-foot (8′) stop is one whose longest pipe pro- and is about 8 feet duces the in length, i. e. a tone *C:* stop whose pipes produce tones corresponding in pitch to the keys depressed ; a 4-foot (4′) stop is an octave-stop ; a 16-foot (16′) stop yields tones an octave below those indicated by the keys touched. The 8-foot octave embraces the 7 tones from *C* upwards (comp. *Pitch*, §1) ; [the pitch is an 8-foot instr. (because the pitch of its tones is the same as that indi-

cated by the notes), while the piccolo is a 4-foot (or octave) instr.—The derivation of the term is as follows : The velocity of sound-waves is estimated at 1056 feet per second ; by dividing this velocity by the vibration-number of the given tone, we obtain the length of one sound-wave of that tone ; for instance, the tone C_2 having 33 vibrations per second, 1056 ÷ 33 = 32 feet, the length of one sound-wave, and likewise the length of an open flue-pipe capable of producing the tone C_2 (CCC).

Foot-key. Pedal-key (of an organ).

Foreign chords or **tones** are such as do not belong to a given key.

Forla'na (It.), **Forlane** (Fr.) A lively Italian dance in 6-8 or 6-4 time.

Form. Form in music is that element, or combination of elements, which, by securing a *proper balance* between contrasting parts, produces *finish of effect*, or *Unity.* What are called the musical forms depend, in varying degree, for their distinctive features, (1) on rhythmical and metrical grouping ; (2) on thematic construction ; (3) on melodic and harmonic contrast ; (4) on contrasting tempi ; and (5) on contrasting moods. Points 1 and 2 cover the ground of (I) *mechanical symmetry ;* the contrasts of melody, harmony, tempo, and mood postulate a more highly developed sense for (II) *æsthetic symmetry.*

I. (1.) The element of metrical grouping is eminently characteristic of ordinary dance-airs and simple songs ; the following example exhibits its simplest form :

Period.

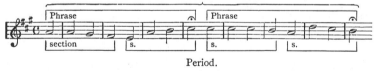

Period.

Analysis of this *Sentence (compound period,* here a period of 16 measures), which contains a musical thought complete in itself, shows it to be composed of 2 simple 8-measure *Periods,* each period being formed by 2 *Phrases,* each

of which embraces 2 *Sections* formed, in turn, of 2 *Measures* each. [The term *motive* for measure is to be rejected as misleading and unnecessarily confusing, except in the qualified shape of *measure-motive.*] The *punctuation* of such a *musical* sentence presents a striking analogy to that of the *grammatical* sentence from which its terminology is in part borrowed : Phrase 1 = subject and predicate [*comma*], Phrase 2 = limiting clause [*semicolon*], Phrase 3, further modification [*comma*], Phrase 4, second limiting clause and conclusion of sentence [*period*] The exact symmetrical balance here observable, of 2+2, 4+4, and 8 + 8, though of very common occurrence, is not the general rule, and would engender wearisome monotony (especially in extended compositions) if regularly adhered to ; the variety of changes caused by triple time, compound measures, the opposition of unequal phrases, the expansion or contraction of periods, etc., etc., is practically limitless. But in all the musical forms in which metrical symmetry is observed, the simple period is, in one shape or another, the *form-element* or *germ-cell*, so to speak, on which their construction is founded.

I. (2.) A theme or melody simply repeated, (formula A + A, or |: A :|), presents no distinctive departure from the simplest form ; repeated in alternation with another |: A + B :| it ex-hibits the peculiar feature of the *song with refrain ;* once repeated, after any digression (interlude, or second theme), it produces the so-called *Song-form* (*Liedform*, A+B+A), or that of the *Minuet with Alternativo.* With 2 distinct themes alternating as follows : (|: A + B :| + B [A] + A + B [in the original key of A]), it has the *Sonata-form*, or *First-movement Form ;* while the *Rondo-form* has the following alternations : (A + B + B [A] + A + B [B2 in same key as A ; development-section in the middle]); or : (A + B + A [in same key as B] + B [same key as A] + A). It must be added, however, that the Song-form, Sonata-form, and Rondo-form, as carried out in practice, present frequent deviations from the above formulas.—A theme repeated or imitated while still progressing, produces the form of the *Canon, Catch,* or *Round ;* one or more themes repeated in conjunction or alternation with an accompanying or contrasting counterpoint, according to a more or less regular formula, the *Fugue.* The following is a fairly exhaustive formula for the construction of a simple 2 part fugue :

I. Exposition :	Theme on 1st deg. (tonic)		Answer on 5th (dominant)
1st Episode :	" " 6th " (in augment.)		" " 3d (in diminut.)
II. First Development :	" " 5th "		" " 1st
2d Episode :	" " 2d " (inverted)		" " 7th (inverted)
III. Second Development :	" " 1st "		" " 5th
Stretto : Theme brought out on the 4th " (with modulation to the subdominant)			
— Coda.			

II. (1.) The element of harmonic contrast is derived in part from contrasting themes, in part from the deliberate choice of keys directly or remotely related to that of the leading theme ; in part, also, from the harmonies accompanying or varying the theme or themes. Dependence on the harmonic variation of repetitions of a single theme, together with the light and shade of varying tempi, is an important principle of the *Theme with Variations.*

II. (2.) In cyclic compositions (the *Cyclical Forms*), contrasting tempi (S = slow, F = fast) in the successive movements are a prominent feature. The old *Suite* originally had the formula (S + F + S + F) ; later a fifth movement, either slow or fast, was inserted after (seldom before) the 2nd slow one. The *Sonata* and *Symphony* are essentially alike in plan ; either (F + S + F), or more commonly (F + S + F + F), or (S + F + S + F) or (F + F + S + F) ; or, in 5 movements, (F + S + F + S + F) ; etc.; a *slow closing movement* rarely occurs.

II. (3.) The foregoing formal schemes are a product of the slow evolution of centuries. First, the primitive dance-song develops into lyric and epic song—love-ditties, ballads,—and into instrumental dance-tunes differently named according to their character or origin ; while a parallel progress is seen in the rise of church-music from the severe Gregorian Chant to the stupendous contrapuntal works of the late middle ages and the chaste style of Palestrina. Instrumental art-music now borrows and develops its forms from the vocal style ; the forms of imitative music (canon and fugue) gradually near perfection, finally attained by J. S. Bach ; through the adoption by artists of the *rhythmic melody* and *monodic style* of the hitherto despised *natural music* (folk-music), and the *recognition of its harmonic basis*, the two currents of art-music and folk-music are slowly merged in one broad stream ; the popular dance-tunes are transformed into art-forms, and combined in the Suite ; the rondo-form and the first-movement (sonata-) form are evolved step by step, and their combination produces the Sonata and Symphony; which latter, discarding the scheme of 4 formal movements, and aspiring to the uninterrupted flow and sweep of an epico-lyrical drama without words, becomes the Symphonic Poem. [Compare also *Passion, Oratorio, Opera, Overture.*]

Forma're il tuono. See *Messa di voce.*

Fort (Ger.) Off; as *Flöte fort* (organ-music).

Fort (Fr.) 1. Forte.—2. Skilful, eminent... *Temps fort*, strong beat... *Fourniture 3 tuyaux forte*, a mixture-stop of 3 ranks.

Fortbien. A keyboard stringed instr. inv. by Friederici in 1758, having a softer tone and lighter touch than the fortepiano then in vogue.

For'te (It.) 1 (*adjective*). Loud, strong (abbr. *f*) ; *più forte* (*pf*), louder ; *poco forte* (also *pf*), rather loud ; *forte piano* (*fp*), accent strongly, diminishing instantly to *piano ; fortemen'te*, loudly, forcibly ; *forte possi'bile*, as loud as possible.—2 (*noun*). (*a*) A passage to be executed loudly or forcibly ; (*b*) in the harmonium, a slide within the chest containing one or more sets of reeds, opened by a stop or knee-lever to produce a *forte* effect ; sometimes divided, one section affecting the treble side and the other the bass side.

Fortepia'no (It.) Same as *Pianoforte.*

Fortis'simo (It., superl. of *forte.*) Very loud, or extremely loud or forcible (abbr. *ff*, or *fff* for the extreme) ; also *forte possi'bile* (*ffff*).

Fort'rücken (Ger., *noun.*) The advance of the hand on a keyboard or fingerboard, as caused by the repetition of a figure with the same fingering but at a different pitch.

Fort'schreiten (Ger.) To progress... *Fort'schreitung*, progression ; *Fort'-schreitung einer Dissonanz'*, resolution.

For'za (It.) Force, vigor ; *con f.*, forcibly, etc.

Forzan'do (It., "forcing, straining".) With force, energy ; indicates that a note or chord is to be strongly accent-ed ; abbr. *fz*...Also *Forza'to, Sforzan'do* (*sfz*).

Forzar' la vo'ce (It.) To force the voice.

Foundation-stops. See *Stop.*

Fourchette tonique (Fr.) Tuning-fork.

Fourniture (Fr.) A mixture-stop.

Four-part. (Ger. *vier'stimmig ;* Fr. *à quatre voix ;* It. *a quat'tro vo'ci.*) Set for, or performed by, 4 parts in harmony.

Fourth. (Ger. *Quar'te ;* Fr. *quarte ;* It. *quar'ta.*) 1. The fourth degree in the diatonic scale ; the subdominant.—2. An interval embracing 4 degrees (see *Interval*). The typical or standard fourth is the *perfect* (or *major*) *fourth*, equal to the interval between the key-note and the 4th tone of ____ its vibrational the diatonic ратио being scale, as *c-f :* ____ *c : f :: 3 : 4*... *Diminished (imperfect, defective, minor*, or *false*) *fourth*, an interval narrower by a chromatic semitone than a perfect fourth... *Augmented (pluperfect, superfluous, or extreme) fourth*, one wider by a chromatic semitone than a perfect fourth.

Française (Fr.) A dance in triple time, resembling the country-dance.

Francamen'te (It.) Freely, with freedom (of delivery), boldly ; frankly, ingenuously.

Franchez'za (It.), **Franchise** (Fr.) Freedom, confidence, boldness... *Con fr.*, see *Francamente.*

Franz'ton (Ger.) " French pitch " ; it is lower than the ordinary *Kammerton.*

Frappé (Fr., " beaten ".) The down-beat ; opp. to *Levé.*

Fra'se (It.) Phrase ; *frase larga =* *largamente*... *Fraseggia're*, to phrase.

Fred'do,-a (It.) Cold... *Freddamen'te*, coldly.

Fredon (Fr.) An obsolete term for a roulade, trill, or tremolo ; also, a sign calling for a florid extension of a single written note... *Fredonnement*, trilling, warbling ; humming... *Fredonner*, to trill, warble ; to hum, sing to oneself.

Free chant. A form of recitative music for the Psalms and Canticles, in which a phrase, consisting of 2 chords only, is applied to each hemistich of the words. [STAINER AND BARRETT.]... *Free fugue*, see *Fugue*... *Free part*, an independent part added to a canon or fugue to complete or enrich the harmony... *Free* *reed*, see *Reed*...*Free style* (of composition), that in which the rules of strict counterpoint are relaxed.

Fregiatu′ra (It.) A grace, an ornament.

Frei (Ger.) Free...*Frei′heit*, a license or liberty.

French Horn, Sixth, Violin-clef. See the nouns.

Fret. (Ger. [equiv.] *Bund;* Fr. *touche;* It. *ta′sto.*) One of the narrow ridges of wood, metal, or ivory crossing the fingerboard of the mandolin, guitar, zither, etc., against which the strings are pressed by the fingers to shorten their vibrating length and thus raise the tone.

Fretel, Fretèle (Fr.) A sylvan pipe; the Pan's-pipe with 7 reeds. Sometimes called *sifflet des chaudronniers*. (Also *fretetel, freteau, fretiau, frestel*.)

Fret′ta, con (It.) With haste, celerity; hurriedly.

Fricassée (Fr.) 1. A sort of popular dance interspersed with pantomime, in vogue in the 18th century in the *théâtres des boulevards* at Paris.—2. A kind of part-song of the 16th century, each part having different words.

Fries (Ger.) Purfling.

Frisch (Ger.) Brisk, lively, vigorous (also *adverb*).

Fröh′lich (Ger.) Glad, joyous, gay, (also *adverb*).

Front′pfeife (Ger.) See *Prospekt*.

Frosch (Ger.) Nut (of a bow).

Frot′tola (It., "comic ditty".) A popular ballad or song intermediate between the villanella and the madrigal; in great vogue during the 16th century.

F′-Schlüssel (Ger.) F-clef.

Fu′ga (Lat. and It.) A fugue...*F. ad octa′vam* [*quin′tam*] (Lat.), fugue at the octave [fifth]...*F. æqua′lis mo′tus* (Lat.), fugue in similar motion, the answer ascending and descending like the subject...*F. al contra′rio* [*rever′so, rove′scio*] (It.), see *F. contraria*...*F. authen′tica* (Lat.), fugue with a subject ascending above the key-note...*F. cano′nica* [*tota′lis*] (Lat.), a canon...*F. compo′sita* (Lat.), a fugue whose subject progresses by conjunct degrees...*F. contra′ria* (Lat.), a fugue having the answer in contrary motion to the subject...*F. del tuo′no* (It.), tonal fugue. ..*F. dop′pia* (It.), double fugue...*F. homopho′na* (Lat.), fugue with answer at the unison...*F. impro′pria* (Lat.), see *F. irregula′ris*...*F. inæqua′lis* (Lat.), see *F. contraria*...*F. incompo′sita* (Lat.), a fugue whose subject progresses by disjunct degrees...*F. in conseguen′za* (It.), a canon...*F. in contra′rio tem′pore* (Lat.), see *F. per ar′sin et the′sin*...*Fuga in no′mine*, a "fugue in name," i. e. a nominal or free fugue. ..*F. inver′sa* (Lat.), a fugue worked throughout in double reversible counterpoint, so that the inversions of the parts may appear in contrary motion. ..*F. irregula′ris* (Lat.), a fugue irregular in form...*F. li′bera* (Lat. and It.), a fugue with free episodes...*F. liga′ta* (Lat. and It.), a fugue without free episodes, strictly developed from its subject and countersubject...*F. mix′ta* (Lat.), a fugue varied in development by employing different contrapuntal devices (augmentation, diminution, inversion, etc.)...*F. obbliga′ta* (It.), see *F. ligata*...*F. partia′lis* (Lat.), a fugue proper, in contradistinction to a canon. ..*F. per augmentatio′nem* [*diminutio′nem*] (Lat.), a fugue in which the answer is in augmentation [diminution] either throughout, or as a rule...*F. per the′sin et ar′sin* (Lat.), a fugue whose subject begins on the strong beat, and the answer on the weak beat, thus shifting the accents throughout...*F. per imitatio′nem interrup′tam* (Lat.), a fugue in which the answer is interrupted by breaks or rests.. *F. per mo′tum contra′rium* (Lat.), see *F. contraria*...*F. perio′dica* (Lat.), see *F. partialis*...*F. perpe′tua* (Lat.), a canon...*F. plaga′lis* (Lat.), a fugue with subject descending below the key-note...*F. pro′pria* (Lat.), see *F. regularis*...*F. rea′le* (It.), a real fugue...*F. rec′ta* (Lat.), see *F. æqualis motus*...*F. redi′ta* or *reddita* (It.), a fugue at the middle or end of which all or some of the parts progress in canon...*F. regula′ris* (Lat.), a fugue in regular form...*F. retrogra′da* (Lat.), a fugue having the answer in retrograde progression; or *F. retrogra′da per mo′tum contra′rium*, when the answer is in retrograde progression and contrary motion...*F. ricerca′ta* (It.), a fugue in whose working-out the rarer and more elaborate contrapuntal devices are "sought out" for display; a long and elaborate master-fugue...*F. sciol′ta* (It.), or *solu′ta* (Lat.), see *F. li′bera*... *F. tota′lis* (Lat.), a canon.

Fuga′ra. (Ger. *Foga′ra, Voga′ra*.) An

organ-stop having metal flue-pipes generally of small scale and 8 or 4-foot pitch ; tone of a sharp, " stringy " quality.

Fuga'to (It., " in fugue style ".) A passage or movement consisting of fugal imitations, but not worked out as a regular fugue.

Fu'ge (Ger.) Fugue.

Fuggi're la caden'za (It.) To avoid the cadence (by interrupting it).

Fughet'ta (It., dimin. of *Fuga*.) A short fugue, usually only a fugue-exposition.

Fugue. (Ger. *Fu'ge ;* Fr. *fugue ;* It. *fu'ga.*) The most highly developed form of contrapuntal imitation, based on the principle of the equality of the parts, a theme proposed by one part being taken up successively by all participating parts, thus bringing each in turn into special prominence. The word fugue is presumably derived from the Latin *fuga*, a flight, which aptly characterizes the chasing and changing of the subject through the several parts.

The elements essential to every fugue are (1) *Subject*, (2) *Answer*, (3) *Countersubject*, (4) *Stretto ;* to these are commonly added (5) *Episode*, (6) *Organ-point*, (7) *Coda ;* the (8) *Codetta* is merely a fortuitous appendage to the actual subject, bridging over the interval sometimes left between the true end of the latter and the entrance of the *Answer*.—The *subject* is usually short and suggestive ; after its proposition by the part taking the lead, it is taken up by the part next following as the *answer*, and at a different interval (usually a fifth higher or a fourth lower than the original one), being then accompanied by a contrast-

ing counterpoint, the *countersubject*, in the first part ; if there are 3 parts, the 3rd resumes the subject at the octave of its original pitch, followed (if there are 4 parts) by the answer in the 4th. This first enunciation of the subject by all the parts in turn, with contrapuntal accomp. in the rest, is called the *Exposition ;* this is commonly succeeded by an *Episode*, which is generally constructed (for the preservation of unity of effect) of motives from the subject and countersubject, with modulation into related keys ; then comes the *First Development*, or *Repercussion*, in which subject and answer are taken up by the several parts in a different order, followed by a second and variously modified episode. Further developments and episodes follow at the composer's pleasure, varied by the contrapuntal devices enumerated above, and generally in freer form, the subject and answer appearing in new keys and at a different interval. The fugue may be concluded by a *Stretto* or *Final Development*, in which the subject and answer overlap each other in consequence of following in closer succession ; the stretto is frequently above an *organpoint ;* or the organ-point is used to support the freer contrapuntal combinations of the *coda*, a general finale or winding-up ; or stretto and coda are identical ; etc., etc.—The modern fugue has 2 principal varieties : (1) The *Real Fugue*, in which the original form of the subject is preserved in the answer (i. e. the latter is an exact transposition of the former) ; and (2) the *Tonal Fugue*, in which the subject is modified in the answer in order to return to the original key ; e. g.

Subject.   Answer (Tonal).   Not :

Further varieties are the *Double Fugue* (with 2 subjects, the exposition of the 1st being followed by that of the 2nd, and finally by the combination of both) ; —the *Triple Fugue* (with 3 subjects) ; etc. ; a fugue with 2 or more subjects is sometimes called a *Manifold Fugue.*—A fugue in which the countersubject is retained and developed together with the subject throughout, is also called a double fugue. The most elaborate fugal form is the *Fuga ricercata* (comp.

Fuga).—Fugues may be written for voices or instr.s, or for solo instr.s (pfte., organ). (Compare *Form* I, 2.)

Fugued, Fuguing. See *Fuga'to*. Written in either strict or free fugal style.

Füh'rer (Ger.) " Leader, dux ", subject (of a fugue.)..*Füh'rung*, leading.

Full anthem. See *Anthem*...*Full band*, a military band, or an orchestra, having all the customary instr.s...*Full cadence*, close, see the nouns...*Full Choir* (direction in organ-playing), draw all stops of the choir-organ...*Full chord*, one represented by all its tones ; also (in concerted music), one in which all the parts unite... *Full Great* (in organ-playing), draw all stops of great organ... *Full orchestra*, see *Full band*...*Full organ*, with all stops and couplers drawn...*Full score*, see *Score*...*Full stop* (in lute-playing), a full chord followed by a pause ; also, a chord in which all available fingers are occupied in stopping the strings...*Full Swell* (organ), draw all stops of swell-organ. ..*Full to fifteenth* (in organ-playing), draw all stops but mixtures and reeds.

Füll'pfeife (Ger.) A dummy pipe... *Füll'quinte*, a very sharp-toned organ-stop of 5⅓-foot pitch, to be drawn only with a strong combination of foundation-stops...*Füll'stelle*, a passage put into "fill out"; padding...*Füll'stimme*, (*a*) a part reinforcing a principal part at the octave or unison ; (*b*) a mutation-stop a third or a fifth above the normal pitch ; (*c*) *pl.*, in polyphonic composition, accessory parts not treated melodically like the principal parts, but brought in occasionally to complete the harmony or mark the rhythm.

Fundamental. 1. The root of a chord. —2. A generator (in this sense also *fundamental bass*, *note* and *tone*)... *Fund. chord, triad*, see *Chord, Triad*. ..*Fund. position*, any arrangement of the tones of a chord in which the root remains the lowest.

Fundamental'bass (Ger.) Fundamental bass...*Fundamental'ton*, root ; keynote, tonic (*Grund'ton, To'nika*).

Funèbre (Fr.), Fu'nebre, Funera'le (It.) Funereal, mournful.

Fünf'fach (Ger.) See *-fach*...*Fünf'-stimmig*, 5-part ; for 5 parts or voices. ..*Fünf'stufige Ton'leiter*, pentatonic scale.

Fuo'co [foo-ô'-co] (It.) Fire, spirit ; *con f.*, or *fuoco'so*, with fire, fiery, spirited.

Fu'ria (It.) Fury, passion ; *con f.*, wildly, passionately.

Furiant, Furie. A rapid Bohemian dance with alternating rhythms and changing accentuation.

Furibon'do (It.) Furious, frenzied.

Furio'so,-a (It.) Furious, passionate ; *furiosamen'te*, passionately ; *furiosis'-simo*, with extreme passion.

Furla'na (It.) See *Forlana*.

Furniture-stop. A mixture-stop.

Furo're (It.) A rage, mania, passionate fondness (for anything)...Also, fury, passion, vehemence ; *con f.*, passionately.

Fu'sa(Lat.), **Fuse** (Fr.) An eighth note, or quaver.

Fusée (Fr.) An ornament consisting of a rapid ascending or descending diatonic series of notes ; a slide.

Fusel (Ger.) Same as *Fusa*.

Fusel'la (Lat.) 32nd-note...*Fusel'lala*, 64th-note.

Fuss (Ger.) Foot ; *-füssig*, the adjective-ending corresponding to -foot, as *8' füssig* (*acht' füssig*), 8-foot...*Fuss'klavier*, pedals (of an organ)...*Fuss'ton*, equivalent to "-foot pitch", e. g. an organ-pipe of 4-foot pitch is said to be of *4-Fusston*.

Füt'terung (Ger.) Linings (of a violin).

G.

G. The fifth tone and degree in the typical diatonic scale of *C*-major...*G.* abbr. for *gauche* (*m. g.* = main gauche) ; *G. O.* (or simply **G**), grand-orgue.

Ga'belklavier (Ger.) A keyboard instr. inv. in 1882 by Fischer and Fritzsch of Leipzig, in which steel tuning-forks are substituted for strings. The somewhat dull timbre, due to the lack of harmonics, has been brightened by adding, for each key, a second fork tuned an octave higher than the first... *Ga'belton*, "fork-tone," i. e. the tone *a*¹ pitched for tuning...*Ga'belgriffe* (pl.), cross-fingerings.—See *Stimmgabel*.

Gagliar'da (It.), **Gagliar'de** (Ger.) A galliard.

Gai (Fr.) Gay, lively, brisk...*Gaiement*, or *gaîment*, gaily, briskly.

Gaillarde (Fr.) A galliard.

Gajamen'te (It.) Gaily, lively...*Ga'jo,-a*, gay.

Ga'la (It.) In the phrase *di gala*, gaily, merrily.

Galamment (Fr.), **Galantemen'te** (It.) Gallantly, gracefully, prettily.

Galant' (Ger.) Free ; e. g. *galan'te Fu'ge*, free fugue ; *galan'ter Stil*, *galan'te Schreib'art*, free style, the homophonous style of composition for the clavichord or harpsichord, in vogue in the 18th century ; opp. to *gebun'dener Stil*, strict style, in which a certain number of contrapuntal parts was adhered to throughout.

Galant,-e (Fr.), **Galan'te** (It.) Gallant, graceful, pretty.

Gal'liard. (Ger. *Gagliar'de ;* Fr. *gaillarde ;* It. *gagliar'da.*) An old French dance for 2 dancers (also called *Romane'sca*), of a gay and spirited character, though not rapid, and in 3-4 time ; like the Pavan, it had 3 reprises of 4, 8, or 12 measures. It was the precursor of the Minuet.

Gal'op. (Fr. *galop*, *galopade ;* Ger. *Galopp'.*) A very lively and spirited round dance in 2-4 time ; supposed to have been derived from the old German *Hop'ser* or *Rutsch'er* (names descriptive of the step). Introduced into France early in the 19th century.

Galoubé, Galoubet (Fr.) A kind of small fife, the shrillest of all wind-instr.s, with 3 holes and a compass of 17 notes ; found only in Provence.

Gam'ba. 1. See *Viola da gamba.*—2. An organ-stop similar in tone to the viola da gamba.

Gam'be (Ger.) Viola da gamba... *Gam'-benstimme*, a gamba-stop... *Gam'benwerk*, piano-violin.

Gam'bist. A player on the viola da gamba.

Gam'ma. The Greek G (Γ). In medieval music from the 10th century onward, the lowest tone of the mus. system then obtaining was called Γ ; the letter was ⌐F⌐ together with the *F*-also used ⌐Γ⌐ clef. Hence, its use as a clef ⌐Γ⌐ to name the entire scale (see *Gamme* and *Gamut*)... *Gamma ut*, name of *G*. in the old system of solmisation.

Gamme (Fr.) A scale (see *Gamma*)... *G. diatonique* (*chromatique*), diatonic (chromatic) scale.

Gam'ut (from *gamma ut*). 1. See *Gamma.*—2. A scale.—3. The staff.—4. In old English church-music, the key of *G*.

Gang (Ger.) Passage. (Plural *Gänge*.)

Ganz (Ger.) 1. Whole... *Gan'ze Note* (*gan'ze Takt'note*), whole note (𝆺)... *Ganz'instrument*, a metal wind-instr., the lowest natural tone of whose tube can be made to speak ; opp. to *Halb'instrument*... *Ganz'schluss* whole cadence... *Ganz'ton*, or *gan'zer Ton*, whole tone.—2. Very.

Gar'bo (It.) Grace, elegance.

Gas'senhauer (Ger.) In the 16th century, a designation for popular songs or folk-songs (*Gas'senhawerlin*) ; the word now signifies a trite and threadbare tune, and at the same time something vulgar and unworthy of art. [RIEMANN.]

Gathering-note. In chanting, an irregular *fermata* on the last syllable of the recitation, to enable the body of the singers to catch up and begin the cadence together.

Gauche (Fr.) Left ; *main g.* (abbr. *m. g.*), left hand.

Gaudio'so (It.) Joyous, jubilant.

Gau'menton (Ger.) A guttural tone.

Gavot'. (Fr. *gavotte ;* It. *gavot'ta.*) An old French dance-form in strongly marked duple time (₵ alla breve), beginning with an *auftakt*, of a lively though dignified character, and resembling the Minuet. (See *Suite*.) The Gavot has latterly been revived as an instrumental piece.

Gaz'el. A piece with a short and oft-recurring theme or refrain.

G-clef. (Ger. *G'-Schlüssel ;* Fr. *clef de sol ;* It. *chiave di soprano.*) The sign determining the position of the note g^1 on the staff. (See *Clef*.)

Geblä'se (Ger.) Bellows (of an organ ; usually *Balg*).

Gebroch'en (Ger.) Broken.

Gebun'den (Ger.) 1. Tied.—2. Legato, tied ; as *gebun'dene Dissonanz'*, prepared dissonance ; *gebun'denes Spiel*, legato playing ; *gebun'dener Stil*, strict style.—3. Having 2 or more digitals to one string (said of clavichords) ; opp. to *un'gebunden* or *bund'frei* (1. e. "fretted" or "fret-free" [GROVE]). (Comp. *Bundfrei*.)

Gedackt' (Ger.) Stopped (of organpipes) ; opp. to *offen.* (Also *gedact, gedakt.*)

Gedämpft' (Ger.) Damped ; muffled ; muted.

Gedeckt' (Ger., "covered".) See *Gedackt.*

Gedehnt' (Ger.) See *Dehnen.*

Gedicht' (Ger.) Poem.

Gefähr'te (Ger.) Answer (in fugal composition).

Gefal'len (Ger.) Pleasure ; *nach G.*, a piacere.

Gefäl'lig (Ger.) Pleasing, attractive, graceful.

Gefühl' (Ger.) Feeling, emotion...*Mit G.*, with feeling, expression (also *gefühlvoll*).

Ge'gen (Ger.) Against, contrary to... *Ge'genbewegung*, contrary motion... *Ge'genfuge*, a fugue in which the answer is an inversion of the subject... *Ge'genharmonie*, counter-subject (in a fugue)...*Ge'gensatz*, (*a*) contrast ; (*b*) contrasting movement or effect...*Ge'genstimme*, contrapuntal part ; countersubject.

Gegit'tertes B (Ger.) *B* cancellatum.

Gehal'ten (Ger.) Held, sustained.

Geh'end (Ger.) Andante.

Gei'ge (Ger.) Violin...*Gei'genclavicymbel*, *Gei'genklavier*, bow-piano...*Gei'genharz*, rosin...*Gei'geninstrument*, bow-instr...*Gei'genprincipal*, violindiapason (organ-stop)...*Gei'genwerk*, piano-violin...*Geigenzettel*, the maker's "label" or "inscription" on a violin.

Geist (Ger.) Spirit, soul ; mind, intellect ; genius ; essence.

Gei'sterharfe (Ger.) Æolian harp.

Geist'lich (Ger.) Sacred ; opp. to *welt'-lich*, secular.

Gelas'sen (Ger.) Calm, composed, placid ; easy. (Also *adverb*.)

Geläu'fig (Ger.) Fluent, voluble ; easy, familiar...*Geläu'figkeit*, fluency, celerity, velocity ; ease, familiarity.

Gemäch'lich (Ger.) Comfortable, easy, commodious, convenient ; slow, gentle. (Also *adverb*.) *Recht gemächlich*, commodetto.

Gemä'ssigt (Ger.) Moderate. (See *Mässig*.)

Gemisch'te Stim'men (Ger.) 1. Mixed voices.—2. In the organ, the mixtures, or mixture-stops.

Gems'horn (Ger., "chamois-horn.") In the organ, a metal flue-stop having tapering pipes of 8, 4, or 2-foot pitch on the manuals and of 16-foot pitch on the pedal, with mellow, horn-like timbre. ...*Gems'hornquinte*, a 5⅓-foot stop of the above type.

Gemüt'(h) (Ger.) Soul, heart, spirit ; mind ; disposition, temperament, nature.

Ge'nera. Plural of *Genus*.

General'bass (Ger.) Thorough-bass ; *General'bassschrift*, thorough-bass notation...*General'pause*, a pause for all instr.s or parts in the midst of a composition, particularly when so introduced as to produce a striking effect. A hold ⌒ over the rest for such a pause renders its duration indeterminate ; i. e. robs it of rhythmic value, as if the beats or counts were suspended for the time being...*General'probe*, full rehearsal.

Generator. (Fr. [*son*] *générateur*.) 1. A root, or fundamental tone.—2. A tone which produces a series of harmonics.

Ge'nere (It.) A mode or key ; a genus.

Genero'so,-a (It.) Generous, free, ample.

Genial' (Ger.) Relating to or exhibiting genius ; talented, gifted, ingenious, clever ; spirited.

Génie (Fr.), **Genie'** (Ger.) Genius.

Genouillière (Fr.) Knee-lever ; formerly used in German grand pftes. as a substitute for the earlier draw-stops, before the general introduction of pedals.

Genre (Fr.) Genus, as *g. diatonique*, *chromatique*, *enharmonique*.—Also, style.

Gentil,-le (Fr.) **Genti'le** (It.) Graceful, delicate, pretty.—*Gentilment* (*gentilmen'te*), gracefully, etc...*Gentilez'za*, *con* (It.), with dignity, refinement, grace.

Ge'nus (Lat.) 1. In ancient music, a system of arranging the notes of a tetrachord ; for *diatonic*, *chrom.*, *enharm. genus*, see *Greek Music*, §2.—2. A mode or octave-scale.

Gera'de Bewe'gung (Ger.) Similar or parallel motion...*Gera'de Takt'art* (*gerader Takt*), duple or quadruple time.

German flute, the cross-flute...*German sixth*, see *Extreme*.

Ges (Ger.) G♭...*Ges'es*, G♭♭.

Gesang' (Ger.) Singing, song ; a song, vocal composition ; melody, air...*Gesang'buch*, a song-book, hymn-book... *Gesangs'kunst*, the art of singing, vocal art...*Gesang'(s)mässig*, melodious ; adapted for singing, for the voice... *Gesang'verein*, singing society, choral society.

Geschlecht' (Ger.) Genus ; mode.

Geschleift' (Ger.) Slurred ; legato.

Geschmack' (Ger.) Taste... *Geschmack'voll*, tasteful(ly).

Geschwänzt' (Ger., "tailed".) Having a hook or hooks (♪ ♬).

Geschwind' (Ger.) Swift, rapid, quick. (Also *adverb.*)

Ges'es (Ger.) See *Ges.*

Gesicht' (Ger.) Front (of organ)... *Gesichts'pfeifen*, front pipes.

Gespon'nen (Ger. "spun".) *Gesponnene Saite*, "covered" string... *Gesponnener Ton*, "son filé" (see *Filar*), an even, sustained tone (voice or violin).

Gestei'gert (Ger.) Intensified; rinforzato.

Gestrich'en (Ger.) 1. Having hooks. —2. In compound words, equivalent to *-lined*, *-accented*, as *ein'gestrichene Okta've*, one-lined (once-accented) octave. —3. Crossed, ⟨notation⟩ or ⟨notation⟩.—4. Cut with a stroke or ⟨notation⟩ (as a scene in line across, as ⟨notation⟩ an opera).

Get(h)eilt' (Ger.) Divided, separated... *Geteil'te Violi'nen*, violini divisi... *Geteil'te Stim'men*, partial stops (organ).

Getra'gen (Ger.) Sostenuto. See *Tragen.*

Geworfener Strich (Ger.) "Thrown stroke"; in violin-technics, a form of the *saltato.*

Ghaz'al, Ghaz'el (Arabic.) See *Gazel.*

Ghiribiz'zo (It.) Whim, fancy, caprice. .. *Ghiribizzo'so*, whimsical, etc.

Gi'ga (It.) See *Gigue.*

Gigeli'ra (It.) Xylophone.

Gigue (Fr.) 1. Early name for the old form of viol, which nearly resembled that of a ham (*gigue*); hence German *Geige*.— 2. Ordinary title in the Suite for the Jig.

Gioche'vole (It.) Playfully, merrily.

Giocon'do,-a (It.) Jocund, gay, playful. .. *Giocondamen'te*, joyously, merrily.

Gioco'so,-a (It.) Playful, sportive, bantering; humorous... *Giocosamen'te*, playfully, etc.

Gio'ja (It.) Joy, delight, pleasure... *Giojan'te*, joyfully, mirthfully... *Giojo'so,-a*, joyful, mirthful... *Giojosamen'te*, joyfully, etc.

Giovia'le (It.) Jovial, cheerful.

Giraffe. An old-style upright grand pfte.

Gi'ro (It.) A turn.

Gis (Ger.) G♯... *Gis'is*, G×.

Giubili'o (It., also *giu'bilo, giubilazio'ne*.) Joy, rejoicing, jubilation... *Giubilo'so,-a*, jubilant.

Giuocan'te (It.) Playful, bantering. .. *Giuoche'vole*, playfully, etc.

Giu'sto,-a (It.) Appropriate, strict, moderate (as *tempo giusto*), exact, precise, correct... *Allegro giusto* (*all.° modto*), moderately fast... *Giustamen'te*, correctly, exactly... *Giustez'za,con*, with precision.

Glas'harmonika (Ger.) *Harmonica* 1.

Glee. A secular composition for 3 or more unaccompanied solo voices, of later origin and less contrapuntal ingenuity than the Madrigal, and peculiar to England. It is of modern character, both with regard to tonality and to its employment of harmonic masses and the perfect cadence. The name *glee* is not properly descriptive of its nature, as *serious* glees are written as well as *merry* ones.

Gleich (Ger.) Equal... *Glei'cher Kon'trapunkt*, equal counterpoint... *Glei'che Stimmen*, equal voices... *Gleich'schwebende Temperatur'*, equal temperament.

Gli (It.) The (masc. pl.).

Glicibarifo'na (It.) A wind-instr. inv. in Italy about 1827 by Catterini; a small 4-octave expressive organ.

Glide. The smooth connection of 2 tones by slurring.

Glissan'do (also *glissa'to, glissican'do, glissica'to;* spurious It. forms imitated from the Fr. *glisser*.) 1. On bowed instr.s, (*a*) calls for a flowing, unaccented, execution of a passage; (*b*) same as *Portamento.*—2. On the pfte., a rapid scale-effect obtained by sliding the thumb, or thumb and one finger, over the white keys, producing either the simple scale, or thirds, sixths, etc. (easier and more effective on the Jankó keyboard).

Glissé (Fr.) 1. *Glissando* 2.—2. A direction indicating that a passage is to be executed smoothly and flowingly.

Glock'e (Ger.; dimin. *Glöck'chen*.) Bell. .. *Glockenist'*, same as *Carillonneur*... *Glock'enspiel*, (*a*) a carillon; (*b*) an instr. consisting of bells or (more recently) of steel bars, tuned diatonically and struck with a small hammer; occasionally used in the orchestra; (*c*) an organ-stop which causes a set of small bells to be sounded by the manual.

Glo'ria. See *Doxology, Mass.*

Gnac'care (It.) Same as *Castagnette.*

Goathorn. See *Gemshorn.*

Gon'dellied (Ger.)　Gondoliera.

Gondolie'ra (It.) See *Barcarole*.

Gong. (*Tam-tam* in Fr. and Ger. use.) An instr. of percussion in the form of a large round slightly concave plate or basin of metal (alloy of 4 parts copper to 1 part tin), with a raised rim. It is struck with a stick having a padded leather head, and is used in the orchestra to intensify melodramatic effects.

Goose. (Fr. *couac*.) A harsh break in the tone of the clarinet, oboe, or bassoon, caused by a defective reed or improper manipulation.

Gorgheggia're (It.)　To execute florid vocal music; also see *Fredonner*... *Gorgheggiamen'to*, art of singing florid passages, etc...*Gorgheg'gio*, a florid passage.

Gospel side. See *Epistle side*.

Goût (Fr.)　Taste.

Grace. (Ger. *Verzie'rung;* Fr. *ornement, agrément;* It. *abbellimen'to, fio- ret'to*.) A vocal or instrumental ornament or embellishment not essential to the melody or harmony of a composition. (The long appoggiatura is an exception; it was formerly written as a small note—grace-note—because careful composers could thus nominally evade the rule prohibiting the entrance of unprepared dissonances.)...*Grace-note*, a note of embellishment, usually distinguished by its smaller comparative size.

The graces for harpsichord, clavichord, pianoforte and voice, enumerated below in alphabetical order, are given according to the following authorities:—J. H. d'Anglebert, 1689 (d'A.); J. S. Bach, 1720 (B.); C. Ph. E. Bach, 1787 (Em B.); Dr. John Blow, 1700 (Bl.); Dr. Thomas Busby, 1786 (Bu.); François Couperin, 1713 (C.); J. W. Callcott, 1817 (Ca.); Etienne Loulié, 1696 (L.); N. de S. Lambert, 1697 (La.); F. W. Marpurg, 1762 (M.); P. J. Milchmeyer, 1797 (Mi.); J. S. Petri, 1782 (P.); Fr. Pollini, 1711 (Po.); J. P. Rameau, 1737 (R.); Christopher Simpson, 1659 (S.); G. F. Wolf, 1783-89 (W.); and J. G. Walther, 1732 (Wa.).

In every case, the special article in the body of the book should also be consulted, the primary intention of this article being to give a *list of signs* for ready reference.

Accent.　Accent and Mordant.　Accent and Trillo.

Acciaccatura.　Anschlag.　Appoggiatura.

Arpège.　Arpègement en descen-en montant.　dant.

Arpègement simple.　figuré.　Arpeggio.

Aspiration.

Backfall.　Double Backfall.　Shaked Backfall.

Back Turn.　Balancement.　Beat.

Shaked Beat. Bebung. Beisser. Brechung.

Cadence.

Doppelt-Cadence.

Doppelt-Cadence and Mordant.

Cadence pleine. Cadence brisée.

Cadent. Shaked Cadent.

Chute. Chute et Pincé. Chute.

Coulé.

Tierce coulée. Coulé.

Doppelschlag. Geschnellter Doppelschlag. Prallender Doppelschlag.

Umgekehrter Doppelschlag. Doppelvorschlag. Doublé.

D. sur une tierce. Doublé. Elevation. Shaked Elevation.

Double Relish. Schleifer. [Coulé.] (S.) [Slide.] (Bu.)

Slide. Springer. Passing Shake.

(R.) (C.) (d'A.) (d'A.) (M.)

Son Suspen- Trem- Tremblem. appuyé. Tremblement.
coupé. sion. blement.

(C.) (P.)

Tremblem. continu. Turn. Doppeltriller mit Nachschlag.

(Bl.) (P.) (Bl.) (Bl.)

Mit Vor- und Nachschlag. Trill without Trill with
after-beat. appogg[a].

Gracieux, Gracieuse (Fr.) Graceful.

Gra'cile (It.) Graceful and delicate ; thin, slender (*vo'ce gracile*).

Grad (Ger.) Degree.

Gradation. An ascending or descending series of diatonic chords.

Grade'vole (It.) Pleasing, agreeable... *Gradevolmen'te*, pleasingly.

Gra'do (It.) Degree, step... *Gr. ascenden'te*, ascending step... *Gr. descenden'te*, descending step... *Di grado*, by a step, stepwise ; opp. to *di salto*, by a skip.

Gradual. (Lat. *gradua'le*.) 1. An antiphon following the epistle ; so called because sung on the step (gradus) of the ambo or pulpit.—2. A *cantatorium* (book of chants) containing the graduals, introits, and other antiphons of the R. C. Mass.

Graduellement (Fr.) Gradually.

Grammatical accent. See *Accent*.

Gran cas'sa (It.) See *Cassa*... *Gran gu'sto*, epithet applied to an eccentric or highly effective composition.

Grand. Technical term for Grand Pianoforte (see *Pianoforte*)... *Grand action*, an action such as is used in grand pftes. ..*Grand barré*, see *Barré*.

Grand (Fr.) Large, great... *Gr. barré*, see *Barré*... *Gr. bourdon*, double-bourdon... *Gr. chœur*, full-organ... *Gr. jeu*,

(*a*) full organ ; (*b*) an harmonium-stop which brings into action the full power of the instr...*A grand orchestre*, for full orchestra... *Grand-orgue*, (*a*) full organ ; (*b*) great organ; (*c*) pipe-organ.

Grandeur (Fr.) Width (of intervals).

Grandez'za (It.) Grandeur, majesty, dignity.

Grandio'so (It.) Grand, pompous, majestic.

Grandisonan'te (It.) Loud or long-sounding, re-echoing ; sonorous.

Granulato (It., " granulated.") Non legato.

Grap'pa (It.) Brace.

Grasseyement (Fr.) A guttural and vicious pronunciation of the *r* and *l* in singing... *Grasseyer*, to pronounce as above.

Gratio'so (It.) Same as *Grazioso*.

Gra've (Fr. and It.) 1. Grave or low in pitch.—2. Heavy, slow, ponderous in movement (see *Tempo-marks*).—3. Grave or serious in expression.

Gravement (Fr.), **Gravemen'te** (It.) Slowly, heavily, ponderously; seriously.

Gravicem'balo (It.) A harpsichord. (Also *Gravecembalo*.)

Grav'is (Lat.) Heavy, ponderous ; see *Accentus eccl.*

Gra'zia (It.) Grace, elegance ; *con gr.,*

gracefully, etc... *Grazio'so,-a*, graceful, elegant... *Graziosamen'te*, gracefully.

Graziös' (Ger.) Graceful(ly).

Great octave. See *Pitch, absolute...*

Great organ, see *Organ.*

Greater. Major.

Grec (Fr.) Greek...A chorus *à la grec* is one introduced at an act-close, in imitation of the ancient Greek tragedy.

Greek music. Without attempting to explain the theoretical and mathematical subtleties of the system, a brief statement of some leading features will be given below.

§1. The Modes, or Octave-scales.

The typical Greek scale was precisely the reverse of our modern *ascending major scale*, being conceived as a *descending minor scale*. Harmony in the modern sense was unknown ; the aim of Greek theory in treating of harmonic intervals was, therefore, to establish the melodic succession of the tones, and the Greeks conceived the scale as constituted of a series of *tetrachords* (4-tone groups with the compass of a perfect fourth).

The primitive Greek modes were simple octave-scales ; the three most ancient forms were (1) the Dorian, (2) the Phrygian, and (3) the Lydian, to each of which were later added 2 attendant modes, making 9 in all :

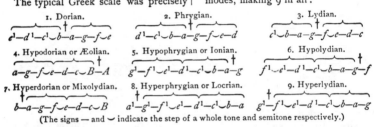

1. Dorian.
2. Phrygian.
3. Lydian.
4. Hypodorian or Æolian.
5. Hypophrygian or Ionian.
6. Hypolydian.
7. Hyperdorian or Mixolydian.
8. Hyperphrygian or Locrian.
9. Hyperlydian.

(The signs — and ‿ indicate the step of a whole tone and semitone respectively.)

The prefix *hypo* signifies "a fifth below"; *hyper*, "a fifth above". (Compare *Mode*.) The character and name of each mode depended (*a*) upon the form of the tetrachord, and (*b*) upon the position of the *diazeuctic tone*. While each of the 3 primitive modes is composed of 2 tetrachords of like name and form, which are *disjoined* (separated) by the diazeuctic tone (marked † ; from *diazeuxis*, a separation), each of its 2 attendant modes is composed of 2 similar *conjoined* tetrachords, united by one common tone, and preceded or followed by the *diazeuxis*. The character of the tetrachord depends on the position of the semitone ; e. g. in the Dorian tetrachord, found in the Dorian and attendant modes, the semitone occurs between the third and fourth tones. This Dorian mode is an exact inversion of the modern major mode :

Major Mode.　　　　Dorian Mode.

§2. The Perfect System is based on the Dorian tetrachord ; it comprises the following two octaves, in which the Dorian mode occupies the central portion:

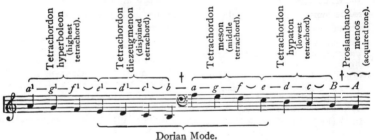

Tetrachordon hyperboleon (highest tetrachord). Tetrachordon diezeugmenon (disjoined tetrachord). Tetrachordon meson (middle tetrachord). Tetrachordon hypaton (lowest tetrachord). Proslambano-menos (acquired tone).

a^1 — g^1 — f^1 ‿ e^1 — d^1 — c^1 ‿ b　†　a — g — f ‿ e — d — c ‿ B — A

Dorian Mode.

This system is formed by adding, at either extreme of the Dorian scale, a conjoined tetrachord, and completing the 2-octave system by the addition of *A* (hence called *Proslambanomenos*, "the acquired tone") in the lower octave, thus forming a complete *a*-minor descending scale. The 2 central tetrachords were therefore disjoined; but, for modulations to the *lower quint* (which to the Greeks was the most natural transition, just as that to the key of the *higher quint* is to us), they used the semitone above the highest tone of the middle tetrachord, and consequently distinguished a special "conjoined tetrachord" (*tetrachordon synemmenon*) d^1-c^1-$b\flat$ ⌣ a, in opposition to the "disjoined tetrachord" (*tetr. diezeugmenon*) d^1-c^1 ⌣ b-a.

Full Names of all Degrees in the Perfect System.

Nete hyperboleon	a^1 (highest of the high)		
Paranete hyperb.	g^1 (next-highest of the high)		
Trite hyperboleon	f^1 (third of the high)		
Nete diezeugmenon	e^1		
(highest of the disjoined)			
Paranete diezeugmenon	d^1 d^1	Nete synemmenon	
(next-highest of the disjoined)		(highest of the conjoined)	
Trite diezeugmenon	c^1 c^1	Paranete synemmenon	
(third of the disjoined)		(next highest of the conjoined)	
Paramese	b $b\flat$	Trite synemmenon	
(the [tone] next the middle)		(third of the conjoined)	
Mese	a a	Mese	
(middle tone)			
Lichanos meson	g (forefinger-tone of the middle)		
Parhypate "	f (next-lowest of the middle)		
Hypate "	e (lowest of the middle)		
Lichanos hypaton	d (forefinger-tone of the low)		
Parhypate "	c (next-lowest of the low)		
Hypate "	B (lowest of the low)		
Proslambanomenos	A (acquired tone) [in no tetrachord]		

(brace: Tetrachordon synemmenon)

The theorists attributed special importance to the middle tone *Mese*, as the tonic of the perfect system. This system also forms the foundation of medieval mus. theory; even the compass given above was not overstepped till the introduction of the *Γ* (gamma). Gregorian music keeps within these limits, and the notation in Latin letters retains this same diatonic scale even to the chromatic alteration of *Paramese* to *Trite synemmenon*. This perfect system (*systema teleion*) was also styled the *systema metabolon*, the "mutable (i. e. modulatory) system," with reference to the modulation to the subdominant made possible by employing the conjoined tetrachord; without this tetrachord it was called the *systema ameta-bolon* (immutable). [This *diatonic* division of the tetrachord into 2 whole tones and a semitone (as a-g-f⌣e), of which the Dorian tetrachord is the normal type, was the distinctive feature of the *diatonic genus* (genus=melodic arrangement of the tones within the tetrachord); the *earlier enharmonic genus* was formed by omitting the *paranete* or the *lichanos* (as a——f⌣e), and the *later*

enharmonic genus by dividing the *trite* or the *parhypate* into 2 tones (as a——$e\sharp$ f⌣e); while the *chromatic genus*, also omitting the diatonic second degree, was expressed by sharping either *trite* or *parhypate* (as a—⌣$f\sharp$⌣f⌣e); etc.]

§3. **Transposing Scales.** While the perfect system remained the standard in theory, the progress of Grecian musical art widened its application in practice until all flat and sharp semitones were employed, and its range likewise extended. The chromatic alterations were expressed in the Greek alphabetical notation by different letters and different positions of the same letter, which were equivalent in effect to our $\sharp$ and $\flat$. E. g., on substituting in the octave-scale d^1—d the conjoined for the disjoined tetrachord (i. e. $b\flat$ for b), this octave-scale is no longer the Phrygian, but becomes the Hypodorian, for the distinction between the modes depends on the position of the semitonic step; moreover, as the Hypodorian octave-scale is to be considered as that extending from the Dorian *mese* to *proslam-banomenos*, this octave-scale d^1—d

with $b\flat$ belongs to a transposed Dorian mode, having not A, but d, for *proslambanomenos*. Greek music was not tied, like the Gregorian, to the diatonic scale A—a^1 without chromatics, but employed transpositions of the perfect 2-octave system parallel to our 12 or more sharp and flat keys; finally, these transpositions numbered 15 in all, those first in vogue bearing the same names as the first 7 octave-scales. In the Greek method of alphabetical notation, the *natural* scale (without chromatics) was the Hypolydian:

$$f^1 \smile e^1 - d^1 - c^1 \smile b - a - g - f \dagger$$

consequently, the 2-octave system A—a^1 without chromatics is called the Hypolydian (being the *natural* scale among the transposing scales, as is C-major among the sharp and flat keys), and the transposing scales are named according to the mode represented by the various chromatic alterations of the octave-scale f^1—f. For instance,

$$f^1 \smile e^1 - d^1 - c^1 - b\flat \smile a - g - f \dagger$$

being a Lydian octave, the 2-octave system (or transposing scale) d—d^2 with one flat is called the Lydian transposing scale. It follows, that the octave f^1—f belongs

without ♯ or ♭ to the system A—a^1 (Hypolydian)
with 1 ♭ to the system d—d^2 (Lydian)
" 2 ♭ " " " G—g^1 (Hypophrygian)
" 3 ♭ " " " c—c^2 (Phrygian)
" 4 ♭ " " " F—f^1 (Hypodorian)
" 5 ♭ " " " $b\flat$—$b^2\flat$ (Dorian)
" 6 ♭ " " " $e\flat$—$e^2\flat$ (Mixolydian, or Hyperdorian)

On the other hand, all the sharp scales (of later origin) show new names; the octave f^1♯—f♯ belongs
with 1♯ to the system e—e^2 (Hyperiastian)
(high Mixolydian)
" 2♯ " " " B—b^1 (Iastian)
(high Dorian)
" 3♯ " " " F♯—f^1♯ (Hypoiastian)
(high Hypodorian)
" 4♯ " " " c♯—c^2♯ (Æolian)
(high Phrygian)
" 5♯ " " " G♯—g^1♯ (Hypoæolian)
(high Hypophrygian)
" 6♯ " " " d♯—d^2♯ (Hyperdorian)
(high Lydian)

The system d♯—d^2♯, with 6 sharps, is enharmonically identical with $e\flat$—$e^2\flat$ with 6 flats; both are named Hyperdorian; here closes the circle of fifths. —The names of the sharp scales re-emerge as those of church-modes (the number of which was increased to 12 in the 16th century); namely, the Ionian (= Iastian) and Hypoionian, Æolian, and Hypoæolian.

Gregorian chant. The forms of mus. worship as revised and established by Pope Gregory I. (the Great, d. 604) for the R. C. Church, and known collectively under the name of Plain Chant. There was probably no essential difference between the Gregorian and Ambrosian styles; St. Gregory's chief work was the careful revision of the ritual music employed at his time, the rejection of redundances and abuses, and the final establishment of the material thus sifted and arranged as the norm for all Western Churches. He was also presumably the arranger, if not the originator, of the 4 Plagal modes parallel to the 4 Authentic modes of St. Ambrose. (See *Mode.*)

Grei'fen (Ger.) To stop (on the violin); to take or play (on other instr.s); to finger; to stretch (*er kann eine De'zime greifen*, he can stretch a tenth).

Griff (Ger.) Stop (on violin); touch, stroke, stretch (*weiter Griff*); fingering...*Griff'brett*, fingerboard...*Griff'-saite*, a string stopped by the fingers; a melody-string.

Grob (Ger., "coarse.") Used as a suffix, it means "of broad scale" (said of organ-pipes, as *Grobgedackt*).

Groove. (Ger. *Kanzel'le.*) One of the separate divisions of the windchest of an organ, serving to conduct the wind to the pipes.

Groppet'to (It.) See *Gruppetto.*

Grop'po (It.) See *Gruppo.*

Gross (Ger.) Great, large, grand; major (as *gro'sse Terz*, major Third)... *Gro'sse Okta've*, great octave.

Grosse-caisse (Fr.) See *Caisse.*

Gros'so (It.) Large, great; full, heavy.

Gros-tambour (Fr.) Bass drum.

Grotte'sco (It.) Grotesque, comic, humorous.

Ground bass. See *Bass.*

Group. I. A short series of rapid notes; specifically, such a series sung to one

syllable; a division or run.—2. A section of the orchestra, or of an orchestral score, embracing instr.s of one class, e. g. the strings.

Groupe (Fr.) 1. Group; specifically, a group of notes with their hooks slurred together; a turn.—2. A unison 2.

Grund (Ger.) Ground, foundation, fundament... *Grund'akkord*, a chord in the fundamental position... *Grund'bass*, fundamental bass... *Grund'lage*, fundamental position (of a chord)... *Grund'stimme*, (*a*) see *Grundbass;* (*b*) a bass part; (*c*) foundation-stop (organ). ..*Grund'ton*, (*a*) root; (*b*) key-note. ..*Grund'tonart*, ruling or principal key in a composition.

Gruppet'to (It.) Formerly, a trill or relish; in modern music, a turn.—Also, a collective term applied loosely to various "groups" of grace-notes, such as:

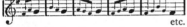

etc.

Grup'po (It.) Group; also, a turn.— Formerly, a grace similar to the trill. (See *Trillo.*)

G'-Schlüssel (Ger.) *G*-clef.

Guara'cha (Span.) A lively Spanish dance, one part of which is in 3-4 or 3-8 time and the other in 2-4 time; usually accompanied on the guitar by the dancer himself.

Gue. An instr. of the violin kind, having only 2 strings (of horsehair), and played like a 'cello; formerly used in Shetland. [CENTURY DICT.]

Guerrie'ro (It.) Martial, warlike.

Gui'da (It.) 1. Subject (of a fugue); antecedent (in a canon or other imitation).—2. A direct.—3. See *Presa.*—4. In solfeggio, a tone or tones through which the voice glides from one interval-tone to the other.

Guide. 1. *Guida* 1 and 2.—2. (Fr.) *Guida* 1 and 4... *Guide-main*, "hand-guide," chiroplast.

Guidon (Fr.) A direct.

Guido'nian hand. The Guidonian Hand was a diagram, for memorizing the solmisation-syllables of the 20-tone diatonic scale (Γ to *ee*), in the shape of an outstretched left hand with the syllables written in regular order on the successive finger-tips and joints. The syllables were called the *Aretinian* or *Guidonian syllables.* (See *Solmisation.*)

Guimbard. (Fr. *guimbarde.*) A jew's-harp.

Guitar'. (Span. *guitar'ra;* Ger. *Guitar're;* Fr. *guitare;* It. *chitar'ra.*) An instr. of the lute family. The modern ("Spanish") guitar has six strings, the 3 highest of gut, the 3 lowest of silk covered with fine silver wire, tuned *E-A-d-g-b-e*[1]:

(or E-B-e-$g\sharp$-b-e[1]); but guitar-music is written an octave higher, in the *G*-clef. The pitch of all 6 strings can be raised a semitone by using the capotasto. Compass (with the 3 octaves harmonics, and a fourth: an octave more). The long fingerboard is furnished with frets on which the strings are stopped with the left hand, while the right plucks the strings with the finger-tips (the thumb taking the 3 lowest, the forefinger *g*, the middle finger *b*, and the ring-finger high *e*), or strikes them with the back of the fingers; the thumb also sweeps the strings with the arpeggio-effect called the *rasgado.*— The body of the guitar has a broad waist, no corners, and a flat face and back. It is used as a solo instr., and in accompanying songs.

Guitare d'amour (Fr.), **Guitar-violoncello.** See *Arpeggione.*

Guiterne (Fr.) Former name for the guitar.

Gu'sto (It.) Taste... *Di buon g.*, in good taste, tasteful... *Gusto'so*, with taste... *Gran gusto*, see *Gran.*

Gut. Gut strings (in the singular Ger. *Darm'saite;* Fr. *corde à* or *de* or *en boyau;* It. *minu'gia*), popularly known as catgut, are ordinarily manufactured from the entrails of sheep, those of young lambs yielding the evenest and finest strings because they do not have to be split. The best are the genuine Roman strings.

Gut (Ger.) Good... *Gu'ter Takt'teil*, strong beat.

H.

H (Ger.) The note *B*... In scores, *H* is an abbr. for *Horn;* in organ-music, for *Heel;* in music for keyboard instr.s, for *Hand* (*r. h., l. h.*)

Hack'brett (Ger.) Dulcimer.

Halb (Ger.) Half; also, "smaller"... *Hal'be Applikatur'*, half-shift...*Halb'-bass*, a double-bass of smaller size than usual...*Halb'cello*, a small 'cello... *Halb'gedeckte Stim'me*, see *Stimme* 3. ...*Halb'instrument*, see *Ganzinstrument*...*Halb'kadenz*, half-cadence... *Halb'mond*, crescent...*Hal'be Note*, half-note...*Hal'be Or'gel*, an organ lacking, even on the pedal, a stop lower than 8-foot pitch...*Hal'be Pau'se*, half-rest...*Halb'prinzipal*, an organ-stop of 4-foot pitch (disused)...*Halb'schluss*, half-close...*Hal'be Stim'me*, a half-stop or partial stop...*Hal'be Takt'note*, half-note...*Halb'ton*, *hal'ber Ton*, semitone...*Halb'violine*, three-quarter violin (for children)...*Halb'violon* [PAUL], see *Halbbass, Deutscher Bass*. ..*Halb'werk*, see *Halbe Orgel*.

Half-cadence, -note, -rest, -shift, -step, -stop, -tone, see the nouns.

Hallelujah. See *Alleluia*.

Hals (Ger.) 1. Neck (of the violin, etc.) —2. Throat (of a singer).—3. Stem (of a note).

Halt (Ger.) A hold (⌒); usually *Ferma'te*.

Hammer. 1. (Ger. *Ham'mer;* Fr. *marteau;* It. *martel'lo.*) That part of the pfte.-action which strikes the strings and evokes the tone.—2. A mallet, used in playing the dulcimer...*Ham'merclavier, -klavier* (Ger.), early name for the pianoforte (opp. to *Federklavier*).

Hanac'ca. A Moravian dance in 3-4 time, resembling the Polonaise in the shifting of the accent, but in more rapid tempo. (Ger. *Hana'kisch.*)—*Alla h.*, in the style of this dance.

Hand, harmonic. See *Guidonian Hand.*

Hand'bassl (Ger.) An obsolete bow-instr., intermediate in size between the viola and 'cello; employed as a bass-instr...*Hand'bildner, Hand'leiter*, a chiroplast...*Hand'stücke*, short and easy exercises or practice-pieces... *Hand'trommel*, tambourine.

Hand-harmonica. Accordion.

Handle-piano. A mechanical pfte. on the principle of the barrel-organ; the studs on the barrel catch levers connected with the hammers, causing the latter to strike the strings, a spring forcing the hammer to recoil instantly. The older instr.s have few or no damp-

ers; more recent ones show an improvement in this regard.

Hand-note. Stopped tone (on the horn).

Hand-organ. A portable barrel-organ.

Hard. (Of tones, touch, execution.) Coarse, rough, harsh; cold, unsympathetic, lacking expression or feeling.

Hardiment (Fr.) Boldly, vigorously, dashingly.—Also, *Avec hardiesse*.

Har'fe (Ger.) Harp...*Har'fenbass*, Albertinian bass...*Harfenett'*, see *Spitzharfe*...*Har'feninstrumente*, stringed instr.s whose strings are plucked either with the fingers or a plectrum...*Har'fenlaute*, dital harp.

Harmoni'a (Gk. and Lat.) Harmony.

Harmon'ic. 1 (*adjective.*) (Ger. *harmo'nisch;* Fr. *harmonique;* It. *armo'nico.*) Pertaining to chords (either consonant or dissonant), and to the theory and practice of harmony; opp. to *melodic*...*H. curve*, the curved figure described by a vibrating string... *H. figuration*, broken chords...*H. flute*, see *H. stop*...*H. hand*, see *Guidonian Hand*...*H. mark*, in music for the violin, etc., a sign (°) over a note, calling for an harmonic tone...*H. note*, see *H. tone*...*H. reed*, see *H. stop*... *H. scale*, see *Harmonic* 2...*H. stop*, an organ-stop having pipes double the ordinary length, and pierced midway, so that a 16-foot pipe yields an 8-foot tone. Various solo stops are thus constructed: An *harmonic flute* is a flute-stop, an *harmonic reed* a reed-stop, made on this principle...*H. tone*, also flageolet-tone, see *Harmonic* 2 (*b*)... *H. triad*, a major triad.

Harmonic. 2 (*noun*). (*a*) (Ger. *O'berton;* Fr. *son harmonique;* It. *suono armonico.*) One of the series of tones sounding with, but higher in pitch and less intense than, its generator (see *Acoustics*).—(*b*) (Ger. *Flageolet'-ton, Harmo'nikaton;* Fr. *son harmonique;* It. *suono armonico.*) A tone obtained, on any stringed instr. which is stopped (violin, guitar, zither, etc.), and also on the harp, by lightly touching with the finger-tip a nodal point of a string; the string, when set in vibration, can then not vibrate as a whole, but only in independent sections, each section corresponding in length to the division of the string cut off by the finger, and each producing one and the same tone—the *harmonic*. Thus, by lightly touching the *G*-string of a violin at its midpoint, it is divided into 2 vibrating sections, each producing the octave of *g*, i. e., *g*^{1} ; by touching it one-third of the distance from nut to bridge, it is divided into 3 vibrating sections, each producing the fifth above the octave of *g*, i. e., *d*^{2} ; etc. Such harmonics, obtained from open strings, are called *natural;* when the string is previously shortened by stopping, and the harmonics then obtained by lightly touching this shortened section, they are called *artificial.* The following table shows the harmonics obtained on a string : By lightly touching

the octave,   we get the octave ;
" fifth,   "   "   "   twelfth ;
" fourth,   "   "   "   fifteenth ;
" third (maj.) "   "   its own 15th ;
" third (min.) "   "   "   "   17th.

The harmonics are distinguished by their soft, sweet, ethereal character, and the " fluty" quality of their tone (hence the epithets *flautato, flageolet*). They are called for by the sign ° (the " *harmonic mark*") over the notes to be touched (*not stopped*).

Harmon'ica. (Comp. Ger. *Harmo'nika.*) **1.** The instr. developed by Benjamin Franklin from the musical glasses, and named by him *Armon'ica.* It consisted of a graduated series of glass bells or basins forming a diatonic scale (lowest tone to the left), and fastened in a row upon a spindle, which was made to revolve by a treadle ; the ends of the spindle were supported by the end-pieces of a trough containing water to moisten the revolving glasses, whose edges were touched by the fingers in playing. Melodies could be performed, and accompanied harmonically by chords as wide as the fingers could stretch.—**2.** See *Mouth-harmonica.*

Harmonicel'lo. A bow-instr. resembling the 'cello, with 5 gut and 10 wire strings ; inv. by Joh. Karl Bischoff of Nuremberg in the 2nd half of the 18th century.

Harmonichord. See *Piano-violin.*

Harmo'nici. Aristoxenos and his followers, who deduced the rules of harmony from musical practice ; opp. to *Canonici* (Pythagoras and his disciples), who derived their rules from the mathematical determination of the intervals.

Harmon'icon. **1.** A mouth-harmonica. **2.**—An orchestrion.—**3.** A keyed har-

monica combined with a flue-stop or stops ; inv. by W. C. Müller.

Harmoni-cor (Fr.) See *Harmoniphon* 2.

Harmonicorde (Fr.) Harmonichord.

Harmo'nicum. An improved form of Bandonion, inv. by Brendel and Klösser of Mittweida (Saxony) in 1893. It is, essentially, an accordion-body fixed in an harmonium-case ; the keyboard is made like either that of the harmonium or bandonion ; the wind-supply is controlled by treadles.

Harmonie' (Ger.) **1.** Harmony ; chord. —**2.** Music for the wind-instr.s (brass and wood); also *Harmonie'musik.*—**3.** The wind-instr.s (brass and wood) collectively.—*Harmonie'eigen,* harmonic, chordal ; (tones) proper to a harmony ; opp. to *harmonie'fremd...Harmonie'-lehre,* theory of harmony...*Harmonie'-trompete,* an instr. between a horn and trumpet, which permitted of the successful use of muted tones ; inv. early in the 19th century [RIEMANN].

Harmonieux,-ieuse (Fr.) Harmonious.

Harmo'nika (Ger.) Accordion ; concertina ;—see also *Holz'harmonika, Mund'harmonika, Zieh'harmonika.*

Harmo'niker (Ger., pl.) Harmonici.

Harmon'iphon. **1.** A keyboard wind-instr. inv. by Panis of Paris in 1837, having a set of reed-pipes in imitation of oboe-tubes ; hence the Ger. name *Klavieroboe.*—**2.** The *harmoni-cor,* inv. by Jaulin of Paris, similar to the above, but with clarinet-tubes ; the wind is supplied through a mouthpiece.

Harmo'nisch (Ger.) Harmonic.

Harmo'nium. Comp. *Reed-organ.*—In harmonium-music, numerals enclosed in circles are used in 'lieu of the stop-names in full, and signify:

Stops on bass side (sign below bass staff.)	Stops on Treble side (sign above or below treble staff.)
① Cor anglais	① Flute
② Bourdon	② Clarinet
③ Clarion	③ Piccolo
④ Bassoon	④ Oboe

Harmonom'eter. An appliance for measuring the harmonic relations of tones (intervals). See *Monochord.*

Har'mony. (Ger. and Fr. *Harmonie'*; It. *armoni'a.*) In general, a combination of tones or chords producing music.—Specifically, a chord, either consonant or dissonant, though usually applied to the former kind, especially to the triad.—Applied to an entire composition, the chordal (harmonic) structure, in contradistinction to the melody and rhythm ; hence, *2-part*, *3-part harmony*, according to the number oi parts present... *Chromatic h.*, that in which many chromatic tones and modulations are introduced ; opp. to *diatonic h...Close h.* (in 4-part writing), that in which the 3 highest parts lie within the compass of an octave ; opp. to *open n... Compound h.*, that in which 2 or more of the tones essential to a chord are doubled ; opp. to *simple h.. .Dispersed, extended h.*, see *Open h... Essential h.*, (*a*) the fundamental triads of a key ; (*b*) the harmonic skeleton of a composition, left after pruning off all figuration and ornaments... *Figured h.*, that in which the simple chords are varied or broken up by foreign and passing tones, anticipations, suspensions, and other devices ; opp. to *plain h... Open h.* (in 4-part writing), that in which the 3 highest parts spread beyond the compass of an octave... *Pure h.*, music performed with pure intonation (motet, string-quartet ;) opp. to *tempered h...Spread h.*, open h... *Strict h.*, composition according to strict rules for the preparation and resolution of dissonances... *Tempered h.*, music performed with tempered intonation (pfte., organ); see *Temperament*.

Harp. (Ger. *Har'fe;* Fr. *harpe;* It. *ar'pa*.) A stringed instr. of ancient origin and wide dissemination, played by plucking the strings with the fingers and thumbs of both hands.—The modern orchestral harp (Erard's double-action harp) has a nearly 3-cornered wooden *frame*; the apex or *foot* of which is formed by an upright *pillar* meeting the hollow *back* (the upper side of which bears the *soundboard*) in the *pedestal;* the upper, divergent ends of pillar and back are united by the curving *neck*. The gut *strings*, stretched vertically between soundboard and neck, and tuned by *wrestpins* inserted in the latter, are 46 (or 47) in number, and variously colored to render them readily distinguishable ; the 8 lowest strings are covered with fine wire. Compass, six and one-half octaves, from $C_1\flat$ to $f'\flat$ (or $g'\flat$):

this is the fundamental diatonic **scale ;** the intermediate chromatic tones are obtained by the use of 7 *pedals* adjusted in the pedestal, each pedal acting on all the strings of the same letter-name in such a way that, when pressed to its *first* position, the pitch of every string affected is raised a semitone, and, when the pedal is pressed down to its *second* position, a semitone higher. Thus, by depressing all 7 pedals once, the scale would be raised from $C\flat$ to $C;$ by depressing them twice, to $C\sharp$ ($D\flat$); by suitable combinations, any desired key may be obtained. The depressed pedals are held in position by notches. As on the Jankó keyboard, the fingering of the scale is the same for every key. Natural harmonics are obtainable ; the first harmonic (the octave of the tone of the open string) is that almost exclusively employed. Music for the harp is written on 2 staves as for the pfte.—In the old *single-action harp* each pedal can change the pitch of its note by only *one* semitone ; scale, $E\flat$; compass, 5 octaves and a sixth, from F_1 to d': A *Double Harp* has 2 rows of strings tuned dissimilarly ; a *Triple Harp* has 3 such rows... *Æolian h.*, see *Æolian. ..Couched h.*, the spinet... *Dital harp*, see *Dital...Double-action pedal-harp*, **see** *Harp... Welsh h.*, a kind of triple harp.

Harpeg'gio, Harpeggie'ren. See *Arpeggio, Arpeggiate*.

Harpicor'do. Same as *Arpicordo*.

Harp-lute. See *Dital harp*.

Harpo-lyre (Fr.) A kind of improved guitar, with 21 strings and 3 necks ; inv. 1829 by Salomon of Besançon.

Harp-pedal. See *Pedal*.

Harp'sichord. (Ger. *Kiel'flügel;* Fr. *clavecin;* It. *arpicor'do, clavicem'balo*.) A keyboard stringed instr. in which the strings were twanged by quills or bits of hard leather (see *Pianoforte*).—*Vis-à-vis harpsichord*, one with a keyboard at either end or side, for 2 performers.

Harp-way tuning. Favorite early English tunings (*scordature*) of the viola da gamba ; termed *harp-way* tunings because admitting of a ready execution of arpeggios :

Sharp :   Flat :

other variants are found in German works.

Hart (Ger.) Hard ; major (usually *dur*) ; abrupt, unprepared (of a progression or modulation)...*Hart vermin'derter Drei'klang*, triad with major third and diminished fifth, as *B-d♯-f.*

Haupt (Ger., "head".) Chief, principal...*Haupt'accent*, primary accent. ..*Haupt'akkord*, fundamental triad. ..*Haupt'gesang*, leading melody (*Haupt'melodie*)...*Haupt'kadenz*, full cadence...*Haupt'manual*, great-organ manual (abbr. *Man. I.*)...*Haupt'note*, (a) principal note ; (b) chord-note ; (c) accented note ; (d) melody-note... *Haupt'prinzipal*, 8-foot diapason (on manual), 16-foot (on pedal)...*Haupt'-probe*, see *Generalprobe*...*Haupt'satz*, principal theme...*Haupt'schluss*, full cadence...*Haupt'septime*, dominant 7th...*Haupt'stimme*, principal part... *Haupt'thema*, first or principal theme. ..*Haupt'ton*, (a) root (of a chord ; in recent theory, the *fifth* of the minor triad) ; (b) key-note ; (c) see *Haupt-note*...*Haupt'tonart*, the principal or ruling key in a composition...*Haupt'-werk* (abbr. *H. W.*), great organ.

Hausse (Fr.) Nut (of a bow)...*Hausser*, to raise (the pitch).

Haut,-e (Fr.) High, acute...*Haute-contre*, high tenor...*Haut-dessus*, high soprano...*Haute-taille*, high tenor.

Hautbois (Fr.) Oboe...*H. d'amour*, see *Oboe*.

Hautboist' (Ger.) A player in a military band.

Haut'boy. Oboe.

Head. 1. Point (of bow).—2. In the violin, lute, etc., the part above the neck, comprising peg-box and scroll.— 3. In the drum, the membrane stretched over one or both ends.—4. In a note, the oval (formerly square or diamond-shaped) part which determines its place on the staff...*Head-tones, Head-voice*, the vocal tones of the head-register ; opp. to *chest-tones*, etc.

Heel. (Ger. *Stöckchen* [des Halses] ; Fr. *talon* [de la manche].) In the violin, etc., the wooden elbow or brace by which the neck is firmly fastened to the body.

Heer'pauke (Ger.) An old and very large form of kettledrum.

Hef'tig (Ger.) Vehement, impetuous,

passionate (also *adverb*)...*Hef'tigkeit*, vehemence, passion.

Heim'lich (Ger.) Secret, mysterious; furtive, stealthy, clandestine. (Also *adverb.*)

Hei'ter (Ger.) Serene, cheerful, glad. (Also *adverb.*)

Hel'dentenor (Ger.) See *Tenor* 1.

Hel'icon. (Ger. *Helikon*.) 1. An ancient instr. for illustrating the theory of the mus. intervals, consisting of 9 strings stretched across a square resonance-box.—2. A brass wind-instr. of recent invention, used chiefly in military music as a bass ; its tube is bent to form a circle, and it is carried over the shoulder. It is constructed in various pitches (*F*, *E♭*, *C*, *B♭*), and of broad scale, so that its lowest natural tone speaks (2 octaves below the notes on the bass-staff 15ᵐᵃ.

Helper. An octave-pipe set beside and sounding with another of 8-foot pitch, for the sake of brilliancy.

Hemidemisemiqua'ver. A 64th-note. ..*H.-rest*, a 64th-rest.

Hemidiapen'te. In Gk. music, a diminished fifth.

Hemidi'tone. In Gk. music, a minor third.

Hemio'la, Hemio'lia (Gk.) 1. In ancient music, quintuple rhythm (5-4, 5-8 time). —2. The interval of a fifth (2 : 3).—3. A triplet (3 : 2).—4. In mensurable notation, see *Notation*, §3, *Color*.

Hem'iphrase. A half-phrase.

Hem'itone. In Greek music, the interval of a half-tone (256 : 243), the modern (diatonic) semitone being 16 : 15.

Hep'tachord. In Greek music, a diatonic series of 7 tones, with one semitone-step between the 3rd and 4th.— 2. The interval of a major 7th.—3. A 7-stringed instr. —4. The 7-tone scale.

Hep'tad, Heptadec'ad. See *Duodene*.

Herab'strich (Ger.) Down-bow.

Herauf'strich (Ger.) See *Hinaufstrich*.

Heroic. (Ger. *hero'isch;* Fr. *héroïque;* It. *ero'ico,-a.*) Grand, imposing, noble, bold, daring (in conception, or construction)...The "Heroic Symphony" (Sinfoni'a ero'ica) by Beethoven is the Third, Op. 55 in *E♭*...*Heroic verse*, (a) in classical poetry, the hexameter ; (b) in Engl., Ger., It. poetry, the iambic of 10 syllables ; (c) in Fr. poetry, the Alexandrine.

Her′strich (Ger., "hither-stroke".) Down-bow (on the 'cello and double-bass).

Herun′terstrich (Ger.) Down-bow (on the violin, etc.)

Her′zig (Ger., "hearty," "heartily".) Same as *Innig*, but perhaps implies greater *naïveté*.

Hes (Ger., "*H♭*.") Unusual for (Ger.) *B* [=(Eng.) B♭]...*Hes′es*, B♭♭.

Heu′len (Ger.) Ciphering.

Hex′achord. 1. In Greek music, (a) a diatonic series of 6 tones ; (b) the interval of a major sixth.—2. See *Solmisation*.

Hexam′eter. The usual hexameter-line has 6 feet, the first 4 being dactyls or spondees, the 5th a dactyl or spondee, and the 6th a spondee or trochee, thus :

—◡◡|—◡◡|—◡◡|—◡◡|—◡◡|—◡

Hidden. See *Octave*.

Hift′horn (Ger.) A kind of wooden hunting-horn producing 2 or 3 tones ; there were 3 varieties, the *Zin′ke* (high), *Halb′rüdenhorn* (medium), and *Rü′denhorn* (low pitch).

Hilfs- (Ger.) Auxiliary...*Hilfs′linie*, leger-line...*Hilfs′note*, auxiliary note. ..*Hilfs′stimme*, mutation-stop.—(Often *Hülfs-*.)

Hinauf′strich (Ger.) Up-bow (on the violin, etc.)

Hin′strich (Ger., "thither-stroke".) Up-bow (on the 'cello, and double-bass).

Hin′tersatz (Ger.) In old German organs, a mixture-stop placed behind the diapason, which it reinforced.

Hip′pius. 1. A metrical foot of 4 syllables, 3 long and 1 short ; called 1st, 2nd, 3rd or 4th hippius according as the short syllable occupies the 1st, 2nd, 3rd or 4th place.—2. Same as *Molossus*.

His (Ger.) B♯...*His′is*, B✕.

Histor′icus (Lat.) Narrator (oratorio).

Hobo′e (Ger.) See *Oboe*.

Hoch (Ger.) High, acute...*Hoch′amt*, high Mass...*Hoch′zeitsmarsch*, wedding-march.

Hock′et. An early form of contrapuntal vocal composition in 2 or 3 parts, characterized by the frequent and sudden interruption, in rapid alternation, of the vocal parts, producing a spasmodic,

"hiccupy" effect ; chiefly in vogue during the 12th and 13th centuries. (Also spelled *hoquet, hocquet, hoquetus, ochetus*, etc.)

Höh′e (Ger.) High pitch, acuteness ; high register (e. g. "*Obo′enhöhe*", highest notes of the oboe).

Hohl′flöte (Ger. ; Fr. *flûte creuse;* the smaller sizes are also called *Hohlpfeifen*.) In the organ, an open flue-stop of broad scale, usually with eared pipes, having a dark, mellow timbre, somewhat hollow (whence the name), generally of 8 or 4-foot pitch, seldom of 16′ or 2′. As a mutation-stop in the fifth it is called the *Hohl′quinte*.

Hold. (Ger. *Ferma′te;* Fr. *point d'arrêt, couronne;* It. *ferma′ta, coro′na*.) The sign ⌢ over, or ⌣ under, a note or rest, indicating the indefinite prolongation of its time-value, at the performer's discretion, in accordance with the rhythm of the composition...In orchestral scores often called (Ger.) *General′-pause*, (It.) *pa′usa genera′le*.—(In England, usually called a *Pause*.)—Placed over a bar or double-bar, the hold indicates a slight pause or breathing-spell before attacking what follows ; opp. in this sense to *Attacca*.

Holding-note. A note sustained in one part while the others are in motion. [STAINER AND BARRETT.]

Holz′bläser (Ger., sing. and pl.) Player(s) on wood wind-instr.s. (Abbr. *Hzbl.*)...*Holz′blasinstrumente*, wood wind-instr.s ; technically, the "wood-wind".

Höl′zernes Geläch′ter ⟩ (Ger.) Xylo-
Holz′harmonika ⟩ phone.

Homophone (Fr.) The enharmonic of a given tone, as *d* of *c*✕, *d♭* of *c♯*, etc.

Homophonic,-ous. (Lit., alike in sound or pitch.) 1. In earlier music, unisonous, in unison ; opp. to *antiphonic*.—2. In modern music, a style in which *one* melody or part, supported to a greater or less extent by chords or chordal combinations, (i. e. an *accompanied melody*), predominates, is called homophonic ; opp. to *polyphonic*...*Homophony*, homophonic music; opp. to *antiphony* and *polyphony*. (See *Monody*.)

Hook. (Ger. *Fah′ne, Fähn′chen ;* Fr. *crochet ;* It. *co′da uncina′ta*.) A stroke attached to the stems of eighth-notes, 16th-notes, etc. (♪ ♬). Also *Flag, Pennant*.

Hoquetus. Hocket.

Ho'ræ cano'nicæ (Lat.) The canonical hours.

Horn. (Ger. *Horn;* Fr. *cor;* It. *cor'no.*) One of a group of brass wind-instr.s distinguished by the following characteristics: Cupped mouthpiece of conical shape; conical tube, narrow and long, variously bent upon itself (the smallest horn generally used, in high B♭, has a tube nearly 9 feet long; that an octave lower in pitch, nearly 18 feet); wide and flaring bell; the tone is rich and mellow, sonorous and penetrating; the compass lies between the 2nd and 16th tones of the harmonic scale. The older *natural* or *French Horn*, yielding only the natural tones supplemented by "stopped tones", has a fairly complete chromatic scale of 2 octaves and a fifth, from the 3rd partial (lowered by stopping) up to the 16th partial; there are 16 crooks in all, giving a total possible compass of 3½ octaves:

but only 8 or 10 are in general use in the symphony-orchestra; the following tones at either end of this scale are difficult:

Thus the highest "safe" tones on the horns in common use would be (according to GEVAERT):

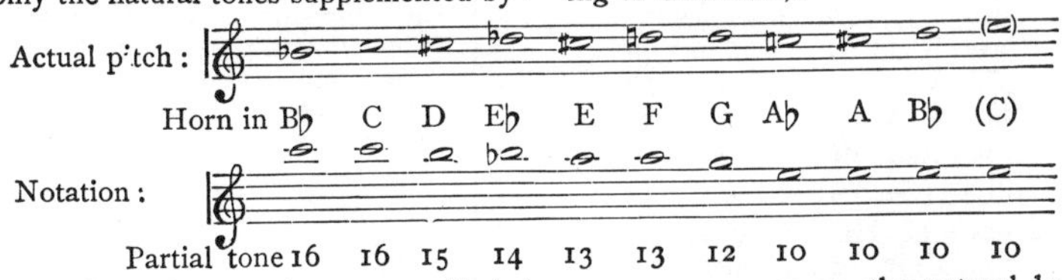
Actual pitch:
Horn in B♭ C D E♭ E F G A♭ A B♭ (C)
Notation:
Partial tone 16 16 15 14 13 13 12 10 10 10 10

The stopped tones have a peculiarly sombre quality, and are often utilized for special effects; they can be produced on the valve-horn in exactly the same manner as on the natural horn (also comp. *Trumpet*). This modern *Valve-horn* is usually constructed in the following sizes [RIEMANN]:

B♭ C D E♭ E F G A♭ A B♭ C
low
high

the given pitch-note being in each case the 2nd partial tone (octave of the generator), and represented in each case by the note:

the horn being a transposing instr.; when the *G*-clef is employed, the notes are written an octave higher than when noted in the *F*-clef, consequently

Horn-band. A band of trumpeters... *Russian horn-band*, a band of performers on hunting-horns, each of which produces but one tone, the number of players and instr.s being equal to that of the scale-tones required by any given piece; e. g. 37 for the chromatic scale of 3 octaves.

Hörner (Ger.) Plural of *Horn*, equiv. to *corni.* (Abbr. *Hr.*)

Horning. A mock serenade with tin horns and other discordant instr.s, performed either in humorous congratulation, as of a newly married couple, or as a manifestation of public disapproval, as of some obnoxious person. (Local U. S.) [CENTURY DICT.]—A callithumpian concert.

Horn'musik (Ger.) See *Harmoniemusik.*

Hornpipe. 1. An obsolete English mus. instr.—2. An old English dance in lively tempo, the earlier ones in 3-2 time with frequent syncopations, and the later in 4-4 time; very popular during the 18th century.

Horn'quinten (Ger., "horn-fifths".) The covered fifths produced by the natural tones of a pair of horns:

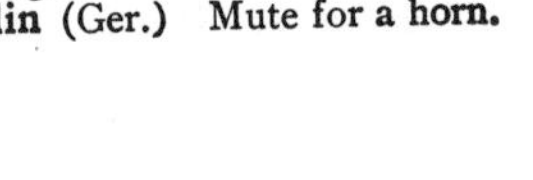

Horn'sordin (Ger.) Mute for a horn.

Hosan'na; Hosian'na (Hebr.) Lit. "save, I pray"; an interjection used as a prayer for deliverance or as an acclamation.—In the Mass, a part of the Sanctus.

Hue'huetl (Aztec.) (Also *huehuitl, vevtl, tlapanhuehuetl.*) Drum of the aborigines in Mexico and Central America, consisting of a section of a log hollowed out, carved on the outside, from 3 to 4 feet in height, as thick as a man's body, and set upon a tripod. The upper end was furnished with a head of leather or parchment which could be tightened or relaxed, thus raising or lowering the tone. It was struck with the fingers, and considerable skill was required to play it. From the indistinct accounts of the old Spanish writers it appears to have yielded, in conjunction with the *Teponaztli*, a rude harmonic bass accompaniment.

Huit-pieds (Fr.) Same as *Halbe Orgel.*

Hülfs- (Ger.) See *Hilfs-.*

Hum'mel, Hüm'melchen (Ger.) 1. A drone.—2. An obsolete organ-stop, by drawing which 2 reed-pipes were caused to sound continuously until it was pushed in.—3. The Balalaïka, which has a sympathetic string.—4. The "drones" of the hurdy-gurdy.

Humoresque. (Ger. *Humores'ke.*) A composition of humorous or fantastic style. See *Caprice.*

Hurdy-gurdy. (Ger. *Dreh'leier, Bau'-ernleier;* Fr. *vielle;* It. *li'ra tede'sca.*) A stringed instr. with a body shaped like that of a lute or guitar, and from 4 to 6 strings, only 2 of which are melody-strings, the others being merely drones tuned a fifth apart. The melody-strings (compass [notation] are stopped by about 2 [notation]) means of keys octaves: [notation] controlled by the left hand; the right hand turns a crank at the tail-end of the instr., which causes a rosined wheel impinging on all the strings to revolve, thus producing the harsh and strident tone. This wheel and the key-mechanism are contained in an oblong box corresponding to the neck of the lute, etc., but set directly on the belly, only the peg-box and head projecting beyond. The melody-strings pass through this box, and are attached to a tailpiece; the drones lie outside. The music produced is of the rudest description.

The hurdy-gurdy was in great vogue from the 10th to the 12th century.

Hur'tig (Ger.) Quick, brisk, swift; *presto.*

Hydrau'licon. An hydraulic organ.

Hydraulic organ. (Ger. *Was'serorgel;* Gk. *hydrau'los;* Lat. *or'ganum hydrau'-licum.*) A small kind of organ, inv. by Ktesibios of Alexandria (180 B. C.), in which the wind-pressure was regulated by water.

Hymn. (Ger. and Fr. *Hymne;* It. *in'no.*) A religious or sacred song; usually, a metrical poem to be sung by a congregation...In foreign usage, a national song of lofty character, such as the *Marseillaise.*

Hy'per (Gk.) Over, above; often occurs in compounds, as *hyperdiapa'son*, the octave above; *hyperdiapen'te*, the fifth above, etc...In the Greek transposing scales (see *Greek music*) *hyper* signified a fourth higher. (Lat. equivalent *super.*)

Hypercatalectic. In dipodic versification, a line having a redundant half-foot (either thesis or arsis) is thus termed; *hypercatalexis* being such state of redundancy.

Hy'po (Gk.) Under, below; frequent in compounds, as *hypodiapa'son*, the octave below, *hypodiapen'te*, the fifth below, *hypodit'onos*, the third below... In the Greek transposing scales (see *Greek music*) and the church-modes (see *Mode*), *hypo* signified a fourth below; in the ancient Greek modes, a fifth below. (Lat. equivalent *sub.*)

I.

I (It., masc. pl.) The.

Iam'bus. A metrical foot of 2 syllables, one short and one long, with the ictus on the long (⏑ —́).

Ias'tian. Same as *Ionian.*

Ic'tus. Accent or stress, either rhythmical or metrical.

Idea. A musical idea is a figure, motive, phrase or strain, with or without harmonic concomitants; also, a fully developed theme or subject.

Idée fixe (Fr.) Berlioz's term for an oft-recurring and characteristic idea or theme; a sort of leading-motive.

I'dyl. (Ger. and Fr. *Idyl'le;* It. *idil'lio.*) A composition of a pastoral or tenderly romantic character.

Il (It., masc. sing.) The.

Imboccatu'ra (It.) 1. Mouthpiece (of a wind-instr.)—2. *Lip* 2.

Imbro'glio (It.) "Embroilment, confusion". A passage in which the rhythm of the different parts is sharply contrasted and perplexing in effect.

Imitan'do (It.) Imitating.

Imitation. (Lat. *imita'tio;* Fr. *imitation;* It. *imitazio'ne;* Ger. *Nach'ahmung.*) The repetition of a motive, phrase or theme proposed by one part (the *antecedent*) in another part (the *consequent*), with or without modification...*I. at the fifth, octave*, etc., that in which the consequent follows the antecedent at the interval of a fifth, octave, etc...*I. by augmentation*, that in which the time-value of each note of the antecedent is increased according to a certain ratio in the consequent $(\quad=\quad$, or $\quad=\quad$. etc). ...*I. by diminution*, that in which the time-value of each note in the antecedent is decreased according to a certain ratio in the consequent $(\quad=\quad$ etc.)...*I. by inversion*, that in which each ascending interval of the antecedent is answered by a like descending interval in the consequent, and descending intervals by ascending ones. ...*Canonic i.*, strict imitation (see *Canon*)...*Free i.*, that in which certain modifications of the antecedent are permitted in the consequent (e. g. augmentation, diminution, reversed imitation, as explained above ; or when certain intervals are answered by others, the time-value of certain notes altered, etc.); opposed to *Strict imitation*, in which the consequent answers the antecedent note for note and interval for interval. ...*Retrograde i.*, that in which the theme is repeated backwards (*recte e retro*); see *Cancrizans.*

Im'mer (Ger.) Always ; continuously ; *immer stärker werdend*, continually growing louder ; *immer langsamer*, slower and slower ; *immer langsam*, slowly throughout.

Immuta'bilis (Lat.) One of the *accentus eccl.*

Impazien'te (It.) Impatient, restless, vehement...*Impazientemen'te*, impatiently, etc.

Imperfect cadence, consonance, interval, measure. See the nouns... *Imp. time*, see *Notation*, §3.

Imperfection. 1. See *Notation*, §3.— 2. In a ligature, the presence of a breve as final note, indicated by using the figura obliqua (◥).

Imperio'so,-a (It.) Imperious, haughty, lofty.

Im'peto (It) Impetuosity...*Con i.*, or *impetuosamen'te*, impetuously...*Impetuosità'*, impetuosity...*Impetuo'so, -a*, impetuous.

Implied discord. An interval which, though not itself dissonant, is contained within a dissonant chord ; e. g. a major third in ... *Implied interval* (in thorough-bass), an interval not indicated by a figure, but understood, e. g. the *sixth* and *fourth* in a chord of the second :

Imponen'te (It.) Imposing, impressive.

Impresa'rio (It.) The agent or manager of a traveling opera or concert-company.—Occasionally, an instructor of singers in opera or concert.

Impromp'tu. 1. An improvisation.— 2. A composition of loose and extemporaneous form and slight development ; a fantasia.

Imprope'ria (Lat., "reproaches".) In the Roman ritual, a series of antiphons and responses forming part of the solemn service substituted, on the morning of Good Friday, for the usual daily Mass.

Impropri'etas (Lat.) A term applied to a ligature when its first note is not a breve, but a long ; indicated, when the second note ascends, by a descending tail to the right or left of the first ; when the second note descends, by the absence of the tail. Opp. to *Proprietas*.

Improvisation. Extemporaneous musical performance.

Improviser (Fr.) To improvise...*Improvisateur (-trice)*, a male (female) improviser.

Improvisier'maschine (Ger.) A melograph.

Improvvisa're (It.) To improvise... *Improvvisamen'te*, extemporaneously. ...*Improvvisa'ta*, an improvisation, impromptu...*Improvvisato're (-tri'ce)*, a male (female) improviser...*All'improvvi'sta*, extempore.

In'betont (Ger.) With *mediate* accent. (See *Abbetont.*)

Incalzan'do (It.) "Pursuing hotly." See *Stringendo.*

Incarna'tus. Part of the Credo. See *Mass.*

Inch of Wind. See *Weight.*

Inchoa'tio (Lat.) The introductory tones or intonation of a plain-song chant.

Incomplete stop. A partial stop (organ).

Incrociamen'to (It.) Crossing.

Indeci'so (It.) Undecided.

Independent chord, harmony, triad. One which is consonant (i. e. contains no dissonance), and is therefore not obliged to change to another by progression or resolution ; opp. to *Dependent.*

Index. Same as *Direct.*

Indifferen'te (It.) Indifferent, careless. ..*Indifferentemen'te,* or *con indifferen'za,* indifferently, etc.

Inferna'le (It.) Infernal, hellish.

Infinite canon. (It. *ca'none infini'to.*) See *Canone.*

Inflati'lia (Lat.) Inflatile or wind-instruments.

Infrabass' (Ger.) Subbass.

Ingan'no (It.) Deceit...*Caden'za d'inganno,* deceptive cadence.

Ingres'sa. Name of the Introit in the Ambrosian rite.

In'halt (Ger.) Contents , idea, conception ; subject-matter.

Inharmonic relation. See *False relation.*

Inner parts. Parts lying between the highest and lowest...*Inner pedal,* a pedal-point in such part or parts.

In'nig (Ger.) Heartfelt, sincere ; fervent, intense ; with deep, true feeling ; equivalent to It. *affettuo'so, con affet'- to; in'timo, intimis'simo...Mit in'- nigem Aus'druck,* with heartfelt expression...*In'nigkeit,* deep emotion or feeling, fervency, intensity...*In'niglich,* same as *Innig.*

In'no (It.) Hymn.

Innocen'te (It.) Natural, unaffected... *Innocentemen'te,* naturally, artlessly... *Innocen'za,* naturalness, artlessness, etc.

In no'mine (Lat., "in the name".) 1. A kind of motet or antiphon.—2. See *Fuga in nomine.*

Inquie'to (It.) Unrestful, restless.

Insensi'bile (It.) Imperceptible...*Insensibilmen'te,* insensibly.

Insisten'do (It.) Insistently, urgently, with strong stress. (Also *con insistenza.*)

In'ständig (Ger.) Urgent, pressing. (Also *adverb.*)

Instan'te (It.) Urgent, pressing...*Instantemen'te,* urgently, etc.

Instrument. (Ger. and Fr. *Instrument';* It. *instrumen'to, istrumen'to, stromen'- to, strumen'to.*) A list of the principal modern instruments is given opposite, according to Gevaert's classification ; the asterisk (*) indicates that the instr. is little used in the orchestra ; the brack. ets ([ ]), that it is obsolete, or nearly so

Instrument (Fr) *I. à archet,* bow-in. strument...*I. à cordes,* stringed instrument...*I. à percussion,* percussive instrument...*I. à vent,* wind-instrument.

Instrumentation. (Ger. *Instrumentie'- rung;* Fr. *instrumentation;* It. *istrumentazio'ne.*) The theory and practice of composing, arranging, or adapting music for a body of instruments of different kinds, especially for orchestra. (See *Orchestra, Orchestration.*)—*Instrumentierung* (Ger.) is a term also occasionally applied to pfte.-music to denote dynamic shading and variety of touch ; sometimes with reference to all, at others to single, parts.

Intavola're (It.) 1. To write out or copy in tablature or score.—2. To set to music...*Intavolatu'ra,* (*a*) tablature ; (*b*) notation ; (*c*) figured bass.

In'teger va'lor nota'rum (Lat.) "Integral value of the notes ", i. e. their absolute duration at an average tempo, a question of high importance before the invention of tempo-marks and the metronome. Michael Prætorius says (1620), that about 80 *tempora* (=breves, the tempus, or unit of measure, then being the breve ▄) should fill 7½ minutes, thus :

80 ▄ =7½ minutes

10⅜ ▄ =1 min.=10⅜ M.M.; hence

◇ =21⅓ M.M.; ◆ =42⅔ M.M.; and

♩ =85⅓ M.M. (♩=85⅓ M.M.)

[RIEMANN.

Intenziona'to (It.) With stress, emphasis.

Interlude. 1. An intermezzo.—2. An

CLASSIFIED LIST OF MUSICAL INSTRUMENTS.

I. Stringed Instruments.

A. Strings, rubbed
- a) by a bow
  - 1. with 4 strings — { Violin, Viola, Violoncello, Double-bass
  - 2. with more than 4 strings — { *Viola d'amore / [Viols, various]
- b) by a wheel turned by a crank — Hurdy-gurdy, Piano-violin

B. Strings, plucked
- a) by the fingers
  - 1. without fingerb. Harp
  - 2. with fingerboard *Guitar, *Mandolin, *Zither, [Lute]
- b) by a keyboard-mechanism — [Harpsichord]

C. Strings, percussed
- a) directly by the player — *Zimbalon (or Tympanon), xylophone
- b) by a keyboard-mechanism — Pianoforte

II. Wind-Instruments.

A. With mouth-hole
- a) lateral — Flutes, Piccolos, Fife
- b) whistle-like — [Flûtes à bec], *Flageolet

B. With reed
- a) cylindrical tube + beating reed — { [Chalumeau], clarinets, *alt-clarinet (basset-horn), bass-cl.
- b) conical tube + beating reed — Saxophones, *octavin
- c) conical tube + double reed — { Oboe,*hautbois d'amour, alt-oboe or cor anglais / *Sarrusophones / Bassoon, quint-bassoon, double-bassoon

C. With mouthpiece
- a) natural — { Horn, natural / Trumpet, natural / *Post-horn / *Bugle, military
- b) chromatic
  - 1. with slide — Trombones, slide-trumpet / [Cornetto, Serpent]
  - 2. with holes (keys) — { *Key-bugle, or key-trumpet / *Ophicleide
  - 3. with valves (pistons) — { Valve-horn / Valve-trumpet / Valve-trombone, (*alto, tenor, *bass) / Cornet à pistons / Valve-bugles or saxhorns ; Tubas or saxhorns

D. Polyphonic
- a) without keyboard ....
- b) with keyboard
  - 1. with tubes — Organ
  - 2. without tubes — Harmonium, *Vocalion

III. Instruments of Percussion.

A. With a membrane
- a) with tones of determinate pitch — Kettledrums
- b) with tones of indeterm. pitch — Bass drum, side-drum, etc.

B. Autophonic
- a) with tones of determinate pitch — Bells, carillons, Glockenspiel
- b) with tones of indeterm. pitch — { Triangle, cymbals, tam-tam, castanets, etc.

instrumental strain or passage connecting the lines or stanzas of a hymn, etc. —3. An instrumental piece played between certain portions of the church service (Lat. *interlu'dium*).

Intermède (Fr.) 1. Interlude 1.—2. An operetta in one act.

Interme'dio (It., dimin. *intermediet'to*.) Interlude 2.

Intermez'zo (It.) *Intermezzi* were originally short mus. entr'actes in the Italian tragedies, of a very simple description, and quite independent of each other ; towards the end of the 16th century they assumed larger proportions ; finally they were treated as separate parts of a whole mus. drama, of a less serious cast than the principal work which they were intended to embellish, their acts alternating with those of the latter.—

Having reached this stage, they merely had to be detached from the larger work to form a self-existent *operetta* or *opera buffa*.—Instrumental music sometimes takes the place of the old *intermezzi* in modern dramas (e. g. that to the "Midsummer-night's Dream," by Mendelssohn)...The term *intermezzo* is also technically applied to many short movements connecting the main divisions of a symphony or other extended work ; sometimes to entire long movements, or even to independent compositions... *Intermez'zi* in the Suite are such dances (movements) as do not form one of its regular constituent parts, but are occasionally introduced for variety's sake, and usually between Sarabande and Gigue.

Interrogati'vus. One of the *accentus eccl.*

Interrot'to (It.) Interrupted...*Inter-ruzio'ne*, interruption.

Interval. (Lat. *interval'lum ;* Ger. *In-tervall' ;* Fr. *intervalle ;* It. *interval'lo.*) The difference in pitch between 2 tones. —For naming the various intervals there are 2 systems in vogue ; both are founded upon and derived from the names of the intervals formed, in the diatonic major scale, between the key-note and the successive ascending de-grees ; in both the 1st degree is called a *Prime* (or *First*), the 2nd a *Second*, the 3rd a *Third* (or *Tierce*), 4th a *Fourth* (or *Quart*), 5th a *Fifth* (or *Quint*), 6th a *Sixth* (or *Sext*), 7th a *Seventh* (or *Sept*), and the 8th an *Octave* (or *Eighth*). In the typical scale of *C*-major the standard intervals are as follows, counting upward from the key-note, *C :*

(*TABLE I.*)

(1) The older system, that in general use, will be explained first ; premising, that intervals are always considered as measured *upwards* from the lower tone to the higher, unless expressly accom-panied with the epithet *below* or *lower.* Table III includes the standard inter-vals and their direct derivatives between

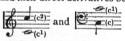

Table III shows (*A*) that each *major* or *perfect* interval, when widened by a semitone, becomes *augmented ;* that each *major* interval, narrowed by a semitone, becomes *minor;* and that each *minor* or *perfect* interval, narrowed by a semitone, becomes *diminished ;* (*B*) that by inverting the intervals :

```
      1  2  3  4  5  6  7  8
      8  7  6  5  4  3  2  1
a Perfect    interval becomes perfect
a Major         "       "     minor
a Minor         "       "     major
an Augmented    "       "     diminished
a Diminished    "       "     augmented ;
```

(*C*) the regular order of the standard intervals according to their pitch (com-pare *Vibration*), both in *Just Intona-tion* and *Equal Temperament*, inter-vals bracketted together being Enhar-

monic ; (*D*) the division of the Octave in Equal Temperament.

(2) In the newer system, all the standard intervals are called *major;* any *major* interval widened by a semi-tone becomes *augmented*, if narrowed by a semitone, it is *minor ;* and any *minor* interval narrowed by a semitone becomes *diminished :*

(*TABLE II.*)

Inter-vals.	Ma-jor.	Aug-mented.	Minor.	Diminished.
Second...	C—D	C—D♯	C—D♭	C—D♭♭ or C♯—D♭
Third...	—E	—E♯	—E♭	—E♭♭
Fourth..	—F	—F♯	—F♭	—F♭♭
Fifth....	—G	—G♯	—G♭	—G♭♭
Sixth....	—A	—A♯	—A♭	—A♭♭
Seventh.	—B	—B♯	—B♭	—B♭♭
Octave..	—C	—C♯	—C♭	—C♭♭

The latter system is simpler and more consistent than the old, and might be advantageously substituted for it if all leading musicians in England and America would agree to adopt it ; other-wise, its occasional use can serve only to increase the confusion unhappily pre-vailing in English musical terminology. In this Dictionary the older system is adhered to throughout. An interval is : —*Augmented*, when wider by a chroma-tic semitone than major or perfect... *Chromatic*, when occurring between a key-tone and a tone foreign to the key. ..*Compound*, when wider than an oc-tave ; thus a Ninth is an Octave plus a Second, a Tenth is an Octave plus a Third, etc... *Consonant*, when not re-quiring resolution (comp. *Consonance*). ..*Diatonic*, when occurring between 2 tones belonging to the same key (ex-ceptions, the *augm.* 2nd and 5th of the harmonic minor scale)... *Dimin-ished*, when a chromatic semitone nar-rower than minor or perfect... *Disso-nant*, when requiring resolution (comp. *Dissonance*)... *Enharmonic*, when both its tones, though having different letter-names, are represented by one and the same tone on an instr. of fixed intona-tion. . .*Extreme*, see *Augmented.* . . *Flat*, see *Diminished.* . .*Harmonic*, when both tones are sounded together... *Imperfect*, see *Diminished*...*Inverted*, when the higher tone is lowered, or the lower tone raised, by an octave (see Table I)...*Major ;* according to Table I, the major intervals of the major scale are the Second, Third, Sixth, and Seventh ; acc. to Table II, all its inter-vals are major...*Melodic*, when the 2 tones are sounded in succession...

B. Inverted Intervals.	(*TABLE III.*) A. Standard Intervals.	C. Vibrational Ratio in Just Intonation.	C. Vibrational Ratio in Tempered Intonation.	D. Division of Octave in Equal Temperament.
Perfect Octave (1 : 2)	Perfect Prime	1 : 1	1 : 1	0.00000
Dimin. Octave (25 : 48)	Augm. Prime (Chromatic Second)*	128 : 135	} $1 : 1\frac{1}{12}$	0.08333
Major Seventh (8 : 15)	Minor Second (Step of Leading-tone)	15 : 16		
Minor Seventh (9 : 16)	Major Second†	8 : 9	$1 : 1\frac{1}{6}$	0.16666
Dimin. Seventh (75 : 128)	Augm. Second	64 : 75	} $1 : 1\frac{1}{4}$	0.25
Major Sixth (3 : 5)	Minor Third	5 : 6		
Minor Sixth (5 : 8)	Major Third	4 : 5	} $1 : 1\frac{1}{3}$	0.33333
Augm. Fifth (16 : 25)	Dimin. Fourth	25 : 32		
Dimin. Sixth (675 : 1024)	Augm. Third	512 : 675	} $1 : 1\frac{5}{12}$	0.41666
Perfect Fifth (2 : 3)	Perfect Fourth	3 : 4		
Dimin. Fifth (25 : 36)	Augm. Fourth	18 : 25	} $1 : 1\frac{1}{2}$	0.5
Augm. Fourth (18 : 25)	Dimin. Fifth	25 : 36		
Perfect Fourth (3 : 4)	Perfect Fifth	2 : 3	$1 : 1\frac{7}{12}$	0.58333
Dimin. Fourth (25 : 32)	Augm. Fifth	16 : 25	} $1 : 1\frac{2}{3}$	0.66666
Major Third (4 : 5)	Minor Sixth	5 : 8		
Minor Third (5 : 6)	Major Sixth	3 : 5	$1 : 1\frac{3}{4}$	0.75
Dimin. Third (225 : 256)	Augm. Sixth	128 : 225	} $1 : 1\frac{5}{6}$	0.83333
Major Second (8 : 9)	Minor Seventh	9 : 16		
Minor Second (15 : 16)	Major Seventh	8 : 15	} $1 : 1\frac{11}{12}$	0.91666
Augm. Prime (128 : 135)	Dimin. Octave	25 : 48		
Perfect Prime (1 : 1)	Perfect Octave	1 : 2	1 : 2	1.00000

* The *greater* chromatic Second ; the *lesser* (e. g. d–d♯) is 24 : 25.
† The *greater* whole tone ; the *lesser* (e. g. d–e) is 9 · 10.

Minor, when a chromatic semitone narrower than major or perfect...*Perfect:* the Prime, Fourth, Fifth, and Octave. ..*Redundant*, see *Augmented.* *Sharp*, see *Augmented*...*Simple*, when not wider than the Octave...*Superfluous*, see *Augmented.*

In'timo, Intimis'simo (It.) Compare *Innig.*

Intona're (It.) To intone.

Intonation. 1. The production of tone, either instrumental or vocal, especially the latter ; when applied to the pitch of the tone produced, it is said to be correct, pure, just, true, etc., in opposition to incorrect, impure, false.—2. The method of chanting employed in Plain Song.—3. The opening notes leading up to the reciting-tone of a chant... *Fixed intonation*, see *Fixed.*

In'tonator. See *Monochord* 1.

Intonatu'ra, Intonazio'ne (It.) Intonation ; pitch.

Intonie'ren (Ger.) To intone ; also, to voice (as organ-pipes) ; voicing.

Intra'da. (It. *intra'ta, entra'ta ;* Ger. *Intra'de ;* Fr. *entrée.*) 1. An instrumental prelude or overture, especially the pompous introduction to the earlier dramas and operas ; hence applied to opening movements of various descriptions. —2. See *Entrée.*

Intre'pido,-a (It.) Bold...*Intrepidamen'te*, boldly...*Intrepidez'za*, boldness.

Introduction. A phrase or division preliminary to and preparatory of a composition or movement ; may vary in length from a short strain up to an extended and independent movement. (It. *introduzio'ne.*)

Intro'it. (Lat. *intro'itus*, " entrance"; It. *intro'ito.*) An antiphon sung while the priest is approaching the altar to celebrate the Mass ; formerly an entire psalm, but abbreviated later.—In the modern Anglican Church, an anthem or psalm.

Invention. A short piece in free contrapuntal style, developing one motive in an impromptu fashion. (Comp. Bach's 30 Inventions.)

Inversion. 1. (Ger. *Um'kehrung ;* Fr. *renversement;* It. *riversamen'to, rivol'to.*) The transposition of the notes forming an interval or a fundamental chord : —(*A*) A *simple interval* is inverted by setting its lower note an octave higher,

or its higher note an octave lower (see *Interval*); *compound* intervals must first be reduced to simple ones, and then inverted :—(*B*) A *chord* is inverted when its lowest note is not the root ; thus any triad has 2 inversions, e. g.:

a is the fundamental position; *b*, *1st inversion*, or chord of the sixth ; *c*, *2nd inversion*, or chord of the fourth and sixth ;--a chord of the seventh has 3 inversions, e. g.:

a, fund. position ; *b*, *1st inversion*, or chord of the fifth and sixth ; *c*, *2nd inversion*, or chord of the third and fourth; *d*, *3rd inversion*, or chord of the second. —2. In double counterpoint, the transposition of 2 parts, the higher being set below the lower, or vice versa; this transposition may be by an octave or some other interval, and is technically termed " inversion in the octave ","in the fifth", " in the tenth ", etc.—3. The repetition of a theme in contrary motion, ascending intervals being answered by descending ones, and vice versa ; also called *imitation in contrary motion*, or *imitation by inversion.*—4. An organ-point is termed inverted when in some other part than the lowest.

Invi'tatory. (Lat. *invitato'rium*.) In the R. C. Church, the variable antiphon to the Venite, at matins ;—in the Greek Church, the triple " O come, let us worship ", preceding the psalm at each of the canonical hours ;—in the Anglican Church, the versicle " Praise ye the Lord " with the response " the Lord's name be praised ", at matins.

Ionian. See *Mode.*

I'ra (It.) Wrath, passion ; *con ira*, wrathfully, passionately...*Ira'to*, wrathful, passionate.

Irlandais,-e (Fr) Hibernian, Irish.

Iro'nico,-a (It.) Ironical...*Ironicamen'te*, ironically.

Irregular cadence. See *Cadence.*

Irresolu'to (It.) Irresolute, undecided, hesitating.

Isorrhyth'mic. (Ger. *isorrhyth'misch.*)

In prosody, an *isorr. foot* is one divisible into 2 parts containing an equal number of rhythmic units, i. e. one having thesis and arsis of equal length ; as the dactyl (—ᵕ ᵕ), anapest (ᵕ ᵕ —), and spondee (— —).

Istes'so tempo, l' (It.) " The same tempo " (or time) ; signifies (1) that the tempo of either the measure or measurenote remains as before, after a change of time-signature ; or (2) that a movement previously interrupted is to be resumed. (Also *Lo stesso tempo*.)

Istrumen'to (It.) Instrument...*Istrumenti a piz'zico* (Ger. *Kneif'instrumente*), stringed instr.s plucked with fingers or plectrum...*Istrumentazio'ne*, instrumentation.

Italian sixth. See *Extreme.*

Italien,-ne (Fr.) Italian ; *à l'italienne*, in the Italian style.

I'te, mis'sa est. See *Mass.*

J.

Jack. 1. In the harpsichord and clavichord, an upright slip of wood on the rear end of the key-lever, carrying (in the former) a bit of crow-quill set at a right angle so as to pluck or twang the string, or (in the latter) a metallic tangent.—2. In the pfte., the escapement-lever, usually called the *hopper* or *grasshopper.*

Jagd'horn (Ger.) Hunting-horn...*Jagd'stück*, hunting-piece.

Jä'gerchor (Ger.) Hunters' chorus ; hunting-chorus.

Jale'o (Span.) A Spanish national dance for one performer, in 3-8 time and moderate tempo.

Jalousie'schweller (Ger.) The " Venetian-blind " swell. See *Swell.*

Jan'izary music. (Ger. *Janitscha'renmusik*, music for triangle, cymbals, and bass drum.) According to GROVE, the Janizary band " contained 1 large and 3 small oboes, and 1 piccolo flute, all of very shrill character ; 1 large and 2 small kettledrums, one big and 3 small long drums, 3 cymbals, and 2 triangles".

Jankó keyboard. See *Keyboard.*

Jeu (Fr.) 1. Style of playing.—2 (pl. *jeux*). A stop of an organ, harmonium, harpsichord, etc...*Jeu à bouche*, flue-stop. ..*Jeu céleste*, see *Céleste*...*Jeu d'anche*, reed-stop...*Jeu d'ange*, vox angelica.

..*Jeu de flûtes*, flute-stop...*Jeu de mutation*, (*a*) mutation-stop ; (*b*) mixture-stop...*Jeu de timbres*, Glockenspiel... *Jeu de violes*, consort of viols...*Jeu de voix humaine*, vox humana...*Grand jeu, plein jeu*, full organ ; full power. ..*Demi-jeu*, half power.

Jew's-harp. (Ger. *Maultrommel;* Fr. *trompe, guimbarde ;* It. *trom'ba.*) A small instr. with a rigid iron frame, within which is adjusted a thin, vibratile metallic tongue ; the frame is held between the teeth, and the metallic tongue, being plucked with the finger, produces tones reinforced in loudness and determined in pitch by the cavity (air-space) of the mouth.—Formerly also *jew's-trump, trump, tromp.*

Jig. (Fr. and Ger. *Gigue;* It. *gi'ga.*) A species of country-dance, though with all conceivable modifications of step and gesture, usually in triple or compound time, and in rapid tempo.—In the Suite, the *Gigue* is generally the last movement.

Jingles. The disks of metal attached at intervals to the hoop of the tambourine.

Jocula'tor (Lat.) See *Jongleur.*

Jo'deln (*verb*), **Jo'dler** (*noun*) (Ger.) A favorite style of singing among the inhabitants of the Alps, characterized by a frequent and unprepared alternation of falsetto tones with those of the chest-register. A *Jodler* is a song or refrain sung as above.

Jongleur (Fr.) A wandering minstrel in medieval France, and also in England under the Norman kings ; later, a juggler or mountebank.

Jo'ta (Span.) A national dance of northern Spain, danced by couples, in triple time and rapid movement, somewhat resembling a waltz, though with innumerable extempore and fantastic variations of step, and accompanied by the castanets and mandolin, with vocal interludes.

Jouer (Fr.) To play (any instrument) ; used with *de, du, de l'.*

Jour (Fr., " day.") A *corde à jour* is an open string.

Ju'ba. A dance of the negroes in the Southern States, forming an essential feature of the breakdown.

Ju'bal. (Ger.) An organ-stop of either 2 or 4-foot pitch.

Ju'belhorn (Ger.) See *Klappenhorn.*

Jubila'te. In the Anglican liturgy, the 100th psalm, following the second lesson in the morning service; named from the first word of the psalm in the Vulgate.

Jubila'tio (Lat.) In the R. C. musical service, the melodic cadence or coda on the last syllable of "alleluia"; also *Jubilus.*

Ju'bilus (Lat.) 1. Same as *Jubilatio.*—2. An extended melodic phrase or ornament sung to one vowel.

Ju'la (Ger.) An obsolete 5⅓-foot organ-stop.

Jump. 1. See *Dump.*—2. A leap.

Jung'fernregal or *Jung'fernstimme* (Ger.) Vox angelica. (Lat. also *vox virginea.*)

Jupiter Symphony. Mozart's 49th (and last) symphony, in *C*-major.

Juste (Fr.) Just, true, accurate (said of intonation)...*Justesse,* purity (of tone); correctness, accuracy (of ear or voice).

K.

Kadenz' (Ger.) Cadence; close; cadenza...*Ab'gebrochene K.,* interrupted cadence...*Auf'gehaltene K.,* the fermata (usually on the ⁶₄ chord) before a cadenza...*Plagal'kadenz,* plagal cadence...*Trug'kadenz,* deceptive cadence...*Un'vollkommene (voll'kommene) K.,* imperfect (perfect) cadence.—Also frequently *Schluss* (close), which see.

Kalama'ika. A Hungarian national dance in 2-4 time and rapid tempo, of an animated and passionate character.

Kalkant' (Ger.) A "bellows-treader" of the older German organs...*Kalkan'-tenglocke,* bell-signal for the blower.

Kam'mer (Ger., imitating It. *camera.*) A private room or small hall...*Kam'-merkantate,* chamber-cantata...*Kam'-merkomponist,* court-composer (for a prince's private band)...*Kam'merkonzert,* (a) chamber-concert, (b) chamber-concerto...*Kam'mermusik,* chamber-music...*Kam'mermusiker,* court-musician...*Kam'mersänger,* court-singer. ..*Kam'merstil,* the style of chamber-music...*Kam'merton,* normal or standard orchestral pitch (now *a¹*=435); see *Chorton*...*Kam'mervirtuos,* court-virtuoso.

Ka'non (Ger.) Canon.

Kanta'te (Ger.) Cantata.

Kanun'. A sort of Turkish dulcimer or zither with gut strings, played with plectra adjusted like thimbles on the finger-tips.

Kanzel'le (Ger.) Groove (in windchest.)

Kanzo'ne (Ger.) Canzone.

Kapel'le (Ger.) 1. Especially in the 18th century, a company of musicians, either instrumentalists or vocalists, or both, maintained as part of the establishment of a court or nobleman, or of some church dignitary.—2. In modern usage, an orchestra...*Kapell'knabe,* choir-boy...*Kapell'meister,* (a) conductor of an orchestra; (b) *Choir-master.* (Sometimes literally translated *chapel-master.*) ..*Kapell'meistermusik,* "band-master music", i. e. music filled with reminiscences from works familiar to the conductor-composer, and hence the reverse of original.

Kapodas'ter (Ger.) Capotasto.

Kassation' (Ger.) Cassazione.

Kastagnet'ten (Ger., pl.) Castanets.

Katalek'tisch (Ger.) Catalectic.

Ka'tzenmusik (Ger., "cat-music".) A callithumpian concert, mock serenade.

Kavati'ne (Ger.) Cavatina.

Kazoo'. A musical (?) toy, consisting of a pasteboard tube furnished with a gut string, which vibrates when the performer sings into the tube.

Keck (Ger.) Bold, confident; pert. (Also *adverb.*)...*Keck'heit,* boldness, confidence.

Keh'le (Ger.) Throat...*Kehl'fertigkeit,* vocal skill...*Kehl'kopf,* larynx. ..*Kehl'schlag* (Fr. *coup de glotte*), sudden, firm attack of a vocal tone, the vocal cords closing and adjusting themselves simultaneously with the emission of air.

Kehrab', Kehraus' (Ger.) Familiar term for the concluding dance at a party or ball.

Ken'ner (Ger.) A connoisseur, expert.

Kent bugle. (Ger. *Kenthorn.*) Key-bugle.

Kerau'lophon. In the organ, an 8-foot partial flue-stop, having metal pipes of small scale, each surmounted by an adjustable ring, and with a hole bored near the top; the tone is soft and reedy. Inv. by Gray and Davidson of England.

Keren. A Hebrew trumpet.

Kes'sel (Ger.) Cup (in mouthpiece of brass instr.s)...*Kes'selpauke*, kettledrum (usually simply *Pauke*).

Ket'tentriller (Ger.) Chain of trills.

Kettledrum. (Ger. *Pau'ke;* Fr. *timbale;* It. *tim'pano.*) The only orchestral drum tuned to accord with other instruments. It consists of a hollow brass or copper hemisphere (the *kettle*) resting on a tripod, with a *head* of vellum stretched by means of an iron *ring* and tightened by a set of *screws* or a system of *cords* and *braces*. It is generally played in pairs, the larger drum yielding any tone from *F* to *c*, and the smaller accord-from , ing as *Bb* to *f*: the head is relaxed or tightened. The *timpani* were formerly noted as transposing instr.s (i. e. in *C*, with the added direction " Timpani in *Eb*, in *Db*," etc.), but now the notes desired are generally written. As used at first, they took only the tonic and dominant of the movement, chiefly as a rhythmical reinforcement ; now they take very various intervals, and are employed to obtain musical and dramatic effects. They are struck with 2 sticks having elastic handles and soft knobs of felt, sponge, and the like.

Key (1). (Ger. *Ton'art;* Fr. *mode, ton;* It. *mo'do, to'no.*) The series of tones forming any given major or minor scale, considered with special reference to their harmonic relations, particularly the relation of the other tones to the tonic, or key-note ; the term " scale" indicates simply their melodic succession. (Comp. *Tonality.*) Each key is named after its key-note, as *C*-major, *a*-minor. See General View, page 108. The following keys :

{ *C*-sharp maj.[=*D*-flat maj.]
{ *A*-sharp min.[=*B*-flat min.]

{ *C*-flat maj.[=*B*-major]
{ *A*-flat min.[=*G*-sharp min.]

are comparatively little used, being enharmonically equivalent to the simpler keys added in brackets...*Attendant keys*, see *Attendant*...*Chromatic key*, one having sharps or flats in the signature ; opp. to *natural* key...*Extreme*

key, a remote key...*Major key*, one having a major third and major sixth. ..*Minor key*, one having a minor third and sixth...*Natural key*, one with neither sharps nor flats in the signature. ..*Parallel key*, (*a*) a minor key with the same key-note as the given major key, or vice versa ; (*b*) same as—*Relative key*, see *Relative*...*Remote key*, an indirectly related key (comp. *Phone*, §4).

Key (2). (Ger. *Tas'te ;* Fr. *touche ;* It. *ta'sto.*) 1. A digital or finger-lever in a pfte., organ, etc.—2. A pedal or footkey in the organ and pedal-piano.

Key (3). (Ger. *Klap'pe ;* Fr. *clé, clef ;* It. *chia've.*) In various wind-instr.s, a mechanical contrivance for opening or closing a hole in the side of the tube, thus shortening or lengthening the vibrating air-column and consequently raising or lowering the pitch of the tone produced. The key here replaces the finger-tip ; it is attached to a lever worked by the finger or thumb, and differs in principle from the *valve* in lying flat outside the tube.

Key (4). A tuning-key.

Key (5). A clef. (Obsolete.)

Key-action. In the pfte. or organ, the entire mechanism connected with and set in action by the keys, including the latter themselves.

Keyboard. (Ger. *Klaviatur';* Fr. *clavier ;* It. *tastatu'ra, tastie'ra.*) The keys or digitals of the pfte., organ, etc., taken collectively. The modern standard keyboard is the product of an evolution extending over 1,000 years.—Its only successful rival at present is the **Jankó keyboard**, inv. by Paul von Jankó of Totis, Hungary, in 1882, which presents to the eye the appearance of six different rows of keys arranged stepwise, one above the other. But the corresponding keys in the 1st, 3rd, and 5th rows are all fixed on one key-lever ; thus, if *C* be struck in the 1st (lowest) row, the corresponding keys in the 3rd and 5th rows are depressed ; further, the 2nd, 4th, and 6th rows are similarly connected ; so that any given tone can be struck in three different places, admitting of the choice of the key most convenient to the position of the hand at any given instant. The 6 rows are therefore arranged in 3 pairs ; in the lower row of any pair the succession of

GENERAL VIEW OF THE KEYS.

Key-signature.	English.	German.	French.	Italian.	
	C-major A-minor	C dur A moll	Ut majeur La mineur	Do maggiore La minore	} Natural keys.
	G-major E-minor	G dur E moll	Sol majeur Mi mineur	Sol maggiore Mi minore	
	D-major B-minor	D dur H moll	Ré majeur Si mineur	Re maggiore Si minore	
	A-major F-sharp minor	A dur Fis moll	La majeur Fa dièse mineur	La maggiore Fa diesis minore	
	E-major C-sharp minor	E dur Cis moll	Mi majeur Ut dièse mineur	Mi maggiore Do diesis minore	} Sharp keys.
	B-major G-sharp minor	H dur Gis moll	Si majeur Sol dièse mineur	Si maggiore Sol diesis minore	
	F-sharp major D-sharp minor	Fis dur Dis moll	Fa dièse majeur Ré dièse mineur	Fa diesis maggiore Re diesis minore	
	G-flat major E-flat minor	Ges dur Es moll	Sol bémol majeur Mi bémol mineur	Sol bemolle maggiore Mi bemolle minore	
	D-flat major B-flat minor	Des dur B moll	Ré bémol majeur Si bémol mineur	Re bemolle maggiore Si bemolle minore	
	A-flat major F-minor	As dur F moll	La bémol majeur Fa mineur	La bemolle maggiore Fa minore	} Flat keys.
	E-flat major C-minor	Es dur C moll	Mi bémol majeur Ut mineur	Mi bemolle maggiore Do minore	
	B-flat major G-minor	B dur G moll	Si bémol majeur Sol mineur	Si bemolle maggiore Sol minore	
	F-major D-minor	F dur D moll	Fa majeur Ré mineur	Fa maggiore Re minore	

---

keys is *C D E* [white] *F♯ G♯ A♯* [black] *c* [white], etc.; in the upper row : *C♯ D♯* [black] *F G A B* [white] *c♯* [black], etc.:

upper row of keys (in pair) **C♯ D♯** F G A B c♯
lower " " " " " C D E F♯ G♯ A♯ c.

Consequently, a chromatic scale is played by the simple alternation between the successive keys of any 2 adjoining rows ; the fingering of all the major scales is uniform, and all minor scales are also fingered alike. The width of an octave on the ordinary keyboard is just that of a tenth on this ; so that large hands can stretch a thirteenth, or even a fourteenth (*c¹–b²♭*).

Key-bugle. See *Bugle.*

Key-chord. The tonic triad.

Keyed violin. A piano-violin.

Key-fall. See *Dip.*

Key-harp. (Fr. *clavi-harpe.*) An instr. resembling a pfte. in form, and with a similar keyboard, but having a set of tuning-forks in lieu of strings. Inv. in 1819 by Dietz and Second. (Comp. *Klaviatur-Harfe.*)

Key-note. The tonic.

Keyship. Tonality.

Key-signature. See *Signature.*

Key-stop. A key (digital) attached to the fingerboard of a violin so as to replace the fingers in stopping the strings; the instr. is then called a *key-stop* (or *keyed-stop*) *violin.* (Comp. *Klavier-Violoncello.*)

Key-tone. Same as key-note.

Key-trumpet. A trumpet provided with keys.

Kicks (Ger.) The " goose ".

Kin. An ancient Chinese instr., consisting of a soundboard with 2 bridges, over which silk strings varying in number from 5 to 25 are stretched ; they are plucked with the fingers.

Kin'derscenen (Ger.) Scenes of Childhood (Schumann)... *Kin'derstücke,* pieces for children.

Kind'lich (Ger.) Childlike ; with fresh, naïve effect.

King. An ancient Chinese instr., consisting of a graduated series of 16 sonorous stones (or plates of metal), suspended by cords and struck with a mallet.

Kir'chenmusik (Ger.) Church-music. ..*Kir'chenton* (pl.-*töne*), a church-mode... *Kir'chenstil,* (*a*) the style of harmonic progression peculiar to the medieval church-modes ; (*b*) the style of sacred music.

Kis'sar. The 5-stringed Abyssinian lyre.

Kit. (Ger. *Ta'schengeige ;* Fr. *pochette ;* It. *sordi'no.*) The small old-fashioned violin used by dancing-masters, with the accordatura *c¹-g¹-d²,* and about 16 inches in length over all.

Ki'thara (Gk.) A harp-like instr. of the ancient Greeks ; ancestor (in name) of the guitar, cithern, zither, etc.

Klang (Ger.) 1. A sound.—2. A composite musical tone (a fundamental tone with its harmonics) ; rendered by Tyndall " clang ".—3. See *Phone,* §1... *Klang'boden,* soundboard (usually *Resonanz'boden*... *Klang'farbe,* " clang-tint ", " tone-color ", quality of tone. ..*Klang'folge,* a progression of chords, viewed from the standpoint of their tonality... *Klang'figuren,* Chladni's figures ; see *Nodal lines*... *Klang'geschlecht,* mode.. .*Klang'schlüssel,* see *Phone,* §6... *Klang'stufe,* degree ; interval... *Klang'vertretung,* see *Phone,*

§3...*Klang'verwandschaft,* chord-relationship.

Klap'pe (Ger.) Key 3...*Klap'penhorn,* key-bugle.

Klarinet'te (Ger.) Clarinet.

Klau'sel (Ger.) Clausula, cadence... *Bass'klausel,* the dominant-tonic skip of the bass at the close.

Klaväoli'ne (Ger.) See *Æolodicon.*

Klavi- (Ger.) See *Clavi-.*

Klaviatur' (Ger.) Keyboard...*Klaviatur-Harfe* (or *Klavier-Harfe*), a piano-harp, i. e. a harp with piano-keyboard, inv. 1893 by Ignaz Lutz of Vienna ; the strings are plucked or twanged by plectra (in lieu of hammers) actuated by the digitals ; the effect closely resembles that of the double-action harp, the tone being even fuller. ..*Klaviatur-Zither,* piano-zither, i. e. a small pfte. in grand shape, the *single* strings of which are twanged by playing on the keyboard ; inv. 1893 by Ignaz Lutz of Vienna.

Klavier' (Ger.) 1. A keyboard.—2. A keyboard stringed instr.; specifically, in the 18th century, a clavichord ; now, a pfte. of any kind...*Klavier'auszug,* (*a*) pfte -arrangement; (*b*) vocal score ..; *Klavier-Harmonium,* a combined pfte and harmon. ; inv. 1893 by F. Woronecki of Przemysl, Galicia, is shaped like a small grand piano, the harmonium-mechanism being attached below and behind the body and controlled by from 5 to 10 draw-stops...*Klavier'hoboe,* harmoniphon...*Klavier'mässig,* suitable for the pfte., in pfte.-style... *Klavier'-satz,* (music in) pfte.-style, pfte.-music, pfte.-writing. .*Klavier'spiel,* pfte.-playing...*Klavier-Violoncello,* the invention, in 1893, of Prof. de Vlaminck of Brussels. To a 'cello, fixed on a horizontal frame about the height of the knee, a keyboard is attached in such a manner, above the strings, that by manipulating it the player's left hand can effect all stops and double-stops. With the bow, all the effects on the 'cello as ordinarily played are obtainable ; while purity of intonation is attained with mathematical accuracy by the aid of the tangents actuated by the keys ; even the *vibrato* effect can be brought out.— *Klavier-Viola,* a viola to which a key-mechanism similar to the foregoing is applied ; when played, it is set on a low table or stand.

Klein (Ger.) Small ; minor... *Klein'-gedackt*, flute (organ-stop).

Kling'ende Stim'men (Ger.) Speaking or sounding stops (of an organ) ; opp. to *stum'me Regis'ter.*

Knee-stop. A knee-lever under the manual of the reed-organ ; there are 3 kinds, used (*a*) to control the supply of wind ; (*b*) to open and shut the swell-box ; (*c*) to draw all the stops.

Kneif'instrument (Ger.) An instr. having strings plucked by the fingers or a plectrum.

Knie'geige (Ger.) Viola da gamba... *Knie'guitarre*, guitare d'amour.... *Knie'zug*, knee-stop.

Knopf'regal (Ger.) See *Apfelregal.*

Kno'te (Ger.) Node...*Kno'tenpunkt*, nodal point.

Kollektiv'zug (Ger.) Composition-pedal.

Kol'lern (Ger.) See *Sgallinacciare.*

Kolophon'. See *Colophony.*

Kombinations'pedal (Ger.) Combination-pedal...*Kombinations'ton*, combination-tone.

Komponie'ren (Ger.) To compose... *Komponiert'*, composed...*Komponist'*, composer.

Kon'trabass (Ger.) Double-bass...*Kon'trafagott*, double-bassoon...*Kon'traoktave*, contra-octave...*Kon'trapunkt*, counterpoint...*Kon'trasubjekt*, counter-subject.

Konzert' (Ger.) Concert ; concerto. (Also *Concert*.) . . . *Konzert'meister*, leader, first violin...*Konzert'oper*, a light opera for concert performance without stage-accessories...*Konzert'-stück*, (*a*) a short concerto in one movement and free form ; (*b*) any short solo piece for public performance.

Kopf'stimme (Ger.) Head-voice.

Kop'pel (Ger.) Coupler...*Koppel ab*, coupler off...*K. an*, draw coupler.

Kornett' (Ger.) Cornet.

Kosa'kisch (Ger.) A national dance of the Cossacks, the melody of which consists of 2 8-measure repeats in 2-4 time.

Ko'to. The Japanese zither-harp, with 13 silk strings stretched over an arching oblong soundboard, each having a separate movable bridge, by adjusting which the string can be tuned. Compass about 2 octaves. The player uses both hands ; the chromatic tones are produced by pressing the strings behind the bridges.

Kraft (Ger.) Force, vigor, energy.. *Kräf'tig*, forceful, vigorous. (Also *adverb*.)

Kra'gen (Ger.) Peg-box (of a lute).

Krakowiak. See *Cracovienne.*

Kräu'sel (Ger.) Mordent.

Krebs'gängig (Ger.) Cancrizans, retrograde...*Krebs'kanon*, canon cancrizans.

Krei'schend (Ger.) Harsh, strident ; screeching, screaming.

Kreuz (Ger., " a cross ".) A sharp (♯). ...*Kreuz'saitig*, overstrung...*Kreuz'-tonart*, a sharp key.

Krie'gerisch (Ger.) Martial, warlike.

Kriegs'lied (Ger.) War-song.

Kro'me (Ger.) Chroma.

Krumm'bogen (Ger.) Crook...*Krumm'-horn*, (*Kromphorn*, *Krumhorn*, hence Fr. *cromorne* and It. *cormorne* ; It. also *cornamu'to tor'to*, or, for short, *stor'to*.) 1. An obsolete wood-wind instr. of the Bombard class, blown by means of a double reed within a cupped mouthpiece, and differing from the bombards by the semi-circular turn of the lower part of the tube and by its remarkably narrow compass (a ninth). In the 16th century it was made in 3 or 4 different sizes, treble, alto, (tenor), and bass, and had 6 ventages on the straight part of the tube. The tone had a melancholy timbre, which was imitated—2. in the organ-stop of the same name (also *cormorne*, *cremona*, *phocinx*), formerly in vogue for small-sized organs and for the echo-work of larger ones (of 8 and 4-foot pitch, on the pedal also of 16-foot pitch as *Krumm'hornbass*) ; a reed-stop, the tubes of which were frequently half-covered, or conical below and cylindrical above. [RIEMANN.]

Krus'tische Instrumen'te (Ger.) See *Schlag'instrumente.*

Kuh'horn (Ger.) The alp-horn...*Kuh'-reigen*, *Kuh'reihen*, Ranz des vaches.

Kunst (Ger.) Art ; science...*Kunst'-fugue*, fuga ricercata...*Künst'ler*, artist. ..*Kunst'lied*, an *art*-song, opp. to *folk*-song (*Volkslied*)...*Kunst'pfeifer*, see *Stadtpfeifer.*

Kurz (Ger.) Short ; crisp(ly)...*Kur'zer Mor'dent*, short mordent...*Kur'ze Ok-*

ta've, short octave...*Kurz und be-stimmt'*, short and decided...*Kur'zer Vor'schlag*, short appoggiatura.

Ky'rie (Gk.,"Lord".) The first word, and hence the opening division, in the Mass.

L.

L. Abbr. for *left* (or Ger. *links*) in the direction *l. h.* (left hand).

La. 1. The 6th Aretinian syllable.—2. (Fr., It., etc.) The note *A.*—3. The (Fr., fem. sing.)...*La bémol*, etc., see *Key 1*, Table.

Labecedisa'tion. See *Bebisation*.

Labial'pfeife (Ger.) A labial (lipped) pipe ; a flue-pipe...*Labial'stimme*, a flue-stop.

Labisa'tion. Same as *Bebisation*.

La'bium (Lat.) Lip (of an organ-pipe). (Plural, in Ger. use, *La'bien*.)

Lacrimo'sa (Lat.) First word in the 8th strophe of the Requiem ; hence, name of a movement or division of the grand musical requiem, usually of a tender and plaintive character.

La'ge (Ger.) Position (of a chord); position, shift (in violin-playing)...*La'-genwechsel*, change of position, shifting. ..*Enge (weite) Lage*, close (open) harmony.

Lagriman'do (It.) Complainingly, plain-tively...*Lagrimo'so*, "tearful", plain-tive, in the style of a lament.

Lah. For *La*, in the Tonic Sol-fa system.

Lamenta'bile (lamentan'do, lamen-te'vole, lamento'so) (It.) In a sad, melancholy, or plaintive style.

Länd'ler (Ger.) A slow waltz of South Germany and Austria (whence the Fr. name *Tyrolienne*), in 3-4 or 3-8 time, and the rhythm

Lang'sam (Ger.) Slow, slowly...*Lang'-samer*, slower.

Language. In a flue-pipe of an organ, an inner partition between foot and body ; see *Pipe 1, a.*

Languen'do, Languen'te (It.) Lan-guishing, plaintive.

Languette (Fr.) 1. The tongue of a harp-sichord-jack, on which the quill was fixed.—2. Tongue of a reed in the harmonium or reed-organ.—3. Pallet

(in the organ).—4. Key (on wind-instr.s).

Languid. Same as *Language*.

Languidamen'te (It.) Languishingly, languidly...*Lan'guido*, languid, lan-guishing.

Lantum. A large kind of hurdy-gurdy, having a rotatory bellows which supplies wind to metallic reeds, and played by pressing buttons adjusted in front.

Lapid'eon. An instr. consisting of a series of flint-stones graduated to the tones of the scale, hung in a frame, and played with hammers ; inv. by Baudry.

Largamen'te (It.) Largely, broadly ; in a manner characterized by breadth of style without change of time. [GROVE.]

Largan'do (It.) "Growing broader", i. e. slower and more marked ; generally a crescendo is implied.

Large. See *Notation*, §3.

Large, Largement (Fr.) Largamente (Ger. *breit*); sostenuto (Ger. *getragen*).

Larghet'to (It.) Dimin. of *Largo;* calls for a somewhat quicker movement, nearly equivalent to *Andantino*.

Lar'go (It.; superl. *larghis'simo*.) Large, broad ; the slowest tempo-mark, calling for a slow and stately movement with ample breadth of style...*L. assa'i*, with due breadth and slowness...*L. di molto*, or *molto largo*, an intensification of *Largo*. . .*Poco largo*, "with some breadth"; can occur even during an *Allegro*.

Larigot (Fr.) Originally, a kind of shepherd's pipe, or flageolet ; hence, an organ-stop of $1\frac{1}{3}$ foot pitch, one of the shrillest registers.

Lau'da (Lat.) A laud (hymn or song of praise)...*Lau'des*, lauds ; together with matins, the first of the 7 canonical hours, taking its name from the 148th, 149th, and 150th Psalms then sung.

Lauf (Ger.) 1. See *Läufer*.—2. Peg-box (usually *Wir'belkasten*).

Läu'fer (Ger.) A run.

Lau'nig (Ger.) 1. With light, gay humor. —2. With facile, characteristic expres-sion.

Laut (Ger.) 1. Loud.—2. A sound.

Lau'te (Ger.) A lute...*Lau'tengeige*, a viol...*Lau'teninstrumente*, see *Knei'f'-instrumente*...*Lautenist'*, lute-player. ...*Lau'tenmacher*, see *Luthier*.

Lavol'ta (It.) An old Italian dance in triple time, resembling the waltz.

Lay. A melody or tune.

Le (Fr. and It.) The.

Lead. 1. The giving-out or proposition of a theme by one part.—2. A cue (comp. *Presa*).

Leader. 1. Conductor, director.—2. In the orchestra, the first violin ; in a band, the first cornet ; in a mixed chorus, the first soprano.—(In small orchestras the leader [1st violin] is still, as was the rule in earlier times, also the conductor.)

Leading. 1 (*noun*). In a composition, the melodic progression of any part or parts.—2 (*adjective*). Principal, chief; guiding, directing... *Leading-chord*, the dominant chord, as leading into that of the tonic... *Leading melody*, principal melody or theme... *Leading-motive*, see *Leitmotiv*... *Leading-note*, *-tone* (Ger. *Leit'ton;* Fr. *note sensible;* It. *no'ta sensi'bile*), the 7th degree of the major and harmonic minor scales ; so called because of its tendency, in certain melodic and chordal progressions, to the tonic.

Leaning-note. Appoggiatura.

Leap. 1. In piano-playing, a spring from one note or chord to another, in which the hand is lifted clear of the keyboard.—2. See *Skip*.

Leben'dig, Leb'haft (Ger.) Lively, animated. (Also *adverb*.)... *Leb'haftigkeit*, animation ; *Mit L. und durchaus' mit Empfindung und Ausdruck*, with animation, and with feeling and expression throughout.

Ledger-line. See *Leger-line*.

Legan'do. (It.) See *Legato*.

Lega'to (It. ; superl. *legatis'simo*.) "Bound"; a direction to perform the passage so marked in a smooth and connected manner, with no break between the tones ; also indicated by the *legato-mark*, a curving line drawn over or under notes to be so executed... *Lega'tobogen* (Ger.), legato-mark, slur.

Legatu'ra (It) A tie ; a syncopation... *L. di voce*, see *Ligature* 2.

Le'gend. (Ger. *Legen'de* ; Fr. *légende*.) A composition based on a poem of lyrico-epic character, the poem serving either as text or program... *Legen'denton, im* (Ger.), in the style of a romance or legend.

Léger, légère (Fr.) Light, nimble... *Légèrement*, lightly, nimbly.

Leg'er-line. (Ger. *Hilfs'linie;* Fr. *ligne ajoutée;* It. *ri'go aggiun'to* or *finto*.) One of the short auxiliary lines used for writing notes which lie above or below the staff. Leger-lines are counted away from the staff, either up or down... *Leger-space*, a space bounded on either side or both sides by a leger-line.

Leggerez'za (It.) Lightness, swiftness. ..*Leggermen'te*, lightly, swiftly...*Legge'ro*, same as *Leggiero*.

Leggiadramen'te. (It.) Neatly, elegantly, gracefully...*Leggia'dro*, neat, graceful, elegant ; in a brisk and cheerful style.

Leggieramen'te, Leggiermen'te (It.) Lightly, swiftly...*Leggie're*, light, etc. ..*Leggierez'za*, lightness, swiftness... *Leggie'ro*, a direction indicating, in piano-technic, that the passage is to be performed with as great lightness as is consistent with the degree of loudness required ; generally in swift *piano* passages with little rhythmical emphasis. It differs from *Legato* in calling for a mere down-stroke of the fingers without pressure, and with a quick, springy recoil...*L. con moto*, lightly and swiftly.

Le'gno, col (It.) "With the stick"; in violin-playing, a direction to let the stick of the bow fall on the strings.

Leicht (Ger.) 1. Light, brisk.—2. Easy, facile...*Leicht bewegt*, (*a*) leggiero con moto ; (*b*) with slight agitation.

Lei'denschaft (Ger.) Passion, fervency, vehemence...*Mit L.*, or *lei'denschaftlich*, passionately, vehemently.

Lei'er (Ger.) Lyre; *L.kasten*, hand-organ.

Lei'se (Ger.) Low, soft, *piano*.

Lei'ter (Ger., "ladder".) Scale (*Ton'-leiter*)...*Lei'tereigen*, proper or belonging to the scale...*Lei'terfremd*, foreign to the scale.

Leit'motiv [-teef"] (Ger.) Leading-motive ; a term brought into special prominence by Wagner's musical dramas, and applied to any striking mus. motive (theme, phrase) characteristic of or accompanying one of the persons of the drama or some particular idea, emotion, or situation in the latter ; the motive recurring reminiscently at suitable stages of the action...Also used of similar motives in recent operas, oratorios, and program-music.

Leit′ton (Ger.) Leading-tone.

Lenez′za, con (It.) In a gentle, quiet manner.

Le′no (It.) Faint, feeble.

Lent,-e (Fr.) Slow... *Lentement,* slowly. ..*Lenteur,* slowness.

Len′to (It.) Slow ; a tempo-mark intermediate between *Andante* and *Largo* (comp. art. *Tempo-mark*). Also used as a qualifying term, as *Adagio non lento*...*Lentamen′te,* slowly...*Lentan′do,* growing slower, retarding ; a direction to perform a passage with increasing slowness (*ritardando, rallentando*). ..*Lentez′za, con,* slowly, deliberately.

Lesser. Minor ; as the *lesser* third... *Lesser appoggiatura,* short appoggiatura. ..*Lesser whole tone,* see *Intervals,* Table III, foot-note.

Lesson. (Fr. *leçon.*) In the 17th and 18th centuries, the name of the several pieces for the harpsichord, etc., 'which, when combined, formed a Suite.

Le′sto (It.) Lively, brisk.

Letter-name. A letter used to designate a tone, note, key, or staff-degree. See *Alphabetical notation.*

Levé (Fr.) 1. Up-beat. 2. Auftakt.

Ley′er (Ger.) Earlier spelling of *Leier.*

Liaison (Fr.) 1. A tie.—2 (*liaison d'harmonie*). A syncopation.—3. See *Ligature* 2.

Libel′lion. An automatic music-box, distinguished by the feature that the notes are represented by perforations in sheets of tough cardboard, which (as they *pass through* the box) can be made continuous, so that compositions of any desired length may be performed.

Liberamen′te (It.), **Librement** (Fr.) Freely.

Libret′tist. A writer of libretti...*Libret′to* (It., pl.-*i.* ; Fr. ditto, or *livret ;* Ger. *Text*). A "booklet" ; specifically, one containing the words of an opera, oratorio, etc. ; also such words or text, whether in book-form or not ; a book.

License. (Ger. *Frei′heit ;* Fr. *licence ;* It. *licen′za.*) An intentional deviation from established custom or rule. *Con alcu′no licenza* (It.), with a certain freedom.

Lice′o (It.) Academy (of music).

Lich′anos (Gk.) See *Lyre* 1.

Lié (Fr.) Tied ; legato.

Lieb′lich (Ger.) Lovely, sweet, charming ; often with names of organ-stops.

Lied (Ger.) Song.—A preëminently German song-form is that of the *durch′-komponiertes Lied,* which differs from the ballad (*Stro′phenlied*) in not repeating the same melody for each stanza, but following closely the sense of the words by changing melody, harmony, and rhythm...*Kunst′lied, Volks′lied, Volks′t(h)ümliches Lied,* see those words...*Lie′dercyclus,* a cycle (set) of songs...*Lie′derkranz,* (*a*) a choral society ; (*b*), also *Lie′derkreis,* a set or series of songs...*Lie′derspiel,* see *Vaudeville*...*Lie′dertafel,* a singing-society of men, of a social character...*Lied′-form,* see *Form.*

Liga′to (It.) Legato.

Lig′ature. (Ger. *Ligatur′* ; Fr. *ligature ;* It. *legatu′ra.*) 1. In mensurable music, a connected group of notes to be sung to one syllable. Ligatures were derived from the compound neumes ; their simplest form is the *Figura obliqua* (q. v.) (Comp. *Proprietas, Improprietas, Perfection, Imperfection.*)—2. In modern music, a group or series of notes to be executed in one breath, to one syllable, or as a legato phrase.—3. A tie ; hence, a syncopation.

Ligne (Fr.) A line...*Ligne ajoutée* (*postiche,* or *supplémentaire*), a leger-line.

Li′mite (It.) Limit.

Lim′ma. See *Apotome.*

Li′nea (It.) A line.

Lin′gua. (It.) Reed (of organ-pipe).

Lingual′pfeife (Ger.) Reed-pipe (usually *Zung′enpfeife*).

Li′nie (Ger.) A line...*Li′niensystem,* the staff.

Linings. (Ger. *Fut′terung ;* Fr. *contre-éclisses.*) In the violin, etc., the strips of pine-wood glued inside the body to the ribs, to stiffen the fixed structure.

Lin′ke Hand (Ger.) Left hand.

Lip. 1. (Ger. *Lip′pe* or [Lat.] *La′bium,* pl. *La′bien ;* Fr. *biseau* [upper lip].) The lips of a flue-pipe are the flat surfaces above and below the mouth, called the upper and lower lip. See *Pipe* 2, *a.*—2. (Ger. *An′satz ;* Fr. *embouchure ;* It. *imboccatu′ra.*) The art or faculty of so adjusting the lips to the mouthpiece of a wind-instr. as to produce artistic effects of tone ; also *lipping*

Lip'penpfeife (Ger.) Flue-pipe (usually *Labialpfeife*).

Li'ra (It.) Lyre (see *Lyre*).—While the ancient lyre was a harp-like instr., the *lira* of the 16th–18th century was a species of viol, a bow-instr. with a varying number of strings, and made in 3 principal sizes...*L. barberi'na*, a small lyre inv. by Doni of Florence in the 17th century...*L. da brac'cio*, "arm-lyre", a bow-instr. first mentioned in the 9th century, and appearing in the 15th as an instr. resembling the viol in form of head and in stringing, though in other points (and finally in the adoption of 4 strings) like the violin (see art. *Violin*, foot-note)...*L. da gam'ba*, knee-lyre...*L. tede'sca*, hurdy-gurdy.

Li'rico,-a (It.) Lyric, lyrical.

Liro'ne (It.) The great bass lyre (also *Accor'do*, *Archivio'la di lira*), with as many as 24 strings.

Li'scio (It.) Smooth, flowing.

L'istes'so. See *Istesso*.

Litany. (Gk. *litanei'a*; Lat. and It. *litani'a*; Fr. (pl.) *litanies*; Ger. *Litanei'*.) A song of supplication; "a solemn form of prayer, sung, by priests and choir, in alternate invocations and responses, and found in most Office-books, both of the Eastern and Western Church" [GROVE]. Litanies were ·originally employed in processional supplications for averting pestilence and other dangers, and later adopted by the Church as portions of the regular service at certain seasons.

Lit'teræ significati'væ (Lat.) Single letters, or abbreviations, of doubtful significance, employed in medieval neumatic notation. (Ger. *Roma'-nusbuchstaben*.)

Liu'to (It.) A lute.

Livre (Fr.) Book...*À livre ouvert*, at sight.

Livret (Fr.) Libretto.

Lo (It.) The.

Lob'gesang (Ger.) Song or hymn of praise.

Loch in der Stimme (Ger.) "Hole in the voice"; said of that part of a register in which certain tones cannot be made to "speak" on account of a morbid state of the vocal organ.

Lo'co (It.) Place; signifies, following

8va, "perform the notes as written". Also *al loco*.

Lo'crian. (Ger. *lo'krisch*.) See *Mode*.

Long. (Lat. *longa*.) See *Notation*, §3; also for *Long-rest*.

Lonta'no (It.) Distant...*Da l.*, or *in lontanan'za*, from a distance, far away

Loop. 1. A vibrating portion of a body, bounded by 2 nodes. See *Node*. —2. The cord fastening tailpiece to button (violin, etc.)

Lö'sung, fort'schreitende (Ger.) Resolution (usually *Auf'lösung*).

Loud pedal. Damper-pedal.

Loure (Fr.) 1. An ancient Fr. bagpipe inflated by the mouth; hence—2. A dance named from the instr., on which it was formerly played, in 6-4 or 3-4 time and slow tempo, the down-beat strongly marked.

Louré (Fr.) Slurred, legato, *non staccato*.

Low. 1. (Ger. *lei'se*; Fr. *douce*; It. *pia'no*.) Soft, not loud.—2. (Ger. *tief*; Fr. *bas,-se*; It. *basso,-a*.) Grave in pitch, not acute.

Lugu'bre (Fr. and It.) Mournful.

Lullaby. Cradle-song, berceuse.

Lun'ga (It.) Long. Written over or under a hold, it signifies that the latter is to be considerably prolonged...*Lunga pa'usa*, a long pause or rest.—*Lunghe* (pl. of *lunga*), drawn out, prolonged; "*note*" (notes) being implied.

Luo'go (It.) Same as *Loco*.

Lur (Danish, from Old Norse *ludr*, a hollowed piece of wood.) 1. A unique pre-historic wind-instr. of bronze (alloy of copper 88.90%, tin 10.61%, nickel and iron 0.49%), numerous well-preserved specimens of which have been found, but only in Denmark, southern Sweden, and Mecklenburg. The long, slender, exactly conical tube, varying in length from 5 ft. to 7 ft. 9¾ in., forms a sweeping, graceful curve (forward from the player's lips, upward and backward over his left shoulder, and forward again over his head), and terminates with a broad circular flat plate (about 10 in. in diam.) in lieu of a flaring bell. This plate is ornamented with bosses in front, and on the rear with several small bronze tassels, depending loosely. The Lur has a cupped mouthpiece, shallower and more nearly V-shaped than that of the trombone.

LUSINGANDO—MACHÊTE. 115

The tone is powerful and mellow.—2. The modern *Lur*, of Norway and Sweden, is usually made of birch bark, and is allied to the Swiss alp-horn.

Lusingan'do, Lusingan'te (It.) Coaxing, caressing ; also *lusinghe'vole*... *Lusinghevolmen'te*, coaxingly, etc... *Lusinghie're*, or *-o*, coaxing, flattering, seductive.

Lus'tig (Ger.) Merry, gay (also *adverb*).

Lute. (Ger. *Lau'te ;* Fr. *luth ;* It. *liu'to.*) A stringed instr., now obsolete, of very ancient origin ; it was brought to Europe by the Moors, who called it *Al' ud* or *Al Oud*...The body has no ribs, the back being, like that of the mandolin, in the vaulted shape of half a pear. The strings, attached to a bridge fixed on the face of the instr., and passing over or beside the fretted fingerboard, were plucked by the fingers, and varied in number from 6 up to 13, the highest or melody-string (*treble, canto*) being single, and the others in pairs of unisons. Bass strings *off* the fingerboard, each yielding but one tone, were generally attached to a second neck ; they were in later times covered with silver wire, the other strings being of gut. These bass strings were introduced in the 16th century, and led to divers modifications in the build of the instr.; the various forms of large double-necked lutes then evolved (*theorbo, archiliuto, chitarrone*) being general favorites, and holding, from the 15th to the 17th century, the place in the orchestra now occupied by the bass violins. Music for the lute was written in tablature, there being 3 systems (French, Italian, and German)...A lute-player is variously called a *lutenist, lutanist, lutinist,* and *lutist.*

Luth (Fr.) Lute...*Lutherie*, the trade of, and also the instr.s made by, a *luthier*...*Luthier*, formerly, a lutemaker ; now, a maker of any instr. of the lute or violin class.

Luttuo'so (It.) Mournful, plaintive... *Luttuosamen'te*, mournfully, etc.

Lyd'ian. (Ger. *ly'disch.*) See *Mode*.

Lyre. I. (Gk. and Lat. *ly'ra;* It. *li'ra;* Fr. *lyre;* Ger. *Lei'er.*) A stringed instr. of the ancient Greeks, of Egyptian or Asiatic origin. The frame consisted of a soundboard or resonance-box, from which rose 2 curving arms joined above by a cross-bar ; the strings, from 3 to

10 in number, were stretched from this cross-bar to or over a bridge set upon the soundboard, and were plucked with a plectrum. The names of the strings (whence were derived the names of most of the tones in the Greek modes) on the 8-stringed lyre were as follows :

Hyp'ate, "uppermost" (as the lyre was held) ; the longest and deepest-toned.
Parhyp'ate, "next to hypate".
Lich'anos, "forefinger-string".
Me'se, "middle string".
Parame'se, "next to Mese".
Tri'te, "third string" (from the lower side).
Parane'te, "next to the last".
Ne'te, "last," or "lowermost" (the highest in pitch).

The *Kithara* may be considered as a large form of the lyre, the *Chelys* as a treble lyre.—The lyre differed from the harp in having fewer strings, and from the guitar, lute, etc., in having no fingerboard ; its compass and accordatura varied greatly. It was chiefly used to accompany songs and recitations.—2. An instr. used in military bands, consisting of loosely suspended steel bars tuned to the tones of the scale and struck with a hammer.—3. See *Rebec*.

Lyric, lyrical. Pertaining to or proper for the lyre, or for accompaniment on (by) the lyre ; hence, adapted for singing or for expression in song.—The term is applied to music and songs (or poems) expressing subjective emotion or special moods, in contradistinction to *epic* (narrative), and *dramatic* (scenic, accompanied by action)...*Lyric drama*, the opera...*Lyric opera*, one in which the expression of subjective feeling, and the lyric form of poetry, predominate... *Lyric stage*, the operatic stage.

M.

M. Abbr. of It. *mano*, and Fr. *main*, (hand) ; in organ-music, of *manual* (usually *Man.*), and Lat. *manua'liter ;* and of *metronome* (usually M. M.) and *mezzo*...ᴔ represents the note *me* (mi) in Tonic Sol-fa notation.

Ma (It.) But ; as in the phrase *vivace, ma non troppo*, lively, but not too much so.

Machête. A small Portuguese guitar (octave-guitar), having 4 strings tuned :

or sometimes *d²* instead of *e²*.

Machine-head. (Ger. *Mecha'nik*.) A rack-and-pinion adjustment substituted for the ordinary tuning-pegs of the double-bass, the guitar, and of the melody-strings of the zither.

Ma'dre, al'la (It.) " To the Mother " ; a superscription of hymns to the Virgin.

Mad'rigal. (Ger. and Fr. *Madrigal'*; It. *madriga'le, madria'le, mandria'le*.) Originally, a short lyrical poem of an amorous, pastoral, or descriptive character.—Hence, a poem of this kind set to music, which is polyphonic, with incessant contrapuntal variations, and based (in the stricter style) on a *cantus firmus*; it is without instrumental accompaniment, and differs from the Motet in being of a secular cast. This style of composition appears to have had its rise in the Low Countries towards the middle of the 15th century, spreading thence to other European States, and cultivated with peculiar success in Italy and England well into the 18th century ; in England the Madrigal Society still flourishes.   Madrigals are written in from 3 to 8 or more parts, and are best sung by a *chorus*, which feature forms one of the chief distinctions between the *M.* and the Glee (for *solo* voices).

Maesto'so (It.) Majestic, dignified... *Maestà' (con), Maesta'de (con), Maestè'vole, Maestevolmen'te, Maestosamen'te,* with majesty or dignity, majestically.

Maestra'le (It.) Occasional term for the stretto of a fugue, when in canonform.

Maestri'a (It.) Mastership, skill, virtuosity.

Mae'stro (It.) A master... *M. al cem'balo,* term formerly applied to the conductor of an orchestra, who sat at the harpsichord instead of wielding the baton... *M. dei put'ti,* " master of the boys", i. e., the choir-master of St. Peter's at Rome... *M. del co'ro,* choirmaster... *M. di canto,* singing-master. ..*M. di cappel'la,* (*a*) choir-master ; (*b*) conductor; (*c*) *Kapell'meister* (conductor of chorus and orchestra).

Mag'adis (Gk.) An ancient Greek instr. with 20 strings tuned in octaves two by two ; hence the term *mag'adize,* to sing in parallel octaves, as boys and men.

Ma'gas (Gk.) Bridge (of a cithara or lyre) ; fret (of a lute).

Magazin'balg (Ger.) Reservoir-bellows (organ).

Maggiola'ta (It.) A May Song.

Maggio're (It.) Major.

Mag'got. A " fancie ", or piece of an impromptu and whimsical character.

Magni'ficat. Name of, and first word in, the " Magnificat anima mea dominum " (my soul doth magnify the Lord), the hymn or song of the Virgin Mary (Luke I, 46-55), sung in the daily service of the Church.

Main (Fr.) Hand... *M. droite (gauche),* right (left) hand... *M. harmonique,* harmonic hand.

Maître (Fr.) Master... *M. de chapelle,* Kapellmeister, conductor... *M. de musique,* (*a*) conductor ; (*b*) music-master, teacher.

Maîtrise (Fr.) In France, prior to 1789, a music-school attached to a cathedral, for the education of young musicians, who were called *enfants de chœur.* Some few were reëstablished, and still exist.

Majestä'tisch (Ger.) Majestical(ly).

Major. (Ger. *dur* ; Fr. *majeur* ; It. *maggio're*.) Lit. " greater", and thus opp. to *minor,* " lesser." (Comp. *Phone, Interval*.)...*Major cadence,* one closing on a major triad...*M. chord* or *triad,* one having a major third and perfect fifth. ..*M. interval, key, mode, scale, tonality,* see the nouns...*M. whole tone,* the *greater* whole tone 8:9 (as *c–d*); opp. to the *lesser* (or minor) whole tone 9:10 (as *d–e*).

Malinconi'a (It.) Melancholy... *Con m.,* with melancholy expression, dejectedly (also *malinconicamen'te*)...*Malinco'nico* (*-nio'so, -no'so*), melancholy, dejected.—Also *Melanconi'a,* etc.

Mancan'do (It.) Decreasing in loudness, dying away, *decrescendo ;* usually, a combination of *decrescendo* and *rallentando* is intended (v. *Tempo-mark*).

Manche (Fr.) Neck.

Mando'la (It.) A large variety of Mandolin.

Man'dolin(e). (It. *mandoli'no*.) An instr. of the lute family, the body shaped like that of a lute, though smaller, having wire strings tuned pairwise, played with a plectrum, and stopped on a fretted fingerboard.   There are 2 chief varieties, (1) the Neapolitan (*mandolino napolita'no*), which has 4 pairs of strings tuned $g–d^1–a^1–e^2$ like those of the violin ;

and (2) the Milanese (*mand. lombar'do*), which has 5 or 6 pairs, tuned *g c¹ a¹ d² e³* (or *g–b–e¹–a¹–d²–e²*). Compass about 3 octaves:

Mandolina'ta (It.) A piece for mandolin, or played with mandolin-effect.

Mando'ra, Mando're. Same as *Mandola.*

Ma'nico (It.) Neck (of a lute, violin, etc.)

Man'ichord. (Lat. *manichor'dium.*) A term variously applied to different forms of obsolete keyboard stringed instr s.

Manier' (Ger.) An *agrément* (harpsichord- or clavichord-grace).

Manie'ra (It.) Style, manner, method. *..Con dolce m.*, in a suave, delicate style.

Manifold fugue. See *Fugue.*

Män'nerchor (Ger.) A male chorus; also, a composition for such a chorus. *..Män'nergesangverein*, men's choral society...*Männerstimmen*, men's voices.

Ma'no (It.) Hand...*M. de'stra* (*sini'-stra*), right (left) hand.

Man'ual. 1. A digital.—2. (Ger. *Manual'; Fr. clavier; It. manua'le.*) An organ-keyboard; opp. to *pedal.* (Compare *Organ.*)...*Manual-key*, a digital. *..Manual'koppel* (Ger.), a coupler connecting 2 manuals.

Manu'brium (Lat.) Knob of a draw-stop; Ger. pl. *Manu'brien*, whence *Manu'brienkoppel*, draw-stop coupler.

Marcan'do (It., "marking".) } With distinctness and emphasis...*Marcatis'simo*, with very marked emphasis.
Marca'to (It., "marked".) }

March. (Ger. *Marsch;* Fr. *marche;* It. *mar'cia.*) A composition of strongly marked rhythm, suitable for timing the steps of a body of persons proceeding at a walking pace, and thus bearing a processional character akin to that of the Polonaise, Entrée, etc. The march-form of the earlier operas and clavier-pieces also resembles that of the old dances, consisting of 2 reprises of 8, (12), or 16 measures. The modern march-form is further developed; it is in 4-4 time, with reprises of 4, 8, or 16 measures, and is followed by a *Trio* (usually in the dominant or subdominant key and of a more melodious character), after which the march is repeated, often with amplifications.— The ordinary *Parade March* (Ger.

Para'demarsch; Fr. *Pas ordinaire*) has about 75 steps to the minute; the Quick-step (Ger. *Geschwind'marsch;* Fr. *Pas redoublé*), about 108; while for a *Charge* (Ger. *Sturm'marsch;* Fr. *Pas de charge*) some 120 steps per minute are reckoned. ..Besides these military marches of a bright and martial character, *Funeral* or *Dead Marches* are composed, slower in movement and more solemn in effect, and sometimes symphonically developed.

Marche (Fr.) 1. A march.—2. Progression...*Marcher*, to progress.

Mar'cia (It.) A march; *alla m.*, in march-style.

Mark. (Often equiv. to *sign.*) *Cadence-mark*, the vertical line separating the words of a chant, dividing those sung to the reciting-note from those in the cadence...*Harmonic mark*, see *Harmonic 2, b...Metronomic mark*, see *Metronome...Mark of expression*, see *Expression-mark...Tempo-mark*, see that word.

Markiert' (Ger.), **Marqué** (Fr.) Marked, accented; *marcato.*

Marseillaise. The French revolutionary hymn, the poem of which was written and set to music during the night of April 24, 1792, by Rouget de Lisle, Captain of Engineers, at Strassburg; first named by its author "Chant de guerre de l'armée du Rhin"; but, soon after its introduction in Paris by the soldiers of Marseilles, it became universally known as "La M.", or "Hymne des Marseillais".

Marteau (Fr.) 1. Hammer (of pfte.-action).—2. Tuning-hammer.

Martelé (Fr.), **Martella'to** (It.) "Hammered"; a direction in music for bow-instr.s, indicating that the notes so marked are to be played with a sharp and decided stroke (usual sign ♭);—in piano-music, that the keys are to be struck with a heavy, inelastic plunge of the finger, or (in octave-playing) with the arm-staccato...*Martellato* notes are generally *mezzo staccato*, and often take the sign > or *sfz.*

Martellement (Fr.) 1. In harp-playing, calls for the *crush-note* (*acciaccatu'ra*) or redoubled stroke.—2. Comp. *Graces.*

Marzia'le (It.) Martial, warlike.

Maschera'ta (It.) Masquerade.

Maschi'nen (Ger., pl.) See *Pistons...Maschi'nenpauken*, kettledrums provided with a mechanism for the rapid adjustment of the pitch.

Mask, Masque. (Ger. *Mas'kenspiel;* Fr. *masque.*) The mus. dramas called masques, so popular during the 16th and 17th centuries, were spectacular plays on an imposing scale and with most elaborate appointments, the subject being generally of an allegorical or mythological nature, and the music both vocal and instrumental.—The masque was the precursor of the opera, but was distinguished from it by the lack of monody.

Mass. (Lat. *mis'sa;* It. *mes'sa;* Fr. and Ger. *Mes'se.*) "Mass" is derived from *missa*, in the phrase "Ite, missa est [ecclesia]" (Depart, the congregation is dismissed), addressed, in the R. C. Church, to persons in the congregation not permitted to take part in the communion service, the Mass itself taking place during the consecration of the elements.—The divisions of the musical mass are (1) the Kyrie; (2) the Gloria (incl. the Gratias agimus, Qui tollis, Quoniam, Cum Sancto Spiritu); (3) the Credo (incl. the Et incarnatus, Crucifixus, Et resurrexit); (4) the Sanctus and Benedictus (with the Hosanna); (5) the Agnus Dei (incl. the Dona nobis). It has passed through very various phases, from the simple unison chant of Plain Song to the most elaborate productions of late medieval counterpoint, with a transition thereafter to the severity of the Palestrina epoch, to the vocal masses in 8, 16, or even 32 parts, and finally to the grand mass with full chorus and orchestra (*missa solem'nis*)...*High mass*, one celebrated on church festivals, accompanied with music and incense...*Low mass*, one without music....*Missa brev'is*, short mass of Protestant churches, incl. only the Kyrie and Gloria.

Mä'ssig (Ger.) Moderate(ly).

Mas'sima (It.) 1. The maxim.—2. A whole note.—3 (*adj.*) Augmented (of intervals).

Master-chord. The dominant chord... *Master-fugue*, fuga ricercata...*Master-note*, leading-note...*Mastersinger*, see *Meistersinger.*

Masure, Masurek, Masurka. See *Mazurka.*

Matelotte (Fr.) An old sailors' dance resembling the hornpipe, in duple time.

Mat'ins. The music sung at morning prayer, the first of the canonical hours.

Maul'trommel (Ger.) Jew's-harp... *Maul'trommelklavier*, the melodicon.

Max'im. (Lat. *max'ima.*) See *Notation*, §3, *Large.*

Mazur'ka. A Polish national dance in triple time and moderate tempo, with a variable accent on the third beat.

Me. For *mi* (Tonic Sol-fa).

Mean. Former name for an inner part (as the tenor or alto), or an inner string (of a viol)...*Mean clef*, the *C*-clef, as used for noting the inner parts.

Mean-tone system. See *Temperament.*

Measurable music. Mensurable music.

Measure. 1. (Ger. *Takt;* Fr. *mesure;* It. *misu'ra.*) A metrical unit, simple or compound, of fixed length (time-value) and regular accentuation, forming the smallest metrical subdivision of a piece or movement; visibly presented by the group of notes or rests contained between two bars, and familiarly called a "bar". (Comp. *Time.*)—2. Occasional for *tempo.*—3. A dance having a stately and measured movement.— *Measure-note*, a note indicated by the time-signature as an even divisor of a measure; $\frac{3}{4}$ thus indicates that each measure has 3 quarter-notes, and a measure-note is then a quarter-note... *Measure-rest*, see *Rest.*

Mécanisme (Fr.) Technic or technique; mechanical skill. (It. *meccanismo.*)

Mecha'nik (Ger.) 1. A mechanism or mechanical apparatus, such as (*a*) the pfte.-action; (*b*) the machine-head of a guitar, zither, etc.—2. In pfte.-playing, (*a*) technique; (*b*) specifically, the mere mechanical action of the fingers and hand, as the lift and down-stroke of finger or wrist, the passing-under of the thumb, etc.; often carelessly translated by *mechanism.*

Mechanism. See *Mechanik* 2 *b.*

Mede'simo (It.) The same.

Me'dial. Proper to the Mediant.

Me'diant. 1. (Ger. and It. *Median'te;* Fr. *médiante.*) The third degree of a scale.—2. In medieval music, one of the 3 pivotal tones of a mode, situated as nearly as possible midway between the Final and Dominant, and ranking next in importance to the latter.

Me'dius. See *Accentus ecclesiastici.*

Mehr (Ger.) More...*Mehr'chörig*, for several (4-part) choruses...*Mehr'fach*, manifold ; *mehr'faches Intervall'*, compound interval ; *mehr'facher Ka'non*, a canon having more than 2 themes ; *mehr'facher Kon'trapunkt*, counterpoint written in more than 2 invertible parts ; *mehr'fache Stim'me* (organ), a compound stop...*Mehr'stimmig*, in several parts ; polyphonic...*Mehr'stimmigkeit durch Bre'chung*, apparent polyphony obtained (especially on the pfte.) by employing broken chords.

Mei'ster (Ger.) Master...*Mei'sterfuge*, fuga ricerca'ta...*Mei'stersinger* (or -*sänger*), in Germany, the successors of the *Min'nesänger* (Troubadours), but, unlike the latter, chiefly artisans, who formed guilds in various cities for the cultivation and propagation of their art, the stringent rules for which were contained in the *Tabulatur'*. Their poems were founded for the greater part on biblical subjects ; the musical treatment was apt to be dry and prosaical.—They originated about the 14th century in Mainz, reached their zenith in the 15th and 16th centuries (notably under Hans Sachs of Nuremberg), and thereafter decayed gradually, the last society becoming extinct in 1839 (Ulm).

Melancoli'a (It.), **Mélancholie** (Fr.) See *Malinconia*.

Mélange (Fr.) A medley, pot-pourri.

Melis'ma (Gk.) 1. A melodic ornament, fioritura, grace ; colorature.—2. A *Cadenza* 1...*Melismat'ic*, ornamented, embellished ; said of vocal or instrumental music abounding in ornaments ; also, specifically, *melismatic song*, that in which more than one tone is sung to a syllable ; opp. to *syllabic song*.

Melo'deon. The original American organs were called melodeons or melodiums. (See *Reed-organ*.)

Melo'dia. (Organ.) A variety of stopped diapason nearly resembling the Clarabella.

Melod'ic. Pertaining to the progression of single tones ; hence, *vocal*, as a *melodic interval*.

Melo'dica. A small variety of pipeorgan inv. in 1770 by Joh. Andr. Stein of Augsburg, having a tone like the *flûte à bec*, and a compass of but 3½ octaves. It was used ordinarily to play the *melody* to a harpsichord- or pfte.-accompaniment ; hence the name. An

excellent crescendo and decrescendo were obtainable by varying the finger-pressure on the keys.

Melo'dico (It.) Equiv. to *Cantando*.

Melo'dicon. A keyboard instr. inv. by Peter Rieffelsen of Copenhagen, in 1800, in which the tones were produced by tuning-forks.

Melo'dik (Ger.) Science or theory of melody.

Melo'diograph. See *Melograph*.

Melo'dion. A keyboard instr. inv. by J. C. Dietz, of Emmerich, in which the tones were produced by vertical steel bars chromatically graduated ; these bars being pressed by the digitals against a rotating cylinder. *Forte* was obtained by a quicker, *piano* by a slower, rotation. Compass, 5½-6 octaves.

Melo'dium. 1. Melodeon.—2. (Ger.) Alexandre organ.

Mel'odrama. 1. Originally, a musical drama.—2. In modern usage, (*a*) stage-declamation with a mus. accomp. ; (*b*) a form of the drama in which the music plays a very subordinate part, and the plot is more or less romantic and sensational.

Mel'ody. (Ger. *Melodie'*; Fr. *mélodie*; It. *melodi'a*.) 1. The rational progression of single tones ; contrasted with *Harmony*, the rational combination of several tones.—2. The leading part in a movement, usually the soprano.—3. An air or tune.

Mel'ograph. Name of various mechanical devices for recording the music played on a pfte. One of the latest and most successful is the *electric m.* or Phonautograph (inv. by Fenby, in England), in which the pressure on the digitals closes an electric circuit, effecting a record on paper as in the Morse system of telegraphy. A cardboard stencil forming an exact copy of the record can be made to reproduce the music when placed in the *Melotrope*, a mechanical attachment to a pfte. by means of which the digitals are depressed as if by the player's fingers.

Mel'ophone. A variety of Concertina.

Melopian'o. A pfte. inv. by Caldera of Turin, in 1870, in which the tone is sustained by rapidly repeated blows of small hammers attached to a bar passing over and at right angles to the strings, the bar being kept in vibration by means of a treadle worked by the player. *Crescendo* and *decrescendo* effects are producible at will, and the tone is of delightful quality.

Mel'oplaste. A simplified method for learning the rudiments of music, inv. by Pierre Galin about 1818. Instead of teaching the notes, clefs, etc., at first, he took merely the 5 lines of the staff, singing familiar airs to the syllables *do, re, mi,* etc., at the same time showing with a pointer the position on the staff of the notes sung. For teaching rhythmical relations he used a double metronome marking both measures and beats.

Me'los (Gk.) "Song". The name bestowed by Wagner on the style of recitative exemplified in his later mus. dramas. (See *Recitative.*)

Mel'otrope. See art. *Melograph.*

Même (Fr.) The same... *À la même,* l'istesso tempo.

Men. Abbr. of *Meno.*

Ménestrel (Fr.) Minstrel (q. v.)

Ménétrier,-trière (Fr.) Originally, a player on any instrument, especially for dancing; now, a vagabond fiddler at fairs and in low places of entertainment, or a village musician.

Me'no (It., abbr. *men.*) Less, not so.— When *Meno* occurs alone as a tempomark, *mosso* is implied... *Meno mosso,* " less moved," i. e., slower.

Mensur' (Ger.) 1. *Mensu'ra,* i. e. the time of a movement (mensurable music). —2. Scale (of organ-pipes).—3. In other instr.s, the various measurements requisite for their true intonation (as length of tube, distance between fingerholes, thickness of strings, etc.)

Mensural'gesang,-musik (Ger.) Mensurable music. (See *Notation,* §3.)

Men'te (It.) Mind, memory ; *alla m.,* improvised, extempore.

Menuet (Fr.), **Menuett'** (Ger.) Minuet.

Me'rula (Lat., "blackbird, ousel".) Same as *Vo'gelgesang.*

Mescolan'za (It.) A medley.

Mes'otonic. Mean-tone.

Mes'sa (It.), **Mes'se** (Ger. and Fr.) Mass.

Mes'sa di vo'ce (It.) The attack of a sustained vocal tone *pianissimo,* with a swell to *fortissimo,* and slow decrease to *pianissimo* again ; thus :

$$pp \mathrel{<\!\!\!-\!\!\!-} ff \mathrel{-\!\!\!-\!\!\!>} pp$$

The attack and increase was formerly called *forma're il tuono ;* the sustaining of the *ff* tone, *ferma're il tuono ;* and the decrease and close, *fini're il tuono.*

Messan'za (It.) A quodlibet.

Me'sto (It.) Pensive, melancholy... *Mestamen'te,* plaintively, grievingly. (Also *con mesti'zia.*)

Mesure (Fr.) Measure ; a measure ; *à la m.,* in time (i. e. *a tempo, a battu'ta*). ...*Mesuré,* measured.—(See *Time*)

Metal'lo (It., "metal".) A ringing, "metallic" quality of voice.

Metal'lophone. A pfte. in which graduated steel bars take the place of strings.—2. An instr. like the xylophone, but with bars of metal instead of wood.

Meter, Metre. 1. Metre in music is the symmetrical grouping of musical rhythms ; a disposition of musical members akin to the arrangement of the poetic strophe. It differs from Form in having to do merely with the rhythmical groupings within compositions ; from Rhythm, in treating of the symmetrical arrangement of the smaller tone-groups, the *articulation* of which produces the rhythm or time. These definitions are, however, not universally binding, *metre* and *rhythm* being used sometimes as interchangeable terms, and sometimes with significations exactly the reverse of those just given. In metre the smallest metrical element (unit of measure) is the Measure ; the combination of 2 measures (either simple or compound) produces the Section ; of 2 sections, the Phrase ; of 2 phrases, the Period (of 8 measures), which may be extended to 12 or 16 measures ; beyond the period of 16 measures the metrical divisions seldom go, i. e. they are not followed by the ear as *metrical,* but as *thematic* divisions (see *Form*).— 2. The metre of English hymns is classified, according to the feet used, as *iambic, trochaic,* or *dactylic ;* in the syllabic schemes below, the figures indicate the number of syllables in each line. Variants are not infrequent in modern hymnology.

A. *Iambic metres :* Common metre (C. M.), 8 6 8 6 ; Long metre (L. M.), 8 8 8 8 ; Short metre (S. M.), 6 6 8 6 ; these have regularly 4 lines to each stanza ; when doubled to 8 lines they are called Common metre double (C. M. D.), Long metre double (L. M. D.), and Short metre double (S. M. D.). They may also have 6 lines in each stanza, and are then named

Common particular metre (C. P. M.), 8 8 6 8 8 6; Long particular metre (L. P. M.), or Long metre 6 lines, 8 8 8 8 8 8; and Short particular metre (S. P. M.), 6 6 8 6 6 8. Besides the above, there are Sevens and Sixes 7 6 7 6; Tens 10 10 10 10; Hallelujah metre 6 6 6 6 8 8 (or 6 6 6 6 4 4 4); etc.
B. *Trochaic metres:* Sixes 6 6 6 6; Sixes and Fives, 6 5 6 5; Sevens 7 7 7 7; Eights and Sevens 8 7 8 7; etc.
C. *Dactylic metres:* Elevens 11 11 11 11; Elevens and Tens 11 10 11 10; etc.
These are most of the metres in general use (comp. *Common*).

—3. In ancient prosody, the science of *Metrics* treated of the *quantity* (length) of the syllables; whereas in modern English poetry all accented syllables are treated as long, the unaccented as short. The metrical unit is a *mora* (time) or *syllable ; syllables* combine to form *feet; feet* to *cola, verses* (i. e., lines), or *periods ; periods* to *strophes ; strophes* to *pericopes ;* and *pericopes* (or *lines,* or *periods*) to *poems.* ..*Syllables* are either short (◡), long (—), or common (⌒); the long being equivalent to 2 short, and the common either long or short according to position. A *Foot* is a combination of 2 or more syllables.

Méthode (Fr.), **Me'todo** (It.) Method.

Metro'metro (It.), **Métromètre** (Fr.) A metronome.

Met'ronome. (Fr. *métronome ;* Ger. *Metronom' ;* It. *metro'nomo.*) A double pendulum, weighted below, actuated by clockwork, and provided with a graduated scale on which a slider can be moved up and down, the slider determining by its height how many beats the pendulum shall make per minute; often with a bell-attachment (*Bell-metronome*). With the slider set at 60 the pendulum makes one beat per second...*Metronome-mark* (*metronom'ic mark*), a mark set at the head of a composition for exactly indicating its tempo; e. g., M. M. ♩ = 60 means, that the time-value of one quarter-note is equal to one pendulum-beat with the slider set at 60; M. M. standing for "Maelzel's Metronome" after its reputed inventor, Maelzel of Vienna (1816).—The *M.* is much used by beginners and students, for learning to play strictly in time, and for timing their practice.

Me'tro (It.), **Me'trum** (Lat.) Metre.

Mct'te (Ger.) Matins (in the R. C. Church).

Mettez (Fr.) Draw, add (organ-music).

Mez'zo,-a (It.) Half...*A mezza a'ria,* see *Aria parlante.*..*Mezzo for'te* (*mf*), half-loud...*Mezzo lega'to,* in pfte-technics, a variety of touch resembling *leggie'ro* in being a down-stroke without pressure, but differing from it in requiring that greater attention be paid to a forcible stroke than to a rapid, springy return of the finger...*Mezza ma'nica,* half-shift...*Mezza orche'stra,* with half the string-band...*Mezzo pia'no* (*mp*), half-soft, less loud than *mezzo forte.*..*Mezzo sopra'no,* the female voice intermediate between soprano and alto, partaking of the timbre of both, and usually of small compass (*a—f²,* or *a—g²*), but very full-toned in the medium register...*Mezzo teno're,* same as *Barytone ;* only the *mezzo tenore* is in quality rather a low tenor than a high bass...*Mezza vo'ce,* with half the power of the voice; nearly equivalent to *mezzo forte,* in singing or playing.

Mi. 1. The third of the Aretinian syllables.—2. Name of the note *E* in France, Italy, etc...*Mi contra fa est diabolus in musica,* "mi against fa [i. e. the tritone] is the devil in music", a theorem of medieval musicians expressive of their abhorrence of the melodic step, and even of the harmonic relation, of the tritone (the *mi = B♮* of the "hard" hexachord and the *fa = F* of the "natural" hexachord).

Middle-C. The one-lined *c'* on the first leger-line below the treble staff or above the bass staff: ...*Middle part* or *voice,* same as inner part.

Militairement (Fr.), **Militarmen'te** (It.) In military style. Also (It.) *Alla militare.*

Militär'musik (Ger.) 1. Military music. —2. A military band.

Military music. The military band differs from the orchestra in being a wind-band (composed solely of wind-instruments), and in admitting the cornet, bugle, saxophones, and other instr.s whose timbre is considered not to blend well with those of the symphony-orchestra. Another peculiar feature is the large reinforcement of the clarinets, which take the place and parts of the violins and violas in the orchestra. Military bands may contain anywhere from 40 to 90 performers;

that of the 22nd Regt., New York, has 66, namely:

2 piccolos	1 contraffagotto
2 flutes	1 Eb cornetto
2 oboes	2 1st Bb cornets
1 Ab piccolo clarinet	2 2nd " "
3 Eb clarinets	2 trumpets
8 1st Bb clarinets	2 flügelhorns
4 2nd " "	4 French horns
4 3rd " "	2 Eb alto horns
1 alto "	2 Bb tenor horns
1 bass "	2 euphoniums
1 sopr. saxophone	3 trombones
˄lto "	5 bombardons
1 tenor "	3 drums
1 bass "	1 pair cymbals
2 bassoons	

In France, in accordance with the official order promulgated Nov. 17, 1892, the regular infantry bands comprise the following instruments:

2 flutes	3 trombones
2 small clarinets	2 alto saxhorns
8 large "	3 alto saxotrombas
2 oboes	5 bass saxhorns
1 sopr. saxophone	1 contrabass saxh.
1 alto "	1 " tuba
1 baryt. "	1 shallow drum
1 tenor "	1 bass drum
2 cornets	1 pair cymbals
2 trumpets	

or 40 in all (14 wood-wind, 23 brass, 3 percussives).—The principal innovations on the former standard (established by imperial decree of March 26, 1860) are (1) disuse of wooden flutes, for which metal flutes are substituted; (2) suppression of 4 saxophones, and substitution of 4 more clarinets; (3) suppression of 2 barytone saxhorns, for which 2 bass saxhorns are substituted.

Mimodrama. (Fr. *mimodrame.*) A pantomimic dramatic performance, often accomp. by music.

Minacce'vole (It.) In a menacing or threatening manner. (Also *minaccevolmen'te, minaccian'do, minaccio'so, minacciosamen'te.*)

Mineur (Fr.) Minor.

Min'im. (Lat. *mi'nima;* It. *mi'nima* or *bian'ca;* Fr. *minime* or *blanche;* Ger. *hal'be No'te.*) 1. A half-note.—2. See *Notation,* §3... *Minim-rest,* a half-rest.

Min'nesinger,-sänger (Ger., sing. and pl.) One of the German troubadours, or lyric poets and singers of the 12th and 13th centuries, who were exclusively of noble lineage; distinguished from their Southern contemporaries by their chaster conception of love (*Min'ne, Frau'endienst*). They accompanied their songs (*Min'negesang,* written chiefly in the Swabian dialect) on the

viol or *arpanetta,* and their rivalry culminated in grand poetical contests, such as the one immortalized by Wagner in "Tannhäuser." Their art originated in Austria, spreading thence to the Rhine, Thuringia, and Saxony; in the hands of their successors, the *Mei'stersinger,* it degenerated past recognition.

Mi'nor. (Ger. *klein, moll;* Fr. *mineur;* It. *mino're.*) Lesser; smaller (comp. *Interval, Major, Phone*)... *Minor tone,* the *lesser* whole tone 10:9.

Minstrel. The minstrels of the middle ages were professional musicians who sang or declaimed poems, often of their own composition, to a simple instrumental accomp. They were followers of the nobility in court and camp. The French *ménestrels* of the 8th century and later were the musical attendants of the *trouvères* and troubadours, having to execute practically the musical conceptions of their noble masters. Thus they occupied from the outset a subordinate position; their art slowly degenerated in England, whither they were transplanted at the Norman Conquest, until they were classed by statute (1597) with "rogues, vagabonds, and sturdy beggars"; in France their guilds were maintained down to the Revolution. In England they coalesced with the Anglo-Saxon "gleemen". Their favorite instr. was the rebec... *Negro Minstrels,* singers and actors portraying (originally) scenes from Southern plantation-life. The chief performers of the troupe are the *middle-man* or *interlocutor* and the two *end-men* (so called from their respective positions in the semi-circle of performers on the stage); the former leads the talk and gives the cues, while the latter preside over the tambourine and "bones", and crack the jokes.

Minuet'. (It. *minuet'to;* Fr. *menuet;* Ger. *Menuett'.*) One of the earlier French dance-forms, supposed to have originated in Poitou; it dates as an art-product from about Lully's period (end of 17th century), and, as such, properly consists of 2 minuets, or a double minuet with contrasted sections of 16 measures each, the second forming the Trio, after which the first is repeated. It is in triple time, and has a slow, stately movement, eschewing all ornamentation. It frequently occurs in the Suite, Sonata, and Symphony; Beethoven was the first to introduce in its stead, in the 2 latter, the livelier and freer Scherzo ; in the Suite it figures, by way of contrast, between the Sarabande and Gigue.

Miracle, Miracle-play. See *Mystery*.

Miscel'la (Lat.) A mixture-stop.

Mise de voix (Fr.) Messa di voce.

Misere're (Lat.) The first word of the Psalm LI (in the Vulgate, L), which begins : "Miserere mei, Domine" (Pity me, O Lord) ; hence, the name of this Psalm, or of a musical setting of it, sung in the Catholic Churches as part of the burial service, at the Communion of the Sick, and the like. During Holy Week it is performed with peculiar solemnity in the Sistine Chapel at Rome.

Mis'sa (Lat.) The Mass...*M. brev'is*, short mass...*M. canta'ta*, chanted mass ..*M. pro defunc'tis*, see *Requiem*. ..*M. solem'nis*, or *solen'nis*, high mass.

Mis'sal. (Lat. *missa'le*.) The R. C. Mass-book, containing the liturgical forms necessary for the celebration of mass the year round.

Miss'klang (Ger.) Discord, cacophony.

Misterio'so (It.) Mysterious...*Misteriosamen'te*, mysteriously.

Mistichan'za (It.) A quodlibet.

Misu'ra (It.) A measure...*Misura'to*, measured, in exact time.

Mit (Ger.) With.

Mit'klang (Ger.) Resonance...*Mit'- klingende Töne*, overtones.

Mit'telkadenz (Ger.) Semi-cadence. ..*Mit'telstimme*, an inner part or voice.

Mixed cadence. See *Cadence*...*Mixed*

canon, one in which the successive parts enter at different intervals...*Mixed chorus, quartet, voices*, vocal music combining male and female voices.

Mixolyd'ian. See *Mode*.

Mixture. (Ger. *Mixtur'*; Fr. *fourniture*; It. *ripie'no, accor'do*.) A compound auxiliary flue-stop with from 3 to 6 ranks of pipes sounding as many harmonics of any tone represented by a given digital. These harmonics are generally octaves and fifths of the fundamental tone ; sometimes a third, or even a seventh, is added; they are higher in comparative pitch for low tones than for high ones, (see *Break* 3) ; e. g. for the tone C the 3-rank mixture would usually contain c^1-g^1-c^2 ; and for c^1, c^2-g^2-c^3 (not c^3-g^3-c^4). In some old German organs mixtures are found having from 8 up to 24 (!) ranks, there being, of course, several pipes to each harmonic. —Mixtures are used to reinforce and " brighten " the upper partials of the heavier foundation-stops.

Mo'bile (It.) With a facile movement, readily responsive to emotion or impulse.

Mode. 1. For Greek modes, see *Greek music*.—2. (Lat. *mo'dus*.) The medieval church-modes were octave-scales, like the Greek modes, and also borrowed their names (see below) from the latter ; but they, and the fundamental diatonic scale A-a, were conceived as *ascending* scales, a distinct departure from ancient theory. They were called *church*-modes because each chant in the Gregorian antiphony was kept strictly within the compass of some one of these octave-scales, without chromatic change save that from $B\flat$ to B, or vice-versa.

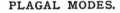

AUTHENTIC MODES.	PLAGAL MODES.

Mode I (Do'rian). Mode II (Hypodo'rian).

Mode III (Phryg'ian). Mode IV (Hypophryg'ian).

Mode V (Lyd'ian). Mode VI (Hypolyd'ian).

Mode VII (Mixolyd'ian). Mode VIII (Hypomixolyd'ian).

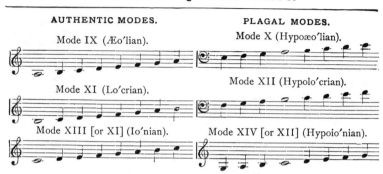

AUTHENTIC MODES.

Mode IX (Æo'lian).

Mode XI (Lo'crian).

Mode XIII [or XI] (Io'nian).

PLAGAL MODES.

Mode X (Hypoæo'lian).

Mode XII (Hypolo'crian).

Mode XIV [or XII] (Hypoio'nian).

In the authentic modes the *Final* (what we should call the *key-note*) is the lowest tone ; in the plagal modes, a fourth above the lowest ; it is marked by a whole note in the Table. Each plagal is derived from a parallel authentic ; St. Ambrose is supposed to have established the first 4 authentic modes, to which St. Gregory added the corresponding plagals ; these 8 were exclusively employed in serious composition down to the 16th century, despite the lack of any scale similar to the (*C-*) major and (*A-*) minor scales of modern music ; then, however, the last 4 modes were added. The *Locrian* (*B-b*) and *Hypolocrian* (*F-f*) were rejected as useless, neither fulfilling the law that each authentic mode should be divisible into a perfect fifth plus a perfect fourth, and each plagal mode into a fourth plus a fifth.—Both the names, and the prefix *hypo-*, are used in a sense different from that of the original Greek modes. the medieval theorists having misinterpreted the Greek nomenclature.

Greek Names.	Octave-scales.	Final Medieval Names.
Hypophrygian	g a b c¹ d¹ e¹ f¹ g¹	Mixolydian (Mode VII, 4th authentic)
Hypolydian	f g a b c¹ d¹ e¹ f¹	Lydian (Mode V, 3rd authentic)
Dorian	e f g a b c¹ d¹ e¹	Phrygian (Mode III, 2nd authentic)
Phrygian	d e f g a b c¹ d¹	Dorian (Mode I, 1st authentic)
	[d e f g a b c¹ d¹]	[Hypomixolydian (Mode VIII, 4th plagal)]
Lydian	c d e f g a b c¹	Hypolydian (Mode VI, 3rd plagal)
Mixolydian	B c d e f g a b	Hypophrygian (Mode IV, 2nd plagal)
Hypodorian (or Æolian)	A B c d e f g a	Hypodorian (Mode II, 1st plagal)

The gradual development of monodic, harmonic, and chromatic music, the evolution of the leading-note, the acceptance of the third as a consonance, and the recognition of the predominance of the tonic triad, with the modern system of transposing tempered scales in the major and minor modes thence resulting, led to the gradual disuse of the church-modes.

Mode hellénique (Fr.; also *troisième*

mode). The inverted major scale, beginning on the 3rd degree :

$$e^1—d^1—c^1\smile b—a—g—f\smile e.$$

so termed by Blainville (1711-69), this being the ancient Dorian mode (see *Greek music*).

Modera'to (It.; superl. *moderatis'simo.*) 1 (*noun*). Moderate ; i. e. at a moderate rate of speed, or tempo.—2 (*adverb*). (Also *moderatamen'te*). Moderately ; as *allegro moderato*, moderately fast.

Moder'no,-a (It.) Modern ; *alla moderna*, in modern style.

Modification. Same as *Temperament.*

Mo'do (It.) Mode ; style.

Mod'ulate. (Ger. *modulie'ren;* Fr. *moduler;* It. *modula're.*) To pass from one key or mode into another ; to effect a change of tonality...*Modulation.* (Ger. and Fr. *Modulation';* Fr. also *transition;* It. *modulazio'ne.*) Passage from one key to another ; change of tonality.
—A modulation may be either *final* or *transient;* it is *final* when the new tonic is permanently adhered to, or still another follows ; *transient* (*transitory, passing*), when the original tonic is speedily reaffirmed by a cadence... *Chromatic modulation*, one effected by the use of chromatic intervals ; *diatonic m.*, one effected by the aid of diatonic intervals ; *enharmonic m.*, one effected through employing enharmonic changes to alter the significance of tones or intervals.

Mod'ulator. See *Tonic Sol-fa.*

Mo'dus (Lat.) Mode.

Moll (Ger.) Minor...*Moll'akkord*, minor chord...*Moll'dreiklang*, minor triad...*Moll'tonart*, minor key... *Moll'tonleiter*, minor scale ; etc., etc.

Mol'le (Lat., "soft".) A term probably first used in the 10th century to designate the *B rotun'dum* (*B molle,*=♭), in opposition to the *B quadra'tum* (*B du'rum*, ♮, the modern B♮). Later it was applied to the hexachord *f—d*, in which *b*♭ was substituted for *b*♮ ; and, finally, to the minor key and triad (with flat third).

Mollemen'te (It.) Softly, gently.

Mol'lis (Lat.) See *Molle.*

Moloss(e). (Lat. *molossus.*) A metrical foot of 3 long syllables (— — —).

Mol'to,-a (It.) Much, very ; as *molto adagio*, very slowly ; *molto allegro*, very fast...*Di molto*, exceedingly, extremely.

Momen'tulum (Lat.) A 16th-rest.

Momen'tum (Lat.) An 8th-rest.

Mon'ochord. (Fr. *monocorde;* It. *monocor'do.*) I. A very ancient instr. for the precise mathematical determination of the intervals, consisting of a single string stretched over a soundboard and provided with a bridge sliding on a graduated scale, by means of which any desired division of the string could

be isolated, and intervals of true pitch obtained.—An instr. of the same name, but furnished with several strings for the purpose of obtaining harmonic effects, was the precursor of the clavichord.—2. The tromba marina.—3. A clavichord.—4. (Ger., recent.) A kind of bow-zither, having one string stretched over a fretted fingerboard attached lengthwise to the top of an oblong resonance-box.

Mon'ody. (Ger. and Fr. *Monodie';* It. *monodi'a.*) A style of composition (*monod'ic* or *monophon'ic*) in which one part, the melody, predominates over the rest, they serving as a support or accomp. to it. It took its rise in Italy about 1600, in the form of a vocal solo with instrumental accomp., the latter being at first a mere figured bass executed on the harpsichord, theorbo, etc. Its novelty lay, not in its newness, but in its employment and recognition by artists. It developed into the opera, cantata, and oratorio on the one hand, and, on the other, into all those forms of instrumental music in which the element of accompanied melody is found, as the suite, symphony, etc. (Also *Homophony, Monophony.*)

Monoph'onous. Capable of producing but one tone at a time ; opp. to *polyphonous*...*Monoph'ony*, see *Monody.*

Mon'otone. I. A single unaccompanied and unvaried tone.—2. Recitation (intoning, chanting) in such a tone.

Monter (Fr.) I. To ascend; *montant*, ascending.—2. To raise the pitch of.—3. To put strings on an instr.; also, to put an instr. together, to set it up.

Montre (Fr.) In the organ, the diapason ; so called because "shown" or set up in the organ-front, away from the soundboard.

Moralities. (Ger. *Moralitä'ten;* Fr. *moralités.*) A later form of the miracleplays or mysteries.

Morceau (Fr.) A piece, composition ; *morceau de genre*, characteristic piece.

Mordant (Fr.) Comp. *Graces.*

Mordent. (Ger. *Mor'dent*, *Bei'sser;* Fr. *pincé;* It. *morden'te.*) A grace consisting of the single rapid alternation of a principal note with an auxiliary a minor second below, thus:

played : 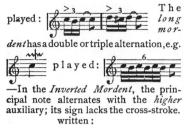 The long mor-

dent has a double or triple alternation, e.g.

played: —In the *Inverted Mordent*, the principal note alternates with the *higher* auxiliary; its sign lacks the cross-stroke.
written :

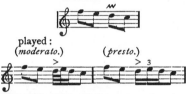

played :
(*moderato*.)   (*presto*.)

Moren'do (It.) Dying away, growing fainter and fainter (v. *Tempo-marks*).

Mormoran'do (It.) Murmuring, murmurous, in a very gentle, subdued tone. Also *mormore'vole*, *mormoro'so*.

Morris-dance. (Also *morrice-dance*, *Moresque*, *Morisco*, etc.) A sort of costume-dance, apparently of Moorish origin, in 4-4 time and of a boisterous character ; now obsolete.—Also, a kind of country-dance still performed in Yorkshire, England.

Mos'so (It., " moved".) Equivalent to "rapid" in the phrases *meno mosso*, less rapid, *più mosso*, more rapid, and *poco mosso*, somewhat rapid (e. g. *Allegretto poco mosso*, a rather lively *allegretto*, nearly *allegro*).

Mo'stra (It.) A direct.

Motet'. (Ger. *Motet'te;* Fr. *motet;* It. *mottet'to*.) A sacred vocal composition in contrapuntal style, without instrumental accomp. In former times the *a cappella* style was not always strictly adhered to. The *motet* resembles the *anthem* in having a biblical prose text, but differs from it in being polyphonic ; compositions in anthem-style are, however, sometimes called motets.—The Latin *mote'tus* is a term of various and sometimes obscure signification.

Motif' (Fr.) A motive.

Motion. I. The progression or leading of a single part or melody ; it is *conjunct* when progressing by steps, *disjunct* when progressing by skips.— 2. The progression of one part considered in relation to that of another ;

contrary or *opposite motion* is that in which one part ascends while the other descends ; *parallel* motion*, that in which both parts ascend or descend by the same interval ; *oblique motion*, that in which one part is held while the other ascends or descends ; *similar* motion*, that in which both parts ascend or descend together by dissimilar intervals ; *mixed motion*, that in which 2 or more of the above varieties occur at once between several parts.

* N.B.—The above fine distinction between *parallel* and *similar* motion is very often not observed, the term *parallel motion* being used indiscriminately for both.

Mo'tive [sometimes pron. *mo-teev'*]. (Ger. *Motiv';* Fr. *motif';* It. *moti'vo*.) I. A short phrase or figure (rhythmic, melodic, or harmonic) used in development or imitation.—2. A theme or subject (see *Leading-motive*).—3. Sometimes used for *Measure*, as the rudimentary element of the *Period*.—*Measure-motive*, one whose accent coincides with the measure-accent.

Mo'to (It.) I. Motion...*M. contra'rio*, contrary motion...*M. mi'sto*, mixed motion...*M. obbli'quo*, oblique motion...*M. perpe'tuo*, perpetual motion. ..*M. ret'to*, similar motion.—2. Movement, tempo...*Con moto*, with an animated and energetic movement...*Moto preceden'te*, at the former tempo.

Motteggian'do (It.) Bantering, facetious.

Mottet'to (It.) Motet.

Mo'tus (Lat.) Motion...*M. contra'rius*, contrary motion...*M. obli'quus*, oblique motion...*M. rec'tus*, similar motion.

Mouth. The opening on the front side of an organ-pipe...*Mouth-harmonica*, a set of graduated metal reeds mounted in a narrow frame, blown by the mouth, and producing different tones on expiration and inspiration...*Mouth-organ*, see Pan's-pipes...*Mouthpiece* (Ger. *Mund'stück;* Fr. *embouchure;* It. *imboccatu'ra*), that part of a wind-instr. which a player places upon or between his lips.

Mouvement (Fr.) Movement, tempo. ..*Mouvementé*. A piece is said to be *bien mouvementé* when its rhythmical structure is elegant and symmetrical.

Movement. I. (Ger. *Bewe'gung;* Fr. *mouvement;* It. *movimen'to*, *mo'to*, *tem'-po*.) Tempo, rate of speed.—2. (Ger.

Satz; Fr. *partie;* It. *tempo.*) A principal and usually separate division or section of a composition, containing themes and a development peculiar to itself.

Muances (Fr.) See *Mutation* 2.

Mund (Ger.) Mouth...*Mund' harmonika,* mouth-harmonica...*Mund' loch,* mouth (of an organ-pipe; usually *Auf'-schnitt*)...*Mund' stück,* mouthpiece.

Mune'ira (Span.) A Galician dance of moderate tempo and in 2-4 time, with an *auftakt* of a quarter-note, and the strong beat marked by the castanet-rhythm.

Mun'ter (Ger.) Lively, animated, gay. (Also *adverb.*)

Murky. A *murky-bass* is one progressing in broken octaves; a harpsichord-piece with such a bass was called a *murky.*

Muse. The mouthpiece or wind-pipe of the bagpipe.

Musette (Fr.) 1. A small and primitive kind of oboe.—2. A variety of bagpipe in which the wind is supplied by a bellows.—3. A short piece of music imitating in style that played on this kind of bagpipe, i. e. of a soft and gentle character and with a drone-bass; hence, the dance-tunes of the same style and name.—4. A reed-stop in the organ.

Mu'sica (Lat. and It.) Music...*M. da ca'mera,* chamber-music...*M. da chie'-sa,* church-music...*M. da tea'tro,* theatre (theatrical) music...*M. di gat'ti,* charivari (see *Katzenmusik*).

Musical box, Music-box. The so-called *Swiss music-box* consists of a metallic cylinder or barrel studded with small pins or pegs, and caused to revolve by clockwork. In revolving, the pins catch and twang a comb-like row of steel teeth arranged in a graduated scale, each tooth producing a tone of very accurate pitch. In the larger instr.s the barrel may be shifted so as to play several tunes, or is made exchangeable for others.—For the newer music-boxes, compare *Symphonion, Libellion.*

Musician. (Ger. *Mu'siker;* Fr. *musicien;* It. *mu'sico, musici'sta.*) One who practises music in any of its branches as a profession.

Music-pen. 1. A soft-nibbed, broad-pointed pen for writing notes, etc.—2.

A 5-pointed pen for drawing the 5 lines of the staff on paper.

Music-recorder. See *Melograph, Phonograph, Phonautograph.*

Music-wire. Steel wire for the strings of mus. instr.s.

Musik' [-zeek'] (Ger.) Music...*Musik'-bande,* see *Bande*...*Musik'diktat,* see *Dictée musicale*...*Musik'direktor,* a conductor...*Musik'fest,* mus. festival. ..*Musik'meister,* conductor of a military band.

Musika'lien (Ger.) Music (i. e. musical compositions). [A trade term.]

Musikant' (Ger.) A vagabond or bungling musician.

Mu'siker, Mu'sikus (Ger.) A musician.

Musiquette (Fr.) Little piece of music; or (collectively) light music.

Mu'ta (It.) "Change!" A direction in orchestral scores indicating a change of crook or instr., or in the tuning of an instr., necessitated by a change of key.

Mutation. 1. (Ger. *Mutie'rung;* Fr. *mue;* It. *mutazio'ne.*) The change of the male voice at puberty.—2. (Ger. *Mutation';* Fr. pl. *mutations, muances;* It. *mutazio'ne.*) In medieval solmisation, the change or passage from one hexachord to another, with the consequent change of syllable (comp. *Solmisation*).—3. In violin-playing, "shifting."

Mutation-stop. In the organ, any stop, except a mixture, whose pipes produce tones neither in unison nor in octaves with the foundation- (8-foot) stops; i. e., all tierce and quint-stops, and their octaves.

Mute. 1. (Ger. *Däm'pfer;* Fr. *sourdine;* It. *sordi'no.*) The mute for the violin, etc., is a piece of brass or other heavy material, having cleft projections which permit of its firm adjustment on the bridge without touching the strings; its weight deadens the resonance of the sound-box. (Recently made in the form of a spring clip.) The direction for putting on the mutes is "con sordini"; for taking them off, "senza sordini".—2. A pear-shaped, leather-covered pad introduced into the bell of the horn or trumpet to modify the tone. Other forms of this mute are (for the horn) a pasteboard cone with a hole at the apex, and (for the trumpet) a cylindrical tube of wood pierced with holes.

Mu't(h)ig (Ger.) Spirited, bold. (Also *adverb.*)

Mutie'rung (Ger.) Mutation 1.

Mysteries. (Ger. *Myste'rien;* Fr. *mys-tères.*) Medieval scenic representations of biblical events, arranged originally by the monks, and generally accompanied by vocal, often by instrumental, music. The *Passion-plays* (still surviving at Oberammergau in Bavaria) are as old as the 7th or 8th century; the *Moralities*, a peculiar form of the Mysteries, in which abstract conceptions were personified, originated about the 13th century. The Mysteries were the precursors of the *Oratorio.*

N.

Nacaire (Fr.) A former kind of kettledrum.

Nac'cara, Nac'chera (It.) 1. See *Nacaire.*—2. (Also *Gnac'care;* pl.) Castanets.

Nach (Ger.) After; according to... *Nach'ahmung*, imitation... *Nach Belie'-ben*, ad libitum... *Nach'druck*, emphasis; *nach'drücklich* (or *mit Nachdruck*), with emphasis, emphatically... *Nach'-lassend*, slackening (in tempo)... *Nach'-lässig*, careless, negligent (also *adverb*). ...*Nach'ruf*, a farewell, leave-taking. ...*Nach'satz*, after-phrase, second phrase or theme, contrasting with *Vor'dersatz. Nach'schlag*, (*a*) the unaccented appoggiatura; (*b*) "after-beat" of a trill (also *Nach'schleife*)... *Nach'spiel*, a postlude... *Nach'tanz*, see *Saltarello* 2... *Nach und nach'*, step by step, gradually.

Nacht (Ger.) Night... *Nacht'horn, Nacht'schall*, a flue-stop in the organ, having covered pipes of 2, 4, or 8-foot pitch, and resembling in tone the Quintatön or the *Hohl'flöte... Nacht'-hornbass*, the same stop on the pedal. ...*Nacht'stück*, a nocturne.

Nænia. See *Nenia.*

Na'gelgeige,-harmonika (Ger.) Nail-fiddle.

Naïf, Naïve (Fr.), **Naiv'** (Ger.) Naive; unaffected, ingenuous, artless... *Naïve-ment*, naively... *Naïveté*, artlessness, simplicity, etc.

Nailfiddle. (Ger. *Na'gelgeige.*) An instr. consisting of a soundboard in which are inserted from 16 to 20 steel or brass pins of graduated length, sounded by means of a bow well smeared with rosin; the tone is like that of the harmonica. Inv. by Johann Wilde of St. Petersburg, toward the middle of the 18th century.

Naked fifth (fourth). A fifth (fourth) without an added third. (Also *bare.*)

Narran'te (It.) In narrative-style; calls for a very distinct declamatory enunciation of the words sung.

Narrator. The personage who, in the earlier passion-plays and oratorios, sings the narrative portions of the text.

Nasard (Fr.; Span. *nasar'do;* Ger. *Nasat'.*) In the organ, the mutation-stop commonly known as the Twelfth (2⅔-foot pitch). The *Gros-nasard* (*Gross'nasat*), is a quint-stop either on pedal (10⅔-ft.) or manual (5⅓-ft.); the *Petit nasard* (*Larigot*), is a double-octave quint-stop (1⅓-ft.) (Also *nasarde, nassart, nasillard, nazad.*)

Nason flute. An organ-stop having stopped pipes of mild, suave tone.

Natur'- (Ger.) Natural... *Natur'horn*, a *Wald'horn*(without valves)... *Natur'-skala*, natural scale... *Natur'töne* (or *natür'liche Töne*), natural harmonic tones, as of the horn, etc... *Natur'-trompete*, a trumpet without valves.

Natural. 1. (Ger. *Auf'lösungszeichen;* Fr. *bécarre;* It. *bequa'dro.*) The sign ♮ (see *Chromatic Signs*).—2. A white digital on the keyboard... *Natural harmonics*, those produced on an open string; opp. to *artificial*, which are produced on a stopped string... *Natural hexachord*, that beginning on *C... Natural horn*, the French horn without valves... *Natural interval*, one found between any 2 tones of a diatonic major scale... *Natural key*, see *Nat. scale... Natural pitch*, that of any wind-instr. when not overblown... *Natural scale*, C-major, having neither sharps nor flats. ...*Natural tone*, a tone producible, on a wind-instr. with cupped mouthpiece, by simply modifying the adjustment of the lips and the force of the air-current, without using mechanical devices for changing the length of the tube (such as keys, valves, or the slide). Such natural tones always belong to the series of higher partials (comp. *Acoustics*). These are the only tones which an instr. having a tube of invariable length (like the natural [French] horn) can yield; they are produced by the division of the vibrating air-column defined by their tube into aliquot (equal) parts of constantly decreasing length. A tube of wide bore in proportion to its length will yield most readily the low and medium tones of the series, including the fundamental; a tube comparatively narrow, the medium and higher tones, omitting the fundamental. Any metal instr. yielding the fundamental tone (e. g. the Tuba) is called a complete instr. (Ger. *Ganz'instrument*); one incapable of yielding it (e. g. the Trumpet), an incomplete instr. (Ger. *Halb'instrument*). With a minimum air-pressure, and the lips most relaxed, the fundamental tone of the tube is sounded.

Natura'le (It.) Natural, unaffected... *Naturalmen'te*, naturally, etc.

Natura'lis (Lat.) Natural... *Can'tus naturalis*, and *hexachor'dum natura'le*, music, and the hexachord, embracing the tones *c d e f g a*.

Naturalist' (Ger.) A natural or self-taught singer; one not trained according to any vocal "method" or "school". ..*Naturalis'tisch*, amateurish.

Naturel,-le (Fr.) Natural.

Neapolitan sixth. A chord of the sixth on the subdominant in minor, with minor sixth: or

Ne'ben- (Ger.) By-, accessory...*Ne'bendominante*, dominant of the dominant, e. g. *D* in the key of *C*...*Ne'bendreiklang*, secondary triad...*Ne'bengedanke*, accessory theme or idea...*Ne'benklang*, accessory tone (either essential, as harmonics, or unessential). ..*Ne'bennote*, auxiliary note...*Ne'benseptimenakkorde*, secondary chords of the 7th (all except the dominant)... *Ne'benstimme*, accompanying or *ripieno* part...*Ne'benwerk* (on 2-manual organ), choir-organ.

Neck. (Ger. *Hals;* Fr. *manche;* It. *ma'nico.*) The elongated projection from the body of an instr. of the viol or lute family, bearing the fingerboard on its upper side, and ending with the head or scroll.

Negligen'te (It.) Negligent, careless. ..*Negligentemen'te*, negligently.

Ne'gli, nei, nel, nell', nel'la, nel'le, nel'lo (It.) In the.

Ne'nia. A funeral song or lament; a dirge.

Neo-German school. The disciples of Schumann and Liszt; the romantic school of composition, and the "programmists".

Ne'te. See *Lyre.*

Nettamen'te (It.) Neatly, cleanly; clearly, distinctly...*Net'to*, neat, clean, clear.

Neu'deutsche Schu'le. See *Neo-German.*

Neu'ma, Neume. 1. In Gregorian music, a melisma.—2. In medieval mus. notation, one of the characters used to represent tones, inflections, and graces. They were of different and fluctuating form and signification, at first with a curious outward resemblance to modern short-hand, later changing to coarse and heavy strokes and flourishes. The earlier neumes (8th to 13th century) can hardly be successfully deciphered, even with the aid of the letters (*litteræ significativæ*) sometimes added, or of the lines (inception of staff-notation) employed, from the 10th century onward, to fix the pitch; for they were less an attempt at exact notation in the modern sense, than an aid to memory, a system of mnemonic signs. They are important as being the first attempt to exhibit the relative pitch of notes by their relative height on the page; they gradually passed over into the *notæ quadratæ* and ligatures of Plain Song.

Neuvième (Fr.) The interval of a ninth.

Nicht (Ger.) Not.

Ni'colo (It.) A large kind of bombardon (17th century); precursor of the bassoon.

Nie'der- (Ger.) Down...*Nie'derschlag*, down-beat...*Nie'derstrich*, down-bow. ..*Nie'dertakt*, down-beat.

Nineteenth. 1. The interval of 2 octaves and a fifth.—2. See *Larigot* (organstop).

Ninth. (Ger. *No'ne;* Fr. *neuvième;* It. *no'na.*) An interval wider by a semitone or a whole tone than a perfect octave; a *compound second;* but distinguished in theory from the second by the fact that it enters into the formation of a chord in the series of ascending thirds...*Chord of the ninth*, a chord practically recognized under 2 principal forms: (1) the *major*, and (2) the *minor* chord of the ninth, each a chord of the dominant seventh with added ninth:

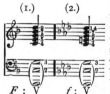

(1.)   (2.)   The former, based on par-tials 2–3–(4)–5–(6)–7–9, is acoustically the more euphonic, though the latter has been often used in practical music. Their inversions are figured according to the ordinary rule. (Comp. *Chord.*)

F : V   *f* : V

No'bile (It.) Noble; refined, chaste... *Nobilmen'te*, nobly... *Con nobiltà'*, with nobility, grandeur.

Noch (Ger.) Still, yet.

Nocturne (Fr.; Ger. *Noktur'ne, Nacht'-stück;* It. *nottur'no.*) A word introduced by Field as a title for piano-pieces of a dreamily romantic or sentimental character, but lacking a distinctive form.

Noc'turns. Services of the Church held during the night, each portion of the Psalm set aside for this purpose being termed a Nocturn.

Nodal figures. The figures corresponding to the nodal lines of a vibrating plate of wood, glass, etc.; rendered visible by strewing fine dry sand on the plate, this sand being tossed by the vibrating portions of the plate to the *nodal lines*, which are points of perfect or comparative rest; the symmetrical figures thus formed are also called *Chladni's figures*, having been discovered by him... *N. point*, see *Node.*

Node. (Ger. *Kno'tenpunkt;* Fr. *nœud;* It. *no'do.*) A point or line in a vibrating body (such as a string, soundboard, trumpet, bell), which remains at rest during the vibrations of the other parts of the body. Opp. to *Loop* 1.

No'dus (Lat., "knot".) An enigmatical canon.

Noël (Fr.) A sort of carol sung in the South of France, chiefly on the day before Christmas, or Christmas eve.

Nœud (Fr.) 1. A turn (usually *groupe*). —2. A node.

Noire (Fr.) A quarter-note.

Nome, Nomos (Gk.) A canon (rule) for mus. composition; hence, a song composed according to the rule.

Non (It.) Not.

No'na (It.), **No'ne** (Ger.) The interval of a ninth.

Nones. The fifth of the canonical hours.

Nonet'. (Ger. *Nonett';* It. *nonet'to.*) A composition for 9 voices or instr.s.

Non'nengeige (Ger.) Nun's-fiddle, tromba marina.

Nono'le (Ger.) Nonuplet.

Non'uplet. A group of 9 notes of equal time-value, executed in the time proper to 6 or 8 of the same kind belonging to the regular rhythm.

Normal'ton (Ger.) Standard pitch... *Normal'tonarten* (pl.), normal keys... *Normal'tonleitern*, normal scales.

No'ta (Lat. and It.) A note... *N. buo'na*, an accented note... *N. cambia'ta (cambita)*, (a) a changing-note; (b) an irregular resolution of a dissonance by a skip... *N. caratteri'stica*, leading-note. .. *N. catti'va*, an unaccented note... *Nota contra notam* (Lat.), note against note, equal counterpoint... *N. d'abbellimen'to*, a grace-note... *N. da passa'gio*, a passing-note... *N. falsa*, a changing-note. .. *N. principa'le*, a principal (essential) note... *N. quadra'ta (quadriquar'ta)*, a Gregorian or plain-song note... *N. roma'na*, a neume... *N. sensi'bile*, the leading-note.

Notation. Musical notation is the art of representing musical tones by means of written characters. Letters, numerals, and signs of different kinds, have been used. The signs now almost universally employed are called notes, and are written on a staff of 5 lines; hence, this system of writing music is termed *Staff-notation* (Comp. also *Alphabetical notation, Neumes, Numerals, Tonic Sol-fa.*)

§1. The lines and spaces of the staff indicate the pitch of the notes. The lines which Hucbald first used (about A.D. 900), served the same end by representing *strings;* in the spaces between, the syllables of the words sung were written, the relative pitch of the successive tones being (sometimes) marked by the letters *t* (=*tonus*, whole tone), and *s* (=*semitonium*, semitone).—This system was also used later for noting the primitive part-music called *or'ganum* or *discant;* increasing the number of lines as far up or down as necessary, and setting the syllables for the several parts vertically one above the other.—An example of one-part notation acc. to Hucbald now follows :

			ta		
		li/ \		lus\	
	Ec\	Isra \ /	in quo \	o/	no\
S	ce\	/	he	do/	on\
	vere /				est

Solution in choral notes:

Ec - ce ve - re Is - ra - he - li - ta, in quo do - lus non est.

Nearly contemporaneously with Hucbald's invention, an innovation appeared in neumatic notation ; a red horizontal line was drawn across the page, and all neumes written on this line were of the same pitch, this pitch being fixed by a letter *f*: set before the line. A second line, but yellow, was soon added for c^1 above the *f*-line (or *below*, for plagal melodies) ; the two greatly facilitated the reading of written music. Another improvement, in a different direction, is shown by an orderly system of lines marked in regular succession by Greek letters set before them, the tones being represented by points or dots on the lines. To Guido d'Arezzo is generally ascribed the systematization and introduction (about 1026) of the *4-line staff*, in which both *lines* and *spaces* were at length utilized ; he retained the red and yellow lines, added a third (black) line between them for *a*, and a fourth (black) line either above or below these three, according to the range of the melody written, for e^1 or *d*; he did not use notes, but either letters or neumes.

§2. A staff being thus established, and affording a firm basis for exactly fixing the pitch of written music, the neumes hitherto in ordinary use gradually lost their hieroglyphical appearance and became transformed into the **Choral Notes** of Plain Chant, the regular square form of which (■) gave rise to the name *nota quadrata* or *quadriquarta*, other shapes occurring only occasionally in certain figures ◆, ◆◆, or ◆◆ ■. The 4-line staff is still retained in Plain Chant ; other staves, having from 6 to 15 or more lines, were arbitrarily em-

ployed down to the 15th century, when the 5-line staff for all vocal music except Plain Chant, and the *6-line staff* for organ-music, were universally adopted ; the present 5-line staff superseded the latter after the invention of music-printing.—All this time the form of the clefs was likewise changing, the original *f* and *c* becoming :

(*f*)   (*c*)

etc.; the *g* also assumed a great variety of fantastic shapes before the modern forms were finally settled.

§3. **Mensurable notation,** differing from that of Plain Chant by expressing a determinate (relative) time-value of the tones in its notes, which were invented for the exact indication of rhythmic relations, appeared near the beginning of the 12th century. The notes in use for some 200 years, and imitated from Plain Chant, were the *Large* (■) or *duplex longa* or *maxima;* the *Long* (■) or *longa;* the *Breve* (■), and the *Semibreve* (◆ or ▼) ; to which were then added the *Minim* (♩) and *Semiminim* (♪). Early in the 15th century the first five were supplanted by the *open* notes (large ⊣, long ⊢, breve ◻, semibreve ◇ or △, minim ♩), the smaller notes which had been gradually added being written in 2 forms :

Semiminima [♩] ♪ or ♩.

Croma or Fusa [♪] ♪ or ◆.

Semicroma or Semifusa [♪] ♪ or ♪

Below are the corresponding **rests** :

Perfect Large-rest.	Imperf. Large-rest.	Perf. Long-rest.	Imperf. Long-rest. (Pausa)	Breve-rest (Semipau.)	Semibr.-rest	Minim-rest (Suspirium) (Semisuspirium).	Semiminim-rest	Croma-rest	Semicr.-rest

—The single notes were often joined in groups (comp. art. *Ligature*).—The angular notes of measured music were not finally supplanted by modern round notes, in music-printing, till about 1700, though in MS. music they had been freely employed since the 16th century.

For determining the relative time-value of the notes, various and often conflicting rules were made for the *Modus* (mode), *Tempus* (time-value of the breve), *Prola'tio* (prolation), *Color*, *Position*, etc.; a brief explanation of the 16th-century rules follows, premising, that the terms *perfect* and *imperfect* refer to the measure or time, *triple* time being regarded (out of reverence for the "Blessed Trinity") as perfect, while *duple* time was held to be imperfect.

MODUS (mode) governed the subdivision of the *Large* into Longs, and of the *Long* into Breves : in the

Modus major perfectus, $1 \text{ } \equiv = 3 \text{ }$

    "   " imperfec., $1 \equiv = 2$

    " minor perfectus, $1 = 3 \equiv$

    "   " imperfec., $1 = 2 \equiv$

TEMPUS (time) governed the subdivision of the *Breve* into Semibreves ; in Tempus perfectum (sign the circle

$\bigcirc$), $1 \equiv = 3 \diamond$

Tempus imperfec. (sign the semic.

C), $1 \equiv = 2 \diamond$

PROLATIO (prolation) governed the subdivision of the *Semibreve* ; in

Prolatio major $1 \diamond = 3 \diamondsuit$

    " minor $1 \diamond = 2 \diamondsuit$

the former marked by a dot in the time-signature ($\odot$ or C), the latter simply by the absence of a dot.*

The usual *mode-signatures* were vertical strokes (long-rests) at the head of the staff ; e. g., with the signs for *tempus* and *prolatio* :

{ Modus maj. perf.
} Modus min. perf.
} Tempus perfectum
{ Prolatio major

---

* The system previously in vogue referred to the relative time-value of the notes in general ; thus, according to de Vitry (13th century) :

I. prolatio : $\blacksquare = 3 \blacklozenge$, and $1 \blacklozenge = 3 \blacklozenge$

II.   " $\blacksquare = 3 \blacklozenge$, " $1 \blacklozenge = 2 \blacklozenge$

III. " $\blacksquare = 2 \blacklozenge$, " $1 \blacklozenge = 3 \blacklozenge$

IV.   " $\blacksquare = 2 \blacklozenge$, " $1 \blacklozenge = 2 \blacklozenge$

{ Modus maj. imperf.
} Modus min. perf.
} Tempus imperfec.
{ Prolatio major

{ Modus maj. perf.
} Modus min. imperf.
} Tempus perfectum
{ Prolatio minor

{ Modus maj. imperf.
} Modus min. imperf.
} Tempus imperfectum
{ Prolatio minor

N.B.—The time-signatures were often written smaller, between the second and third, or third and fourth, lines, etc.—The mode-signatures were also drawn from the fourth line down to the lowest ; as a rule, they were omitted altogether, leaving the reader to ascertain the mode from conventional peculiarities in the notation called *sig'na impli'cita* or *intrin'seca* (implied signs), in contradistinction to the *signa indicia'lia* (indicatory signs) ; as, in the *greater mode perfect*, a group of 3 black larges (see *Color*, below), or, in the *lesser mode perfect*, a group of 2 black longs, or 2 breve-rests at the beginning of a modal unit.

POSITION (i. e. the order in which the notes stood) was very important. A long followed by a long, or a breve by a breve, was always *perfect* (tripartite) *by position;* whereas a long preceded or followed by a breve, or a breve preceded or followed by a semibreve, was always *imperfect* (bipartite) *by position*. After the minim was invented, the semibreve also became similarly influenced by its position ; the minim and lesser notes were always perfect.

COLOR was the general designation for notes differing in color from those ordinarily used ; the red note (*no'tula ru'bra*) of the 14th century generally marked a change from perfect to imperfect time, or vice versa ; the white note (*notula alba*) was at first used like the red, but soon obtained the fixed and definite signification of *imperfection* in opposition to the ordinary black note (of the 14th century); finally, the black note (*notula nigra*) of the 16th and 17th centuries, when the *white* notes were universally adopted, in its turn indicated imperfection ; thus, from the 15th century onward, groups of 2 or more black notes had the *proportio hemiolia* to the surrounding white notes, i. e. their time-value stood to that of the latter in the ratio of 2 to 3,—hence their name *Hemiola* or *Hemiolia* (q. v.)

AUGMENTATION AND DIMINUTION. Terms used loosely to express any increase or decrease in the time-value of the notes ; but signifying, specifically, (*augmentatio*) a retarding of the tempo, generally doubling the *integer valor;*

and (*diminutio*) an acceleration of the tempo, generally reducing the *integer valor* by one-half.—The *diminutio* was first expressed by a vertical line through the tempus-signature (⊘ ⊄ ⊕ ⊄), or by inverting the semicircle (⊃)*;* also by adding to the *tempus*-signature, in the midst of a composition, numerals or fractions (3, 2, $\frac{2}{1}$, $\frac{3}{1}$, $\frac{4}{1}$,); 2 or $\frac{2}{1}$ then signified that 2 *tactus* (semibreves ◇) were equal to 1 ◇ of the preceding tempo; etc., etc.—*Augmentatio* was generally employed to reverse a preceding *diminutio;* the sign for which was simply annulled by the usual sign for the *integer valor* (○, ⊂) or by the inversion of the fraction ($\frac{1}{2}$, $\frac{1}{3}$, etc.) These fractions, however, were properly termed *signs of Proportion.*

PROPORTION. The theory of *Proportio*, from the 15th century onward, treats of the different time-signatures and tempo-marks applied to several parts progressing simultaneously; for instance, in a 4-part composition the *integer valor* might be marked for the discant in *tempus perfectum* ○, and for the bass in *tempus imperfectum* ⊂, the alto might be in *tempus imperfectum diminutum* ⊄, while the tenor had *diminutio in tripla* ⊄ 3; further, changes might be made in any or all parts in the course of the piece, and were indicated by fractions (the *signs of proportion;* compare *Augmentation,* above).

ALTERATION (*alteratio*) was the doubling of the time-value of the second of 2 equal notes, and occurred either when the next largest kind of note was perfect, and the 2 (smaller) notes stood between two such large ones, or when the 2 notes were separated from a following note of equal or smaller value by a *punctum divisionis;* e. g. ⊨ ◇ ◇ ⊨ in *tempus perfectum* (○) would be expressed thus in modern notation (○ · | ◇ ○ | ○ ·).

The *Punc'tum* or *Punc'tus* (point, dot) had various uses; (*a*) *Punctum augmentatio'nis,* equivalent to our dot of prolongation; (*b*) *Punctum alteratio'nis,* which, placed before the first of 2 short notes lying between 2 long ones, doubled the value of the second short note and restored the perfection of the 2 long ones; (*c*) *Punctum perfectio'nis,* used in prolation, and also to restore the perfection of a note made imperfect by position; and (*d*) *Punctum divisio'nis* or *imperfectio'nis,* written between 2 short notes lying between 2 long ones, indicated the imperfection of both the latter.

None of these rules or signs were invariably followed or employed; the above remarks will serve, however, to give a correct general idea of the intricacies of Mensurable Notation. (Also see *Figura obliqua.*)

Note. (Ger. and Fr. *No'te;* It. *no'ta.*) One of the signs used to express the relative time-value of mus. tones. (Comp. *Notation.*) The notes employed in modern notation are the following:

	English.	**German.**	**French.**	**Italian.**
⊨ , ⊨ or ‖⊒‖	{ Breve, or { Double note	Brevis	Brève, or Carrée	Breve
○	{ Semibreve, or { Whole note	{ Ganznote, or { ganze Taktnote	{ Semi-brève, or { Ronde	Semibreve
⊘	{ Minim, or { Half-note	{ Halbnote, or { halbe Note	Blanche	{ Minima, or { Bianca
⊿	{ Crotchet, or { Quarter-note	{ Viertel, or { Viertelnote	Noire	{ Semiminima, or { Nera
⊿	{ Quaver, or { Eighth-note	{ Achtel, or { Achtelnote	Croche	Croma
⊿	{ Semiquaver, or { Sixteenth-note	{ Sechzehntel, or { Sechzehntelnote	Double-croche	Semicroma
⊿	{ Demisemiquaver, or { Thirty-second-note	{ Zweiunddreissig- { stel(note)	Triple-croche	Semibiscroma
⊿	{ Hemidemisemiquaver, { or Sixty-fourth-note.	{ Vierundsechzig- { stel(note)	Quadruple-croche	Quattricroma

Black note, one having a solid head (⊿); opp. to *white note* (⊿). Also, a black digital or key...*Changing note,* see *Changing-note*...*Character-notes,* notes varying in shape from those in common use, employed to present characteristic qualities of the tones other than their time-values... *Choral-note*, see *Notation,* §§1 and 2...*Crowned note,* one with a hold (⌒) over it... *Double note,* a breve (= 2 ○)...*Driving-note,* a syncopated note... *Essential note,* a chord-note, or melody-note... *Grace-note,* see *Grace.* ..*Harmonic note,* a chord-note...*Hold-*

ing-note, a tone sustained in one part while the other parts move...*Leading note*, *Master-note*, see *Leading-note*... *Open note*, a white note...*Passing note*, see *Passing-note*...*Reciting-note*, see *Reciting*...*White note*, see *Black note*.

Note (Fr.) A note...*N. accidentée*, an accidental...*N. d'agrément*, or *de goût*, grace-note...*N. sensible*, leading-note. ...*Notes surabondantes* (pl.), groups like triplets, quintuplets, etc., etc.—The French names for the 7 notes of the scale are (1) *ut, ré, mi, fa, sol, la, si;* and (2) *tonique, sus-tonique, médiante, sous-dominante, dominante, sus-dominante, sensible*.

Noten (Ger. pl.) 1. Notes.—2. Music (i. e. compositions, pieces).

No'tenfresser (Ger.) Same as *Croque-note*.

No'tograph. See *Melograph*.

Nottur'no (It.) Nocturne ; dimin. *Notturni'no*.

Nourri (Fr., " nourished ".) *Un son nourri*, a full or well-sustained tone.

Novellette. A name probably first bestowed by Schumann (Op. 21) on a style of instrumental composition free in form, bold in harmonic structure, romantic in character, and specially characterized by a variety of contrasting themes and by considerable length. (Sometimes *Novelette*.)

Novemo'le (Ger.) A nonuplet.

Nowel. (Fr. *Noël*.) A Christmas carol, especially one in polyphonic style.

Nuance (Fr.) A shading or inflection in vocal delivery or instrumental rendering, affecting either timbre, tempo, or dynamic effect, to a greater or less degree.

Null. A naught or cipher. (See *O*.)— In thorough-bass, a cipher calls for *tasto solo*.

Number. 1. A principal division or movement of an extended composition, like an opera or oratorio ; or any smaller and more or-less complete portion of a large work, as a song, aria, interlude, etc.; or, finally, any single piece on a program.—2. Equivalent to *Opus-number*.

Numerals. For the employment of *Arabic numerals*, comp. *Abbreviations* 2, *Fingering*, *Harmonium-music*, *Organ*, *Phone* §6, *Pitch* §2, *Tablature*, *Thorough-bass*.—As abbreviations, *2-time*, *3-time*, are equivalent to duple

time, triple time ; *4tte, 5tte,* to quartet, quintet...(It.) 3ᵃ, 4ᵃ, 5ᵃ, 6ᵃ, 7ᵃ, contractions of Terza, Quarta, Quinta, Sesta, and Settima respectively; *8* or *8ᵛᵃ*, " all' ottava " ; *15ᵐᵃ*, " alla quindecima." ..(Fr.) 2p, 4p, 8p, 16p, equiv. to 2-foot, 4-foot, etc...*Roman numerals* are used, in mus. theory, to mark fundamental chords, thus showing at a glance from what triad any given inversion is derived (comp. *Chord*, and *Phone*, §§5, 6).

Nu'merus (Lat.) 1. Number.—2. Rhythm.

Nunc dimit'tis. The first 2 words in the Canticle of Simeon (Luke II, 29-32) " Nunc dimittis servum tuum, Domine, ...in pace" (Now, O Lord, lettest thou thy servant depart in peace) ; a text frequently used by composers, and forming portions of special services in the Catholic and Anglican Churches.

Nun's-fiddle. Tromba marina.

Nuo'vo,-a (It. [noo-ô'vo].) New...*Di nuovo*, anew, again.

Nut. 1. (Ger. *Sat'tel;* Fr. *sillet;* It. *capota'sto*.) The ridge over which the strings pass at the end of the fingerboard next the head of a violin, lute, etc.—2. (Ger. *Frosch;* Fr. *talon*.) The movable projection at the lower end of the violin-bow, to which the hair is attached, and by which it is tightened or slackened.—3. The *lower nut* on the violin, etc., is the ridge between the tailpiece and tailpin (or button).

O.

O. A circle (○) was the medieval sign for *tempus perfectum* (see *Notation*, §3); enclosing figure (①), see *Harmonium-music*...A small circle signifies, in modern notation, (*a*) an open string ; (*b*) the harmonic mark ; (*c*) the diminished fifth ; (*d*) in thorough-bass, *tasto solo;* (*e*) in old German clavier-music, marks notes to be played with the thumb.

O (It.) Or. (Also *od*.)

Obbliga'to (It.) Required, indispensable. An *obbl. part* is a concerted (and therefore essential) instrumental part; the term is specially applied to an instrumental part accompanying and vying with a vocal solo, very numerous examples of which may be found in the music of the 18th century.

Obbli'quo (It.) Oblique.

O′ber (Ger.) Over, above, higher... *O′-berdominan′te*, the dominant (opp. to *Un′terdominante*, the subdominant)... *O′berlabium*, upper lip (organ-pipe)... *O′bermanual*, upper manual... *O′ber-stimme*, highest part... *O′bertaste*, black key... *O′bertöne*, overtones, harmonics; *pho′nischer Oberton*, the 15th partial... *O′berwerk* (in Germany), *choir*-organ (when organ has 2 manuals); *swell*-organ (when organ has 3); *solo*-manual (when organ has 4 manuals). (Abbr. Obw., or O. W.)

Obligat′,-o (Ger.), Obligé (Fr.) Obbligato.

Oblique motion. See *Motion*... *Oblique pfte.*, an upright pfte. with strings running diagonally instead of vertically.

Obli′quus (Lat.) Oblique... *Figura obliqua*, see *Figura*... *Motus obliquus*, oblique motion.

O′boe. (Ger. *Obo′e;* Fr. *hautbois;* It. *oboè.*) 1. An orchestral instr. with conical wooden tube, having from 9 to 14 keys, and a double reed held by the player directly between his lips, he thus completely controlling the expression. Compass 2 octaves plus a seventh :
is formed by octaves of the fundamental tones, as in the flute, the fingering of which is also similar to that of the oboe. The tone is very reedy and penetrating, though mild, and equally suited for scenes of pastoral gaiety or of lonely melancholy. —The oboe family is incomplete, only 2 instr.s, the ordinary *treble oboe* (formerly *oboè pic′colo*) and the *alt-oboe* (*cor′no ingle′se*) being now used, the former as a non-transposing instr. written in the *G*-clef, the latter as a transposing instr. The bass for the oboe is furnished by the bassoon. The *oboè d'amo′re* (Fr. *hautbois d'amour*) is at present played only in the historical concerts of the Brussels Conservatory ; its pitch is a minor third below the treble oboe, and it differs from the obsolete *oboè bas′so* (Fr. *grand hautbois*) in having a spherical bell with a narrow aperture, whereby the tone is sensibly subdued.—The parent instr. of the oboe was the *shawm*. (See APPENDIX.)

Oboi′sta (It.) Oboist.

Ocari′na. A small wind-instr., an improvement of the toy 2-tone cuckoo-pipe. It has an elongated bird-shaped terra-cotta body 5 or more inches long, provided with a varying number of finger-holes, and with a mouthpiece like a whistle projecting from the side. The tone is mellow and fluty. The better kinds are provided with a tuning-slide.

Occhia′li (It.) Same as *Brillenbässe.*— Also, recent name for the white notes (𝄰 and 𝅘𝅥).

Ochet′to (It.), Oche′tus (Lat.) See *Hocket.*

Octachord. 1. An 8-stringed instr.—2. A series of 8 consecutive diatonic tones.

Octave. 1. (Ger. *Okta′ve;* Fr. *octave;* It. *otta′va.*) 1. A series of eight consecutive diatonic tones.—2. The interval (1:2) between the 1st and 8th tones of such a series. (Comp. *Interval.*)—3. The 8th tone of such a series, considered in its relation to the 1st ; or *vice versa.* The 8th is called the higher octave of the 1st, the 1st the lower octave of the 8th.—4. One of a number of arbitrary divisions of the entire range of tones employed in practice, made for the sake of convenience in referring to and establishing the absolute pitch of each tone. (Comp. *Pitch.*)—5. In the organ, a stop whose pipes sound tones an octave higher than those represented by the digitals touched ; like the Principal... *At the octave*, see *Ottava, all′.* ..*Broken octaves*, see *Broken*... *Concealed, covered,* or *hidden octaves*, parallel octaves *suggested* by the progression of 2 parts in similar motion to the interval of an octave... *Rule of the octave,* a system of harmonizing the diatonic scale taken as a bass ; much employed in tuition before the laws governing harmonic progression had been formulated... *Short octave,* in organ-building, the lowest octave of the keyboard, when abbreviated by the omission of all digitals not needed for the bass of the simpler harmonies, the digitals remaining being set side by side as if forming the regular series ; this was done to save expense and space... *Octave-coupler,* see *Coupler... Octave-flute,* (*a*) the piccolo ; (*b*) an organ-stop of 4-foot pitch... *Octave-scale,* see *Mode... Octave-stop,* same as *Octave* 5.

Octavia′na. See *Ottavino.* (Also *octavin, octavina, octavina.*)

Octavin′ [-veen]. 1. See *Ottavino.*—2. A wind-instr. inv. in 1893 by Oscar

Adler of Markneukirchen, Saxony. It has a single reed, and a wooden tube of conical bore; the keys are so arr. that the fingering is similar to that of the clarinet, oboe, etc. The tone is quite powerful; the timbre between oboe and horn. Made in 2 sizes, $B\flat$ and C; compass 3 octaves, c^1—c^4.

Octavo attachment. See *Octave-pedal*, under *Pedal*.

Octet'. (Ger. *Oktett'*; Fr. *octette*; It. *ottet'to*.) A composition for 8 voices or instr.s.

Octo-basse (Fr.) The octo-bass, an immense 3-stringed double-bass 4 metres in height, provided with a mechanism of digitals and pedals for stopping the strings; it is a third lower in pitch than the ordinary double-bass (C_1-G_1-C), and its tone is smooth and powerful. Inv. by J. B. Vuillaume in 1851.

Octochord. See *Octachord*.

Octo'le (Ger.) Octuplet.

Oc'tuor. Same as *Octet*.

Oc'tuplet. A group of 8 equal notes having the same time-value as 6 notes of the same kind in the regular rhythm.

Ode. A lyric poem intended for singing, and expressive of lofty and fervent emotion; it has no set characteristic metrical form.—Also, the musical setting of such a poem.

Ode'on. (Gk. *odei'on*; Lat. *ode'um*.) A public building in which musical contests were held.

O'der (Ger.) Or, or else.

Ode-symphonie (Fr.) A choral symphony, symphony with chorus.

Œuvre (Fr.) Work, composition.

Off. In organ-music, a direction to push in a stop or coupler; as *Sw. to Gt. off*...*Off the pitch*, false in pitch or intonation.

Of'fen (Ger.) 1. Open (of organ-pipes). —2. Parallel (fifths, octaves).

Of'fenbar (Ger.) Open, manifest...*Of'fenbare Okta'ven, Quin'ten*, open or parallel octaves, fifths.

Of'fertory. (Lat. and Ger. *Offerto'rium*; Fr. *offertoire*; It. *offerto'rio*.) In the R. C. Mass, the verses or anthem following the Credo and sung by the choir while the priest is placing the unconsecrated elements on the altar, during which the offerings of the congregation are collected. The daily offertory of the Gregorian antiphonary is now

usually supplemented by a motet on the same or different verses; such offertories are also composed with instrumental accomp.

Oficle'ide (It.) Ophicleide.

Oh'ne (Ger.) Without.

Oh'renquinten (Ger., "ear-fifths".) Covered fifths, the ill effect of which the ear detects (or is supposed to detect); sometimes used to designate mere theoretical finicalities.

Okta've (Ger.) Octave...*Oktavie'ren*, to produce, when overblown, the higher octave of the lowest natural tone of the tube (wind-instr.s)...*Oktäv'chen, Oktav'flöte*, piccolo...*Okta'vengattungen*, octave-scales...*Okta'venverdop'pelungen, Oktav'folgen,-paralle'len*, parallel or consecutive octaves...*Oktav'-Waldhorn*, a new species of Waldhorn, inv. by Eichborn and Heidrich of Breslau, of particularly full tone in the high and low parts of its range.

Oktavin'. See *Octavin* 2.

O'lio. A medley, or mus. miscellany.

Olivettes (Fr.) Dances after the olive-harvest.

Om'bra (It.) A shade, shading, nuance.

Om'nes, Om'nia (Lat.) All. See *Tutti*.

Om'nitonic. (Fr. *omnitonique*.) Having or producing all tones, chromatic; as *cor omnitonique*, chromatic (valve-) horn.

Once-accented. See *Pitch*.

Ondeggiamen'to (It.) Undulation... *Ondeggian'te*, undulating, wavy.

Ondulation (Fr.) Undulation...*Ondulé*, undulated, wavy.

One-lined. See *Pitch*.

Ongare'se (It.) Hungarian.

Onzième (Fr.) The interval of an eleventh.

Open diapason, *harmony, note, order, pedal, pipe*, etc.; see the nouns.

Op'era. (It. *O'pera* [*se'ria, buf'fa*, etc.], *dram'ma per mu'sica*; Fr. *opéra*; Ger. *O'per, Musik'drama*.) Modern opera, a form of dramatic representation in which vocal and instrumental music forms an essential and predominant element, took its rise towards the close of the 16th century in the striving of Italian (Florentine) composers and æstheticians to emancipate vocal music from the fetters of contrapuntal form. Their efforts led to the adoption of Monody (*q. v.*) as an art-style, and its application to dramatic purposes. The first opera given was probably "Dafne" (music by Peri and Caccini, book by Rinuccini) in 1594, which was lauded to the skies as a successful return to the musical declamation of the ancient Greek tragedy. The dry *stilo rappresentativo* of the earliest operas was improved upon by Monteverde (1568-1643), who employed vocal and orchestral resources with a freedom undreamed of up to his time, justly earning him the title of "father of the art of instrumentation". His orchestra for the opera "Orfeo" (1608) is given below:

2 Gravicembani, 2 Contrabassi di Viola, 10 Viole da Braccio, 1 Arpa doppia, 2 Violini piccoli alla francese, 2 Chitarroni, 2 Organi di legno, 3 Bassi da gamba, 4 Tromboni, 1 Regale, 2 Cornetti, 1 Flautina alla 22da, 1 Clarino, con 3 Trombe sorde.

With Alessandro Scarlatti (1659-1725) begins the era of modern Italian opera ; the sensuous charm of melody asserts itself more and more strongly ; the singer becomes master of the situation, and operas are written to his order. This tendency, early transplanted with Italian opera to France and Germany, was combatted by leading composers of those countries ; Lully (1633-1687) and Gluck (1714-1787) were reformers of the musical drama in ridding vocal dramatic music of superfluous melismas and coloraturas, making it follow throughout the course and sense of the action.—The *grand* or *heroic opera*, with its full choruses and finales, its arias and recitatives, and all varieties of ensemble (duets, trios, quartets, etc.) is a growth due to the grafting of Italian opera upon the French musical stock, and is the style especially affected by modern French composers ; the formal plan of Italian opera was likewise adopted by the great German composers, but with an infusion of artistic potency and sincerity which raise their productions far above the earlier level (Mozart, Beethoven), and a tinge of German romanticism which lends them a truly national color (Weber, Marschner). In comedy-opera the Italians were also pioneers (Pergolesi, Cimarosa) ; then follow the French (Grétry), and lastly the Germans (Mozart), all in the 18th century. Recent Italian operas show a distinct reaction against the old type, and bear witness to the strong influence of Germany (par-

ticularly of Wagner). France continues in the footsteps of her national composers (Grétry, Méhul, Boieldieu, Adam, Hérold, Halévy, Auber, Meyerbeer, Gounod).—To the purification, or rather annihilation, of the quasi-dramatic form of the grand opera, Richard Wagner (1813-1883) devoted all the powers of his marvelous genius. The guiding principle in his "Musikdramen" (musical dramas) is the harmonious coöperation of the dramatic, poetic, scenic, and musical elements ; thus, the action of the drama must never be checked or veiled by purely musical episodes, however charming in themselves ; the music must illustrate the (emotional) course and effects of the action, and nothing else. Hence the discontinuance of cut-and-dried movements and leveling of traditional forms, the rarity of full cadences and harmonic sequences, the richly modulated flow of inspired *melos*, the absence of "vain repetitions" of words and phrases, the uninterrupted dramatic interpretation by the orchestra of scenes and moods.—Both the grand opera and the Wagnerian drama find zealous advocates and imitators ; these, together with operettes of most various complexion, are the typical forms of musico-dramatic composition at present. The *comedy-opera* varies the form of grand opera by the interpolation of spoken dialogue... *Opéra bouffe* [formerly *bouffon*] (Fr.), light comic opera... *Opera buffa* (It.), Italian opera of a light and humorous cast,—comic opera in which the dialogue is carried on in *recitativo secco*, instead of being spoken... *Opéra comique* (Fr.), comedy-opera... *Opera seria* (It.), serious (grand, heroic, tragic) opera ; opp. to *opera buffa.*

Operet'ta (It.; Ger. and Fr. *Operet'te.*) A "little opera", with reference either to duration or style of composition. The text is in a comic, mock-pathetic, parodistic, or anything but serious vein; the music light and lively, in many cases interrupted by dialogue. The English *Ballad-operas* and the German *Singspiele* are varieties of the operetta. Modern masters of this style are Öffenbach, Lecocq, Strauss, Sullivan, etc.

Oph'icleide. (It. *Oficle'ide.*) The bass instr. of the key-bugle family (brass instruments with keys), now little used; it was made in various sizes and of different pitch ; (1) as *bass ophicleide* in *C,*

B♭, and *A♭*, compass 3 octaves and a semi-tone,chromatically ascending from: same, but only from: (2) as *alt-ophicleide* in *F* and *E♭*, compass the upward, (3) as *contrabass ophi-cleide* in *F* and *E♭*, compass only 2½ octaves, pitched an octave lower than the alt-ophicleide. Only the bass ophicleide was for a time in comparatively general use. (RIEMANN.) Now superseded in the orchestra by the bass tuba in *E♭*.

Opposite motion. Contrary motion.

Oppu're (It.) Or, or else; abbr. *opp.* See *Ossia.*

O'pus (Lat.) A work; abbr. *Op.* or *op.*

Orato'rio. (Fr. and It. ditto; Lat. and Ger. *Orato'rium.*) An extended composition of dramatic type, for vocal soli and chorus with orchestral accomp., usually having a text based on Scripture. It is distinguished from Opera mainly by the absence of scenic decoration and of stage-play by the performers, the action being contained *implicite* in the words. The oratorio takes its name from the *oratory* in which the monk Neri (d. 1595) held discourses, illustrated by sacred songs, on biblical history; similar productions of a mystical character, and a growing preponderance of the musical element, led up to the first known oratorio employing the *recitative* (E. del Cavaliere's "Anima e Corpo", 1600), which is also a distinctive feature of the opera. At this period oratorios were given with scenery and dramatic action (*azio'ne sacra*); the adoption by Carissimi (d. 1674) of the epical part of the *Narrator*, rendered both superfluous. The modern oratorio, with full orchestra, recitatives, lyrical soli, and the grand choruses (in their solemn and majestic breadth the fundamental characteristic of oratorio-style), is a product of the early 18th century (Haydn, Händel). (Comp. *Mysteries, Passion, Opera.*)—Rubinstein's "geistliche Opern" (sacred operas, *Paradise Lost, Tower of Babel, Moses, Christus*) are also called oratorios, although adapted for stage-performance, for which reason they are playfully termed "Operatorios."

Or'chestra. (Ger *Orches'ter;* Fr. *orches-*

tre.) 1. A place reserved (*a*) in the ancient Greek theatre, for the chorus, between audience and stage; (*b*) in ancient Rome, for seats for distinguished personages, in the same place; (*c*) in the modern theatre, for the band of instrumentalists, placed in front of the stage, and either just below the level of the lowest seats in the auditorium, or (as in the Wagner theatre at Bayreuth) sunk still lower, and provided with a half-roof concealing the musicians from the audience. Hence—2. (*a*) A company of musicians performing on the instr.s commonly used in the theatre or concert-hall in opera, in oratorio, etc., or in symphony-concerts; (*b*) the instr.s so played on, taken collectively; as *Wagner's orchestra*, a *symphony-orchestra.*—The orchestral instr.s (compare *Instruments*) are classified in 4 main groups: (1) The *strings* or *string-band* (violin, viola, violoncello, double-bass); (2) the *wood-wind* (flute, piccolo, English horn, oboe, bassoon, double-bassoon, clarinet, basset-horn); (3) the *brass-wind* (French horn, trumpet, trombone, saxhorns, bass tuba, cornet, [ophicleide]); (4) the *percussives* (kettle-drums, bass drum, snare-drum, cymbals, triangle, bells, gong, and likewise the harp and pfte., though the latter is not generally reckoned as an orchestral instr.)—The *full orchestra*, in which all the above groups are represented, may be either a *grand orchestra* (*symphony-orchestra*) or *small orchestra;* the former should contain 2 flutes, 2 oboes, 2 clarinets, 2 bassoons, 2 trumpets, 4 horns, 3 trombones, and a pair of kettledrums, to balance which there should be, in the "string-quartet", about 14 1st violins, 14 2nd violins, 9 violas, 9 violoncelli, and 6 double-basses (orchestra of the *Gewandhaus*, Leipzig); this basic grand orchestra may be enlarged *ad libitum* (as for the modern opera) by doubling the principal instr.s or by adding others. On the other hand, by leaving out the trombones, 2 of the horns, and even the kettledrums and clarinets, we get the *small orchestra.*—Groups 2 and 3 constitute what is called the "wind-band".

Orches'tral flute. An organ-stop closely imitating the flute in timbre.

Or'chestrate. (Ger. *orchestrie'ren;* Fr. *orchestrer;* It. *orchestrare.*) To write or arrange music for orchestra...*Or-*

thestra'tion, the art of writing music for performance by an orchestra; the science of combining, in an effective manner, the instr.s constituting the orchestra. [The best treatises on the instr.s and on orchestration are by Gevaert, Berlioz, and Riemann.]

Orchestre. (Fr.) Orchestra...*À grand orchestre*, for full orchestra.

Orchestri'na di ca'mera. One of various small keyboard free-reed instr.s, each constructed with the compass and timbre of some orchestral instrument which it was intended to replace, such as the clarinet, oboe, or bassoon; inv. by W. E. Evans, about 1860.

Orchestri'no. A kind of piano-violin imitating in tone the violin, viola d'amore, and 'cello; inv. by Pouleau of Paris in 1808.

Orches'trion. The modern *o*. is a large stationary barrel-organ (*q. v.*), generally with a self-acting mechanism, and imitating, by means of a variety of stops, various orchestral instr.s.—The *orch.* of Abbé Vogler (inv. towards the end of the 18th century) was a "simplified" organ, in which the complicated key-action and registers were abolished, the pipes standing directly behind the keys governing them, while the mixtures and numerous other adjuncts were done away with; it also had a Venetian swell, and for the 16-foot stops he substituted a combination of an 8-foot stop and a fifth (5⅓-ft.)—an idea still of utility.

Ordina'rio. (It.) Common, ordinary... *Tempo o.*, common (4-4) time.

Or'gan. (Lat. *or'ganum;* Ger. *Or'gel;* Fr. *orgue;* It. *or'gano*.) The largest and most powerful among musical instr.s, and of great antiquity, trustworthy accounts reaching back to the 2nd century B. C. Up to the 10th century A. D. the organ appears to have been a very primitive instr., with a diatonic compass of 2 octaves at most; the pipes were all flue-pipes, constructed in much the same manner as at present; reed-pipes were not introduced until the 15th century. But as early as 980 we hear of an organ at Winchester, England, which had 400 pipes and 2 manuals, each with a compass of 20 keys, and with 10 pipes to each key. The keys of the early organs were so broad, and the whole action so clumsy, that in

playing the plain-song melodies the clenched fists, or even the elbows, were used to depress them. Improvement has been steady, and chiefly due to German, English, and French organ-builders.—The *pipe-organ* (see also *Reed-organ*) is a keyboard wind-instr. consisting of few or many sets of pipes controlled by one or more keyboards. It has 3 distinct mechanisms: (1) The *wind-supply*, incl. bellows, windtrunk, windchest, etc.; (2) the *pipes*, called collectively the *pipe-work;* (3) the *keyboards*, *pedals*, and *stops*, called collectively the *action*, and under the player's direct control.—(1) The wind (compressed air) is obtained from a weighted *storage-bellows* filled by *feeders;* from the storage-bellows the wind is driven, by pressure of the weights on the storage-bellows, through a hollow wooden canal, the *windtrunk*, into the *windchest*, a wooden wind-reservoir beneath the *soundboard* on which the pipes are set; the wind passes up through the soundboard by way of *grooves* separated by *bars*, and leading directly to the pipes; the grooves are closed below by *pallets* (air-tight valves) opened by depressing the keys, and above by *sliders* opened by pulling out the draw-stops. —(2) The pipes are divided into 2 principal groups, *flue-pipes* and *reed-pipes* (which see; also comp. *Stop*). They are held in position over the soundboard by the *upper-board*, into which the *noses* of the pipes are inserted, and the *pipe-rack*, a board pierced with holes to admit the *feet* of the pipes and to support the latter. Each set of pipes (a *stop* or *register*) is ranged in one or more rows above a *slider*, which is a long, narrow strip of wood with holes corresponding in size and relative position to those in the feet of the pipes, and pushed back and forth by a *draw-stop;* when the latter is *on* (out, or drawn) the slider-holes come exactly under the pipe-feet, so that wind can pass from the grooves into the pipes; when the draw-stop is *off* (i. e. in) the slider-holes are out of position, and the pipes cannot speak.—(3) The *action* : (*a*) The *draw-stop action* is that acting upon the sliders by means of a system of levers; combination-pedals (see *Pedal*) are compound draw-stops...(*b*) The *keyboard-action* acts upon the pallets closing the grooves; when a key is depressed, its rear end rises, forcing up an upright wooden wand called a *sticker*, which raises the front end of a horizontal lever called a *backfall*, whose rear end in turn goes down, and pulls with it a *tracker*, a thin, vertical strip of wood bearing on its upper end the *pull-down* or *pallet-wire*, a wire attached to a *pallet* (valve) closing the lower side of a *groove;* this pull-down thus pulls down the pallet and admits the compressed air to the groove from the windchest; if a draw-stop is on, so that the wind can enter a pipe, the pipe will speak which corresponds to the key depressed. This is a common variety of key-action; *squares* and *roller-boards* are also often interposed between the stickers and trackers; more recent inventions are the *pneumatic* and the *electric actions*, in which the depression of a key simply forms a connection setting the compressed air or electric current at work. ..(*c*) *Couplers* are mechanical stops acting to connect 2 manuals, or pedal with manual, so that when one is played on, the other is combined with it. A 4-manual organ often has as many as 8, namely, 4 *manual-couplers* (Ch. to Gt.,

Sw. to Gt., Solo to Gt., Sw. to Ch.), and 4 *pedal-couplers* (Gt. to Ped., Ch. to Ped., Sw. to Ped., Solo to Ped.) The organ-keyboards are usually called *manuals;* there may be from 1 to 5 (see list below) with or without *pedal-keyboard*. Usual compass of manuals, 4 octaves and a fifth, with 56 keys (sometimes 5 full octaves), from C to g^3:

Compass of pedal, up to 2 octaves and a fourth, with 30 keys:

This notation, however, expresses only a part of the full compass, the lowest pedal-pipes), yielding C_2 (2 octaves below and the highest manual-pipes (piccolo 1-foot) producing g^6 (3 octaves higher than the total compass of the organ thus being 9 octaves and a fifth (C_2 to g^6).—The stops belonging to each manual are set on a separate soundboard or set of soundboards, and constitute a *partial organ.*—The names of the manuals follow :

ENGLISH.	GERMAN.	FRENCH.	ITALIAN.
Gt. org. manual	Haupt'werk (Man. I.)	Grand-orgue (1ᵉʳ clavier)	Principale.
Choir manual	Un'terwerk (Man. II.)	Positif (2ᵉ clavier)	Organo di coro.
Swell manual	Schwell'werk (Man. III.)	Clav. de récit (3ᵉ clavier)	Organo d'espressione.
Solo manual	So'loklavier (Man. IV.)	Clav. des bombardes (4ᵉ clav.)	Organo d'assolo.
Echo manual	E'choklavier (Man. V.)	Clav. d'écho (5ᵉ clavier)	Organo d'eco.

Organet'to (It.) A bird-organ ; a barrel-organ.

Organier (Fr.) Organ-builder.

Organi'sta (It.) Organist.

Organis'trum (Lat.) Hurdy-gurdy.

Or'gano (It.) Organ (*q. v.*)...*O. pie'no*, full organ...*O. porta'bile*, a portable organ.

Organochor'dium. A combined pfte. and pipe-organ (Fr. *piano organisé*); the idea originated with Abbé Vogler.

Organ-point. (Ger. *Or'gelpunkt ;* Fr. *point d'orgue ;* It. *pun'to d'or'gano.*) A tone sustained in one part to harmonies executed by the others. It is ordinarily a bass note (usually the tonic or dominant, or even both combined), and is also called a *pedal-point*, or *pedal;* but a tone so sustained in a higher part is more properly termed a *holding-note*, or simply a *sustained tone*, and the organ-point is then sometimes termed *inverted.* —*Pastoral organ-point*, tonic and dominant sustained together in the bass.

Or'ganum (Lat.) 1. An instrument ; later, an organ.—2. The earliest attempts at harmonic or polyphonic music, in which the parts progressed in parallel fifths and fourths. The excruciating effect of this diaphony on the modern ear has led investigators to make the most of any historical evidence going to show that these progressions were not simultaneous, but of an antiphonal character ; it appears to be established, however, that they were really the connecting link between the earlier chanting in octaves, and the later contrapuntal forms slowly developed out of the oblique and contrary motion in certain forms of the *organum*, due to the occasional introduction of harmonic seconds and thirds.—Though the *organum* was, properly, the part added *below* the *cantus firmus*, the term is generally applied to all the first rude attempts at harmonic composition, whether in 2 parts (*diaphonia*), 3 parts (*triphonia*, the added third part being called *triplum*.

whence our *treble*), or 4 parts (*tetrapho-nia*). The examples are quoted from

AMBROS, and are of the time of Huc-bald (A.D. 840–930):

(1)

Tu pa - tris sem - pi - ter - nus es fi - li - us.

(2)

Tu pa - tris sem - pi - ter - nus es fi - li - us.

Or'gel (Ger.) Organ... *Or'gelgehäuse*, organ-case... *Or'gelmetall*, organ-metal. ..*Or'gelpunkt*, organ-point... *Or'gel-register*, organ-stop ..*Or'gelwolf*, ciphering (also *Heu'len*).

Orgue (Fr.) Organ...*O. de Barbarie*, or *à cylindre*, barrel-organ...*O. expres-sif*, (*a*), an harmonium; (*b*) swell-organ...*O. à percussion*, a form of reed-organ constructed by de Provins and Alexandre, Paris.

Orguinette. A mechanical wind-instr. having 1 or more sets of reeds, and an exhaust-bellows ; by turning a crank the bellows is operated, and a perforated strip of paper attached to 2 rollers is made to pass over the reeds, the perforations admitting wind to the reeds and thus producing music.

Ornament. (It. *ornamen'to;* Fr. *orne-ment;* Ger.*Verzie'rung*.) A grace, embellishment... *Ornamental note*, an accessory note.

Ornatamen'te, Orna'to (It.) Embellished, ornamented.

Orpha'rion. See *Orpheo'reon.*

Orphéon. 1. In France, a singing-society composed of men...*Orphéoniste*, a member of such a society.—2. A piano-violin.

Orpheo'reon, or **-ron.** A variety of cither, having a flat back, and ribs with more than one incurvation on either side.

Or'pheusharmonika (Ger.) Same as *Panharmonikon.*

Oscillation. (Ger. *Oszillation'*.) Vibration, or beating.

Osservan'za, con (It.) With care, and attention (to the signs)...*Osserva'to*, carefully observed ; *sti'le osservato*, strict style.

Ossi'a (It.) Or; or else ; indicates an alternative or facilitated reading (or fingering) of a passage. (Also *oppure*, *ovvero*.)

Ostina'to (It.) Obstinate...*Basso o.*, a

ground bass ; hence the use of *ostinato* substantively, as a technical term for the incessant repetition of a theme with a varying contrapuntal accomp.

Otez (*ôtez*) (Fr.) Off (in organ-mus.)

Otta'va (It.) Octave...*All'ottava* (usually abbr. ta *8va* or *8* or *8 a~~*), "at the octave", an octave higher.—Also signifies, in scores, that one instr. is to accompany another in the higher octave. ..*Coll'ottava*, "with the octave," i. e. in octaves...*O. alta*, the higher octave...*O. bassa* (*8va bassa*), the lower octave, an octave below...*O. rima*, an Italian strophe of 8 lines, each in the heroic metre of 11 syllables, the first 6 rhyming alternately and the last 2 forming a couplet.

Ottavi'na (It.) 1. An octave-spinet.— 2. A harpsichord-stop controlling a set of strings tuned an octave higher than the rest.

Ottavi'no (It.) The piccolo (*fla'uto piccolo*).

Ottemo'le. An octuplet.

Ottet'to (It.) An octet.

Otto'ne (It.) Brass.

Ou (Fr.) Or. (See *Ossia*.)

Ouïe (Fr.) Sound-hole.

Ouvert,-e (Fr.) Open...*Accord à l'ou-vert*, a chord produced on open strings of stringed instr.s...*À livre ouvert*, at sight.

Ouverture (Fr.), **Ouvertü're** (Ger.) Overture.

Overblow'. With wind-instr.s, to force the wind through the tube in such a way as to cause any of the harmonics to sound. Metal instr.s (horn, trumpet) are in most cases overblown ; wooden instr.s (flute, clarinet) are overblown in the higher octaves.

O'ver-chord. See *Phone, §*1.

Overspun'. (Ger. *überspon'nen*.) Used

for *covered* (strings), the correct technical term.

Overstring'. To arrange the strings of a pfte. in 2 sets, so that one set lies over and diagonally crossing the other ; a pfte. so strung is called an *overstrung* pfte. (Ger. *kreuz'saitig*), in contradistinction to *vertical*.

O'vertone. See *Acoustics.*

O'verture. (Ger. *Ouvertü're;* Fr. *ouverture;* It. *overtu'ra, sinfoni'a*.) A mus. prelude or introduction. The first Italian *opera-overtures* were simple vocal (sung) prologues, or instrumental preludes in vocal (madrigal-) style ; with Scarlatti the *overture* or *sinfonia* assumed a purely instrumental character, and was written in three divisions (I allegro, II slow, III vivace, presto) ; hence the *overture in sonata-form*, with 2 or 3 contrasting themes following a short and slow introductory passage, and repeated after a more or less extended development-section, but differing from the true sonata-form in lacking the characteristic reprise before the development. This overture in sonata-form is the parent both of the modern Symphony and of the *Concert-overture* (a term derived from the custom of performing real opera-overtures as separate concert-pieces), in which latter the above form is usually adhered to.—*Opera-overtures* not in this form are either *potpourris* of leading mus. numbers taken from the body of the work, or *preludes* (*symphonic poems*) treating and blending themes occurring in the musical drama in the form of an independent composition, with the intention of preparing the hearers for the coming action ; such preludes have neither a regular key-plan, nor any conventional formal method of construction.

Ov'vero (It.) Or. (See *Ossia*.)

P.

P. Abbr. of *Pedal* (P. or Ped.) ; *piano* (*p*) ; *pp*, or *ppp*, *pianissimo;* P. F., *pianoforte; pf*, (*a*) *più forte* (louder), (*b*) *poco forte* (rather loud) ; *fp*, *fortepiano* (i. e. loud, instantly diminishing to soft) ; *mp*, *mezzo-piano* (half-soft) ; of *Pointe* (Fr., = toe) ; and, in Fr. organ-music, P stands for *Positif* (choir-organ).

Padiglio'ne (It.) Bell (of horn, etc.)

Padova'na (It.) Same as *Pavane*. (Also *Padovane, Paduana, Paduane*, etc.)

Pæ'an (Gk.) A hymn to Apollo ; a hymn of invocation or thanksgiving to Apollo or other help-giving god.

Pæ'on (Gk.) A metrical foot of 4 syllables, 1 long and 3 short. It has 4 forms according to the place occupied by the long syllable ; namely, *first pæon* (— ‿ ‿ ‿), *second* (‿ — ‿ ‿), *third* (‿ ‿ — ‿), and *fourth pæon* (‿ ‿ ‿ —).

Paired notes. A proposed equivalent, in pfte.-technic, for the term double-stops on the violin, and for the Ger. *Dop'pelgriffe;* i. e. 2 parallel series of notes played with one hand, as thirds, sixths, and octaves.

Palala'ïka. See *Balalaïka.*

Pal'co (It.) A stage ; a box (theatre).

Palestri'nastil (Ger., "Palestrina-style".) Equiv. to *a cappella* style (It. *alla Palestrina*).

Palettes (Fr., pl.) The white keys of the keyboard ; opp. to *feintes*, the black keys.

Palimbac'chius. See *Antibacchius* and *Bacchius.*

Pan'dean Pipes. (Also *Pan's-pipes, Syrinx*.) A simple wind-instr., known in slightly varying forms from earliest antiquity ; it consists of a set of graduated reeds or tubes arranged in a row and blown by the mouth. The Grecian instr. usually had 7 tubes.

Pando'ra, Pandu'ra, etc. See *Bandola.*

Pan'flöte (Ger.) Pandean pipes. (Also *Pansflöte.*)

Panharmon'icon. A variety of self-acting orchestrion, inv. by J. N. Mälzel of Vienna in 1800.

Panmelo'dion. A keyboard instr., the tone of which was produced by the friction of wheels on metal bars ; inv by Fr. Leppich, in 1810.

Panorgue (Fr.) A miniature reed-organ attached beneath and played by the keyboard of a pfte.; the combined instr. is named a *panorgue-piano*. Inv. by J. Jaulin of Paris.

Pantal'eon, Pan'talon. An improved dulcimer, inv. in 1690 by, and named after, Pantaleon Hebenstreit; a precursor of the pfte. It was 4 times as large as the ordinary dulcimer, and oblong in shape; had 2 soundboards, as of 2 instr.s standing close together; was strung on one side with steel and brass wires, and on the other with gut; the 2 wooden mallets in the player's hands were sometimes used with the softer face, sometimes with the harder.

Pantalon (Fr.) The first figure or movement in the old quadrille.

Pan'talonzug (Ger.) "Pantalon-stop"; a harpsichord-stop which neutralized the action of the damping mechanism, and thus produced the confused effect peculiar to the Pantalon.

Par'allel. See *Interval, Key, Motion.* ..*Parallel'bewegung* (Ger.), parallel (and also similar) motion...*Paralle'len* (Ger., pl.), (*a*) sliders (in the organ); (*b*) consecutives...*Parallel'tonart* (Ger.), a relative (major or minor) key.

Par'aphrase. A transcription or rearrangement, of a vocal or instrumental composition, for some other instr. or instr.s, with more or less extended and brilliant variations.

Parfait (Fr.) Perfect (of intervals); complete (of cadences); true, pure (of intonation); strong, accented (of beats).

Parhyp'ate. See *Lyre* 1.

Parlan'do, Parlan'te (It.) "Speaking"; a style of singing resembling recitative in clear enunciation, the vowel-sounds being markedly "thrown forward."

Part. (Ger. *Part, Stim'me;* Fr. *partie, voix;* It. *par'te, vo'ce.*) In concerted music, the series of tones written for and executed by a voice or instr., either as a solo or together with other voices or instr.s of the same kind; a melody so performed.

Part-book. 1. (Ger. *Stimm'buch.*) A written or printed part for a single performer, like those in vogue during the 15th and 16th centuries.—2. (Ger. *Chor'buch.*) A book of that period, containing 4 vocal parts (sometimes with added instrumental accomp.), not, as at present, in score, but each on a separate staff side by side with the others (*can'tus latera'lis*), and on opposite pages; the fragments of the several parts so corresponding, of course, that the leaf could be turned for all at the same time. Some were so printed, that singers on opposite sides of the table could read from the same open book. The diagrams give a notion of this peculiar arrangement:

Soprano	Tenor
Alto	Bass

ɹoua⊥	ouɐɹdoS
Alto	Bass

Par'te (It.) 1. Part...*Colla parte*, a direction to accompanists to follow yieldingly and discreetly the solo part or voice.—2. A movement.

Partial stop. See *Stop*...*Partial tone*, see *Acoustics*...*Partial turn*, see *Turn* 1.

Participating-tone. See *Accessory*.

Particular metre. See *Metre*.

Partimen'to (It.) A figured bass... *Partimenti* (pl.), exercises, generally written on a figured bass, for training students to read and accompany from such a bass.

Parti'ta (It.), **Partie'** (Ger.) 1. See *Suite*.—2. A set of variations.

Partiti'no (It.) A supplementary score, appended to the body of the score when there are too many parts for all to be written on one page.

Partition (Fr.), **Partitur'** (Ger.), **Par-**

titu'ra (Lat. and It.) A partition, score...*Partitura cancella'ta*, a system of staves *scored* (hence Engl. *Score*) by the vertical lines of the bars drawn from top to bottom.

Part-music. Concerted or harmonized music; a term properly applied to vocal music of this description. (See *Part-song*.)

Part-singing. The singing of part-music; as generally understood, without instrumental accomp.

Part-song. A composition for at least 3 voices in harmony, without accomp. [and for equal or mixed voices].—The first requisite of the music is well-defined rhythm, and the second unyielding homophony...Tunefulness in the upper part or melody is desirable, and the attention should not be withdrawn by elaborate devices of an imitative or contrapuntal nature in the harmonic substructure...The part-song being essentially a melody with choral harmony, the upper part is in one sense the most important...The words may be either amatory, heroic, patriotic, didactic, or even quasi-sacred in character...The part-song...is one of three forms of secular unaccompanied choral music, the others being the madrigal, and the glee...Like the madrigal and unlike the glee, the number of voices to each part may be multiplied within reasonable limits. [GROVE.]

Part-writing. The art and practice of counterpoint.

Pas (Fr., *noun.*) A step; also, a solo dance in a ballet...*Pas de deux*, a dance performed by 2 dancers...*Pas redoublé*, quickstep...*Pas seul*, a solo dance...(*Adverb.*) Not; as *pas trop lent*, not too slow.

Paspy. See *Passepied.*

Passaca'glia, or **-glio** (It.; Fr. *passacaille;* Ger. *Gas'senhauer.*) An old Italian dance in triple time and stately movement, written on a ground bass of 4 measures, whose theme sometimes appears in a higher part. It was always in minor, and is hardly distinguishable, as an instrumental piece, from the *Ciaccona.*

Passacaille (Fr.) Passacaglia.

Passage. 1. A portion or section of a piece, usually short.—2. A rapid repeated figure, either ascending or descending. A *scale*-passage is usually called a *run*...*Notes de passage* (Fr.), grace-notes.

Passag'gio (It.) Passage 1.—2. A modulation.—3. A flourish or *bravura* embellishment, either vocal or instrumental.

Passamez'zo (It.) An old Italian dance in duple time, and similar to the Pavane except in having a more rapid movement.

Passant (Fr.) Slide (of bow).

Passepied (Fr.) A paspy, an old French dance in 3-8 or 6-8 time, generally beginning with an eighth-note on the weak beat, and having 3 or 4 reprises in an even number of measures, the third reprise being short, and sportive or toying; like the minuet in movement, but quicker.

Passing-notes,-tones. Notes or tones foreign to the chords which they accompany, and passing by steps from one chord to another. They differ from suspensions in not being prepared, and in entering (usually) on an unaccented beat.

Passion, Passion-music. A musical setting of a text descriptive of Christ's sufferings and death (passion). Its beginnings are traceable back to the 4th century; the oldest music extant is a solemn plain-song melody of uncertain date (*can'tus passio'nis*). In a quasi-dramatic form the passion is of later origin; and possibly directly derived from the ancient custom of chanting the scriptural text of the passion, during passion-week, to Gregorian melodies. It is certain, that from early in the 13th century (1) the words spoken by Christ, (2) the connecting narrative, and (3) the exclamations of the apostles, the populace, the high priest, etc., were recited by 3 different singers (impersonating *Christ,* the *Evangelist,* the *Disciples,* etc.) The evolution of the Passion as an art-form is, after the 16th century, nearly parallel with that of the *Oratorio* (which see); from its resemblance to the latter it is sometimes styled "passion-oratorio". It differs from it however, by a distinct infusion of an element of pious contemplation and subjective emotion, expressed in hymns of praise and choral songs, devotional arias and choruses. The crowning work of this kind is Bach's "Matthä'uspassion" (Passion according to St. Matthew).—The full dramatic form of the Passion, with stage-setting and dramatic action, still survives in the German Passion-plays at Oberammergau.

Passionatamen'te (It.) Passionately in an impassioned style...*Passiona'to,· a,* passionate, impassioned...*Passio'ne,* passion, fervent emotion; *con p.*, same as *appassionato.*

Passionné (Fr.) Passionato.

Pastic'cio (It.), **Pastiche** (Fr.) A mus. medley or olio consisting of extracts (songs, arias, recitatives) from different works, pieced together and provided with new words so as to form a "new" composition, as an opera (Ger. *Flick-oper*), etc.

Pastoral. (It. and Fr. *pastora'le.*) 1. A scenic cantata representing pastoral or idyllic life; a pastoral opera.—2. An instrumental composition imitating in style and instrumentation rural and idyllic scenes.—*Pastoral organ-point*, see *Organ-point*.

Pastori'ta. See *Nachthorn*.

Pastourelle (Fr.) 1. A bucolic song, as sung by the troubadours.—2. A figure in the quadrille.

Pateticamen'te (It.), **Pathétiquement** (Fr.) Pathetically... *Pate'tico* (It.), *pathétique* (Fr.), pathetic.

Patimen'to (It.) Suffering, grief ; *con espressio'ne di p.*, with mournful or plaintive expression.

Patouille (Fr.) Same as *Claquebois*.

Patte (Fr., "paw".) 1. A music-pen 2.—2. A special key on the clarinet.

Pau'ke (Ger.) Kettledrum... *Maschinenpauke*, see *Maschinen*.

Pa'usa (It.) A rest ; a pause.

Pause. 1. A rest.—2. A hold (⌒).—3. (Fr.) A whole rest, semibreve-rest.

Pav'an,-e. A stately dance of Italian or Spanish origin, in slow tempo and alla-breve time. [Probably of Italian origin, the It. *pava'na* (abbr. of *padova'na*) referring to a peasant-dance of the province of Padua.]

Paventa'to (It.) Afraid, fearful.

Pavillon (Fr.) Bell (of a wind-instr). ..*P. chinois*, a crescent...*Flûte à p.*, an organ-stop, the pipes of which have a flaring top... *Pavillon en l'air*, " turn the bell upwards " ; a direction to horn-players.

Peal. 1. See *Change* 3.—2. A chime of bells ; a carillon.

Pearly. (Ger. *per'lend;* Fr. *perlé.*) In piano-technic, a style of touch producing a clear, round, and smooth effect of tone, especially in scale-passages ("like a string of pearls").

Pedal. (Ger. *Pedal'* ; Fr. *pédale;* It. *peda'le.*) 1. A foot-key ; opp. to *digital* (see *Organ* and *Pedal-piano*).—2. A foot-lever ; as the swell-pedal of the organ, the loud and soft pedals of the pfte., or the pedals of the harp.—3. A treadle, as those used for blowing the reed-organ, etc.—4. A stop-knob or lever controlled by the foot, as a combination-pedal in the organ.—5. Contraction of *Pedal-point.*—*Pedal-action*, the entire mechanism directly connected with a pedal or set of pedals ... *Pedal-check*, a bar under the organ-pedals which can be so adjusted (often by a stop-knob) as to prevent them from

being depressed...*Pedal-coupler*, see *Coupler*...*Pedal-keyboard*, the organ-pedals (see *Organ*)...*Pedal-note*, see *Pedal-tone*...*Pedal-organ*, the set of stops (partial organ) controlled by the pedal-keyboard in playing...*Pedal-piano*, a pfte. provided with a pedalier... *Pedal-pipe*, *-soundboard*, *-stop*, one belonging to the pedal-organ...*Pedal-point*, see *Organ-point*...*Pedal-tone*, a sustained or continuously repeated tone. ..*Combination-pedal*, a metal foot-lever placed above the pedal-keyboard of an organ, and giving the player control over a certain combination of stops. It is *single-acting* when it only draws out new stops in addition to those already drawn, or pushes in some of the latter ; and *double-acting*, when it always produces the same combination, whatever stops were or were not previously drawn. Comb.-pedals are of 3 kinds : (1) The *forte pedal*, drawing all the stops of its keyboard ; (2) the *mezzo pedal*, drawing the chief 8-foot and 4-foot stops of its keyboard ; and (3) the *piano pedal*, pushing in all but a few of the softest stops...*Composition-pedal*, a combination-pedal... *Coupler-pedal*, see Pedal-coupler...*Crescendo-pedal*, a pedal mechanism drawing all the stops successively up to "full organ". (Also, occasional for swell-pedal.)...*Damper-pedal*, the right pfte.-pedal, on depressing which the dampers are raised from the strings...*Diminuendo-pedal*, the reverse of crescendo-pedal, retiring successively the stops drawn by the latter...*Extension-pedal*, see *Loud pedal*...*Harp-pedal*, same as soft pedal...*Loud* or *open pedal*, the damper-pedal on the pfte...*Octave-pedal* (A. B. Chase Co.'s, for pfte.), acts, when depressed, in such a way that when a key is struck, the higher octave of the tone is also sounded. (Usually *Octavo attachment.*)...*Prolongation-pedal*, see *Sustaining-pedal*...*Reversible pedal*, a pedal-coupler...*Sforzando-pedal*, a pedal in the organ which brings out the full power of the instr for the production of a sudden and forcible accent...*Soft pedal*, the left pedal. of the pfte....*Sustaining-pedal*, a piano-pedal acting to hold up any dampers already raised by the damper-pedal, by this means prolonging the tone of all strings affected...*Swell-pedal*, a foot-lever in the organ, by depressing which the shutters of the swell-box can be opened ; they close when the pedal is released.—*Balance swell-pedal*, the modern form of organ swell-pedal :—a lever in the shape of an iron plate made to fit the shoe-sole, and placed above the centre of the pedal board. Depression of the toe-end of the plate opens the swell-shutters ; depression of the heel-end closes them. Called *balance* s.-p. because it remains at rest (balanced) wherever the foot leaves it.

Pédale (Fr.) 1. A pedal-key, the pedal-keyboard being *clavier des pédales*.—2. Pedal (of the pfte.) ; *petite pédale*, soft pedal, "una corda".—3. A pedal-point.

Peda'le dop'pio (It.) Same as *Doppio pedale*.

Pedal'flügel (Ger.) A grand piano provided with a pedalier.

Ped'alier. (Fr. *pédalier*.) A set of pedals, either (1) so adjusted as to play the low octaves of the pfte. after the manner of organ-pedals, or (2) provided with separate strings and action, to be placed underneath the pfte. and played with, but not affecting the action of, the latter. (Sometimes *Pedalion*.)

Pedalie'ra (It.) A pedal-keyboard.

Pedal'klaviatur (Ger.) A pedal-keyboard ; either a pedalier, or for the organ.

Peg. 1. (Ger. *Wir'bel;* Fr. *cheville;* It. *bi'schero*.) In the violin, etc., one of the movable wooden pins set in the head, and used to tighten or slacken the tension of the strings...*Peg-box*, the hollow part of a violin-head in which the pegs are inserted.—2. A tuning-pin.

Pennant. Same as *Hook*.

Pensieroso (It.) Pensive, contemplative, thoughtful.

Pentachord. 1. A 5-stringed instr.—2. A diatonic series of 5 tones.

Pentam'eter. A form of dactylic verse, differing from the hexameter by the ellipsis of the second half of the 3rd and 6th feet :

⌒ ⌒⌒ | ⌒ ⌒⌒ | ⌒ |⌒⌒⌒|⌒⌒⌒| ⌒

Pentatone. An interval embracing 5 whole tones ; an augmented sixth... *Pentaton'ic*, having, or consisting of, 5 tones ; *pentatonic scale*, see *Scale*.

Per (It.) For, by, from, in, through... *Per l'or'gano*, for the organ...*Per il flauto solo*, for solo flute.

Percussion. 1. The striking or sounding of a dissonance, contradistinguished from its preparation and resolution.—2. The act of percussing, or striking one body against another. The instruments of percussion are the various drums, the tambourine, cymbals, bells, triangle, etc., and the dulcimer and pianoforte. ..*Percussion-stop*, a reed-organ stop used to strike the reed a smart blow simultaneously with sounding it, thus rendering its vibration prompter and stronger.

Percussive. An instr. of percussion.

Perden'do, Perden'dosi (It.) Dying away ; *morendo* or *diminuendo*, together (in modern music) with a slight *rallentando*.

Perdu'na. Bourdon (organ-stop).

Perfect. (Ger. *rein;* Fr. *parfait;* It. *perfet'to*.) See *Interval*.

Perfection. 1. See *Notation*, § 3.—2. In ligatures, the presence of a *longa* as final note (*ul'tima*), which occurred when a higher penultimate note was not joined with the final as a *figura obliqua* (◣), or when, after a lower penultimate note, the final took a descending tail to the right (since the 15th century ; from the 12th to the 14th this tail signified a *plica*, and to secure the perfection of the final note it was written vertically over the penultimate). (See *Figura obliqua*, ex. in black notes ; also *Notation*, § 3.)

Périgourdine (Fr.) An old Flemish dance in 6-8 time.

Period. See *Form*.

Perlé (Fr.), **Per'lend** (Ger.) Pearly.

Perpe'tuo (It.) Perpetual ; infinite.

Pes (Lat., "foot".) An harmonic accomp. or ground bass to a round, the round itself being called *rota*.

Pesan'te (It.) Heavy, ponderous ; calls for a firm and vigorous execution of the passages so marked.

Petite (Fr.) Small...*Petite flûte*, the piccolo...*Petite mesure à deux temps*, 2-4 time...*Petites notes*, grace-notes... *Petite pédale*, soft pedal.

Pet'to (It.) The chest...*Di petto*, from the chest, i. e. in a natural voice, not falsetto... *Voce di petto*, chest-voice.

Peu à peu (Fr.) Little by little, gradually... *Un peu*, a little.

Pez'zo (It.) 1. A piece... *Pezzi concertan'ti*, concerted pieces.—2. A number (of an opera, etc.)

Pfei'fe (Ger.) A pipe ; specifically, an organ-pipe. The technical name of the 1-foot stops is *-pfeife*, as *Bau'ernpfeife.*

Phantasie' (Ger.) Fancy, imagination. ..*Phantasie'stück*, a fantasia ; in modern music, a short piece of a romantic and intensely subjective cast, without distinctive formal structure... *Phantasie'ren*, to improvise... *Phantasier'-maschine*, any kind of melograph.

Philomèle. See *Bow-zither*, under *Zither.*

Phonau'tograph. An electric music-recorder for keyboard instr.s, inv. by Fenby, in which a stud attached under each key makes an electric connection when the key is depressed, and thus marks, on paper, lines corresponding in length to the duration of the notes... Another, inv. by the Abbé Moigno, records the tones (sounded or sung) by the aid of a pencil fitted to a sort of drum, the membrane of which vibrates to the tones.

Phone. §1. It forms no part of a compiler's work to introduce new words on his personal responsibility ; but the terms "tone", "clang", and "sound" being already appropriated, a distinctive and exact equivalent had to be employed in rendering the German " Klang" as used in modern musical theory. The Greek word φωνή, in the English form phone, appears to be a fairly acceptable neologism.—A *phone*, then, will be understood as signifying not only a tone with its overtones and undertones (Tyndall's " clang"), but specifically the *major triad* (generator and *higher* partials [2] 3 [4] and 5) or *over-phone*, and the *minor triad* (generator and *lower* partials [2] 3 [4] and 5) or *under-phone*. [N.B. Over-phone and under-phone are also called *over-chord* and *under-chord* respectively.— In the subjoined statement of the modern theory of chords, RIEMANN is followed.]

§2. There can be no doubt, that the consonance of the major triad (major consonance) is referable to the series of higher partials (see *Acoustics*), i. e. that a major triad, however the tones may be set or inverted, is to be conceived as a consonance in which certain higher partials of the root are reinforced by actual tones. E. g.,

Moreover, the generator accompanying each phone represented above, is always present as a resultant tone. But the series of partials not only completes itself *downwards* to the generator by means of the resultant tones, but continues itself *upwards* by the aid of the upper partials of the primary overtones. Those overtones, above the 8th, which are represented by composite numbers ($9=3 \times 3$, $15=3 \times 5$, etc.), are conceived as *overtones of overtones* (*secondary* overtones); i. e. as integral constituents of the *primaries* (the 9th overtone as the 3rd of the 3rd primary, the 15th as the 5th of the 3rd primary, etc.), and, sounded as notes of an actual chord, appear as *dissonances*; that primary overtone, whose overtones they are, has the character of a *generator*, 2 overphones thus being simultaneously represented. Only the ratio of the octave (2:1) is never dissonant. Striking out from the series of overtones the doublings in the octave, there remain, to represent the major consonance of the over-phone, only (1) the *generator*, (2) the *twelfth*, and (3) the *fifteenth*; hence, the primitive form of the major triad is not, properly speaking, the triad in close harmony: open harmony: —The consonance of the minor triad is not derivable from the series of higher partials, but is referable to a series of lower partials (undertones) diametrically opposed to the former (comp. *Acoustics*). The lower partials 1, 2, 3, 4, 5, 6, 8, 10, 12, 16, etc., in fact all tones of the lower series corresponding to lower octaves of the 1st, 3rd, and 5th lower partials, are constituents of the minor triad below *c*, of the *C* under-phone: in just the same sense as the same numbers in the higher series are constituents of the *C* over-phone: its dissonances also have a parallel explanation.

§ 3. PHONIC REPRESENTATION (*Klang' vertretung*) is the peculiar significance attaching to any tone or interval, according as it is conceived as belonging to a particular phone. For instance, the tone *C* has a very different meaning, in the logic of progression, when conceived as *tierce* in the *A♭*-major chord, from that as *tierce* in the *A*-minor chord; in the former case, it is most closely related to *D♭* and the *D♭*-major chord; in the latter, to *B*, and the chords of *E*-major and *E*-minor. Every tone may form an integral part of 6 different phones; for instance, the tone *C* in the *C* over-phone (*C*-major chord) as major root, in the *F* over-phone as major quint (over-quint), in the *A♭* over-phone as major tierce (over-tierce), in the *C* under-phone (*F*-minor chord) as minor root, in the *G* under-phone (*C*-minor chord) as minor quint (under-quint), and finally in the *E* under-phone (*A*-minor chord) as minor tierce (under-tierce):

Major chords (*read up*). **Minor chords** (*read down*).

Whenever the tone *C* enters into any other chord as a dissonant-tone, or is substituted for some chord-tone as a suspended or altered tone, it is nevertheless always to be conceived as belonging to one of the above 6 phones, i. e. to the one most nearly related in any given case.

§ 4. THE RELATION OF TONES is a modern conception, based on the affinity of tones belonging to the same phone. Tones *belonging to the same phone* are *directly* related; to *c*, for instance, are directly related *g*, *f*, *e*, *a♭*, *a*, and *e♭*; for *c* : *g* belongs to the chord of *C*-major or *C*-minor, *c* : *e* to the chord of *C*-major or *A*-minor, *c* : *a♭* to the chord of *A♭*-major or *F*-minor, *c* : *a* to the chord of *F*-major or *A*-minor, and *c* : *e♭* to the chord of *A♭*-major or *C*-minor. *Directly related* tones are *consonant;* all other, or *indirectly related*, tones are *dissonant*. The mutual relation of the former is more easily understood than that of the latter. Directly related phones are (1) those *similar* ones (both either major or minor) in which the phonic root of the one is directly related to the phonic root of the

other [phonic root = generator, i. e. the *fundamental tone* in a major triad, or the *quint* in a minor triad]; (2) those *dissimilar* ones (one major and the other minor) of which the one is the under-phone of some chord-tone of the other; namely, for the major chord, the under-phones (*minor phones*) of its *phonic* root, quint, and tierce; for the minor chord, the over-phones (*major phones*) of its *phonic* root, quint, and tierce; to which must be added the under-phones of the respective leading-tones. Thus, the following chords are directly related to the *C*-major chord:— *G*-major, *F*-major, *E*-major, *A♭*-major, *E♭*-major, *F*-minor, *C*-minor, *A*-minor, and *E*-minor; whereas, to the *A*-minor chord, are directly related the chords of :—*D*-minor, *E*-minor, *F*-minor, *C♯*-minor, *C*-minor, *F♯*-minor, *E*-major *A*-major, *C*-major, and *F*-major.—The relation of the tones depending on that of the the tonics (tonic phones), it follows, that any key is directly related to *C*-major (or *A*-minor), whose tonic is one of the phones (chords) given above as directly related to the chord of *C*-major (or *A*-minor).

§ 5. PHONIC PROGRESSION (*Klang'-folge*) is the progression between two chords with reference to their significance as phones. The ordinary method of marking the phones (major and minor triads) by the Roman numerals I, II, III, IV, etc. (comp. *Chord*) is inadequate from the standpoint of free tonality; e. g. this passage:

C : I   V⁷   I
f : V   III
     c : VI
       G : V⁷

is hardly intelligible with such a figuring; although it in no way signifies a modulation into another key, one must perforce consider the *A♭*-chord as in *f*-minor, and the *D*-chord as in *G*-major. For such progressions, a figuring with reference to a scale is simply impossible; they are referable to *free tonality*, an idea but recently recognized, whose scope extends far beyond the bounds of diatonic harmony. Tonality knows neither diatonic nor foreign chords, but only a *tonic phone* and *referable* (related) *phones*. In the above example, the *C*-major triad is throughout the tonic phone, to which the others are referable ; the *A♭*-major chord is its under-tierce phone, the *D*-minor chord is its second over-quint phone, and the *G*-major chord its over-quint phone. The first progression (*C*-major to *A♭*-major) reaches over to the undertone side ; the second (*A♭*-major to *G*-major) springs across to the overtone side ; the other two lead back to the tonic phone. If we term a progression between 2 similar phones a *stride* (*Schritt*), and one between 2 dissimilar phones a *change* (*Wechsel*), we can distinguish 4 species of phonic progression in which the mutual relation of the roots is a quint-relation. It is of widely different significance for the tonality, whether a stride from the tonic goes to overtone side or to the undertone side ; starting from a major chord the *latter*, and from a minor chord the *former*, signifies a contradiction of, or opposition to, the phonic principle ; strides or changes to *contraphones* (i. e. phones belonging to the opposite side) will be indicated by the prefix *contra*. Thus (1) the progression from *C*-major to *G*-major, or *A*-minor to *D*-minor (= *E* underphone to *A* under-phone) is a simple quint-stride ; (2) *C*-major to *F*-major, or *A*-minor to *E*-minor (*E* under-phone to *B* under-phone) is a contraquint-stride ; *c*-*°g*, or *°e*-*a* (see § 6), is a simple quint-change ; *c*-*°f*, or *°e*-*b*, is a contraquint-change. In all species of phonic progression the simple changes are, like that above, easily intelligible ; whereas the contra-changes are much more difficult to understand.—The tierce-progressions are, for example, the simple tierce-stride *c*-*e*, or *°e*-*°c* ; contratierce-stride, *c*-*a♭*, or *°e*-*°g♯* ; simple tierce-change, *c*-*°e*, or *°e*-*c* ; contratierce-change, *c*-*°a♭*. Any direct progression to a remoter phone makes the want of an (omitted) connecting link sensibly felt ; it will be easy to *modulate* to such an intermediate phone, i. e. to transfer to it the significance of a tonic phone.

§ 6. PHONIC FIGURING (*Klang'-schlüssel*) [according to RIEMANN]. (1) No scale-degrees are marked or taken note of ; small letters are used to mark the root-tones of the phones, with an ° prefixed for an under-phone ; thus *c* =

C-major triad, *°c* = *F*-minor triad.—(2) To these letters are affixed numerals, marking intervals added to the phones ; not, however, counting from the bass note, but from the phonic root ; Arabic numerals [read up !] for over-phones (major triads), Roman numerals [read down !] for under-phones (minor triads). Thus 1 (I) = phonic root ; 2 (II) = major second ; 3 (III) = major tierce ; 4 (IV) = perfect quart ; 5 (V) = perfect quint ; 6 (VI) = major sext ; 7 (VII) = major sept.—(3) The sign < after a numeral denotes the raising of the interval by a semitone ; > denotes its lowering by a semitone. Examples :

Pho'nikon. A metal wind-instr. with a globe-shaped bell ; inv. by B. F. Czerveny of Königgrätz in 1848.

Phonom'eter. (Fr. *phonomètre*.) An instr. for recording the number of vibrations made by a sonorous body in a given length of time.

Phor'minx (Gk.) An ancient stringed instr. resembling the cithara or the lyra.

Phrase. 1. See *Form*.—2. Any short figure or passage complete in itself and unbroken in continuity...*Phrase-mark*, in mus. notation, a curved line connecting the notes of a phrase 2.

Phrasing. (Ger. *Phrasie'rung*, from *phrasie'ren*, to phrase.) 1. The bringing-out into proper relief of the phrases (whether motives, figures, subjects, or passages), both as regards their individual melodic and rhythmic characterization and their relative importance.—2. The signs of notation devised to further the above end.

Phryg'ian. See *Mode*.

Physharmon'ica. 1. A small reed-organ inv. in 1818 by Anton Häckel of Vienna, and designed for attachment beneath a piano-keyboard to sustain the tones of melodies. It was the precursor of the harmonium.—2. (Ger.) A free-reed stop on the organ.

Piace're, a (It.) "At pleasure"; a direction equivalent to *ad libitum*, signifying that the expression of the passage so marked is left to the performer's discretion.—Also marks the introduction of a cadenza. (Sometimes *a piaci-men' to*.)

Piace'vole (It.) Pleasant, agreeable; calls for a smooth, suave rendering, free from forcible or passionate accents. ...*Piacevolmen'te*, smoothly, suavely.

Piacimen'to (It.) Equiv. to *Piacere*.

Pianette. A low form of upright piano.

Piangen'do (It., "weeping, tearful.") Wailing, plaintive. (Also *piange'vole*, *piangevolmen'te*.)

Piani'no (It., dimin. of *piano*.) An upright pianoforte.

Piani'sta (It.) 1. A pianist.—2. A mechanical pianoforte.

Pia'no (It.) Soft, softly (sign *p*)...*Piano pedal*, the soft or left pedal of the pfte...*Pianis'simo* (superl. of *piano*), very soft (sign *pp* or *ppp*).

Piano. (Abbr. of *Pianoforte*)...*Boudoir p.*, a short style of grand pfte... *Cabinet p.*, an old form of upright pfte. ..*Cottage p.*, see *Cottage*...*Dumb p.*, a pfte.-keyboard without action or strings, used for silent mechanical practice. (See *Virgil Practice-Clavier*.)...*Electric p.*, one whose strings are set in vibration by electro-magnets instead of hammers...*Grand p.*, see *Pianoforte*. ...*Pedal-piano*, see *Pedal*...*Piccolo p.*, a small upright piano introduced by Wornum of London in 1829...*Semi-grand p.*, same as *Boudoir*...*Square*, *Upright p.*, see *Pianoforte*.

Piano (Fr.) A pianoforte...*P. à archet*, piano-violin...*P. à claviers renversés*, a grand pfte. having 2 keyboards, one above the other, the ascending scale of the upper one running from *right* to *left*...*P. à queue*, grand pfte.; *à queue écourtée*, boudoir grand pfte...*P. à secrétaire*, cabinet pfte...*P. carré*, square pfte...*P. droit* (*oblique*, *à pilastres*, *vertical*), upright pfte...*P. éolien*, see *Anemochord*...*P. harmoni-corde*, a combined pfte. and harmonium, inv. by Debain...*P. mécanique*, a mechanical piano...*P. muet*, dumb pfte... *P. organisé*, a pfte. with physharmonica-attachment.

Pian'oforte. (Ger. *Klavier'* [in Ger. *Pianofor'te* usually means "square

piano"]; Fr. *piano* [more rarely *piano-forté* or *forté-piano*, very seldom *forté*]; It. *pia'no, pianofor'te*.) A keyboard stringed instr. of percussion, the tones being produced by hammers striking the strings.—The principal parts are (1) the Frame, (2) the Soundboard, (3) the Strings, (4) the Action, and (5) the Pedals.—According to the shape of the case, pftes. are classed as GRAND (harp-shaped; Ger. *Flü'gel;* Fr. *piano à queue;* It. *pia'no a co'da*), with horizontal strings and built in several sizes, as *Concert Grand, Parlor Grand, Boudoir;* —SQUARE (oblong; Ger. *Pianofo'rte*, or *ta'felförmiges Klavier';* Fr. *piano carré;* It. *pianofor'te a tavoli'no*) with horizontal strings;—and UPRIGHT (buffet-shaped; Ger. and It. *Piani'no;* Fr. *piano droit*) with vertical or slanting strings.

(1) The *Frame* is now generally of iron cast in one piece (Broadwood's pftes. form the most notable exception to this rule), and braced with *cross-bars* and *trusses* to resist the string-tension, which varies from about 12 up to nearly 20 tons.—(2) Below the frame is the *Soundboard*, near the front end of which is a *bridge* of hard wood over which the strings are stretched.—(3) The *Strings* are attached at one end by *hitchpins* to the *stringplate*, and at the other to *wrestpins* (*tuning-pins*) set in the *wrest-plank;* they are of steel wire, the bass strings of a steel core covered (coiled) with copper wire; 8 or 10 of the lowest bass tones have one string, about 1½ octaves above have 2 strings, and the remaining 5 octaves 3 strings, to each tone; such pairs or triplets of strings to one tone are called *unisons*.—(4) The *Action* consists essentially of the *key* (*digital*, finger-lever); the *hopper* on the rear end of the key, raising the hammer when the key is depressed, and allowing the instant escape of the latter after propelling the hammer, which can therefore immediately rebound into position after striking the string; the *hammer*, hinged at the *butt*, with a slim round *shank*, upon which is fixed the *head* (the hammer proper) made of felt and sometimes covered with leather.— (5) The *Pedals* are 2 (sometimes 3) in number: (*a*) *Damper-pedal*, (*b*) *Piano pedal*, (*c*) *Sustaining-pedal* (comp. art. *Pedal*).

The idea of the *key-mechanism* was derived indirectly, through the monochord, spinet, harpsichord, and clavichord, from that of the organ ; the idea of a *hammer-action* (which constitutes the essential difference between the Pianoforte and its precursors) was, perhaps, derived from the dulcimer in its perfected form the *Pantalon*. The hammer-action was first *practically* developed by Bartolommeo Cristofori of Padua in 1711, whose action is the same, in essentials, as that now manufactured by Broadwood (English action).

Pian'ograph. A form of music-recorder.

Piano-harp. See *Klaviaturharfe*.

Piano-organ. Same as *Handle-piano*.

Piano-violin. (Ger. *Bo'genflügel, Gei'-genwerk;* Fr. *piano à archet, piano-quatuor*.) The English name covers the results of a long series of experiments, and of improvements of the hurdy-gurdy, the prototype of the class. —In the *Geigenwerk* inv. by Heiden of Nuremberg (about 1600) the keys, when touched, pressed their corresponding wire strings against small rosined wheels made to revolve by a treadle ; the tone was similar to that of a bow-instr.—The *Gambenwerk* was made by Risch of Ilmenau (about 1750), and improved by the substitution of gut strings for wires.—Hohlfeld's *Bogen-flügel* (1754) had gut strings, beneath which was a bow furnished with horsehair ; on pressing the keys, the strings were drawn by little hooks against the bow, whose slow or rapid movement was controlled by a pedal-stop.—C. A. von Meyer, of Knownow, provided a separate horsehair bow for each string (1794).—The *clavecin harmonique* of Hübner (Moscow, about 1800) accurately reproduced the sound of a string-quartet.—Pouleau's *orchestrine* was a further improvement of the *clavecin harmonique*.—H. C. Baudin of Paris invented an instr. called the *piano-quatuor*, patented in England in 1865 under the name of *piano-violin*. It has for each tone one wire string, at or near a nodal point of which is attached a piece of stiff catgut projecting about an inch. Above these gut ties, a rosined roller is caused to revolve rapidly by a treadle ; on touching the keys, these ties are carried up against the roller, the tones thus produced having the timbre of tones from gut strings. The instr. is capable of rapid execution and articulation.

Piat'ti (It., pl.) Cymbals.

Pi'broch. A set of variations for the bagpipe on a theme called the *urlar*, generally 3 or 4 in number, and increasing in difficulty and speed up to the closing quick movement (the *crean-luidh*). This is the highest and most difficult form of bagpipe-music.

Piccanteri'a, con (It.) With piquant sprightly expression.

Picchetta'to, Picchietta'to (It.) Detached. See *Piqué*.

Picco pipe. A small pipe with a flageolet-mouthpiece, and 3 ventages, 2 above and 1 below ; named after the Italian peasant Picco, whose extraordinary virtuosity on his instr. introduced it to the general public (London, 1856), and who obtained from it a compass of 3 octaves.

Pic'colo. (It. *fla'uto pic'colo;* Fr. *petite flûte;* Ger. *Oktav'flöte, Pick'elflöte*.) The octave-flute. See *Flute*.

Pic'colo (It.) Small...Used as a noun, equiv. to (1) *Flauto piccolo*, and (2) *Piano piccolo*, a small style of upright pfte.

Pick (*verb*). To pluck or twang (as the strings of a guitar, mandolin, etc.) ; (*noun*), a plectrum.

Piece. 1. A composition.—2. An instrument, taken as a member of an orchestra or band (usually in pl.)

Pièce (Fr.) A piece (ordinarily of instrumental music)...*Suite de pièces*, a set of pieces.

Pie'no (It.) 1. Full.—2. Mixture-stop.

Pieto'so (It., "pitiful, moving".) Calls for a sympathetic and expressive delivery ; nearly same as *espressivo*.

Piffera'ro (It.) A player on the piffero.

Pif'fero (It., dimin. *pifferi'no*.) 1. A fife ; also, the name of a primitive kind of oboe or shawm.—2. An organ-stop (see *Bifara*).

Fikie'ren (Ger.) Same as *piquer*. See *Piqué*.

Pincé (Fr , " pinched".) 1. Plucked or twanged, as the strings of the harp, zither, etc.—2. Pizzicato (in violin-playing).—3 (*noun*). A mordent; sign ⅂ or ⅃...*Pincé étouffé*, acciaccatura ; *pincé renversé*, inverted mordent.

Pipe. 1. A primitive wind-instr., a rude flageolet or oboe.—2. An organ-pipe. (Ger. *Or'gelpfeife;* Fr. *tuyau d'orgue:*

It. *can'na d'or'gano*.) (*a*) FLUE-PIPES are those in which the tone is produced by the vibration of a column of air within a tube or "body", the vibration being set up by an air-current forced through a narrow aperture and impinging on a sharp edge. A flue-pipe may be of metal or wood ; the part resting on the pipe-rack is the *foot*, which is divided from the *body* by an aperture in front called the *mouth*, having an upper and a lower *lip*, and *ears* on either side ; within the mouth a projecting shelf or ledge called the *block* (when thick) or *language* (when thin) deflects the wind rushing through the foot, forming below a channel called the *throat*, and above (between language and lower lip) a narrow passage called the *windway;* the wind passing out of the latter impinges on the sharp edge of the *leaf* (bevelled portion of the upper lip), setting the air-column within the body in vibration and thus producing a tone. The body of an open metal pipe is provided at the top with flaps called *tuners*, that of a wooden pipe with small movable wooden boards, by adjusting which the pipes can be tuned—("voiced"). —Flue-pipes are *open* or *covered* (stopped, plugged) ; an *open pipe* produces a tone proportioned in pitch to the length of the body, hence the terms 8-foot tone, 16-foot tone, etc. (Compare *Harmonic stop*.) A *stopped pipe* yields a tone an octave lower than an open pipe of like length.—(*b*) REED-PIPES are those in which the tone is produced by a reed ; the tone may be modified in quality, but not in pitch, by the shape and size of the body or tube. A reed-pipe has a *boot* (corresponding to the *foot* of a flue-pipe), within which is the *block*, a circular plate of metal with 2 apertures, one holding the *tuning-wire* and the other the *reed*. A *reed* consists of 2 parts, a metal tube (called the *shallot*) of conical form, widest below, with a

lengthwise opening along one side covered by the *tongue* (the vibrating reed proper), an elastic strip of metal made fast at the top, but free below to vibrate ; across its upper portion passes the bent end of the *tuning-wire*, which can be raised or lowered so as to allow a longer or shorter part of the tongue to vibrate, and thus alter the pitch. The tube is fixed above the block, and may be of metal or wood, and in very various forms.

Pipe-metal. The metal of which the metallic flue-pipes in the organ are made ; generally an alloy of tin and lead, the tone improving as the proportion of tin increases. Pure tin, lead, or zinc, or all 3 in varying proportions, have also been used.

Pipe-organ. See *Organ*.

Pique (Fr.) Peg or standard of a 'cello.

Piqué (Fr.) In violin-playing, the *mezzo-staccato* called for by a slur with staccato dots, notes so marked to be played in one bow (*picchietta'to*)...*Piquer*, to execute *picchiettato*.

Pirolino (It.) Button (on violin, etc.)

Piston. See *Valve*.

Piston-Solo (Ger.) Solo for the *cornet à pistons*.

Pitch. (Ger. *Ton'höhe;* Fr. *hauteur du ton;* It. *diapason*.) The position of a tone in the musical scale.—Pitch is relative, or absolute. The *relative pitch* of a tone is its position (higher or lower) as compared with some other tone. (See *Interval*.) Its *absolute pitch* is its fixed position in the entire range of musical tones.

§ 1. For ordinary purposes the mus. scale´ is divided, to indicate *absolute* pitch, into a fixed series of octaves, which are named and lettered, in English usage, as follows :

NAMES OF THE OCTAVES IN ABSOLUTE PITCH.

Double contra-octave (32-foot octave, organ)	Contra-octave (16-foot oct.)	First octave (Great octave) (8-foot oct.)
C₂ D₂ E₂ F₂ G₂ A₂ B₂	C₁ D₁ E₁ F₁ G₁ A₁ B₁	C D E F G A B

Second octave (Small octave) (4-foot oct.)	Third octave (One-lined oct.) (2-foot oct.)	Fourth octave (2-lined oct.) (1-foot oct.)
c d e f g a b	c¹ d¹ e¹ f¹ g¹ a¹ b¹	c² d² e² f² g² a² b²

NOTE.—The double contra-octave is often written CCC, DDD, etc., and the contra-octave CC, DD, etc.; also, instead of small figures, accents or lines are employed to mark the letters, as C͵͵ D͵͵ or C̄ D̄ for C₂ D₂ etc.;—c′ d′, or c̄ d̄, for c¹ d¹ etc.;—c″ d″, or c̿ d̿, for c² d² etc.;—hence the terms *one-lined* octave, *two-lined* octave, and *once-accented* octave, *twice-accented* octave, etc.

§ 2. For scientific purposes, and to ascertain the *relative* pitch of the tones of the scale, the above system is modified, *C* being retained as the starting-point or standard tone, while the distinction between lower and higher octaves is disregarded, and lines (in this case not marking different octaves) are drawn above or below the letters to distinguish between *Quint-tones* (i. e. tones whose relative pitch is determined by reaching them through ascending or descending, from the standard tone *C*, by skips of successive perfect fifths), and *Tierce-tones* (i. e. tones determined by reaching them through skips of major thirds). For instance, the tone *e* may be reached either as the fourth quint above C (C-G-D-A-E), or by ascending one tierce to *e;* in the former case E, as the third of C, is a *quint-tone*, whereas in the latter case it is a *tierce-tone*, the difference in pitch being noted by a line under the tierce-tone E, signifying that it is lower than the quint-tone E by a syntonic comma (80 : 81). This syntonic comma represents the ratio between the Pythagorean tierce of C (=E, the fourth quint), and the major tierce of C (=E) of just intonation (E : E :: 80 : 81); for every tierce-skip taken upward, a line is added below the letter, and for every tierce-skip downward, a line is added above the letter ; showing by how many commas the tierce-tone obtained is lower or higher than the corresponding quint-tone.

Table (after RIEMANN).

	4th quint below	3d quint below	2d quint below	1st quint below		1st quint above	2d quint above	3d quint above	4th quint above	
4th tierce above				g×	d×	a×	e×	b×	f×♯	
3d tierce above.			a♯	e♯	b♯	f×	c×	g×	d×	
2d tierce above.		b	f♯	c♯	g♯	d♯	a♯	e♯	b♯	
1st tierce above.	c	g	d	a	e	b	f♯	c♯	g♯	
	a♭	e♭	b♭	f	**C**	g	d	a	e	
	f♭	c♭	g♭	d♭	a♭	e♭	b♭	f		1st tierce below.
	d♭♭	a♭♭	e♭♭	b♭♭	f♭	c♭	g♭			2d tierce below.
	b♭♭♭	f♭♭	c♭♭	g♭♭	d♭♭	a♭♭				3d tierce below.

(bottom column labels, left to right: 4th quint below, 3d quint below, 2d quint below, 1st quint below.)

In this Table each skip horizontally is a quint-skip, and each skip vertically is a tierce-skip ; the major triads are grouped thus, $\frac{c}{a\flat}$ $\frac{}{e\flat}$ and the minor triads thus $\frac{c\ g}{e\flat}$.

In just intonation the major scale would be represented thus :

C D E F G A B c

and its parallel minor scale thus :

C D E̅♭ F G A̅♭ B c

§ 3. The **absolute pitch** of a tone is determined by the number of vibrations it makes per second, and is stated as a *vibration-number*. The standard *French pitch*, universally adopted in France in 1859, gives the tone a^1 435 (double) vibrations per second, c^3 having 522. Formerly there was no recognized standard, the pitch varying in different instr.s (organs) and localities by as much as a fourth. The inconveniences resulting led to the establishment, early in the 17th century, of a mean pitch (a^1 averaging about 420 vibrations), which held its own for some 200 years ; this has been called the *classical pitch*, it having obtained throughout the era of classical composition. After this, the growing tendency to force the pitch upwards led to numerous deliberations by scientists and musicians ; the German congress at Stuttgart adopted the pitch $a^1 = 440$; but the French pitch mentioned above is, in point of fact, the only real standard, and, since its formal adoption by the Vienna Congress in Nov., 1887, is frequently termed the *international pitch*. It is called *low pitch*, as opposed to the *high pitch* (*concert-pitch*) in vogue till lately in concerts and operatic performances. The so-called *philosophical standard of pitch* is obtained by taking, for Middle-*C*, the nearest power of 2, giving 256 vibrations for c^1, and nearly 427 for a^1 ; it has frequently served as a basis in theoretical calculations.

Pitch-pipe. A small metal or wooden reed-pipe producing, when blown, one or more tones of fixed pitch, according to which an instr. may be tuned, or the correct pitch ascertained for the performance of a piece of music.

Più (It.) More.—When *Più* stands alone as a tempo-mark, *mosso* is implied.

Pi′va (It.) 1. A bagpipe.—2. A piece imitative of bagpipe-music.

Pizzica′to (It., "pinched".) Plucked with the finger ; a direction, in music for bow-instr.s, to play the notes so marked by plucking the strings. The succeeding direction *coll 'arco* (with the bow) indicates the resumption of the bow for playing. (Abbr. *pizz.*)

Placidamen′te (It.) Tranquilly, smoothly ; from *pla′cido*, placid, tranquil.

Pla′cito (It.) Pleasure...*A be′ne placito*, at (the performer's) pleasure ; means that the tempo may be altered, graces or cadenzas added, or that certain specified instr.s may be used or not, as fancy may dictate.

Plagal cadence, mode, see *Cadence, Mode*...*Plagal melody*, one whose range extends about a fourth below and a fifth above its tonic or final.—*Plagal* is opp. to *Authentic* in all senses.

Plain chant, Plain song. (Lat. *can′tus pla′nus, cantus chora′lis*.) The unisonous vocal music of the Christian Church, probably dating from the first centuries of the Christian era, the style being still obligatory in the R. C. ritual. Handed down at the beginning by oral tradition, it was first regulated by St. Ambrose (see *Ambrosian chant*), and later revised by St. Gregory (*Gregorian chant*). The comparatively modern name *cantus planus* distinguished this style from that of the strictly rhythmical *cantus mensura′bilis*, which originated early in the 12th century, after which period plain chant began to be sung in notes of equal length ; in its earlier form, however, the tone-values of plain chant were determined by rules very similar to those for poetical metre. Just as a poem consists of lines, the lines of feet, and the feet of 2 or more syllables, a melody was divided into so-called *distinctions* consisting of a more or less extended group of *neumes* (notes), a distinction being in turn divided into single neumes (single notes), each neume, finally, representing one or more *tones*. Thus a metrical *line* corresponded to a musical *distinction*, a metrical *foot* to a musical *neume*, and a *syllable* to a *tone*. (Comp. *Notation,* § 3.)

Plainte (Fr.) A lament.

Plaisanterie (Fr.) A *divertissement* for harpsichord or clavichord.

Planchette. 1. A board studded with pins or pegs, an essential part of the mechanism of the *piano mécanique.*—2. See *Pianista* 2.

Plantation. In the organ, the disposition or arrangement on the soundboard of the pipes composing a stop.

Plaqué (Fr.) Struck at once ; as *un accord plaqué*, a " solid " chord ; opp. to *arpégé*, arpeggio'd, broken.

Plec'trum (Lat.; Gk. *plectron.*) A small piece of ivory, tortoise-shell, or metal, held between the forefinger and thumb, or fitting to the latter by a ring, and used in playing certain instr.s to pluck or twang the strings (mandolin, zither ; the zither-plectrum is called the "ring").

Plein-jeu (Fr.) 1. A stop or combination of stops bringing out the full power of the organ, harmonium, etc.—2. Same as *Fourniture.*

Pli'ca (Lat.) One of the neumes.

Plus (Fr.) More.

Pneu'ma (Gk. "breath".) The long coloratura or vocalise on the last syllable of the Alleluia (early Christian Church), so called because taxing the singers' lungs ; a jubilation.

Pneumatic action. See *Organ...Pneumatic organ*, the ordinary pipe-organ, as contradistinguished from the early hydraulic organ.

Pochette (Fr.) A kit.

Po'co (It.; superl. *pochis'simo;* dimin. *pochetti'no, pochet'to;* abbr. *po'*.) A little...*Poco a poco*, little by little, gradually...*Poco allegro*, rather fast ; *poco largo*, rather slow.

Poggia'to (It.) Leaned or dwelt upon.

Po'i (It.) Then, thereafter.

Point. 1. See *Notation*, § 3.—2. A dot. —3. A staccato-mark.—4. The attack by, or entrance of, an instrumental or vocal part bringing in a prominent motive or theme.—5. Head (of a bow).

Point (Fr.) A dot (*point d'augmentation*). ..*Point d'arrêt, de repos*, a hold (⌒). ..*Point final*, final pause...*Point d'orgue*, (*a*) a hold ; (*b*) an organ-point ; (*c*) a solo cadenza or flourish...*Points détachés*, staccato-dots...*Point sur tête*, dot above (or below) the head of a note.

Pointe (Fr.) 1. Point or head (of a bow). —2. Toe (in organ playing ; abbr. *p;* —*t p* = *talon pointe;* Engl. *h t* = heel toe,—but compare *Signs* [o ∨]).

Pointé (Fr.) Dotted.

Pointer (Fr.) 1. To dot.—2. To execute staccato.

Poitrine (Fr.) Chest ; *voix de p.*, chest-voice.

Polac'ca (It.) Polonaise...*Alla p*, in the style of a polonaise.

Polichinelle (Fr.) A grotesque clog-dance ; also, the tune to which it is performed.

Polka. (Bohemian *pulka.*) A lively round dance in 2-4 time, originating about 1830 as a peasant-dance in Bohemia...*Polka-mazurka*, a form of mazurka accommodated to the steps of the polka.

Polonaise (Fr.; Ger. *Polonä'se;* It. *polac'ca.*) A dance of Polish origin, in 3-4 time and moderate tempo, formerly in animated processional form, but in the modern ball-room merely a slow opening promenade, supplanting the old *Entrée.* The rhythm is characterized by the commencement on the strong beat with a sharp accent |⟩ ♪♪♪♪ |, and by the close on the last beat |♪♪♪ ⟩ ♪ ⁊|.

Polska. A Swedish dance in triple time, somewhat like the Scotch reel, and generally in minor.

Polychord. ("Having many chords [strings]".) An instr. in the shape of a bass viol, with movable fingerboard and 10 gut strings ; played either with a bow or by plucking with the fingers. Inv. by Fr. Hillmer of Berlin, first half of 19th century. It never became popular.

Polymor'phous. Having, or capable of assuming, many forms...*P. counterpoint*, a style of contrapuntal composition admitting of a manifold variation of the theme (as in the fugue by inversion, augmentation, diminution, etc.)

Polyphon'ic. 1. Consisting of 2 or more independently treated parts ;— contrapuntal ;—concerted ; opp. to *homophonic* and *harmonic.*—2. Capable of producing 2 or more tones simultaneously, as the pianoforte, harp, or organ ; opp. to *monophonous*, and equivalent to *polyphonous.*

Pol'yphony. In mus. composition, the combination in harmonious progression of 2 or more independent parts (as opp.

to *Homophony*) ; the independent treatment of the parts (as opp. to *Harmony*) ; —*counterpoint* in the widest sense ;—concerted music. (Also pron. *polyph'-ony*.)

Pom'mer (Ger.) See *Bombard*.

Pompe (Fr.) A tuning-slide (in the trombone, horn, and various other instr.s).

Pompo'so (It.) Pompous, majestic, dignified...*Pomposamen'te*, in a broad and dignified style.

Ponctuation (Fr.) Phrasing...*Ponctuer*, to phrase.

Pondero'so (It.) Ponderous, heavy, very strongly marked.

Ponticel'lo (It.) 1. The bridge of bow-instr.s...*Sul p.*, near the bridge ; a direction to play near the bridge, the tones resulting having a more or less strident and metallic sound ; abbr. *s. pont.*; opp. to *sui tasto.*—2. The break in the voice.

Pont-neuf (Fr.) Generic title for popular street-songs in Paris.

Portamen'to (It.; equiv. to *portar' la voce*, to carry the voice ; see *Port de voix*.) A smooth gliding from one tone to another ; an effect attained in great perfection on bow-instr.s, the melody-strings of the zither, and with the human voice. It differs from the *legato* not only in its more deliberate execution, but also in the actual (though very rapid and slurring) sounding or passing-through the intermediate tones, without a noticeable break, or a pause on any tone. It may be written thus :

Portan'do (It., "carrying".) Usually in the phrase *p. la voce*, carrying the voice, i. e. *portamento*.

Portata (It.) Staff.

Portatif (Fr.), **Portativ'** (Ger.) Portative organ, i. e. a small organ convenient of transportation ; opp. to *positif*.

Port de voix (Fr.) 1. Portamento.—2. See *Accent, Chute*.

Portée (Fr.) The staff.

Porter la voix (Fr.) See *Portamento*.

Portunal flute. An open wooden flue-stop in the organ, with pipes wider at top than at the mouth.

Portu'nen (Ger.) Bourdon (org.)

Posa'to (It.) Sedate, dignified.

Posau'ne (Ger.) 1. Trombone.—2. A reed-stop in the organ, having metal pipes of broad scale and 8-foot pitch (manuals) or 16-foot pitch (pedal) ; the 32-foot stop is called the *contra-posaune*.

Poschet'te. Ger. form of *Pochette*.

Posément (Fr.) *Posato*.

Poser la voix (Fr.) To attack a vocal tone with clearness and precision.

Positif (Fr.), **Positiv'** (Ger.) A "positive" or stationary organ ; opp. to *portatif*.—Also, the French term for choir-organ ; and (in German) a small partial organ in front of the main instr. was often called *Rückpositiv*, because usually *behind* the organist.

Position. 1. (Ger. *La'ge;* Fr. *position;* It. *posizio'ne*.) The place of the left hand on the fingerboard of the violin, etc. In the *1st pos.*, the forefinger stops the tone or semitone above the open string ; by shifting up (see *Shift*) so that the 1st finger takes the place previously occupied by the 2nd, the *2nd pos.* is reached ; and so on for each succeeding position. There are 11 positions in all, but only 7 are commonly employed.—The *half-position* is the same as the 1st pos., except that in it the 2nd, 3rd, and 4th fingers occupy the places taken, in the 1st pos., by the 1st, 2nd, and 3rd fingers.—2. The arrangement of notes in a chord with reference to the lowest part ; in the *1st*, or *fundamental, position* the lowest part takes the root ; in the *2nd position* it takes the third, etc.—3. Close and open position, see *Harmony*.

Possi'bile (It.) Possible ; *pianissimo possibile*, as soft as possible ; *il più presto possibile*, as rapid as possible.

Post-horn. The straight horn used by postmen. See APPENDIX.

Post'lude. (Lat. *postlu'dium;* Ger. *Nachspiel;* Fr. *clôture*.) A concluding voluntary on the organ, closing a church-service.

Pot-pourri (Fr.) A musical medley, all kinds of tunes or parts of tunes being juxtaposed in an arbitrary manner, often with very flimsy connecting-links.

Poule (Fr.) The 3rd movement or figure in the quadrille.

Poussé (Fr., "pushed".) Up-bow.

Präch'tig (Ger., "splendid".) Grand, majestic, dignified. (Also *adverb*.)

Præcen'tor (Lat.) Precentor.

Prall'triller (Ger.) An inverted mordent. (Also *Pral'ler*,)

Präludie'ren (Ger.) To prelude.

Präzis' (Ger.) Precise, exact.

Pream'bulum (Lat.) A prelude, introduction.

Pre:en'tor. In the Anglican Church, a director and manager of the choir and of the musical services in general, ranking after the Dean, and sitting on the side of the choir opposite to the latter, whence the terms *cantoris* (i. e. the precentor's) and *decani* (the Dean's) side.

Precipitan'do, Precipitatamen'te (It.) Precipitately; calls for a rapid and bold execution of the figure or passage so marked; *precipita'to* (also *precipito'so*), (Fr. *précipité*), precipitate.

Precisio'ne, con (It.) With precision. ...*Preci'so*, precise, exact.

Preghie'ra (It.) A prayer; a modern title for certain melodious salon-pieces of a more or less devotional character.

Prel'ude. (Lat. *prælu'dium;* It. *prelu'dio;* Fr. *prélude;* Ger. *Vor'spiel*.) A piece of music introductory or preparatory to another and more extended movement or composition, or to a dramatic performance, church-service, etc. The prelude has no distinctive form or independent character, being adapted to what is to follow it. (Comp. *Overture*.)—The short piano-pieces by Chopin, entitled "Préludes", are anomalous, not having been intended for introductory pieces.—An *organ-prelude* to the church-service is commonly called a *voluntary*.

Premier (Fr., fem. *première*.) First... *Premier dessus*, first soprano... *Première fois*, first time... *A première vue*, at first sight... *Première* (*noun*), the first production of a dramatic work.

Preparation. (Ger. *Vor'bereitung;* Fr. *préparation;* It. *preparazio'ne*.) The *p*. of a dissonance consists in the presence, in the preceding chord and same part, of the tone forming the dissonance. (Comp. *Percussion, Counterpoint*, and *Substitution*.)

Prepare. 1. See *Preparation*.—2. To introduce by a grace-note or figure; e. g. a prepared trill is one prefaced by a turn or other grace.

Pre'sa (It.) A sign marking the successive entrance of the parts of a canon, having various forms (·*S*· *S*+ ✕ etc.)

Pressan'te (It.) Accelerando, stringendo.

Pressez (Fr.) Accelerando, stringendo; *pressez un peu*, poco stringendo.

Pressure-note. A note marked thus ≳, indicating a sudden pressure or crescendo following the attack.

Prestant (Fr.) An open flue-stop in Fr. and Ger. organs, generally of 4-foot pitch; equiv. to Engl. *Principal*.

Prestez'za, con (It.) With rapidity (of movement or execution).

Prestissimamen'te, Prestis'simo (It.) Very rapidly, as fast as possible.

Pres'to (It.) 1. Fast, rapid; indicates a degree of speed above *allegro* and below *prestissimo*...*P. assa'i*, very rapid. —2. A rapid movement, most frequently concluding a composition.

Prick. In earlier terminology, the dot or mark forming the head of a note; *to prick* meaning, to write music. Hence, *prick-song*, (*a*) written music, opp. to extemporized; (*b*) the counterpoint to a *cantus firmus*, the *point against point*.

Primary accent. The down-beat or thesis; the accent beginning the measure, directly following the bar... *Primary triad*, one of the 3 fundamental triads of a key (those on the 1st, 5th, and 4th degrees).

Prime. 1. The first note of a scale.—2. See *Interval*...*Prime tone*, same as *generator*.—3. The 2nd of the canonical hours.

Prim'geiger (Ger.) Leader (1st violin).

Pri'mo,-a (It.) First...*Prima buf'fa*, the leading female singer in comic opera ..*Prima don'na* ("first lady"), the leading soprano singer in the opera. ..*Prima vi'sta*, at first sight...*Prima vol'ta*, the first time (abbr. *Ima volta*, or simply I, or 1.); indicates that the measure or measures under its bracket are to be played the first time, before the repeat; whereas, on repeating, those marked *secun'da volta* (abbr. *IIda volta*, or simply II, or 2.) are to be performed instead.—*Tempo primo*, at the first or former rate of speed...*Primo uo'mo*, the first male singer (*castra'to*), or first tenor. (Obsolete in both senses.)

Pri'mo (It., *noun*.) A first or leading part, as in a duet.

Prim'zither (Ger.) Treble zither.

Principal. 1. In the organ, a flue-stop of open metal pipes, of 4-foot pitch on the manual, and 8-foot pitch on the pedal. (In Ger., *Prinzipal* is the open diapason.)—2. Theme of a fugue (obsolete).

Principal chords. The basic chords of a key, i. e. the triads on the tonic, dominant, and subdominant, with the dom. chord of the 7th. (Also called *fundamental, primary*, etc.)

Principa'le (It.) 1. Diapason (organstop).—2. Principal, chief; also, principal or leading part.—3. Sometimes found, in old scores, for *tromba* (trumpet).

Princ²pal-work. See *Stop (noun)* 2.

Princi'pio (It.) Beginning, first time. [In Beethoven, Op. 27, No. 2, 1st movem.: "più marcato del principio," more marked than the first time.]

Prise du sujet (Fr.) Entrance of the subject.

Pro'be (Ger.) Rehearsal... *General'probe*, full rehearsal.

Proceed. (Fr. *procéder*.) To progress.

Pro'gram. (Ger. *Programm'*; Fr. *programme*; It. *program'ma*.) A list of compositions to be performed at a concert...*Program-music*(Ger.*Programm'-musik*), a term of modern invention, applied to a class of instrumental compositions intended to represent distinct phases of emotion, or actual scenes or events; sometimes made synonymous with "descriptive music". The "program" of such a composition may be merely its title; or occasional interpolated remarks; or a concise summary of its poetic subject-matter, appended as a description for the better comprehension of the music.

Progress'. (Ger. *fort'schreiten*; Fr. *procéder, marcher*.) To advance or move on; in melody, from one tone to another; in harmony, from one chord to another...*Progression* (Ger. *Fort'-schreitung*; Fr. *progrès, marche*; It. *progressio'ne*), the advance from one tone to another, or from one chord to another; the former is *melodic*, the latter *harmonic*, progression.

Progressive stop. A compound organ-stop in which the number of ranks increases as the pitch rises.

Prolation. (Lat. *prola'tio*.) See *Notation, §3*.

Prolongement (Fr.) 1. A mechanical attachment in the reed-organ for holding down single keys after the fingers are raised.—2. Sustaining-pedal.

Promptement (Fr.), **Prontamen'te** (It.) Promptly, swiftly.

Pron'to,-a (It.) Prompt, speedy.

Pronunzia'to (It.) Pronounced, marked; *ben pr.*, well, clearly enunciated.

Proportion. (Lat. *propor'tio*.) See *Notation* § 3, and *Nachtanz*.

Propo'sta (It.) Theme of a fugue.

Propri'etas (Lat.) A term applied to a ligature when the first note was a breve. It was indicated, when the 2nd note was the lower, by a descending tail on the left (seldom on the right) of the first note; when the 2nd was the higher, by the absence of the tail. *Oppo'sita proprietas* occurred when the first 2 notes of the ligature were semibreves, —indicated by an ascending tail to the left of the first note... *Si'ne proprietas*, same as *Impropri'etas*.

Prose. (Lat. *pro'sa*.) See *Sequence*.

Proslambanom'enos (Gk.) See *Greek music*, p. 89.

Prosody. (Lat. and It. *prosodi'a*; Fr. and Ger. *Prosodie'*.) Metrics, or the science of metre; specifically, the science of the quantity of syllables, and of accentuation, as affecting versification.

Prospekt' (Ger.) The front of an organ. ..*Prospekt'pfeifen*, front or display-pipes; also *Frontpfeifen*.

Pro'va (It.) Rehearsal.

Psalm-melodicon. A wood-wind instr. with 8 finger-holes and 25 keys, having a compass of 4 octaves, and so constructed that from 4 to 6 tones could be produced at once. Inv. by Weinrich of Heiligenstadt in 1828; improved by Leo Schmidt in 1832, by whom it was called the *Apollo-Lyra*.

Psal'tery. (Lat. *psalte'rium*; It. *salté rio*; Fr. *psaltérion*; Ger. *Psal'ter*.) An instr. of very ancient origin, and in use down to the 17th century, known to the Hebrews as the *kinnor*, to the Germans as the *Rotta*; a kind of harp-zither, with a varying number of strings plucked by the fingers or with a plectrum. The strings were stretched over a soundboard, as in the dulcimer.

Psaume (Fr.) A psalm.

Psautier (Fr.)   Psalter.

Pul'satile instruments.   Instr.s of percussion (Lat. *pulsatilia*).

Pulse.   A beat or accent.

Punc'tus, or **Punc'tum** (Lat.)   1. A dot.
—2. A note...*Punctus contra punctum*, counterpoint.

Punkt (Ger.)   A dot...*Punktiert'*, dotted.

Pun'ta (It.)   Point (of the bow).

Pun'to (It.)   Dot...*Punta'to*, dotted ; staccato'd.

Pupitre (Fr.)   Music-desk.

Purf'ling.   The ornamental border on the bellies and backs of violins, etc.

Put'ti (It., pl.)   Boys, choir-boys.

Pyramidon.   An organ-stop having short covered pyramidal pipes more than 4 times as wide at top as at mouth, and of 16' or 32' tone.

Pyr'rhic, Pyrrhich'ius.   A metrical foot consisting of 2 short syllables (‿ ‿).

Pyth'ian metre, verse.   The dactylic (or spondaic) hexameter (— —|— — |— —|— —|— |— —).

Q.

Quadrat' (Ger.)   A natural (♮).—(Engl.) In medieval music, a breve (Lat. *quadra'tum*).

Quadrici'nium (Lat.)   A composition in 4 parts.

Quadrille.   (It. *quadri'glia*.)   A square dance consisting of 5 (or 6) figures named *le Pantalon, l'Été, la Poule, la Pastourelle, (la Trenise)*, and *la Finale*. The time alternates between 3-8 (6-8) and 2-4.

Quadruple counterpoint.   See *Counterpoint*...*Q. croche* (Fr.), a 64th-note... *Q. rhythm* or *time*, that characterized by 4 beats to the measure.

Quad'ruplet.   A group of 4 equal notes to be executed in the time of 3 or 6 of the same kind in the regular rhythm ; written ♩♩♩.

Quality of tone.   (Ger. *Ton'farbe;* Fr. *timbre;* It. *timbro.*)   That characteristic peculiarity of any vocal or instrumental tone which distinguishes it from the tone of any other class of voices or instr.s.

Quantity.   In metrics, prosodic length,

i. e. the time-value of a syllable.—In English versification this is apt to be disregarded, accented and unaccented syllables taking the place of long and short ones.

Quart.   The interval of a fourth.

Quart (Fr.)   Quarter...*Q. de soupir*, a 16th-rest.

Quar'ta (Lat. and It.)   The interval of a fourth...*Q. modi (toni)*, the subdominant.

Quar'te (Ger. and Fr.)   The interval of a fourth...*Q. du ton* (F♮) the subdominant.

Quar'tenfolgen (-parallelen) (Ger.)   Consecutive or parallel fourths.

Quarter-note.   (Ger. *Vier'telnote, Vier'-tel;* Fr. *noire;* It. *ne'ra*.)   A crotchet (♩).   (Sometimes abbrev. to *Quarter*.)
—*Quarter-rest*, a rest equivalent in time-value to a quarter-note (𝄾, or ♩).   (Also called *quarter-note rest*, and *crotchet-rest*.)

Quartet'.   (Ger. *Quartett';* Fr. *quatuor;* It. *quartet'to*.)   1. A concerted instrumental composition for 4 performers, in symphonic form.—2. A comp. or movement, either vocal or instrumental, in 4 parts.—3. The 4 performers themselves.

Quart'fagott (Ger.)   See *Bassoon*... *Quart'flöte*, see *Flöte*. . *Quart'geige*, see *Violin*...*Quartsext'akkord*, chord of the fourth and sixth (⁶₄ chord).

Quarto d'aspetto (It.)   A 16th-rest.

Quarto'le (Ger.)   A quadruplet.

Qua'si (Lat. and It.)   As if, as it were ; like ; nearly, approaching.   E. g., *Andante quasi allegretto*, andante approaching allegretto.

Qua'ter.   See *Bis* 3.

Quatorzième (Fr.)   The interval of a fourteenth.

Quatre (Fr.)   Four...*À quatre mains*, for 4 hands.

Quat'rible.   In medieval music, a counterpoint progressing in parallel fourths to the *cantus firmus;* a *quinible* progressed in parallel fifths.

Quatrici'nium (Lat.)   A composition in 4 parts.

Quattricro'ma (It.)   A 64th-note.

Quat'tro (It.)   Four...*À quattro mani*, for 4 hands.

Quatuor (Fr.)   A quartet, vocal or instrumental.

Quaver. An eighth-note.

Quer′flöte (Ger.) Orchestral flute...
Quer′pfeife, a fife...*Quer′stand*, false
or inharmonic relation. *Quer′strich*,
the thick stroke substituted for the
hooks of hooked notes when grouped.

Queue (Fr., " tail ".) 1. Stem of a note.
—2. Tailpiece...*Piano à queue*, see
Piano (Fr.)

Quickstep. See *March.*

Quie′to (It.) Calm, quiet ; opp. to *agi-
ta′to.*

Quinde′cima (It.) A fifteenth (either
the interval or the organ-stop)...*Alla
q.* (abbr. *15ma*), two octaves higher (or
lower).

Quinde′zime (Ger.) The interval of a
fifteenth.

Quin′ible. See *Quatrible.*

Quin′quegrade. Same as *Pentatonic.*

Quint. 1. The interval of a fifth.—2.
A 5⅓-foot organ-stop, sounding a fifth
higher than the normal 8-foot pitch.—
3. The *E*-string of the violin.—4. See
Violin...*Quint-stride*, the (*a*) harmonic
or (*b*) melodic progression of a fifth :

Quin′ta (Lat. and It.) The interval of a
fifth...*Q. de′cima*, the int. of a fifteenth.
..*Quinta fal′sa* ("false fifth"), the
prohibited melodic interval between *mi*
in the *hexachordum durum* and *fa* in
the *hex. naturale :* the modern diminished fifth...*Q. mo′di* (*to′ni*), the dominant (comp. *Quintus*)...*Alla quinta*,
at or in the fifth.

Quint′absatz (Ger.) A half-close, in
the midst of a piece, on the dominant ;
same as *Halbkadenz.*

Quintatön′ (Ger.) In the organ, a covered flue-stop of 8, 16, or 32-foot pitch.

Quinte (Fr.) See 1 and 2 below...
Quintes cachées, covered fifths.

Quin′te (Ger.) 1. The interval of a fifth.
—2. See *Quint* 2.—3. The *E*-string of
the violin (Fr. *chanterelle*)...*Quin′ten-
folgen, -parallen*, consecutive fifths...
Quin′tenrein, an epithet applied to
strings of bow-instr.s, signifying that
they produce " true fifths " to the neighboring strings throughout their length.
..*Quin′tenzirkel*, circle of fifths.

Quin′terne. See *Lute* A species of
lute or guitar extremely popular in Italy
some 200 years ago, with a body resembling a violin and from 3 to 5 pairs of
gut strings, to which were sometimes
added 2 wire-covered single strings.

Quintet′. (Ger. *Quintett′ ;* Fr. *quintuor ;*
It. *quintet′to.*) 1. A concerted instr′l
comp. for 5 performers, in symphonic
form.—2. A comp., movement, or number, vocal or instr′l, in 5 parts

Quintie′ren (Ger.) To overblow by a
twelfth, like the clarinet and other instr.s
with single reed.

Quintoier (Fr.) 1. To quinible (also
quintoyer).—2. See *Quintieren.*

Quinto′le (Ger.) Quintuplet.

Quinton (Fr.) 1. The 5-stringed treble
viol, or (acc. to ROUSSEAU) the tenor
viol.—2. See *Saxhorn.*

Quint′stimme (Ger.) A quint (organ-
stop)...*Quint′töne*, quint-tones (see
Pitch, § 2).

Quintuor (Fr.) A quintet.

Quintuple rhythm, time. That characterized by 5 beats to the measure.

Quin′tuplet. A group of 5 equal notes
to be executed in the time of 4 of the
same kind in the regu-
lar rhythm ; written :

Quintus (Lat.) " The fifth " part, in
compositions of the 16th century written in 5 or more parts ; it might be set
for any one of the usual 4 classes of
voices, and even wander from one to
the other, whence the name *quintus
vagans*, "wandering fifth "...Also
Quinta (vox).

Quintvio′le (Ger.) 1. See *Quinton* 1.—
2. In the organ, a mutation-stop (see
Gambenstimme).

Quinzième (Fr.) The interval of a fifth.

Quire. Obsolete for *Choir*...*Quirister*,
ditto for *Chorister.*

Quod′libet (Lat., " what you please " ;
also *Quot′libet*, " as many as you
please " ; It. *messan′za, mistichan′za*,
a mixture.) A humorous combination
of various airs, performed either simultaneously or one after the other ; the
latter mode differing from the pot-pourri
in lacking the connecting interludes ;
a favorite device in the 16th and 17th
centuries, and occasionally employed
even now.

R.

R. Abbr. for *right* (Ger. *rechte*); *r. h.=* right hand (*rechte Hand*); for *ripieno;* ℟ stands in Catholic church-music for *Responsorium;* RG, for *Resp. Graduale;* **R,** in Fr. organ-music, stands for *clavier de récit* (swell-manual).

Rab'bia, con (It.) With passion, frenzy; furiously.

Rackett' (Ger.; also *Ranket.*) 1. An obs. wood-wind instr. of the bombard class, with the tube bent many times and, in consequence, a very weak tone; improved by Chr. Denner, who reduced the number of bends and made it more like the bassoon, whence the later name *Rackett* (*Fagott'*, *Stock'fagott*). —2. An organ-stop with a tone resembling the above.

Racler (Fr.) To scrape, saw; *racleur*, a bungling fiddler.

Raddolcen'do, Raddolcen'te (It.) Growing calmer and gentler...*Raddolcia'to*, gentler, calmer.

Raddoppiamen'to (It.) 1. Doubling chord-notes.—2. Manifolding copies of parts.—*Raddoppia'to*, doubled.

Ra'del (Ger.) See *Rundgesang.*

Radiating pedals. A pedal-keyboard in which the pedals are set in fan-shaped arrangement, spreading out to the rear from in front, and concave (i. e. somewhat higher at the sides).

Radical bass. A fundamental bass... *Radical cadence*, see *Cadence.*

Rad'leier (Ger.) Hurdy-gurdy.

Ra'dlmaschine (Ger.) Piston-mechanism.

Rallentamen'to (It.) A slackening in tempo...*Rallentan'do*, gradually slackening the tempo, growing slower and slower ; equiv. to *ritardando*. (Abbr. *rall.*)—Also *rallenta'to*...*Rallenta're*, to grow slower ; *senza rallentare*, without slackening the pace.

Rang (Fr.) Rank.

Rank. A row of organ-pipes. A mixture-stop is said to have 2, 3, or more ranks according to the number of pipes sounded by each digital.

Rant. An old dance ; a name given to the tunes of various country-dances, and also to reels (e. g. the Cameronian Rant).

Ranz des vaches (Fr.; Ger. *Kuh'-*

reigen, Kuh'reihen.) One of the airs, or variations on an original air, sung, or played on the Alpine horn, in the Swiss Alps as a call to the cattle. It is characterized by oft-repeated figures, rising and falling broken chords, and (when sung) by the frequent employment of the *Jodler.*

Rapidamen'te (It.) Rapidly...*Rapidità', con,* with rapidity...*Ra'pido*, rapid.

Rapsodie (Fr.) 1. Rhapsody (see *Rhapsodie*).—2. A composition of bizarre and desultory form, lacking unity and consistency.

Rasch (Ger.) Fast, rapid, swift... *Noch rascher*, still faster...*So rasch wie mö'glich*, as fast as possible.

Rasga'do (Span., "a rasping"). In guitar-playing, the sweeping the strings with the thumb ; hence, the arpeggio effect so obtained.

Ras'tral, Ras'trum. (Ger. *Rastral'*.) 1. Music-pen 2.—2. A 5-pointed claw or graver used by music-engravers for scoring the lines of the staff in the zinc plates.

Rät'selkanon (Ger.) Enigmatical canon.

Rattenen'do, rattenu'to (It.) See *Ritenuto.*

Rauh (Ger.) 1. Harsh(ly), rough(ly).— 2. Hoarse(ly).

Rau'scher (Ger.) A rapidly repeated note, as on the pianoforte.

Rausch'quinte (Ger.) In the organ, a mixture-stop of 2 ranks, combining pipes of 5⅓ and 4-foot pitch, or of 2⅔ and 2-foot pitch, without a break (Also *Rausch'flöte*, *-pfeife*, *-quarte -werk.*)

Ravvivan'do (il tempo) (It.) Accelerating the tempo.

Ray. For *Re*, in the Tonic Sol-fa system.

Re. Second of the Aretinian syllables, and name of the note *D* in Italy, etc.— In French, *Ré.*

Re'bec(k). The primitive violin of medieval Europe, known in Italy as the *ribe'ba* or *ribe'ca*, and in Spain as the *rabe, rabel.* The body was shaped like a half-pear ; it had 3 gut strings, which yielded a powerful, strident tone.

Rechange (Fr., "exchange"). The *corps* or *tons de rechange* are the crooks of the horn, etc.

Recht (Ger.)   Right ; *rechte Hand*, right hand.

Récit (Fr.)   1. A vocal or instrumental solo part.—2. The leading part in a piece of concerted music.—*Clavier de récit*, swell-manual.

Recital.   In the usual acceptation of the term, a concert at which either (*a*) all the pieces are executed by one performer [as a *pfte.-recital*], or (*b*) all pieces performed are by one composer.

Recitan'do (It.)   In declamatory style.

Récitant,-e (Fr.)   One who sings or plays a solo.

Recitati've(teev').   It. *Recitati'vo;* Fr. *récitatif;* Ger. *Recitativ'*.   A style of declamatory singing, dating from 1600 (the earliest operas), and springing from the efforts to emancipate dramatic song from the contrapuntal forms then in vogue.   The first recitatives had a very simple accompaniment, a mere figured bass (*recitativo sec'co*) ; this broadened into the *recitativo accompagna'to* (or *obbliga'to, stromenta'to ;* Fr. equiv. *obligé, accompagné*), in which the instrumental parts were invested with more life, variety, and musical importance.— Unless marked *recitativo a tempo*, the recitative may be performed *ad libitum*. The connecting-link between the *rec.* of the opera and oratorio and the *A'ria* is found in the *Ario'so*.— *Wagner's rec.* differs from the earlier forms in the perfectly natural musical inflection of the vocal part (the ancient cadences, etc., being abolished), and the richly instrumented and marvelously pregnant accompaniment (comp. *Melos*).

Réciter (Fr.)   To sing or play a *récit.*

Reciting-note.   That tone, in any Gregorian mode, on which the greater portion of every verse in a psalm or canticle is continuously recited ; i. e. the dominant of the mode.

Recorder.   An obsolete species of flageolet, having 7 finger-holes on the upper side and one below, with an extra hole near the mouthpiece covered with a thin membrane (goldbeaters'-skin), and probably influencing the quality of the tone.   Compass about 2 octaves, from *f*¹: upward.

Recte et retro (Lat., "forwards and backwards").   Direction for performing a *canon cancrizans.*

Rectus (Lat.)   See *Motus.*

Reddi'ta, Redi'ta (It.)   A repeat.

Redoubled interval.   A compound interval.

Red'owa.   A   dance   derived from Bohemia, and, like the Mazurka, though less strongly accented, in 3-4 time and lively tempo.   In Bohemia there are 2 varieties, the *Rejdovak* in 3-4 or 3-8 time, and the *Rejdovacka* in 2-4 time.

Réduire (Fr.), **Reduzie'ren** (Ger.)   To reduce the volume of a composition by rearranging it for a smaller number of instr.s, while preserving its form as far as possible.

Redundant.   Same as *Augmented* (of chords and intervals).

Reed.   (Ger. *Roh'blatt, Zung'e ;* Fr. *anche ;* It. *an'cia, lin'gua*.)   A thin strip of cane, wood, or metal, so adjusted before an aperture as nearly to close it, fixed at one end, and set by an air-current in vibration, which it communicates either to an enclosed column of air (organ-pipe, oboe, etc.), or directly to the free atmosphere, thus producing a musical tone.   There are 2 classes of reeds, (1) *Free Reeds*, which vibrate within the aperture without striking the edges ; and (2) *Beating* (or *striking, or percussion*) *Reeds*, which strike on the edges ; in either class, the elasticity of the reed causes its return-stroke after it is borne down by the air-current.— *Double Reed*, two beating reeds which strike against each other (oboe, bassoon). (Also comp. *Pipe 2, b, Reed-organ, Regal.*)

Reed-instrument.   One whose tone is produced by the vibration of a reed in the mouthpiece ; the orchestral instr.s of the oboe and clarinet groups.

Reed-organ.   The precursor of the reed-organs now in use was the Regal, which contained beating reeds similar to those in the reed-pipes of church-organs. The present reed-organs have free reeds ; there are 2 principal classes : (1) The *Harmonium*, the bellows of which forces compressed wind outwards through the reeds ; and (2) the *American organ*, in which an exhaust or suction-bellows draws the air in through them. Until the invention of the *Vocalion*, a variety of reed-organ having compression-bellows like those of the harmonium, the tone of the second class was generally superior to that of the first.—The wind-supply is ordinarily obtained by the aid of a pair of treadles operated by the performer. There may be one or many sets of reeds or vibrators, each controlled by a stop and slider-mechanism. The timbre of the various orchestral instr.s is now very successfully imitated.—Common mechanical devices are the *percussion-stop*, *expression-stop* (harmonium), *knee-swell* (Amer. org.), *tremulant*, *double-touche*, and *prolongement*.—The first reed-organ was invented by Grénié in 1810, and named by him *orgue expressif* on account of the *crescendo* and *decrescendo* obtainable on it ; other inventors constructed the *æoline*, *æolodikon*, *phys-harmonica*, etc.; the *Harmonium*, the first instr. of the class having several stops, was patented in Paris by A. Debain in 1843.

Reed-pipe, Reed-stop. See *Pipe 2, b.*

Reed-work. See *Stop (noun)* 2.

Reel. A lively dance, probably of Celtic origin, still in vogue in Scotland and Ireland, and usually in 4-4 (sometimes in 6-4) time, with reprises of 8 measures; danced by 2 couples.

Refrain'. A burden.

Re'gal. (Ger. *Regal'*.) 1. An obsolete kind of portable organ with one or two sets of reed-pipes (beating reeds), a keyboard for the right hand, and a bellows worked by the left. According to the number of pipes sounded by each digital, it was called a *single* or *double regal*. The old English name was *regall*, or a *pair of regalls*. (See *Harmonium*.) A *Bibelregal* (Ger.) was one folding up like a large bible ; a bible-organ.—2. (Ger.) An obsolete suffix distinguishing reed-stops ; e. g. *Har'-fenregal*, *Gei'genregal*.—3. An old species of xylophone.

Re'gel (Ger.) A rule.

Re'gens cho'ri (Lat.) Choir-master.

Regier'werk (Ger.) In the organ, the mechanism of the keys and draw-stops, taken collectively.

Reg'ister. 1. (Ger. *Regis'ter*.) A set of pipes or reeds controlled by one draw-stop ; in this sense synonymous with stop (organ-stop).—2. A board with perforations for guiding and steadying the trackers of an organ-action.—3. A portion of the range and compass of the voice, and of certain instr.s ; (*a*) see *Voice ;* (*b*) comp. *Chalumeau.*

Regis'ter (Ger.) Register 1 and 3.— *Regis'terknopf*, stop-knob...*Regis'ter-* *stange*, stop-lever...*Regis'terzug*, draw-stop mechanism...*Stum'me Register* (pl.), mechanical stops ; *tönende Register* (pl.), speaking stops.

Registre (Fr.) 1. A stop-knob.—2. Register 3.

Registration. 1. The art of effectively employing and combining the various stops of the organ.—2. The combination or combinations of stops employed for any given composition.

Registrie'ren (Ger.) To registrate or register (see *Registration*).—*Registrie'-rung*, registration.

Règle (Fr.) Rule.

Rein (Ger.) Perfect (of intervals) ; just, true, correct (of pitch or intonation).

Rein'greifen (Ger.) Accurate stopping (violin) ; accurate playing (in general).

Rei'tertrompete (Ger.) Clarion, clarina, clarino. (Medieval trumpet, with straight tube about 30 inches long.)

Rela'tio non harmo'nica (Lat.) Inharmonic relation.

Relation. (Ger. *Verwand'schaft;* Fr. *relation;* It. *relazio'ne.*) The degree of affinity between keys, chords, and tones. The simplest explanation of relationship is that promulgated by the neo-harmonists (comp. *Phone*, § 4).— Also *Relationship*, *Tone-relationship* (Ger. *Ton'verwandschaft*).

Relative key. (Ger. *Parallel'tonart;* Fr. *mode relatif;* It. *tono relati'vo.*) A minor key is relative to that major key, the tonic of which lies a minor third above its own ; a major key is relative to that minor key, the tonic of which lies a minor third below its own. (N. B. *Relative* is sometimes used for *related*, in qualifying keys and chords.)

Religiosamen'te, Religio'so (It.) In a style expressive of religious or devotional feeling.

Relish. One of the "shaked graces" of the old harpsichord-music ; in 2 forms, namely, the Single Relish :

and the Double Relish : played:

Remote key. An unrelated key. (See *Relation.*)

Remo'tus (Lat.) Remote, far apart ; as *harmonia remota*, open harmony.

Remplissage (Fr., "filling"). The *parties de r.* are the inner parts.—The word *r.* is also used as a term of reproach for superfluous or cumbrous parts in the works of novices—"padding" ; also, for non-concerted parts.

Rendering. Artistic interpretation or reproduction. (Preferable to the term "rendition".)

Rentrée (Fr.) Reëntrance of a part or theme after a rest or pause.

Renverser (Fr.) To invert ; *renversé;* inverted ; *renversement,* inversion.

Renvoi (Fr.) The sign (e. g. 𝄋) directing the performer to return to and repeat from a similar sign.

Repeat. (Ger. *Wieder ho'lungszeichen;* Fr. *bâton de reprise;* It. *re'plica.*) The sign 𝄇: :𝄆 or 𝄇:𝄆 or 𝄇:𝄆, the first signifying that the division between the dotted double-bars is to be repeated ; the second and third, that the preceding and also the following division is to be repeated ; the dots always being on the same side of the bar as the division to be repeated.—Comp. *Da Capo,* and *Dal Segno.*

Repeating action. See *Repetition* 2.

Repercussion. (Lat. *repercus'sio.*) 1. The repetition of a tone or chord.—2. The regular reëntrance, in a fugue, of the subject and answer after the episodes immediately following the exposition.—3. In Gregorian music, the dominant of the mode, as being the tone most reiterated.

Repetie'ren (Ger.) 1. To break (see *Break* 3)...*Eine repetie'rende Stim'me*, a mixture-stop with a break.—2. To repeat.

Repetition. 1. The very rapid reiteration of a tone or chord, producing almost the effect of a sustained sound. —2. Repeating action, one in which the rebound of the hammer admits of the instant restriking of the key and repetition of the tone (pfte.)

Répétition (Fr.) Repetition ; rehearsal.

Repetition' (Ger.) *Repetition* 1 and 2 ; also, a *Break* 3...*Repetitions' mechanik*, repeating action (pfte.)

Repeti'tor (Ger.) The trainer or conductor of an opera-chorus. (Fr. *chef du chant.*)

Repetizio'ne (It.) Repetition.

Re'plica (It.) A repeat...*Replica' to*, (*a*) repeated ; (*b*) doubled.

Rep'licate. A tone one or more octaves above or below a given tone.

Replik' (Ger.) A complementary interval.

Réplique (Fr.) 1. A replicate (unused). —2. Answer (usually *réponse*).—3. A complementary interval.—4. A cue.

Reply. Answer.

Répons (Fr.) A response.

Réponse (Fr.) An answer.

Report. Same as *Answer.*

Repos (Fr.) The end of a phrase, marked by a full cadence.

Reprise (Fr.) 1. A repeat.—2. The revival of a work.—3. Break 3.—4. The repetition of the first theme, in a short movement, after an episode.—5. Same as *Rentrée.*

Re'quiem. The first word in the Mass for the Dead, which begins with the antiphon *Requiem æternam dona eis, domine;* hence, the title of the musical setting of that Mass. Its divisions are as follows: (1) Requiem, Kyrie ; (2) Dies iræ, Requiem ; (3) Domine Jesu Christe ; (4) Sanctus, Benedictus ; (5) Agnus Dei, Lux æterna.

Resin. See *Rosin.*

Resolution. (Ger. *Auf'lösung;* Fr. *résolution;* It. *risoluzio'ne.*) The progression of a dissonance, whether a simple interval or a chord, to a consonance.

Resoluzio'ne, con (It.) See *Risoluto.*

Res'onance-box. A hollow resonant body, like that of a violin or zither.

Resonanz'boden (Ger.) Soundboard or belly...*Resonanz' kasten*, resonance-box. ..*Resonanz'saite*, sympathetic string.

Respi'ro (It.) A 16th-rest.

Respond. See *Responsory* 3.

Response. (Lat. *respon'sum.*) 1. The musical reply, by the choir or congregation, to what is said or sung by the priest or officiant, either in the Anglican or R. C. Church.—2. See *Responsory.* —3. Same as *Answer.*

Respon'sory. (Lat. *responso'rium.*) 1. That psalm, or part of one, sung be-

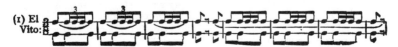

tween the missal lessons.—2. The Gradual.—3. A Respond; i. e. a part of a psalm (formerly an entire psalm) sung between the lessons at the canonical hours.

Ressort (Fr.) Bass-bar.

Rest. (Ger. *Pau'se;* Fr. *silence;* It. *pa'usa.*) (1) A pause or interval of silence between two tones; hence (2) a sign indicating such a pause.—The rests equivalent in time-value to the several notes are as follows:

I. 2. 3. 4. 5. 6. 7.

Rests:
Time-value:

ENGLISH.	GERMAN.	FRENCH.	ITALIAN.
1. Whole rest.	Taktpause. [Pause.	Pause.	Pausa della semibreve.
2. Half-rest.	Halbe (*or* Zweitel-)	Demi-pause.	" " minima.
3. Quarter-rest.	Viertelpause.	Soupir.	" " semiminima (*or* Quarto).
4. Eighth-rest.	Achtelpause.	Demi-soupir.	" " croma (*or* Mezzo-quarto).
5. 16th-rest.	Sechzehntelpause.	Quart de soupir.	" " semicroma (*or* Respiro).
6. 32nd-rest.	Zweiunddreissigstelp.	Demi-quart de s.	" " biscroma.
7. 64th-rest.	Vierundsechzigstelp.	Seizième de s.	" " semibiscroma.

...*Breve-* ▬ equal in time-value *rest*, a rest ▬ to 1 breve (⏸), or 2 semibreves or whole notes (⏹⏹). ...*Large-rest, Long-rest*, see *Notation*, §3, p. 131...*Measure-rest*, a pause throughout a measure. The *whole rest* is often used as a measure-rest, regardless of the measure-value expressed in the time-signature; the 2-measure rest is then writ- ▬ the 3-measure ten thus: ▬' rest thus: ▬ the 4-measure ▬ etc. ▬' rest thus: ▬' But, for rests longer than one measure, any one of the following conventional signs is usually employed, with a numeral above to show the number of measures rested:

3   8   4   6
▬▬▬▬▬▬, etc.

Restric'tio (Lat.) Stretto (of a fugue).

Resultant tones. See *Acoustics*, §3.

Retard. To suspend...*Retarded progression*, same as *Retardation* 2.

Retardation. A holding-back, decreasing in speed.—2. A suspension resolving upward; opp. to *Anticipation*.

Retraite (Fr.) The tattoo.

Retrograde. (Lat. *retrogra'dus;* It. *retrogra'do*). See *Imitation*.

Ret'to (It.) Direct, straight. See *Moto*.

Reveille (Engl. and Ger.; from Fr. *ré-veil*.) A military signal for rising.

Reverie. An instrumental comp. of a dreamy cast, without characteristic form.

Reversion. See *Imitation, retrograde*. ..*Reverse motion*, same as Contrary motion.

Rhapsodie (Fr.) In ancient Greece, rhapsodies were fragments from the great epics, sung by the *rhapsodes* to the cithara. In modern music, the rhapsodie is generally an instrumental fantasia on folk-songs or motives taken from primitive national music; an exception is Brahms' Op. 53. (Also *Rhapsody*.)

Rhythm. (Ger. *Rhyth'mus;* Fr. *rythme;* It. *rit'mo.*) 1. The measured movement of similar tone-groups; i. e., the effect produced by the systematic grouping of tones with reference to regularity both in their accentuation and in their succession as equal or unequal in time-value.—*A* Rhythm is, therefore, a tone-group serving as a pattern for succeeding groups identical with it as regards the accentuation and duration of the tones. The rhythm, being thus a thing apart from tonal melody or harmony, is reducible to a formula of notes without pitch, merely representing an orderly series of pulsations; take, for instance, the castanet-rhythm of 3 Spanish national dances:

(1) El Vito:

(2) Fandango:

(3) Bolero:

etc.

The vertical bars divide the *measures;* the slurs connect notes forming one *rhythmic group* or *rhythm.* The difference between a *measure* and a *rhythm* is apparent ; the former is the sum of the time-values of notes (or rests) between 2 bars, whatever be their arrangement ; the latter *may* be contained (1) within a measure, but at (2) embraces 2 measures, and at (3) begins before the bar.—*Time,* on the other hand, is the division of each measure into equal fractional parts of a whole note, corresponding (at least in the simple times) to the same number of regular beats to a measure ; with which regular beats the pulsations of the rhythm are by no means required to coincide.—It must be added, however, that the above definitions are not universally accepted, and that great confusion prevails in this department of English mus. terminology, as in others ; they are given simply as valid for this Dictionary.—2. Rhythm, in a wide sense, is the accentuation marking and defining *broader mus. divisions* in the flow and sweep of a composition *by special emphasis at the entrance or culminating points of motives, themes, phrases, passages, sections,* etc. (Comp. *Accent* 2.)

Ribs. (Ger. *Zar'gen ;* Fr. *éclisses ;* It. *fa'scie.*) The curved sides of the violin and similar instr.s, connecting belly and back.

Ribattu'ta (It.) A device for beginning a trill. (Comp. *Trill.*)

Ribe'ba, Ribe'ca (It.) Rebec.

Ricerca're, Ricerca'ta (It.) 1. Originally vocal, and later also instrumental, compositions of the 16th and 17th centuries, in fugal form more or less highly developed, usually built up as a sort of fantasia on original motives.—2. See *Fugue.*

Riddle-canon. See *Canon, enigmatical.*

Ridot'to (It.) 1. Reduced (see *Réduire*). —2. A reduction.

Rigadoon'. (Fr. *rigaudon.*) An animated, often grotesque dance of French origin, generally in 4–4 time (sometimes 2–2, rarely 6–4) with an *auftakt* of a quarter-note ; it consists of 3 or 4 reprises, the third falling in as if by chance at a lower pitch and frequently without a regular close, to enhance the contrast with the succeeding division.

Ri'go (It.) The staff. (Also *banda, portata, sistema, tirata,* or *verto.*)

Rigo're (It.) Rigor, strictness... *Con r., al r. di tempo,* in strict time. (Also *rigoro'so.*)

Rilascian'do, Rilascian'te (It.) Rallentando.

Rimetten'do (It.) "Resuming" the former tempo (after *accel.* or *rall.*).

Rinforza're (It.) To reinforce (by additional stress) ; to emphasize... *Rinforzamento,* reinforcement ; *rinforzan'do* or *rinforza'to,* with special emphasis ; indicates a sudden increase in loudness, either for a tone or chord, or throughout a phrase or short passage (abbr. *rinf., rfz., rf.*) ; *rinfor'zo,* reinforcement ; *per rinforzo,* by way of reinforcement.

Ripercussio'ne (It.) Repercussion.

Ripetizio'ne (It.) Repetition.

Ripie'nist. (It. *ripieni'sta.*) A musician playing a *ripieno* part.

Ripieno (It. ; lit. " full, filling up ; supplementary.") 1. A *ripieno* part in instrumental music is one reinforcing the leading orchestral parts by doubling them or by filling in the harmony, and is thus opposed to *solo, concertante,* and *obbligato ;* such parts are termed *ripie'ni* (noun).—2. In scores, *ripieno* is a direction calling for the entrance of the full string-band (or, in military music, the clarinets, oboes, etc.), being equivalent to *Tutti.* (Also *v.* APPENDIX.)

Ripien'stimmen (Ger.) Ripieni.

Ripiglia're (It.) To resume ; *ripiglian'do,* resuming.

Ripren'dere (It.) To resume ; *riprenden'do,* resuming.

Ripre'sa (It.) A reprise or repeat : also the sign 𝄋.

Rise. Same as *Plain-beat.*

Risenti'to (It.) Energetic, vigorous; expressive.

Risoluzio'ne (It.) 1. Energy, decision. —2. A resolution...*Risolu'to*, energetic, decided, strongly marked...*Risolutamen'te*, with energy, decision.

Risonan'za, Risuonan'za (It.) Resonance.

Rispo'sta (It.) Answer (in a fugue); consequent (in a canon).

Riss in der Stimme (Ger., "crack in the voice".) A break (when the passage from one register to another cannot be smoothly effected).

Ristret'to (It.) A stretto.

Risveglia'to (It.) Lively, animated.

Ritardan'do (It.) Growing slower and slower (abbr. *ritard., rit.*)—Also *ritarda'to*...*Ritar'do*, retardation.

Ritenen'do, Ritenen'te (It.) Same as *Rallentando.*

Ritenu'to (It.) Properly, held back, in slower tempo; but often used incorrectly for *rallentando.*—Abbr. *riten., rit.* (See *Tempo-marks.*)

Rit'mo (It.) Rhythm...*R. di due (tre) battu'te* [= 2-measure (3-measure) rhythm], a phrase indicating that not one measure, but 2 (3) measures, are to be considered as forming a great measure or metrical unit. [An identification of *rhythm* with *metre;* comp. *Rhythm* 2.]

Ritornel'lo (It.) 1. In accompanied vocal works, such as songs, arias, oratorios, or operas, an instrumental prelude, interlude, or postlude (refrain); or, a *tutti* in a concert-piece.—Also *ritornelle* (Fr. *ritournelle*).—2. A repeat.—3. The burden of a song.

River'so (It.) 1. Reversed.—2. Retrograde. (Comp. *Rovescio.*)

Rivolgimen'to (It.) Transposition of the parts in invertible counterpoint.

Rivol'to (It.) Inversion...*Rivolta'to*, inverted.

Robu'sto (It.) Firm and bold...*Robustamen'te*, firmly and boldly.

Rock-harmonicon. An instr. consisting of a series of rock-crystals, graduated to the tones of the scale, and played with hammers.

Roger de Coverly. See *Sir Roger.*

Rohr, Rohr'blatt (Ger.) 1. Reed; the latter is applied specifically to the reeds of the oboe and bassoon (*dop'peltes Rohrblatt*), and of the clarinet (*ein'faches Rohrblatt*). *Zung'e* is the usual term for *Reed...Rohr'flöte* (Fr. *flûte à cheminée;* Engl. *reed-flute*), a half-covered flue-stop in the organ, with a hole or chimney in the cover, and of 8, 16, or 4-foot pitch; the tone is brighter than when the pipes are wholly covered; the lower half of the rank, however, is wholly covered. Of 2 or 1-foot pitch, it is usually called *Rohr'schelle.* The *Dop'pelrohrflöte* is one with double mouth, the *Rohr'quinte* a reed-flute of 2⅔-foot pitch. The English *clarionet-flute* resembles the *Rohrquinte...Rohrwerk*, reed-work.—2. Tube (of a wind-instr.) [only *Rohr*].

Roll. 1. (Ger. *Wir'bel;* Fr. *roulement;* It. *rollo.*) A tremolo or trill on the drum, produced (a) on the *kettledrum* by rapid alternate single strokes; (b) on the *side-drum*, by striking alternately 2 strokes with the left hand and 2 with the right. The sign in notation is:

..*Long roll*, the prolonged and reiterated drum-signal to troops, either for the attack, or the rally.—2. In organ-playing, a rapid arpeggio.—3. On the tambourine, the rapid and reiterated hither-and thither-stroke with the knuckles.

Rol'le (Ger.) A succession of rapid undulatory (ascending and descending) runs or passages consisting of repetitions of the same figure.

Rol'lo (It.) *Roll* 1.

Roller. 1. The cylinder or barrel of a music-box, or of a carillon.—2. A roller-board; a wooden bar resting on gudgeons and provided with 2 arms, one pulled by a tracker from a key, which makes the other draw a tracker opening a valve (organ)...*Roller-board action*, the mechanism belonging to the roller-boards of an organ.

Romance. (It. *roman'za;* Ger. *Roman'ze.*) Originally, a ballad, or popular tale in verse, in the Romance dialect; the name, being later transferred to stories of love and knightly adventure, which were often set to music, has been employed in modern times as the title of epico-lyrical songs, and, by further transference, of short instrumental pieces of a sentimental or romantic cast, and without definite form (see *Ballade*).—The French *romance* is a simple love-ditty expressive of tender melancholy ; *Romances sans Paroles* are " Songs without Words."

Romane'sca (It.) The Italian form of the Galliard, so called because coming from Rome.

Romantic. The opposite of *classic* (which denotes an accepted and comprehended type, in which form and spirit blend to form an harmonious whole). *Romantic* was an epithet originally derived from Romance poems of the early middle ages, and applied to very various products of a lively, gloomy, or heated imagination down to the German revival of Romantic literature during the 18th century. All late romantic poems having something of exalted mysticism, visionary enthusiasm, or strong subjective and sentimental emotion of an uncommon type, the term *romantic* was naturally transferred to composers and their works that depart from the beaten track, and aim at expressing emotion in a style and with means differing from those employed by their predecessors. Thus, old forms are broadened, new forms and types created, and also many eccentric and ill-conceived productions brought to light. Hence it comes, too, that the *Romanticists* of to-day are the *Classicists* of to-morrow ; that Haydn and Mozart, — Beethoven, — Weber, Chopin, and Schumann,—Berlioz, Liszt, and Wagner,—are all in turn decried, listened to, tolerated, admired, worshipped,—and imitated. And the imitators of original genius are simply post-classicists, who, in full accord with the form and mode of expression employed by their models, seek to elaborate and finish both in a manner suited to their own needs. It might be said, that any great original composer remains a romanticist until he is thoroughly understood. Berlioz, Liszt, Wagner and their following are generally classed as the neo-romantic school.

Roma'nusbuchstaben (Ger.) The *literæ significativæ.*

Ronde (Fr.) A whole note.

Ron'do. (It. *rondò* [dimin. *rondinet'lo, rondinet'to, rondi'no, rondolet'to*] ; Fr. *rondeau.*) A form of instrumental composition, the characteristic feature of which, a return of the leading theme, is derivable from the construction of the old French poetical form of the *rondeau.* While in the earlier rondos the digressions from the 1st theme were of an irregular and desultory character, the episodes of the modern form assume the shape of well-defined contrasting themes, somewhat in the following order: I–II (dominant)–I–III–I–II (tonic)–Coda. (See *Form.*)

Root. The lowest note of a chord in the fundamental here g^1 is the position; e.g. root of the triad g^1–b^1–d^2.

Rosa'lia (It.) A melodic form consisting of the repetition of a phrase or figure several times, each time transposed one degree higher, or simply (as more loosely interpreted) on various degrees. (Ger. *Rosa'lie ;* also *Schu'sterfleck,* and *Vet'ter Mi'chel.*)

Rose. (Ger. *Ro'se ;* Fr. *rosette ;* It. *ro'sa.*) The ornamental pattern bordering the sound-hole in the belly of the guitar, mandolin, etc. ; often used not merely as an ornament, but as a trade-mark.

Rosin. (Ger. *Kolophon' ;* Fr. *colophane ;* It. *colofo'nia.*) The residue of turpentine, after distillation to obtain the oil of turpentine. That used for violin-bows is the refined article.

Ro'ta. 1. A round, rondeau, or piece of similar construction.—2. (Also *Rote, Rotta, Rotte.*) See *Crowd.*

Roton'do (It.) Round, full (of a tone).

Roulade (Fr.) A grace consisting of a run or arpeggio from one principal tone to another ; a vocal or instrumental flourish.

Roulement (Fr.) Roll.

Round. 1. A species of vocal rhythmical canon at the unison, differing from the regular canon in having no coda, thus being infinite ; a favorite style of composition in England, from early times (the celebrated round " Sumer is i-cumen in" is supposed to date from the middle of the 13th century) down to the present day. It differs from the catch (with which it was formerly identical) in eschewing the comical effects of the latter.—The round proper sometimes has an harmonic support or accompaniment called the *pes.*—2. A circle-dance, or round dance.

Roundel. A dance in which the participants form a circle or ring.

Roundelay. A lay or song containing some continued reiteration or refrain.— Also, a roundel.

Rovesciamen'to (It.) 1. Reversion, contrary motion ; retrograde motion.— 2. Inversion.

Rove'scio (It., " reverse, wrong side".) *Al r.* signifies : (*a*) Imitation by contrary motion ; (*b*) a movement so constructed that it may be performed backwards (*cancrizans*).

Ruba'to (It., "robbed".) Used in the phrase *tempo rubato* as a direction, in passages calling for the display of intense or passionate feeling, that the performer should modify the strict rhythmical flow of the movement by dwelling on, and thus (often almost insensibly) prolonging, prominent melody-notes or chords, this in turn requiring an equivalent acceleration of less prominent tones, which are thus *robbed* of a slight portion of their time-value.

Rubèbe (Fr.) Rebec.

Rück'fall (Ger.) A backfall.

Rück'gang (Ger.) Return (i. e. a transition from one theme to the repetition of a preceding theme).

Rück'positiv (Ger.) See *Positiv.*

Rück'ung (Ger., "a shifting".) 1. Syncopation.—2. Enharmonic change (*enharmonische Rückung*).

Rück'weiser (Ger.) The sign 𝄉.

Ruh'ezeichen (Ger.) See *Pause* (Ger.)

Ruh'ig (Ger.) Quiet, calm, tranquil. (Also *adverb.*)

Rüh'rung (Ger.) Emotion.

Rule of the octave. See *Octave.*

Rullan'te (It.) Rolling ; *tambu'ro rullante*, a side-drum.

Run. 1 (*noun*). A rapid scale-passage ; in vocal music, usually applied to such a passage sung to one syllable.—2 (*verb*). The wind in the windchest (organ) is said to *run* when it leaks into a groove ; this *running* causes a more or less distinct sounding of the pipes on that groove, and is a serious defect.

Rund'gesang (Ger.) A solo song, with refrain for chorus.

Russ'pfeife (Ger. ; Dutch *Ruispipe.*) See *Rauschquinte.*

Ru'stico (It.) Rustic, pastoral.

Rutsch'er (Ger.) Old Ger. name for the Galop.

Ru'vido (It.) Rough...*Ruvidamen'te*, roughly, coarsely.

Rythme (Fr.) Rhythm.

Rythmé (Fr.) In rhythm, measured ; *bien r.* (It. *ben ritmato*), with due rhythmic emphasis; or (of a composition) well-balanced and effective in rhythmical construction.

S.

S. Abbr. of *Segno*, in the phrases *al Segno, dal Segno ; Senza*, in the phrases *senza Pedale, senza Sordini ;* of *Sinistra; Solo; Sordini* ; and of *Subito*, in the phrase *volti subito.*

Sabot (Fr.) 1. In the double-action harp, one of the movable disks, each provided with 2 projecting studs, which make a partial revolution on depressing a pedal, the studs engaging and thus shortening the string.—2. An inferior fiddle.

Saccade (Fr.) In violin-playing, a firm stroke of the bow by which 2 or more strings are so pressed down as to sound together.

Sackbut. 1. Earlier form of the trombone.—2. In the Bible (author. vers.), the translation of *sabbeka*, which is supposed to have been a harp-like instr. (Also *Sacbut.*)

Sack'pfeife (Ger.) Bagpipe.

Sacque-boute (Fr.) See *Saquebute.*

Sacred music. (Ger. *Kir'chenmusik;* Fr. *musique d'église;* It. *mu'sica religio'sa.*) Church-music, or music for devotional purposes ; opp. to *secular music.*

Sa'crist. A person retained in a cathedral, whose office it is to copy out the music for the use of the choir, and take care of the books. [BUSBY.]

Sagbut. Same as Sackbut.

Sai'te (Ger.) A string...*Sai'tenchor*, a unison of strings (group of 2 or 3 tuned in unison)...*Sai'tenfessel*, usually *Sai'tenhalter*, tailpiece...*Sai'tenharmonika*, a keyboard stringed instr. inv. by J. H. Stein in 1788, with *diminuendo* attachment...*Sai'teninstrumente*, stringed instr.s...*Sai'tenorgel*("string-organ"), a keyboard stringed instr. inv. by Carl Gümbel of Kroffdorf, near Giessen, Prussia, in 1890. The sustained tone (organ-tone) is obtained by adding to each unison a fourth string, which is set in continuous vibration by the rapid blows of an harmonium-reed furnished with a leathern head ; the action of these reeds (whose vibration-numbers coincide with those of the corresponding unisons struck by the ordinary hammers) is controlled by wind, supplied by bellows filled by a pair of treadles worked by the player.—By means of various stops and combinations, the *S.* can be played (1) as a pfte.; (2) as an organ ; (3) with pfte.-tone and organ-tone combined ; (4) the bass side as an organ, and the treble side as a pfte., or vice versa ; (5) with *crescendo* and *decrescendo* effects, and all imaginable gradations of tone-power.—The combined timbre partakes of the qualities of the string-band, organ, and pfte. —Built in 2 styles, upright and grand.

Sal'icet, Sali'cional. An organ-stop having open flue-pipes of metal, generally of 8-foot pitch, sometimes of 4, 2, and (on the pedal) 16-foot pitch, with a mellow, reedy tone like the Dulciana.

Salmi (Fr.) Quodlibet.

Sal'mo (It.) Psalm.

Salon'flügel (Ger.) Parlor grand (pfte.) .. *Salon'stück*, a piece of *salon*-(parlor-) music.

Saltarel'la, Saltarel'lo (It.) 1. A jack. —2. In many dance-tunes of the 16th century, the second part (Ger. *Hop'peltanz, Nach'tanz;* Lat. *propor'tio;* Fr. *tourdion*), which was in triple time, the first being in duple time ; the skipping step was marked in the rhythm:

etc.—3. A Roman (or Venetian [?]) dance in 3-4 or 6-8 time.—4. *In saltarello*, a term formerly applied to a *canto fermo* accompanied by a counterpoint in sextuplets.

Salta'to (It.) In violin-technic, a variety of the " springing bow ".

Salteret'to (It.) The rhythmical figure

Salte'rio, Salte'ro (It.) 1. Psaltery.— 2. Dulcimer (*salterio tede'sco*).

Sal'to (It.) A skip, leap...*Di salto*, (progressing) by skips or leaps.

Salva're (It.) To resolve (*salvar' una dissonan'za*).

Salvation (Fr.) Resolution (of a dissonance).

Sal've Regi'na (Lat., " Hail ! Queen [of heaven] ".) One of the antiphons to the "Blessed Virgin Mary", sung, in the R. C. service, after lauds or complin from Trinity Sunday to Advent.

Sambu'ca. One of the most ambiguous instrument-names of the middle ages, usually employed in the sense of the Greek σαμβύκη (Lat. *sambuca*) for a kind of small psaltery (*Spitz'harfe*), but also occurring (as if derived from the Lat. *sambu'cus*, alder) for a species of pipe ; and finally, as a corruption of *symphonia* (*samponia, zampogna*) for the bagpipe and hurdy-gurdy (*sambuca rota'ta*), and, instead of *sacqueboute*, for instr.s of the trombone class. *Sambut, Sambiut*, are German forms of *sambuca* in the sense of a psaltery. [RIEMANN.]—Also *Sambuke*.

Sampo'nia. See *Sambuca*, and *Zampogna*. (Also *cf.* APPENDIX.)

Sampo'gna (It.) A rustic reed, or flageolet.

Sanctus (Lat.) A division of the Mass.

Sanft (Ger.) Soft, low...*Sanft'gedackt*, a flue-stop in the organ, having stopped pipes of soft intonation.

Sanglot (Fr., " sob ".) An obsolete *agrément*, consisting of an accent or *chute* sung to an interjection :

[RIEMANN.]

Sans (Fr.) Without.

Saquebute (Fr.) Sackbut.

Sar'aband. (Ger. and Fr. *Saraban'de;* It. *saraban'da*.) A stately dance of Spanish or Oriental origin, for a single dancer, though later changed (in England) to a sort of country-dance. The instrumental saraband has, as a rule, 2 8-measure reprises, in slow tempo and triple time, generally beginning on the down-beat, with a stress on or prolongation of the second beat (♩ ♩ ♩ | ♩ ♩), and often highly embellished. Its place in the Suite, as the slowest movement, is before the Gigue.

Sarrusophone. A brass wind-instr., inv. (1863) by and named after the band-master Sarrus of Paris, with a *double reed* like the oboe and bassoon; herein differing from the single-reed

Saxophone, from which its key-mechanism is in great part borrowed. Like the saxophone, it is made in 6 principal sizes, with the addition of a rare sopranino in E♭ and a contrabass in E♭. Its tone partakes in quality of that of the nearly-related *oboè da caccia*, double-bassoon, and bombar i.—Little used outside of France.

Sat'tel (Ger.) Nut... *Sattel ma'chen*, in 'cello-playing, firm pressure of the thumb on a string, in the higher positions, for obtaining harmonics, the thumb acting as a temporary nut... *Sat'tellage*, half-position (in violin playing).

Satz (Ger.) 1. A theme or subject.—2. A phrase, i. e. half a period of 8 measures, the 1st half being the *Vor'dersatz*, the 2nd the *Nach'satz* (sometimes translated "fore-phrase" and "after-phrase").—3. A chief division of a movement.—4. A *Movement* 2.—5. The science of harmony and counterpoint; art or style of composition; e. g. *rei'ner Satz*, strict style (of writing).—6. A passage or separate portion of a composition.

Saut (Fr.) Skip... *Sauter*, to overblow. ..*Sautereau*, a jack.

Sauver (Fr.) To resolve (a dissonance).

Saxhorn. A brass wind-instr. inv. in 1842 by Adolphe Sax, a Belgian. It is essentially an improved key-bugle or ophicleide, having from 3 to 5 valves instead of keys. Saxhorns are constructed in 7 different sizes, forming a complete series alike in timbre and method of playing, and named according to their fundamental tone or their relative pitch and compass. They are not fitted for the use of crooks. Though extensively employed in military music, only two, the Euphonium and Contrabass-tuba, have achieved a place in the orchestra.—The nomenclature of the saxhorn family being sadly confused, a list with the various appellations is annexed :

1. Sopranino saxh. (petit saxh., petit bugle à pistons, Piccolo in *Es*.
2. Soprano saxh. (contralto saxh., bugle-ténor, Flügelhorn in *B*).
3. Alto saxh (Althorn in *Es*).
4. Tenor saxh. (baryton en *si♭*, Tenorhorn in *B*, Bassflügelhorn).
5. Bass saxh. (tuba-basse en *si♭*, Basstuba, Euphonium, Baryton, Tenorbass in *B*).
6. Low bass saxh. (bombardon en *mi♭*).
7. Contrabass saxh. (bombardon en *si♭* grave, Kontrabasstuba).

Saxhorns 1 to 4 are classed as *bugles à pistons;* while 5 to 7 are classed as *tubas* or *bombardons.*—Their extreme compass is :

1. in *E♭*.　2. in *B♭*.　3. in *E♭*.　4. in *B♭*.　5. in *B♭*.　6. in *E♭*.　7. in *B♭*.

For the orchestra there are also made a bass in *C*, a contrabass in *C*₁, and a low bass in *F*₁; and all members of the family are also constructed a semitone lower in pitch than shown above.

Saxophone. An instr. of a type inv. about 1840 by Adolphe Sax of Dinant-sur-Meuse, Belgium. It is a wind-instr. of metal, having a conical tube with recurved bell, and clarinet-mouthpiece with single reed, the key-mechanism and fingering also being similar to those of the clarinet. It is an "omnitonic" (chromatic) instr., with a mellow and penetrating tone of veiled quality partaking of that of the clarinet, *cor anglais*, and violoncello, but very sonorous, and of remarkable homogeneity in all registers and sizes; 6 principal sizes are made, at intervals of a fourth and fifth apart, each size

in turn comprising 2 individuals a whole tone apart :

1. Sopranino saxophone in *F* (and *E♭*).
2. Soprano   "   " *C* (" *B♭*).
3. Contralto   "   " *F* (" *E♭*).
4. Tenor   "   " *C* (" *B♭*).
5. Baryton   "   " *F* (" *E♭*).
6. Bass   "   " *C* (" *B♭*).

The notation for this transposing instr. is alike for all sizes; the compass is: Chiefly used in military bands.

Saxotrom'ba. A valve instr. of the trumpet family, inv. by Ad. Sax, intermediate in quality of tone and scale of tube between the Horn and Saxhorn constructed, like the latter, in 7 sizes.

Sbal'zo (It.) A skip or leap... *Sbalza to.* dashingly impetuously.

Sbar'ra (It.) Bar ; *sb. dop'pia*, double-bar.

Scagnel'lo (It.) Bridge.

Scale. 1. (Ger. *Ton'leiter ;* Fr. *échelle, gamme;* It. *sca'la.*) For the ancient scales compare *Mode, Greek music, Octave-scale.*—A modern scale is simply the series of tones, taken in direct succession, which form (*a*) any major or minor key (diatonic scale), or (*b*) the chromatic scale of successive semitonic steps. (Comp. *Key.*)..*Pentaton'ic scale,* a "5-tone" scale found in primitive melodies of certain peoples (Scotch, Chinese), in which the step of a semitone is avoided by omitting the 4th and 7th degrees in major and the 2nd and 6th in minor. It can be played on the piano by touching 5 successive black keys, beginning on *F♯* for major, and on *E♭* for minor. The ancient Greek chromatic scale also had five tones.—2. The series of tones producible on various wind-instr.s is also called a *scale,* whether the series is diatonic or not ; the term is also used for the compass or range of a voice or instr.—*Harmonic scale,* the series of higher partial tones (see *Acoustics*).—3. (Ger. *Mensur';* Fr. *étalon.*) In the tubes of wind-instr s, especially organ-pipes, the ratio between the width of bore and the length ; this varies in organ-pipes from about 1 : 10 to 1 : 24, a *broad scale* yielding a mellow, sonorous tone, and a *narrow scale* yielding a sharp and thrilling, or a thin, stringy tone.

Scannet'to, Scannel'lo (It.) Same as *Scagnello.*

Seman'do (It.) See *Diminuendo.*

Sce'na (It.) 1. In the opera, a scene (Fr. *scène,* Ger. *Auf'tritt*), i. e. a division marked by the entrance or exit of one or more performers.—2. An accompanied solo of a dramatic character, consisting of arioso and recitative passages, and frequently terminating with an aria, then being termed *scena ed a'ria.*—3. A stage.

Scena'rio (It.) 1. The plot of a dramatic work.—2. A skeleton libretto of such a work, sketching the course of the plot, and giving entrances and exits of leading personages, serving as a guide to stage-managers, actors, etc.—3. A play-bill.—4 (pl.) *Scena'rii,* scenes, side-scenes, decorations.

Scena'rium. An opera-libretto contain-ing the full dialogue, and directions for the actors, etc.

Scene. 1. A division of a dramatic performance marked by a change of scenery.—2 (the preferable usage). Same as *Scena* 1.

Schablo'ne (Ger.) A stencil, pattern ; hence, *Schablo'nenmusik, schablo'nen-hafte Musik',* uninspired composition written to fit a cut-and-dried form, or in mere imitation of any style; "stereotyped" music.

Schä'ferlied (Ger.) Shepherd's song, pastoral ditty...*Schäferpfeife,* shepherd's pipe, shawm...*Schä'fertanz,* shepherd's dance.

Schalk'haft (Ger.) Roguish, sportive, wanton. (Also *adverb.*)

Schall (Ger.) Sound, resonance, resounding, ringing...*Schall'becher,* Bell 2... *Schall'becken,* cymbals...*Schall'loch,* (*a*) *f*-hole; (*b*) sound-hole...*Schall'-stab,* triangle...*Schall'stück, -trichter,* Bell 2.

Schalmei', Schalmey' (Ger.) Shawm; chalumeau.

Schanzu'ne (Ger.) Corruption of *Chanson.*

Scharf (Ger.) Sharp. See *Acuta.*

Schau'rig (Ger.) In a style expressive of (or calculated to inspire) mortal dread ; weirdly.

Schel'lenbaum (Ger.) Crescent.

Scherzan'do (It.) In a playful, sportive, toying manner. Also *scherzan'te, scherze'vole, scherzo'so.*

Scherz'haft (Ger.) Sportive ; jocose, burlesque. (Also *adverb.*)

Scher'zo (It., dimin. *scherzi'no.*) A joke, jest.—1. An instrumental solo piece of a light, piquant, humorous character : hence applied to very various compositions in which an animated movement and sharp and sudden contrasts are leading features.—2. A movement in a sonata, concerted composition, or symphony, usually in triple, sometimes in duple, time, introduced chiefly by way of contrast with slower movements, consequently of a bright, vivacious, often humorous character, with strongly marked rhythm, and sharp and unexpected contrasts in rhythm and harmony, requiring delicate phrasing and shading. Its forerunner in the symphony was the *Minuet* of Haydn ; Beethoven named this movement, which had entirely lost its original slow and stately character, *Scherzo*, nothing of the Minuet being left but the (much extended) form. The Beethoven Scherzo is usually the 3rd movement; but under different conditions the scherzo may with equal propriety take the second place.

Schiet'to, Schiettamen'te (It.) Plain, simple, unembellished (also *adverb*).

Schis'ma (Gk.) The difference between the third tierce of the 8th quint (see *Temperament*) and the octave of the given tone (*b♯* : *c* = 32805:32768); one-eleventh of a syntonic comma.

Schlag (Ger.) A beat, pulse ; blow, stroke... *Schlag'feder*, a plectrum... *Schlag'instrument*, instr. of percussion. ..*Schlag'manieren* (pl.), the various strokes in drum-playing... *Schlag'-zither*, the ordinary zither played with plectrum and fingers; opp. to *Streich'-zither* (bow-zither).

Schlä'gel (Ger.) Drumstick ; mallet, small hammer.

Schlecht (Ger., " bad "). Weak ; as *schlech'ter Takt'teil*, weak beat.

Schleif'bogen (Ger.) Slur... *Schlei'fen*, to slur... *Schlei'fer*, (*a*) a slide ; (*b*) a slow German waltz, Ländler... *Schleif'-zeichen*, slur.

Schlep'pen (Ger.) To drag, retard... *Schlep'pend*, dragging.

Schluss (Ger.) Conclusion, end; close, cadence... *Schluss'fall*, a cadence... *Schluss'kadenz*, final or closing cadence... *Schluss'note*, final note... *Schluss'satz*, concluding movement, Finale... *Schluss'striche*, double-bar... *Schluss'zeichen*, (*a*) the double-bar ; (*b*) the hold ⁀.

Schlüs'sel (Ger., " key "). A clef... *Schlüs'selfiedel*, nail-fiddle. ..*Schlüs'sel-G*, the note *g*¹ on the treble-clef line:

Schmei'chelnd (Ger.) Flattering ; in a coaxing, caressful style.

Schmerz (Ger.) Pain ; grief, sorrow. ..*Schmerz'haft*, *schmerz'lich*, painful, sorrowful, plaintive. (Also *adverb*.)

Schna'bel (Ger., " beak " ; Fr. *bec*). A mouthpiece like that of the clarinet or flageolet... *Schnabelflöte*, flûte à bec.

Schnarr'werk (Ger.) The reed-work of an organ, or a single reed-stop.—Also, a Regal.

Schneck'e (Ger., " snail "). Scroll.

Schnell (Ger.) Fast, quick, rapid. (Also *adverb*.)... *Schnel'ler*, (*a*) faster; as *nach und nach schneller*, gradually faster ;—(*b*) an inverted mordent.

Schot'tische. (Ger. *Schot'tisch*, "Scotch, Scottish "). A round dance in 2-4 time, a variety of the Polka ; the *Écossaise* is a country-dance.

Schräg (Ger.) Oblique.

Schreib'art (Ger.) Style.

Schrei'end (Ger.) Strident ; screaming, screeching, squeaking.

Schrei'erpfeife (Ger.) See *Schryari* 2.

Schryari. 1. An obs. wind-instr. described by Prætorius in the " Syntagma ".—2. The sharpest mixture-stop, usually in 3 ranks and tuned in octaves, beginning 3 octaves above the key struck.

Schub (Ger.) Slide (of bow).

Schuh (Ger.) Bridge (of a tromba marina)... *Schuh'plattltanz*, a kind of clog-dance in the Austrian and Bavarian Alps.

Schul'tergeige (Ger.) Viola da spalla; opp. to *Kniegeige*.

Schu'sterfleck (Ger.) Rosalia.

Schwach (Ger.) 1. Weak, as *schwach'er Taktteil*, weak beat.—2. Soft, faint, low; *schwäch'er*, fainter, softer.

Schwär'mer (Ger.) A *Rauscher*.

Schwe'bung (Ger.) 1. In mus. acoustics, a *Beat* 4.—2. Same as *Tremulant*.

Schwe'gel (Ger.) 1. Any wind-instr.— 2. A pipe, especially a flue-pipe in the organ, the *Schwe'gelpfeife* being an open stop of 8 or 4-foot pitch, the pipes slightly tapering at the top.

Schwei'gezeichen (Ger.) A rest.

Schweins'kopf (Ger., " pig's-head "). Obsolete term for *Flügel*.

Schwei'zerflöte (Ger.) 1. Fife.—2. In the organ, an 8-foot metal flue-stop of penetrating tone ; the same of 4-foot pitch is called *Schwei'zerpfeife;* of 16-foot pitch, on the pedal, *Schwei'zer-flötenbass*... *Schwei'zerpfeiff*, earliest name of the German flute.

Schwel'len (Ger.) See *Anschwellen*.

Schwel'ler (Ger.) Swell (of the organ).

Schwell'ton (Ger.) Messa di voce.

Schwell'werk (Ger.) Swell-organ.

Schwer (Ger.) 1. Heavy, ponderous

(see *Pesante*).—2. Difficult... *Schwer'-mütig*, melancholy, sad.

Schwie'gel (Ger.) See *Schwegel*.

Schwin'dend (Ger.) Dying away, *morendo*.

Schwing'ung (Ger.) Vibration.

Schwung'voll (Ger.) With sweep and passion.

Scialumò' (It.) Chalumeau.

Scintillan'te (It. and Fr.) Brilliant, sparkling.

Scioltamen'te (It.) Freely, fluently, nimbly... *Scioltez'za*, freedom, fluency· ...*Sciol'to,-a*, free, fluent, agile; *fuga sciolta*, free fugue, opp. to *fuga obbliga'ta*.

Scorda'to (It.) 1. Discordant, out of tune.—2. Tuned in a manner deviating from the ordinary one... *Scordatu'ra*, an alteration of the ordinary *accordatura* of a stringed instr. for the attainment of special effects; e. g. Paganini's tun- in which the ing of G-string was the violin: raised a minor and a major third respectively ; such an alteration is sometimes called *solo pitch*.

Score. (Ger. *Partitur'*; Fr. *partition;* It. *partitu'ra, partizio'ne*.) A systematic arrangement of the vocal or instrumental parts of a composition one above the other, tones sounded together being in the same vertical line, to facilitate reading... *Close* or *compressed score*, see *Short score*...*Full* or *orchestral score*, one in which each vocal and instrumental part has a separate staff assigned to it (see *Orchestra*)...*Pianoforte-score*, one having the vocal parts written out in full, generally on separate staves, the pfte.-accomp. being arranged or compressed (from the full instrumental score) on 2 staves below the rest... *Organ-score*, arr. like *pfte.-score*, except that a third staff for pedal-bass is often added below the others... *Short score*, (*a*) any abridged arrangement or skeleton transcript ; (*b*) 4-part vocal score on 2 staves... *Supplementary score*, see *Partitino*... *Vocal score*, (*a*) score of an *a cappella* composition ; (*b*) same as *pfte.-score*.

Scoring. Same as *Instrumentation*, or *Orchestration*.

Scorren'do (It.) Flowing, gliding. (Also *scorre'vole*.)

Scotch snap or **catch.** The rhythmic mo- frequently recurring in many tive ' Scotch airs (the reverse of the common motive .

Scozze'se (It.) Scotch ; *alla s.*, in the Scotch style.

Scroll. (Ger. *Schnecke;* Fr. *volute;* It. *voluta*.) The terminal curve of the head in the violin, etc.

Sde'gno (It.) Scorn, disdain ; wrath indignation... *Sdegnosamen'te*, scornfully, etc... *Sdegno'so*, scornful, etc.

Sdrucciolan'do (It.) Sliding... *Sdrucciola're*, to slide, by pressing down the pfte.-keys in a rapid sweep with the finger-nails.

Se (It.) If... *Se biso'gna*, if necessary ; *se pia'ce*, if you please. (Comp. *Si*.)

Sea-trumpet. Tromba marina.

Sec (Fr.), **Sec'co** (It.) Dry ; simple, unembellished (see *Recitative*).

Sechs (Ger.) Six... *Sechsach'teltakt*, 6-8 time... *Sechs'er, sechs'taktiger Satz*, a passage, period, or theme comprising 6 measures... *Sechsvier'teltakt*, 6-4 time.

Sech'(s)zehn (Ger.) Sixteen... *Sech'zehntel* (*note*), 16th-note... *Sech'zehntelpause*, 16th-rest.

Second. 1 (*noun*). (Ger. *Sekun'de;* Fr. *seconde;* It. *secon'da*.) The interval between 2 conjunct degrees (see *Interval*).—2. The alto part or voice. —3. (*adj*.) (Ger. *zweit-er,-e,-es;* Fr. *second,-e;* It. *secondo,-a*.) (*a*) Performing a part lower in pitch than first ; as *second bass, second violins;* (*b*) lower in pitch, as *second string;* (*c*) higher, as *second line* of staff.

Secondaire (Fr.) A *temps secondaire* is a weak beat.

Secondary chords. Subordinate chords.

Seconde dessus (Fr.) Second soprano.

Secon'do,-a (It.) Second (*adj.*); as *seconda don'na*, the female singer taking the leading parts after the *prima donna; violi'ni secondi*, second violins. ..(*Noun.*) *Secondo*, a second part or performer in a duet.

Section. In the wider sense, a short division (1 or more periods) of a composition, having distinct rhythmic and harmonic boundaries ; specifically, half a phrase (see *Form*).

Secular music. Music other than that

intended for worship and devotional purposes.

Secun'de (Ger.) See *Sekunde.*

Sede'cima (Lat. and It.) 1. The interval of a sixteenth.—2. Obs. name of the fifteenth (organ-stop).

See'le (Ger., "soul"). Soundpost.

Se'gno (It.) A sign... *Al segno,* to the sign ; *Dal segno,* from the sign,—directions to the performer to turn back and repeat from the place marked by the sign (., , ⊕, §, etc.) to the word *Fine,* or ⏜ In place of the to a double- 𝄇. words, the sign bar with hold: 𝄇 alone is sometimes set.

Se'gue (It.) Follows ; as *segue l'aria,* the aria follows... *Seguen'do, seguen'te,* following.—Also, same as *Simile.*

Seguen'za (It.) Sequence.

Seguidil'la (Span) Spanish dance in triple time, some varieties slow and stately, others lively; usually in minor, acc. by guitar, and voice, and at times by the castenets

Sehn'sucht (Ger.) Longing, yearning. ...*Sehn'süchtig,* in a style expressive of intense yearning.

Sehr (Ger.) Very.

Se'i (It.) Six.

Sei'tenbewegung (Ger.) Oblique motion... *Sei'tensatz,* a second or secondary theme, as in the sonata and rondo.

Sekun'de (Ger.) A second.

Semibiscro'ma (It.) A 32nd-note.

Sem'ibreve. (Lat. *semibrev'is.*) A whole note.

Semicadence. A half-cadence.

Semicro'ma (It.) A 16th-note.

Sem'icrome. A semicroma ; but formerly sometimes used for quaver.

Semicrotch'et. A quaver.

Sem'idemisemiqua'ver. A 64th-note.

Semidiapa'son. Diminished octave... *Semidiapen'te,* diminished fifth... *Semidiates'saron,* diminished fourth.

Semidi'tas (Lat.) The diminution caused by a vertical stroke through the time-signature.

Semi-di'tone. (Lat. *semidi'tonus.*) The minor third... *Semiditonus cum diapente,* minor 7th.

Semifu'sa (Lat.) Semiquaver.

Semi-grand. A small grand piano

Semiminim. (Lat. and It. *semimi'nima.*) A crotchet, or quaver.

Semipau'sa (Lat.) A semibreve-rest.

Semiqua'ver. A 16th-note.

Semisuspi'rium (Lat.) A crotchet-rest.

Semitone. (Ger. *Halb'ton;* Fr. *demiton;* It. *semituo'no.*) The narrowest interval employed in modern music. (See *Interval.*)

Semi-tonique (Fr.) Same as *chromatique.*

Semito'nium (Lat.) A semitone... *S. fictum,* a chromatic semitone... *S. modi,* the leading-note... *S. natura'le,* a diatonic semitone.

Sem'plice (It.) Simple, plain, unaffected. ...*Semplicemen'te,* simply, etc... *Semplicità',* *con,* in a simple, unaffected style.

Sem'pre (It.) Always, continually ; throughout.

Sensi'bile (It., "sensitive").—*Nota sensible,* or *la sensibile,* leading-note.

Sensibilità', con (It.) See *Espressivo.*

Sensible (Fr.) The leading-note ; also *note sensible.* (In English the leading-note is sometimes called "sensible note".)

Sentence. See *Period, Form.*

Sentimen'to, con (It.) With feeling, expressively.

Senti'to (It., "felt"). With feeling, expression, special stress.

Sen'za (It.) Without. (Abbr. *S.*)... *S. passio'ne,* with avoidance of all marked accents and passionate expression... *S. piat'ti,* "drum alone" (where one performer plays the cymbals and bass drum)... *S. sordi'ni,* see *Sordino...S. tem'po,* not in strict tempo, *ad libitum.* ...*S. di slentare,* without retarding. [*Senza* is often followed by a bare infinitive, which is then to be translated as a participial substantive ; e. g. *senza rallentare,* without retarding.]

Separation. 1. An obs. term for a passing-note between 2 tones forming a tierce.—2. In the organ, a mechanical device for preventing the great-organ action from sounding its stops ; used when the action is pneumatic and coupled to other manuals of heavier touch.

Sept-chord. Chord of the 7th.

Septde'zime (Ger.) A seventeenth.

Septet'. (Ger. *Septett';* Fr. *septuor;* It.

settimi'no.) A concerted composition for 7 voices or instr.s.

Septième (Fr.), **Sep'time** (Ger.) The interval of a 7th... *Sep'timenakkord* (Ger.), chord of the 7th.

Septimo'le, Septo'le (Ger.) Septuplet.

Septuor (Fr.) Septet.

Sep'tuplet. A group of 7 equal notes to be performed in the time of 4 or 6 of the same kind in the regular rhythm; written:

Se'quence. (Lat. *sequen'tia;* It. *seguen'za;* Ger. *Sequenz'*.) 1. The repetition, oftener than twice in succession, of a melodic motive, the repetitions ascending or descending by uniform intervals. The *harmonic sequence* is merely the grouping of chords necessitated by the reiteration of the melodic figure. A *diatonic* or *tonal sequence* employs only tones proper to the key ; a *chromatic* or *modulatory sequence* is one in which accidentals are used more or less freely ; a sequence progressing by a whole tone or semitone is called a Rosalia. (Also *Progression*.)—2. In the R. C. Church, a kind of hymn ; such were founded on the melodies of the *sequentiæ* (the jubilations of the Alleluia following the epistle, words being in time set to the melodies instead of the original syllables a-e-u-i-a), whence the name. They originated in the 9th century, and multiplied to such an extent that Pius V. in 1568 expunged all but 5 (Victimæ paschali ; Veni Sancte Spiritus ; Lauda Sion ; Stabat Mater ; Dies iræ). (Also *Prose* [Lat. *prosa*].)

Seraphi'na, Ser'aphine. A precursor of the harmonium, inv. by John Green in 1833 ; owing to its harsh tone, it was speedily superseded by the latter.

Serenade'. (Ger. *Ständ'chen;* Fr. *sérénade;* It. *serena'ta*.) 1. An "evening song ;" specifically, such a song sung by a lover before his lady's window.— 2. An instrumental composition imitating the above in style.—From these was evolved the

Serena'ta (Fr. and It. ditto ; Ger. *Serena'de*.) 1. A species of dramatic cantata greatly in vogue during the 18th century.—2. An instrumental composition, midway between the Suite and Symphony, but freer in form than either, consisting of 5, 6, or more movements for very various combinations of instr.s,

and in chamber-music style. The earlier serenatas were invariably concerted pieces ; they were also called *Cassations* and *Divertimenti.*

Sere'no (It.) Serene, calm, tranquil.

Serinette (Fr.) A bird-organ (small barrel-organ used in training song-birds).

Se'rio,-a (It.) Serious... *O'pera seria,* grand or tragic opera ; opp. to *Opera buffa.. Tenore serio,* dramatic tenor.

Serio'so (It.) In a serious, grave, impressive style.

Serpent. (It. *serpen'te*.) A nearly obs. wood-wind instr., still used in some French churches, but seldom met with in the orchestra ; inv. by Canon Guillaume of Auxerre in 1590. It belongs to the *Zinke* (*Cornetto*) family ; the modern forms have a recurvate bell, and a cupped mouthpiece set in a brass crook forming a right angle with the first bend of the serpentine tube. The tube is of wood, covered with leather, about 8 feet long, and provided with 6 finger-holes and a varying number of additional keys. Compass : the serpent being a transposing instr., in *B♭*, the notes are written a degree higher. The tone is variously described by French authorities as "harsh and savage", and as a "cold, horrid howling". It is replaced, in the modern orchestra, by the bass tuba (or ophicleide).—The *Serpentcleide* resembles the ophicleide, but retains the wooden tube.—The *Contra-serpent* produces 16-foot *E♭*.—Some old organs have reed-stops named *serpent.*

Service. In the Anglican Liturgy, a complete series of mus. settings of the canticles, etc., the free composition of which is sanctioned by usage. Versicles, responses, chants, and anthems, are excluded. The full list for morning and evening prayer, and communion, includes the Venite exultemus, Te Deum, Benedicite, Benedictus (dominus), Jubilate, Kyrie, Credo (Nicene Creed), Sanctus, Agnus Dei, Benedictus (qui venit), Gloria, Magnificat, Cantate domino, Nunc dimittis, and Deus misereatur; all composed for chorus and soli, with or without accomp by organ or orchestra.

Sesquial'tera (Lat., " one-half more ".)

1. A perfect fifth, its ratio to the prime being $1 : 1\frac{1}{2} = 2 : 3$.—2. In mensurable music, the proportion marked by the signature $\frac{9}{2}$, indicating that the time-value of 3 minims is then equivalent to that of 2 before.—3. A mixture-stop in the organ ; the name is properly applicable to a mutation-stop a fifth above the fundamental tone or some given octave of the latter, but is ordinarily used to designate a compound stop producing the 3rd, 4th, and 5th partial tones, or their octaves ; it has from 2 to 5 ranks.

Sesquino'na. The lesser whole tone, its ratio being $9 : 10$.

Sesquiocta'va. The greater whole tone, its ratio being $8 : 9$.

Sesquiquar'ta. The major third, its ratio being $4 : 5$.

Sesquiquin'ta. The minor third, its ratio being $5 : 6$.

Sesquiter'tia. The perfect fourth, its ratio being $3 : 4$.

Ses'quitone. A minor third, i. e. $1\frac{1}{2}$ tone.

Sestet'. (It. *sestet'to*.) A sextet.

Sesti'na (It.) A sextuplet.

Se'sto,-a (It.) Sixth... *Sesta* (*noun*). interval of a sixth.

Ses'tole, Ses'tolet. A sextuplet.

Settimi'no (It.) A septet.

Set'timo,-a (It.) Seventh... *Set'tima* (*noun*), interval of a 7th.

Setz'art (Ger.) Style of composition... *Setz'kunst*, art of composition... *Setz'-stück*, crook.

Seul,-e (Fr.) Alone, solo.

Seventeenth. 1. Interval of 2 octaves plus a tierce.—2. Same as *Tierce* (organ-stop).

Seventh. (Ger. *Sep'time;* Fr. *septième;* It. *set'tima*.) See *Interval*... *Seventh-chord*, a chord of the 7th, composed of a root with its third, fifth, and seventh.

Severamen'te (It.) Strictly, with rigid observance of tempo and expression-marks.

Sext. 1. The interval of a sixth.—2. The office of the fourth canonical hour. —3. A compound organ-stop of 2 ranks (a twelfth and a seventeenth) a sixth apart.

Sex'ta (Lat.) Sixth... (*Noun.*) The interval of a sixth ; also, a sixth part (see *Quintus*).

Sex'te (Ger.) A sixth.

Sextet'. (It. *sestet'to:* Fr. *sextuor;* Ger. *Sextett'*.) A concerted composition for 6 voices or instr.s ; or for 6 obbligato voices with instrumental accomp.

Sex'tole, Sex'tolet. A sextuplet.

Sex'tuplet. A group of 6 equal notes to be performed in the time of 4 of the same kind in the regular rhythm. In the *true sextuplet* the 1st, 3rd, and 5th notes are accented ; the *false sextuplet* is simply a double triplet.

Sex'tus (Lat.) A sixth part (see *Sexta*).

Sfoga'to (It., "exhaled"). In vocal music, a direction to render the passage so marked in a light and airy manner. ..*Soprano sfogato*, a high soprano; compass from c^1 to c^3 (f^3).

Sforzan'do (It., "forcing, pressing"). A direction commonly applied to a single tone or chord, indicating that it is to be performed with special stress, or marked and sudden emphasis. Abbr. *sfz., sf.*; sign $>$, $\wedge$, $\big\rvert$ (Also *Sforza'to*.)

Sfuggi'ta (It.) Avoided, eluded ; as *cadenza sfuggita*.

Sgallinaccia're (It.) To sing with a harsh, uneven, quavering voice. (From *gallinac'cio*, a turkey-cock.)

Shade. "Shading of pipes", the placing of anything so near the top of an organ-pipe as to affect the vibrating column of air which it contains. [Stainer and Barrett.]

Shake. Same as *Trill*... *Shaked graces* (obs.), the shaked Beat, Backfall, Cadent, and Elevation, and the Double Relish.

Shalm. A shawm.

Sharp (*noun*). (Ger. *Kreuz;* Fr. *dièse;* It. *die'sis*.) The sign ♯, which, set before a note or on a degree of the staff, raises its pitch by a chromatic semitone ..*Double-sharp*, the sign $\times$ (formerly also ✕, ✕, etc.), raising the pitch of its note by 2 chromatic semitones ($= 1$ tone on tempered instr.s).

Sharp (*adj.*) 1. (Of tones or instr's.) Too high or acute in pitch.—2. (Of intervals.) Major or augmented.—3. (Of keys.) Having a sharp or sharps in the signature.—4. (Of organ-stops.) Shrill. —5. (Of digitals; pl.) The black keys; also any white key a semitone above another.

Shawm. (Ger. *Schalmei'.*) An obs. double-reed wind-instr., the precursor of the oboe, the prime difference between them being that the reed of the shawm was set in a cupped or globular mouthpiece, whereas the oboe-reed is held directly betwixt the lips.—The chanter of the bagpipe is probably the sole surviving form of the ancient shawm. (Also *Shalm.*) [N. B. The Fr. *chalumeau* had a *single* reed.]

Shift. A change in the position of the left hand, in playing the violin, etc., from the first position, in which the forefinger stops its string a semitone or tone higher than the pitch of the open string, according to the scale; the 2nd position is called the *half-shift*, the 3rd the *whole shift*, and the 4th the *double shift.* When out of the 1st position the player is said to be "on the shift", and *shifting up* or *down*, as the case may be. (See *Position.*)

Shutter. In the organ, one of the blinds forming the front of the swell-box.

Si. 1. (It.) One, it; often written in directions, as *si leva il sordino*, take off the mute; *si le'vano i sordini*, take off the mutes; *si pia'ce*, *si libet* (Lat.), at pleasure; *si repli'ca*, repeat (= Da Capo); *si segue*, proceed; *si tace*, be silent; *si volta*, turn over. [Beethoven writes (*E*♭ Quartet, op. 74): "Si ha s'immaginar'la battuta di $\frac{6}{8}$", meaning: "Imagine the time to be $\frac{6}{8}$."]—2. The 7th of the solmisation-syllables; hence, name of the note *B* in France and Italy...*Si contra fa*, see *Mi.* (Compare *Key*, and *Solmisation.*)

Sicilia'na (It.), **Sicilienne** (Fr.) Dance of the Sicilian peasants; a kind of pastorale in moderately slow tempo and 6-8 or 12-8 time, frequently in minor, and common (especially in the 18th century) as an andante movement in sonatas or vocal music. (Not *Sicilia'no*)...***Alla siciliana***, in the style of the above.

Side-drum. See *Drum.*

Sieb (Ger.) Soundboard of the organ (Lat. *cribrum*).

Sifflet (Fr.) Whistle...*S. de Pan*, Pandean pipes...*Sifflet-diapason*, pitch-pipe.

Sif'flöt (Ger.) In the organ, an open metal flue-stop of broad scale and 1 or 2-foot pitch.—Also *Suf'flöt*, *Sub'flöt*, *Weit'pfeife.*

Sight-reader. A musician capable of correctly performing a piece of music at sight.

Signs. (Compare *Abbreviation*, *Notation*, *Segno.*) [Italicized terms indicate that the signs are no longer in use.]

·	Dot. Staccato. *Sforzato.*
–̣	Forte tenuto.
⌒ .... /	*Bebung* Mezzo staccato.
o	(See Dot 3.)
———— or	(under notes to be sung to one syllable; in Tonic Sol-fa, a line under the letters).
𝄐	Hold.
⊙ ☾	(Notation, §3.)
𝄎	(Abbreviation.)
·S· 𝄋	Presa.
𝄋 𝄋 ⊕	Segno.
∴ ∴	*Double relish.*
※ ※ ♯	*Double-sharp.*
𝄂 𝄆 𝄇 𝄆𝄇	Repeat.
:‖: :‖‖:	*Repeats* (2 and 4 times).
:‖:	*Repetition of words.*
× or +	Thumb (pfte.-music).
×♩	Double-sharp.
,	Breathing-mark. *Backfall, Coulé, Pincé, Tremblement.*
,,	*Double Backfall.*
—	Tenuto. Pesante.
⌒ – – –	Mezzo legato.
⌒	Bind. Slur. Tie.
(	*Accent. Coulé. Port de voix.*
)	*Pincé.*
‿	*Tasto solo.*
( )	*Double Appoggiatura.*
⌃	*Suspension.*
\	*Cadent.*
/	*Plain beat.*
\ or /	*Accent. Nachschlag. Portamento. Schleifer.*
\	*Chute.*
/	*Port de voix.*
\ (\\)	*Backfall* (*Double Backfall*).
/	*Springer.*
♪	*Acciaccatura. Arpeggio.*

I (II) — Single (Double) Relish.

≡≡≡ — (Abbreviations.)

◁ — Crescendo.

▷ — Decrescendo.

' , — Staccatissimo. Martellato.

> — Forte piano (fp).

> or < — Rinforzando.

∧ ∨ > — Sforzato.

V v — Up-bow. Breathing-mark. Martellement. *Port de voix. Aspiration.*

∧ — Down-bow (violoncello-music).

∧ ∨ — Heel and toe (organ-music; better as given below).

W VV — *Martellement double* and *triple.*

⌢ — Nachschlag.

⌐ ⌐⌐ — Down-bow.

□ — Pesante.

[— Arpeggio. Acciaccatura. —In modern pfte.-music, signifies that 2 notes so connected are to be played (a) with the same hand, (b) with one finger.—In vocal music, signifies *voci divise:*

⌐⌐ ⌐⌐ — Bind. Organ-music, pedal; notes so connected are to be played with alternate toe and heel of same foot.

∿ — *Bind.*

⌠ — Brace.

•~•~•~ — Trill. All'ottava. (A mark of continuation.)

⋀⋀⋀⋀ — *Balancement. Tremblement.*

⋀⋀⋀ — *Tremblement.*

⌇ — Arpeggio.

/ or \ — from one staff to another, shows (a) in pfte.-music that notes so con-

nected are to be played with the same hand ; (b) that a part is transferred from one staff to another.

ᴡ, ᴧᴧ or ∿ — Direct.

ᴧᴧ — Inverted Mordent. *Cadence.*

ᴧᴧ — Mordent.

tr ᴧᴧ) ᴧᴧ etc. — Trill.

∾ (∾ ⅜ ⅜) — Turn (*Back-turn*).

✳ — Take damper-pedal (obsolete).

✳ ⊕ + — Release damper-pedal.

o — Sign of the dimin. triad (e. g. vii°).

o or O — Harmonic mark. Open string.

O — Tasto solo (Thorough-b.).

Ȯ — *Triple time* (see Notation, §3).

ȣ — Thumb-positions (violoncello-playing).

o ∧ (or ᴗ ∨) — Heel and toe (organ-music). Over notes for right foot, under notes for left foot.

∧ — ∨ — Change toes on organ-pedal.

∧ ᴗ ∧ — Slide same toe to next note.

Examples:

1, 2, 3, 4, etc. (See Numerals.)

①, ②, etc. (See Harmonium-music.)

𝄃, 𝄃, 𝄃, etc. (See Chord, Thorough-bass.)

I II₇ III' (See Chord.)

2' 4' 8' 16' (See Foot.)

a' b'' c'''
a¹ b² c³
_ = ≡ etc. (See Pitch, §1.)
a b c
A₁ B₁ C₂

Γ — Gamma.

♩ ♩ ♩ ⅌ ⅌ ⅌ (See Tambourine.)

M. M. ♩ = 60 (See Metronome.)

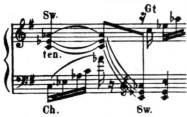

In organ-music, signifies " change hands on chord ".

In pfte.-music, signifies " hold chord with pedal ".

Signal'horn (Ger.) A bugle.

Signature. The signs set at the head of the staff at the beginning of a piece or movement, indicating the key and measure in which it is written. The chromatic sign or signs are termed the *key-signature;* the figures or signs indicating the measure, the *time-signature,* or rhythmical signature.

Signatu'ren (Ger., pl.) The figures and signs employed in thorough-bass notation.

Signe (Fr.) Sign.

Sig'num (Lat.) Sign... *Signa impli'cita, indicia'lia, intrin'seca,* see *Notation,* §3, *Modus.*

Siguidil'la (Span.) See *Seguidilla.*

Sil'bendehnung (Ger.) Slurring a syllable, i. e. singing it to more than one tone.

Silence (Fr.), **Silen'zio** (It.) A rest. (Comp. *Pause, Soupir.*)

Sillet (Fr.) Nut; specifically, *petit sillet,* nut at upper end of neck; *grand sillet,* nut at tailpiece.

Similar motion. See *Motion.*

Si'mile (It., " similarly, in like manner.") A direction to perform the following passage or passages in the same style as a preceding similar passage; used to save the trouble of repeating phrase-marks and other signs... *The simile-mark* is ⸺ (*see Abbreviation*). [*Simile,* being an adverb, is indeclinable,

and has no plural form *simili;* the Lat. term is *similiter.*]

Simple. (Of tones and intervals.) Not compound.—(Of counterpoint, imitation, rhythm etc.) Not compound or complex, undeveloped, not varied.

Sin' (It.) Abbr. of *Sino.*

Sinfoni'a (It.) 1. A symphony.—2. An overture (to the earlier Italian operas).

Sinfonie' (Ger.) Symphony (usually *Symphonie'*).

Sing'akademie (Ger.) A choral singing-society.

Sing'bar (Ger.) Singable; *cantabile... Sehr singbar vor'zutragen,* perform in a very singing style.

Sing'end (Ger.) Singing, melodious, *cantabile.*

Sing'etanz (Ger.) Dance accomp. with song.

Sing'fuge (Ger.) Vocal fugue.

Singhiozzan'do (It.) Sobbingly, catching the breath.

Sing'manieren (Ger., pl.) Vocal graces.

Sing'schule (Ger.) Singing-school.

Sing'spiel (Ger.) The German national form of the opera, established during the 2nd half of the 18th century by J. A. Hiller, whose guiding rule was to give simple, folk-songlike melodies to singers representing plain characters, whereas to " gentlefolk" he gave arias; the instrumental accomp. is also kept subordinate to the vocal parts.—The term is also used for any light opera or operetta with spoken interludes; likewise, by extension, for more pretentious operas and mus. dramas.

Sing'stimme (Ger.) The singing-voice, the voice.

Sini'stra (It.) Left; *mano s.,* left hand; *colla s.,* with the left hand.

Sink-a-pace. See *Cinque-pace.*

Si'no (It.) To, up to, as far as, till; *sino* (or *sin*) *al fine,* to the end.

Si'ren. (Ger. *Sire'ne;* Fr. *sirène.*) An acoustical apparatus for determining the vibration-number of a given tone.

Sir Roger de Coverley. An ancient English dance-tune in 9-4 time, still in vogue as a country-dance.

Siste'ma (It.) Staff.

Sis'trum (Lat.) An ancient mus. instr. of Egypt and the East; a sort of rattle,

consisting of loose metal rods set in an
oval frame, and shaken by a handle.

Sitole. See *Citole.*

Sitz (Ger.) Seat ; situation, place.

Sixième, Sixte (Fr.) Sixth ; *sixte
ajoutée*, added sixth.

Sixteenth-note. (Ger. *Sech'zehntel
[-note]; Fr. double-croche; It. semicro'-
ma.*) A semiquaver (♪). Sometimes
abbr. to *Sixteenth... 16th-rest*, a semi-
quaver-rest (♩). Comp. *Note, Rest.*

Sixth. (Ger. *Sex'te;* Fr. *sixte;* It.
se'sta.) See *Interval...Chord of the
sixth*, first inversion of a triad... *Chord
of the added sixth* (Fr. *accord de la
sixte ajoutée*), the sub-
dominant triad with
sixth added, e. g.:
...*Chord of the extreme sixth*, see *Extreme.*

Sixtine (Fr.) Sextuplet.

Sixty-fourth-note. (Ger. *Vierund-
sech'zigstel [-note]; Fr. quadruple
croche; It. quattricro'ma.*) A hemi-
demisemiquaver ( ); sometimes abbr.

to *Sixty-fourth...64th-rest,* (𝄾).

Skip. (Ger. *Sprung;* Fr. *saut;* It. *sal'-

to.) Melodic progression by an interval wider than a second ; disjunct (or
discrete) progression.

Skiz'ze (Ger.) Sketch ; a short characteristic piece, or bit of salon-music,
without fixed form.

Slan'cio, con (It.) With vehemence,
impetuously. (Sometimes written *islancio*, for the sake of euphony.)

Slargan'do, Slargan'dosi (It.) Growing slower ; comp. *Largando.*

Slentan'do (It.) See *Slargando.*

Slide. 1. A movable U-shaped tube in
the trombone (sometimes in the trumpet
and French horn), which is pushed in
and out to alter the pitch of the tones
while playing. It is a more perfect
device than the valve, because it changes
only the length of the vibrating air-
column, not the direction and form of
the wind-current ; and also because perfect purity of pitch is obtainable [comp.,
however, art. *Trumpet*, last sentence];
but it is technically more difficult of
manipulation.—2. In the organ, a
slider.—3. A grace (Ger. *Schlei'fer;*
Fr. *coulé*), either (*a*) a diatonic series
of 2 or more tones rapidly ascending or
descending, the notation of which varies
greatly :

or (*b*) a portamento.

Slide-horn. See *Slide-trumpet.*

Slider. See *Organ,* (1).

Slide-trombone,-trumpet. One played
by the use of a slide instead of keys or
valves.

Sliding relish. An old harpsichord-
grace written : played :

Slissa'to (It.) Slurred.

Slur. 1. (Ger. *Lega'tobogen;* Fr. *liaison;*
It. *legatu'ra.*) A sweeping curve drawn
over or under 2 or more notes, signifying that they are to be executed *legato.*
—2. In vocal music, the slur unites 2
or more notes to be sung to the same
syllable and in one breath ; the notes

so sung are also called a slur... *Slurred
melody*, one in which 2 or more tones
are sung to one syllable ; opp. to *syllabic melody.*

Small octave. See *Pitch...Small orchestra*, see *Orchestra.*

Smanian'te, Smanio'so (It.) In an
impetuous, passionate style.

Sminuen'do, Sminui'to (It.) Diminishing and decreasing (in speed and
force).

Smoren'do (It.) Dying away.

Smorfio'so (It.) With affected expression.

Smorzan'do (It.) " Fading away";
equiv. to *Morendo.*

Snap. See *Scotch snap.*

Snare-drum. See *Side-drum,* under
Drum.

Soa've (It.) Suave, sweet, soft... *Soavemen'te*, suavely, etc.

Socket. In a clarinet, the short, rounded joint connecting the mouthpiece with the "top-joint".

Sogget'to (It.) Subject, theme.—This term is properly applied to a homogeneous theme of moderate length, a longer one being called an *andamento*, and a short, motive-like theme **an** *attacco* (though this last term is practically obsolete).

Sognan'do (It.) Dreaming, in a dreamy manner.

Soh. For *sol*, in the Tonic Sol-fa system.

Sol. I. The fifth of the Aretinian syllables.—2. Name of the note *G* in France, Italy, etc.

Solem'nis (Lat.) Solemn.

Solen'ne (It.) Solemn; splendid, pompous... *Solennemen'te*, solemnly, etc... *Solennità'*, solemnity, pomp.

Solfà' (It.) I. Scale, gamut.—2. Music in general; *bat'tere la solfà*, to beat time.—3. A conductor's baton.

Sol-fa (Engl.) I (*verb*). To sing *solfeggi;* specifically, to sing to the solmisation-syllables.—2 (*noun*). Solmisation, and the syllables employed in it; a solfeggio on those syllables.— *Tonic Sol-fa*, see *Tonic*.

Solfeggia're (It.) To sol-fa.

Solfeg'gio (It., pl. *solfeg'gi;* Fr. *solfège*.) A vocal exercise, either on one vowel, or the syllables of solmisation, or to words.

Solid chord. One the tones of which

are performed simultaneously; opp. to *broken.* ("*Flat chord*" is preferable.)

So'lito (It.) Accustomed, habitual... *Al solito*, as usual, in the customary manner.

Solmisation. A method of teaching the scales and intervals by syllables, the invention of which is ascribed to Guido d'Arezzo (b. 990 ?). It is based, in opposition to the Greek theory of *tetrachords*, on the *hexachord* or 6-tone scale : the first six tones of the natural major scale, *c d e f g a*, were named *ut, re, mi, fa, sol, la*, (the initial syllables of the successive phrases of a hymn to St. John beginning *Ut queant laxis*, these syllables happening to fall on these 6 tones), forming the *natural* hexachord (*hexachor'dum natura'le*) with the semitonic step at *mi-fa;* the syllables were further applied to 2 other hexachords, the *hard* hexachord (*hex. du'rum*) *g a b c d e* (so called because constructed with the hard *B* = *B♮* or *B durum*), and the *soft* hexachord (*hex. mol'le*) *f g a b♭ c d* (with the soft *B* = B♭ or *B molle*); in each, the step *mi-fa* was in the same relative position. The entire mus. scale, extended beyond that of Greek theory by adding I tone below (Gamma Γ = *G*), and 4 above, embraced 7 hexachords, the higher ones being mere reduplications of the original 3. In the following View, the solmisation-names of the notes will be found by reading up from (and including) the letter-name ; thus low *G* was called *Gamma-ut*, its octave *G sol re ut*, and its double-octave likewise *G sol re ut;* *B*, however, was called only *B fa* or *B mi*, ac cording as it occurred in the soft or hard hexachord.

VIEW OF THE GUIDONIAN HEXACHORDS.

VII. Hex. durum (with B mi)											ut	re	mi	fa	sol	la		
VI. Hex. molle (with B fa)										ut	re	mi	fa	sol	la			
V. Hex. naturale									ut	re	mi	fa	sol	la				
IV. Hex. durum (with B mi)							ut	re	mi	fa	sol	la						
III. Hex. molle (with B fa)						ut	re	mi	fa	sol	la							
II. Hex. naturale					ut	re	mi	fa	sol	la								
I. Hex. durum	ut	re	mi	fa	sol	la												
Modern letter-name	G	A	B	c	d	e	f	g	a	b	c¹	d¹	e¹	f¹	g¹	a¹	b♮¹	c²	d² e²
Medieval "	Γ	A	♮ / ♭	C	D	E	F	G	a	♮ / ♭	c	d	e	f	g	aa	♮/♭	cc	dd ee

When a melody overstepped the compass of one hexachord, a transition, termed a *mutation*, was made from one

set of syllables to another; the change of syllables was preferably effected between the natural and soft, or natural and hard, hexachords (a direct transition from hard to soft, or vice versa, being less smooth because of the clashing significance of $B\natural$ and $B\flat$), and usually after *fa* (*sol* = *re*) in ascending and after *mi* (*re* := *la*) in descending. These mutations exhibit a dawning of the modern idea of modulation, the final victory of which, in establishing the major and minor modes and freely transposable scales, disposed of the system of hexachords.—During the supremacy of the medieval modes, this system sufficed for the composer's needs; but after the recognition of the leading-note, and the general adoption of a corresponding 7th syllable *si* early in the 17th century, the modern 7-tone scale, or *heptachord*, gradually superseded the hexachord in theory and practice. Many proposed changes in the syllable-names met with merely local and transient favor; among them, those of Waelrant of Antwerp in 1550 (bo, ce, di, ga, lo, ma, ni), called *Bocedisation* or *Bobisation*), Pedro d'Urenna in 1620 (ni for si), Hitzler of Stuttgart in 1628 (la, be, ce, de, me, fe, ge, called *Bebisation*), Graun in 1750 (da, me, ni, po, tu, la, be, called *Damenisation*). In Italy, and afterwards in all Europe excepting France, the syllable *do* (presumably first used in 1673, by Bononcini) has ousted the original *ut* (comp. *Do*). In both France and Italy the *syllables* have, in everyday usage, quite supplanted the *letter-names* of the notes, which are employed in Germany, Holland, England, and the United States.

So′lo (It., "alone".) Properly, a piece or passage for a single voice or instr.; by extension, any non-concerted piece or passage in which a single voice or instr. predominates. As an orchestral direction, *Solo* (or simply I) marks a passage where one instr. (1st violin, 1st flute, etc.) takes a leading part.—In a 2-hand arr. of a pfte.-concerto, *Solo* marks the entrances of the solo pfte. —*Violino solo* signifies, according to circumstances, either "violin alone", or "1st violin" (accompanied).—*Solo organ*, see *Organ*...*Solo pitch*, a *scordatura* temporarily employed by a solo player for obtaining unusual effects... *Solo quartet*, (*a*) a quartet consisting of 4 singers (4 "solo voices"); (*b*) a composition or passage in 4 parts for 4 singers; (*c*) a non-concerted composi-

tion for 4 instr.s, one of which has a leading part...*Solo stop*, see *Stop*.

So′losänger (Ger.) A solo singer.. *So′lospieler*, a solo player...*So′lostimme*, a solo part or voice.

Sombrer (Fr.) In vocal music, to give to the tones, for dramatic effect, a sombre, veiled, yet intense expression.

Som′ma (It.) Utmost, highest, extreme; greatest.

Som′merophone. An instr. of the bombardon or saxhorn class, inv. by Sommer of Weimar in 1843; also called *Euphonion*, *Euphonic Horn*.

Sommier (Fr.) Windchest.

Son (Fr.) Sound; tone...*Son harmonique*, an harmonic; *son plein*, a round, full tone.

Sona′bile (It.) Resonant, sounding.

Sonan′te (It.) Sounding, resounding; sonorous, resonant.

Sona′re (It.) To sound; to play (on an instr.)...*Sonare alla men′te*, to improvise.

Sona′ta (It.; Fr. and Ger. *Sona′te*.) The original Italian word, meant any instrumental "sound-piece" in contradistinction to a *canta′ta* (vocal composition). The old *sonata da camera* and *sonata da chiesa* were such instrumental pieces, for secular and sacred use respectively.—The modern Sonata (comp. *Form*) is an instrumental composition in 3 or 4 extended movements contrasted in theme, tempo, and mood...*Sonata-form*, see *Form*... *Double sonata*, a duo for 2 solo instr.s, in sonata-form.

Sonatil′la (It.) A short, easy sonata.

Sonati′na (It.), **Sonati′ne** (Fr. and Ger.) A short sonata in 2 or 3 (seldom 4) movements, the first having the characteristic first-movement form, though the development-section is either very short, or quite omitted.

Sonato′re (It.) A player on any instr.

Sone′vole (It.) Same as *Sonabile*.

Song. 1. (Ger. *Gesang;* Fr. *chant;* It. *can′to*.) Vocal musical expression or utterance.—2. (Ger. *Lied;* Fr. *chanson;* It. *canzo′ne*.) A short lyrical or narrative poem with a musical setting characterized by a structure in simple periods. Songs may be divided, according as they are classed as spontaneous popular productions or the result of artistic inspiration, in 2 broad groups, *folk-songs* and *art-songs*, though the former were doubtless originally conceived by specially gifted singers of earlier times, and the latter are frequently written with studied simplicity (*volks'thümlich*). Further, art-songs are either *strophic* (i. e. each strophe sung to the same tune, with a deviation at most in the final one), or *composed-through* (see *Durch'komponieren*).— The so-called *song-form* (Ger. *Lied'-form*), either vocal or instrumental, has 3 sections and 2 themes, the second contrasting theme occupying the 2nd section. (See *Form.*)

Sonnante (Fr.)   Same as *Stahlspiel*, or *Lyre* 2.—The steel bars are sometimes replaced by fixed bells.

Sonner le tambour (Fr., " to beat the drum "; also *rouler*.)   Said of the *G*-string on a 'cello when a jarring sound is given out on playing certain notes.

Sonnerie (Fr.)   1. Same as *Carillon* (peal or chime of bells).—2. A military call or signal.

So'no (It.)   Sound ; tone.

Sonom'eter.   An apparatus for acoustic experiments with strings, consisting of a sounding-board provided with bridges over which 2 strings may be stretched.

Sonoramen'te (It.)   Sonorously, resonantly, resoundingly.

Sono'ro (It.)   With a sonorous, ringing tone... *Sonoramen'te*, sonorously, resonantly, resoundingly... *Sonorità'*, con, sonorously, ringingly... *Sono're*, sonorous, resonant (pl.; *le note* implied).

Sonor'ophone.   A variety of bombardon.

So'nus (Lat.)   Sound ; tone.

So'pra (It.)   On, upon ; above, over, higher... *Sopradominan'te*, dominant. .. *Soprato'nica*, supertonic... *Sopra una corda*, on one string... *Co'me sopra*, as above... *Nella parte di sopra*, in the higher (or highest) part.

Sopran' (Ger.)   Soprano... *Sopran'-schlüssel*, treble-clef... *Sopran'stimme*, soprano voice or part.

Sopra'na corda (It.) . The chanterelle. (ST. AND B.)

Soprani'sta (It.)   A soprano singer ; specifically, a male soprano (*castra'to*).

Sopra'no (It.; Ger. *Sopran'*; Fr. *dessus*.) The highest class or division of the human voice.—The female soprano, or

treble, has a normal compass from c^1 to a^2 all tones of which, except the extremes, are common to both the chest-register and head-register ; solo voices often reach above c^3, and phenomenal ones up to g^3 or even c^4. There are also boy-soprani, and male soprani (of these latter 2 classes, the *falsetti* [*alti natura'li, tenori'ni*], and *castra'-ti*).—*Soprano dramma'tico*, a female soprano of dramatic power... *Soprano leggie'ro*, a light soprano... *Mezzo-soprano*, see *Mezzo*... *Soprano natura'-le*, natural soprano, a male singer having an unusually developed falsetto of soprano quality... *Soprano sfoga'to*, see *Sfogato*... *Soprano-clef*, the *C*-clef on the first line... *Soprano string*, the chanterelle.

Sordamen'te (It.)   With a veiled, muffled tone.

Sordelli'na (It.)   An Italian variety of the musette (bagpipe), provided with 4 pipes which could be opened and closed at will.

Sordi'no (It., pl. *sordini;* Ger. pl. *Sordi'-nen.*)   1. A mute ; *con sordini*, with the mutes ; *senza sordini*, without the mutes; *si le'vano i sordini*, take off the mutes.—2. Damper (of the pfte.); *senza sordini*, with damper-pedal ; so used by Beethoven, who employed *con sordini* to express the release (raising) of the damper-pedal, instead of ✿.—3. A kit.

Sor'do,-a (It.)   Muted ; as *clarinetto sordo*, *tromba sorda*.

Sordo'no (It.; Ger. *Sordun'*; Fr. *sor-done*.)   1. An obs. wood-wind instr. resembling the bombard, with a double reed and 12 ventages, constructed like a bassoon, and in 5 different sizes.—2. An obs. reed-stop in the organ, with a perforated foot and a chimney, of 4, 8, or 16-foot pitch and muffled tone.

Sordun' (Ger.)   See *Sordono*.—Also, a mute for the trumpet, in the shape of a perforated disk of wood.

Sorg'fältig (Ger.)   Careful, cautious. (Also *adverb*.)

Sorti'ta (It.)   1. A closing voluntary. —2. The first number sung by any of the leading characters in an opera.

Sospiran'do (It., " sighing, sobbing".) A vocal effect produced by interposing a rest between two tones in such a way as to interrupt a word of 2 or more syllables, the singer catching his breath as if deeply moved.

Sospire'vole, Sospiro'so (It.) Sighing deeply ; plaintive, mournful.

Sostenen'do, Sostenen'te (It.) See *Sostenu'to.*

Sostenu'to (It., abbr. *sost.; superl. sostenutis'simo.*) "Sustained, prolonged"; sometimes implying a tenuto, at others a uniform rate of decreased speed ; e. g. *andante sostenuto...Più sostenuto,* equiv. to *meno mosso.*—Standing alone, as a tempo-mark, it is nearly equiv. to *andante.*

Sostinente pianoforte. A pfte. in which some device is employed for "sustaining" or prolonging the tones, such as the numerous piano-violins, the lyrichord, celestina, claviol, etc.

Sot'to (It.) Below, under... *Sottovoce,* in an undertone, aside...*Sottodominan'te,* subdominant.

Soubasse (Fr.) Subbass.

Soubrette (Fr.) In comedy and comic opera, a maid-servant or lady's-maid, of an intriguing and coquettish character ; applied, by extension, to various light rôles of this or a similar type.

Soufflet (Fr.) The bellows (of an organ, harmonium, etc.)...*Souffler,* to blow. ...*Soufflerie,* the bellows with all adjuncts...*Souffleur,* (*a*) organ-blower ; (*b*) prompter (fem. *souffleuse*).

Sound. See *Acoustics.*

Soundboard. 1. (Ger. *Resonanz'boden;* Fr. *table d' harmonie;* It. *ta'vola armo'nica.*) The thin plate of wood placed below or behind the strings of various instr.s, to reinforce and prolong their tones by reflecting them from its broader surface by means of molecular vibration. The *s.* of the pfte. is sometimes, that of the violin generally, called the *belly.* —2. (Ger. *Pfeifenstock;* Fr. *pied du tamis d'orgue;* It. *casso'ne.*) In the organ, the cover of the windchest, in which the feet of the pipes are inserted.

Sound-body, Sound-box. Same as *Resonance-box...Sound-bow,* the thick rim of a bell, against which the clapper strikes...*Sound-hole,* a hole cut in the belly of a stringed instr. to enhance the resonance...*Soundpost.* (Ger. *See'le, Stimm'stock;* Fr. *âme;* It. *a'nima.*) In the violin, etc., the small cylindrical wooden prop set inside the body, between belly and back, just behind (near-

ly beneath) the treble foot of the bridge. Its function is not only to brace the belly against the strong string-tension, but also to transmit the vibration of the strings from belly to back, thus rendering the whole body of the instr. resonant.

Soupape (Fr.) Valve.

Soupir (Fr.) A quarter-rest...*Demisoupir,* an eighth-rest...*Huitième de soupir* (or *demi-quart de soupir*), 32nd-rest... *Quart de soupir,* a 16th-rest...*Seizième de soupir,* a 64th-rest.

Sourdeline (Fr.) Same as *Sordellina.*

Sourdine (Fr.) 1. A mute.—2. A stop in the harmonium, which partially intercepts the wind-supply, so that full chords can be played softly.—3. Same as *pédale céleste* (of the pfte.)—4. Formerly, a spinet (or lute) of veiled, muffled tone.

Sous (Fr.) Under, below...*Sous-chantre,* subcantor...*Sous-dominante,* subdominant...*Sous-médiante,* submediant...*Sous-tonique,* subtonic, leadingnote.

Space. (Ger. *Zwisch'enraum;* Fr. *espace;* It. *spa'zio.*) In the staff, the interval between 2 lines or leger-lines. (See *Leger-space.*)

Spal'la (It.) Shoulder... *Vio'la da spalla,* see *Viola.*

Spa'nischer Rei'ter (Ger.) See *Durchstecher...Spanisches Kreuz,* sign (×) of the double-sharp.

Spar'ta, Sparti'ta, Sparti'to (It.), **Spar'te** (Ger.) A partitura.

Sparti're (It.) To write out in score.— The Ger. form *spartie'ren* signifies, to copy out old scores into modern notation.

Spassapensie'ro (It.) A jew's-harp.

Spass'haft (Ger.) Scherzando.

Spa'tium (Lat.), **Spa'zio** (It.) A space.

Sperr'ventil (Ger.) See *Ventil* 2.

Spezza'to (It.) Divided.

Spiana'to,-a (It., "leveled".) Smooth, even, tranquil ; nearly equiv. to *senza passione.*

Spicca'to (It., " separated".) See *Springing bow.*

Spiel (Ger.) Playing ; style (of playing). ..*Spiel'art,* (*a*) style or method of playing ; (*b*) touch (of a keyboard instr.). ..*Spiel'bar,* handy to play (on vio-

lin); playable (as a passage or piece).
.. *Spie'len*, to play ; *Spie'ler*, player. ..
Spiel'leute, (*a*) wandering fiddlers, etc.,
of the middle ages ; (*b*) the drummers
and fifers of a military band ; opp. to
Hautbois'ten. .. *Spiel'manieren*, instrumental graces. .. *Spiel'oper*, light opera,
comic opera. .. *Spiel'tenor*, light tenor,
as for comic opera or oper₁ tta.

Spi'na (Lat.) Quill (of a spinet).

Spin'et. (It. *spinet'ta;* Fr. *épinette;*
Ger. *Spinett'*.) An obs. keyboard instr.
like a harpischord, but smaller. Also
called *Virginal* (*pair of Virginals*),
and *Couched Harp.*

Spi'rito, con (It.) With spirit. Also
spiritosamen'te, spirito'so, with animation and energy.

Spit'ze (Ger.) 1. Point (of the bow).
Often abbr. *Sp.*—2. Toe (in organ-
playing).

Spitz'flöte (Ger.) In the organ, an open
flue-stop of organ-metal, tin, or wood,
of 8, 4, 2, and 1-foot pitch ; tone somewhat thin, but pure and reedy. The
pipes are conical, whence the name.
(Also *Spill'flöte, Spin'delflöte;* Lat.
ti'bia cus'pida.)

Spitz'harfe (Ger ; It. *arpanet'ta*.) A
small triangular harp (psaltery) to be
set on a table ; it had an upright soundboard with strings on both sides of it,
the bass strings on one side and the
treble strings on the other. Also called
*Harfenett', Flü'gelharfe, Zwit'scher-
harfe.* [RIEMANN.]

Spitz'quint (Ger.) The quint of the
Spitzflöte.

Spon'dee. A metrical foot consisting of
2 long syllables (——).

Spread harmony. See *Harmony.*

Springing bow. In violin-playing, a
style of bowing in which the bow is allowed to drop on the string, its elasticity then causing it to rebound and quit
the string between each two tones.
There are 2 varieties : (1) the *Spicca'to*,
indicated by dots over the notes, and
played near the middle of the bow with
a loose wrist, for rapid passages in
equal notes :—(2) the *Salta'to*, with a
longer fall and higher rebound, generally employed when several equal notes
are to be taken in one bow.

Sprung (Ger.) A skip, a leap ; *sprung-
weise*, by skips or leaps.

Square pianoforte. See *Pianoforte.*

Squillan'te (It., from *squil'la*, a little
bell.) Ringing, tinkling.

Sta'bat Ma'ter. See *Sequence.*

Sta'bile (It.) Steady, firm.

Stacca're (It.) To make staccato.

Stacca'to (It.; superl. *staccatis'simo;*
abbr. *stacc.*) " Detached, separated";
noting a style in which the tones played
or sung are more or less abruptly disconnected. The ordinary staccato is
marked by round dots over or under
the notes ; a sharper staccato, by wedge-
shaped dashes (the *martelé* of violin-
playing); the *mezzo-staccato*, in which
the tones are nearly run together, has a
slur over the staccato-dots.—*Staccato-
mark*, a dot or wedge-shaped stroke.

**Stadt'musikanten, -pfeifer, -zinke-
nisten** (Ger., pl.) Salaried town-musicians, belonging to a privileged guild
which originated in the 15th (?) century,
and under obligations to furnish music
for civic ceremonies ; their leader had
the title of *Stadt'musikus.* (Also *Amts'-
pfeifer, Kunst'pfeifer.*)

Staff, Stave. (Ger. *Li'niensystem, System';* Fr. *portée;* It. *ri'go.*) The 5 (in
Gregorian music 4) parallel horizontal
lines used in musical notation. .. *Grand*
or *Great staff*, one of 11 lines, middle-
C occupying the sixth. .. *Staff-notation*,
the staff and the system of musical
signs connected with it ; opp. to *Alphabetical notation* (q. v.). Compare *Notation.*

Stagio'ne (It.) Season.

Stahl'harmonika (Ger.) An instr. consisting of small steel bars caused to
sound by diminutive bows ; inv. by
Nöbe in 1796. .. *Stahl'spiel*, see *Lyre* 2.

Stamentienpfeife (Ger.) See *Schwegel.*

Stamm'akkord (Ger.) Any chord of a
key, in its fundamental position ; also
sometimes denotes any fundamental or
inverted chord belonging to the given
key, i. e. any chord not altered or suspended. .. *Stamm'ton*, natural tone. ..
Stamm'tonleiter, the typical diatonic
scale of *C*-major.

Stampi'ta (It.) A song with instrumental accomp.

Ständ'chen (Ger.) A serenade.

Stanghet'ta (It.) Bar.

Stan'za (It.; Fr. *stance;* Ger. *Stan'ze.*)
A group of more than 2 lines, arranged
according to a regular plan as regards

either metrical length, or rhyme, or both, and forming, in connection with similar groups, a poem, or a part of one.

Staple. In the oboe, etc., the metallic tube which carries the double-reed, and conveys the vibr. of the latter to the body of the instr.

Stark (Ger.) Loud, forcible, vigorous ; forte. (Also adverb.). .Stär'ker, louder, stronger; più forte.

Stave. See Staff.

Steam-organ. The Calliope.

Stec'ca (It.) A vicious vocal effect,— the choked or interrupted tone caused by pressing the root of the tongue too far back into the pharynx.

Stech'er (Ger.) A sticker.

Steg (Ger.) Bridge.

Stem. (Ger. Hals; Fr. queue; It. gam'-bo.) The vertical line attached to a note-head (♩ ♪, etc.)—Also Tail.

Stentan'do (It.) Dragging and heavy, ritenu'to e pesan'te.—Also Stenta'to.

Step. (Ger. Schritt.) A melodic progression of a second (either major, minor, or augm.)—Also, often used as synonymous with degree ; and, further, as equiv. to whole tone and semitone, in the phrases whole step and half-step. . .Chromatic step, the progression of a chromatic second. . .Diatonic step, a progression between conjunct degrees of the diatonic scale.

Ster'bend (Ger., "dying"). Morendo.

Ste'so (It.) Extended, prolonged ; steso moto, a slow movement.

Stes'so (It.) The same.

Sthen'ochire. An apparatus designed for increasing the strength and dexterity of the hands and fingers of players on keyboard instr.s.

Sticca'do, Sticca'to (It.) Xylophone.

Sticker. See Organ.

Stie'fel (Ger.) Boot (of a reed-pipe).

Stiel (Ger.) Stem ; neck (of violin.)

Stil (Ger.), **Sti'le** or **Sti'lo** (It.) Style.

Still'gedackt (Ger.) A soft-toned stopped organ-register.

Sti'lo (It.) Style. . .S. osserva'to, strict style, especially of pure vocal music. . . S. rappresentati'vo, dramatic monodic song with instrumental accomp. in chords ; a style originating toward the close of the 16th century.

Stim'me (Ger.) 1. Voice.—2. Part ; mit der Stimme, colla parte.—3. Organ-stop (generally in compounds).—4. Soundpost. . . Stimm'ansatz, the attack of a vocal tone. . . Stimm'bänder, vocal cords. . . Stimm'bildung, training or development of the voice. . . Stimm'bruch, breaking of the voice, mutation. . . Stimm'buch, part-book. . . Stim'men, to tune ; to voice (an organ). . . Stim'mer, (a) tuner ; (b) drone (of bagpipe). . . Stimm'flöte, pitch-pipe. . . Stimm'führer, leader in a chorus. . . Stimm'führung, leading of the parts. . . Stimm'gabel, tuning-fork. . . Stimm'hammer, tuning - hammer. . . Stimm'holz, -hölzchen, soundpost. . . Stimm'horn, tuning-cone. . . Stimm'keil, tuning - wedge. . . Stimm'krücke, tuning-wire. . . Stimm'mittel, vocal powers, capacity. . . Stimm'pfeife, pitch-pipe. . . Stimm'ritze, glottis. . . Stimm'stock, soundpost (violin) ; wrest-plank (pfte.). . . Stimm'umfang, compass of the voice. . . Stim'mung, (a) tuning ; accordatura ; (b) pitch ; Stimmung halten, to keep in tune; (c) a mood, frame of mind ; Stim'mungsbild, a "mood-picture", short characteristic piece. . . Stimm'werkzeuge, vocal organs.

Stinguen'do (It.) Dying away.

Stiracchia'to, Stira'to (It.) Dragging, retarding the tempo.

Stock (Ger.) Bundle of 30 strings.

Stöck'chen des Hal'ses (Ger.) "Heel" of violin, etc.

Stock'fagott (Ger.) Same as Rackett. . .Stock'flöte, same as Czakan.

Stol'len (Ger.) See Strophe.

Stonan'te (It.) Dissonant.

Stone-harmonicon. See Lapideon.

Stop (noun). 1. (Ger. Regis'terzug; Fr. registre; It. regi'stro.) That part of the organ-mechanism controlling the admission of wind to the grooves beneath the pipes.—2. (Ger. Regis'ter; Fr. jeu d'orgue(s); It. regi'stro.) A set or row of organ-pipes of like character, arranged in graduated succession. These are called speaking or sounding stops; they are classed as Flue-work (having flue-pipes), and Reed-work, (having reed-pipes) ; the flue-work has 3 sub-classes, namely (a) Principal-work, having cylindrical flue-pipes of diapason-quality, i. e. the characteristic organ-tone ; (b) Gedackt-work, having covered (stopped or plugged) pipes ; and (c) Flute-work, including all flue-stops having flue-pipes of a scale too broad or too narrow to produce the diapason-tone, together with such stopped pipes as have chimneys, and all 3- or 4-sided wooden pipes...*Complete stop*, one having at least one pipe for each key of the keyboard to which it belongs...*Compound stop*, see *Mixture-stop*...*Divided stop*, one in which the lower half of its register is controlled by a different stop-knob from the upper, and generally bears a different name...*Flue-stop*, one composed of flue-pipes. ..*Foundation-stop*, one of normal 8-foot pitch...*Half-stop*, *incomplete* or *imperfect stop*, one producing (approximately) half the tones called for by the full scale of its manual...*Mechanical stop*, one not having a set of pipes, but governing some mechanical device ; such are the couplers, tremulant, bell-signal, and the like...*Mixture-stop*, one with 2 or more ranks of pipes, thus producing more than one tone for each key (as the *Mixture, Carillon, Cornet, Cymbal*)...*Mutation-stop*, one producing tones a major 3rd or perfect 5th (or a higher octave of either) above the 8' stops (as the *Tierce, Twelfth, Quint*)...*Partial stop*, see *Half-stop*. ..*Pedal-stop*, a stop on the pedal... *Reed-stop*, one composed of reed-pipes. ..*Solo-stop*, any organ-stop adapted for the production of characteristic melodic effects, whether on the solo organ or not...*Sounding* or *speaking stop*, a stop proper, having pipes and producing musical tones.—3. On a violin, etc., pressure of a finger on a string, to vary its pitch ; a *double-stop* is when 2 or more strings are so pressed and sounded simultaneously ;—on wind-instr.s with finger-holes, the closing of a hole by the finger or a key, to alter the pitch ;—on wind-instr.s of the trumpet family, the partial closing of the bell by inserting the hand, thus raising the pitch and modifying the quality of the tone.

Stop (*verb*). To vary the pitch of instr.s as described under *Stop* 3 above... *Stopped notes*, notes obtained by stopping ; opp. to *open*...*Stopped pipes*, organ-pipes closed (plugged or covered) at the top ; opp. to *open*.

Stop'fen (Ger.) To stop (bell of horn with the hand)...*Stopf'töne*, stopped tones, " hand-notes " (horn).

Stop-knob. The projecting handle of a *Stop* 1.

Stoss'zeichen (Ger.) Staccato-mark.

Straccicalan'do (It.) Babbling, prattling.

Strain. In general, a song, tune, air, melody ; also, some well-defined passage in or part of a piece.—Technically, a period, sentence, or short division of a composition ; a motive or theme.

Strascican'do (It.) Dragging, drawling. (Also *strascinan'do; strascinando l'arco*, drawing the bow so as to bind the tones.)

Strathspey. An animated Scotch dance, somewhat slower than the reel, and like it in 4-4 time, but progressing in dotted eighth-notes alternating with 16ths, the latter frequently preceding the former, then producing the peculiar jerky rhythm of the Scotch snap.

Stravagan'te (It.) Extravagant, eccentric, fantastical.

Stravagan'za (It.) An extravaganza.

Straw-fiddle. See *Strohfiedel*.

Strei'chen (Ger.) 1. To bow (draw the bow across).—2. To cut (as a scene in an opera)...*Strei'chend* (Ger.; lit. " drawing [as a bow]"), the quality of tone called in English *stringy* (opp. to *reedy, fluty*, etc.)...*Streichende Regis'ter*, in the organ, stops with string-tone...*Streich'instrumente*, bow-instr.s. ..*Streich'orchester*, string-orchestra, " the strings "...*Streich'quartett, -trio*, string-quartet, -trio...*Streich'zither*, bow-zither.

Streng (Ger.) Strict, severe. (Also *adverb*.)

Stre'pito (It.) Noise...*Strepitosamen'te, strepito'so*, in a noisy, boisterous, impetuous style.

Stretch. On a keyboard or fingerboard, a wide interval whose tones are to be taken simultaneously by the fingers of one hand.

Stret'ta, commonly **Stret'to** (It.; Fr. *strette;* Ger. *Eng'führung*.) " Narrow, drawn together". 1. A division of a fugue (usually a final development, for the sake of effect) in which subject and answer follow each other in such close succession as to overlap...*S. maestra'le*, one constructed in strict canon...*Alla stretta*, in, or after the manner of, a stretto...*Andante stretto*, same as *andante agitato*.—2. A concluding passage taken, to enhance the effect, in faster tempo.

Strette (Fr.) Stretto... *S. magistrale*, same as *Stretto maestrale*.

Strich (Ger.) 1. Stroke; *Strich'art*, Bowing 2.—2. A line, dash, or stroke. —3. A "cut".

Striden'te (It.; "noisy," "harsh".) In pfte.-playing, equiv. to *martellato* (comp. Beethoven, op. 76, Var. VI).

String. (Ger. *Sai'te;* Fr. *corde;* It. *cor'-da*.) The materials chiefly used for manufacturing musical strings are *gut* (entrails of lambs and sheep), *cast steel* (drawn out for piano-strings, etc.), *silver* (mostly for covering or winding spirally around a *core*—steel wire or silk cord—to make the string thicker and heavier in proportion to its length, and consequently deeper-toned), and *silk* (as a core in covered strings, especially for the guitar and zither). Copper and brass are also employed... *The Strings*, technical term for the string-group in the orchestra... *First string*, the highest of a set... *Open string*, one not stopped or shortened... *Silver string*, one covered with silver wire... *Soprano string*, the chanterelle.

Stringed instruments. (Ger. *Sai'ten-instrumente;* Fr. *instruments à cordes;* It. *strømen'ti da cor'da*.) All musical instr.s whose tones are produced by strings, whether struck, plucked, or bowed. See *Instruments*.

Stringen'do (It.) Hastening, accelerating the movement, usually suddenly and rapidly, with a *crescendo*.

String-gauge. A gauge for measuring the thickness of strings.

String-organ. A keyboard instr., provided with a series of free reeds connected by rods with ordinary piano-strings of corresponding pitch, which are sympathetically affected by the vibrations of the reeds. The tone is pure and sweet, the instr. combining in a degree the qualities of the harmonium and pfte.—Also compare art. *Saitenor-gel*.

String-quartet. A quartet for 1st and 2nd violin, viola, and 'cello; hence, the instr.s themselves, or the players on them; and, by extension, the string-group in the orchestra (see *String-quintet*).

String-quintet. 1. A quintet for 2 violins, 2 violas, and 'cello; or for 2 violins, 1 viola, and 2 'celli; or for 2 violins, viola, 'cello, and double-bass.

These are the most usual combinations, which may be variously extended to form string-sextets, septets, etc.—2. The string-group in the orchestra, when considered as composed of (1) 1st and (2) 2nd violins, (3) violas, (4) 'cellos, and (5) double-basses; called string-*quartet* when considered as composed of (1) violins, (2) violas, (3) 'cellos, and (4) double-basses.

Stringy. Having the quality of tone ("string-tone") peculiar to bow-instr.s.

Striscian'do (It.) Gliding, smooth, *legato*.

Stro'fa (It.) Strophe.

Stroh'bass (Ger.) The deep, husky tone of the lower chest-register (male voice) produced by forcing the breath between the vocal chords when the latter, though brought near together, are in a state of relaxation... *Stroh'fiedel*, the xylophone.

Stroke. The sweep (fall and rise) of a digital or pedal.

Strombetta're (It.) To sound a trumpet... *Strombettie're*, trumpeter.

Stromenta'to (It.) Instrumented.

Stromen'to (It.) Instrument... *S. da arco*, bow-instr... *S. da corda*, stringed instrument... *S. da fia'to (di vento)*, wind-instr... *S. da ta'sto*, keyboard instr... *S. di le'gno*, wooden instr... *S. di metal'lo*, metal instr.

Stro'phe. (Gk., "a turning round".) 1. In the Greek drama, the song of the chorus when turning from right to left, the *antis'trophe* being what was sung when turning from left to right, the *ep'ode* then following.—2. A recurrent group of lines in a poem, arranged according to a fixed metrical system or plan; equivalent to *stanza* in modern poetry.—3. The former of two such groups, the latter then being called the *antistrophe* (see above)... The Strophe, Antistrophe, and Epode of the Greek tragic chorus and Pindar's odes, closely correspond to the 2 *Stollen* and the *Abgesang* of the German *Meistersinger;* the *Bar* being the group formed by the 2 *Stollen* and the *Abgesang*.

Stück (Ger.) A piece; a number (as on a program).

Study. (Ger. *Stu'die* [pl. *Stu'dien*], or *Etü'de* [pl. *Etü'den*]; Fr. *étude;* It. *stu'dio*.) See *Étude*.

Stu'fe (Ger.) A degree... *Stu'fenweise*

Fort'schreitung, diatonic or conjunct (" stepwise") progression.

Stumm (Ger.) Dumb... *Stum'mes Kla-vier'*, dumb piano... *Stum'me Pfei'fe*, dummy pipe... *Stum'mes Regis'ter*, mechanical stop.

Stür'misch (Ger., "stormy".) Impetuous, passionate. (Also *adverb.*)

Stür'ze (Ger.) Bell (of wind-instr.s)... *Stür'ze in die Höh'e*, "turn the bell upwards!"

Stuttgart pitch. That proposed by Scheibler at the Stuttgart Congress in 1834, the a^1 to make 400 vibrations per second at a temperature of 69° Fahrenheit. (Comp. *Pitch, Absolute.*)

Stutz'flügel (Ger.) Boudoir grand, "baby" grand (pfte.)

Su (It.) On, upon ; by, near... *Arco in su*, up-bow.

Suabe flute. A sweet-toned organ-stop.

Sua've (It.) See *Soave... Suavità', con*, suavely, sweetly.

Sub (Lat.) Under.

Subbass', Subbour'don. An organ-stop of 16 or 32-foot pitch, generally on the pedal and stopped.

Subcantor. A deputy cantor or precentor, supplying the place of his chief in the latter's absence. Also *Succentor.*

Subdiapen'te. In medieval music, the fifth below a given tone.

Subdom'inant. The under-dominant, i. e. the tone below the dominant in a diatonic scale ; the 4th degree.

Subitamen'te, Su'bito (It.) Suddenly, quickly... *Volti subito* (abbr. V. S.), turn over quickly... *p subito* (after *f*), an abrupt [change to] *piano*, without gradation.

Subject. (Ger. *Subjekt'*; Fr. *sujet;* It. *sogget'to.*) A melodic phrase or motive on which a composition or movement is founded ; a theme ; opp. to *answer*. (Also *antecedent, dux, guida, proposta*, etc.)—Compare *Soggetto*.

Subme'diant. The third scale-tone below the tonic ; the 6th degree.

Suboc'tave. The octave below a given tone.—*Suboctave-coupler*, an organ-coupler bringing into action keys an octave below those struck, either on the same manual or another.

Subordinate chords. Chords not fun-damental or principle ; the triads on the 2nd, 3rd, 6th, and 7th degrees, and all chords of the seventh but the dominant chord.

Subprincipal. A subbass (pedal-) stop of 32-foot pitch, of the open diapason class.

Subsemifu'sa (Lat.) A 32nd-note(medieval).

Subsemitone. The subtonic, or leading-tone (Lat. *subsemito'nium modi*).

Substitution. In contrapuntal progression, the resolution (or preparation) of a dissonance by substituting, for the proper tone of resolution (preparation), its higher or lower octave in some other part.

Substitution (Fr.) Change of fingers.

Subtonic. The leading-note.

Succentor (Lat.) A subcantor ; also, the singer of a lower or bass part.

Succession. 1. Progression.—2. Sequence.

Suf'flöte (Ger.) See *Sifflöte*.

Suffoca'to (It., "suffocated".) Damped, muffled.

Su'gli, Su'i (It.) On the (comp. *Sul*).

Suite (Fr.) A cyclical instrumental composition consisting of a set or series of pieces in various idealized dance-forms. It originated, presumably, in the practice of the town-bands, during the later middle ages, of stringing together a succession of dance-tunes, differing in character and form but alike in key. These are the characteristic features of the old Suite, which was taken up in the 17th century by composers as a form of clavier-composition under the name of *Partie* or *Partita*. The extension of the primitive forms, naturally resulting from instrumental treatment at the hands of Italian and German musicians, was cut short by Couperin (1668-1733), who in many respects served Bach as a model ; the *Kammersuiten* of the latter mark the culmination of the old suite-form.—The earlier artistic Suites have 4 principal movements or divisions : The Allemande, Courante, Saraband, and Gigue; other forms introduced at will (*intermezzi*) are the Bourrée, Branle, Gavotte, Minuet, Musette, Passepied, Loure, Pavane, etc.; such an *intermezzo* was usually brought in between the Saraband and Gigue, rarely before the former.—The *modern orchestral Suite* can hardly be called a revival of the old form, as the separate movements are not necessarily or generally in danceform, nor do they keep to one key; it more nearly resembles the *Divertimento*, both in character and form.

Suivez (Fr., "follow".) Same as *Colla parte.*—Also, "continue," "go on" (i. e., in like manner); *simile.*

Sujet (Fr.) Subject.

Sul, sull', sul'la, sul'le (It.) On the, near the (all contractions of *su*, on, with the definite article)... *Sulla corda La*, on the *A*-string... *Sulla tastie'ra*, near or by the fingerboard... *Sul ponticel'lo*, near the bridge (*see Ponticello*).

Summational tone. See *Acoustics*, §3, *b*.

Suona're (It.) Same as *Sonare*... *Suona'ta*, see *Sonata*... *Suo'no*, sound, tone; *suoni armo'nici*, harmonics, flageolet-tones.

Super (Lat.) Above, over.

Superdominant. The 6th degree of any major or minor scale.

Superfluous. (Fr. *superflu.*) See *Augmented.*

Supe'rius (Lat.) Formerly, the highest part.

Superoctave. 1. An organ-stop pitched 2 octaves higher than the diapasons (i. e. of 2-foot pitch).—2. An organ-coupler bringing into action keys an octave above those struck, either on the same manual or another.—3. The octave above a given tone.

Supertonic. The 2nd degree of a diatonic scale.

Suppliche'vole, Supplichevolmen'te (It.) In a style expressive of supplication, entreaty, pleading.

Support. An accompaniment, or subordinate part.

Supposed bass. See *Bass.*

Sur (Fr.) On, upon, over... *Sur une corde*, see *Sopra una corda.*

Surabondant (Fr.) See *Note* (Fr.)

Suraigu, -ë (Fr.) Superacute.

Surdeli'na (It.) See *Sourdeline.*

Surprise cadence. See *Cadence.*

Sus-dominante (Fr.) Superdominant.

Suspended cadence. See *Cadence.*

Suspension. (Ger. *Vor'halt;* Fr. *suspension;* It. *sospensio'ne.*) A disso-nance caused by suspending (holding back) a tone or some tones of a chord while the other tones progress; the dissonance of a seventh or second, occurring immediately before a chord which would have entered entire were it not for the suspension; e. g.

—Double (triple) suspension, one in which 2 (3) tones are suspended.—The suspended tone itself is also termed a suspension.

Suspi'rium (Lat.) A quarter-rest; in mensurable notation, a minim-rest.

Süss (Ger.) Sweet(ly).

Sustain. To hold during the full time-value (of notes); specifically, to perform in *sostenuto* or *legato style*... *Sustained note*, see *Organ-point.*—*Sustaining-pedal*, see *Pedal.*

Sus-tonique (Fr.) Supertonic. (Also *Sutonique.*)

Susurran'do, Susurran'te (It.) In a whispering, murmurous tone.

Sveglia'to (It.) Lively, animated, brisk.

Svel'to (It.) Light, nimble.

Swell. 1. In the organ, a contrivance for producing a *crescendo* and *diminuendo*. By enclosing a partial organ (swell-organ) in a box, the front of which could be opened or shut at will, this end was attained. In the modern (so-called *Venetian*) swell the front of the swell-box is composed of movable parallel shutters (swell-blinds); when these shutters are horizontal, they are usually opened by a lever (swell-pedal) worked by the organist's right foot, and close automatically when the lever is released (but comp. *Balance swell-pedal*); when vertical, they are closed by a spring.—Formerly other devices were employed, notably the *nag's-head swell*, a single broad shutter in front of an echo-organ, to be raised or lowered.—On the harpsichord a swell was obtained by a movable cover.—2. A crescendo (◁——▷), or crescendo and diminuendo (◁—— ——▷)... *Swell-keyboard*, the manual controlling the swell-organ, generally the one next above the great-organ manual... *Swell-organ* (Ger. [compare *Oberwerk*]; Fr. *clavier de récit;* It. *organo d'espressione*), see *Swell* 1, and *Organ.* (In organ-music abbr. *Sw.,* or *Swell.*)

Syl'be (Ger.) Syllable.

Syllabic melody. One each tone of which is sung to a separate syllable (Ger. *silla'bischer Gesang;* Fr. *chant syllabique*); opp. to *Slurred melody.*

Syllable-name. A syllable taken as the name of a note or tone, as *Do* for *C;* opp. to *Letter-name.*

Sympathetic string. A string (e. g. the octave-strings stretched over the unisons in Blüthner's "aliquot grands") adjusted so as to be affected by the vibrations of other strings or resonant bodies, and not by being itself struck, plucked, or bowed.

Symphone'ta (Lat.) Polyphony, polyphonic writing.

Symphoni'a (Gk. and Lat.) 1. In Greek music, a consonance.—2. (Medieval.) A name formerly applied to various different instr.s, as the hurdy-gurdy and virginal.—3. A symphony.

Symphon'ic. (Ger. *sympho'nisch;* Fr. *symphonique;* It. *sinfo'nico.*) Relating or pertaining to a symphony... *Symphonic poem* (Ger. *sympho'nische Dich'tung;* Fr. *poème symphonique*), an orchestral composition allied, both in its length and in the power and variety of its instrumentation, to the symphony; but radically differing from the latter by discarding the orthodox form (division into the regular movements), and in being directly based on and receiving its inspiration from a *program* (the *poem;* i. e., it is conceived as an instrumental poem, depicting events, scenes, or moods like a word-poem). This "fairest flower" of program-music can necessarily have no fixed form, but its continuous flow is moulded into a sort of unity by the repetition of the same theme variously modified and transformed.

Symphonie (Fr.) 1. Symphony.—2. Harmony, euphony.—3. An instrumental accomp.—4. The string-group in the orchestra.—5. Orchestra.

Symphonie-Ode (Ger.) A symphonic composition combining chorus and orchestra (Fr. *ode-symphonie*).

Sympho'niker (Ger.) A composer for full (symphony- or opera-) orchestra.

Sympho'nion. 1. A pfte. combined with an organ flute-stop, inv. in 1839 by Fr. Kaufmann of Dresden.—2. A music-box, consisting essentially of a graduated comb-like series of steel teeth, and a thin flat metallic disk caused to rotate by clockwork, and in which the notes are punched in such a manner that short tongues of metal project from the lower side of the disk ; in rotating over the steel teeth, these tongues engage a series of small wheels furnished with projecting studs, which twang the teeth in the same way as the studs on the cylinder of the ordinary Swiss music-box. The instr.s are made in all sizes, and as the note-disks are interchangeable, the repertory is limited only by their number (now several thousand).

Symphoniste (Fr.) 1. A composer.—2. A symphony-writer.—3. A member of a symphony-orchestra.

Sym'phony. (Ger. *Symphonie', Sinfonie';* It. *sinfoni'a;* Fr. *symphonie*, from the Gk. *symphoni'a,* "consonance", i. e. consonant interval.) 1. A form of instrumental composition developed from the *Overture* (*q. v.*), the 3 divisions of which latter were separated towards the middle of the 18th century, by composers writing purely orchestral pieces, into 3 distinct movements ; the 4th (the Minuet) being introduced by Haydn, who thus consummated the modern 4-movement form. This form is identical with that of the Sonata (comp. *Form*). For the Minuet, Beethoven substituted the *Scherzo*, which since then has been the typical form of the 3rd movement. Haydn also transferred the "first-movement" form of the sonata to the symphony, and utilized the individual timbres of the various instr.s for contrasts in orchestration ; the perfection of instrumental individualization is the work of Mozart and Beethoven, and the latter enlarged the symphony-orchestra to its modern status (comp. *Orchestra*). The usual plan of the symphony is now I (*Allegro* [in first-movement form, often with a slow introductory division]) ; II (*Adagio*); III (*Scherzo*); IV (*Allegro* or *Presto*).—Its latest development is the Symphonic Poem.—2. Same as *Ritornello* 1.—3. A medieval name for several instr.s, as the Hurdy-gurdy, Bagpipe, etc.

Syn'copate. To efface or shift the accent of a tone or chord falling on a naturally strong beat, by tying it over from the preceding weak beat ; a tone or chord so robbed of its accent is termed *syncopated.*

Syncopa'tion. (Ger. *Syn'kope;* Fr. *syncope;* It. *sin'cope.*) The tying of a weak beat to the following strong beat, effacing the accent naturally falling on the latter and in most cases shifting it to the (naturally unaccented) weak beat. Syncopation may take place in one, several, or all parts ; in the first two cases as an anticipation, a suspension, or a resolution of either (as a resolution the accent is weakest, or quite elided, particularly when concluding a phrase) ; in the third case, or in anticipation, the accent is apt to have a *sforzando* character.

Synem'menon. See *Greek music.*

Syn'kope (Ger.) Syncopation... *Synkopie'ren,* to syncopate.

Synonyme (Fr.) Same as *Homophone,* which latter term is more correct.

Synton'ic comma. See *Comma.*

Syntonolyd'ian. Same as *Hypolydian* (see *Mode*).

Syringe (Fr.) Syrinx.

Syr'inx. See *Pandean pipes.*

System. 1. A number of staves braced together for writing out a full score... 2. (Ger.) See *Liniensystem.*

Syste'ma 1. (Gk.) In Greek music, a comparatively wide interval filled out by intermediate tones ; e. g. a tetrachord.—2. (Lat.) The staff.—3. The series of tones constituting a hexachord.

Système (Fr.) 1. The whole range of musical tones.—2. The compass of any given instr.

Syzygi'a (Lat.) A chord ; specifically, a triad... *S. compo'sita,* triad with doubled tone... *S. perfec'ta,* triad... *S. propin'qua,* chord in close harmony. ...*S. remo'ta,* chord in open harmony. ...*S. sim'plex,* the simple triad without doubled tones.

T.

T. An abbr. of *Talon, Tasto* (*t. s.* = tasto solo), *Tempo* (*a t.* = a tempo), *Tendre, Tenor, Toe* (in organ-music), *Tre* (T. C. = tre corde), and *Tutti.*

Tabal'lo (It.) See *Timpano.*

Tab'lature. 1. (Ger. *Tabulatur'.*) The rules and regulations for the poetry and song of the Meistersinger.—2. (Ger. *Tabulatur' ;* Fr. *tablature;* It. *intavola-tu'ra.*) An obsolete system of musical notation employed chiefly for the lute, viol, and organ, and most in vogue from the 15th century till early in the 18th.—The *organ-tablature* (also called *German t.*) used for keyboard instr.s was a system of alphabetical notation based on the division of the mus. scale into the octaves *C—H* (= *B*), *c—h* (= *b*), etc.; the melody (highest part) was often noted on a staff, the accompanying chords being expressed by vertical rows of letters. In the *lute-tablatures* (excepting the German) the tones were represented by letters (*French* or *English t.*) or numerals (earlier *Italian t.*) indicating the frets at which the strings were to be stopped, and were written on the lines or in the spaces of a kind of staff, said lines or spaces showing the number of strings on the instrument. The pitch of the tones represented by the letters or figures would therefore vary with the size of the lute, and was not a staff-notation in the modern sense.—Three leading features were common to nearly all systems of tablature : (1) The vertical disposition of the characters representing one chord ; (2) the use of bars to divide the measures ; (3) a system of signs for marking the time-value of the tones called for by letters or figures (or of the corresponding rests), these signs being written either above or below the latter, and signifying:

Note-Signs.	Rest-Signs.	Time-Value.
•	⸬	Brevis (𝄺)
ı	⊥	Semibrevis (𝅝)
⌐	⌐	Minima (𝅗𝅥)
⌐	⌐	Semiminima (𝅘𝅥)
⌐	⌐	Fusa (𝅘𝅥𝅮)
⌐	⌐	Semifusa (𝅘𝅥𝅯)

The hooks of consecutive equal notes were often run together thus ▬▬▬

or ⊣⊥⊢. Arbitrary variations from these general rules were, however, of frequent occurrence.—A new development of tablature is the Tonic Sol-fa system of notation.

Table (Fr.) Soundboard ; belly. (Also *table d'harmonie.*)... *Table de dessous*, back.

Table-music. See *Tafelmusik.*

Tabor. A small drum, like a tambourine without jingles ; formerly much used by pipers, who beat the tabor with the right hand as an accompaniment to a flageolet or pipe manipulated by the left... *Taboret, Tabret*, a small tabor.

Tab'ulature. See *Tablature.*

Ta'cent (Lat.) " Are silent". See *Tacet.*

Ta'cet (Lat.), **Ta'ce** or **Ta'ci** (It.) " Is silent"; signifies that an instrumental or vocal part so marked is omitted during the movement or number in question.

Tac'tus (Lat.) A beat.—In medieval music its time-value was styled *tactus major* when it marked a breve to a measure, and *tactus minor* when a semibreve.

Ta'felklavier (Ger.) A square pfte.— Also *ta'felförmiges Klavier'* ... *Ta'felmusik*, "table-music"; (a) music performed during repasts; (b) music so printed that several performers, sitting around a square table, could read their several parts from the same book. See *Part-book.*

Tail. Same as *Stem*... *Tailpiece.* (Ger. *Sai'tenhalter;* Fr. *cordier*, *queue*.) In the violin, etc., the piece of wood (usually ebony) to which the strings are attached behind the bridge.

Taille (Fr.) Tenor voice (now used only for church-music ; otherwise *ténor*). Also, the tenor violin... *Taille de basson*, same as *Oboè da caccia.*

Takt (Ger.) 1. A beat.—2. A measure. —3. Time... *Takt'accent*, measure-accent, primary accent... *Takt'art*, time, measure, rhythm... *Takt'erstickung*, syncopation... *Takt'fach*, a space. .. *Takt'fest*, steady in time... *Takt'glied*, measure-note... *Takt'halten*, to keep time ; keeping time... *Tak'tieren*, to beat time... *Tak'tierstab*, a baton. .. *Takt'mässig*, in time... *Takt'messer*, metronome... *Takt'note*, whole note. .. *Takt'pause*, measure-rest... *Takt'schlagen*, to beat time... *Takt'stock*, a

baton... *Takt'strich*, a bar... *Takt' teil*, beat, count ; *guter Taktteil*, strong beat ; *schlechter Taktteil*, weak beat. .. *Takt'vorzeichnung*, *Takt'zeichen*, time-signature... *Ein Takt wie vorher' zwei* (" one measure like two before "), same as *Doppio movimento*... *Im Takt*, a tempo.

Talon (Fr., " heel"). 1. Nut (of the bow.)—2. In pedal-playing, heel ; abbr. *t* (compare *Pointe* 2).—*Talon de la manche* (in the violin, etc.), heel (end of neck joining the body).

Tambour (Fr.) 1. A drum.—2. A drummer (also Ger.)—*Tambour chromatique*, see *Timbalarion*... *T. de basque*, tambourine... *T. roulante*, the long drum.

Tambou'ra, Tambu'ra. An Oriental instr. of the lute kind, having a round body, fretted fingerboard, and 3 or 4 strings.

Tambourin (Fr.) 1. A sort of tabor. —2. A French peasants' dance, in 2-4 time and lively tempo, often accomp. by the *tambourin* and *galoubet* (tabor and pipe).

Tambourine'. (Ger. *Tamburin'*; Fr. *tambour de basque;* It. *tamburi'no.*) A small drum played by striking it with the right hand, consisting of a shallow circular hoop of wood or metal with one head of parchment ; in apertures made around the hoop are fastened several pairs of loose metallic plates, called *jingles* from the noise they produce. Used principally in Spain and southern France as an accomp. to dancing ; occasionally employed in the (operatic) orchestra. In tambourine-music, notes with wavy stems ♪ ♪ ♪ call for the *roll;* notes with short vertical strokes over them ♩ ♩ ♩ for the *jingles.*

Tamburel'lo (It.) Tabor.

Tamburi'no (It.) 1. A drummer.—2. Tambourine.

Tambu'ro (It.) Side-drum... *Tamburo'ne*, the big drum, bass drum (also *Cassa grande*).

Tamis (Fr.) Pipe-rack (organ).

Tam-tam. 1. A gong.—2. A Hindu drum of elongated form. (Also *Tom-tom.*)

Tän'delnd (Ger.) In a toying, bantering style.

Tangent. (Ger. *Tangen'te.*) In the clavichord, a brass wedge fixed in the jack on the rear end of a key ; on depressing the key, the tangent struck and rubbed across the string, and remained bearing on it until the finger was lifted, thus both producing the tone and fixing its pitch... *Tangen'tenflügel* (Ger.), a clavichord shaped like a grand piano.

Tanti'no (It.) A little ; very little.

Tan'to. (It.) As much, so much ; too (much); *allegro non tanto*, not too fast (here equiv. to *troppo*); *a tanto possi'- bile*, as much as possible.

Tanz (Ger.) A dance... *Tanz'lieder*, dance-songs ; *Tanz'stücke*, dance-tunes (instrumental); the former were the original form of dance-music (*Tanz'- musik*), the latter being at first mere imitations of them. (Comp. *Form* II, 3.)

Tarantel'la (It.), **Tarentelle** (Fr.) A dance of southern Italy, in 6-8 time, the rate of speed gradually increasing, and the mode alternating irregularly between major and minor.—In modern music, an instrumental piece in 3-8 or 6-8 time, very rapid tempo (*presto*), and bold and brilliant style.

Tardamen'te (It.) Slowly, lingeringly. ...*Tardan'do*, *Tarda'to*, see *Ritardan- do*... *Tar'do*, slow, lingering.

Tartini's tone. A differential tone (comp. *Acoustics*).

Tasch'engeige (Ger.) A kit.

Tasseau (Fr.; Ger. *Herz.*) The "mould" on which ribs and blocks of a violin are set up.

Tastatur' (Ger.), **Tastatu'ra** (It.) Keyboard, fingerboard.

Tas'te (Ger.) Key (digital or pedal)... *Tas'tenstäbchen*, fret. (The usual term, *Bund*, means literally the *space between two frets*.)

Tastie'ra (It.) Keyboard ; fingerboard. ...*Sulla t.*, near the fingerboard (direction in violin-playing).

Ta'sto (It.) 1. Key (digital).—2. Fret.—3. Touch.—4. Fingerboard ; *sul tasto*, same as *sulla tastiera*... *Tasto solo* (abbr. *t. s.*), "one key alone"; a direction in thorough-bass, signifying that the bass part is to be played, either as written or in octaves, without chords (sign **0**, or ‿).

Tattoo'. Military drum-signal or bugle-call for retiring at night.

Te. For *si*, in the Tonic Sol-fa system.

Té (Fr.) C♯ (for *ut dièse*).

Tech'nic, Technique'. (Ger. *Tech'nik.*) All that relates to the purely mechanical part of vocal or instrumental performance.—In some German works treating on pfte.-technique, a distinction is made between *Mecha'nik* (the merely mechanical drill of fingers and wrist, apart from its application in playing), and *Technik* (the acquired skill and dexterity in actual performance).

Tech'nicon. A finger-gymnasium, or apparatus for training and strengthening the hands and fingers of players on keyboard instr.s ; inv. in 1889 by J. Brotherhood of Montreal, Canada.

Techniphone. Earlier name of the (improved) Virgil Practice-Clavier (q. v.)

Tede'sco,-a (It.) German...*Alla te- desca*, in the German style ; "the term '*tedesca*', says Bülow, has reference to waltz-rhythm, and invites changes of time". [Quoted from GROVE.]...*Lira tedesca*, hurdy-gurdy.

Te deum. See *Ambrosian Hymn.*

Teil (Ger.) A part... *Teil'töne*, partial tones.

Telephone-harp. An instr. so connected with a telephone as to render music performed at a distance audible to an audience.

Telltale. See APPENDIX.

Te'ma (It.) Theme.

Temperament. (Ger. *Temperatur'*; Fr. *tempérament*; It. *temperamen'to.*) A compromise between the acoustic purity of theoretically exact intervals, and the harmonic discrepancies arising from their practical employment.—E. g., taking the tone *C* as a starting-point, and ascending by quint-strides through a series of 12 perfect fifths (*C...B♯*), we reach a tone (*B♯*) which, on instr.s of fixed intonation (like the pfte.), is identical in pitch with the sixth octave of *C* (*c⁵*), but which, as an acoustic interval, is by $^{74}/_{73}$ higher than *c⁵*. A similar result is obtained by descending through 12 fifths to *D♭♭*, which proves to be lower by $^{74}/_{73}$ than the corresponding lower octave of C. Now, by setting *C = B♯ = D♭♭*, and equally distributing the deviation $^{74}/_{73}$ among the 12 quint-tones in either series, i. e. by *tempering* each fifth, the deviation for each becomes practically unnoticeable on keyboard instr.s ; such equal distribution is called *equal temperament.*— Another example : The tone *A♭*, as

the major tierce below C, has the ratio
$4:5$; the tone $G\sharp$, as *tierce of the
tierce* of C, has $25:32$; that is, $G\sharp$ is
by $\frac{125}{128} = \frac{5}{4} \div \frac{25}{32}$ lower than $A\flat$.—If
it be attempted, as formerly, to take
note of and employ in practice even
only the most noticeable of the different shades of intonation (e. g. by building keyboards with separate keys for
$c\sharp$ and $d\flat$, $d\sharp$ and $e\flat$, etc., etc.), the
tones in each octave of our keyboard
instr.s would evidently have to be
greatly increased in number beyond the
ordinary chromatic scale of 12 degrees.
However, a perfect fifth ($^3/_2$) differs
from a tempered one by only about $\frac{885}{884}$
[HELMHOLTZ], an interval close to the
extreme limit of perceptible differences
in pitch, and the use of such an interval instead of a perfect fifth can in very
few cases be regarded as objectionable.
In the system of equal temperament
the series of fifths, instead of going on
indefinitely, returns to the starting-
point C, thus forming a circle, as it
were; this progression from end to
end of the series is called the *Circle of
Fifths*:

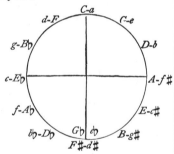

Unequal temperament is a system in
which the excess in the series of fifths
is not equally apportioned, some intervals being purer, and others less pure,
than in equal temperament. In the
mean-tone system, once extensively employed, the major thirds were tuned
true, and divided into two equal tones
forming a mean between the greater
and lesser whole tone, hence the term
mean-tone; each fifth was ¼ comma
too flat, making the 12th in the series
about 2 commas out of tune, this
error being usually laid upon the fifth
the system also had 4 thirds
which were too sharp by nearly the same interval. The

discordant effect produced by chords
containing any of these anomalous intervals was called the "wolf".

Tempestosamen'te (It.) Impetuously,
passionately; *tempesto'so*, impetuous,
impassioned.

Tempête (Fr., "tempest".) A lively
dance of modern (Parisian) origin, in
2-4 time, and danced like a quadrille,
with some modifications of the steps.

Tem'po (It.; Ger. *Zeit'mass*.) 1. Rate
of speed, Movement 1. (Compare
Tempo-marks.)—2. Time, measure;
beat...*A tempo*, or *tempo primo*, return
to the original tempo...*Tempo alla
bre've*, see *Breve;* alla semibre've*, see
T. ordina'rio...*Tempo bina'rio*, duple
time...*Tempo com'modo*, at a convenient pace...*Tempo de'bole*, weak beat.
..*Tempo di Ballo, Bole'ro, Minuet'to*,
etc., see *Ballo*, etc...*Tempo di primo
par'te*, in the tempo of the first part...
Tempo for'te, strong beat...*Tempo
giu'sto*, see *Giusto*...*Tempo maggio're*,
same as *t. alla breve*...*Tempo mino're,
T. ordina'rio*, (*a*) 4-4 time of 4 beats
to the measure; opp. to *t. alla breve;*
(*b*) same as *t. primo*...*Tempo perdu'to*,
irregular, unsteady tempo...*Tempo
primo, primie'ro*, see *A tempo*, above.
..*Tempo reggia'to*, same as *Colla parte*.
..*Tempo ruba'to*, see *Rubato*...*Tempo
terna'rio*, triple time...*L'iste'so tempo*,
or *Lo stesso tempo*, the same tempo;
indicates, at a change of rhythm, that
the pace remains the same. (Comp.
Istesso.)..*Senza tempo*, same as *a
piace're*.

Tempo-mark. (Ger. *Tem'pobezeichnung*.)
A word or phrase indicating the pace
or speed of a movement, and thus
establishing the absolute time-value of
the notes.—Generally accepted tempo-
marks were hardly known before the
beginning of the 17th century, and
were used sparingly until the 18th.—
There are 3 classes: (1) indicating a
steady rate of speed; (2) indicating
acceleration; (3) indicating a slackening
of the pace.—They do not in themselves indicate a fixed and positive rate
of speed, but only the general character
of the movement; consequently, for
the sake of precision, a metronome-
mark is often added to the tempo-mark;
e. g. "*Adagio*, M. M. $\flat= 56$," signifies a tranquil movement in which a
quarter-note has the time-value of one
beat of the metronome set at 56. Fur-

thermore, various qualifying words are added (comp. the several Key-words).

CLASS I.
(Indicating a steady rate of speed.)

Larghis′simo, molto largo **Lar′go** (broad, stately) Largamen′te Larghet′to **Gra′ve** (heavy, dragging) **Len′to** (slow) Adagis′simo **Ada′gio** (slow, tranquil) Adagiet′to	Group I. General signification of terms is SLOW.
Andanti′no **Andan′te** (moving, going along) [Modera′to] Allegret′to Allegramen′te **Allegro** (brisk, lively) [con mo′to, viva′ce] [agita′to, appassiona′to] **Pre′sto** (rapid) [con fuo′co, velo′ce] Prestis′simo	Group II. General signification of terms is FAST.

CLASS II.
(Indicating acceleration.)

Acceleran′do (gradually accelerating)
Stringen′do
Affrettan′do } (suddenly accelerating, usually with a crescendo.)
Incalzan′do
Dop′pio movimen′to (twice as fast)
Più mos′so } (a steady rate of speed, *faster*
Velo′ce } than preceding movement)

CLASS III.
(Indicating a slackening in speed.)

Rallentan′do
Ritardan′do
Largan′do
Tardan′do } (gradually growing slower)
Slentan′do
Strascinan′do
Ritenu′to } (a sudden drop to a slower rate
Me′no mos′so } of speed)
Calan′do
Deficien′do
Mancan′do
Moren′do } (growing slower and softer)
Sminuen′do
Smorzan′do

Temporiser (Fr.) To play an accomp. *colla parte.*

Temps (Fr.) Beat... *T. faible (secondaire)*, weak beat; *t. fort (sensible)*, strong beat.

Tempus (Lat., "time".) In medieval music, the *tempus* was simply *the time-value of the breve* (except in case of Alteration). The *tempus perfectum* (sign $\bigcirc$), was the original kind, in which the breve was equal to 3 semibreves; in the tempus imperfectum (sign C) later introduced, the breve had the value of 2 semibreves. (Comp. Notation, § 3.).. *Tempus bina′rium (terna′rium)*, duple (triple) time.

Ten′ebræ (Lat. pl., "gloom, darkness".)

In the R. C. Church, the lamentations (matins and lauds) sung especially on Good Friday in the Sistine Chapel, while the candles burning at the altar are extinguished one by one.

Te′nero,-a (It.) Soft, tender, delicate. .. *Teneramen′te*, or *con tenerez′za*, tenderly, delicately; nearly equiv. to *dolce*, but with somewhat more of passion.

Teneur (Fr.) The *canto fermo* in a choral or hymn-tune.

Ten′or. (Ger. *Tenor′;* Fr. *ténor* or *taille;* It. *teno′re.*) 1. The high natural male voice. The Germans distinguish 2 classes of tenors, the *Hel′dentenor* (dramatic tenor), and *ly′rischer Tenor* (lyric tenor) ; the compass of the former is from *c* to *b′♭* the voice full and powerful throughout, with a barytone timbre ; the range of the latter is the about from *d* to *c²* (*c²♯*) lowest tones usually rather weak, the high tones brilliant, and the timbre generally bright and pleasing. The Italian terms nearly corresponding to the above are (1) *teno′re robu′sto, tenore di for′za*, and (2) *tenore di gra′zia, t. leggie′ro;* but they are very variously and arbitrarily employed.—2. The part taken by a tenor voice ; hence, by transference, a prefix to names of instr.s taking parts of similar compass, as *tenor trombone;* specifically, the tenor violin (viola).—3. Tenor (from Lat. *tenere*, to hold), originally "a holding, holding fast", was applied to the melody (as the unchanging part) of the Gregorian chants sung by men, and hence to the high male voice.—4. In medieval music, tenor also signified (*a*) a hold ; (*b*) ambitus (of a mode) ; (*c*) the initial tone of the EVOVAE.— *Tenor-C*, small *c... Tenor-clef*, see Clef... *Tenor violin*, the viola.

Teno′re (It.) Tenor 1... *T. buf′fo*, a tenor who sings comic roles... *T. contralti′no*, a light tenor voice resembling the contralto in timbre... *T. di for′za, di gra′zia, leggie′ro, robu′sto*, see *Tenor* 1.— *T. di mezzo carat′tere*, a tenor voice of barytone timbre (see *Heldentenor*, under *Tenor* 1).

Tenori′no (It.) A falsetto tenor voice or singer ; specifically, a *castrato*.

Tenorist′ (Ger.; Fr. *ténoriste;* It. *tenori′sta.*) Tenor-singer.

Tenoroon'. The *oboè da caccia.*

Tenor'schlüssel, -zeichen (Ger.) Tenor-clef.

Tenth. (Ger. *De'zime;* Fr. *dixième;* It. *de'cima.*) 1. An interval of an octave plus 2 degrees.—2. Same as *Decima* 2.

Tenu, -e (Fr.) Held, sustained.

Tenue (Fr.) A sustained tone, or organ-point.

Tenu'to (It., "held".) A direction signifying (*a*) generally, that a tone so marked is to be sustained for its full time-value; and (*b*) occasionally, *legato.* ..*Forte tenuto* (*ften.*), *forte* throughout... *Tenuto-mark,* a short stroke over a note, with signification as at (*a*).— *Tenute* [*le note* implied], [the notes] sustained or held.

Tepidamen'te (It.) In an even, unimpassioned style.

Teponaz'tli (Aztec.) A species of drum still used by the aborigines of Central America and Mexico. It consists of a section of a log (left round in the ruder specimens, but carefully squared in the more artistic ones) in a horizontal position, from 2 to 5 feet long, hollowed out on the under side so as to leave the ends 3 or 4 inches thick and the top part (belly) a few lines through; in the belly 2 parallel incisions are made lengthwise, and connected by a shorter one crosswise, the 3 assuming the shape of the letter ⌶. The 2 tongues left between, when struck by the sticks, yield 2 different tones, at an interval—in various instr.s—of a third, fourth, fifth, sixth, or octave apart. It serves to mark the rhythm, and as an imperfect bass, in the aboriginal music. It is played with 2 sticks, the heads of which are covered with wool or an elastic gum.

Ter (Lat.) Thrice; indicates that a passage, or (in songs) a verse or part of one, is to be repeated twice. (Also comp. *Bis.*)... *Ter unca,* the 3-hooked semifusa.

Terce. 1. See *Tierce* 4.—2. The 3rd of the canonical hours.

Tercet (Fr.) A triplet;—in poetry, a group of 3 rhyming lines.

Ter'nary. (Fr. *ternaire;* It. *terna'rio.*) Composed of, or progressing by, threes. ..*Ternary form,* Rondo-form... *Ternary measure,* simple triple time.

Terpo'dion. A six-octave keyboard instr., similar to Chladni's clavicylinder, with wood substituted for glass as the tone-producing medium; inv. by J. D. Buschmann of Berlin in 1816.

Ter'tia (Lat.) A third or tierce... *Tertia modi,* 3rd degree of a scale.

Tertian'. (Ger. *Tertian zwei'fach.*) An organ-stop consisting of a tierce and larigot combined.

Terz (Ger.), **Ter'za** (It.) The interval of a third... *Terza ma'no* (It., "third hand"), an octave-coupler... *Terzade'cima* (It.), *Terzde'zime* (Ger.), the interval of a thirteenth... *Terzdezimo'le* (Ger.), a tredecuplet... *Terzett'* (Ger.), *Terzet'to* (It.), properly, a vocal (seldom an instrumental) trio; now generally called *Trio*... *Terz'flöte* (Ger.), a small transverse flute pitched a third above the ordinary flute... *Terzi'na* (It.), a triplet... *Terzo suo'no* (It.), a differential tone... *Terzquartsext'ak-kord* (Ger.), chord of the third, fourth, and sixth ($^6_4$)... *Terzquintsext'akkord* (Ger.), chord of the (third), fifth and sixth ($^6_3$)... *Terz'töne* (Ger., pl.), tierce-tones.

Tessitu'ra (It., "web, framework"). The region covered by the main body of the tones of a given part, infrequent high or low tones not included. The nearest English equivalent is to say that the part "lies" high or low.

Te'sto (It.) 1. See *Soggetto.*—2. Same as *Libretto.*

Tête (Fr.) Head (of a note); scroll.

Tet'rachord. 1. A 4-stringed instr.—2. The interval of a perfect fourth.—3. The scale-series of 4 tones contained in a perfect fourth (comp. *Greek music*). ..*Tetrachor'dal,* relating to or consisting of tetrachords... *Tetrachordal system,* the original form of the Tonic Sol-fa system.

Tetrachor'don (Gk.) 1. A tetrachord. —2. A variety of the piano-violin.

Tet'rad. A name suggested, but not to any extent adopted, for *chord of the seventh;*—analogous to *Triad.*

Tetradiapa'son. The interval of 4 octaves. (Also *quadruple diapason, octave,* or *eighth.*)

Tet'raphone. See *Tetratone.*

Tetrapho'nia. See *Organum.*

Tet'raphony. (Medieval.) Diaphony for 4 parts.

Tet′ratone. An interval embracing 3 whole tones ; an augm. fourth.

Text. The words of vocal music.

Theil (Ger.) See *Teil.*

Thematic composition. A style based on the contrapuntal treatment or development of one or more themes.

Theme. (Ger. *The′ma;* Fr. *thème;* It. *te′ma.*) Same as *Subject.*—Specifically, a theme is an extended and rounded-off subject with accompaniment, in period-form, proposed as a groundwork for elaborate variations (*tema con variazio′ni*).

Theor′bo. (Ger. *Theor′be;* Fr. *théorbe,* It. *tior′ba, tuor′ba.*) One of the various double-necked bass lutes so popular in the 17th century, the bass strings (accompaniment-strings, diapasons) of which were not stopped on the finger-board, but were stretched beside it to a separate peg-box, which latter, in the theorbo, lay next to the other, though somewhat higher up in the head. In its day it was an important member of the orchestra. (Comp. *Lute.*)

The′sis (Gk.) The down-beat, strong beat.

Third. (Ger. *Terz;* Fr. *tierce;* It. *ter′za.*) See *Interval.*—The third in a diatonic scale is also called the *mediant.*

Thirteenth. An interval embracing an octave and a sixth ; a compound sixth.

Thirty-second-note. (Comp. *Note.*) A note having half the time-value of a 16th-note ; a demisemiquaver...*32nd-rest,* a rest (𝄿) corresponding in value to the above.

Thorough-bass. (Ger. *General′bass;* Fr. *basse chiffrée;* It. *basso conti′nuo.*) A species of mus. shorthand in which chords are indicated by figures written over a running bass (briefly explained under *Chord*). It originated in Italy (*basso continuo,* or, for short, *continuo*) toward the close of the 16th century, and for 200 years was the common method of notation for accompaniments by the organ or cembalo. It is now principally employed in mus. theory, in teaching the science of chords.

Three-lined octave. See *Pitch, abso lute.*

Three-quarter fiddle. See *Violino piccolo,* under *Violino.*

Three-time, 3-time. Triple time.

Thren′ody. A song of lamentation ; a dirge.

Thrice-accented octave. See *Pitch, absolute.*

Thumb-position. One of the high positions in 'cello playing, in which the thumb quits the neck of the instr.

Thumb-string. Melody-string of the banjo.

Tib′ia (Lat.) The direct flute ; also, the name of various organ-stops... *T. utricula′ris,* the bagpipe... *Tibi′cen* (pl. *tibi′cines*), a flute-player.

Tie. (Ger. *Bin′debogen;* Fr. *liaison;* It. *fa′scia.*) A curved line joining 2 notes of like pitch which are to be sounded as one note equal to their united time-value... *Tied notes,* (*a*) notes joined by a tie ; (*b*) notes (like eighth-notes, 16th-notes, etc.) the hooks of which are run together in one or more thick strokes, e. g. ♫♫.

Tief (Ger.) Deep, low, grave.

Tier. Same as *Rank* (organ).

Tierce. 1. Same as *Third.*—2. The fourth harmonic of a given tone.—3. In the organ, a mutation-stop pitched 2⅗ octaves above the diapason ; now used, if at all, as a component of a mixture-stop.—4. One of the canonical hours. .. *Tierce-tones,* see *Pitch,* §2.

Tierce (Fr.) Tierce 1 and 4... *T. de Picardie,* a major third in the closing chord of a minor movement... *T. cou-lée* (slurred third), a grace written (*en montant*), or (*en descendant*); see *Slide.*

Tige (Fr.) Stick (of bow); also *baguette.*

Timbalarion (Fr) A set of 8 drums of different sizes, each furnished with a pedal, on which diatonic and chromatic scales, and some chords, can be played. Also *Tambour chromatique.*

Timbale (Fr.), **Timbal′lo** (It.) Kettle-drum.

Timbre (Fr.; It. *tim′bro.*) 1. Quality of tone.—2. A fixed bell without a clapper, struck from outside by a hammer. ..*Jeux de timbres,* Glockenspiel (*b*).— 3. Snare (of a drum).

Timbrel. A tambourine.

Time. 1. Same as Tempo.—2. (Ger. *Takt, Takt′art;* Fr. *mesure;* It.

tem'po.) The division of the measure into equal fractional parts of a whole note (𝅝), forming a standard for the accentuation or regular rhythmic flow of the movement. The sign for time is called the *time-signature*, and is usually in the form of a fraction set immediately after the clef at the beginning of the movement, the numerator indicating the number of notes of a given kind in each measure, while the denominator shows the kind of notes taken as the unit of measure; e.g. $\frac{3}{4}$ (three-four time) means 3 quarter-notes to a measure, | ♩ ♩ ♩ |; $\frac{12}{16}$ (twelve-sixteen time) means 12 sixteenth-notes to a measure, | ♬♬ ♬♬ |, etc. Among the numerous systems of nomenclature the ordinary *English method* is still that most in use, and is employed throughout this Dictionary; some others are appended for the purpose of comparison.—There are 2 classes of time, *Duple* and *Triple*.

In *Duple* time the *number of beats* to the measure is divisible by 2; in *Triple* time, by 3. There are also 2 subclasses, *Compound Duple time*, and *Compound Triple time*. In *compound duple time* the number of beats to each measure is still divisible by 2, but *each beat* contains, instead of an ordinary note divisible by 2, a dotted note (or its equivalent in other notes or rests) divisible by 3; hence the term *compound*, each simple beat being represented by a dotted or compound note divisible by 3, instead of a simple note divisible by 2. In *compound triple time* not only the number of beats in each measure is divisible by 3, but also each beat, as above. (See Table on p. 201.)

Another English classification is the following; it contains the times ordinarily employed, to which should be added *simple octuple time* $\frac{8}{8}$, and *compound octuple time* ($\frac{24}{16}$), both with eight beats to the measure:

(From Troutbeck & Dale's Music Primer.)

	Duple.	Triple.	Quadruple.
Simple	¢ or $\frac{2}{2}$ 𝅗𝅥 𝅗𝅥	$\frac{3}{2}$ 𝅗𝅥 𝅗𝅥 𝅗𝅥	¢ or $\frac{4}{2}$ 𝅗𝅥 𝅗𝅥 𝅗𝅥 𝅗𝅥
	$\frac{2}{4}$ ♩ ♩	$\frac{3}{4}$ ♩ ♩ ♩	C or $\frac{4}{4}$ ♩ ♩ ♩ ♩
	$\frac{2}{8}$ ♪ ♪	$\frac{3}{8}$ ♪ ♪ ♪	$\frac{4}{8}$ ♪ ♪ ♪ ♪
Compound	$\frac{6}{4}$ 𝅗𝅥. 𝅗𝅥.	$\frac{9}{4}$ 𝅗𝅥. 𝅗𝅥. 𝅗𝅥.	$\frac{12}{4}$ 𝅗𝅥. 𝅗𝅥. 𝅗𝅥. 𝅗𝅥.
	$\frac{6}{8}$ ♩. ♩.	$\frac{9}{8}$ ♩. ♩. ♩.	$\frac{12}{8}$ ♩. ♩. ♩. ♩.
	$\frac{6}{16}$ ♪. ♪.	$\frac{9}{16}$ ♪. ♪. ♪.	$\frac{12}{16}$ ♪. ♪. ♪. ♪.

A proposition made in the above work, to indicate the *compound* times by the same signatures as those of the *simple* times, merely *adding a dot* to the denominator to show the **tripartite** division:

Compound	$\frac{2}{2\cdot}$ 𝅗𝅥. 𝅗𝅥.	$\frac{3}{2\cdot}$ 𝅗𝅥. 𝅗𝅥. 𝅗𝅥.	$\frac{4}{2\cdot}$ 𝅗𝅥. 𝅗𝅥. 𝅗𝅥. 𝅗𝅥.
	$\frac{2}{4\cdot}$ ♩. ♩.	$\frac{3}{4\cdot}$ ♩. ♩. ♩.	$\frac{4}{4\cdot}$ ♩. ♩. ♩. ♩.
	$\frac{2}{8\cdot}$ ♪. ♪.	$\frac{3}{8\cdot}$ ♪. ♪. ♪.	$\frac{4}{8\cdot}$ ♪. ♪. ♪. ♪.

Triple Time.   Duple (or Common) Time.

Compound.   Simple.   Compound.   Simple.

Time-signature.	No. of beats in meas.	English.	German.	French.	Italian.
2 or ₵	2	Two-two (alla breve)	Zweizweiteltakt	Deux-deux	A cappella (or alla breve)
2/4	2	Two-four	Zweivierteltakt	Deux-quatre	Due-quarti (or quattro-due)
2/8	2	Two-eight	Zweiachteltakt	Deux-huit	Due-ottavi (or otto-due)
4/2	4	Four-two	Vierzweiteltakt	Quatre-deux	Quattro-mezzi (or due-quattro)
4/4 or C	4	Four-four (common)	Viervierteltakt	Quatre-quatre	Quattro-quarti (or quattro-quattro) (also binario, or ordinario)
4/8	4	Four-eight	Vierachteltakt	Quatre-huit	Quattro-ottavi (or quattro-otto)
4/16	4	Four-sixteen	Viersechzehnteltakt	Quatre-seize	Quattro-sedicesimi (or sedici-quattro)
8/8	8	Eight-eight	Achtachteltakt	Huit-huit	Otto-ottavi (or otto-otto)
6/2	2	Six-two	Sechszweiteltakt	Six-deux (or due-sei)	Sei-mezzi (or due-sei)
6/4	2	Six-four	Sechsvierteltakt	Six-quatre	Sei-quarti (or quattro-sei)
6/8	2	Six-eight	Sechsachteltakt	Six-huit	Sei-ottavi (or otto-sei)
6/16	2	Six-sixteen	Sechssechzehnteltakt	Six-seize	Sei-sedicesimi (or sedici-sei)
12/4	4	Twelve-four	Zwölfvierteltakt	Douze-quatre	Dodici-quarti (or quattro-dodici)
12/8	4	Twelve-eight	Zwölfachteltakt	Douze-huit	Dodici-ottavi (or otto-dodici)
12/16	4	Twelve-sixteen	Zwölfsechzehnteltakt	Douze-seize	Dodici-sedicesimi (or sedici-dodici)
24/16	8	Twenty-four-sixteen	Vierundzwanzig-sechzehnteltakt	Vingt-quatre-seize	(Sedici-ventiquattro)
3 or 3/1	3	Three-one	Dreieinteltakt	M. à trois un	(Uno-tre)
3/2	3	Three-two	Dreizweiteltakt	M. à trois deux	Tre-mezzi (or due-tre)
3/4	3	Three-four	Dreivierteltakt	M. à trois quatre	Tre-quarti (or quattro-tre)
3/8	3	Three-eight	Dreiachteltakt	M. à trois huit	Tre-ottavi (or otto-tre)
9/4	3	Nine-four	Neunvierteltakt	M. à neuf quatre	Nove-quarti (or quattro-nove)
9/8	3	Nine-eight	Neunachteltakt	M. à neuf huit	Nove-ottavi (or otto-nove)
9/16	3	Nine-sixteen	Neunsechzehnteltakt	M. à neuf seize	Nove-sedicesimi (or sedici-nove)
5/4	5	Five-four	Fünfvierteltakt	M. à cinq quatre	Cinque-quarti (or quattro-cinque)
5/8	5	Five-eight	Fünfachteltakt	M. à cinq huit	Cinque-ottavi (or otto-cinque)

German groupings: Einfacher. / Zusammengesetzter. / Einfacher. / Zusammenges. — Gerader Takt. — Ungerader Takt (or Tripeltakt).

French groupings: Division binaire. / Division ternaire. — Mesures à deux ou quatre temps. / Mesures à trois temps.

Italian groupings: Semplici. / Composti. / Semplici. / Composti. — Tempi pari. / Tempi dispari.

is deserving of notice as an ingenious way of marking the number and position of the beats ; the measure-note being found in each case by multiplying the denominator by 2. Still another, and highly ingenious, system, by Mr. Frederick Niecks, is given below ; for the terms duple and triple he substitutes *binary* and *ternary*, referring, not to the number of beats, but to the grouping of the measure-notes in twos and threes.

Simple Times.

Simple Binary Time	$\frac{2}{1}$ $\frac{2}{2}$ $\frac{2}{4}$ $\frac{2}{8}$
" Ternary "	$\frac{3}{2}$ $\frac{3}{4}$ $\frac{3}{8}$ $\frac{3}{16}$

Compound Times.

Duple Binary Time	$\frac{4}{2}$ $\frac{4}{4}$ $\frac{4}{8}$
" Ternary "	$\frac{6}{2}$ $\frac{6}{4}$ $\frac{6}{8}$ $\frac{6}{16}$
Triple " "	$\frac{9}{4}$ $\frac{9}{8}$ $\frac{9}{16}$
Quadruple " "	$\frac{12}{4}$ $\frac{12}{8}$ $\frac{12}{16}$

Finally, a system has been suggested in which the word *rhythm* is substituted for *time; duple* and *triple* retained for the *simple forms* of the measure ; while the *complex forms* are called *quadruple rhythm, sextuple rhythm, octuple rhythm*, etc.—However, the desideratum of any new system, i. e. the plain expression of the number of beats to the measure as well as of the number of notes of a given kind, is not yet attained ; and well-meant half-reforms serve only to make confusion worse confounded...*2-time, 3-time*, abbreviations of *duple* and *triple time* respectively.

Timidamen'te (It.) See *Ängstlich.*

Timidez'za, con (It.) In a style expressive of timidity or hesitation.

Timoro'so (It.) Timorous, fearful... *Timorosamen'te*, timorously, etc.

Tim'pano (It., pl. *tim'pani*.) Kettledrum... *Timpani coper'ti*, muffled drums.

Tintinna'bulum (Lat.), **Tintinna'bolo** (It.) A small bell.—Also, an ancient rattle, formed of little bells or small disks of metal.

Tintinnamen'to, Tintinni'o (It.) A tinkling or jingling.

Tin'to, con (It.) With shading ; *espressivo.*

Tior'ba (It.) Theorbo.

Tirade (Fr.) An extended slide ; a rapid run connecting two melody-notes.

Tirant (Fr.) 1. Stop-knob... *T. à accoupler*, coupler.—2. Button.—3. Cord of a drum.

Tirar'si, da (It., "to be drawn out".) Equiv. to the prefix "slide-" in the phrase *tromba da tirarsi* (slide-trumpet) and the like.

Tirasse (Fr.) In small organs, a pedal-keyboard having no pipes of its own, acting only on the lower keys of the manual ; also, a pedal-coupler.

Tira'ta (It.) See *Tirade.*

Tira'to (It.) Down-bow (*arco in giù*).

Ti'ra tut'to (It.) A combination-pedal or draw-stop bringing on the full power of an organ. (Fr. *grand jeu*.)

Tiré (Fr., "drawn.") Down-bow. Also *tirez*, "draw."

Tisch'harfe (Ger., "table-harp".) A variety of autoharp.

Tocca'ta (It., from *tocca're*, to touch.) An early species of composition for keyboard instr.s, originating in Italy toward the close of the 16th century. In style it is free and bold, approaching the (old) fantasia ; it has no distinctive form, but consists of runs and passages alternating with fugued or contrapuntal work, built up in the more elaborate specimens on a figure or theme, generally in equal notes, with a flowing style and lively, rapid movement.— *Toccati'na, Toccatel'la*, diminutives of *Toccata.*

Tocca'to (It.) In trumpet-music, a fourth (bass) trumpet-part added as a substitute for the kettledrums.

To'(d)tenmarsch (Ger.) Dead-march.

Ton (Ger.) A tone ; pitch ; key, mode, octave-scale...*Den Ton angeben*, to give the pitch ; *den Ton halten*, to keep the pitch... *Ton'abstand*, interval... *Ton'art*, Key 1 ; *Ton'artenverwandschaft*, key-relationship... *Ton'bestimmung*, the (mathematical) determination of tones... *Ton'bildung*, (a) production of tone ; (b) vocal culture... *Ton'dichter*, composer ; *Ton'dichtung*, composition .. *Ton'fall*, see *Ton'schluss*... *Ton'farbe*, "tone-color", timbre, quality. .. *Ton'folge*, series or succession of of tones... *Ton'führung*, melodic leading or progression... *Ton'fuss,* (a) a rhythm ; (b) a measure... *Ton'gebung,* production of tone ; intonation... *Ton'-geschlecht,* mode ; "the distinguishing of a chord or key (tonality) as major or minor" [RIEMANN]... *Ton'höhe,* pitch. .. *Ton'kunde,* science of music... *Ton'-kunst,* art of music, musical art ; music. .. *Ton'künstler,* musician... *Ton'lage,* pitch ; register... *Ton'leiter,* a scale ; *fünfstufige Tonleiter,* pentatonic scale. .. *Ton'loch,* a ventage... *Ton'malerei,* "tone-painting", imitative music, pro-gram-music... *Ton'messer,* monochord; sonometer ; siren... *Ton'messung,* see *Ton'bestimmung...* *Ton'rein* (of violin-strings), true to pitch, true fifths... *Ton'satz,* composing ; composition... *Ton'schluss,* cadence... *Ton'setzer,* com-poser... *Ton'setzkunst,* art of composi-tion... *Ton'sprache,* the language of tones (i. e. music)... *Ton'stück,* piece of music, composition... *Ton'stufe,* degree (of a scale)... *Ton'system,* sys-tem or theory of musical tones... *Ton'-umfang,* compass... *Ton'unterschied,* interval... *Ton'verwandschaft,* relation or affinity of tones... *Ton'verziehung,* tempo rubato... *Ton'werkzeug,* a mu-sical instr., either natural (voice) or arti-ficial... *Ton'zeichen,* a note or other sign representing a tone.

Ton (Fr.) 1. Tone ; pitch ; *donner le ton,* to give the pitch.—2. Mode.—3. Scale, key.—4. A crook (*ton de re-change*).—5. (Formerly) a tuning-fork. .. *Ton bouché,* stopped tone (horn)... *Ton d'église,* church-mode... *Ton de rechange,* crook... *Ton entier,* whole tone... *Ton feint,* see *Fictum...* *Ton majeur* (*mineur*), a major (minor) key. .. *Ton ouvert,* open or natural tone (on a wind-instr.)... *Ton relatif,* related key... *Ton générateur,* one of the 7 natural tones.

Tonal. Pertaining to tones, or to a tone, mode, or key... *Tonal fugue,* see Fugue... *Tonal imitation,* imitation not overstepping the limits of the key of a composition ; non-modulating imi-tation.

Tonal'ity. (Ger. *Tonalität';* Fr. *tonal-ité.*) The term *Tonality,* as contrasted with *Key,* is distinguished by its broader significance and wider scope. *Key* de-notes simply the *mode* (of a piece) and the pitch of that mode ; strictly, it re-fers solely to the harmonies constructed from the tones of its own diatonic scale.

On quitting these harmonies, even by touching an "altered chord", it tres-passes on the domain of *tonality* ; for—here is the dividing line—*key* embraces the *diatonic harmonies* referable to *one tonic chord* as the point whence they depart and whither they return, whereas *tonality,* taking this same tonic chord as a starting-point, includes any and every harmony related to it, so long as no actual change of tonic is brought about by a modulation. *Tonality* might therefore be briefly defined as the chords grouped around and attracted by one central tonic chord, and thus appears as founded upon the relations of chords independent (in a measure) of key. (Comp. *Phone,* § 4.)

Tone. (Ger. *Ton;* Fr. *son, ton;* It. *tuo'no, suo'no.*) See *Acoustics... Tone-color,* quality of tone.

Tongue. 1 (*noun*). Same as *Reed;* but, in the so-called reed of an organ-pipe, the *tongue* is the vibratile slip of metal producing the tone.—2 (*verb*). To employ the tongue in producing, modifying, or interrupting the tone of certain wind-instr.s... *Tonguing,* the production of effects of tone, on wind-instr.s, by the aid of the tongue. *Single-tonguing,* the effect obtained by the re-peated tongue-thrust to the nearly in-audible consonant *t* or *d;* *Double-tongu-ing,* that obtained by the repetition of *t k; Triple-tonguing,* by *t k t;* etc. With reed-instr.s, single-tonguing only is applicable.

Ton'ic. (Ger. *To'nika;* Fr. *tonique;* It. *to'nica.*) 1. The key-note of a scale.—2. In the new system of harmony, the *tonic chord* (in *C*-major the major triad on *C;* in *C*-minor the minor triad on *C*) is designated as the tonic. (Comp. *Phone.*).. *Tonic chord,* one having the key-note as root... *Tonic pedal,* organ-point on the key-note... *Tonic section,* a section or sentence in the key in which a composition began, with a cadence to the tonic of that key... *Tonic Sol-fa,* a method of teaching vocal music, inv. by Miss Sarah Ann Glover of Norwich, England, about 1812, and perfected by the Rev. John Curwen, who became acquainted with the method in 1841.—Its formal basis is the "movable-Do" system ; the 7 usual solmisation-syllables are employ-ed, but Englished as follows

doh ray me fah soh lah te

each is represented in notation by its initial letter (d r m etc.), to which a vertical dash is added above or below when a higher or lower octave is entered ; thus s, d d' in a soprano part would be equivalent, in *G*-major, to

For teaching the tones and modulation, these tone-names are arranged in a musical chart called a Modulator :

d¹	f¹	
t	— m¹	— l
l	= r¹	— s
s	— DOH¹	— f
	TE	— m
f	ta le	
m	— LAH	= r
	la se	
r	— SOH	— d
	ba fe	
		t₁
d	— FAH	
t₁	— ME	— l₁
	ma re	
l₁	= RAY	— s₁
	de	
s₁	— DOH	— f₁
	t₁	— m₁
f₁		
m₁	— l₁	= r₁
r₁	— s₁	— d₁
		t₂
d₁	— f₁	—
t₂	— m₁	— l₂

This arrangement shows the exact position of each tone in its relation to the key-tone ; in fact, the fundamental principle of the method is key-relationship, and that the character of every tone is decided by the relation which it holds to its tonic, the name Tonic Sol-fa signifying "solfaing according to the tonic principle" The system of tonic sol-fa insists upon the mental effect of each tone in relation to the tonic, i. e. the pupils are taught to recognize the tones of the scale by observing the mental impressions peculiar to each.—The parallel columns of the Modulator show the relation of key to key, and may be extended through all the sharp and flat keys, the former lying to the right, the latter to the left of the central column. Sharped tones take the sharp vowel *e*, flat tones the broad vowel *a* (ah). In modulating, so-called *bridge-tones* are added in the notation in the form of small letters indicating the relation of the modulating tone to the key just left, the large letter showing the relation of the tone to the new tonic ; thus ˢd means, that *soh* of the old key is *doh* of the new, as in modulating from *C*-major to *G*-major. For a mere chromatic passing-note, however, or a transient modulation, the chromatic syllables are employed. In the printed notation, equal spaces represent equal times, and fractions of time are shown by fractions of space ; the beats ("pulses") are represented by regular intervals of space. A thick bar marks the primary accent (strong pulse) ; the weak pulse is preceded by a colon ; a shorter bar marks the secondary accent ; a dot midway in a pulse-space marks a half-pulse ; and quarter-pulses are marked by commas. The continuation of a tone is indicated by a dash, while a rest (silence) is left simply as a blank space.—In lieu of protracted explanations, the hymn "America" is here appended in the Tonic Sol-fa notation :

GOD SAVE THE QUEEN.

(America.)

Key A.   Arr. by HARRY BENSON.

S.	d	: d	: r	t₁	: – .d	: r	m	: m	: f	m	: – .r	: d
C.	s₁	: s₁	: l₁	s₁	: – .fe₁	: s₁	d	: d	: d	d	: – .t₁	: d
	God	save	our	gra -	cious	Queen,	Long	live	our	no -	ble	Queen,
T.	m	: d	: f	r	: – .r	: r	s	: l	: l	s	: – .f	: m
B.	d₁	: m₁	: f₁	s₁	: – .l₁	. t₁	d	: l₁	: f₁	s₁	: – .se₁	: l₁
	(My	coun -	try,	'tis	of	thee,	Sweet	land	of	li -	ber -	ty.)

```
r  : d  : t| | d  : —  : —  | s  : s  : s   | s   :—.f  : m
l| : s| : s| | s| : —  : —  | d  : d  : d   | d   :—.t| : d
God  save  the| Queen.       | Send  her  vic-| to - ri - ous,

f  : m  : r  | m  : —  : —  | m  : m  : m   | m   :—.r  : d
f| : s| : s| | d| : —  : —  | d| : m| : s|  | d   :—.d  : d
Of   thee  I  | sing.        | Land  where  my| fa - thers  died,

f  : f  : f  | f  :—.m  : r  | m  : f.m  : r.d | m  :— .f : s
t| : r  : t| | t| :—.d  : t| | s| : s|   : s|.d | d.l| : s|.f| : m|
Hap - py  and| glo - ri - ous,| Long  to  reign| o -  ver  us,

r  : s  : s  | s  :—.s  : s  | d  : t|.d  : r.m | d  :— .r : m
s| : t| : r  | s| :—.s| : s| | d  : r.d  : t|.l| | s|.f| : m|.r| : d|
Land  of  the| pil - grims' pride,| From  ev' - ry| moun - tain - side
```

rallentando

```
l.s,f: m  : r  | d  : —  : —
d  : d  : t|  | d  : —  : —
God  save  the| Queen!

f.l : s  : f  | m  : —  : —
f| : s| : s|  | d| : —  : —
Let  free - dom| ring!)
```

Despite strenuous opposition, the Tonic Sol-fa method continues to spread ; and it deserves to, having triumphantly proved its thorough excellence both in principle and practice.

To'nisch (Ger.) Tonic, i. e. pertaining to the tonic.

To'no (It.) Tone ; key.

To'nos (Gk.), **To'nus** (Lat.) 1. A tone (whole tone, major second).—2. A mode.

Toquet (Fr.) Toccato.

Tostamen'te (It.) Rapidly and boldly.

To'sto (It.) The phrase *più tosto* is used by Beethoven in the sense of "rather", "quasi"; as *Allegro molto, più tosto presto*, "very fast, nearly presto."

Touch. (Ger. *An'schlag;* Fr. *toucher;* It. *ta'sto.*) The method and manner of applying the fingers to the digitals of keyboard instr.s.

Touche (Fr.) 1. A key (digital).—2. A fret.—3. A fingerboard, either with or without frets.

Toucher (Fr.) 1 (*verb*). To play, as *toucher le piano*. (*Jouer* is the universally applicable and more modern term.) —2 (*noun*). Touch, manner of manipulation.

Touchette (Fr.) Fret.

Toujours (Fr.) Same as *Sempre.*

Tourmenté,-e (Fr.) Overdone ; as by an overplus of eccentricity, ornamentation, unusual or disconnected harmonies, oddities of instrumentation, and the like.

Tourniquet (Fr.) Plug or cap.

Toy Symphony. (Ger. *Kin'dersinfonie;* Fr. *Foire des Enfants.*) The original toy symphony was written by Haydn in 1788, with parts for 6 toy instr.s (a cuckoo-pipe, playing *c* and *g*, a quail-call in *f*, a trumpet and drum in *G*, a whistle, and a triangle), with 2 violins and a double-bass. Key, *C*-major.—It has been variously imitated.

Trackers. (Ger. *Abstrak'ten;* Fr. *abrégés.*) See *Organ.*

Tract. (Lat. *tractus.*) An anthem on verses usually taken from the Psalms, substituted, from Septuagesima to

Easter eve, for the Gradual, or for the Alleluia following the Gradual, in the R. C. and some other services.

Tradot'to (It.) Arranged ; transposed.

Tra'gen der Stimme (Ger.) Port de voix.

Traîné (Fr.) Slurred... *Traînée*, same as *Schleifer* (*b*).

Trait (Fr.) 1. Tract.—2. Passage ; vocal or instrumental run... *T. de chant*, melodic phrase... *T. d'harmonie*, a chord-passage.—3. An old form of the trill-sign (∿) ; also *plique*.

Traktur' (Ger.) In the organ, the interior key-action, especially the trackers.

Tranché,-e (Fr.) Cut, crossed... *C-tranché* (obsolete ; now *C-barré*), the sign ₵

Tranquillamen'te (It.) Tranquilly, in a quiet style; also *con tranquillità'*... *Tranquil'lo*, tranquil ; often (with Beethoven) equiv. to *moderato*.

Transcription. 1. The arrangement or adaptation of a composition for some voice or instr. other than that for which it was originally intended.—2. (Fr.) *Transcription uniforme*, the uniform notation of transposing instr.s, peculiar to the French military bands, attained by noting them all in the *G*-clef, i. e. an octave higher than the ordinary method.

Transient. Passing, not principal ; intermediate ; as a *transient modulation.* —*Transient chord*, in modulation, an intermediate chord foreign both to the key left and that reached... *Transient modulation*, a temporary modulation soon followed by a return to the key left.

Transition. (Lat. *transi'tio;* Fr. *transition.*) 1. Modulation ; specifically, a transient one.—2. In Tonic Sol-fa, a modulation without change of mode.

Tran'situs (Lat.) "A passing-through". —*Tr. regula'ris*, progression by passing-notes ; *tr. irregula'ris*, progression by changing-notes.

Transpose. (Ger. *transponi'ren;* Fr. *transposer;* It. *variar' il tuo'no.*) To perform or write out a composition in a different key... *Transposed mode*, one of the medieval modes transposed (by a *B♭* in the signature) a fourth above or fifth below its regular pitch. An added

E♭ raised the new pitch by a fourth, i. e. lowered the original pitch by a tone.

Transposing Instruments. 1. Those the natural scale of which is always written in *C*-major, regardless of the actual pitch.—2. Instruments (chiefly with keyboards, as the pfte., harpsichord, etc.) having some device by which the action or strings can be shifted so that higher or lower tones are produced than when they are in the normal position... *Transposing scales*, see *Greek music*.

Transpositeur (Fr.) 1. A transposer.— 2. A mechanism attached to the valvehorn as a substitute for the numerous crooks generally used ; inv. by Gautrot.—3. The transposing keyboard of the *piano transpositeur*, inv. by Auguste Wolff of Paris in 1873.

Transposition. See *Transpose*... *Transpositions'skalen* (Ger.), transposing scales.

Transverse flute. See *Flute.*

Trascinan'do (It.) Same as *Strascinando.*

Trasporta'to (It.) Transposed... *Chia'-vi trasportati*, see *Chiavette.*

Trattenu'to (It.) Held back, retarding the tempo. (Abbr. *tratt.*)

Trau'ermarsch (Ger.) Funeral march.

Trau'rig (Ger.) Sad, melancholy.

Travailler (Fr.) "To work". An instrumental part is said to *travailler* when it leads while the others act as an accompaniment or filling... *Musique travaillée*, music abounding in passages and bristling with difficulties.

Travel. To carry ; said of sound.

Travers'flöte (Ger.) 1. Flauto traverso.—2. A 4′ organ-stop resembling the orchestral flute in timbre.

Traversière (Fr.), **Traver'so** (It.) Transverse.—*Traverso* (for *flauto traverso*) occurs in scores.

Tre (It.) Three... *A tre*, for 3 voices or instr.s ; *a tre voci*, for 3 parts... *Tre corde*, see *Una corda.*

Treb'le. See *Soprano*... *Treble-clef*, *G*-clef.

Trede'zime (Ger.) A thirteenth.

Trei'bend (Ger.) Urging, hastening ; *accelerando, stringendo.*

Treizième (Fr.) A thirteenth.

Treman'do, Tremolan'do (It.) With a tremolo-effect.

Tremblant (Fr.) Tremulant.

Tremblement (Fr.) Trill; tremolo... *Trembler*, to execute a trill or tremolo.

Tre'molo (It., "a quivering, fluttering;" comp. *Vibrato*.) 1. In singing, a tremulous fluctuation of tone, effective in highly dramatic situations, though frequently a mere mannerism or vocal defect.—2. On stringed instr.s, an effect

produced by the extremely rapid alternation of down-bow and up-bow, marked —3. On the pfte., the rapid alternation of the tones of a chord, e. g. written: or

played:

(2 examples from Gade, Op. 51):

1. Written: played:

2. Written: played:

(This last is simply a trill without afterbeat.) [N. B. The pfte.-tremolo is not always written as an exact abbreviation (comp. *Abbreviation* 2); e. g., may signify instead   , in case the tempo is slow enough to admit of the former reading.]—4. A fluttering effect produced by the tremolo-stop or tremulant.—5. A tremulant.

Tremolo'so (It.) With a tremulous, fluttering effect.

Tremulant. A mechanical device in the organ for producing a tremolo. It consists of a valve or arm of thin metal which, when set in action by a drawstop, partially checks the inflow of wind, by which latter it is forced to oscillate rapidly, the consequent alternate checking and admission of the wind to the pipes causing a tremulous tone.— Organ-pipes producing a similar tone without the tremulant are those of the *Piffaro, Unda maris*, etc.

Tremulie'ren (Ger.) To execute a trill or tremolo; also sometimes used (as a noun) for *vibrato*.

Trenchmore. An old English country-dance, in lively tempo and triple or compound duple time.

Trenise (Fr.) A figure in the quadrille.

Trepo'dion. See *Terpodion*.

Très (Fr.) Very; *molto*.

Triad. (Ger. *Drei'klang*; Fr. and It. *tria'de*.) A "three-tone" chord composed of a given tone (root) with its third and fifth in ascending diatonic order...*Harmonic triad*, a major triad.

Triangle. (Ger. *Triang'el;* Fr. *triangle;* It. *trian'golo*.) An orchestral instr. of percussion, consisting of a steel rod bent into triangular shape, one corner being left slightly open; it is struck with a metal wand. The rhythm alone being noted, the triangle-part is usually written on a single line, headed by the *time*-signature only.

Tri'as (Lat.) A triad.

Tri'brach. A metrical foot of 3 short syllables, having the ictus on either the first or second, thus: (‿ ‿ ‿ or ‿ ‿́ ‿).

Tri'chord. A 3-stringed instr.— *Trichord pfte.*, one having 3 strings (unisons) to each tone throughout the greater part of its compass.

Trich'ter (Ger.) Tube (of a reed-pipe); bell (of a horn or trumpet). Often *Schall'trichter*.

Trici'nium (Lat.) An *a cappella* composition for 3 voices.

Tridiapa'son. A triple octave.

Trill. (Ger. *Tril'ler;* Fr. *trille;* It. *tril'lo*.) (Also *Shake*.) [Sign 𝄮 or 𝄮 ⁓⁓; obs. *t.*, +, ⁓⁓, or (⁓⁓, ⁓⁓, ⁓⁓ etc.] A grace occupying the entire time-value of the principal note.

being the rapid and even alternation of the latter with a higher auxiliary (the maj. or min. second above); except when the time for its execution is so brief as to reduce it to a mere turn, or an inverted mordent.—In modern mu-sic, the trill generally begins on the principal note (*a*), and ends with an after-beat (*b*), which should be written out ; if to be begun on the auxiliary, an appoggiatura should be set before the principal note (*c*).

A dotted quarter-note would call for one more group of 4 16th-notes ; a 𝅗𝅥 for 2 such additional groups ; etc.

These are the typical forms of the *long trill ;* they differ in different kinds of time ; e. g.

or when preceded by an ascending appoggiatura :

the tempo also exercises a controlling influence, the [music] per-following trill: formed :

Andante.
[music], passing over into

[music] (Allegro), [music] or

(Presto). The last is one form of the *short trill*, which might, in turn, be-come a long trill in *presto*, when the

time-value of the principal note per-mits of such extension, e.g.

[music]

No. 6, written thus :

(All°. commodo) [music]

would be executed : [music]

The after-beat may be modified **chro-**matically, as at No. 3, or thus :

It is often in place when not written out (comp. Ex. *b* under *chain of trills*); its introduction is then either a matter of taste, or depends on what follows, it being usually required where the trill is followed by an accented note ; though the next three examples require no after-beat :

Successive trills, even though alike in notation, may differ in execution by reason of the notes immediately preceding them :

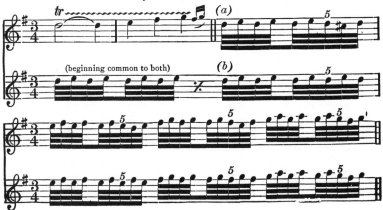

A trill on several tones in direct succession is called a *chain of trills ;* it may be performed with or without an after-beat :

though in case any step is merely a chromatic alteration of a principal note, the after-beat is best omitted :

the following requires short trills like inverted mordents :

—The only rule now universally appli-

—In the 17th and 18th centuries, and early in the 19th, a common practice was to *begin* the trill on the *auxiliary*, and end on the principal note.— For varieties of the trill indicated by the signs ＼ⅿ ⌒ⅿ ⅿ⌒ ⅿ⌒ etc., compare *Graces, Mordent, Signs...Double* and *Triple Trills*, in alternate thirds, sixths, etc., for both hands, frequently occur in modern pfte.-music.

cable to the execution of the trill is one equally applicable to all other graces ; namely, that it must exactly fill out the time allotted to it, neither accelerating nor retarding the rhythm.—A peculiar mode of commencing the trill, called the *ribattuta*, and still sometimes employed by vocalists, flutists, and violoncellists on account of the smoothness attainable thereby, has the following forms :

Tril′lerkette (Ger.) Chain of trills.

Tril′lo (It.) Trill. (N. B. The *trillo* described in Caccini's Singing Method (1601) " consists of the rapid repetition of a *single note*...He also mentions another grace which he calls the Gruppo, which closely resembles the modern shake :

GROVE.)... *Trillo capri′no*, see *Bockstriller.*

Trine. A 3-tone group, or triad, composed of any given tone (the *root*) with its major thirds above and below (as *A♭-C-E*). Compare *Duodene.*

Trink′lied (Ger.) Drinking-song.

Tri′o (It.) 1. A composition for 3 voices or parts. (*a*) The *Instrumental Trio*, usually in sonata-form, is most commonly either a *Pianoforte Trio* (pfte., violin, 'cello), or a *String Trio* (violin, viola, 'cello ; or 2 violins and 'cello). Compositions for 3 concerted instruments, accompanied by a fourth playing a *basso continuo*, were formerly also styled trios...An *Organ Trio* is a 3-part organ-piece for 2 manuals and pedal, the registration of the manuals being strongly contrasted.—(*b*) The *Vocal Trio* is usually in song-form or aria-form.—2. In minuets, marches, scherzi, etc., the trio or *alternativo* is a

division set between the first theme and its repetition, and contrasting with it by a more tranquil movement and *cantabile* style ; called " trio" because written in 3 parts, in contrast to the ordinary 2-part style of the principal subject.

Trio′le (Ger.), **Triolet** (Fr.) Triplet.

Triomphale (Fr.), **Trionfa′le** (It.) Triumphal.

Triomphant (Fr.), **Trionfan′te** (It.) Triumphant.

Trip′elfuge(Ger.) Triple fugue... *Trip′-elkonzert*, triple concerto (for 3 solo instr.s with orchestral accomp.)... *Trip′-eltakt*, triple time... *Trip′elzunge*, triple-tonguing.

Tripho′nia. See *Organum.*

Tri′pla (It.) 1. A triplet.—2. Triple time... *Tripla di mi′nima*, 3-2 time.

Triple *counterpoint, fugue, time.* See the nouns.

Triple-croche (Fr.) A 32nd-note.

Trip'let. (Ger. *Trio'le;* Fr. *triolet;* It. *tri'pla.*) A group of 3 equal notes to be performed in the time of 2 of like value in the regular rhythm ; written

♪♪♪ or ♪♪♪.

Trip'lum (Lat.) In medieval music, a third part added to the original Altus and Bassus of the *organum*, and generally the highest of the 3 ; hence, Engl. *treble.*

Tri'pola (It.) Same as *tripla.*

Trisemito'nium (Lat.) Minor third.

Tristez'za (It.) Sadness, melancholy ; from *tri'sto,-a*, sad, afflicted.

Tri'te (Gk.) The third tone from above in the conjoined, disjoined, and extreme tetrachords. See *Greek music.*

Tri'tone. (Lat. and Ger. *Tri'tonus;* Fr. *triton;* It. *tri'tono.*) The interval of 3 whole tones, or an augmented fourth ; as

Tritt (Ger.) Treadle or pedal... *Tritt'-harfe*, pedal-harp.

Tri'tus (Lat.) The third authentic church-mode (*Lydian*).

Tro'chee. (Lat. *trochæ'us.*) A metrical foot of 2 syllables, long and short, with the ictus on the first (– ⏑).

Trois (Fr.) Three... *Mesure à trois-deux*, 3-2 time ; *à trois-huit*, 3-8 time ; *à trois-quatre*, 3-4 time.

Troll. A round or catch.

Trom'ba (It.) A trumpet... *Tr. croma'-tica*, chromatic trumpet, valve-trumpet. ..*Tromba mari'na* (*Sea-trumpet, Marine trumpet, Nun's-fiddle;* Ger. *Non'nengeige, Trum'scheit*), a very ancient single-stringed bow-instr., having for a body a long thin wooden shell made of several staves, a flat belly, short neck, and 1 thick gut string generally tuned to *C* (sometimes one or more additional strings as drones). One foot of the bridge rests loosely on the belly, the harsh vibration thus induced rendering the tones very powerful, so that the instr. was formerly used in the English navy for signalling. The natural harmonics have a far more pleasing quality of tone, which accounts for the comparative popularity of the instr., in Germany, from the 14th to the 16th century, in German churches and convents (whence the name "*Nonnengeige*",

nun's-fiddle). It occasionally had an additional octave-string, and some specimens were provided with sympathetic strings *within* the body... *Tr. sorda*, muted trumpet... *Tr. spezza'ta*, earlier name for the *tromba bassa* (bass trumpet).

Trombet'ta (It.) 1. (Also *trombettato're, trombettie're, trombetti'no.*) A trumpeter.—2. A small trumpet (dimin. *trombetti'na*).

Trombone'. 1. (It. and Fr. *trombo'ne;* Ger. *Posau'ne.*) An orchestral wind-instr. of metal, belonging to the trumpet family, with the distinctive feature of the slide-mechanism (see *Slide*), in which shape it dates probably from the 15th century. It is constructed in 4 sizes (alto, tenor, bass, and the more recently added contrabass); the *tenor trombone* is the one in most general use. Gevaert suggests that the *tromba da tirarsi* of Bach's scores was possibly a *soprano tr.*, the place of which was usually supplied by the *cornetto.*—It is a non-transposing instr., and is written in the *C*-clef (alto or tenor) for the alto and tenor instr.s, and in the *F*-clef for the bass and contrabass. In playing, there are 7 positions, obtained on successive descending semitonic degrees by gradually drawing out the slide, the *1st pos.* being when the slide is pushed completely in, i. e. when the tube is shortest ; in each position the tones which can be regularly made to speak are the partials 2 to 8. Utilizing all 7 positions, the tenor trombone in B♭ has a chromatic compass of 2½ octaves, from *E* to *b*♭ chestral compass, above which are the 4 difficult tones *b*[1], *c*[2], *c*[2]♯. and *d*[2]; while below, separated by a tritone from the rest of the scale, are the so-called pedal-tones. The orchestral compass of the *alto trombone* is *A—e*♭; that of the *bass trombone B*₁*—f*[1].—The valve-trombone possesses greater agility than the slide-trombone, but is apt to be inferior to it in purity of tone. (Comp. art. *Trumpet*, last sentence.)—2. In the organ, a powerful reed-stop (same as *Posaune*).

Trom'mel (Ger.) A drum... *Trom'mel-bass*, the rapid reiteration of a bass tone (a term of disparagement)... *Trom'melklöppel* or *-stöcke*, drumsticks... *Gro'sse Tr.*, bass drum... *Militär'trommel*, military drum, side-drum... *Roll'trommel*, tenor drum... *Wir'beltrommel*, side-drum.

Trompe (Fr.) A hunting-horn; formerly, a trumpet... *Tr. de Béarn*, or *tr. à laquais*, jew's-harp.

Trompe'te (Ger.) Trumpet... *Trompe'-tengeige*, tromba marina... *Trompe'-tenregister,-werk,-zug*, trumpet-stop... *Trompe'ter*, trumpeter.

Trompette (Fr.) 1. Trumpet... *Tr. à coulisse*, slide-trumpet... *Tr. harmonieuse*, trombone... *Tr. d'harmonie*, orchestral trumpet... *Tr. marine*, tromba marina.—2. Trumpeter; bugler (for cavalry).

Trope. (Lat. *tro'pus*, pl. *tro'pi;* Ger. pl. *Tro'pen.*) One of the numerous formulas, in the Gregorian chant, for the close of the lesser doxology following the introit. Originally, there was but one for each mode; the different formulas are now termed *differentiæ*.

Trop'po (It.) Too, too much; *allegro, ma non troppo*, rapid, but not over-rapid.

Troubadour (Fr.; Span. *trovador';* It. *trovato're;* comp. *Trouvère*.) One of a class of poet-musicians originating in Provence, and flourishing in southern France, northern Spain, and Italy from the 11th century till toward the close of the 13th. The chief theme of their lyrical effusions was love (comp. *Meistersinger*). Their art, at first cultivated by princes and knights, gradually decayed, passing into the hands of their former attendants, the *Ménestrels*.

Troupe (Fr.) A band or company of musicians.

Trouvère, Trouveur (Fr.) One of a class of medieval bards in northern France, especially Picardy, contemporary with the *troubadours* and often confounded with them, though their poems were chiefly of an epic character and in strong contrast to the elegant lyric verse of the latter. We owe to the *trouvères*, besides their grand epics and the *fabliaux, chansons de geste*, etc., the origination of the prose tales of chivalry (the famous Round Table cycle).

Trüb(e) (Ger.) Gloomy, dismal; sad, melancholy.

Trug'fortschreitung (Ger.) Progression of a dissonant chord to a dissonance instead of its resolution to a consonance... *Trug'schluss*, deceptive cadence.

Trump. 1 (obs.) Trumpet.—2. Jew's-harp.

Trumpet. 1. (Ger. *Trompe'te;* Fr. *trompette;* It. *trom'ba*.) An orchestral metal wind-instr. having a tube of somewhat narrow scale, and a cupped mouthpiece; the convolutions of the tube are straighter than in the horn, and the bell is much smaller; length of tube, for the typical pitch in D, is about 7 ft. 3¼ in. By the aid of crooks the pitch of the prime tone in the natural trumpet may be modified to any degree of the 12-tone chromatic scale (A, $B\flat$, B, C, $D\flat$, D, $E\flat$, E, F, $F\sharp$, G, $A\flat$; and also to high A and $B\flat$). The natural trumpet has the following scale

which, by combining the tones obtained by using the various crooks, gives the following complete compass:

The tone is brilliant, penetrating, and of great carrying power; the stopped tones, however, are so disagreeable as to be practically useless. The trumpet is a transposing instr., and its music is written in the *G*-clef.—The chromatic or valve-trumpet is provided with 3 valves (comp. *Valve*). [N. B. With regard to the assumed inferiority in tone of the valve-trumpet and valve-horn, as compared with the natural instr.s, no less an authority than Gevaert writes: " The chromatic horns and trumpets, when well constructed, possess all the qualities of timbre proper to the natural instr.s, in addition to their own resources".]—2. In the organ, an 8-foot reed-stop of powerful tone.

Trum′scheit (Ger.) Tromba marina.

Tu′ba. 1. The straight trumpet of the Romans.—2. A name applied to the 3 lowest members of the saxhorn family. —The original tubas inv. by Wieprecht of Berlin in 1835, are of broad scale and have 4 valves, giving a complete chromatic scale of about 4 octaves. The *bass tuba* in $B\flat$, and *contrabass tuba* in $B_1\flat$, are the ordinary orchestral sizes in Germany ; these, and also some others, are in general use in military bands... *Tuba curva*, a species of natural trumpet of very limited compass, taught in the Paris conservatory at close of 18th century.—3. In the organ, a reed-stop (*tuba mira′bilis*) on a heavy pressure of wind, of very powerful and thrilling tone.

Tu′bicen (Lat.) A blower of the trumpet or tuba.

Tucket. A flourish of trumpets.

Tumultuo′so (It.) Vehement, impetuous ; agitated.

Tun. Drum of the aborigines of Yucatan.

Tune. An air, melody ; a term chiefly applied to short pieces or familiar melodies of simple metrical construction.

Tuner. 1. (Ger. *Stim′mer;* Fr. *accordeur;* It. *accordato′re.*) One who tunes instr.s as a profession.—2. Same as *Tuning-cone.*—3. The adjustable flap or incision at the top of an organ-pipe, by setting which the pitch is regulated.

Tuning. 1. The act or process of bringing an instr. into tune.—2. The accordance or *accordatura* of a stringed instr... *Tuning-cone*, a hollow cone of

metal, used in tuning metal flue-pipes in the organ. Their tops are "coned out " by inserting the point of the cone, this increasing the flare and raising the pitch ; and " coned in " by pushing the inverted cone down over their tops, decreasing the flare and lowering the pitch... *Tuning-crook*, a crook... *Tuning-fork*, a 2-pronged instr. of metal, yielding one fixed tone (usually a^1 ; Tonic Sol-fa, c^2), and employed to give the pitch for tuning an instr., beginning a vocal performance, etc... *Tuning-hammer*, a hand-wrench used in tuning pftes... *Tuning-horn*, a tuning-cone... *Tuning-key*, a tuning-hammer. .. *Tuning-slide*, a sliding U-shaped section of the tube in certain brass instr.s, used to adjust their pitch to that of other instr.s... *Tuning-wire*, comp. *Pipe* 2, *b.*

Tuo′no (It.) A tone ; a mode.

Tur′ba (Lat., "crowd, throng"). In medieval passions, the chorus representing the Jewish populace, or the heathen, and taking part in the action of the play.

Tur′co,-a (It.) Turkish... *Alla turca*, in Turkish style, with a boisterous and somewhat monotonous harmonic accomp.

Turkish music. See *Janizary music.*

Turn. (Ger. *Dop′pelschlag;* Fr. *groupe;* It. *gruppet′to.*) Sign ∾; obs. ᗡ, 𝄐 , 𝄐 (*back turns*). A melodic grace consisting, in what may be termed the typical form (the *direct turn*), of 4 notes, a *principal note* (twice struck) with its *higher and lower auxiliary* (the maj. or min. second above and below, each struck once). The sign is set either after, or over, the note modified ; a chromatic sign over or under the turn-sign alters the higher or lower auxiliary respectively.

I. **Turn-sign after the note.**

adagio   presto   or [easier]

Except in extremely rapid movements, the principal note is dwelt on,

before the turn, for one-half or ¾ of its
time-value :

and the turn is executed in equal
notes. But a *dotted* principal note

usually loses a larger proportion of its
value :

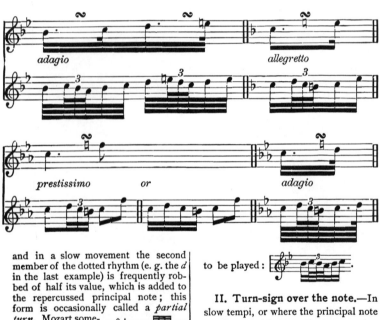

and in a slow movement the second
member of the dotted rhythm (e. g. the *d*
in the last example) is frequently robbed of half its value, which is added to
the repercussed principal note ; this
form is occasionally called a *partial
turn*. Mozart some-
times carelessly
wrote the turn thus :

to be played :

II. Turn-sign over the note.—In
slow tempi, or where the principal note
requires special stress, the turn may begin on the principal note, as in :

this last ornament was called the *shaked turn* (Ger. *prallender Doppelschlag*).

Commonly, however, this turn begins immediately on the higher auxiliary:

III. The Back Turn (sign the inverted or vertical turn-sign ∽ ⁏) begins on the lower auxiliary, and the principal note is generally dwelt on after the turn ·

IV. The sign for the *Double Turn* (𝆑) calls for a turn in 2 parts at once.

Tusch (Ger.) A thrice-repeated flourish of trumpets accomp. by the roll of the drums, or a flourish by the wind-instr.s in the orchestra, in token of applause or welcome.

Tut'to,-a (It.) All, whole; *con tutta la for'za*, with full power or strength. ..*Tutti* (pl.), in scores, indicates the entrance of the whole body of instrumentalists or vocalists after a solo (comp. *Solo*)... *Tutto arco*, whole bow.

Tuyau (Fr.) A pipe; a tube (as of the trumpet)... *T. à anche*, reed-pipe... *T. à bouche*, flue-pipe... *T. d'orgue*, organpipe.

Twelfth. 1. The interval of an octave plus a fifth; a compound fifth.—2. A mutation-stop in the organ, pitched a twelfth higher than the diapasons.

Twenty-second. A triple octave.

Twice-accented (a″, b″, etc.) See *Pitch, absolute*.

Two.—*Two-time*, *2-time*, duple time... *Two-lined octave*, also $\bar{\bar{a}}$, $\bar{\bar{b}}$, etc.; see *Pitch, absolute*.

Tympan. 1. A timbrel or drum.—2. An obsolete Irish instr., probably a kind of crowd.

Tym'pano (It.) See *Timpano*.

Tympanon (Fr., from Gk.) 1. Dulcimer.—2. Same as *tympanum*.

Tym'panum (Lat.) An ancient drum, sometimes having one head like a tambourine, sometimes two, closed and rounded below like a kettledrum, and beaten with a stick or the hand.

Ty'pophone. A keyboard instr., the tones of which are produced by steel wands and a hammer-action similar to that of the pfte. Compass 4 octaves (chromatic) from c^1 to c^5 inclusive. Tone sweet and sustained, resembling that of the harmonic flute.

Tyrolienne (Fr.) A Tyrolese dance or dance-song, a peculiar feature of the latter being the *Jodler*, especially as a refrain.—Hence, a modern round dance in 3-4 time and easy movement.

U.

Ü'ben (Ger.) To practise.

Ü'ber (Ger.) Over, above... *Ü'berblasen*, to overblow ; overblowing... *Ü'bergang*, a transition, modulation... *Ü'bergeführte Stimmen*, divided stops (organ)... *Ü'bergreifen*, (*a*) to cross the hands in pfte.-playing ; (*b*) same as *Démanché; übergreifendes System*, in Hauptmann's theory of harmony, a key-system (i. e. a chain of 3 fundamental triads) formed by adding to the given key-system a new link or triad on the dominant or subdominant side ; e. g. adding to $d/F\text{-}a\text{-}C\text{-}e\text{-}G\text{-}b\text{-}D/f$ the triad $D\text{-}f\sharp\text{-}A$, and thus forming the new key-system $a/C\text{-}e\text{-}G\text{-}b\text{-}D\text{-}f\sharp\text{-}A/c$..*Ü'berleitung*, transitional passage... *Ü'bermässig*, augmented (of intervals)... *Ü'berschlagen* (*a*) to cross hands (on a keyboard instr.); (*b*) to overblow (of organ-pipes and wind-instr.s); (*c*) see *Umschlagen*... *Ü'bersetzen*, to pass over (as a finger over the thumb on the keyboard, or one foot over the other on the pedals)... *Ü'bersteigen*, to rise above ; said of a vocal part which temporarily ascends above one naturally higher.

Ü'bung (Ger.) Exercise ; practice.

Ugua'le (It.) Equal, like, even... *Ugualità'*, equality, conformity... *Ugualmen'te*, equally, alike, evenly.

Uma'no,-a (It.) Human... *Voce umana*, (*a*) vox humana ; (*b*) cor anglais.

Um'fang (Ger.) Compass.

Um'kehrung (Ger.) Inversion.

Umo're (It.) Humor.

Um'schlagen (Ger.) 1. Of the voice, to break ; *umschlagende Stimme*, voice alternating between chest-tones and falsetto.—2. Of wind-instr.s, to overblow ; also compare *Goose*.

Um'stimmung (Ger.) 1. A change of pitch or key in wind-instr.s or the kettledrums, called for in scores by the word *Muta*.—2. A *scordatura* of stringed instr.s.

Un, une (Fr.) A, or an... *Un peu plus lent*, a little slower.

Un, u'no, u'na (It.) A, or an... *Una corda*, with the soft pedal (pfte.) ; *Tre corde* then signifies that the soft pedal is to be released.

Unaccented octave. The small octave (see *Pitch*, § 1).

Unacknowledged note. An unessential or passing-note.

Un'ca (Lat.) Hooked ; hence, an eighth-note (♪); *bis unca* (twice hooked), a sixteenth-note(♬).

Uncoupled. (Ger. *Koppel ab*.) In organ-music, a direction to push in a coupler previously drawn. (Usually "off" ; as *Gt. to Ped. off*.)

Un'da ma'ris (Lat., "wave of the sea".) In the organ, an 8-foot flue-stop pitched a trifle lower than the surrounding foundation-stops, the interference of its tone with theirs producing beats and a wavy, undulatory effect of tone.

Unde'cima (Lat. and It.) The interval of an eleventh.

Undec'uplet. A group of 11 equal notes to be performed in the time of 8 (or 6) of like value in the regular rhythm.

Under-chord. See *Phone*, §1... *Undersong*, burden, refrain... *Undertones* (from Ger. *Un'tertöne*), the lower partials. (See *Acoustics*.)

Unde'zime (Ger.) The interval of an eleventh.

Undezimo'le (Ger.) An undecuplet.

Undulazio'ne (It.) On bow-instr.s, the *vibrato* effect.

Un'eigentliche Fu'ge (Ger.) Fuga irregularis.

Un'endlich (Ger.) Infinite.

Unequal temperament. See *Temperament*... *Unequal voices*, voices different in compass and quality ; mixed voices.

Unessential note. One forming no essential part of the harmony or melody, as passing-notes, changing-notes, many graces, etc.

Ung'arisch (Ger.) Hungarian.

Un'gebunden (Ger.) See *Gebunden*.

Un'geduldig (Ger.) Impatient.

Un'gerader Takt (Ger.) Triple time.

Un'gestrichene Okta've (Ger.) Unaccented octave (the "non-lined," or *small*, octave).

Un'gestüm (Ger.) Impetuous(ly).

Un'gleich (Ger.) Unequal... *Un'gleichschwebende Temperatur'*, unequal temperament.

Un'harmonisch (Ger.) Inharmonic.

Unichord. (Lat. *unichor'dum.*) 1. Monochord.—2. Tromba marina.

Unio'ne (It.) Coupler.

Unison. (Lat. *uniso'nus;* Ger. *Unison';* Fr. *unisson;* It. *uni'sono.*) Properly, a tone of the same pitch as a given tone; by extension, a higher or lower octave of a given tone; as *all'unisono* (It.), *à l'unisson* (Fr.), in unison, at the unison, progressing in unison (in this latter sense often found in scores, as where a double-bass part is written out and the 'cello has merely the direction *col basso all'unisono* [*c. B. all'unisono*], i. e., the same part an octave higher).—Also, in the pianoforte, a group of 2 or 3 strings struck by one hammer and yielding one tone; one such string is called a *unison-string.*—Finally, sometimes equiv. to *Prime.*

Unitamen'te (It.) Unitedly, together with... *Uni'to,-a*, united, joined.

U'no (It.) See *Un.*

Un'rein (Ger.) Impure, false, out of tune.

Un'ruhig (Ger.) Restless(ly), unquiet(ly).

Un'schuldig (Ger.) Innocent(ly).

Un'ter (Ger.) Under, below, sub-... *Un'terbass*, subbass... *Unterbroch'en*, interrupted... *Un'terdominante*, subdominant... *Un'terleitton*, dominant seventh... *Un'termediante*, submediant. .. *Un'tersatz*, subbass... *Un'tersetzen*, to pass under (see *Übersetzen*)... *Un'terstimme*, lowest part; bass part... *Un'tertaste*, a key (digital) belonging to the lower or white row; a white key. .. *Un'tertöne* (pl.), *Un'tertonreihe*, the series of lower harmonics of a given tone; the *undertones;* opp. to *Obertöne.*

Un'vollkommen (Ger.) Imperfect.

Uo'mo (It.) Man. (See *Primo.*)

Up-beat. (Ger. *Auf'takt;* Fr. *levé:* It. *leva'ta.*) 1. The raising of the hand in beating time; opp. to *down-beat.*—2. An unaccented part of a measure.

Up-bow. (Ger. *Hinauf'strich;* Fr. *poussé;* It. *arco in su.*) In playing bow-instr.s, the stroke of the bow in the direction from point to nut; sign V or Λ, which is called the *up-bow mark.*

Upright piano. See *Pianoforte.*

Ut. 1. The first of the Aretinian syllables (see *Solmisation*).—2. Name in France of the note *C*...In the French system of marking the absolute pitch, the several octaves are marked as follows:

| French system begins on → | Octave_2 *ut*_2 | octave_1 *ut*_1 | octave₁ *ut*₁ | octave₂ *ut*₂ | octave₃ *ut*₃ | octave₄ *ut*₄ | octave₅ *ut*₅ |
| English system | C_2 | C_1 | C | c | c^1 | c^2 | c^3 |

Thus Middle-*C* is marked c^1 in the English system, and *ut*₃ in the French.

Ut (Lat.) As, just as, like; *ut supra*, as above.

V.

V. An abbrev. for *Vide* (v. s. = vide sequens), *Violino*, *Volti* (V. S. = volti subito), *Voce* (m. v. = mezza voce.)— V^e, or V^cello, *Violoncello;* V^la, *Viola;* V or 𝒱, *Versicle;* Vv., *violini.*

Va (It.) Go on, continue... *Va crescendo*, go on increasing (the power).

Vacillan'do (It.) Vacillating; noting a passage to be performed in a wavering, hesitating style.

Va'gans (Lat.) See *Quintus.*

Va'go (It.) Vague, dreamy.

Valeur (Fr.), **Va'lor** (Lat.), **Valo're** (It.) Value, i. e. time-value. (Ger. *Werth.*)

Valse (Fr.) Waltz; *valse chantée*, waltz-song; *valse de salon*, a salon-piece in waltz-time for pfte.

Value. (See *Valeur.*) The value (or, better, the *time*-value) of a note or rest, is its length or duration as compared (*a*) with other notes in the same movement, or (*b*) with the standard whole note 𝅝 or any fractional note.

Valve. 1. (Ger. *Ventil';* Fr. *piston;* It. *val'vola*, *pisto'ne.*) In certain **brass** wind-instr.s, a device for diverting the air-current from the main tube to an additional side-tube, thus lengthening the air-column and lowering the pitch of the instrument's entire scale. By the aid of valves, *natural* instr.s **are**

altered to *chromatic* instr.s commanding a chromatic scale throughout their compass. (Compare *Horn, Trumpet;* also *Key* 3.)—The valves are operated by the fingers of the right hand ; their usual number is 3, No. 1 lowering the pitch by (approximately) 1 tone, No. 2 by a semitone, and No. 3 by 1½ tones. Two systems are in ordinary use ; the *Piston-valve,* and the *Rotary Valve.*—(*a*) The *Piston-valve* is a cylindrical plunger working in an air-tight cylinder, terminating in a short rod surmounted by a button, and pierced crosswise by 2 round holes ; the enclosing cylinder is similarly pierced, on either side, one perforation communicating with the main tube, the other with the side-tube. When the piston is not depressed, one of its holes is opposite to those in the cylinder which communicate with the main tube, so that the open (natural) tone of the tube can be sounded ; on depressing the piston with the finger, communication with the main tube is cut off, but opened with the side-tube, so that the lower tone sounds. On releasing the piston, a spiral spring causes its return to the original position. —The *Rotary Valve* is " a four-way stop-cock turning in a cylindrical case in the plane of the instrument, 2 of its 4 ways forming part of the main channel, the other 2, on its rotating through a quadrant of the circle, admitting the air to the side-tube ". Its manipulation is lighter than that of the piston, but it is more liable to derangement.—2. In the organ, the principal valves are the *suction-valves* or *suckers* admitting wind to the bellows and preventing its escape ; the *waste-pallet,* relieving the bellows of an over-supply of wind ; and the *key-valves* or pallets.

Variamen'te (It.) Variously, differently.

Varian'te (It. and Fr.) A variant ; another (optional) reading. See *Ossia.*

Variation. (Ger. and Fr. *Variation';* It. *variazio'ne.*) One of a set or series of transformations of a theme by means of harmonic, rhythmic, and melodic changes and embellishments. In the *Doubles,* or earlier form, the variations left the melody, key, and rhythm of the theme intact, merely embellishing it with new and growingly elaborate figuration ; whereas the modern *tema con variazioni* (beginning with Haydn and

Mozart, and fully developed by Beethoven) may employ the strongest contrasts of rhythm, harmony, and tonality, the sole limitation being that a memory —so to speak—of the theme shall in one way or another be kept alive throughout.

Varia'to (It.), **Varié** (Fr.) Varied... *Air varié, thème varié,* same as *tema con variazoni.*

Varsovienne (Fr.; It. *Varsovia'na.*) A dance in moderate tempo and 3-4 time, with *auftakt* of a quarter-note, the downbeat of every second measure being strongly marked ; presumably invented in France about 1853, as a variant of the Polish polka, mazurka, and redowa.

Vaudeville (Fr.) Originally, a popular convivial or satirical street-song, or song sung about town ; by the introduction of such verses into light plays and operas the way was paved for the modern *vaudeville,* a light comedy, often a parody, in which dialogue an' pantomime alternate with witty and satirical couplets generally set to well-known popular airs.

Veemen'te (It.) Vehement, passionate. ..*Veemen'za, con,* with vehemence, passion.

Veil. In singing, an obscuration of tone, either natural or superinduced by outward causes, detracting from clear and bell-like vocalization. A *veiled voice* is called in It. *vo'ce vela'ta,* in Fr. *voix sombrée* or *voilée.*

Vela'to (It.) Veiled (see *Veil*).

Velluta'to (It.) Velvety.

Velo'ce (It.) Rapid, swift ; usually applied to a passage to be performed more swiftly than those before and after, thus being the opposite of *ritenuto... Velocemen'te,* rapidly... *Velocissimamen'te, velocis'simo,* with extreme swiftness, *presto... Velocità',* velocity.

Ventage. (Ger. *Ton'loch.*) In windinstr.s having finger-holes or keys, any hole to be stopped by a finger or key.

Ven'til. 1. Valve.—2. In the organ, a cut-off or shutter within the windtrunk, for shutting the wind off from, or admitting it to, certain stops or partial organs ; often controlled by a drawstop or pedal... *Ventil'horn* (Ger.), valve-horn ; *Ventil'kornett,* cornet à pistons.

Venu'sto (It.) Graceful, elegant.

Vêpres (Fr.) Vespers.

Verän'derungen (Ger.) Variations.

Verbin'dung (Ger.) Binding, tying, connection; combination... *Verbin'- dungszeichen*, tie.

Verdeckt' (Ger.) Covered, concealed.

Verdop'pelt (Ger.) Doubled... *Verdop'- pelung*, doubling.

Vereng'ung (Ger.) 1. See *Verkür'- zung.*—2. Harmonic compression of a theme by substituting in the imitation a narrower interval for a wider one.

Vergnügt' (Ger.) Cheerful, cheery.

Vergrö'sserung (Ger.) Augmentation (of a theme).

Verhal'len (Ger.) To die away... *Ver- hal'lend*, dying away.

Verkeh'rung (Ger.) Inversion (of the intervals of a theme); i. e. imitation by inversion, or by contrary motion.

Verklei'nerung (Ger.) Diminution.

Verkür'zung (Ger.) Diminution 1.

Verläng'erungszeichen (Ger.) Dot of prolongation.

Verlö'schend (Ger.) Dying away.

Vermin'dert (Ger.) Diminished (of intervals).

Vermit'telungssatz (Ger.) Episode.

Verrillon (Fr.) An *Harmonica* 2.

Verschie'bung (Ger.) Shifting pedal, soft pedal; *mit Versch.*, una corda; *ohne Versch.*, tre corde.

Verschwin'dend (Ger.) Vanishing; dying away.

Verse. A portion of a service or anthem sung by solo voices; opp. to *chorus.* ..*Verse-anthem*, see *Anthem... Verse- service*, a choral service for solo voices.

Verset . (It. *verset'to;* Fr. *verset.*) 1. Same as *Versicle.*—2. A short prelude or interlude for the organ.

Verset'zen (Ger.) To transpose... *Ver- set'zung*, transposition; *Verset'zungs- zeichen*, a chromatic sign.

Versicle. In liturgics, a short verse generally forming, together with its response, but one sentence; e. g.

Vers. O Lord, save Thy people,
Resp. And bless Thine inheritance.

Ver'so (It.) 1. A verse or stanza.—2. An air or tune.

Verstimmt' (Ger.) Out of tune; out of humor, depressed.

Ver'te (Lat.) Turn over. (See *Volti.*)

Vertical. Lying in one plane (said of pfte.-strings); opp. to *overstrung.*

Verve (Fr.) Spirit, animation, vigor, energy.

Verwandt' (Ger.) Related; *verwan'dte Tonarten*, related keys... *Verwandt'- schaft*, relation(ship).

Verwech'selung, *die enharmo'nische* (Ger.) The enharmonic change.

Verwei'lend (Ger.) Delaying; *ritenuto.*

Verziert' (Ger.) Ornamented... *Ver- zie'rung*, ornament, grace.

Verzö'gerung (Ger.) Retardation.

Verzwei'flungsvoll (Ger.) Despairing(ly); with desperation.

Vespers. (It. *ve'spero;* Fr. *vêpres;* Ger. *Vesper.*) "Even-song." The 6th of the canonical hours.

Vezzo'so (It.) Graceful; elegant... *Vezzosamen'te*, gracefully, etc.

Vibran'te (It.) With a vibrating, agitated effect of tone.

Vibration. (It. *vibrazio'ne;* Fr. *vibra- tion ;* Ger. *Schwing'ung.*) The rapid oscillation of any tone-producing body, as a string, an air-column, the vocal cords, etc...*Amplitude of vibration*, the widest departure of a tone-producing body, towards either side, from a point of rest...*Amplitude of a single vibra- tion*, properly, the departure of the tone- producing body from the middle point towards one side only; but frequently made to comprehend the entire width of the excursion from side to side... *Double vibration*, the excursion of a tone-producing body (as a string) from one side to the other and back again... *Vibration-number*, a figure representing the number of vibrations (usually estimated by *double* vibrations) made by a tone.

Vibra'to (It.) 1. On bow-instr.s, the wavering effect of tone obtained by the rapid oscillation of a finger on the string which it is stopping.—2. In singing, a tremulous effect, differing from the *tremolo* in not fluctuating from the pitch, partaking of the nature of a thrill, or series of very rapid partial interruptions of the tone. [Not to be confounded with *Tremolo* in either sense.] The ill-managed vibrato degenerates to a *trillo caprino* (*q. v.*)

Vibrator. A free reed.

Vicen′da (It.) Change... *Vicende′vole*, changeably, vacillatingly.

Vi′de (Lat.), **Vi′di** (It.) See...**Vi- de**, in scores, a sign that a "cut" has been made, directing the performers to skip from **Vi-** over to **de**.

Vide (Fr., "empty".) Open (said of strings)...*Corde à vide*, open string; opp. to *corde à jouer*, a string to be stopped.

Viel (Ger.) Much, great...*Mit vie′lem Nach′druck*, with strong emphasis... *Viel′chörig*, for several choirs or (divided) choruses...*Viel′facher Kon′-trapunkt*, polymorphous counterpoint. ..*Viel′stimmig*, polyphonic.

Vièle (Fr.) A modernized spelling of *vielle*.

Vielle (Fr.) Hurdy-gurdy. (Also *viel′la*.)

Vier (Ger.) Four...*Vierach′teltakt*, 4-8 time... *Vier′doppelter Kon′trapunkt*, quadruple counterpoint... *Vier′fach*, see *fach*...*Vier′füssig*, 4-foot... *Vier′-gestrichen*, see *Gestrichen 2*...*Vier′-händig*, for 4 hands ... *Vier′klang*, chord of the 7th... *Vier′tel* (-*note*), quarter-note ... *Vier′telpause*, quarter-rest... *Viervier′teltakt*, 4-4 time... *Vierzwei′teltakt*, 4-2 time.

Vif, *m.*, **Vive**, *fem.* (Fr.) Brisk, lively.

Vigorosamen′te (It.) With vigor, energy... *Vigoro′so*, vigorous, energetic.

Vihue′la. Primitive form of the Spanish guitar.

Villanci′co (Span.) A sacred vocal composition resembling the English anthem, sung in Spain at the principal festivals of the Church.

Villanel′la (It.) An Italian folk-song of the 16th century, differing from the artistic *madrigal* by simple harmonization and the more rustic, humorous, and sometimes loose character of the poem.

Villarec′cio (It.) Rustic, rural.

Vi′na. An ancient stringed instr. of the Hindus. The body is a section of bamboo, over which are stretched lengthwise 4 strings, tuned in the order *dominant, leading-tone, tonic, subdominant;* the 18 movable frets can be adjusted to coincide with any one of the Hindu scales. There are also 3 sympathetic strings. Two gourds, fixed at either end of the bamboo, act as resonance-boxes.

Vina′ta (It.; dimin. *vinet′ta*.) A vintage song, or drinking-song.

Vi′ol. (It. *vio′la*; Ger. and Fr. *Vio′le*.) Name of a very ancient type of bow-instr., now obsolete; the prototype of the violin tribe (but comp. *Lira*), from which it differed by having a fretted fingerboard, a variable number of strings (from 5 to 8 or more, though the usual number for all sizes was *six*), and in the shape of the body. Both belly (usually) and back (always) were flat, the ribs high, the bouts nearly semicircular, the sound-holes like half-circles, and the upper half of the body narrow and pointed. The bridge being but slightly arched, and having to support so many strings, those in the middle could scarcely be touched separately with the bow; this circumstance, however, together with the number and peculiar tuning of the strings, greatly facilitated chord-playing, in which the violin is comparatively at a disadvantage. The tuning was as follows:

Viola alta.	Viola tenore.	Viola bassa.	Violone.
(Treble viol.)	(Alto or Tenor viol.)	(Bass viol.)	*8va bassa......* (Contrabass viol.)

i.e. in *fourths* with one *third* midway.— The viols formerly held, in conjunction with the lutes, the position in the orchestra now occupied by the violin, etc., and were not fairly ousted by the latter till the beginning of the 18th century. The *Bass Viol* (i. e. in viol-shape, but with fewer strings) is, indeed, still found in England, though superseded elsewhere by the double-bass of violin-type. The violin first supplanted the treble viol; gradually the larger violin-types were invented, with the above-mentioned result. During the transition, the frets were gradually discarded.

Vio′la (It.) 1. The tenor violin.—2. A viol... *V. alta*, (*a*) treble viol; hence (*b*) tenor violin (obsolete name)...*V. bastar′da*, an enlarged *viola da gam′ba*, originally with 6 or 7 stopped strings, to which were added later an equal number of sympathetic strings stretched beneath bridge and fingerboard... *V. da brac′cio*, " arm-viol " (hence Ger. *Bra′tsche*), a viol held on the arm while playing ; opp. to *v. da gamba*... *V. da gamba*, " leg-viol," a large viol held, like the 'cello, between the knees ; the bass instr. of the viol family... *V. d'amo′re* (Fr. *viole d'amour*), a tenor viol similar to the *v. bastarda* in stringing and construction, but of course smaller. .. *V. da spalla*, " shoulder-viol," a somewhat enlarged *v. da braccio*... *V. di bardo′ne*, see *Barytone* 2... *V. pomposa* (*violoncel′lo pic′colo*), a large kind of violin inv. by J. S. Bach, midway in size between a tenor violin and 'cello, with 5 strings tuned *C-G-d-a-e¹*... *Contrabbas′so di vio′la*, see *Viol.*

Vio′le (Ger.) Viol.

Viole (Fr.) Formerly, a viol ; now, a viola... *Viole d'amour*, see *Viola d amore.*

Violentamen′te (It.) Violently, impetuously... *Violen′to*, violent.

Violet. The *viola d'amore.* (Sometimes *English Violet.*)

Violette (Fr.) Small viola.

Violet′ta (It.) Small viol... *Violetta marina*, a bow-instr. inv. by Pietro Castrucci, soli for which were written by Händel in *Orlando* and *Sosarme.*

Violin′. (Ger. *Violi′ne;* Fr. *violon;* It. *violi′no.*) A 4-stringed bow-instr. of comparatively modern type (an improved viol*), and the leading orchestral instr.; constructed in 4 principal sizes (the so-called string-quartet of the orchestra), with the following *accordature:*

Violin.   Viola.   Violoncello.   Double-bass.   (written :)

A description of the treble violin, the typical instr. of the family, will suffice for all its members.—The *resonance-box*, or *body*, is formed by a vaulted *belly* (bearing the *bridge*) and *back*, joined by narrow sides called *ribs;* the *waist* is the narrow middle portion between the incurving *bouts*, at the *corners* of which, and also at other points within the body, are glued triangular pieces of wood called *blocks*, to strengthen the frame. Also inside, just beneath the treble foot of the bridge, is set a round wooden prop, the *soundpost*, placed there to resist the tension of the strings and to communicate their vibration directly to the back ; the *bass-bar* further strengthens the belly. The curved apertures cut in either side of the belly are the *f-holes*, or *sound-holes*. At the bass of the body is the *button*, to which the wooden *tailpiece* is attached by a *loop* of gut ; from the tailpiece the *strings* are stretched across the bridge and over the *fingerboard* (which lies partly upon the *neck* and partly over the belly) to the *nut*, and thence each to a separate *peg* in the *peg-box* or *head*, which ends in the *scroll.*—The word violin is from the It. *violino*, a diminutive of *viola*, meaning literally " small viol ". Violin-music is written in the *G-clef* (*violin-clef*). The strings are numbered 1 2 3 4 from highest to lowest, because the highest string is that next the bow-hand. (Compare also *Bow, Bowing, Position, Shift.*)... *Violin-clef*, the *G-*clef... *Violin-diapason*, a diapason-stop of narrow scale and stringy tone.

Violi′na. A metal flue-stop in the organ, generally of 4-foot pitch, of small scale and stringy timbre.

Violinette. 1. A kit.—2. Same as *violino piccolo.*

Violi′no (It.) Violin... *V. di fer′ro*, nail-fiddle... *V. pic′colo*, a violin smaller and tuned a fourth higher than the ordinary violin... *V. pompo′so*, a violin with an additional string (*c³*).. *V. primo* (*secondo*), first (second) violin.

Violin′schlüssel (Ger.) *G-*clef.

Violiste (Fr.; formerly *violier.*) Viola-player.

Violon (Fr.) 1. Violin.—2. The violin-diapason (organ-stop).

Violonar (Fr.) Recent name for the double-bass.

Violonaro (Fr.) Same as *Octo-basse.*

Violoncel′lo (It.; Ger. *Violoncell′;* Fr. *violoncelle.*) A 4-stringed bow-instr. of

*A. HADJECKI, in his essay on "The Italian Lira da braccio," contends very plausibly that the violin was derived, not from the *viol*, but from the *lira da braccio*.

violin-type (see *Violin*), dating in its present form from the latter half of the 16th century. The word is a diminutive of *violone*, the It. augmentative of *viola*, thus meaning literally a "little big viol". The 'cello, as it is familiarly called, required more than a century to become popular, taking at first very subordinate parts, whence its designation, in many scores of the 17th century, as *Basso* or *Bass*. It slowly conquered the esteem of artists, and supplanted the *viola da gamba*, like which it is held, for playing, between the knees, while firmly supported on the floor by its pointed *peg* or *standard*. Violoncello-music is written in 3 clefs

for convenience of notation, and now invariably according to the actual pitch; but the classic masters, who also frequently used the *G*-clef in chamber-compositions, wrote the notes in this clef an octave higher than they actually sounded... *Violoncello pic'-colo*, see *Viola pomposa.*

Violo'ne (It., "great viol".) 1. See *Viol.*—2. In the organ, a stop on the pedal, of 16-foot pitch and violoncello-like timbre.

Violoniste (Fr.) Violinist.

Vir'ga. Same as *Virgula.*

Virgil Practice-Clavier. A toneless keyboard instr. for mechanical pfte.-practice, inv. by A. K. Virgil, of New York, in 1883 (see *Techniphone*). It differs essentially from the old dumb piano in 2 features: (1) The depression, and also the release, of a digital produces a mild click like that of a telegraph-key; this furnishes a means for accurately timing the practice, for acquiring promptness of down-stroke and up-stroke, and for determining the different styles of touch (e. g. for the strict *legato* the click on depressing one digital exactly coincides with the release-click of the one preceding); (2) it affords, by a simple mechanical adjustment, 6 gradations in the weight of the touch, from 2 to 20 ounces—i. e. from the very lightest pfte.-touch up to 5 times that of the average pfte.-action, or more than the heaviest organ-touch.

Vir'ginal. A small kind of harpsichord: often written in the plural form as "a pair of virginals", signifying merely a single instr. (Comp. *Pianoforte.*)

Vir'gula. One of the *Neumes.*

Virtuos' (Ger.; fem. *Virtuo'sin.*) 1. A virtuoso. (Fr. *virtuose.*)—2. Virtuose; i. e., possessing or exhibiting the qualities of a finished artist; also *virtuo'-senhaft... Virtuosität'*, virtuosity.

Virtuo'so,-a (It.; pl. *virtuosi,-e.*) A finished instrumentalist or vocalist.

Vis-à-vis (Fr.) A harpsichord or pfte. having 2 opposed keyboards, for 2 players.

Vi'sta (It.) Sight; *a* (*prima*) *vista*, at (first) sight.

Vi'stamente (It.) Briskly, animatedly. .. *Vi'sto*, lively, animated.

Vite (Fr.) Quick(ly).

Viva'ce (It.) A tempo-mark which, used alone, calls for a movement equalling or exceeding allegro in rapidity; when used as a qualifying term, it denotes a spirited, bright, even-toned style... *Vivacemen'te, con vivacez'za, vivamen'te, con vivacità'*, are terms nearly synonymous with *vivace... Vivacis'simo*, with extreme vivacity, *presto... Vivacet'to*, less lively than *vivace*, about *allegretto.*

Vive. See *Vif.*

Viven'te (It.) Lively, brisk, animated.

Vi'vido, vi'vo (It.) Lively, spirited. (*Vivace.*)

Vocal. Pertaining to the voice; specifically, proper for the singing-voice... *Vocal cords*, 2 opposed muscles or ligaments in the larynx, whose vibration, due to expulsion of air from the lungs, produces vocal tones . *Vocal glottis* (Lat. *rima vocatis*), aperture between the v. cords when approximated for the production of tones.. *Vocal music*, music written for or executed by the voice, as a solo or with accompaniment... *Vocal registers*, see *Voice... Vocal score*, reduction of orchestral score with voice-part(s) to piano-score with same.

Voca'lion. See *Reed-organ.*

Vocalisation (Fr.) The art of singing prolonged and sustained tones on vowels only... *Vocaliser*, to sing according to the rules of vocal art, using only the vowels *a* and *e... Vocalises*, vocal exercises or études, generally sung to the vowels, but also, in advanced études, to words.

Vocalizza're, Vocaliz'zi (It.) Same as *Vocaliser, Vocalises.*

Vo'ce (It., pl. *voci.*) Voice ; part... *V. ange'lica*, vox angelica... *V. bian'ca* ("white voice"), term applied to the voices of women and children, and to the tones of certain instr.s of similar quality... *V. di ca'mera*, a voice of comparatively slight volume... *V. di go'la*, throaty or guttural voice... *V. di pet'to*, chest-voice... *V. di ripie'no*, a *ripieno* part (see *Ripieno*)... *V. di te'sta*, head-voice... *V. grani'ta*, a powerful, round voice... *V. pasto'sa*, a full, soft, flexible voice... *V. principa'le*, leading part... *V. spicca'ta*, a voice characterized by clear enunciation... *A due (tre) voci*, for 2 (3) parts, voices ; in 2 (3) parts... *Colla voce*, see *Col canto*... *Messa di voce*, see *Messa*... *Mezza voce, sottovoce*, see *Mezza, Sotto.*

Vo'ces (Lat.) Plural of *Vox.*

Vo'gelflöte,-pfeife (Ger.) A bird-call, like that played on by Papageno in *The Magic Flute*... *Vo'gelgesang*, a merula, or set of small pipes standing in water, the passage of the wind through the latter producing a "warbling" tone. (Also *Vogelsang.*)

Voice. (Lat. *vox*; It. *vo'ce;* Fr. *voix;* Ger. *Stim'me*, specifically *Sing'stimme.*) For the several classes of the human voice comp. *Soprano, Mezzo-soprano, Contralto, Tenor, Barytone, Bass.*— The word voice is often made synonymous with "part", in imitation of foreign usage ; the practice cannot be recommended... **Vocal registers.** There is hardly any subject on which opinions are more irreconcilably opposed, than this ; but if we accept E. Behnke's definition (in his treatise : "Mechanism of the Human Voice") of the term *register*—"a series of tones which are produced by the same mechanism"—we arrive at his conclusion ; namely, that there are 3 principal vocal registers in the female voice, and 2 in the male, the chief "break" occurring in both at — (This is the the tone — transition from *f*^{1} or *f*^{1}♯ "chest"-voice to falsetto in tenor voices.) The second principal break in the female voice occurs — an octave higher at — In bass and barytone voices, the chief — In tenbreak occurs at — ors, also, there is a break at this point. (Comp. the above-mentioned treatise.)

Voice-part. 1. A vocal part [Grove, II, p. 526*b*, l.17 ; and IV, p. 49*b*, l.15 ; E. Prout, "Harmony", p. 58, l.7.]—2. A part. [An awkward and equivocal neologism.]

Voicing. Tuning, or regulating the pitch and tone of, an organ-pipe.

Voilée (Fr.) Veiled.

Voix (Fr.) Voice ; part... *V. angélique*, vox angelica... *V. céleste*, an organ-stop with 2 ranks, of the *unda maris* type... *V. de poitrine*, chest-voice... *V. de tête*, head-voice... *V. humaine*, vox humana... *A deux (trois) voix*, for 2 (3) voices ; in 2 (3) parts.

Vokal' (Ger.) Vocal... *Vokal'musik*, vocal music, with or without accomp... *Vokal'stil*, a cappella style ; vocal style.

Volan'te (It., "flying".) Light, swift.

Vola'ta (It.; Ger. *Vola'te* ; Fr. *Volatine.*) A short vocal run, or trill ; a run, or division ; a light and rapid series of notes... Dimin. *volati'na.*

Volks'lied (Ger.) Folk-song... *Volks'-t(h)ümlich* (Ger.), in a style characteristic of or imitating that of the (German) folk-song, or popular music in general ; opp. to *Kunstlied.* A *volks'-thümliches Lied* is a product of art in the style of the folk-song... *Volks'ton, im*, in the style—having the general character —of a folk-song. (It. *in mo'do popola're.*) ... *Volks'weise*, same as *Volkslied.*

Voll (Ger.) Full... *Voll'es Orches'ter*, full orchestra ; *vol'les Werk*, full organ ; *mit vol'lem Cho're*, with full chorus... *Vollgriffig* ("with full hands"), in full chords or harmonies... *Voll'kommen*, perfect(ly)... *Voll'stimmig*, (*a*) in full harmonies ; (*b*) for many parts, polyphonous. [*Voll* frequently occurs as a suffix with the sense of the Engl. *-ful;* e. g., *gedan'kenvoll*, thoughtful(ly), *stim'mungsvoll*, full of (characteristic) expression ; etc.]

Vol'ta (It.) A turn or time... *Prima volta* (or *Ima volta, Ima, I* a., *1.*), first time ; *secunda volta* (or *IIda volta*, etc.), second time ; *una volta*, once ; *due volte*, twice.

Volteggian'do (It.) Crossing hands (on a keyboard); from *volteggia're.*

Vol'ti (It.) "Turn over !"... *Volti su'bito* [V. S.], "turn over instantly".

Volubilmen'te (It.) Fluently.

Vol'untary. An organ-solo before, during, or after divine service; also o casionally applied to an anthem or other choral piece opening the service.

Volu'ta (It.), **Volute** (Fr.) Scroll.

Vom (Ger.) From the... *Vom An'fang,* =da capo ; *vom Blat'te* ("from the page"), at sight.

Voraus'nahme (Ger.) Anticipation.

Vor'bereitung (Ger.) Preparation.

Vor'dersatz (Ger.) First subject or theme ; fore-phrase [PROUT].

Vor'geiger (Ger.) Leader, 1st violin.

Vor'halt (Ger.) Suspension... *Vor'halts-lösung,* resolution of a suspension.

Vor'her (Ger.) Before, previous(ly).

Vor'ig (Ger.) Preceding, previous ; as *vor'iges Zeit'mass,* =tempo primo.

Vor'sänger (Ger.) Precentor.

Vor'schlag (Ger.) Collective name for the various forms of the accented appoggiatura ; opp. to *Nach'schlag,* or unaccented appoggiatura... *Lang'er* (*kur'zer*) *Vor'schlag,* long (short) appoggiatura.

Vor'setzzeichen (Ger.) Chromatic sign.

Vor'spiel (Ger.) Prelude, introduction ; overture.

Vor'trag (Ger.) Rendering, interpretation, performance, style, delivery, execution... *Vor'tragsbezeichnung, Vor'-tragszeichen,* expression-mark ; tempomark.

Vor'zeichnung (Ger.) Signature.

Vox (Lat., pl. *vo'ces;* see below). Voice. ...*Vox ange'lica* (angelic voice), a 4-foot organ-stop corresponding to the 8-foot *vox huma'na*...*Vox antece'dens* (*con'sequens*), the antecedent (consequent)... *Vox huma'na* (human voice), an 8-foot reed-stop in the organ, the tone of which has a [fancied] resemblance to the human voice ; a solo stop, usually drawn with the tremulant.— Also occurs, especially in Italy, as a flue-stop, and occasionally in 2 ranks, one of reed-pipes, the other of flue-pipes...*Vox virginea,* same as *Vox angelica*... *Vo'ces æqua'les,* equal voices. ...*Vo'ces Areti'næ,* the Aretinian syllables... *Vo'ces bel'gicæ,* the Belgian solmisation-syllables *bo ce di ga lo ma ni bo.*

Vue (Fr.) Sight ; *à première vue,* prima vista.

Vulga'ris (Lat.) In the organ, a flute-stop, *tibia* being implied.

Vuo'to,-a (It.) 1. Open, as *corda vuota,* open string. 2. Empty.

W.

W (as a double V, in Fr. usage). Marks violin-parts copied from a score.

Waits. [Also *Waytes, Wayghtes,* etc.] Originally, a class of street-watchmen in England, who gave notice of their approach by sounding horns or other instr.s. The name then appears to have been transferred to town-musicians, and still later to various irregular bands of indifferent music-makers, in which latter application it is not yet obsolete. —Whether the instr. chiefly affected by these musicians (a species of shawm or oboe) derived its name from them, or vice versa, is a moot point.

Wald'flöte (Ger., "forest flute" ; Lat. *tib'ia silves'tris.*) In the organ, an open metal flute-stop of broad scale and usually of 2 or 4-foot pitch, having a suave, full, resonant tone.

Wald'horn (Ger.) The French horn without valves. (Also *Jagd'horn, Natur'horn.*)

Waltz. (Ger. *Wal'zer;* Fr. *valse;* It. *valzer.*) A round dance in 3-4 time, and in tempo varying from slow to moderately fast,—from the primitive *Ländler* and ordinary German waltz up to the sprightlier *trois-temps* (ordinary waltz) and *deux-temps* (rapid waltz). The steps of these waltzes vary thus:

Slow German

Ordinary Waltz (trois temps, Wiener Walzer)

Quick waltz (deux-temps, Zweitritt)

The origin of the waltz is variously ascribed to Bohemia, Germany (*Ländler*), and France (*volte*)... *Waltz* is also the title of numerous effective instrumental pieces in triple time, but not meant for dance-music... *Waltz-song,* a song in waltz-rhythm.

Wal'ze (Ger., "roller"). An undulating figure (see *Rolle*).

Wan'kend (Ger.) Wavering, hesitating.

Warbler. On the bagpipe, a term applied to various forms of melodic embellishment (graces).

Wär'me (Ger.) Warmth ; *mit gro'sser Wärme*, with great warmth.

Was'serorgel (Ger.) Hydraulic organ.

Waste-pallet. See *Valve*.

Water-organ. Hydraulic organ.

Wayghtes. See *Waits*.

Weak accent, beat, pulse. See *Accent*.

Wech'selgesang (Ger.) Antiphonal (responsive) singing or song... *Wech'-selnote*, changing-note.

Weh'mut(h) (Ger.) Sadness, melancholy... *Weh'müt(h)ig*, sad, mournful, melancholy. (Also *adverb*.)

Weich (Ger.) 1. Soft, tender ; mellow, suave (also *adverb*).—2. Minor.

Weight of wind. The tension of the compressed air supplied by the organ-bellows to any stop or group of stops ; the mean pressure raises a column of water in a U-tube to the height of about 3 inches, hence the technical expression "an inch" or "two inches" of wind ; a stop is said to be "voiced on a 3, 6, or 10-inch pressure," etc.

Wei'nend (Ger.) Weeping.

Wei'sse Note (Ger.) A "white," or open, note.

Weit (Ger.) Broad ; open (of harmonies).

Wel'le (Ger.) Roller (organ)... *Well-atur'*, system of rollers... *Wel'lenbrett*, roller-board.

Well-tempered. In equal, and consequently satisfactory, temperament ; as J. S. Bach's Well-tempered Clavichord (Ger. *Wohl'temperirtes Clavier'*).

We'nig (Ger.) Little ; *ein klein wenig lang'samer*, a very little slower.

Werk (Ger.) In the organ, (*a*) the set of stops controlled by one keyboard ; (*b*) a stop or register.

Wert(h) (Ger.) Value, time-value.

We'sentlich (Ger.) Essential... *We'-sentliche Dissonanz'*, a dissonant chord-tone, in contradistinction to a dissonance produced by a passing or changing-note.

Wet'terharfe (Ger.) Æolian harp.

Whistle. The smallest and most primitive type of instr. with a flageolet or flue-pipe mouthpiece. Comp. *Piccopipe*.

White keys. The continuous lower row of digitals on a keyboard ; formerly they were black, the now black keys then generally being white... *White note*, one having an open (not solid) head ($\flat$ $\downarrow$).

Whole note. See *Note*... *Whole shift*, see *Shift*... *Whole step*, (*a*) a step of a whole tone ; (*b*) a whole tone... *Whole tone* (Ger. *Ganz'ton* ; Fr. *ton plein ;* It. *tcno intero*), see Footnote, p. 103.

Wie (Ger.) As... *Wie o'ben*, as above ; *wie vor'her*, as before, as at first ; *wie aus der Fer'ne*, as from a distance.

Wie'der (Ger.) Again... *Wie'dergabe*, performance, production, rendering, interpretation, reading... *Wiederher'stellungszeichen*, see *Auf'lösungszeichen*. .. *Wiederho'lung*, repetition ; *W.s-zeichen*, repeat.

Wiegenlied (Ger.) Cradle-song, lullaby ; *berceuse*.

Wind-band. 1. A company of performers on wind-instr.s.—2. The wind-instr.s in the orchestra ; also, the performers on, or parts written for, the same... *Windchest*, see *Organ*... *Wind-gauge*, an apparatus for measuring the wind-pressure in the windchest of an organ. It consists of a twice-bent glass tube, having water in the U-shaped end, the other end being fixed in a socket ; on setting the socket in a hole in the soundboard, and letting the wind on, the water rises in the outer arm of the U-shaped tube, indicating the wind-pressure by the height in inches to which it is forced. (Comp. *Weight*.) ... *Wind-instruments* (Ger. *Blas'instrumente;* Fr. *instruments à vent ;* It. *stromen'ti da fia'to*), instruments, the tones of which are produced by *wind* (i. e. compressed air), the vibrations excited in the latter being transmitted to an air-column enclosed in a tube (e. g. an organ-pipe, or any orchestral instrument blown by the mouth), or directly to the open air (e. g. free reeds without tubes). The vibrations of the wind are excited (*a*) by its impinging on a sharp edge (flageolet, flute, organ-pipe), (*b*) by the interposition of a vibratile reed (clarinet, oboe, reed-pipe), or (*c*) by the vibration of the player's lips (horn, trumpet, trombone). (Comp. art. *Instruments*.)... *Windtrunk*, see *Organ*.

Windharfe (Ger.) Æolian harp... *Wind'-kasten*, windchest... *Wind'lade*, soundboard (organ)... *Wind'wage*, **wind**-gauge.

Wir'bel (Ger.) 1. Peg ; *Wir'belkasten*,

peg-box.—2. Roll (on a drum).—3. Same as *Schlägel*, the more usual term.

Wohl'temperirt (Ger.) See *Well-tempered*.

Wolf. 1. A discord induced in certain keys, on keyboard instr.s (especially the organ), by inequality of temperament, such as was inherent in the so-called "meantone" system. (Not synonymous with the Ger. *Or'gelwolf.*)—2. In bow-instr.s, the *wolf* is the imperfect or jarring vibration of some particular tone or tones, and is presumably due to some defect in the build or adjustment of the instrument.

Wolf (Ger.) Wolf; specifically, the 12th fifth in the circle of fifths, being the one which causes the main difficulty.

Wood-wind. The orchestral wood-instr.s collectively; or the performers on them.

Working-out. Same as *Development*.

Wrest. A tuning-hammer.

Wrestblock, Wrestplank. See *Pianoforte*.

Wuch'tig (Ger.) Weighty, weightily, ponderous(ly), with strong emphasis, *risoluto*.

Wür'de (Ger.) Dignity; *mit W.*, or *wür'-devoll*, dignified.

Wü'thend (Ger.) Furious, frantic; *furioso*.

X.

Xanor'phica. (Ger. *Xänor'phika*.) A variety of the piano-violin, and the most complicated of all, there being a separate bow for each string; inv. by K. L. Röllig of Vienna in 1797.

Xylharmon'ica. (Ger. *Xylharmo'nikon*). A keyboard instr. inv. by Utho of Sangerhausen in 1810, and resembling Chladni's Euphonium, but with wooden wands instead of glass rods; an improved Xylosistron.

Xyl'ophone. (Lat. *lig'neum psalte'rium;* Ger. *Stroh'fiedel, Holz'harmonika, Holz'- und Stroh'instrument, höl'zernes Geläch'ter;* Fr. *claquebois, échelette, patouille, xylorganon;* It. *gigeli'ra, sticca'do*.) A very ancient and widely disseminated instr. (Europe, Africa, America), consisting of a diatonically graduated series of flat wooden bars adjusted horizontally upon 2 cords (which are sometimes made of twisted straw), and played on with 2 mallets; a wooden dulcimer, capable of pleasing effects in the hands of a skilful player. Usual compass 2 octaves, or a little more.

Xylosis'tron. The parent instrument of the xylharmonikon; inv. by Utho in 1807.

Y.

Yang Kin (Chinese.) A Chinese instr. resembling the dulcimer, with brass strings.

Yodel, Yodler. English spellings of *jodeln, jodler.*

Z.

Za. Former syllable-name for $B\flat$, in solmisation.

Zählen (Ger.) To count; *zähle*, count... *Zählzeit*, a count.

Zale'o. See *Jaleo.*

Zampo'gna (It.) 1. Bagpipe. — 2. Shawm.

Zapatea'do (Span.) A Spanish dance, in which the dancers mark the rhythm by stamping.

Zap'fenstreich (Ger.) The tattoo.—The *gro'sser Zapfenstreich* is an imposing mus. finale of a military review, commencing with a grand *crescendo* roll on the drums of the combined regimental bands.—The *Z.* was originally a blow (*Streich*) struck on the bung (*Zapfen*) of the cask of beer or wine, signifying that drinking in camp must cease for the night; hence, a musical signal to drive the bung into the bung-hole, to attain that end.

Zaraban'da (Span.) Saraband.

Zar'gen (Ger., pl.) Ribs.

Zart (Ger.) Tender, soft, delicate; slender... *Mit zar'ten Stim'men*, with soft-toned stops... *Zart'flöte*, in the organ, a 4-foot flute-stop of very delicate intonation, the pipes having, instead of the block, a windway reaching up from the foot, and directed against the upper lip.

Zärt'lich (Ger.) Tender(ly), caressing(ly).

Zarzue'la (Span.) A two-act drama with incidental music, resembling a vaudeville; so called because first performed in the royal castle of Zarzuela, in the 17th century.

Zeffiro'so (It.) Zephyr-like.

Zei'chen (Ger.) A sign.

Zeit (Ger.) Time. Also, same as *Takt-teil*. . . *Zeit'mass*, tempo ; *im ersten* (or *vor'igen*) *Zeitmass*, = tempo primo. . . *Zeit'messer*, metronome. . . *Zeit'wert*(*h*), time-value.

Zelosamen'te (It.) Zealously, enthusiastically. . . *Zelo'so*, zealous, enthusiastic, ardent ; marking passages to be performed with energy and fire. Also *con ze'lo*.

Zerstreut' (Ger.) Dispersed, open.

Zieh'harmonika (Ger.) Accordion.

Ziem'lich (Ger.) Somewhat, rather.

Zier'lich (Ger.) Neat, delicate ; graceful, elegant. (Also *adverb*.)

Zif'fer (Ger.) Figure. . . *Bezif'fert*, figured; *Bezif'ferung*, figuring.

Zigeu'nerartig (Ger.) Gypsy-like. . . *Zigeu'nermusik*, Gypsy music.

Zim'balon. An improved dulcimer much employed in Hungarian music, provided with dampers, and having a chromatic scale of 4 octaves : Prolongation of a tone is obtained by its rapid reiteration, marked ⌣.

Zim'belstern (Ger.) A sort of toy-stop in some old organs, consisting of a star hung with little bells, placed conspicuously in front of the organ, and caused to sound by a current of air controlled by a draw-stop.

Zingare'sca (It.) A Gypsy song or dance; specifically, a song sung by maskers during the Carnival.

Zingare'sco,-a (It.) Pertaining to Gypsies, Gypsy-like. . . *Zingare'se*, *alla*, in Gypsy style. . . *Zi'ngaro,-a*, a Gypsy ; *alla zi'ngara*, in Gypsy style.

Zin'ke (Ger.; It. *cornet'to*). (Also *Zink*, *Zinken*.) See *Cornetto*.

Zir'kel (Ger.) Circle. . . *Zir'kelkanon*, infinite canon.

Zi'ther (Ger., pron. *tsit'ter;* Engl. pronun. *zith'er*.) [The Ger. *Zither* is a very different instr. from the old Engl. *cither* or *cittern;* to prevent confusion, it would be well to adopt the Ger. spelling for the modern instr.]—1. (*Schlag'zither*, i. e. *plucked zither*.) The zither, as developed from the primitive peasant-instr. of the German Alps, has 32 or more strings stretched over a shallow wooden resonance-box, which is provided with a soundhole, and bears a bridge near the right end and a fretted fingerboard on the side next the player. Above the fingerboard are 5 melody-strings stopped by the left hand, tuned the 2 *A*'s being steel, the *D* brass, the *G* steel silver-covered, and the *C* brass copper-covered. These 5 are plucked with a metal or tortoise-shell ring worn on the right thumb and having a projecting spur. The accompaniment-strings, tuned in fourths as follows :

are plucked by the fore-, middle, and ring-fingers of the right hand, the little finger resting behind the bridge to steady the hand. They are of gut, or covered silk, variously colored to guide the player's eye and fingers. The 3 ordinary sizes of zither are the *Treble Zither* (*Prim'zither*), *Concert-Zither*, and *Elegie'-Zither* (also called *Alt-* or *Liederzither*, and tuned a fourth below the *Prim-* and *Concertzither*).— 2. (*Streich'zither*, i. e. *Bow-zither*.) The earlier bow-zithers were heart-shaped ; of the newer ones, the *Viola-Zither* has the form of a viola, while the *Philomèle* has a more pointed body and shallower bouts ; they are varieties of the *viol*, with short neck,

fretted fingerboard, and 4 strings in violin-tuning, the *E* and *A* of steel, the *D* of brass, and the *G* of silk silver-covered ; but the bow-zither is held quite differently from the viol, its head being furnished with a little foot which rests on the edge of the table before the player, who holds the body in his lap.

Zit'ternd (Ger.) Trembling, tremulous.

Zö'gernd (Ger.) Hesitating, lingering, retarding.

Zolfà' (It.) Sol-fa.

Zop'po,-a (It.) " Halting, limping ".— *Alla zoppa*, syncopated ; as the rhythm 4/4 ♩ ♩ ♩ ♩ ♩ ♩ ; also applied to Magyar music with the rhythm :

$\frac{4}{8}$ ♩. ♪♩♪. | ♩. ♪♩ | ♩. ♪♩♪. | ♪♩ ♪♩ | etc.

Zoulou (Fr., "Zulu".) A style of pianette.

Zu'fällig (Ger.) Accidental(ly)...*Zu'-fälliges Verset'zungszeichen*, accidental.

Zuf'folo (It.) A small flageolet, such as is employed in training singing-birds. (Also *Zu'folo*.)

Zug (Ger.) 1. Same as *Regis'terzug.*—2. A pedal (pfte.)—3. A slide (of a trombone, etc.)...*Zug'trompete*, slide-trumpet...*Zug'werk*, tracker-action (in the organ).

Zu'kunftsmusik (Ger.) Music of the future ; a term first used (according to R. Wagner) about 1850, by Dr. L. Fr. Chr. Bischoff, in a satire on Wagner's essay upon "The Art-work of the Future" [Das Kunstwerk der Zukunft]. The word has been adopted, by enthusiastic disciples of the neo-German cult, as an epithet of distinction, with the meaning "music *with* a future"—a definition whose correctness can hardly be successfully disputed.

Zu'nehmend (Ger.) Increasing, *crescendo*.

Zung'e (Ger., "tongue"). Reed... *Zung'enpfeife*, reed-pipe...*Zung'enstimme*, reed-stop...*Zung'enwerk*, "the reeds," reed-stops of the organ, considered collectively...*Auf'schlagende Zunge*, beating reed ; *durch'schlagende Zunge*, free reed...*Dop'pelzunge*, etc., see *Tonguing*.

Zurück'halten (Ger.) To retard...*Zurück'haltend*, ritardando ... *Zurück'-haltung*, retardation...*Zurück'schlag*, same as *Ribattu'ta*.

Zusam'men (Ger.) Together, simultaneous(ly); *bei'de Chö're zusammen*, both

choruses (choirs) *together*...*Zusam'menklang*, a sounding together, simultaneous sounding of 2 or more tones ; a "solid" chord...*Zusam'mengesetzt*, combined, compound ; *zusam'mengesetzte Takt'art*, compound time... *Zusam'menschlag*, acciaccatura...*Zusam'menspiel*, playing together ; ensemble-playing...*Zusam'menstreichen*, to slur (either by means of the sign called a slur, or by joining the hooks of hooked notes); *Zusam'menstreichung*, slurring.

Zwei (Ger.) Two...*Zwei'chörig*, for 2 choruses (or divided chorus)...*Zwei'-fach*, (*a*) double, as counterpoint ; (*b*) in 2 ranks, as organ-stops ; (*c*) compound, as intervals...*Zwei'füssig*, 2-foot...*Zwei'gesang*, a duet...*Zwei'-gestrichen*, see *Gestri'chen*...*Zwei'-halbe Takt*, 2-2 time...*Zwei'händig*, for 2 hands...*Zwei'stimmig*, for 2 voices ; in or for 2 parts...*Zwei'tel* (-*note*), a half-note...*Zwei'tritt*, see *Waltz*...*Zweiunddrei'ssigstel* (-*note*), a 32nd-note...*Zweivier'teltakt*, 2-4 time. ..*Zwei'zähliger Takt*, duple time... *Zweizwei'teltakt*, 2-2 time.

Zwerch'flöte, **Zwerch'pfeiff** (Ger.) The cross-flute, or German flute.

Zwisch'en (Ger.) Between, intermediate...*Zwisch'enakt*, an entr'acte ; *Zwisch'enaktsmusik*, act-tune(s)... *Zwisch'enharmonie*, see *Zwisch'ensatz*. ..*Zwisch'enraum*, space...*Zwisch'ensatz*, episode...*Zwisch'enspiel*, interlude, intermezzo.

Zwit'scherharfe (Ger.) See *Spitz'harfe*.

Zwölf (Ger.) Twelve...*Zwölfach'teltakt*, 12-8 time...*Zwölf'saiter*, see *Bissex*.

APPENDIX

OF

ADDITIONS AND CORRECTIONS

APPENDIX.

A.

Abbandonan'dosi (It.) Yielding wholly to emotion ; with a burst of passion.

Abbandona're (It.) To leave, to quit ; *sen'za abbandona're la cor'da*, without quitting the string.

***Abbreviations.** Add to former list : c.f. Canto fermo ; cantus firmus. Div. Divisi, divise. incalz. Incalzando. Mov^to. Movimento. ovv. Ovvero. po' poco.

A'bendunterhaltung (Ger.) Pupils' concert (in a music-school ; given for ensemble-practice or *quasi* public performance). (Also *Übungsabend*.)

Ab'langen [eines Tones] (Ger.) Taking [a tone] by extension (in violin-technic).

Ab'schleifer (Ger.) Staccato-dash (❜ ❜).

Accenta'te (It.; plural form of *accenta'ta*, "le note" being implied.) 1. Accented, marked.—2 (imperative, pl.). Accent ! Emphasize !

Accentua're (It.) To accent...*Accentuan'do*, accenting...*Accentua'to,-a*, accented.

Accessit (Fr.) Honorable mention.

Accord'zither (Ger.) See *Zitherharfe*.

Æo'lian. A reed-organ of the American type, the air being *drawn* through the reeds. It has a keyboard, and may be played like an ordinary organ ; but its distinguishing feature is a mechanical arrangement for executing music without using the keyboard. Motive-power and wind are supplied by two pedals (treadles) worked by the feet ; the time-value of the notes is controlled by perforations in a gradually unrolling sheet of paper, the music-roll ; the tempo is regulated by a stop called the *Motor ;* and the expression is regulated (*a*) by the pedal-movement, (*b*) by two knee-swells, and (*c*) by the registration. In the largest instr.s there are ten speaking stops, and a *Tremolo*. The *Æolian* is remarkable, not merely for extreme technical precision, but for the great variety and artistic finish of musical effects, both tempo and expression being wholly at the player's command.—The "*Æolian*" and the keyboard (which has 4 independent stops) may also be played together, the keyboard being used to play an accompaniment to the *Æolian*. The instr., which is the product of long evolution, became known under its present name about the year 1883, in New York. Its repertory includes all classes of music, and at present (1900) comprises about 20,000 numbers. It has a scale of 58 semitones (the keyboard has 6 octaves) ; and all its music-rolls also fit the *Pianola* (*q.v.*).

Affretta're (It.) To hasten, to accelerate. ..*Senza affrettare*, without hastening.

A fior' di lab'bra (It.; Fr. *au bout des lèvres ;* Ger. *gehaucht*.) Very lightly and softly sung or spoken.

Aggiun'to,-a (It.) Added, interpolated. ...*Arie aggiunte* (pl.), airs interpolated in an opera, etc., to which they did not originally belong.

Air coupé (Fr.) An air of set form.

Album-leaf. (Ger. *Albumblatt;* Fr. *Feuillet d'album ;* It. *Pagina d'album*.) Title of a short and (usually) simple vocal or instr.l piece.

Alexandrine verse. "An iambic hexapody, or series of six iambic feet.— French Alexandrines are written in couplets, alternately acalectic with masculine rimes and hypercatalectic with feminine rimes...The cesura occurs at the end of the third foot. The second line of the following extract is an example :
' A needless Alexandrine ends the song,
That, like a wounded snake, drags its slow
    length along.'—(Pope.)"
                [THE CENTURY DICT.]

Allarga'te (It. ; imperative.) Slower and broader.

Amu'sia. Loss of the musical faculty. [BRITISH MEDICAL JOURNAL, Dec. 22, 1894.]

Anco'ra pia'no (It.) Still [sing or play] softly; equiv. to *sempre piano.*

Andan'do (It.) Same as *Andante.*

An'denken (Ger.) Recollection, souvenir.

*A'nima (It.) 3. Core (of a covered string).

A par'te (It.) Aside; e.g., *sottovoce a parte.*

*Aper'to,-a (It.) Open (of organ-pipes).

Appe'na (It.) Hardly, very little; *appena animando,* a very little faster; *appena meno,* a trifle slower.

Appoggiamen'to (It.) Chin-rest.

Appuyer (Fr.) To sustain.

A quat'tro par'ti (sole) (It.) For four (solo) parts.

Arched viall. [Bow-viol?] Pepys' Diary (Oct. 5, 1664) describes this instr. as "being tuned with lute strings and played on with keys like an organ; a piece of parchment is always kept moving, and the strings, which by the keys are always pressed down upon it, are grated in imitation of a bow, by the parchment; and so it is intended to resemble several vialls played on with one bow, but so basely and so harshly that it will never do. But after 3 hours' stay it could not be fixed in tune, and so they were fain to go to some other musique of instruments."

Arcichitar'ra (It.) A modern *Chitarrone.*

Ardo're, con (It.) With ardor, warmth.

*A'ria (It.) *Aria d'entra'ta,* the first air allotted to a leading singer (in opera) on entering the stage...*Aria di sorti'ta,* an air, at the conclusion of which the singer makes his exit. [The *Sortita* is, however, also the name for the first number sung by any of the leading characters in an opera]...*Arie aggiun'te,* see *Aggiunto...Aria* also signifies wind (in the organ, etc.).

*Ariet'ta alla venezia'na (It.) Little air in "Venetian" style; i.e., a barcarola.

Arietti'na (It.) A brief or trifling arietta.

Armag'gio (di corde) (It.) Set of strings. (Also *Montatura.*)

Ascenden'te (It.) Ascending.

Aspirant' (Ger.) A young musician in an orchestra, on half-pay, "aspiring" to full membership.

A'spro,-a (It.) Harsh, rough.

Assie'me (It.) Same as *Ensemble...Pezzo d'assieme,* a concerted piece.

Astuc'cio (It.) Music-roll, music-case.

Auda'cia, con (It.) With boldness.

Auf'hebungszeichen (Ger.) The "cancel" or natural (♮).

Auf'legestimmen (Ger.) The separate parts of an orch.l composition, to be "laid on" the music-desks.

Auf'löser (Ger.) The "cancel" or natural (♮).

Auf'schwingend (Ger.) Soaring(ly), impetuous(ly); *con impeto.*

Auf'schwung (Ger.) Lofty flight, soaring impetuosity; *mit A.,* in a lofty, impetuous, impassioned style.

Aus'geführter Choral' (Ger.) A "worked out" choral; a choral with free counterpoint; or, with contrapuntal working-out; or, contrapuntally worked out (developed).

Aus'stattungsstück (Ger.) Spectacle, spectacular play or opera.

Autoar'pa Wagner (It.; "Wagner Autoharp.") An improved autoharp (*Akkordzither*) inv. 1896 by E. Gläsel of Markneukirchen, the mechanism of which permits playing in any of the ordinary keys.

Autre (Fr.) Other; another, different.

Avec âme (Fr.) Same as *con anima.*

Avec le chant (Fr.) Same as *col canto.*

À volonté (Fr.) Same as *a piacere.*

B.

Babillage (Fr.) Babbling, chatter.

Badinerie (Fr.) Same as *Badinage.*

Bagatel'la (It.) Bagatelle.

Baglio'ra (It.) Flash of light; title for a swift, light and piquant composition.

Balancel'la (It.; Fr. *balancelle.*) A piece of music imitating the easy rocking of a sailboat.

Baldamen'te (It.) Boldly.

*Ballabi'le (It.) 2. Ballet-music.

Ballatel'la (It.) A short ballad.

Bassanel'lo (It.) 1. An obsolete wood-wind instr. allied to the bassoon, with double-reed in a conical mouthpiece carried by an S-shaped crook.—2. A 4-foot or 8-foot reed-stop in old organs.

*Bass'horn (Ger.) A wood-wind instr.

inv. by Frichot in 1804, and already obsolete, allied to the Serpent, but with a brass bell, and a cupped mouthpiece on an S-crook. Compass 4 octaves (C to c^3).

Bassist' (Ger.) Bass singer.

***Bas'so** (It.) 3. An 8-foot pedal-stop on the organ.

Basso'ne (a lingua) (It.) A 16-foot reed-stop on the swell-organ.

***Bassoon** (compass). The A_1 below $B_1\flat$ is occasionally used (Raff).

Bavardage (Fr.) Chatter, tittle-tattle.

Bel canto (It.) The art of beautiful song, as exemplified by the finest Italian singers of the 18th and 19th centuries, and their pupils or imitators. The term is used especially in contradistinction to the "declamatory" style of dramatic vocalism brought into such prominence by Wagner.

Bien chanté (Fr.) Same as *molto cantabile*.

Biril'lo (It.) Peg.

Block (verb). A hammer in the pianoforte-action "blocks" when it remains against the string after impact, instead of recoiling, thus "blocking" (deadening) the tone.

Bluette (Fr.; "spark," "flying sparklet.") 1. A light, playful comedietta.— 2. Hence, a light, sparkling pianopiece of no fixed form.

Botto'ne (da cordie'ra) (It.) Button (on the violin).

Bouts [pl.]. The incurvations on either side of instr.s of the violin-type, forming the "waist."

***Bridge.** A violin-bridge with 4 feet has been inv. (1894) by Edwin Bonn, of Brading, Isle of Wight ; one foot under each string.

Brisé, le (Fr.) In violin-technic, short, detached strokes of the bow.

Budel'lo (It.) Gut. (Also *minugia*.)

Bu'co (It.; pl. *bu'chi*.) Finger-hole (of a mus. instr.).

Büh'ne (Ger.) Stage. ...*Büh'nenmusik''*, (*a*) dramatic music ; (*b*) music played on the stage.

Bun'te Rei'he (Ger.) The phrase means, literally, the alternation, in a company seated at table, of a lady with a gentleman ; hence, as a mus. title, a series of contrasted characteristic pieces.

C.

C. In recent Italian music "1 C." and "3 C." are abbreviations of "*una corda*" and "*tre corde*" respectively.

Cade're (It.) To fall.—*Cadenza* (cadence) means literally a "falling back" to the tonic from the dominant ; Beethoven uses the word jocularly, in the phrase "*Cadenza ma senza cadere*" (heading his Cadenza No. 1 to the 1st movem. of the G-major Pfte.-Concerto), which may be translated : "Fall back, but don't fall down."

Cahier (Fr.) Book.

Camor'ra (It.) Paid *claqueurs* in Italian theatres.

Campagnuo'lo,-a (It.) Pastoral, idyllic ; rustic.

Campes'tre (It.) Pastoral, rural, idyllic ; as *danza campestre*.

Cano'nico,-a (It.) In canon-form.

Canticchian'do (It.; Fr. *en fredonnant.*) Trilling, warbling ; humming.

***Canti'no** (It.) *E*-string. (In mercantile Italian the strings of the violin are named *cantino*, *seconda*, *terza* and *quarta*.)

***Canto,** written in a score over the *blank* part for any instr., means that the latter is to play in unison with the vocal (or melody-bearing) part.—Written over an instr.l part, it signifies that at that point the vocal melody reënters after a *ritournelle* or interlude.

Capo-ban'da (militare) (It.) Bandmaster.

Capoco'mico,-a (It.) See *Striese*.

***Capo d'astro.** [An English corruption of *capotasto*.] In the pianoforte, the "capo d'astro bar" is a transverse metallic bar placed above the strings near the wrestplank. Its name is derived from the fact that it bears down on the strings of the three highest octaves (more or less), and is supposed to add to the brilliancy and carrying-power of their tone. It is, however, not removable, like a real *capotasto*, but fixed.

Capo-mu'sica (It.) Conductor ; bandmaster.

Capo-orches'tra (It.) Conductor of an orchestra.

Capophone. A set of musical glasses inv. by M. F. Coelho, on which he produced remarkable effects.

Caratteris′tico,-a (It.) Characteristic.
...*Pezzo caratteristico*, characteristic piece.

Cas′sa (It.) Body (of violin, etc.).

***Catch.** (It. *cac′ce*, from *cac′cia*, a chase.) The term occurs as early as the 14th century, in a composition by Fr. Landino. [*Cf.* AMBROS, "Geschichte der Musik," vol. iii, p. 470.]

Causerie (Fr.) Chat, conversation.

Cavi′glia (It.) Peg.

Cello′ne. A bow-instr. intended to replace the 'cello (in conjunction with the *Violotta* [*q. v.*]) in the string-quartet. In dimensions it resembles the 'cello, but the accordatura is a fourth lower, namely, G_1-D-A-e. Tone like that of the 'cello (though stronger), being far more prompt in speaking, flexible and mellow than that of the double-bass.

Cer′to,-a (It.) Certain ; *con una certa espressione parlante* [Beethoven], with a certain declamatory expression.

Ce′tra ad accor′di (It.) Autoharp.

Champêtre (Fr.) Same as *Campestre.*

Charme, avec (Fr.) With charm, gracefully (It. *vezzosamente*).

Chin-rest. "An oval plate of ebony, slightly hollowed on its upper surface to receive the curve of the jaw, fastened to the edge of the violin to the left of the tailpiece, and extending over, but not touching, the belly." [KREHBIEL.]

Chitarra′ta (It.) Piano-piece imitative of the guitar.

Chord of Nature. The series of harmonics sounding with a generator. (See *Acoustics.*)

Chord-bar. One of the bars crossing the strings of the autoharp ; being pressed down, it allows only the strings of one special chord to vibrate. (Ger. *Pedal.*)

Clavi-harpe (Fr.) A harp played by a pianoforte-keyboard ; inv. by Dietz of Brussels in 1887, and used with good effect in the orch. of the Monnaie Theatre there in 1888.

***Clef.** The following is a form of tenor-clef now (1896) used in Italy. [From the Milan "Gazzetta Musicale", Dec. 17, 1896.]

Tenori 1mi

Tenori 2di

Colori′to (It.) Same as *Colorit.*

***Col′po** (It.) Stroke ; e. g., *colpo di campanel′lo*, stroke of a bell.

***Co′me pri′ma** (It.) Standing alone, as a tempo-mark, it means that the previous tempo is to be resumed (after a digression) ; also written *tornando come prima...Ritenuto come prima*, held back (retarded) as before.

Co′me re′tro (It.) As before.

Composed-through. A frequent translation of the German term *durchkomponiert* (see *Durchkomponieren*), the correct English equivalent for which is "progressively composed," as contrasted with "strophic composition" (see *Song* 2).

Comprima′rio,-a (It.) In theatrical parlance, a part (rôle) of importance, though not one of the leading parts (*prime assolute*).

Concentran′do (It.) "Concentrating", an expression-mark in vocal music, calling for a dark, veiled, intense effect of tone.

***Concerti′sta** (It.) 2. Concert-giver.

Confet′ti (It.) Sugarplums.

Confinal. Compare *Final.*

Conical mouthpiece. See *Cupped.*

***Contrab(b)as′so** (It.) Sub-bass (organ-stop).

Corde filée (Fr.) Covered string.

Cordie′ra (It.) Tailpiece.

Cordo′metro (It.) String-gauge.

Cordonophon. A keyboard-instr. imitating the tones of bells ; inv. Paris, 1890. The tone is produced by hammers striking on a graduated 2-octave series of hollow bronze cylinders.

Cori′sta (It.) Chorus-singer...*C. capo-fila*, a chorus-leader ; especially one to whom a minor solo part is entrusted (see *Pertichino*).

Cornement (Fr.) Running (of wind in an organ).

***Cornet à pistons.** Even in the symphony-orchestra the cornet is not infrequently used ; but its employment as a *substitute* for the *valve-trumpet* is to be condemned, these instr.s being too dissimilar in tone.

Cornet′ta (It.) Cornet à pistons...*Cornetti′na*, a small cornet.

Cor′to,-a (It.) Short. "*La cadenza sia*

corta" [Beethoven], the cadenza should be short.

*Coulé (Fr.) 3. A slur.

Counting. When a part "rests" for several measures, precision of reëntrance is facilitated by counting

(e. g., for )

thus: 123, 223, 323, 423, 523.

Coupure (Fr.) A "cut".

Cravat'tentenor'' (Ger.) A tenor who sings as if his necktie were too tight.

Cupped mouthpiece. The shallower form of mouthpiece for brass wind-instr.s (Ger. *kes'selförmiges Mund'-stück*), in contradistinction to "conical mouthpiece," the deeper form (Ger. *trich'terförmiges Mund'stück*).

D.

Decimaquin'ta (It.) 1. Interval of a fifteenth.—2. The Fifteenth (organ-stop).

Declama'to,-a (It.) Declaimed; in declamatory style.

Deliran'te (It.) Raving; frenziedly.

*Demi-jeu (Fr.) In violin-technic, the persistent employment of short strokes of the bow.

Dichiarazio'ne (It.) Declaration (title of a composition).

Discenden'te (It.) Descending.

Discretez'za, con (It.) With discretion; discreetly, cautiously.

Dispa'ri (It.) Unequal (voices); triple (times).

Divagazio'ne (It.) A ramble, excursion; rambling, strolling.

Divette (Fr.; diminutive of *diva*.) Leading lady in operetta.

Divi'se. This (the *fem. pl.*) form is properly applied to instr.s of the feminine gender (in Italian), such as *tromba*; also to vocal parts (*voci divise*); it may likewise be expressed by numerals, e. g.

Dodinette, Dodino, Dodo (Fr.) Lullaby.

Do'rico (It.) Doric, Dorian.

Dugazon (Fr.; Ger. *erste Liebhaberin*.) French designation for the leading soprano in comedy-opera, operetta, etc.;

named after Louise-Rosalie Dugazon, a celebrated singer (1753-1821).

Dum'ka (Polish.) A sort of romance, vocal or instr.l, of a melancholy cast; a lament or elegy.

*Du'o. A composition in 2 parts *for one instrument;* e. g., a *violin-duo*, in contradistinction to a *violin-duet* for two violins.

Duologie' (Ger.) Duology (a series of two stage-plays, operas, or oratorios).

E.

Échancrures (Fr. pl.) Bouts.

Eck'satz (Ger.) "Corner movement"; i. e., the opening or closing movement in a cyclical composition.

Éclat (Fr.) Same as *Brio*.

Eguaglian'za (It.) Smoothness, evenness; *con molta eguaglianza*, very smoothly, evenly.

*Ein'lage (Ger.) Extra number; incidental number. (See *Arie aggiunte*.)

Élan (Fr.) Impetuosity, vehemence... *Avec élan*, same as *Con slancio*.

Élargissez (Fr.) Same as *Allargate*.

Enchaînez (Fr.) "Go on directly"; same as *Attaccate*.

En élargissant (Fr.) Same as *allargando*, or *più largamente* (Ger. *breiter werdend*).

En enlevant (Fr.) Raising, lifting; detaching (notes).

Enigmatical Canon. See *Canon*.

Enim'ma (It.; pl. *enimme*.) Enigma; hence, enigmatical canon.

En mesure (Fr.) "In measure," i. e., *a tempo*, or *a battuta*.

Enrégisseur Rivoire. A phonautograph for attachment to a pianoforte; inv. by Rivoire in 1895.

Ensem'blestück (Ger.) A concerted piece (Fr. *pièce* [or *morceau*] *d'ensemble*).

Entusias'mo, con (It.) With enthusiasm.

Erin'nerungsmotiv'' (Ger.) A mus. motive attached to and recalling a past scene, emotion, personage, etc.; in so far, a *Leitmotiv*.

Eroico'mico,-a (It.) Mock-heroic.

Erzäh'lung (Ger.) Story, tale, narration.

Esclama'to,-a (It.) Exclaimed; *declamato con forza*.

Esem'pio (It.) Example.

Espansio'ne, con (It.) With exalted or intense feeling.

Espansi'vo (It.) Same as *con espansione*.

*__Espressio'ne__ (It.) Expression-stop.

Esquisse (Fr.) Sketch.

Estre'mo,-a (It.) Extreme...*Estremamen'te*, extremely.

Etichet'ta (It.) Maker's " label " on a violin.

Étoffer (Fr.) To stuff, fill out ; to " pad."

Exaltation, avec (Fr.) Same as *con esaltazione*.

Exhibition. A scholarship at an English university or music-school, independent of the foundation ; as the Potter Exhibition at the Royal Acad. of Music, London.

*__Expression-marks.__ The mark *p sf* over an arpeggio signifies " begin *piano* with a swift *crescendo*, the highest note *sf*."

F.

Fah'ne (Ger.) A " flag " or hook (♮).

Fallboard. Same as *Fly*.

*__Fantasi'a, con__ (It.) With fancy; spiritedly, vividly.

Fantasi'na (It.) Short fantasia.

Fantasticheri'a (It.) A light, fantastic composition.

Fascia're (It.) To cover, to wind (strings)...*Corde fascia'te*, covered strings.

Féerie (Fr.) Fairy-opera, fairy-play.

Fervo're, con (It.) With fervor, warmth.

Feuille (Fr.) A leaf ; *feuilles volantes*, flying leaves.

Feuillet (Fr.) A leaf, leaflet...*Feuillet d'album*, album-leaf.

Fia'ba (It.) Fable, fairy-tale.

*__Fia'to__ (It.) Wind ; *strumen'to a fiato* (or *da fiato*), wind-instr.

Fi'la (It. ; pl. *file.*) Rank (of organ-pipes) ; e. g., " *Pieno, 3 file XV, XIX, XXII*" signifies " Mixture, 3 ranks (Fifteenth, Nineteenth, and triple octave)".

*__Filer un son__ (Fr.) Also means to sustain a tone *with* a gradual *crescendo* and *decrescendo*.

Fi'lo di voce (It.) The very softest and lightest vocal tone.

Fingered octaves. In pfte.-technic, octaves played with the 1-5 and 1-4 fingers alternately.

*__Fingering.__ Alternative fingerings may be written thus :

or thus :

A change of fingers, temporarily delayed, may be indicated thus :

A trill on the pfte. is sometimes fingered thus : $\frac{2}{1}$, or $\frac{3}{2}$, or $\frac{4}{2}$, etc.

Firing. The ringing of all the bells belonging to a chime at once, in contradistinction to *chiming*.

Fisarmo'nica (It.) Physharmonica.

Fixing the voice. Conscious artistic control, in singing, of the act of expiration.

Flessibilità' (It.) Flexibility.

Flies'send (Ger.) Flowing(ly), smooth(ly) ; *scorrendo*.

Flute-stop. Any flue-stop on the organ (except stops of diapason-tone) made of metal or wood, closed or open, and of any pitch from 1⅗-foot (Terzflöte) to 16-foot (Flautone), may be called a " flute " of some kind, either on account of its tone, or after the builder's taste or fancy. Descriptions of the ordinary styles will be found under their respective names. (Also see *Flute-work*, under *Stop* 2.)

Flûtet (Fr.) Same as *Galoubet*.

Fo'glio (It. ; pl. *fogli.*) A leaf...*F. d'album*, album-leaf...*Fo'gli volan'ti*, flying leaves.

Folâtrerie (Fr.) Whim, caprice, bizarre fancy.

For'te genera'le (It.) The full-organ combination - stop...*Forte l'appoggiatura*, accent the appoggiatura strongly.

*__Fort'schreitung einer Dissonanz'__ (Ger.) Is not *necessarily* the *resolution* of the dissonance, as one dissonance may progress to another ; *Auflösung* is the exact German equivalent of "resolution."

Fortténor (Fr.) Dramatic tenor.

Fouetté (Fr. ; "whipped.") See *Whipping bow*.

Frammen'to (It.) Fragment.

Fra se (It.) Aside.

Frau'enchor (Ger.) 1. A female chorus. —2. A composition for such a chorus. ..*Frau'enstimmen*, women's voices.

Freddez'za, con (It.) With coldness ; coolly, indifferently.

Fremen'te (It.) Furiously.

Frettolo'so (It.) Hurried...*Frettolosamen'te*, hurriedly.

Fri'gio (It.) Phrygian.

Frog. The German word *Frosch* means both "frog" (the animal) and "nut" (of a violin-bow) ; translators of German mus. works into English, often mistakenly use the word "frog" instead of the proper technical term "nut."

Fuo'ri di se (It.) Absently ; dreamingly, as if dreaming.

Furberi'a del can'to (It.) The vocal effect of the *bocca chiusa* (humming).

Für sich (Ger.) Aside.

G.

Garba'to (It.) With simple grace, elegance.

Gefeil'ter Strich (Ger.) Detached bowing (violin-technic).

Gehaucht' (Ger.) Very softly and lightly sung or played.

Gemen'do (It.) Moaning.

Gemes'sen (Ger.) Measured(ly), moderate(ly) ; *misurato*.

Gepei'tschte Strich'art (Ger.) Whipping bow.

Geris'sen (Ger.) Thrown off (in pfte.-technic) by a rapid, deft lift of the wrist ; as *ein gerissener Akkord*.

Gesang'reich (Ger.) Very singingly ; *cantando, cantabile*.

Gezo'gen (Ger.) "Drawn out"; *largamente, sostenuto*.

Gio'co, con (It.) Playfully.

Giovialità', con (It.) With joviality, jovially.

Gix'er (Ger.) Same as *Kicks*.

Glottis. See *Vocal glottis*.

Gosier (Fr.) Throat...*Isthme du g.*, isthmus of the throat.

*Graces. In "La Poule" (a piece for harpsichord, by Rameau), the following grace occurs :

In the "Rappel des oiseaux : "

The former is d'Alembert's *Chute et Pincé*, or J. S. Bach's *Accent und Mordant* (Bach gives a different sign) ; the latter is Fr. Couperin's *Pincé simple*, but with a different sign.

Gradatamen'te (It.) By degrees, gradually.

Grandement (Fr.) With grandeur ; with breadth, dignity and force. (It. *con grandezza*.)

Grand'or'gano (It.) Great organ.

Gravità', con (It.) With gravity, dignity ; ponderously.

*Gruppet'to ascenden'te (It.) Back turn...*G. discenden'te*, ordinary turn.

H.

Habane'ra (Sp.) A species of contradance comprising two 8-measure periods in 6-8 time. It is a typical Cuban dance ; hence called the "contradanza criolla" (Creole contradance).

Hack'e (Ger.) Heel. (Abbreviated, in organ-technic, H.)

Harmony, false. 1. The inharmonic relation.—2. Discord produced by imperfect preparation or resolution.—3. Discord produced by wrong notes or chords.

Havanaise (Fr.) A *Habanera*.

Hin'ter der Sze'ne (or **Sce'ne**) (Ger.) Behind the scenes.

Hoch'format (Ger.) The ordinary shape of music-paper, higher than it is broad (See *Querformat*.)

Holding. The burden of a song. (Obsolete.)

Huitième de soupir (Fr.) A 32nd-rest.

I.

Il più (It.) The most.

Im (Ger.; contraction of *in dem*.) In the.
...*Im Tempo*, in the (regular) tempo ; *a tempo*.

Inci'so,-a (It.) Incisive, sharp ; sharply emphasized ; *inci'se* [*le note*], [the notes] sharply marked.

Ingenuamen'te (It.) Ingenuously, naturally.

Ingranag'gio (It.) Gear, gearing ; machine-head.

Insceni'rung, Inszenie'rung (Ger.) See *Mise en scène.*

Intar'sio, Intar'zio (It.) Purfling.

Interligne (Fr.) Space (between lines of staff).

Intermez'zi sinfo'nici (It.) Incidental music (interludes) for orchestra.

Ipo- (It.) Hypo- ; e.g., *ipofri'gio*, Hypophrygian ; *ipoli'dico*, Hypolydian.

Islan'cio (It.) See *Slancio.*

Isthme (Fr.) Isthmus.

Istrumentato're (It.) Instrumenter ; orchestrater ; composer for orchestra.

J.

Jingling Johnny. Formerly a popular name, in London, for the Turkish *crescent.*

Jonction (Fr.) Blending (of the vocal registers) ; also *l'union des registres.*

Juste (Fr.) Perfect (said of intervals).

K.

Kan'tor (Ger.) Cantor ; the director and trainer of a choir or chorus in a church or school.

Ker'nig (Ger.) With firmness, decision ; *con fermez'za, deciso.*

Kes'selförmiges Mund'stück (Ger.) Cupped mouthpiece.

Klavier'abend (Ger.) Piano-recital in the evening. Also *Clavierabend.*

Klavier'harfe (Ger.) Same as *Klaviatur' harfe.*

Kna'benchor (Ger.) Boy-chorus, boy-choir ; also, a composition for such a chorus or choir...*Kna'benstimmen,* boys' voices.

Kokett' (Ger.) Coquettish(ly).

L.

Lamen'to (It.) Lamentation, dirge, elegy.

Lam'penfieber (Ger.) Stage-fright.

Languo're, con (It.) With languor, languidly.

Larghez'za, con (It.) Same as *Largamente.*

Leer (Ger.) 1. Empty, hollow (of a tone). —2. Open (of a string).

Legan'do (It.; "binding.") 1. Equivalent to *Legato.*—2. An expression-mark, in vocal or instr.l music, calling for the smooth execution of two or more consecutive tones by a single "stroke of the glottis" (vocal), in one bow (violin, etc.), by a single stroke of the tongue (wind-instr.s), or *legatissimo* (on organ or pfte.).

Lega'te (It.; pl. form of *lega'ta*, the words "*le note*" being implied.) Slurred ; played (or sung) evenly and smoothly.

*Legatu'ra (It.) 2. A slur.

Leggen'da (It.) Legend.

Leggeris'sime (It.; pl. of *leggerissima,* "*le note*" being implied.) [Play or sing the notes] very lightly.

Leg'gio (It.) Music-stand.

Le'gni (It.; pl. of *le'gno*, wood.) Woodwind.

Les ff (Fr.) The *f*-holes.

Lice'o (It.) Lyceum ; Conservatory.

Lie'derabend (Ger.; "song-evening.") A song-recital (by one singer).

Lie'derdichter (Ger.) A writer of songs (poems) to be set to music.

Lie'derspiel (Ger.) 1. Ballad - opera, vaudeville.—2. A concert-piece for vocal soli, chorus, and pfte.-accompaniment, with dramatic and local color; invented by Schumann in his "Spanisches Liederspiel," op. 74.

Liuta'io (It.) Same as *Luthier.*

Liuti'sta (It.) Lute-player.

Lontanis'simo (It.) Very far away ; equivalent to *piano possibile.*

Lun'ga e diminuen'do [morendo] (It.) Long sustained and diminishing in force. (Here "*nota*" is implied.)

M.

Macchinet'ta (It.) Machine-head.

Madrile'ña (Sp.) A dance of Madrid.

*Mandolina'ta (It.) 2. Title for a mandolin-piece of a quiet character, such as a serenade or nocturne.

Mandoloncel'lo, Mandolo'ne (It.) Large styles of the mandolin.—" Mandolina, Mandola, Mandoloncello and Mandolone do not differ one from the other in form, but only in size." [GAZZETTA MUSICALE.]

Manua'liter (Lat.) On the manual(s) alone (organ-music).

Marca'te (It.; pl. of *marca'ta*.) A direction signifying : " The notes are to be marked"; the words "*le note*" being implied.

Mar'kig (Ger.) " Marrowy "; with strong emphasis; sturdy, strong, vigorous. (Also *adverb*.)

Mediation. See *Chant* 3.

Melo'logo (It.; pl. *melo'loghi*.) Melodrama ; a spoken dramatic scene accompanied or illustrated by music.

Mes'sa da re'quiem (It.) Requiem mass.

Mes'sa in sce'na (It.) Same as *Mise en scène*.

*Mesuré (Fr.) Equivalent to *moderato ;* e.g., *Allegro mesuré*.

Metro'mano-piano (It.) A finger-exerciser for pianists, inv. by Luigi Pizzamiglio in 1897, and commended by a special committee of the Milan Conservatorio. It has a short keyboard, and various springs and other accessories.

*Mez'zo (It.; *adjective*.) Occurring alone, it refers to the dynamic sign next preceding (either *f* or *p*)...*Mezzo respiro*, half-breath (i.e., a [rapid] partial inspiration).

Mez'zo (It. ; *noun*.) Middle ; *nel mezzo del arco*, in the middle of the bow.

Milieu (Fr.) Middle.

Minu'gia (It.) Gut. (Also *Budello*.)

Mise en scène (Fr.; It. *messa in scena ;* Ger. *Inszenierung*.) Setting of a play on the stage ; stage-setting, mounting.

Moderatamen'te (It.) With moderation (either of tempo or emotion) ; also *con moderazione*.

Mol'to sot'tovoce (It.) Very softly indeed.

Mon'do picci'no (It.) " Little Folks," " Little People"; title equiv. to the German " Kinderszenen," " Kinderstücke."

Montatu'ra (di corde) (It.) Set of strings.

Mor'bido (It.) Soft, tender ; *morbidissimo*, very soft... *Con morbidezza*, with tenderness, softly.

*Morden'te. G. NAVA, in his " Elements of Vocalization," calls an unaccented double-appoggiatura (e. g.,

) a *mordente*.

*Mos'so (It.) Occurring alone as a tempo-mark, *Mosso* is equiv. to *Con moto*. [Verdi : " Aïda," pf.-score, p. 285.]

Mu'sica fic'ta (Lat.; " feigned music.") Mediæval name for scales transposed by the use of the ♮ or ♭ ; such scales being considered irregular (" feigned ") in contrast with the regular ones.

Musical Dictation. See *Dictée musicale*.

Mu'sico (It.) An artificial male soprano ; a *castrato* or *evirato*.

Musique de scène (Fr.) Incidental music.

Musurgia (Gk.) The art of correctly employing the musical consonances and dissonances.

N.

Nach'gebend, Nach'giebig (Ger.) Yielding(ly), slower and slower, *rallentando*...*Nach'giebiger*, more yielding. ly, *più sostenuto*.

Na'ker. Ancient name of the kettledrum.

Naset'to (It.) Point (of bow). Also *punta*.

Naufra'gio (It.; " shipwreck.") Modern equivalent of *Fiasco*.

Negligen'za, con (It.) With negligence, carelessly.

Ni'colo. An ancient style of bombard, the *alto* of the oboe.

Nien'te (It.) Nothing. (The phrase *quasi niente* signifies " inaudible, as it were," i.e., barely audible.)

Nin'na-nan'na ⎰ (It.) Lullaby.
Ninnerel'la ⎱

*Notation. In the following example [Rubinstein, op. 3, No. 4] for pfte., the two notes with convergent stems, $g\flat$ and $g\natural$, are to be played simultaneously :

Notturni'no (It., dimin. of *Notturno.*) A short nocturne.

*Numerals. The Roman numerals I., II., III., IV., in violin-playing, indicate the string to be played on, the E-string being I.—1ª, 2ª, 3ª, and 4ª (for *prima, seconda, terza* and *quarta* **corda**, respectively), are also written.—A single *8* under a bass note signifies that the note should be doubled in the lower octave.—*1 C.* and *3 C.*, in modern Italian piano-music, stand for *Una corda* and *Tre corde* respectively.—Also *cf. Divise* and *Fingering*, in Appendix.

Nymphale (Fr.) A French portable organ of the 16th century.

O.

*Oboe (compass). 1. The usual orchestral compass is only to f^3...*Oboe da cac'cia* (It.), the tenoroon oboe (corno inglese)...*Oboe lunga*, same as oboe d'amore.—2. In the organ, an 8-foot reed-stop, with conical pipes surmounted by a bell and cap...*Orchestral oboe*, a stop accurately imitating the orch.l instr.

Obo'er (Ger.) Oboist.

Officle'ide (It.) Alternative spelling of *Oficleide.*

*Opérette [with *é*] is the correct spelling of the French word.

Operi'sta (It.) Opera-composer.

Order. The arrangement of chord-tones above a given bass, "open" and "close order" being equiv. to "open" and "close harmony".

Orecchian'te (It.) One judging of music "by ear" ; one lacking theoretical and practical training in the art.

Orfeo'nico (It.) Pertaining to the Orphéons.

*Organet'to a manu'brio (It.) Hand-organ. (Also *O. di Barbaria.*)

Organ-metal. Same as *Pipe-metal.*

Or'gano espressi'vo (It.) Swell-organ.

Otto'ni (It. ; pl. of *otto'ne*, brass.) Brass-wind.

P.

ppppp. Young Italy occasionally indulges in five *p*'s to indicate a barely audible musical murmur.

Pa'gina d'album (It.) Album-leaf.

Parabrac'cio (It.) Arm-rest.

Parallel intervals are formed by the progression of two parts in the same direction and at exactly the same interval.

Pa'ri (It.) Equal (of voices ; "*voci pari*") ; duple (of times ; "*tempi pari*").

*Parlan'te (It. ; "speaking.") In pfte.-technic, this direction calls for a clear, crisp *non legato.*

Parla'to (It.) Spoken.

Parolier (Fr.) Same as *Liederdichter.*

Partie (Fr.) Part...*Parties séparées,* separate parts...*Partition et parties,* score and parts.

Partitionnette (Fr.) A little (or slight) score.

Pas'so (It.) 1. Step ; e. g., *Valzer a due passi.*—2. Measure ; time ; *passo ordina'rio,* common time ; *passo doppio composto,* compound duple time.

Pau'ken (Ger.) To thump ; thumping, pounding, banging (rough piano-playing).

Pau'ra (It.) Fear, dismay...*Pauro'so,* fearful, timid.

Pedal' dop'pelt (Ger.) "The pedal-part in octaves" (organ-technic ; It. *pedale doppio*)...*Pedal ein'fach,* a direction following the foregoing, and signifying that the pedal-part is no longer to be doubled...*Pedal'koppel,* pedal-coupler.

Peda'le o'gni battu'ta (It.) "Take pedal with each measure."

Pedalet'to (It.) A mechanical stop on the organ ; e. g., *p. di accoppiamen'to,* coupler ; *p. di combinazio'ne,* combination-stop.

Pedali'no (It.) Same as *Pedaletto.*

Pedal-sign. A sign for the loud pedal, written (a) ⌐‾‾‾‾‾⌐ (b) , has been introduced by Arthur Foote of Boston ; *a* showing the precise point at which the pedal should be depressed, and *b* where it should be raised.

Pei'tschend (Ger.) See *Whipping bow.*

Pel (It.) Contraction of *per il,* "for the" ; e. g., *pel mandolino,* for the mandolin.

Pen'na (It.) Pick, plectrum.

Pensie'ro (It.) Thought ... *Pensiero del(la)* —, Souvenir of —, Recollections of —.

Penso'so (It.) Pensive, thoughtful.

Perce (Fr.) Bore (of wood-wind instr.s).

Per interval'li giu'sti (It.) By exact intervals (in a canon ; i. e., the theme is repeated interval for interval, strictly).

Pertichi'no (It.) The singer of an extremely subordinate operatic part ; a part often taken by the chorus-leader.— In German such a singer has been jocularly termed a *So'lochor''sänger*, "solo chorus-singer". (See *Corista*.)

Petac'cha (It.) Plectrum.

Pezzet'to (It.) Little piece.

Pez'zi stacca'ti (It.) *Airs détachés.*

Phrasé (Fr.; *noun.*) Phrasing.

Piano'la. A mechanical piano-player, invented by E. S. Votey of New York, in the year 1897. It is furnished with 4 stops, *Piano, Forte, Tempo* and *Accent*, by whose skilful manipulation the most artistic effects may be produced at will. The motive-power is supplied by two pedals (treadles) worked by the feet ; these pedals actuate (*a*) a revolving music-roll of perforated paper, whose perforations control the time-value of the notes ; and (*b*) the pneumatic action, consisting of 65 felt-covered levers, or automatic fingers, which command a compass of five octaves and four semitones (from A_1 to c^{4}♯♯), and act with all the delicacy and precision of a trained pianist's digits, besides being able to play any 4-hand pieces. The apparatus is not attached to the pianoforte, but set in front of it in such a position that the 65 automatic fingers engage the proper keys.—The repertory, comprising at present (1900) about 20,000 numbers, embraces all grades of popular, romantic, and classic pianoforte - music and arrangements. (*Cf. Æolian.*)

Pib-corn (Welsh.) A hornpipe.

Piffera'ta (It.) Air for the fife, or in imitation (as on the pfte.).

Placidez'za, con (It.) With placidity ; tranquilly, calmly.

Plain-beat. An obsolete English harpsichord-grace ;

Written:

Played:

Plein (Fr.) Full ; *à plein son*, with full tone (*sonoramente*).

Plet'tro (It.) Plectrum, pick.

Pluperfect. Augmented (of intervals).

Po'co me'no (It.) When this phrase occurs alone as a tempo-mark, *mosso* is implied ; i. e., *poco meno mosso*, a little less fast [slower]...*Poco più*, standing alone, also implies *mosso* ("a little faster")...*Poco più lento della I^{ma} volta*, somewhat slower than the first time.

Poemet'to (It. ; "little poem.") A slight musico-dramatic work.

Pointing. See *Chant* 3.

Pol'ca (It.) Polka.

Polchet'ta (Polketta?) (It.) Little polka.

Polifo'nico,-a (It.) Polyphonic.

Pol'nisch (Ger.; "Polish.") Polacca (as the title of a piece).

Polone'se (It.) Polonaise. (*Polacca*.)

Pom'pa, con (It.) With pomp, pompously, loftily.

Porta-mu'sica (It.) Music-roll, portfolio.

Porta'te la vo'ce (It.) "Carry the voice"; a direction to *more than one* singer to sing *portamento*.

Post-horn. A horn without valves or keys, capable of producing the natural harmonics of its fundamental tone ; used on post-coaches.

Premier dessus (Fr.) Soprano.

Pressan'do (It.) Same as *Pressante*.

Prestissimamen'te (It.) With extreme rapidity (equiv. to *Prestissimo*).

Pre'sto parlan'te (It.) "Speaking rapidly (volubly)"; a direction in recitatives, etc.

Principali'no (It. ; "small diapason.") An 8-foot stop on the swell-organ.

Prinzipal'stimme (Ger.) Leading part ; solo part.

Profa'no,-a (It.) Secular ; as *oratorio profano, musica profana*.

Programmist. 1. A musician who writes music to fit a "program", which latter may be either expressed or implied.—2. A theorist or critic who favors composing according to program.

Progressive composition of a song is the English equivalent for *Durchkomponieren* (*q. v.*).

Prolongement (Fr.) Sustaining-pedal.

Pronunzia'to,-a (It.) Pronounced, emphasized.

Protagoni'sta (It.), **Protagoniste** (Fr.) Singer of the leading rôle in an opera.

***Pro'va** (It.) Rehearsal...*P. in costu'-me*, dress-rehearsal...*P. genera'le*, full rehearsal.

Pult (Ger.) Desk...*Erstes (I.) Pult*, and *Zweites (II.) Pult*, in a score, indicate, respectively, *Division 1* and *2* of a group of orch.1 instr.s playing *divisi*.

Pult'virtuos (Ger.; Fr. *virtuose de pupitre*.) A " virtuoso of the desk " (i. e., conductor's desk); a conductor of celebrity, like Hans Richter, von Bülow, Weingartner, *et al.*, who either travels with his own orchestra, or conducts different orchestras at various places.

Pun'to corona'to (It.) Hold (⌒).

Q.

Qua'dro (It.) Picture, tableau.

Quer'format (Ger.) Oblong (shape of music-paper, broader than long).

Quitter (Fr.) To quit, leave ; *sans quitter la corde*, without quitting the string.

R.

Raccoglimen'to (It.) Collectedness of mind, composure.

Raccol'ta (It.) Collection.

Raccon'to (It.) Tale, story.

Rallenta'te (It., imperative.) Go slower.

Recessional. A hymn sung in church during the departure of the choir and clergy after a service.

Redite (Fr.) Repetition.

Reduce (It. *ridur're*.) Same as *Réduire*. ...*Reduction* (Ger. *Reduktion'; Fr. *réduction ; It. *riduzio'ne*), a reduced composition (see *Réduire*).

Reif'tanz (Ger.) Same as *Schäfflertanz*.

Reminiscen'ze (It. pl.) Recollections.

Résolument (Fr.) Same as *Risolutamente*.

Restez (Fr. ; " stay there ! ") In music for bow-instr.s this direction means : (1) " Play on the same string ", or (2) " Remain in the same position (shift)".

***Rests.** A pause of several measures is often written thus :

Retenu (Fr.) Same as *Ritenuto*.

Retrosce'na (It.) Behind the scenes.

Revue (Fr.) A review in musico-dramatic form, and generally humorous, of the striking events in a season or year just closing.

***Ribattu'to,-a** (It.) Restruck, repeated ; *note ribattute*, repeated notes.

Ric'cio (It.) Scroll.

Ricochet (Fr.) In violin-technic, a variety of staccato differing from the *sautillé (saltato)* in not employing the wrist (in the *saltato*, up-stroke, a separate wrist-movement is made for each detached tone).

Rifiormen'to (It.) Same as *Adornamento*.

Rimembran'za (It. ; pl. *rime: an'ze*.) Recollection, souvenir, memory.

Ripieni'no (It.) A 4-foot stop on the swell-organ.

***Ripie'no** (It.) A combination-stop in the organ drawing all registers of any given manual.

Ripi'glio (It.) Repetition, reprise.

Ripo'so (It.) Repose...*Riposa'to*, reposeful, restful...*Riposatamen'te*, reposefully.

Ripren'dere (It.) To resume ; *stringendo per riprendere il I° tempo*, hastening, in order to regain the former tempo.

Risolutezza, con (It.) With resolution, decision.

Rispet'to (It.) Love-ditty.

Rit. is given on p. 2 as an abbreviation of *Ritenuto*, and is often so used, though more frequently for *Ritardando.*—In view of the difference in meaning between *Ritenuto* and *Ritardando*, it is advisable always to write *Ritenuto* out in full, when that nuance is desired.

Ritardan'za (It.) Retardation.

Ritardazio'ne (It.) Retardation, dragging.

Rit'mico (It.) Rhythmical...*Rit'mico*, written after a recitative, is also equivalent to " *a tempo* " or *misurato*.

Rit'ter-Bra'tsche (Ger.) A large style of viola, the *Viola alta*, inv. by Hermann Ritter of Würzburg ; a performer on it is sometimes called a " Ritter-Bratschist'."

Rivi'sta (It.) Same as *Revue*.

Rola'ta (It.) A roulade.

Roman'za sen'za paro'le (It.) Song without words.

Romanze'ro (It.) A suite or cycle of romantic pieces for pfte.

S.

Sag'gio (It.) Examination.. (*Concerto di saggio*, pupils' concert given for practice in ensemble, or *quasi* public, performance ; equivalent to the German *Übungsabend* or *Abendunterhaltung*).

*****Sampo'gna** (It.) A variety of the Italian bagpipe, having (in a specimen examined in the United States) 2 drones, and 2 melody-pipes fingered by the right and left hands respectively ; on it was played the accompaniment to a shrill reed-pipe which the performers called a *cornamusa*. The bag is inflated by the breath and squeezed by the right arm.

Sans (Fr.) Without.

Sautillé (Fr.) Saltato.

Sauvement (Fr.) Resolution (of a dissonance).

Saxofo'nia (It.) Saxophone.

*****Scale.** 4 (of a piano). Compass ; i.e., the range of tones represented by the keyboard.

Schäfflertanz (Ger.) Festival procession and dance, probably of great antiquity, of the Coopers' Guild at Munich ; held every 7 years.

Schie'ber (Ger.) Same as *Schub*.

Schiettez'za, con (It.) Simply ; neatly, deftly.

Schla'ger (Ger.) A "hit" ; brilliantly successful piece or play.

Schmach'tend (Ger.) Languishing(ly), longing(ly).

Scintil'la (It.; pl. *scintil'le*.) A spark.

Scivolan'do (It.) Same as *Glissando*, in pfte.-technic.

Scoop. Vocal tones are said to be "scooped" when taken, instead of by firm and just attack, by a rough *portamento* from a lower tone.

Secondan'do (It.) Supporting, following ; *secondando la voce* (or *il canto*), yieldingly following the principal part (with the accompaniment).

Second dessus (Fr.) Mezzo-soprano.

Semitril'lo (It.) Inverted mordent.

Sentimenta'le (It.) Feelingly.

Sen'za misu'ra (It.) "Without meas-

ure" ; i.e., not in strict time ; equivalent to the tempo-mark *a piacere*, and opposed to *misurato*... *Senza suono*, "without tone" ; i.e., spoken.

Sept'akkord (Ger.) Seventh-chord. (Also *Sep'timenakkord*.)

Serenatel'la (It.) Little serenade.

Serenità', con (It.) With serenity, serenely, tranquilly.

Serietà', con (It.) Seriously.

Settimi'no (It.) A piece for 7 performers.

Severità', con ; Seve'ro (It.) In a severe (stern, austere) manner.

Sfuma'to (It.; pl. *sfuma'te* [*le note* implied].) Very lightly, like a vanishing smoke-wreath... *Sfumatu'ra*, "Smoke-wreath" (title of a light, airy composition).

*****Signs.** 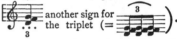 Instead of the misleading short slur, with figure, for doublets, triplets, etc., modern French music sometimes has a dotted slur (as shown above), which is an improvement.

 another sign for the triplet

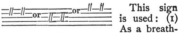 This sign, at the end of a staff, shows that the measure is unfinished, so that no bar is required.

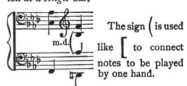 The repeat-s i g n is some-times written at a *single* bar.

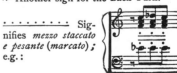 The sign (is used like [to connect notes to be played by one hand.

=||=||= This sign is used : (1) As a breathing-mark ; (2) to mark a very brief pause, together with the interruption caused by taking breath.

~ Another sign for the Back Turn.

· · · · · · · · · Signifies *mezzo staccato e pesante* (*marcato*) ; e.g. :

⌐ ∧ In organ-pieces, signs for pedal-
ling are sometimes written thus :
For right foot, heel ⌐ , toe ∧
" left " " ⌐ " ∨

⌐ ⌐ In piano-playing a note to be
taken by the right hand is sometimes marked thus : ⌐ ; for the left
hand : ⌐.

(Also *cf.*, in APPENDIX, the articles *Notation,
Numerals, Time* and *Turn.*)

*Silen′zio (It.) 2. A pause, silence ; as
lungo silenzio.

Simplement (Fr.) Simply, semplice ;
très simplement, semplicissimamente.

*Sinfoni′a (It.) This term is *still* used
in Italy to designate an opera-overture ;
e.g., *la sinfonia del Tannhäuser.*

Sinfoni′sta (It.) A writer of symphonies, or for symphony-orchestra.

Sing′amt (Ger.) See *Singmesse...Sing′-
en,* to sing, warble...*Sing′gedicht,* a
poem for mus. setting...*Sing′kunst,* art
of singing...*Sing′lehrer,* singing-teach-
er...*Sing′leiter,* gamut, vocal scale...
Sing′märchen, vocal ballad...*Sing′-
meister,* singing-master...*Sing′messe,*
a-cappella mass...*Sing′saite,* treble
string, chanterelle...*Sing′stunde,* sing-
ing-lesson, vocal instruction...*Sing′-
übung,* singing-exercise...*Sing′verein,*
singing-society.

Singhioz′zo (It.) Sob.

Slancian′te, Slancia′to (It.) " Thrown
off " lightly and deftly, or forcibly and
vehemently.

Slarga′to (It.) Slower, *più sostenuto.*

*Slide. 4. On a violin-bow, that part of
the nut which slides along the stick.

Solmizza′re (It.) Same as *Solfeggiare.*

Sopranist′(in) (Ger.) Soprano singer.

Sorri′so (It.) A smile.

*Sorti′ta (It.) See *Aria* in APPENDIX.

Soutenu (Fr.) Same as *Sostenuto.*

Specification. (Ger. *Disposition.*) An
enumeration of the various stops composing any given organ, giving number,
kind, and arrangement.

Spianar′ la vo′ce (It.) To render the
voice even ; to blend the registers.

*Spicca′to (It.) In violin-technic, a variety of staccato differing from the *saltato* in employing the wrist-stroke
throughout, for each detached note.

Spie′gelkanon (Ger.) A canon to be
performed backwards ; i.e., as it appears
when held before a mirror (" Spiegel ").

Spigliatez′za (It.) Agility, dexterity,
briskness...*Spigliatez′ze* (pl.), short,
lively pieces or studies requiring dexterity.

Stanchez′za (It.) Weariness ; *con st.,*
wearily, very dragging.

Stan′co,-a (It.) Weary.

*Stentan′do (It.) Means literally, " delaying, retarding, dragging " the tempo.
...*Stenta′to,* delayed, retarded, dragged.

Stiria′na (It.) See *Styrienne.*

Stornel′lo (It.) A form of song in which
each 8-line stanza rhymes thus : 1-3 2-4
5-6 7-8.

Strambot′to (It.) Folk-song ; rustic
love-ditty. (Also *Strambot′tolo.*)

Strappa′re (It. ; " to pluck off.") In
piano-technic, to throw off a note or
chord by a rapid, light turn of the
wrist...*Lo strappare,* the throwing-off.
...*Strappato,* thrown off (Ger. *gerissen*).

Strascina′re la vo′ce (It.) To sing a
portamento with an exaggerated dragging or drawling.

Strei′cher (Ger.) Player(s) on any bow-
instr.s.

Stret′ta (It.) A closing passage (coda)
in swifter tempo than the movement
preceding.

Strich′-Staccato (Ger.) A staccato indicated by wedge-shaped dashes (❘ ❘).

Strict style (of composition). See *Counterpoint, strict.*

Strie′se (Ger. ; It. *capoco′mico.*) The
leading comic actor or singer in a company, either gentleman or (It. *capoco′-
mica*) lady.

Strimpella′ta (It.) Strumming, scrap-
ing.

Strin′gere (It.) To hasten ; *senza strin-
gere,* without hastening.

Strophic composition. See *Song 2.*

Styrienne (Fr. ; It. *Stiriana.*) An air in
slow movement and 2-4 time, often in
minor, with *Jodler* after each verse,
for vocal or instr.l solo.

Super′bo,-a (It.) Superb ; proud, lofty.
...*Superbamen′te,* proudly, loftily.

Svilup′po (It.) Development.

Sviz′zera, alla (It.) In Swiss style.

T.

Table du fond (Fr.) Back (of violin).

Ta'glio (It.) A " cut."

Tallo'ne (It.) Nut (of bow).

Tarantelli'na (It.) Little tarantella.

Telltale. A small weight moving vertically in a groove, and so connected with the bellows of an organ that, by rising and falling, it shows the organist or " blower" the amount of wind in the bellows.

Terzetti'no (It.) A short terzet.

Tetralogie' (Ger.) Tetralogy ; a series of 4 stage-works or oratorios.

Three-step. (Ger. *Dreitritt ;* It. *Valzer a tre passi ;* Fr. *trois-temps.*) The ordinary (Vienna) waltz. (See *Waltz.*)

Timballo'ne (It.) A 16-foot pedal-stop in the organ.

Timbrel (Hebr.) A tambourine or tabor.

*Time. In French notation the large 3 is still sometimes employed instead of ¾.

Ti'mido (It.) Timid, timorous... *Timo're, con,* with timidity ; timorously, fearfully, anxiously.

Tonan'te (It.) Thundering, thunderous.

Ton'figuren (Ger., pl.) " Tone-figures " ; i.e., " nodal figures " (*q.v.*).

Toni'metro (It.) Tuning-fork (*t. a percussione*) ; pitch-pipe (*t. a fiato*).

*Ton'satz (Ger.) 2. Arrangement (e.g., of the vocal or instr.l accomp to an ancient melody).

Tornan'do (It.) Returning ; *t. al primo tempo* (or *t. come prima*), returning to (resuming) the original tempo.

Traduzio'ne (It.) Arrangement.

Trascrizio'ne (It.) Transcription.

Traspor'to, con (It.) With transport, ecstatically.

Treff'übung (Ger.) A singing exercise on the " attack," as regards either pitch, or time of entrance (in duets, canons, etc.).

Treman'te (It.) Trembling ; i.e., with a tremolo effect.

Trial (Fr.) Buffo (or comic) tenor.

Trich'terförmiges Mund'stück (Ger.) Conical mouthpiece.

Trilogie' (Ger.) Trilogy ; a series of 3 stage-works or oratorios.

Trisser (Fr.) To demand a number for the third time ; to " encore" for a second time.

Trito'nikon (Ger.) A modern form of double-bassoon, made of metal.

Trom'ba rea'le (It.; "royal trumpet.") An 8-foot trumpet-stop in the organ.

Trompe des Alpes (Fr.; It. *tromba delle Alpi.*) " The hollowed trunk or branch of a tree, from which the old mountaineers draw strange tones." [Reintroduced lately into Switzerland by Prof. Heim of Zurich.]

Tron'co,-a (It.) Cut off short ; stopped abruptly... *Suoni tronchi,* tones cut off suddenly.

*Tuba. The bass tuba in $E_{1}\flat$ is extensively employed in the modern orchestra.

*Turn. Example of turn-sign over a dotted note ; from Beethoven, op. 14, No. 1, showing the dot as he himself wrote it :

Tut'ta for'za (It.) Abbreviation of " *con tutta la forza,*" with full force.

Two-step (Ger. *Zweitritt ;* It. *Valzer a due passi ;* Fr. *deux-temps.*) The rapid waltz. (See *Waltz.*)

U.

U'bungsabend (Ger.) See *Abendunterhaltung,* in APPENDIX.

U'bungsstück (Ger.) See *Vortragsstück,* in APPENDIX.

Um'gekehrt (Ger.) Reversed ; *umgekehrter Doppelschlag,* back turn.

Um'schmeissen (Ger. theatrical slang.) To break down in a rôle, so as to necessitate a general stoppage and the recommencement of the passage.

*Un'gebunden (Ger.) Unconstrained ;

mit ungebundenem Humor, with uncon-strained humor, *burlando*.

Union des registres (Fr.)   Blending of the (vocal) registers.

Uni'ti (It., pl.)   " United " ; this direc-tion in a score, after *divisi*, signifies that the instr.s or voices again perform their part in unison.

Unvocal.   1. Not suitable for singing.— 2. Not vibrating with tone ; *unvocal air* is breath escaping with a more or less audible sigh or hiss, due to unskilful management of the vocal apparatus.

V.

Val'zer (It.)   Waltz.

Veris'mo (It.)   Naturalism... *Veris'tisch* (Ger.), pertaining to or affected by naturalism ; naturalistic.

Verstär'ken (Ger.)   To reinforce.

*Vibra'to,-a (It.; pl. *vibrate* [*le note* im-plied].)   Strongly accented, and dimin-ishing in intensity (⊴ ; vocal or instr.l). ... *Vibrazio'ne di voce*, the attack of a tone *forte* or *sf*, and diminishing while holding it.

Vi'de se'quens (Lat.)   " See the follow-ing."

Vielle à roue (Fr.)   Hurdy-gurdy.

Vigo're, con (It.)   With vigor.

Vio'la al'ta.   A large viola, inv. by Her-mann Ritter of Wismar, Germany, and described in his pamphlet, " Die Ge-schichte der Viola alta und die Grund-sätze ihres Baues " (1877).   It has a fuller and freer tone than the ordinary viola, and has been quite extensively introduced into German orchestras.

Vio'la di bordo'ne.   The barytone (instr.).

Violina'ta (It.)   1. A piece for violin.— 2. A piece for another instr., imitating the violin-style.

Violinzo'li (It.)   An 8-foot stop on the swell-organ.

Violi'sta (It.)   Viola-player.

Violoncelli'sta (It.)   'Cellist.

Violot'ta.   A bow-instr. of violin-type, inv. 1895 by Dr. Alfred Stelzner, Dres-den, and intended to fill the hiatus in the string-quartet between viola and 'cello. It is played like the viola, and has the same dimensions ; but its accordatura is *G-d-a-e¹*, a fourth lower than the viola.

Tone full in lowest register, mellow and tender in the medium, and the *E*-string well-adapted for sustained melody.   Suc-cessful concerts have been given with the *Violotta* and *'Cellone* (*q.v.*) in Dres-den.—Dr. S. claims to have obtained the most equable and powerful reson-ance from instr.s of the violin-type.

Virtuose de pupître (Fr.)   See *Pultvir-tuos*.

Vitesse (Fr.)   Rapidity, swiftness.

Vivement (Fr.)   Same as *Vivace*.

*Vocal cords.   " The free median bor-ders of 2 folds of mucous membrane within the larynx, bounding the ante-rior two-thirds of the glottis on either side.   Each is formed by the free me-dian edge of an elastic (inferior thyro-arytenoid) ligament running from the angle of the thyroid cartilage to the vocal process of the arytenoid, and cov-ered with thin and closely adherent mucous membrane."—[CENTURY DICT.]

*Vo'gelgesang (Ger.)   2. A stop in an organ (" bird-stop ").

Voile du palais (Fr.)   Veil of the palate.

Vor'setzungszeichen (Ger.)   Chromatic sign.

Vor'tragsstück (Ger.)   A piece for per-formance before an audience (in con-tradistinction to *Übungsstück*, a prac-tice-piece) ; a concert-piece ; a show-piece.—2. *V. übung*, study intended for concert performance.

Vor'wärts (Ger.)   Forward(s) ; *etwas v. gehend*, somewhat faster, *poco più mosso*.

*Vuo'to,-a (It.)   2. Empty ; *scena vuota*, the stage [remains] empty.

W.

Whipping bow.   (Fr. *fouetté ;* Ger. *ge-peitschte Strichart.*)   A form of violin-technic in which the bow is made to fall with a certain vehemence on the strings.   Chiefly employed when it is desired to mark sharply single tones in rapid tempo ; e.g.,

Not infrequent in modern orchestral music ; but avoided by the classic com-posers on account of its rough, harsh effect.

Z.

Zaramel'la (It.) Rustic pipe, with double-reed held between the player's lips, 7 finger-holes, and bell-mouth; plays melodies to the accompaniment of the Neapolitan *sampogna* (*q.v.*; AP-PENDIX).

Ziem'lich bewegt' und frei im Vor'-trag (Ger.) Quite animated and free in delivery (style).

Zi'therharfe (Ger.) A species of auto-harp in which dampers actuated by digitals are used to damp the strings. Müller's *Accordzither* (inv. 1894 ?) is an example.

Zit'tera (It.) Zither.

SUPPLEMENT.

English-Italian Vocabulary

for

Composers.

A.

Above. Sopra...*Above the right hand,* sopra la mano destra.

Accelerated. Accelerato ; *accelerating,* accelerando ; stringendo ; pressante... *Accelerating the tempo,* ravvivando il tempo. [See *Enliven.*]

Accented. Marcato; enfatico, con enfasi.

Accompaniments. Accompagnamenti. ..*Accompaniment very soft throughout,* sempre pp. gli accompagnamenti.

Affected(ly). Smorfioso ; affettato (con affettazione).

Affectionate(ly). Affettuoso (affettuosamente). [See *Tender.*]

Afraid. Paventato. [See *Fearful.*]

Again. Ancora, ancor.

Agility. Agilità ; velocità.

Agitated(ly). Agitato (con agitazione); tumultuoso (tumultuosamente) ; vibrante.

Agreeable. Gradevole ; piacevole. [See *Pleasing.*]

Air. [See *Melody.*]

All together. Tutti.

Also. Anche.

Alternatively. Alternamente.

Always. Sempre...*Always swift and soft,* sempre con agevolezza e sottovoce.

And. E, ed (before a vowel).

Angry. Adirato ; *angrily,* con ira.

Animated(ly). Animato (con anima) ; allegro (allegramente) ; vivace (vivacemente) ; vivido, vivo (vivamente) ; vivente ; visto (vistamente); con moto ; svegliato ; risvegliato... *With growing animation,* animandosi.

An octave higher. All'ottava (*8va⸻*, or *8⸻* , or *8va alta*).

An octave lower. All'ottava bassa (*8va bassa*).

Anxious(ly). Ansioso (ansiosamente), affanoso (affanosamente) ; timoroso (timorosamente ; con timore).

Ardent(ly). Ardente (con ardore) ; fervente (con fervore).

Artless(ly). Innocente (innocentemente); semplice (semplicemente) ; naturale (naturalmente).

As. Come.

As above. Come sopra.

As before. Come avanti ; come prima

As far as. Fino, *or* fin'; sino, *or* sin'.

Aside. In disparte.

As if. Quasi.

As usual. Al solito.

As written. Come sta ; loco (after *8va⸻* ; or simply terminate dotted line with a down-stroke).

At a distance. In distanza ; in lontananza ; da lontano.

At pleasure. A piacere ; ad libitum ; a bene placito ; senza tempo ; a suo arbitrio.

At sight. A prima vista.

Attack. Attacca, attaccate (*pl.*) ; *attack instantly,* attacca(te) subito.

At the former tempo. A tempo, *or* Tempo I ; moto precedente.

B.

Babbling. Straccicalando.

Back to the sign. Dal segno (𝄋). ..*Back to the beginning,* da capo.

Backwards. Al rovescio.

Begin (to). Attaccare...*Begin!* attacca, attaccate... *To begin again,* ripigliare.

Beginning. Principio ; capo.

Below. Sotto ; *below the left hand,* sotto la mano sinistra.

Bitter(ly).   Amarevole (con amarezza).

Bizarre(ly).   Bizzarro (bizzarramente, con bizarreria).

Boisterous(ly).   Strepitoso (strepitosamente, con strepito) ; brioso (con brio); tempestoso (tempestosamente).

Bold(ly).   Ardito (con arditezza); fiero (fieramente ; con bravura ; francamente; con fierezza); intrepido (intrepidamente, con intrepidezza ; tostamente).

Bound.   Legato.

Brilliantly.   Brillante ; scintillante.

Brisk(ly).   Vivo (vivamente); visto (vistamente) ; allegro (allegramente) ; lesto ; vivace.

Broad(ly).   Largo (largamente, con larghezza); (frase larga) ; *very broad(ly)*, larghissimo (molto largamente); *growing broader*, largando, allargando... *Broader*, più largamente.

Brusquely.   Bruscamente.

Burlesque(ly).   Burlesco (burlescamente).

But.   Ma.

By.   Da ; *by leaps* or *skips*, di salto.

C.

Calm(ly).   Tranquillo (tranquillamente, con tranquillità) ; placido, (placidamente) ; quieto... *Growing calmer*, calmando ; calando ; raddolcendo, raddolcente.

Caprice.   Capriccio ; *capricious*, capriccioso, vicendevole ; *capriciously*, a capriccio, vicendevolmente.

Carefully.   Con diligenza ; con osservanza ; con precisione.

Careless(ly).   Negligente (negligentemente).

Caressing(ly).   Carrezzando, carrezzevole (carezzevolmente); accarrezzevole (accarrezzevolmente).

Certain (adj.).   Alcuno,-a.

Change !   Muta.

Chant.   [See *Melody*.]

Charming(ly).   Vezzoso (vezzosamente).

Chaste.   Nobile.

Clear(ly).   Chiaro (chiaramente) ; netto (nettamente).

Coaxing(ly).   Lusingando, lusinghevole (lusinghevolmente).

Cold(ly).   Freddo (freddamente, con freddezza).

Comic(ally).   Buffo,-a ; buffonesco (buffonescamente)

Complaining.   Lamentando, lamente vole ; lagrimando, lagrimoso.

Connectly.   Legato.

Consoling(ly).   Consolante.

Continually.   Sempre.

Continue.   Va.

Contra-dance.   Contraddanza.

Coquettishly.   Con civetteria.

Country-dance.   Contraddanza.

Cradle-song.   Ninna-nanna ; ninnerella.

D.

Dark.   Cupo.

Dashing.   Sbalzato ; precipitato.

Decided(ly).   Deciso ; fermo (con fermezza) ; energico (con energia).

Declamatory.   Declamando ; narrante ; parlando.

Decreasing (*in force*).   Decrescendo ; diminuendo ; raddolcendo ; diluendo.

Decreasing (*in speed*).   Rallentando ; ritardando ; ritenente ; tardando ; lentando ; slentando ; strascinando ; rilasciando ; rilasciante.

Decreasing (*in force and speed*).   Calando ; deficiendo ; mancando ; morendo ; sminuendo ; smorzando.

Deliberate(ly).   Deliberato (deliberamente).

Delicate(ly).   Delicato (delicatamente, con delicatezza) ; tenero (teneramente, con tenerezza).

Desperate(ly).   Disperato (con disperazione).

Detached.   Staccato, distaccato ; picchettato ; *very detached*, staccatissimo.

Determined.   Determinato ; risoluto.

Devotional(ly).   Devoto (devotamente, con devozione) ; religioso (religiosamente).

Dignified.   Posato ; grave.

Discreet(ly).   Discreto (con discrezione).

Disdain.   [See *Scorn*.]

Distant.   Lontano ; *at a distance*, da lontano, in lontananza, in distanza.

Distinct(ly).   Chiaro (chiaramente) ; ben marcato ; distinto (distintamente).

Distressed.   Appenato.

Divided.   Divisi.

Doleful(ly). Dolendo,dolente (con dolore, dolentemente).

Dragging. Stentando ; strascinando ; strascicando ; stirato.

Drawling. Strascicando.

Dreaming. Sognando.

Dreamy. Vago... *Dreamily,* quasi sognando.

Drinking-song. Brindisi.

Droll. Buffonesco.

Dry. Secco.

Dwelt upon. Tenuto, sostenuto.

Dying away. Morendo ; smorzando ; mancando ; perdendosi ; diluendo ; espirando ; estinguendo, stinguendo.

E.

Easy. Agevole ; commodo ; disinvolto ; facile ; mobile... *Easily,* con agevolezza, agevolmente ; agiatamente ; commodamente ; facilmente ; con disinvoltura.

Echo. Ecco... *Like an echo,* quasi ecco.

Elegant(ly). Garbato (con garbo). [See *Graceful.*]

Emphatic(ally). Enfatico (con enfasi) ; marcato ; sforzato.

End. Fine... *To the end,* sin' (*or* fin') al fine.

Energetic(ally). Energico (energicamente, con energia) ; risentito ; risoluto (risolutamente, con risoluzione).

Enlivening (tempo). Ravvivando il tempo ; animandosi, animando.

Enthusiastic(ally). Zeloso (con zelo ; con entusiasmo).

Entreating(ly). Supplichevole (supplichevolmente).

Equal(ly). Eguale (egualmente) ; equabile (equabilmente).

Even(ly). Eguale (egualmente) ; uguale (ugualmente) ; tepido (tepidamente) ; spianato.

Exact. Esatto... *With exactness,* con esatezza. [See *Precise.*]

Expiring. Espirando. [See *Dying away.*]

Expressive(ly). Espressivo (con espressione); sentito, risentito; pietoso; sentimentale ; (con sentimento ; con sensibilità).

Extempore. All'improvvista ; alla mente... *Extemporaneously,* improvvisamente.

Extinct. Estinto.

Extravagant(ly). Stravagante (stra vagantemente).

Extreme. Sommo,-a.

Extremely. Molto, di molto ; -issimo.

F.

Fading away. [See *Dying away.*]

Faint. Fiacco ; debile ; estinto.

Fantastic. Fantastico.

Fast. Allegro ; vivace ; vivo ; presto. .. *Very fast,* allegro molto, allegro assai, allegro vivo ; vivacissimo ; prestissimo.. *Rather fast,* allegretto, allegro moderato... *Not too fast,* non troppo allegro... *Twice as fast,* doppio movimento ; *not so fast,* meno mosso.

Faster. Più mosso ; più allegro ; più presto ; veloce... *Faster and faster,* sempre accelerando ; pressando, pressante.

Fearful(ly). Paventato ; timido (timidamente) ; timoroso (timorosamente ; con timore).

Feeble. Debile, debole.

Feelingly. [See *Expressively.*]

Fervent(ly). Fervente (con fervore) ; ardente (con ardore).

Festive(ly). Festivo (festivamente).

Fierce(ly). Feroce (con ferocità) ; fiero (fieramente) ; barbaro.

Fiery. Fuocoso ; con fuoco ; ardente.

Firm(ly). Fermo (fermamente, con fermezza).

First part. Primo (*in a duet*) ; *first time,* prima volta (|1. |).

Flattering(ly). Lusingando, lusinghevole (lusinghevolmente).

Flowing(ly). Scorrendo, scorrevole ; disinvolto (con disinvoltura) ; sciolto (scioltamente); andante (andantemente).

Fluently. Volubilmente. [See *Flowing.*]

Flying. Volante.

Following. Seguente, seguendo.

Fond(ly). Amorevole (amorevolmente, con amore) ; amoroso (amorosamente).

For. Per... *For voices alone,* a cappella.

Forcibly. Con forza ; bruscamente ; con tutta forza.

Forcing. Forzando, sforzando.

Free(ly). Disinvolto (con disinvoltura francamente, con franchezza ; liberamente); generoso; sciolto (scioltamente).

Frenzy. Delirio ; *frenzied(ly)*, delirante (con delirio ; con rabbia).

From. Da... *From the beginning*, Da capo... *From the sign*, Dal segno ; *from the sign to the sign*, Dal segno al segno.

Full. Pieno,-a.

Funereal. Funebre.

Furious(ly). Furioso (furiosamente ; con rabbia) ; *with extreme fury* or *passion*, furiosissimamente.

G.

Gay. Gajo ; giojoso... *Gaily*, gajamente, giojosamente.

Gliding. Glissando ; portamento, portando ; scorrendo ; strisciando.

Gondola-song. Gondoliera.

Go on ! Va.

Graceful(ly). Grazioso (graziosamente, con grazia ; con garbo) ; disinvolto (con disinvoltura) ; galante (galantemente) ; elegante (elegantemente) ; vezzoso (vezzosamente) ; venusto... *Gracefully and sweetly*, affabile, amabile.

Gradually. A poco a poco ; gradatamente.

Grand(ly). Grandioso ; nobile (nobilmente, con nobiltà).

Grave(ly). Grave (gravemente, con gravità).

Grotesque(ly). Grottesco ; burlesco (burlescamente).

Growing. [See *Decreasing* and *Increasing*.]

H.

Half. Mezzo,-a... *Half-loud*, mezzo forte; *half-soft*, mezzo piano, mezza voce.

Hammered. Martellato.

Harsh(ly). Aspro (con asprezza); duro (duramente) ; stridente.

Harshness. Asprezza ; durezza.

Hastening. Accelerando ; stringendo ; affrettando ; calcando.

Haughty. Fiero... *Haughtily*, fieramente.

Heartfelt. Intimo, intimissimo ; affettuoso, con affetto.

Heavy. Ponderoso ; pesante ; grave... *Heavily*, pesantemente, gravemente.

Held back. Ritenuto ; trattenuto ; meno mosso.

Held down. Tenuto.

Heroic. Eroico,-a.

Hesitating(ly). Irresoluto ; timido (timidamente) ; vacillando.

High. Alto,-a... *Highest*, il più alto, altissimo... *In the higher octave*, ottava alta (*8va* · · · · · · ·).

Hoarse(ly). Fioco (con fiochezza).

Holding back (*tempo*). Ritenente ; ritardando.

Humorously. Con umore.

Hurried(ly). Affrettoso (con fretta) ; frettoloso (frettolosamente).

Hurrying. Affrettando ; stringendo

I.

If. Se.

Imitating. Imitando ; quasi.

Impassioned. Appassionato, appassionatamente; con abbandono, abbandonatamente ; caloroso.

Impatient(ly). Impatiente (impatientemente).

Imperceptible. Insensibile ; *imperceptibly*, insensibilmente.

Imperious(ly). Imperioso (imperiosamente).

Impetuous(ly). Impetuoso (con impeto, impetuosamente, con impetuosità) ; sbalzato ; tempestoso (tempestosamente).

Imposing. Imponente.

In a festive manner. Con festività.

In a gentle, quiet manner. Con lenezza

In a sweet manner. Con dolce maniera.

Increasing (*in speed*). Accelerando ; stringendo ; affrettando ; incalzando ; ravvivando il tempo; doppio movimento.

Increasing (*in force*). Crescendo ; accrescendo ; rinforzando.

Increasing (*in force and speed*). Stringendo ; affrettando ; incalzando.

In declamatory style. Declamando, recitando ; narrante ; parlando.

In devotional style. Devoto, con devozione.

Indifferent(ly). Indifferente (indifferentemente ; con indifferenza) ; tepido (tepidamente).

Infernal. Infernale.

In haste. Con fretta.

In military style. Militarmente.

In modern style. Alla moderna.

In octaves. Doppio pedale (organ-pedal) ; coll'ottava (coll' 8· ·······).

Insinuating. [See Flattering.]

Intense(ly). Intenso (intensamente, con intensità).

In the same manner. Simile.

In the same time. L'istesso tempo ; moto precedente.

In the style of a. Alla.

In time. A tempo; Tempo I⁰; misurato (after a recitative).

Ironical(ly). Ironico (ironicamente).

Irresolute(ly). Irresoluto (con irresoluzione).

J.

Jesting(ly). Scherzando ; giocoso (giocosamente).

Jovially. Con giovialità.

Joyous(ly). Giojoso (giojosamente) ; gaudioso.

Jubilant(ly). Giubiloso (con giubilio, con giubilazione).

Judicious(ly). Discreto (con discrezione).

L.

Lamenting. Lamentando, lamentabile, lamentoso ; piangendo.

Languid(ly). Languido (con languore, languidamente).

Languishing(ly). Languendo (languidamente).

Left hand. Mano sinistra.

Leisurely. Adagietto ; moderato... Rather leisurely, commodetto.

Less. Meno.

Light(ly). Leggero or Leggiero (leggeramente, con leggerezza ; agilmente) ; sfogato ; svelto.

Lingering(ly). Tardo, tardando (tardamente).

Little by little. A poco a poco.

Lively. Vivace, vivacemente ; vivo, vivamente ; allegro, allegramente ; visto, vistamente ; con allegrezza ; svegliato ; lesto ; desto.

Lofty. Nobile ; fastoso : pomposo ; elevato...Loftily, con nobiltà ; con pompa.

Longingly. Con desiderio.

Loud. Forte ; con forza ; very loud, fortissimo ; extremely loud, con tutta forza, forte possibile (fff) ; half-loud, mezzo forte ; loud, suddenly decreasing to soft, forte piano (fp).

Louder. Più forte ; crescendo ; rinforzando.

Love. Amore.

Loving(ly). Amorevole, amoroso (con amore, amorosamente) ; amabile.

Lullaby. Ninnerella, ninna-nanna.

Lyric. Lirico.

M.

Majestic(ally). Maestoso, maestevole (maestosamente, con maestà) ; pomposo (con pompa) ; fastoso (fastosamente).

Manner. Maniera ; in a quiet manner, con dilce maniera. [See In.]

Marked. Marcato ; con forza ; rinforzato, rinforzando ; enfatico ; sforzato sforzando (sfz).

May song. Maggiolata.

Measured. Misurato.

Medley. Mescolanza ; olio ; pasticcio.

Melancholy. Malinconico ; with melancholy, malinconicamente, con malinconia.

Melody. La melodia. Il canto. La parte...Mark (or accent) and "carry" the melody, Marcando e portando la melodia (il canto) ; ben e precisamente portando la melodia ; la melodia (il canto) ben portando ed espressiva.

Menacing(ly). Minaccevole (minaccevolmente).

Mildly. Dolce ; (dolcemente, con dolcezza) ; piacevole ; affabile.

Moderate(ly) (speed). Moderato (moderatamente) ; non troppo allegro.

More. Più ; more slowly, più lente; più adagio.

Most. Il più.

Mournful(ly). Mesto (mestamente), addolorato ; amarevole (amarevolmente) ; flebile ; funebre : lugubre ; (con espressione di patimento) ; dolente

Mouth. Bocca ; with closed mouth, con bocca chiusa.

Moved. Concitato. [See Agitated.]

Movement. Movimento.

Much. Molto.

Muffled. Coperto ; suffocato ; sordo (sordamente); con sordini.

Murmuring. Mormorando ; susurrando.

Muted. Con sordino (*pl.* con sordini).

Mysterious(ly). Misterioso (misteriosamente) ; cupo.

N.

Natural(ly). Naturale (naturalmente). [See *Simple.*]

Nearly. Quasi.

Neat(ly). Netto (nettamente) ; leggiadro (leggiadramente).

Negligent(ly). Negligente (negligentemente, con negligenza).

Night-piece. Notturno.

Nimble. Agile ; svelto ; sciolto... *Nimbly*, agilmente, con agilità ; scioltamente ; allegramente.

Nobly. Nobilmente, con nobiltà.

Noisy. [See *Boisterous.*]

Not. Non...*Not so*, meno ; *not so fast*, meno mosso, meno allegro ; *not too*, non troppo ; non tanto.

O.

Obliged (necessary). Obbligato.

Obscure. Cupo ; misterioso.

Of. Di.

On. Su ; sopra (*above*).

Or. O, od (*before a vowel*); **or else,** ossia ; oppure ; ovvero.

Other. Altro,-a.

P.

Passionate(ly). Passionato (passionatamente) ; appassionato (appassionatamente) ; (con passione) ; ardente (con ardore) ; fervente (con fervore) ; furioso (con furore) ; caloroso (con calore).

Pastoral. Pastorale ; rustico; campestre.

Pathetic(ally). Patetico (pateticamente) ; doloroso (dolorosamente, con dolore).

Pensive. Pensieroso.

Phrase (to). Fraseggiare ... *W e l l phrased*, ben fraseggiando.

Piece. Pezzo.

Piquantly. Con piccanteria.

Placid(ly). Placido (placidamente). [See *Tranquil.*]

Plaintive(ly). Lamentando ; dolendo, dolente, doloroso (con dolore, dolorosamente) ; addolorato ; flebile ; piangendo. [See *Mournful.*]

Playful(ly). Giuochevole, giuocante ; (con giuoco) ; giocoso (giocosamente) ; scherzoso, scherzando.

Pleading(ly). Supplicando, supplichevole (supplichevolmente).

Pleasing(ly). Piacevole (piacevolmente), compiacevole ; gradevole (gradevolmente).

Pompous(ly). Pomposo (con pompa) ; fastoso (fastosamente).

Ponderous. Ponderoso ; pesante.

Possible. Possibile ; *as fast as possible*, presto possibile ; *as loud as possible*, forte possibile ; con tutta forza.

Prattling. Straccicalando.

Prayer. Preghiera.

Precipitate(ly). Precipitato, precipitoso, precipitando (precipitatamente).

Precise(ly). Preciso (con precisione).

Pressing (*tempo*). Stringendo, pressante; (*expression*) insistendo.

Prompt(ly). Pronto (prontamente, con prontezza).

Pronounced. Pronunziato.

Proud(ly). Fiero (fieramente) ; altiero (altieramente, con alterezza).

Psalm. Salmo.

Q.

Quiet(ly). Quieto ; tranquillo (tranquillamente ; con lenezza). [See *Tranquil.*]

R.

Rapid(ly). Rapido (rapidamente, con rapidità) ; celere ; veloce (velocemente, con velocità, velocissimamente) ; mosso (*in phrases like* meno mosso, più mosso, etc.) ; tosto (tostamente). [quanto.

Rather. Quasi ; piuttosto ; poco ; al-

Refined. Nobile (nobilmente).

Religious(ly). Religioso (religiosamente) ; devoto (devotamente).

Reposeful(ly). Riposato (riposatamente).

Resonant(ly). Sonoro ; sonante (con risonanza ; sonoramente, con sonorità).

Restless. Inquieto.

Resume (to). Ripigliare ; riprendere.

Reverie. Meditazione.

Rhythmized. Ben ritmato.

Right hand. Mano destra.

Ringing(ly). Sonoro (sonoramente, con sonorità).

Romping. Burlando.

Rough(ly). Aspro (con asprezza); ruvido (ruvidamente); (bruscamente).

Rustic. Rustico; campestre; pastorale.

S.

Sad(ly). Tristo (tristamente, con tristezza); mesto (mestamente, con mestizia); languendo, languente; dolente.

Same (the). Medesimo; detto; stesso.

Scorn. Sdegno; *scornful(ly)*, sdegnoso (sdegnosamente).

Second part. Secondo (*in a duet*).

Second time. Seconda volta. ([2.   ].)

Serious(ly). Serioso (con serietà).

Sighing. Sospirando, sospirevole, sospiroso.

Similarly. Simile.

Simple. Semplice; schietto; naturale.
..*Simply*, semplicemente, con semplicità; schiettamente, con schiettezza; naturalmente.

Singing. Cantando; melodico...*In a singing style*, cantabile.

Sketch. Bozzetto.

Sliding. Sdrucciolando.

Slow(ly). Adagio; lento (lentamente, con lentezza); *very slow*, lento molto, adagissimo; grave; largo; *rather slow*, andante, andantino, adagietto, moderato.

Slower. Meno mosso; più adagio; più lento. [See *Decreasing.*]...*Slower and slower*, a poco a poco rallentando (*or* ritardando).

Slurring. Legato; portamento, portando; slissando.

Smooth(ly). Legato; eguale (egualmente); piacevole (piacevolmente); slissato; soave (soavemente); strisciando.

Sobbing. Singhiozzando.

Soft(ly). Piano; dolce (dolcemente; mollemente); *very soft*, pianissimo; dolcissimo; estinto.

Softer. Meno forte. [See *Decreasing.*]

Solemn(ly). Solenne (solennemente, con solennità).

Somewhat. Poco; quasi.

Song. [See *Melody.*]

Sonorous(ly). Sonoro (sonoramente, con sonorità).

Sorrowful(ly). Afflitto (con afflizione); mesto (mestamente); doloroso (dolorosamente).

Sparkling. Brillante; scintillante.

Spirited(ly). Spiritoso (spiritosamente, con spirito); brioso (con brio).

Sportive. [See *Playful.*]

Sprightly. Desto.

Springing. Saltando.

Stern(ly). Duro (duramente).

Sternness. Durezza.

Stifled. Suffocato; con voce suffocata.

Still. Ancora; *still faster*, ancor più mosso; *still slower*, ancor più lento, ancor più moderato.

Strict(ly). Giusto (giustamente, con giustezza); severo (severamente)... *Strictly in time*, a (*or* al) rigore di tempo; tempo rigoroso; misurato; aggiustamente; andare a tempo; a battuta. (Ben misurato. Ben ritmato).

Strident. Stridente.

Style. Stilo; modo...*In the style of a*, alla; in modo.

Suave(ly). Soave (soavemente, con soavità); dolce (dolcemente, con dolcezza, con dolce maniera).

Sublime. Elevato; nobile.

Suddenly. Subito, subitamente; di colpo.

Supplicating(ly). Supplicando, supplichevole (supplichevolmente).

Sustainedly. Sostenuto, sostenendo, sostenente.

Sweet(ly). Dolce (dolcemente); affabile, amabile. [See *Suave.*]...*Very sweetly*, dolcissimo.

Swelling. Crescendo.

Swift. [See *Rapid.*]

Sympathetic(ally). Pietoso (con pietà).

T.

Tasteful(ly). Gustoso (con gusto).

Tearful(ly). Lagrimoso, lagrimando; piangendo; flebile; (con pianto).

Tempestuous(ly). Tempestoso (tempestosamente).

Tender(ly). Tenero (teneramente, con tenerezza); dolce (dolcemente, con dolcezza); affettuoso (affettuosamente, con affezione); amabile; amorevole, amoroso; lirico.

Than. De.

Then. Allora ; poi.

Thoughtful. Pensieroso.

Threatening(ly). Minacciando, minaccioso, minaccevole (minaccevolmente).

Timid(ly). Timido (timidamente, con timidezza).

Timorous. Timoroso (timorosamente, con timore).

Tinkling. Squillante.

To. A, ad (*before a vowel*)... *To the sign*, al segno.

Together. Unisono ; tutti.

Too. Anche (*also*); troppo ; *not too fast*, non troppo allegro ; *not too slow*, non troppo lento.

Tranquil(ly). Tranquillo (tranquillamente, con tranquillità) ; placido (placidamente, con placidezza) ; spianato. [See *Quietly.*]

Trembling(ly). Tremolo ; tremolando, tremoloso (tremolosamente).

Triumphant(ly). Trionfante (trionfalmente).

Tune. [See *Melody.*]

Turn over quickly. Volti subito.

Twice as fast. Doppio movimento.

U.

Under. Sotto ; *under the right hand*, sotto la mano destra.

Undulating. Ondeggiante ; tremando, tremoloso.

Uneasy. Affannato, affannoso; *uneasily*, affannosamente.

Unimpassioned. Tepido.

Unrestful. Inquieto.

Until. Fino (fin') ; sino (sin').

Upon. Su ; sopra.

Up to. [See *Until.*]

Urgent(ly). Insistendo (con insistenza); instante (instantemente).

V.

Vague. Vago.

Vehement(ly). Veemente (con veemenza) ; acciaccato ; sforzando ; feroce (con ferocità ; con islancio); smaniante.

Very. Molto ; assai ; ben(e)... *Very slow*, molto lento ; *very moderate*, molto moderato; *very fast*, molto allegro, allegro assai ; presto, prestissimo, prestissi-

mamente ; *very marked*, ben marcato, marcatissimo ; *very soft*, pianissimo, dolcissimo ; (*vocal*) a fior di labbra; *very loud*, fortissimo.

Vibrant, Vibrating. Vibrante.

Vigorous(ly). Vigoroso (vigorosamente, con vigore).

Violent(ly). Violento, violente (violentemente). [See *Impetuous.*]

Vivacious. [See *Animated.*]

Voice. Voce, canto, parte ; *with the voice*, colla voce, colla parte, col canto.

W.

Wailing. Lamentando ; piangendo.

Warlike. Guerriero ; bellicoso ; *in warlike style*, bellicoso, bellicosamente.

Warmly. Con calore, caloroso.

Wavering. Tremolando ; vacillando.

Weak. Debile, debole.

Well. Bene, ben... *Well marked*, ben marcato, *or* ben pronunziato ; *well rhythmed*, ben ritmato ; *well sustained*, ben tenuto, *or* ben sostenuto... *Well phrased*, ben fraseggiando.

Whim. Ghiribizzo ; capriccio ; fantasia.

Whimsical. Ghiribizzoso.

Whispering. Susurrando, susurrante.

Wild(ly). Feroce (ferocemente) ; fiero (fieramente).

With affectation. Smorfioso.

With affection (pathos). Con affetto.

With anger. Con ira, irato.

With anguish. Angoscioso, angosciosamente.

With ardor. Con affetto ; con ardore.

With boldness. Con fiducia.

With breadth. Largo, largamente.

With confidence. Con fiducia.

With constantly increasing warmth. Sempre incalzando.

With decision. Deciso.

With deliberation. Con lentezza; lentamente.

With desperation. Con disperazione.

With discretion. Con discrezione, discreto.

With distinctness. Distintamente, distinto ; con chiarezza ; marcato, marcando.

With ease. Con agevolezza.

With emotion. Con affetto ; con affezione.

With energy. Con energia.

With expression. Con espressione, espressivo; sensibile, sentito.

With facility. Con agevolezza.

With feeling. Sensibile, sentito.

With fervor. Con calore.

With firmness. Con fermezza.

With frenzy. Con delirio, con rabbia.

With grace. Con grazia, con eleganza, grazioso, elegantemente.

With grandeur. Con grandezza, grandioso.

With grief. Con duolo, con dolore.

With growing animation. Animando, animandosi ; ravvivando.

With impetuosity. Con impeto.

With intensity. Con intensità.

With lightness. Con leggerezza, leggermente ; con disinvoltura.

With longing. Con desiderio.

With mandolin-effect. Mandolinata.

With much passion. Con molta passione.

With nobility. Con nobiltà.

With promptness. Con prontezza.

With rapidity. Con prestezza.

With resolution. Con risoluzione.

With resonance. Con sonorità.

With sadness. Con tristezza.

With spirit. Con spirito ; con anima ; con brio.

With sweetness. Con soavità.

With tears. Piangendo ; lagrimando.

With the bow. Coll'arco ; arcato.

With the fingers. Pizzicato (*violin*).

With the left hand. Colla mano sinistra (usually simply *m. s.*), *or* colla sinistra (*c. s.*)

With the loud pedal. Ped.; tre corde (*after* una corda) ; *with pedal through out*, sempre pedale.

With the octave. Coll'ottava (*coll'8·········*).

With the right hand. Colla mano destra (usually simply *m. d.*), *or* colla destra (*c. d.*)

With the soft pedal. Una corda.

With the stick. Col legno.

With the voice. Colla voce ; colla parte ; col canto.

With warmth. Con calorosità ; con calore.

With wrath. Con ira ; irato.

Without. Senza.

Without accelerating. Senza accelerare.

Without altering. Senza alterare

Without growing slower. Senza rallentare.

Without interruption. Senza interruzione.

Without repeating. Senza ripetizione.

Without retarding. Senza ritardare; senza di slentare.

Without stopping. Senza fermarsi.

Without taking breath. Senza re spirare.

Without the mutes. Senza sordini.

Wrathful(ly). Adirato (con ira).

Z.

Zealous(ly). Zeloso (zelosamente, con zelo).

Zephyr-like. Zeffiroso.